THE MAMMALS OF ANCIENT EGYPT

A hunting scene on the first pylon of the Mortuary Temple of Ramses III, Dynasty XX, Medinet Habu, Thebes. Source: Louis Grivetti. In the uppermost section the partly damaged animals include beisa oryx, asses, and hares. Ahead of the upper charioteer are eight beisa oryx, several with heads reversed, and one pierced with an arrow facing left. Below the oryx are eight hartebeests, three with heads reversed, and one falling and headed left. Below are 13 wild asses in various postures and on the far upper right a hare. In the lower scene, Ramses III has successfully speared three aurochs in the marsh.

THE NATURAL HISTORY OF EGYPT: Vol. IV

Dale J. Osborn
with Jana Osbornová

THE MAMMALS OF ANCIENT EGYPT

OXBOW | books
Oxford & Philadelphia

This edition published in the United Kingdom in 2024 by
OXBOW BOOKS
81 St Clements, Oxford OX4 1AW

and in the United States by
OXBOW BOOKS
1950 Lawrence Road, Havertown, PA 19083

Paperback Edition: ISBN 979-8-88857-077-7
Digital Edition: ISBN 979-8-88857-078-4 (epub)

First published in 1998 by Aris & Phillips Ltd

Oxbow Books is grateful to the Petrie Museum for their collaboration in bringing out these new editions

Printed in the United Kingdom by CMP Digital Print Solutions

For a complete list of Oxbow titles, please contact:

UNITED KINGDOM
Oxbow Books
Telephone (0)1226 734350
Email: oxbow@oxbowbooks.com
www.oxbowbooks.com

UNITED STATES OF AMERICA
Oxbow Books
Telephone (610) 853-9131, Fax (610) 853-9146
Email: queries@casemateacademic.com
www.casemateacademic.com/oxbow

Oxbow Books is part of the Casemate Group

Front cover: Fragment of the Tehenu (Tjhenu) 'Libyan Tribute' palette showing oxen, donkeys, gazelles and olive trees, from Abydos (Protodynastic period *c.* 3100 BC). Grey schist, 190 × 220 mm (Cairo Mus. C.G. 14238; image: Zeinab Mohamed, reproduced under Creative Commons Attribution-Share Alike 2.0 Generic license)

Contents

Preface

This book was not intended to be a taxonomic treatise, but there are so many discrepancies in zoological names that special attention had to be given to that discipline. Many Latin names used in early Egyptological literature are now obsolete and sometimes common names are incorrectly used. For example, horned mammals were often generally referred to as gazelles, antelopes or deer. A gazelle is a kind of antelope, but an antelope is not a gazelle, and neither of them are deer. Some recent dictionaries, however, do not make clear distinctions between these names. The ancient inclusive 'small cattle', which was used by Brewer *et al.* (1994: 90) in reference to sheep and goats, would have been more proper than 'deer' in reference to rows of hoofed mammals.

Ancient Egyptian artists sometimes erred also and applied the wrong hieroglyph or drew some parts of animals incorrectly.

There have been attempts to systematize the mammals of the Dynasties. Hartmann's (1864, 1869) was the first. His early work was without illustrations; the second dealt with identification of mammals in the Dynasty V Tomb of Ptah-hetep. Paton's (1925) book is full of errors, crudely illustrated, and has a difficult format. Other authors limited their examples to special groups (von Bissing, 1905; Borchardt, 1913; Hilzheimer, 1913, 1926; Dawson, 1934; Macramallah, 1935; Boessneck, 1953, 1981b; Haltenorth, 1959, 1961a; Brentjes, 1965; and Carrington, 1972). Boessneck's (1988) recent work is a valuable reference source, but information on mammals is limited. Lack of an index, as noted by Janssen (1990: 43), is a hindrance to researchers and some important species are not included in the text. The recent book on cats by Malek (1993) is very useful and interesting. The book came into my hands too late for communication herein. The same holds for Houlihan's (1996) book on animals of the pharaohs.

Diverse publications of Keimer (1926 *et seq.*) on identification of various portrayals are important contributions. Others are mentioned in discussions of individual species.

Although I have not acknowledged all references in the *Lexikon der Ägyptologie*, it has been a valuable bibliographical source.

Herein, the English name in most common use is given for each species, plus the Latin zoological name. Hieroglyphs, if available, are provided together with the transcription and English pronunciation.

Additional names in English E, French F, German G, and Arabic A are added.

Latin, Greek, and other derivatives of names can be found in Nybakken (1959) and Gotch (1979).

Topographic names follow the map 'Nile Valley, Land of the Pharaohs', Atlas pl. 58, May 1965, drawn in the Cartographic Division of the National Geographic Society.

Descriptions and information on natural history and habitats are necessarily limited herein, but for the reader interested in further descriptions, data on measurements, and details on natural history and distribution of contemporary mammal species, the following books are recommended: Harrison (1964, 1968, 1972), Dorst (1970), Kingdon (1977), Haltenorth and Diller (1980), and Osborn and Helmy (1980).

A remark by Janssen (1990: 48) is worth inserting here: "Egyptian reliefs and paintings, so many times praised for their realism, are actually not so clear as we should wish."

I can also add that although artists are careful in copying ancient Egyptian art, mistakes occur occasionally. Wherever possible I have compared drawings with photographs and the drawings of different artists. Sometimes this has led to further confusion.

For these reasons, and because of lack of biological knowledge, many errors and discrepancies appeared in Egyptological literature dealing with mammals. Therefore, I have listed obvious faults with the hope of improving future research in this field and to encourage authors to be cautious when repeating the biological conclusions of their predecessors or adding new faunal data.

In a booklet that I wrote some years ago on *Animals of the Pharaohs*, a number of errors are present. The reason for this was that I took historical information from a book or two as factual without making further investigation. This is how errors and discrepancies are perpetuated and passed on from author to author. Any findings of errors and discrepandcies in this work will be gratefully accepted.

Dale J. Osborn

Prague, 1998

Acknowledgements

I am deeply indebted to Prof. Dr. Miroslav Verner, Director of the Czech Institute of Egyptology of Charles University, Prague for allowing me free use of their rich Library and for assistance in locating information. Dr. Jiřina Růžová and other members of the staff were also of great help in this respect.

Two staff members, Jaromír Krejčí and Miroslav Bárta were very helpfull in providing all the hieroglyphs and their translations.

Photographers Kamil Voděra and Milan Zemina copied and printed many of the illustrations. The latter also provided me with some good photographs of animals in tombs.

Dr. John McArdle, Director of the Zoological Research Service, Minneapolis, helped me in obtaining literature and also making editorial comments on the earlier chapters of the manuscript.

Dr. Pavel Červíček of Darmstadt also helped me in obtaining literature and in clarifying some difficult translations. His publications of rock drawings have been very useful.

Ms. Marsha Hill, Assistant Curator, of the Metropolitan Museum of Art, N.Y. supplied me with various photographs from publications and gave me copyright privileges. For allowing copying of illustrations and quotations I am also indebted to Dr. Douglas J. Brewer and Dr. Louis Grivetti.

Mr. Ibrahim Helmy of Cairo was most helpful in providing me with a list of mammal names in Arabic.

Dr. C. S. Churcher, University of Toronto, Canada, provided me with many important reprints.

Mr. Martin Kosina and Ing. Zdeněk Kosina kindly assisted in all neccessary computer work.

Last, but not least, I must thank Adrian Phillips, Director of Aris and Phillips Ltd. for publishing this book and, most of all, for his patience in awaiting its completion.

All illustrations are credited in their captions and references are included in the Bibliography.

The following copyright holders are thanked for their kind permission to reproduce and publish illustrations and quotations:

American University in Cairo Press, fig. 13–156.

Augustin, J.J., GmBh, Glückstadt, figs. 7–213 and –214.

Bibliographisches Institut & Brockhaus, F.A., AG, Mannheim, fig. 11–1.

Brewer, D.J., figs. 7–119 and –133.

Brill, E.J., Leiden [Asselberghs 1961] figs. 1–2a,b, 1–5a,b, 1–9, –10, 6–13, 7–89, –200, 10–23, 12–7 and 13–13.

Brooklyn Museum, N.Y., figs. 1–7 and 8–1.

Brunner–Traut, E., figs. 2–16, –17, 5–2, –9, 7–70, –82, –136, –137, –138, –168, 13–215 and –216.

Carnegie Institution, Washington D.C., fig. 7–97.

Churcher, C.S., figs. 7–20 and –25.

Committee of the Egypt Exploration Society, London, figs. 1–1, –19, –20a,b, 2–2 to 2–5, 3–4, 4–3, –18, –29, 5–1, –6, 6–11, 7–9 to –11, –14, –17, –27 to –29, –33, –34, –38, –45, –57, –62, –66, –69, –74, –77, –78, –86, –90, –120, –123, –126, –143, –160, –180, –199, –211, –217, –219, –225, 10–9, –12, –13, –14, –16, –18, 12–3 to –5, –11, –21, –25, 13–4, –12, 15, –31, –34, –35, –36, –42, –43, –57, –60, –67, –74, –81, –82, –101, –111, –113, –122, –132 to –135, –138, –141, –192, –194, –204, –207, –211, –214, –217 and –228.

Droste von, V., figs. 2–10 and –11.

Duncker & Humblot, GmBh, Berlin, figs. 4–34, 7–107, –150 and 13–213.

Fisher, Gustav, Verlag, Jena, fig. 7–1.

Griffith Institute, Ashmolean Museum, Oxford, figs. 1–28, 7–41, –79, –146, –166, –206, 12–6, 13–58, –183, –190 and –230.

Illustrated London News Picture Library, for using text material of I.E.S. Edwards' description of the Pitt Rivers knife handle.

Kaplony, P., fig. 7–131.

Kohlhammer, W., Verlag, GmbH, Stuttgart, figs. 4–24 and 13–49.

Kunsthistorische Museum, Wien, figs. 7–115 and –116.

Metropolitan Museum of Art, N.Y., figs. 1–14a–g, 6–5, 7–43, 7–187; and permission to use own copies of MMA material for figs. 1–23, 4–32, 7–63, –67, –68, –179, –188, –205, –216a,b, –226, –229, 12–8, –19, –20, 13–5, –21, –22, –59, –152, –173, –177, –188, –205.

Museum of Fine Arts, Boston, figs. 7–83, –87, –153 and –156.

Murray, John, London, fig. 7–189a, b.

Náprstek Museum, Prague, fig. 13–100.
Oriental Institute of the University of Chicago, figs. 1–26, 4–33, –38, 7–52, –109, –173, –178, –181, –182, 13–40, –112 and –201.
Österreichische Akademie der Wissenschaften, Wien, fig. 7–157 and 13–93.
Quaritch, Bernard, Ltd, London, figs. 1–6e, –15, 4–1, 7–18, –21, –22, –56, –94, –130, –141, –155, –158, –167, –197, –212, 10–24, 13–11, –37, –64, –88, –89, –110, –126, –129, –148, –171, –196 and –227.
Redford, D., figs. 7–15, 10–1, –2, 13–68 to –70, –83 and –108.
Steiner, Franz, Verlag, (Wiesbaden) Stuttgart, figs. 4–39, –40, 5–2, 7–8, –13, –55, –70, –73, –105, –196, –220, 9–1, 10–3, –4, –5, –6, –7, –8, –10, –11, 12–2, –14, –15, –16, –17, –22, 13–8, –9, –28, –29, –30, –32, –33, –50, –62, –63, –73, –84, –85, –86, –104, –105, –106, –107, –119, –127, –130, –139, –140, –146, –147, –166, –186, –198, –199, –200, –215 and –221.
University of California Press, Berkeley, figs. 4–35 and 7–51.
University College, Oxford, The Estates Bursar and Christ's College, Cambridge, figs. 4–13, 7–185 and 13–222.
University of South Carolina, The Hierakonpolis Expedition, fig. 1–6a.
Vandenhoeck & Ruprecht, Göttingen, figs. 2–16, –17, 5–2, 7–136, –137 and –138.

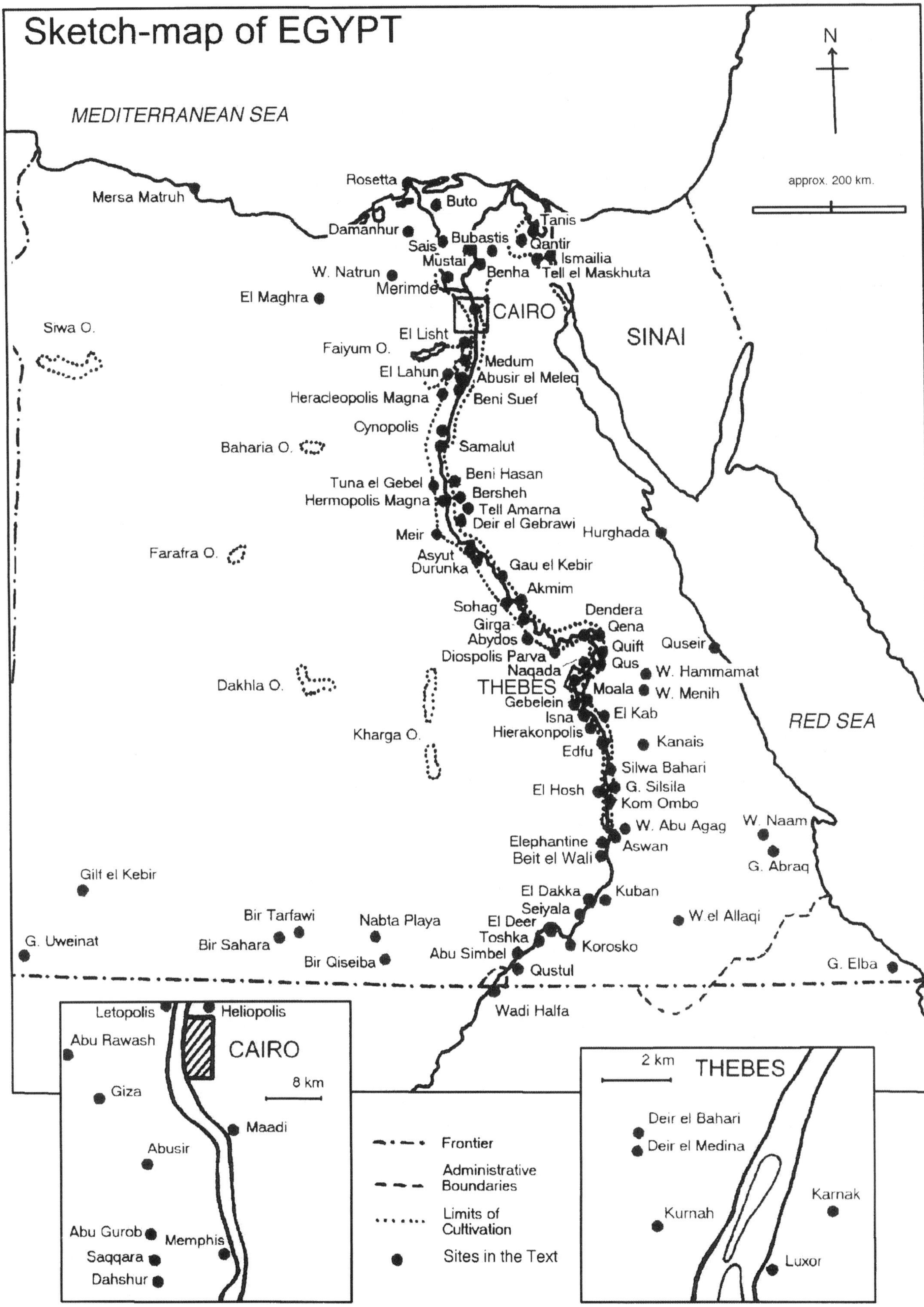
Sketch-map of EGYPT
N
approx. 200 km.
MEDITERRANEAN SEA
Mersa Matruh
Rosetta
Buto
Damanhur
Sais
Bubastis
Tanis
Qantir
Ismailia
Tell el Maskhuta
Mustai
Benha
W. Natrun
Merimde
El Maghra
CAIRO
SINAI
Siwa O.
El Lisht
Faiyum O.
Medum
El Lahun
Abusir el Meleq
Heracleopolis Magna
Beni Suef
Cynopolis
Baharia O.
Samalut
Beni Hasan
Tuna el Gebel
Bersheh
Hermopolis Magna
Tell Amarna
Deir el Gebrawi
Hurghada
Meir
Farafra O.
Asyut
Durunka
Gau el Kebir
Akmim
Sohag
Dendera
Girga
Qena
Abydos
Quift
Quseir
Diospolis Parva
Qus
Naqada
W. Hammamat
THEBES
Moala
W. Menih
Dakhla O.
Gebelein
Isna
El Kab
Hierakonpolis
RED SEA
Kharga O.
Kanais
Edfu
Silwa Bahari
El Hosh
G. Silsila
Kom Ombo
W. Abu Agag
W. Naam
Elephantine
Aswan
Beit el Wali
G. Abraq
Gilf el Kebir
El Dakka
Kuban
Seiyala
Bir Tarfawi
Nabta Playa
El Deer
W. el Allaqi
G. Uweinat
Bir Sahara
Toshka
Korosko
Bir Qiseiba
Abu Simbel
Qustul
G. Elba
Wadi Halfa
Letopolis
Heliopolis
Abu Rawash
CAIRO
8 km
Giza
Maadi
Abusir
Abu Gurob
Memphis
Saqqara
Dahshur
Frontier
Administrative Boundaries
Limits of Cultivation
Sites in the Text
2 km
THEBES
Deir el Bahari
Deir el Medina
Karnak
Kurnah
Luxor

Preface to the 2024 Edition

In the 1970s, a much-anticipated new series of publications illustrated objects and themes related to the excavations of the archaeologist William Matthew Flinders Petrie (1853–1942) in Egypt, and aspects of the collection of University College London's Petrie Museum of Egyptian and Sudanese Archaeology. A young couple setting up in business in the early 1970s, Aris and Phillips published these works, written by members of the UCL Egyptology Department, in their *Modern Egyptology* series. Building on Petrie's own observations, the authors of these volumes aimed to complete the great task of publishing the Petrie Museum of Egyptian and Sudanese Archaeology's vast collection, and to present some of the research that Petrie himself was not able to address in his own published works during his lifetime. As the current Curator of the Petrie Museum, it is a great privilege for me to support Oxbow Books in their mission to republish the series, which remains a key source of information for all those interested in object-based approaches to the study of the ancient world.

The Petrie Museum, part of University College London (UCL), is home to one of the largest and most significant collections of Egyptian and Sudanese archaeology in the world. Free to visit, this extraordinary collection tells stories about the lives of ordinary people who lived along the Nile Valley thousands of years ago. Originally set up as a teaching collection, the Petrie Museum comprises over 80,000 objects housed together with an internationally important archaeological archive. It is a collection of world firsts and 'oldests': the oldest woven garment; the oldest worked iron objects; the first known depiction of loom weaving; the oldest known written document about women's health; the earliest veterinary treatise; the oldest will on paper. The Museum has Designated Status from Arts Council England, meaning that it is considered to have outstanding resonance and national cultural significance. The collection has a substantial, visible international reputation for research, supporting hundreds of researchers every year, both remotely and in person.

The Petrie Museum is named after Flinders Petrie, who was appointed in 1892 as the first Professor of Egyptian Archaeology and Philology in the UK at UCL. Over three-quarters of the material in the Museum comes from excavations directed or funded by Petrie, or from purchases he made for university teaching. In 1880 at the age of 26, Petrie travelled to Egypt to survey the Great Pyramid. For the next five decades he was at the forefront of the development of archaeology in Egypt and later in Palestine, and his detailed methodological approach continues to shape the discipline today.

Petrie worked at more sites, with greater speed, than any modern archaeologist: seeing his life as a mission of rescue archaeology, Petrie aimed to retrieve as much information as possible from sites that were shrinking dramatically in size as Egypt modernised during the late 19th and early 20th centuries. He published a large part, but not all, of the finds from his excavations in his illustrated typological volumes, arranged according to object types and themes. Today, much of the Petrie Museum's collection is displayed and stored in a way which reflects these publications: for example, several storage cupboards are dedicated to the material illustrated in the 'Objects of Daily Use' volume, and objects in the drawers are arranged according to the order of the published plates. This offers a unique opportunity for researchers to engage with Petrie's typological and methodical approach to archaeology, as well as with the history of museum collections.

The first catalogue to be published in the *Modern Egyptology* series was *Amarna: City of Akhenaten and Nefertiti* in 1972 by Julia Samson, Petrie Museum Honorary Research Assistant. As official publishers to the UCL Egyptology Department the series went on to produce facsimile reprints of eight of Flinders Petrie's most important site reports and many of his object catalogues, originally published through the British School of Archaeology in Egypt. The substantial annual royalties from these reprints were paid into the 'Petrie Fund' at the time, which provided special grants to students in financial need.

In many ways, the new reprints of this classic series can be seen as the latest layer in a vast 'publication stratigraphy' of the thousands of finds from Flinders Petrie's excavations, which now live in museum collections around the world. On reading these volumes, I hope that readers will also be inspired to learn more about the Petrie Museum collection and its fascinating history.

Dr Anna Garnett
Petrie Museum of Egyptian and Sudanese Archaeology, University College London
January 2023

Publisher's Preface

Oxbow Books is pleased to present this title in our *Classics in Egyptology* series. This series of facsimile re-issues is comprised of two sub-series. The first consists of 16 typological catalogues produced by W.M. Flinders Petrie based on his massive collection of Egyptian artefacts. Mostly excavated by Petrie during many seasons of campaign in the last years of the 19th and early decades of the 20th century, they now reside in the Petrie Museum at University College London. Published between 1898 and 1937 and long out of print, the catalogues were re-issued in facsimile by publishers Aris and Phillips in the 1970s. These were followed in the next 15 years or so by publication of a number of newly commissioned titles, based on more recent examination of elements of the Petrie Collection by contemporary experts, under the name *Modern Egyptology*. A selection of these additional titles forms the second component of our own series.

The archaeology of Egypt continues to fascinate. Multi-disciplinary investigation and research continues unabated, encompassing methodologies, scientific and data processing techniques, theoretical approaches, and even whole paradigms that were unheard of in the 1970s and undreamt of when Petrie was working in Egypt. Yet all the titles included in this series continue to be invaluable sources of basic data, providing an unparalleled resource that can easily be cross-referenced with the actual materials they describe and discuss. They remain within the Petrie Collection where they may be accessed and re-examined as new research flourishes. As historic documents, the Petrie catalogues stand as exemplars of the craft of typological classification, the backbone of modern archaeology – much of which, though refined by absolute dating and another 100 years of research, still stands the test of time.

A note on presentation

The facsimile titles of Petrie's catalogues re-issued in the 1970s were produced from scans of the original publications. Scanning technology at that time was not of the standard or resolution of today. The scans are no longer available, nor has it been possible to obtain, and in doing so destroy, original copies of the Petrie catalogues. These titles have therefore, of necessity, been rescanned from the 1970s re-issues. Where necessary the pages have been digitally enhanced for clarity of reading and to ensure the good quality of the plates, though inevitably a few are not of the standard we might wish, because of the quality of the previous scan, and occasional blocks of text are not precisely 'straight' or evenly situated on the page. However, some pages in the 1970s re-issues had been inserted in the wrong order and this has been corrected. The originals were produced at a folio size. The pages have been reduced slightly to standard A4 for ease of shelving and because this has the effect of slightly improving the scanned images. In some cases, illustrations were presented to scale and the original scale is given on the plate. There were also no digital files available for titles included in the *Modern Egyptology* series, so these too have been scanned from printed copies.

I

Introduction

The Egyptians have animals always living with them, whilst all other men pass their lives separate from animals.

Herodotus, 450 B.C.

1-1 *Rock drawings of early Nile valley dwellers in Wadi Gash (Qash) 60 km east of Qena. Source: Winkler (1938 i: pl. XIV, 1). On the left is a hippopotamus hunted by men. Other animals are a pariah dog and a crocodile. Above, from left to right, are a pariah dog, an ibex, giraffe, aurochs (?), Barbary goat, elephant, hippopotamus, and a pariah dog.*

All ancient peoples were closely associated with animals, but none illustrated this more spectacularly than the Egyptians.

Depictions of the mammalian fauna of Egypt predate Dynastic art, however, and one must look at prehistoric and predynastic art as the predecessors of some pharaonic Egyptian versions.

We can also see influences in early, as well as in late Egyptian art, from the Assyrian, Babylonian, and Mycenian civilizations. Basically, aside from the carry-overs from the Predynastic, the Egyptians developed an art of their own in depicting animals, which was, except for strictly symbolic, religious, and decorative purposes, much more accurate than contemporaneous art.

Rock drawings (peckings and engravings) and paintings include the oldest representations of Egyptian or northeast African mammals (fig. 1-1). They give us a fairly clear idea about the larger mammals which lived there in Prehistoric times, but they cannot be used for determining the exact limits of distribution of species.

Rock drawings occur in much of the southern two-thirds of the Eastern Desert, the eastern and western borders of the Nile Valley in Upper Egypt, along the Ghubari Road east of Dakhla Oasis, and at Gebel Uweinat and Gilf el Khebir in the southwestern corner of Egypt and adjoining Libya and Sudan. They were created by various groups of early Nile Valley and desert dwellers during the Paleolithic, Neolithic, Pre- and Protodynastic, and well into the Dynasties. Major publications dealing with Egyptian rock art are Winkler (1937, 1938, 1939), Dunbar (1941), Rhotert (1952), Červíček (1974, 1976, 1986), and Leclant and Huard (1980). Goyon (1957) illustrated numerous Dynastic drawings of Egyptian gods and sacred animals in Wadi Hammamat in the Eastern Desert and Redford and Redford (1989) recorded drawings in areas bordering the road between El Laqeita and Bir Hammamat.

Many drawings depict the hunting and capture of animals; therefore, Zarins (1982: 20) and others concluded that the art "served to ensure the success of a hunt, a ritualistic practice common among many ancient societies."

Not only were hunted animals depicted, but also dogs, domestic goats, and cattle, which are pictured and discussed in later chapters.

There is also a hypothesis that certain animal designs on Predynastic funerary pottery would by 'magico-religious' means provide the deceased with a supply of the food in the pots "or at least the meat of the animals depicted" (Hornblower, 1930: 11). A similar belief may explain the purpose of the offering processions in Dynastic tombs, but a totally different interpretation has been given for Dynastic hunting scenes (see below).

Ostrich?
Hyena Dog
Dorcas Gazelle
Hyena Dog

Hyena Dog

2 longnecked Serpopards

Saluki
Soemmering's (?) Gazelle

Ibex, Beisa Oryx

2 Salukis

Hartebbest

2 Dorcas Gazelles

2 'Asian' Lions

Beisa Oryx

Serpopard

Barbary Goat
Leopard

Hyena Dog

Hartebeest

Akheck

Wildebeest

Man disguised

Ibex

Giraffe

Two outstanding pieces of late Predynastic carving set the stage for early Dynastic art: the 'Hierakonpolis', 'Oxford' or 'Hyena Dogs' Palette and the 'Hunters' or 'Lion Hunt' Palette.

The Hierakonpolis Palette (fig. 1-2a,b) was said to be surrounded by two jumping dogs and was called the 'Big Animals Palette' by Asselberghs (1961: 330, pl. LXX). Petrie (1953: 10) called it the 'Two Dogs Palette'. It has also been called the 'Wild Dogs Palette'. The most accurate name is 'Hyena Dogs Palette'.

On this palette twelve kinds of wild animals are shown in action: An ostrich (?), eight species of ungulates, three carnivores, plus saluki hounds, and three different fabulous beasts, along with what was probably supposed to have been a man wearing a fox- or jackal- head mask and tail, who is playing a flute. Legge (1909: 303) said the flute player might be a man in jackal disguise or possibly an ape or monkey. Vandier (1952 I: 582) considered it to be a fox, and Nibbi (1979: 151) called it "a man imitating a wild ass". The fabulous beasts are of Mesopotamian origin. Likewise, the lions are of Asian type with much longer and more extended manes than African lions. Some of the animals that were native to Egypt at that early date, such as the hyena dog (hunting dog), giraffe, and gnu or wildebeest (it is not a buffalo nor an ur) are, with a few exceptions, missing from later scenes of animal life in Egypt.

An amazing aspect of this palette is how so much action and diversity of animals, real and imaginary, symmetrical and naturalistic, were incorporated into such a limited space without creating the ugliness of incongruity. Of course there are conflicting interpretations. Emery (1961: 167) referred to it as a "confused mass of animal life".

Legge (1909: 303) interpreted the scene as having come from the territory of the jackals (to him the hyena dogs were jackals), where the lion is subduing the less warlike tribes represented by the oryx, Barbary goat, etc., and the fabulous beasts of the desert were called upon to assist.

Westendorf (1968: 18 f.) gave a slightly different interpretation: "The palette shows the battle of the animal powers; the attack of the large carnivorous felines and canines on the enemies of the sun, usually represented by various species of antelope". He referred to the snake-necked

1-2a *Obverse of the Hierakonpolis, Oxford or Hyena Dogs Palette of green slate. Provenance: Gebel Ain, Hierakonpolis, Late Gerzean, about 3200 B.C. Actual size: 42x22 cm. Source: Asselberghs (1961: pl. LXX, fig. 127). A pair of hyena dogs (Lycaon pictus) with their forepaws together surmont the palette.*

1-2b *Reverse of the Hierakonpolis Palette. Source: Asselberghs (1961: pl. LXXI, fig. 128).*

panthers (serpopards) stripping off the flesh of a prostrate gazelle, an enemy of the sun, with their rough tongues. The circular depression for grinding cosmetics probably represents the sun.

There is certainly something symbolic about this palette, but, aside from the predation by wild and fabulous beasts, it also includes hunting by humans in the depiction of the flute player disguised as a decoy (Smith, 1969: 312 f.) and, on the obverse, three lop-eared saluki hounds with collars, pursuing the gazelle (red fronted ?), ibex, oryx, and hartebeest.

The Hunters Palette (fig. 1-3) illustrates several possible narrations. Firstly, it depicts two groups of hunters intent on killing two lions and capturing some other animals. Aspects of realism appear where one of the arrow-pierced lions is attacking a hunter, one hunter has lassoed a hartebeest (not a gazelle, as some authors have said), and another hunter in the opposite row is about to throw a lasso at a gazelle.

Legge (1909: 299) suggested this was a scene of war in which almost every animal was engaged, and a defeat of the Lion Tribe.

At one end of the palette there is a "small shrine and a curious double-headed bull, perhaps symbolizing that the hunt is taking place in the IIIrd nome of the Delta" (Aldred, 1965: Ill. 38).

Childe's (1958: 81) interpretation was that the scene took place in the Western Desert and symbolized a victory over the Lybians. The setting could be justified by the lack of mountain species, ibex and Barbary goats, which are present on the Hierakonpolis Palette (fig. 1-2a,b).

Whether or not the long-maned lions on these palettes truly represent the Asian race is questionable. Since both long and short maned lions are depicted during the Predynastic period, those with long manes which were not of Mesopotamian origin either represented long-maned survivors or were the only examples with which the artists were familiar.

On the 'Battlefield Palette' (fig. 1-4a) a battle scene is represented in which the defeated enemies are "being devoured by a lion and birds of prey" (Aldred, 1965: 42, ill.30). Here again the lion has a mane that extends along its belly. The animals for which this palette was named the 'Two Gazelles Palette' (fig. 1-4b), are neither gerenuks nor dibatags, but giraffes. The sloping backs and presence of manes are diagnostic of the giraffe. This palette is definitely Egyptian in origin and was dated to the Late Predynastic, but its provenance is unknown. The similarities between this palette and the palm and two giraffes on the Four Dogs Palette (fig. 1-5a) was discussed by Spinage (1968: 33 f.) who said that one is a copy of the other.

Four hyena dogs dominate the palette in Figure 1-5a,b, which includes a limited number of animals. On the obverse are an ibis, a lion, and a fabulous serpopard. On the reverse a pair of giraffes face a palm tree. Asselberghs (1961: 287), in attempting to decipher the meaning of this palette, concluded that it had some relation to a transition from one period to another and the palm tree was a symbol of peace.

Nevertheless, it indicates that the hyena dog was still well known into the Late Predynastic.

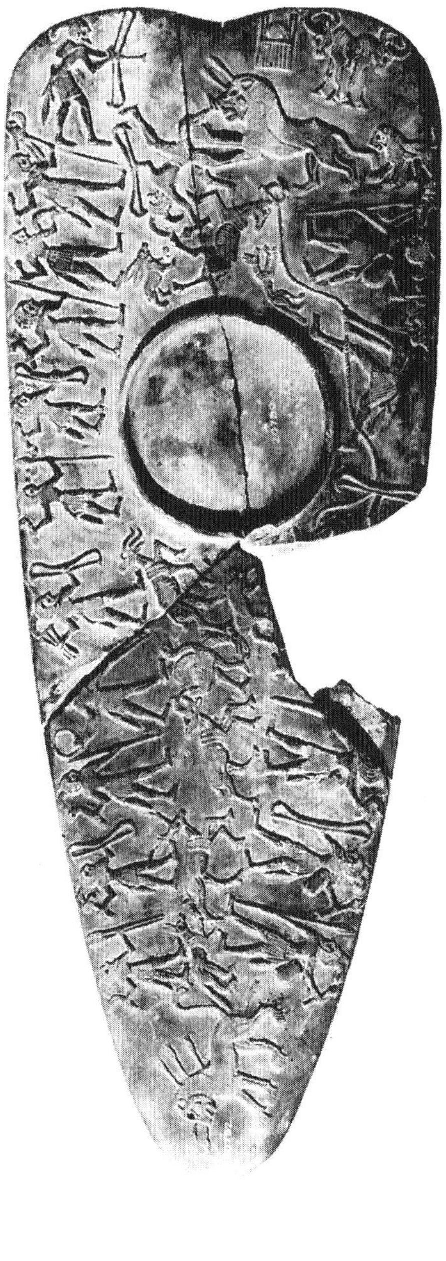

1-3 *Hunters or Lion Hunt Palette. Late Predynastic, provenance unrecorded. Actual length: 62 cm. Source: Spencer (1980: pl. 63, no.575).*

1-4a *Obverse of the 'Battlefield Palette' from the Late Predynastic; provenance not known. Source: Spencer (1980: pl. 64, no. 576). The animals are discussed in the text.*
1-4b *Reverse of the 'Battlefield Palette'. Source: Spencer (1980: pl. 64, no. 576).*

1-5a *Obverse of the 'Four Dogs Palette' from Lower Egypt dated to the Late Gerzean. Source: Asselberghs (1961: pl. LXXII, fig. 129). The animals are discussed in the text.*
1-5b *Reverse of the 'Four Dogs Palette'. Source: Asselberghs (1961: pl. LXXIII, fig. 130).*

A few mammal figures have been found that were produced from flint by pressure flaking, a technique dating from Neolithic times and used for making knives, arrow- and spearheads (Schweinfurth, 1903a: 805). The hippopotamus (fig. 1-6a) is a late Predynastic surface find near Tomb I at Hierakonpolis (Hoffman, 1982: 146, pl.VII,1). The hartebeest, ibex and Barbary goat (figs 1-6b,c,d) came from El Kab, Dynasty V-VI, near Hierakonpolis (Schweinfurth, 1903b: figs 87-89). The poorly pictured pariah dog (fig.1-6e) is from Predynastic Naqada (Petrie, 1920: fig. VII, 2).

Ivory handles of flint knives from the Late Gerzean were sometimes decorated with rows of animals. The best example is the Brooklyn handle from Abu Zaidan, near Edfu (fig. 1-7; Table I), on which the animals were reclassified by Churcher (1984). In addition, he included identifications of others who had examined this artifact.

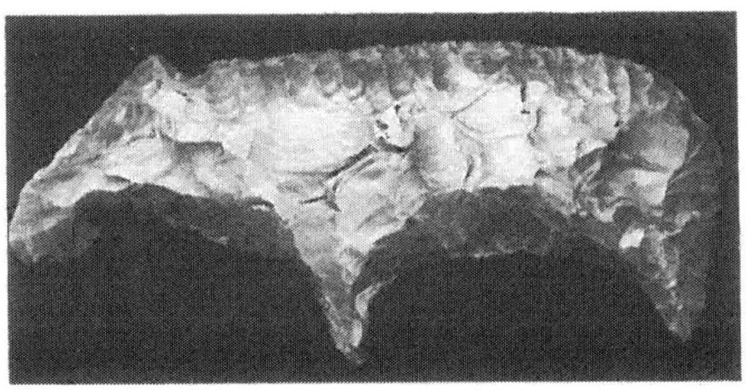

a

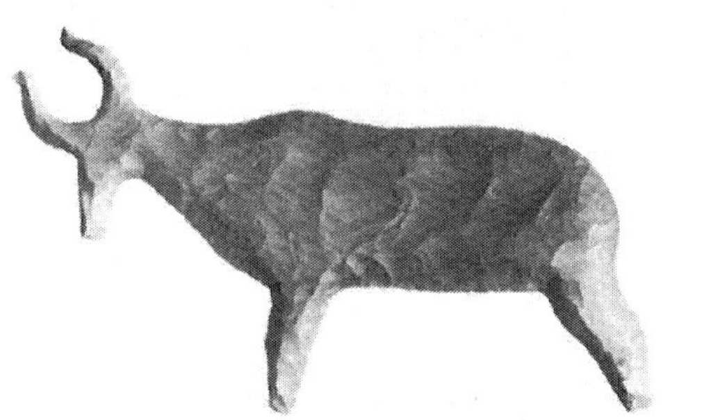

b

c, d, e

1-6a-e *Predynastic and Early Dynastic flint animals produced by pressure flaking: a) hippopotamus, b) hartebeest, c) ibex, d) Barbary goat, e) pariah dog. Notes on provenances and sources are in the text.*

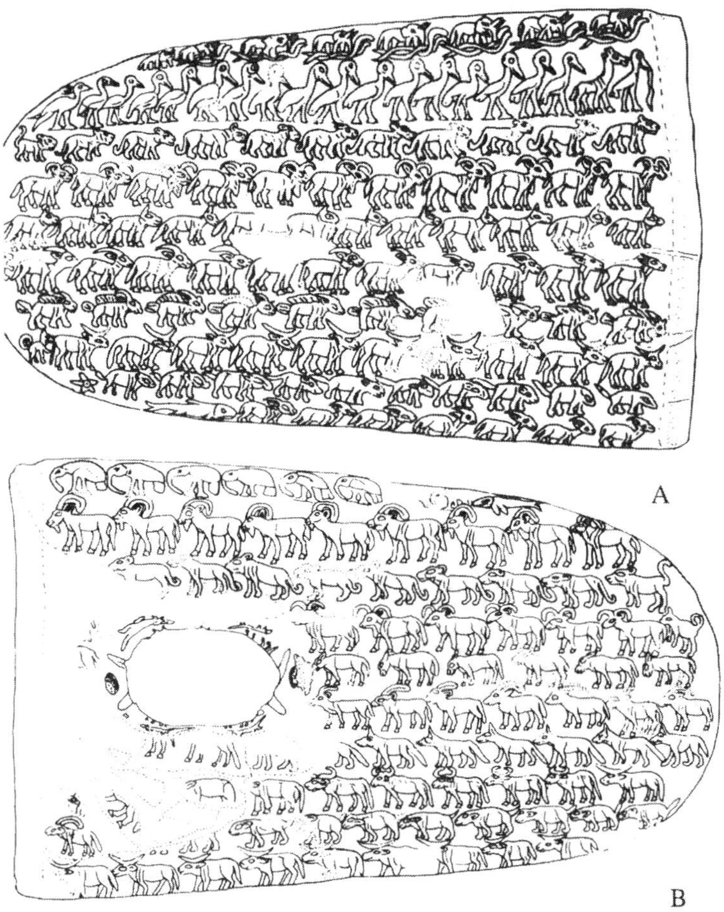

1-7 Brooklyn knife handle of elephant ivory from a burial at Abu Zaidan about 16 km south of Edfu (Idfu) and dated by Needler (1984: 124 ff.) to Naqada III, about 3200-3000 B.C. Actual size is 98x58x12 cm. Source: The Brooklyn Museum, N.Y. See Table 1 for identifications.

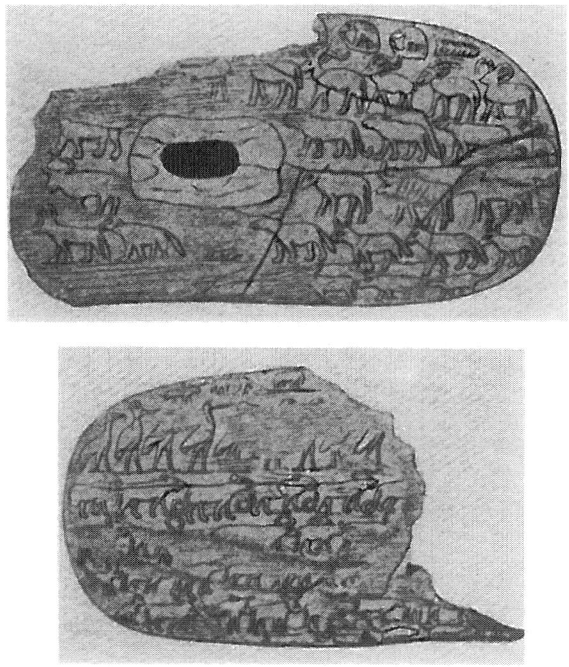

1-8 Pitt Rivers ivory knife handle of Late Gerzean origin from Sohag. Source: Bénédite (1918: fig. 1). Animals are listed from left to right.

Obverse (top): Row 1: Elephants on snakes and a fish (?); Row 2: Two partly destroyed bovids, dama deer, dorcas gazelle, scimitar oryx, and Barbary goat; Row 3: Four leopards and a saluki hound; Row 4: Four aurochs and a fish (?); Row 5: Six jackals; Row 6: Two aurochs and a saluki hound.

Reverse (bottom): Row 1: A long-horned aurochs and two elephants; Row 2: Secretary bird, crowned crane, seven maribou storks; Row 3: Six lionesses; Row 4: Five short-horned cattle; Row 5: Six jackals; Row 6: A saluki hound (?) and six aurochs; Row 7: A line of ratels.

A few of Churcher's comments are worth repeating, because they indicate the difficulties of modern interpretation of these ancient artifacts: "The significance of the isolated faunal elements (giraffe, secretary bird, fish, and pendent serpent) is unclear, as is the reason for selecting the animals shown from the then available fauna .... The faunal sample illustrated on the knife handle therefore represents local faunal elements, including probably domesticated cattle and dogs and possibly domesticated oryx and Barbary sheep" (*op. cit.*, 166). The common dorcas gazelle and hartebeest are missing.

Other handles, known as the Pitt Rivers (fig. 1-8) and Carnarvon (fig. 1-9), plus the Davis Ivory Comb (fig. 1-10) , "... all show to some extent the species and arrangement of animals observed on the Brooklyn knife handle ..." (*op. cit.*, 167).

There are contradictory opinions on the significance of these handles. Hayes (1953 I: 28) said, "The motif is clearly more than mere decoration, and it has been suggested that the animals were totems or emblems of a confederation of prehistoric Egyptian clans or districts to which the owners of the ivories belonged."

Edwards (1955:1061), in a special discussion of the Pitt Rivers handle, discarded a popular theory that animals on knife handles symbolized a confederation of clans, and wrote: "If, as it seems likely, the knife came from a tomb, perhaps, by a processs of imitative magic, it was intended to provide its owner with a plentiful supply of game and a ready quarry in his life after death. It would thus represent the beginning of a development which reached its zenith some centuries later when the nobles decorated their tombs with elaborate scenes of hunting and fowling which were considered to possess these magical properties."

Two other knife handles of Late Gerzean origin show features common to Mesopotamia. The Gebel el Arak (Araq) handle (fig. 1-11) was described by Aldred (1965: 34, ills. 23, 24) as having "a distinctly alien appearance." The upper boats on the obverse, he said are like those of the Tigris, but the lower ones look like Egyptian boats of Gerzean date. One has an ibex head on the prow. On the other side, below the boss, is what appears to be a hunting scene. Above the boss, Onuris the god of This, who resembles Gilgamesh, the Mesopotamian 'Lord of the Beasts,' is subduing

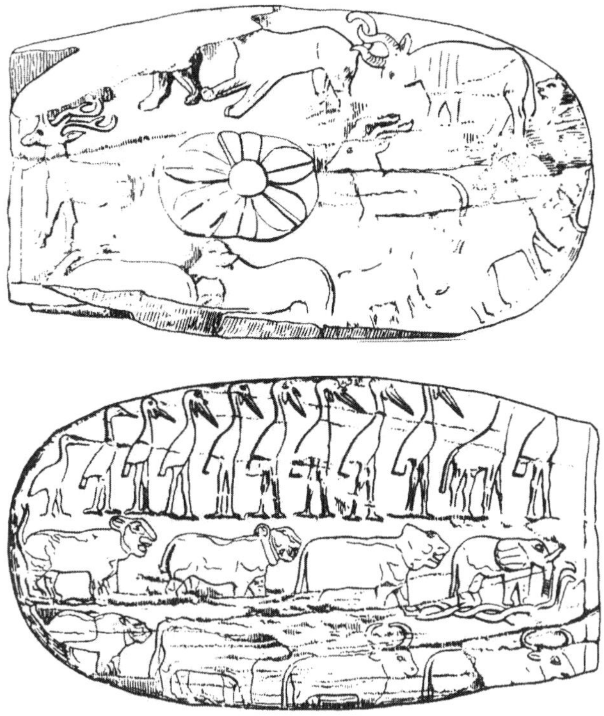

1-9 *Carnarvon ivory knife handle from the Late Gerzean. Provenance unknown. Source: Asselberghs (1961:104, fig. 17).*
On the side with the boss, the first animal in the upper row might be a bear, because the legs are short and stout. It has been called a bovid represented by hoofs, but the feet are certainly not hoof-like. Behind are a headless pariah dog, a lyre-horned aurochs, and another dog. To the left and right of the boss are dama deer. The third row includes a scimitar oryx attacked by a dog and behind them an unidentifiable bovid and a beisa oryx (?).
On the side without boss, there is a heron (?) and a row of nine storks with a giraffe. In the second row are three lions and an elephant treading on intertwined serpents. In the third row a lion follows three aurochs.

two long-maned lions. A similar figure appears in the Hierakonpolis wall paintings (fig. 7-197).

Asselberghs (1961: 261, 277) assumed that this handle and the Gebel el Tarif handle (fig. 1-12) may have been trade items from Mesopotamia, because both show features common to that region. The latter pictures various Mesopotamian mammals. The attack from the rear was, according to Asselberghs (*op. cit.*), typical of Mesopotamian art, and likewise, the intertwined snakes on the reverse side (*loc. cit.*, pl. XXXIII).

Another combination of animals similar to the above examples is on a Dynasty I gold mace handle (fig. 1-13). Some of them are difficult to identify; particularly the hyena. One animal is present that appears nowhere else in Predynastic or Dynastic art, the eland.

Amulets and so-called ivory wands were another source of variation in animal forms. Amulets were believed to protect houses, tombs, temples, those who wore them, and the mummies on which they were placed, from evil spirits and

1-10 *Davis ivory comb of Late Gerzean origin. Provenance unknown. Source: Asselberghs (1961: fig. 14).*
Top row: elephants on snakes. Second row: storks apparently holding snakes followed by giraffes, three more storks, and a heron or crane. Third row: a pariah dog and three lions on one side; four hyenas on the other side. Fourth row: four scimitar oryx, the first with short horns, on one side; four longhorn aurochs on the other. Fifth row: a star and four ratels on one side; four ratels on the other side.

1-11 *Gebel el Arak ivory knife handle of Late Gerzean origin from near Abydos. Source: Bénédite (1918: pl. XXXII).*
Figures are a man dompting two Asian lions, two pariah dogs facing each other over the boss, a hartebeest (?), and an ibex on opposite sides of the boss, an ibex behind a lioness that is attacking an aurochs bull, and a leashed pariah dog behind another bovid.

1-12 *Gebel el Tarif ivory knife handle of Late Gerzean origin from near Abydos. Source: de Morgan (1896: fig. 136). Animals represented are a leopard and another felid (?) attacking a deer, an Asian lion attacking an Arabian oryx, a bear attacked by a pariah dog; an akhekh, and an ibex. The horns of the ibex are in typical Mesopotamian style.*

1-13 *Copy of animals on a Dynasty I gold mace handle from Seiyala ruins west bank of the Nile in Nubia. Source: Firth (1927b: 205, fig. 8).*

dangerous animals, such as scorpions, snakes, and savage beasts.

Amulets of animals or their heads were also worn with the hopes of absorbing the courage, strength, cunning, swiftness, or vision of the original.

Knife-shaped ivory wands (fig. 1-14) were placed around or under beds and also used to draw magic circles on the floor to prevent harmful creatures from reaching a dead or sleeping person.

"The fact that the points of the knives are often worn away on one side suggests that they were used repeatedly to draw circles around the living and sleeping places of their owners to render them safe" (Hayes, 1953 I:249). Animals, both real and fantastic, and various symbols can be recognized on the wands in Figure 1-14 a-g) , which are from left to right as follows:

a) Fox head; Buto, cobra goddess; Taurt, hippopotamus goddess and ?; lion spewing fire on victims; Buto with wings; Sa emblem; god Set; and ?.

b) Leopard attacking a prisoner; snake ?; winged leopard with human head on its back; ? holding two hares; Taurt; lion biting a snake ; ? with snakes on legs and arms; serpopard; snake; and fox head.

c) Leopard; winged leopard with a hawk's head; three braziers and a serpopard; lion biting a snake; ? with snakes on legs and arms; part of Taurt; part of a crocodile.

d) Lion sitting; part of a snake and crocodile; wild cat biting a snake; two Sas and symbol of rule; double Sphinx with human heads with ram horns and ostrich plumes; Heket, frog goddess; and a tortoise.

e) Fox head; Heket; double Sphinx with human heads, snake above, cat below; Taurt; ? with snakes; Taurt, snakes above; and rear half of a cat.

f) Buto; symbol of power; serpopard; brazier; Nekhebet, vulture goddess holding a scepter; brazier; winged leopard with a hawk's head and a human head between the wings; symbol of power; rear half of a leopard and a snake above.

g) Crocodile; ? ; serpopard; mythological beast; lion ?; symbol of power; Taurt; and ?.

For further interpretation of the symbols on these ivories see Hayes (1953 I: 249).

An interesting feature common to rock art, pottery (fig. 1-15), flint flaking, palettes, ivories, and Dynastic reliefs and paintings is the style of showing the horns of certain species, such as Barbary goat, hartebeest, cattle, domestic screw-horned sheep, and often goats, in frontal view, whereas the heads are, with a few exceptions, always in profile.

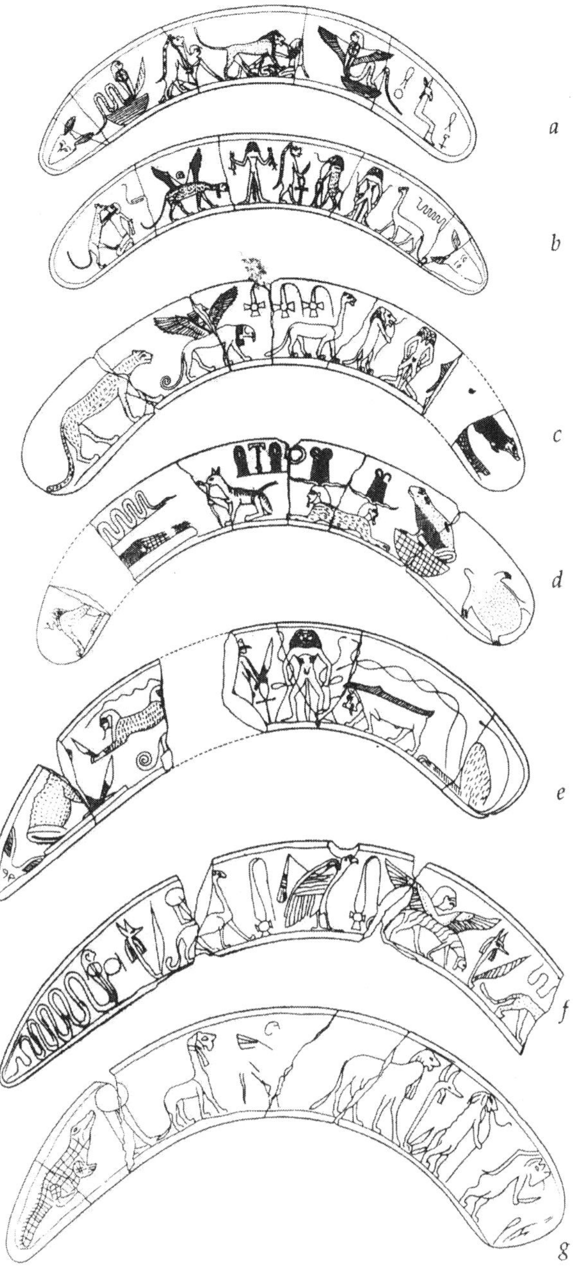

1-14a-g Magic ivory wands used for protection from dangerous creatures and evil spirits. Dynasty XII, El Lisht. Source: Metropolitan Museum of Art, N.Y. The animals and figures are listed in the text.

1-15 A Barbary goat and an ibex on Predynastic white cross-lined pottery. Source: Petrie (1920: pl. XVIII, 73).

Both horns of oryx, ibex, and dorcas gazelles were shown in profile and more or less parallel while the stylization of early Dynastic art developed. From the late Middle Kingdoms single horns in profile were depicted. The horns of domestic goats, however, continued to be shown in frontal view or in parallel.

Horns are most important in identification and extreme stylizations developed for species of gazelles, hartebeest, and ibex.

During the Dynasties we find a great number of mammal figures in the forms of gods and goddesses, sacred animals, and fetishes molded from clay and faience (porcelain), and carved from clay, ivory, stone, wood, and bronze. The outstanding representations are those depicted in reliefs and murals. Therein we can trace from the earliest Dynasties particular styles that continued into the Ptolemaic Period.

Four major themes that were repeated in the decorated tombs of the Dynasties included the majority of mammals commonly known to them or brought from foreign lands. These are the so-called hunt scenes, trophies of the hunt, offering processions, and tribute scenes. In addition, we can observe many wild mammals, particularly of the horned varieties, being fattened (fig. 1-16).

Animals that were fed and fattened in a state of semi-domestication and led or carried as offerings were usually indicated with the hieroglyph [hieroglyph] *rn* (ren) followed or preceded by their names (fig. 1-16).

Griffith (1892: 38) said that this inscription above an oryx being brought as an offering meant, perhaps, "stall fed" and Bissing (1905 I: 25) translated it as meaning "young". Paton (1925: 23) called a hyena in a fattening scene, "stable reared", which is synonymous with stall fed.

Simpson (1976b: 11, pl. D) translated *rn* as "young" for the obviously adult bovids and cervid in an offering procession. Badawy (1978: 27, fig. 35) did the same for a large, longhorn aurochs, a long-horned scimitar oryx, and an oversized female gazelle suckling its foal. Moussa and Altenmüller (1977: 161 f., pls. 82-85) and also Badawy (1978) referred to all animals labelled *rn* as "young".

James (1953: 61) and Vachala (1987: 91) commented that the exact meaning of *rn*, whether "young animal" or "well fed", was not settled. Boessneck (1988: 44) considered it to mean "fattened".

The interpretation of *rn* in *Wb*.II, 429 is "young (of an animal)". Animals that are labeled *rn* are not strictly young animals, however, but adults that had doubtless been tamed and fed in captivity when young and, in some cases, really fattened for offerings and human consumption (fig. 1-16).

1-16 A row of bovids picketed and fed in the Mastaba of Mereruka, Dynasty VI, Saqqara. Source: Osborn (1977). The animals are (left to right) dorcas gazelle, Nubian ibex, addax, hartebeest (bubal), and scimitar oryx. Above each animal the name in hieroglyphs, not always correct, is followed by the sign rn.

1-17 Donkeys pressing grain in the Tomb of Ti, Dynasty V, Saqqara. Source: Wild (1966 III: pl. CXXXVIII B).

Agricultural portrayals (fig. 1-17) provide us with much information about the domesticated animals that furnished the Egyptians with many products as well as special assistance. There are also many portrayals of pet animals that provided entertainment: wild and domesticated cats, cheetahs, lions, dogs, monkeys, ibex, and gazelles, which appear in appropriate chapters.

The standard hunt scene portrays the deceased tomb owner in exaggerated size shooting arrows from behind a stockade or net at wildly leaping game being chased and attacked by hounds (fig. 1-18).

Within the hunt scenes expressiveness and realism gradually developed. According to a rule established in the Old Kingdom, walking animals and humans were always pictured advancing "that foot or arm which is the further from the spectator ..." (Erman, 1894: 400). In contrast to standing or walking, Old Kingdom artists conceived a posture to represent running. The front and hind feet were depicted together and extending forward and backward, although remaining solidly on the ground. Undulations of the ground line also helped to give some impression of movement (fig. 1-19).

Edgerton (1936: 185) observed: "Not until the Middle Kingdom do we meet with a perfectly unambiguous example of a running animal with two feet off the ground". A pair of hartebeest have their forefeet raised and a hare is coming down on both front feet, in a Dynasty XII hunting scene (fig. 1-20a, b) .

By the XVIIIth Dynasty some animals were depicted with all four feet outstretched and off the ground (figs 1-18,-21). Edgerton (*op. cit.*,188, fig. 3) concluded that this posture, "The flying gallop is not an imaginary but a real posture". He did not think it was borrowed from Cretan art as Kantor (1947: 156) and others have assumed, because it appeared to have developed independently numerous times in Oriental art.

One truly independent rendition of the flying gallop, or "flying leap" as it was called later by Groenewegen-Frankfort (1951: 84), is in a predynastic rock drawing at Gebel Uweinat (fig. 1-22).

A well-known example of the so-called flying gallop is in the Dynasty XVIII Tomb of Puyemre (fig. 1-23) along with another posture described by Kantor (*op. cit.*, 156) as the "reverse twist". The history of this much discussed manner of depicting swift action was summarized by Smith (1958: 155), who also discussed changes in the depictions of landscapes in the hunt scenes.

1-18. *A hunting scene in the Tomb of Amenemhet, Dynasty XVIII, Thebes, Sheikh Abd el Gurnah. Source: Wreszinski (1923 I: 53b).*
Behind the king two men are carrying a live striped hyena trussed on a pole. One of them holds a live hare in his hand. Below, another man carries a live hare and a young ibex, which has its horns carved in reverse. Below the king another man holds a saluki hound on a leash.
Animals of the hunt:
Register 1: A female and male striped hyenas; below, a dorcas gazelle on its knees; a Soemmering's gazelle (?), a hare, and a beardless ibex; a saluki hound grasping the throat of a Loder's gazelle; and another beardless ibex.
Register 2: A jackal leaps beside an ibex that is grasped by a saluki hound; another saluki is on the back of a bearded dorcas gazelle; below, a hyena lies on its back; and next a hare leaps above two hornless ungulates with differing tail lengths, one of which is attacked by a saluki hound. The animal with the longer tail could be a deer without antlers and the other might be an imported female Persian goitered gazelle.
Register 3: A saluki chases a fox and an oversized hedgehog calmly eats an insect. Below are an aurochs bull and two cows. The bull is attacked by a saluki hound.
Register 4: A saluki hound grasps one of three ostriches, which look more like swans, and another saluki grasps the nose of a beisa oryx, behind which is a somersaulting dorcas gazelle (with a beard) above a hiding hare. On the right a fox sits on a hillock and another peers out of its den.

The flying gallop became the commonly depicted gait of chariot horses (Frontispiece), but it is a totally false impression, because the only time most animals assume such a posture is when leaping over an obstacle or across a space (e.g., horses and greyhounds in hurdle races).

The only wild mammals known to the Egyptians that normally leaped or bound with all four legs extended and feet off the ground were hares and gazelles. Examples can be found in many hunting scenes, but perhaps the only true example is the hare (fig. 1-20b).

Animals on the Hierakonpolis and Hunters Palettes (figs 1-2,-3) are shown with legs bent, a foot

1-19 *(above) Impression of movement, represented by a 'galloping' hartebeest grabbed by a greyhound. Tomb of Antefoker, Dynasty XII, Thebes. Source: Davies and Gardiner (1920: Frontispiece and pl. VI).*

a

b

1-20a,b *Hartebeest (a) and hare (b) in true galloping postures with two feet off the ground. Tomb of Senbi, Dynasty XII, Meir (Mir). Source: Blackman (1914 I: pls. VII and VIII).*

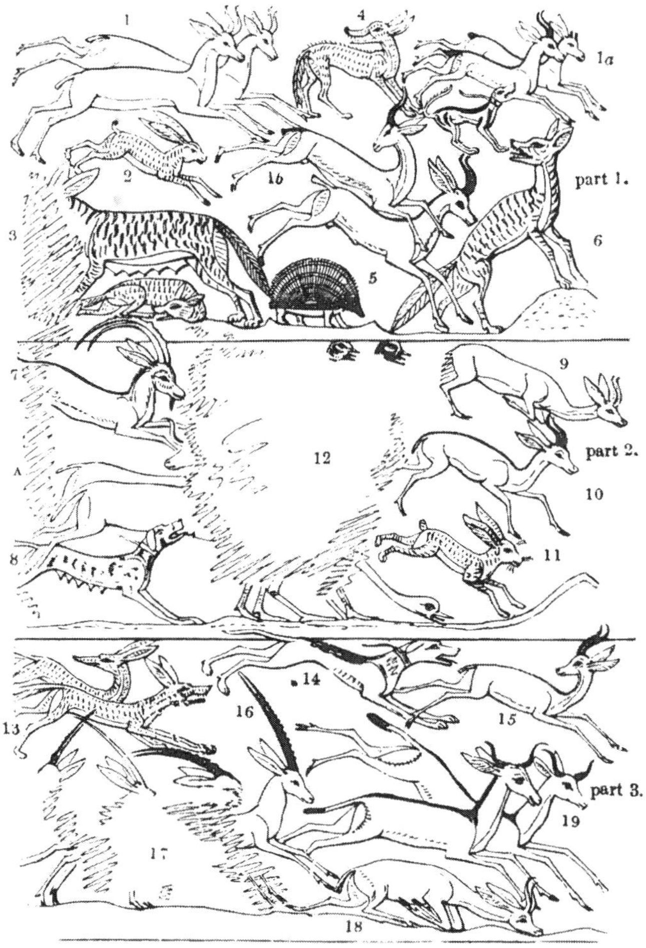

1-21 A desert hunt in a Theban Tomb, Dynasty XVIII. The hunter in a chariot on the left was defaced. Source: Wilkinson (1878 II: 92, No. 357). Animals are listed by numbers: Dorcas gazelles 1, 1a, 1b, 9, 10, 15, 18; hares 2, 11; female hyena with young 3; foxes 4, 13; hedgehog 5; hyena 6; ibex 7; saluki hounds 1a, 8, 14; ostriches 12A (defaced); beisa oryx 16, 17; hartebeest 12A (partly defaced), hartebeest 19.

1-22 Rock drawing of a hunting scene in Karkur Tahl, Gebel Uweinat, showing a Barbary goat and pariah dogs in 'flying gallop' or 'flying leap'. Source: Rhotert (1952: pl. XII, 7).

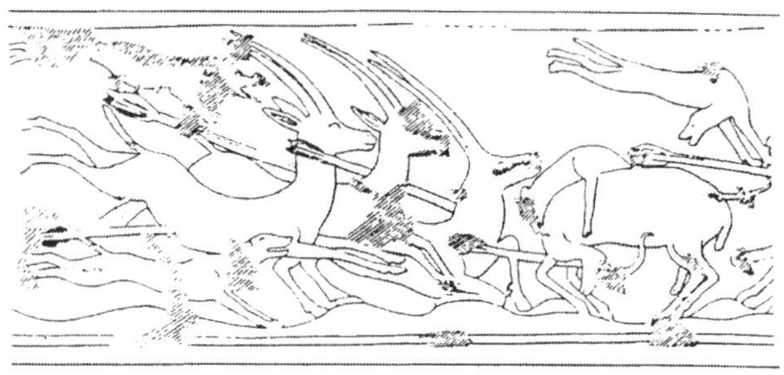

1-23 Saluki hounds and oryx (left) in the flying gallop pose and a saluki in the upper right in the reverse twist. Tomb of Puyemre, Dynasty XVIII, Thebes. Source: Davies (1922: pl. VII).

raised, and in various positions of movement. Several have their heads turned in realistic "reverse twist" positions.

Portrayals of the 'hunt' indicate that the game was either captured and released or driven into enclosures at intervals for the pleasure of the 'hunters'. The conglomerations of species are evidence of this. Predators are portrayed together with prey species. Many species that would normally not be seen together, such as ibex of the mountains are running together with typical plains species, oryx and gazelles, along with savanna hartebeest and wild cattle; all in combination with nocturnal hyenas and an oversized hedgehog walking calmly in the midst of the confusion (figs 1-18,-21). In some scenes animals are hiding (figs 7-69,-125). Contrastingly, there are many hunting scenes in which animals are mating (figs 1-29, 13-41), giving birth (figs 1-30, 4-29, 7-29,-38, 12-5), and suckling young (figs 7-27,-29).

Methods of capturing animals alive are not commonly shown, but we know that the bola (figs 1-3, 7-29), lasso (figs 13-30,-34), leg snare or spiked wheel trap (fig. 12-4), and nets (figs 7-38, 13-78) were used, and probably the cage trap (fig. 7-218).

Generally the significance of the hunt is interpreted to be a display of the power and accuracy of the deceased and to provide the tomb owner with similar experiences in his afterlife. Westendorf (1968: 122) offered a mythological or religious meaning: "Over and beyond reality, slaying the animals of the desert signified to the Egyptians the victory over evil and hostile powers".

Montet (1958: 76 f.) evaluated desert hunts, not as major sources of food, but as a pastime for the wealthy, and a sacrifice of wild animals as a reminder of the past. (Copied from Darby *et al.*, 1977 I: 230).

Following the hunt scene there is usually a panel in which the trophies of the hunt are

1-24 Hunting scene and trophies of the hunt in the Tomb of Neferhotep, Dynasty XVIII, Thebes. Source: Keimer (1940: pl.III).
Animals of the hunt:
Register 1: An aurochs bull, cow, and calf (above); a hyena attacked by a saluki hound; and a short tailed cat, Felis chaus *(above).*
Register 2: Two saluki hounds and four beisa oryx, three hartebeest, and an ostrich attacked by a saluki.
Register 3: A lop-eared mastiff that has been called a hyena with pendant ears, a jackal attacked by a saluki hound, a saluki attacking one of four gazelles, another lop-eared canid pierced by an arrow, and an ichneumon (?) crouched on a hillock.
Register 4: Two hartebeests standing and two galloping, one of which is bitten on the stomach by a saluki; two other bovids with horns missing, the short tail on the near one indicates it is a gazelle; and below, a falling ostrich with an arrow in its neck.
Trophies of the hunt:
Register 1: A man carrying a young oryx, identifiable from a gazelle by the long tail; a beisa oryx with a short tail; an animal with dark pelage and horns destroyed is probably a hartebeest, said by Cailliaud (1831) to perhaps be a dama deer; and a beisa oryx with a normal tail.
Register 2: An ostrich, plumes and eggs; a striped hyena suspended from a pole; and a beisa oryx.
On the left of registers, with the hunters, are two saluki hounds on leashes.

displayed (fig. 1-24). This is a procession including animals on leashes or controlled by hand and some carried over men's shoulders or lashed to poles carried between two men (figs 1-18; 7-159). Primarily, these are symbolic scenes, because no wild animals, except those that were bound could have been carried and led or handled in such a manner. Animals being led or freely carried, if these were true scenes from life, would have been substitutes from previous captures that had been tamed or semi-domesticated.

In offering processions men or women are pictured carrying various foods or other gifts and leading or sometimes carrying animals. In many of these processions the mammals are dwarfed (fig. 1-25). This has led some Egyptologists to believe that dwarf animals were actually developed and bred in Ancient Egypt. Murray (1905 I: 13 f.) was

1-25 *Offering procession with dwarfed animals in the Tomb of Ptah-hetep II, Dynasty V, Saqqara. Source: Murray (1905: pl. XII). A dwarfed calf and a goose of normal size are carried. On leashes are dwarfed ibex, scimitar oryx, dorcas gazelle, and a calf.*

convinced that these small figures of adult animals were truly special breeds of dwarf or 'toy' animals developed for the pleasure of wealthy Egyptians.

Aside from the bones of a dwarf goat from Gerzean middens at Toukh (Lortet and Gaillard, 1905: 282), there is little evidence that Egyptians were familiar with dwarf animals or ever produced them (see *The Dynastic period* in Domestic Goat chapter). The short-legged (brachymely) dogs in Figures 7-52,-53 cannot be considered as dwarfs. Human dwarfs, however, were very popular as caretakers of pet animals (figs 4-33,-34,-35).

Why then were such portrayals made? This is a difficult question to answer. One cannot simply say it was irresponsible use of artists licence for the sake of effect, because some effect was apparently purposely planned. The only evident effect is exaggeration of the bearers of gifts and animal attendants in order to signify their importance ... "and allows them to carry other offerings and still have control of the animal ... or young animals given adult characteristics to emphasize their identities". (Hobbs, 1980: 83).

In one of these offering processions in the Mastaba of Kagemni (Gemni-kai) dwarfed animals are in pairs in which two heads, doubled horns, and four front legs are shown. But in most cases only one pair of hind legs is depicted. This can be seen in a portion of the scene reproduced in Figure 13-213.

Tribute bearers from foreign lands brought ivory, skins, food animals, and exotic animals, including giraffes, baboons, monkeys, elephants, bears, Syrian ibex, and Arabian oryx. Some animals that were extant in Egypt, such as lions, leopards, and cheetahs, were sometimes included (fig. 1-26), because if tamed they were highly prized by Pharaohs and other men of means (Naville, 1894: 25).

Other sources for mammals that were known to the Ancient Egyptians are the dramatic scenes of marsh life showing not only the hunting of birds and fishing, but also various small carnivores climbing papyrus stems and raiding birds' nests

1-26 *Part of a tribute procession of Nubians including a gazelle, a longhorn cow with one horn deformed, a beisa oryx, a genet skin (?), and a lion. Temple of Ramses II, Dynasty XIX, Beit el Wali. Source: Ricke et al. (1967: pl. 7).*

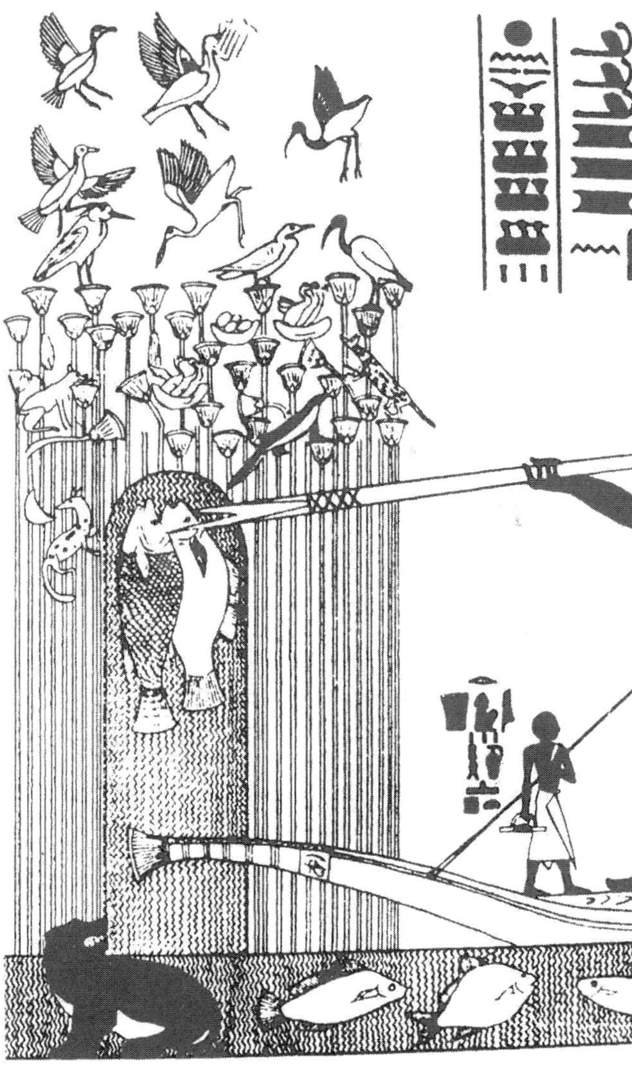

1-27 *Part of a fishing, fowling, and hunting scene in the Tomb of Chnemhotep, Dynasty XII, Beni Hasan. Source: Newberry (1893 I: pl. XXXIV). The mammals include a wild cat, two genets, an ichneumon, and a hippopotamus.*

(fig. 1-27). In some scenes, according to Montet's (1964: 118) interpretation, civets, mongooses, and wild cats were released from cages and would climb the stalks. "When they reached the nests, the parent birds went for them with their beaks and claws, but at the same time became an easy target for the hunters". In the water, the mighty male hippopotamus (fig. 1-28) was harpooned without religious scruples, "... and men of rank of all times liked to have representations of hippopotamus hunting in their tombs" (Erman, 1894: 240).

The greatest variation of animals in hunt scenes appears in the Beni Hasan Tombs of Baqt (fig. 1-29) and Chnemhotep (figs 1-30,-31). Janssen (1990: 47), in reference to these scenes, and to the canids in particular, said they "are too unreliable in their details, and contain fabulous figures".

Nevertheless, the majority of the animals in the Tomb of Baqt (fig. 1-29) can be identified and names in hieroglyphics are above most of them. The list begins from the upper left and continues from left to right. Additional illustrations and discussions on identifications are presented in later chapters.

Copies of the hunt scene in the Tomb of Chnemhotep by Newberry (fig. 1-30) and Lepsius (fig. 1-31) show some obvious discrepancies. Legs are longer in Figure 1-30 and there are numerous variations in horns and lengths and shapes of tails.

On the left side of Figure 1-30, behind and between the bowmen, there are several aurochs, a lop-eared saluki hound, a jerboa (fig. 7-39), and a pair of beisa oryx, which are not shown in Figure 1-31.

Comparison of the two reproductions can be made from the following animals listed from left to right in the four registers.

Register 1: Genet, fox ?, cheetah or leopard (longer neck in Newberry, but broken spots in Lepsius), hedgehog (head drawn correctly in Newberry), chimera, jerboa, serval, hare.

Register 2: Greyhound sniffing at a young hartebeest (horns lacking in Newberry; tail short), two adult hartebeests, male lion, aurochs, three dorcas gazelles (tail lengths varying).

Register 3: Two lynxes (variation in postures and tail lengths), fox or genet (?), hyena (?), long-tailed dorcas gazelle giving birth, hedgehog, genet (?).

Register 4: Greyhounds grasping legs of beisa oryx and of one of two ibex (tails longer, horns double, and a leg missing in Lepsius), fox (tail fox-like in Newberry), beisa oryx foaling (horns straight in Newberry, slightly curved and longer in Lepsius), beisa oryx held by a man (tail short in Newberry, long in Lepsius).

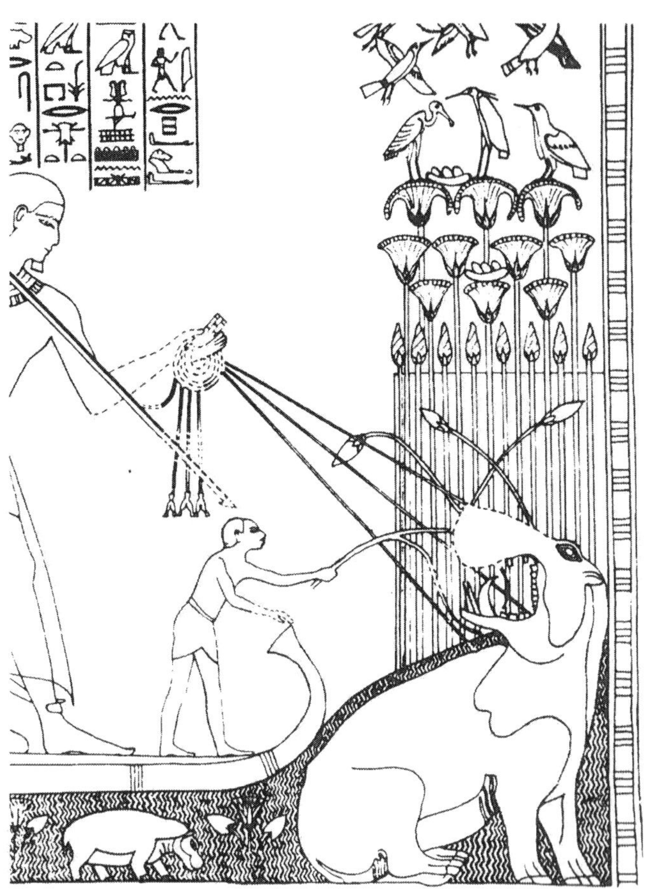

1-28 A hippopotamus hunt in the Tomb of Antef, Dynasty XVIII, Thebes. Source: Säve-Söderbergh (1957: pl. XIV B).

In the Tomb of Amenemhat (fig. 1-32) all animals have exceptionally long legs and some are named with uncertainty.

They are: (A bowman), greyhound, two hartebeests, dorcas gazelle, leopard knocking down a hartebeest, Barbary goat outside the net, hartebeest, two dorcas gazelles, beardless ibex with a long tail, beisa oryx and hare outside the net, (bowmen), hartebeest, dorcas gazelle, ibex outside the net, (two hunters), greyhound, lassoed aurochs, hartebeest outside the net, beisa oryx, fox, gazelle outside the net, cheetah, dorcas gazelle, beisa oryx outside the net, and a roan antelope.

The few photographs from these Beni Hasan tombs that were reproduced by Hobbs (1980: figs 15, 16, 18, 29, 32), although they were indicative of the extremely poor condition of the paintings, did reveal that Newberry's copies were more accurate representations of the originals than those of Lepsius. Additional errors and discrepancies appear between the Newberry and Lepsius copies of a part of the offering scene in the Beni Hasan Tomb of Chnemhotep (figs 1-30,-31).These could be clarified with photographs or additional copies.

In Figure 1-33 the hieroglyphs for *rn ghs'* indicate that a 'stall fed' gazelle is being brought

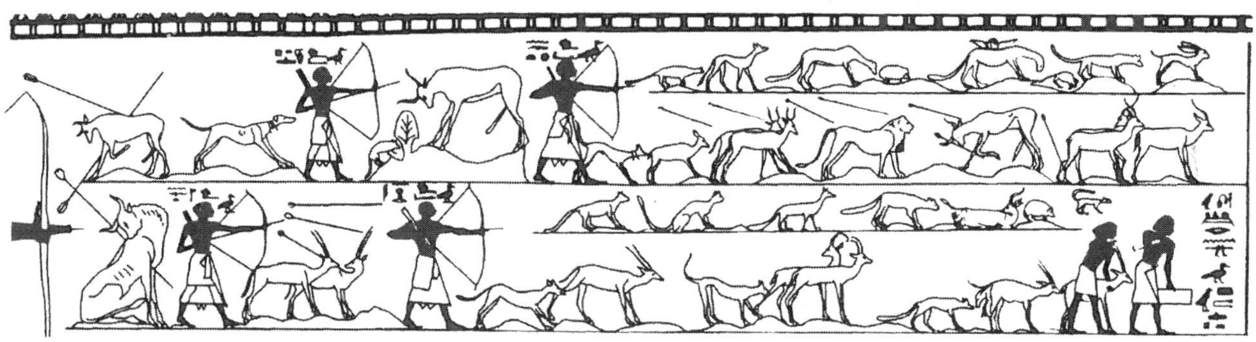

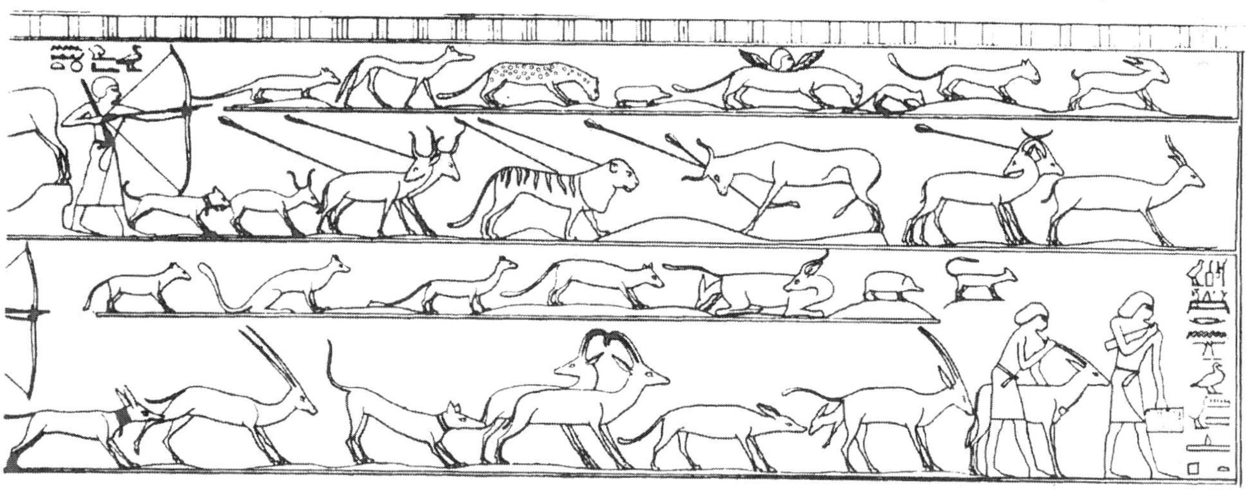

1-29 *(top) A hunting scene in the* ***Tomb of Baqt, Dynasty XII, Beni Hasan****. Source: Newberry (1893 II: pl. IV). The animals are discussed in the text. The animals are: (top) Dorcas* ***gazelle, beisa oryx mating,*** *lioness subduing an ibex, unicorn (?), serpopard, Akhekh, Seth, (a bowman), tesem hound, aurochs with an arrow in its neck, leopard, (centre) two roan antelopes, two dama deer, (a bowman), hare, tesem hound, three hartebeests, two lionesses, two foxes, (bottom) two jackals, two Barbary goats, (a bowman), a man with a bola on an aurochs, lioness, ostrich, two oryx, a young dorcas gazelle and three adults.*

1-30 *(centre) A hunting scene in the Tomb of Chnemhotep, Dynasty XII, Beni Hasan. Source: Newberry (1893 I: pl. XXX). The animals are discussed in the text.*

1-31 *(bottom) A hunting scene in the Tomb of Chnemhotep, Dynasty XII, Beni Hasan. Source: L.D. II, pl. 131. The animals are discussed in the text.*

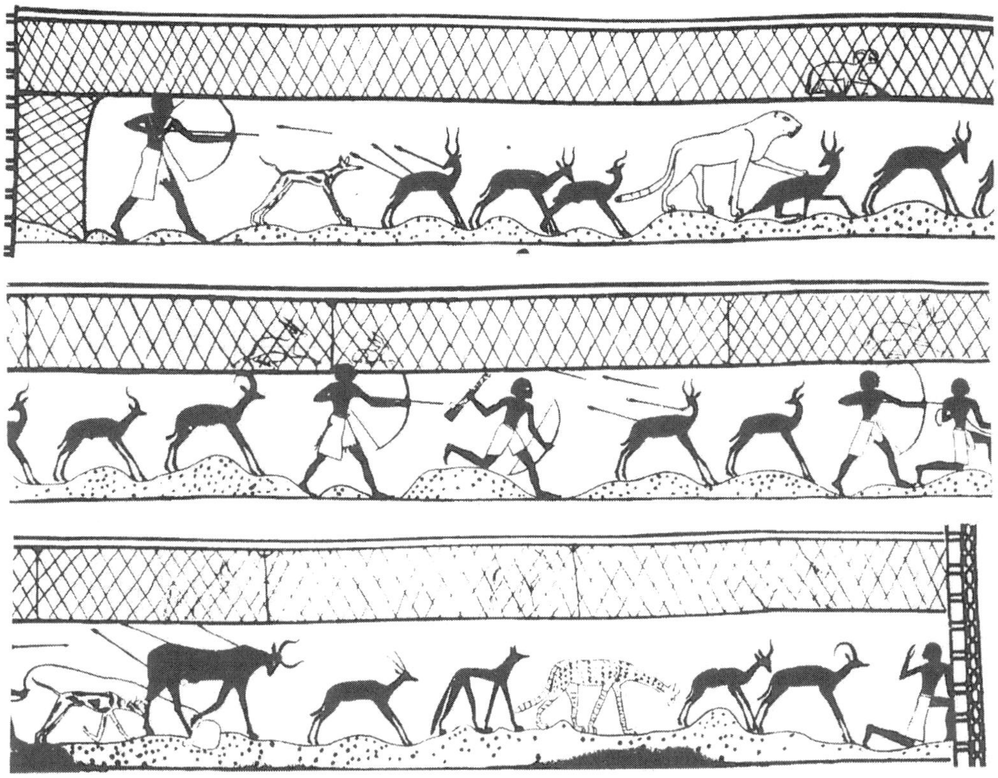

1-32 *A hunting scene in the Tomb of Amenemhat, Dynasty XII, Beni Hasan. Source: Newberry (1893 I: pl. XIII). The animals are discussed in the text.*

forward. Judging from the relatively straight horns it is a Loder's gazelle.

In Lepsius' copy (fig. 1-34), instead of a gazelle, there is a beardless ibex held on a short leash. The leash is missing in Figure 1-33.

The ibex (left) in Figure 1-35 is indicated as a male by the hieroglyph for *nj3*, but it has rather short horns and a beard like a female. It has an obvious scrotum, but no penis, and the tail is very long. The oryx has more or less straight horns.

In Lepsius' copy (fig. 1-36) the ibex has very long horns, which clearly indicate a male, although the penis is also missing. The tail is of normal length. The oryx has distinctly curved horns.

The reader will probably notice several other differences between these figures that were not mentioned.

Animals mating and giving birth were portrayed in some of the hunting scenes (figs 1-29,-30,-31). In addition to adding some naturalism, these portrayals were probably intended to magically provide the tomb owner with animals and food in his future hunts, just as the belief that animals on pots assured the deceased or his Ka with food in the after-life.

Ikram (1991) listed a large number of animal matings, but was unable to identify many of the species correctly. Most of these errors should be apparent in the following chapters.

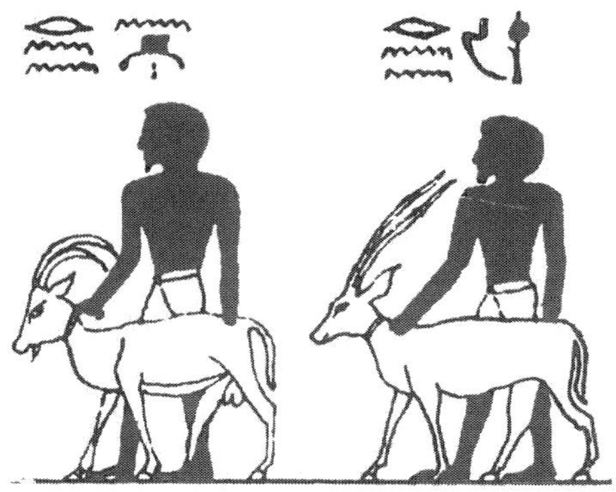

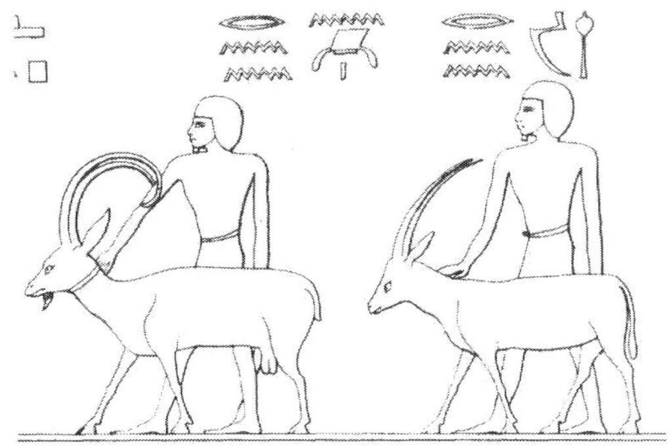

1-33 (top left) Part of offering scene from the Tomb of Chnemhotep, Dynasty XII, Beni Hasan. The animals are (left to right) a Loder's (?) gazelle , with hieroglyph for gazelle, and two hedgehogs and a hare in cages. Source: Newberry (1893 I: pl. XXXV).

1-34 (bottom left) The same scene as in Figure 1-33, except that the gazelle is replaced by a beardless ibex. Source: L.D. II, pl. 128.

1-35 (top right) Part of offering scene from the Tomb of Chnemhotep, Dynasty XII, Beni Hasan. The animals are (left to right) an ibex and a beisa oryx. Source: Newberry (1893 I: pl. XXXV).

1-36 (bottom right) The same scene as in Figure 1-35, except that the ibex has longer horns and a tail of normal length and the oryx has curved horns. Source: L.D. II, pl. 129.

Table I List of animals on the Brooklyn knife handle in Figure 1-7.
Rows A 1-10, face A, upper figure, side away from boss. Rows B 1-10, face B, lower figure, side with boss. Boss: list of figures on boss. Animals are listed from left to right. After Churcher (1984: 155 ff.) with some changes.

Rows A
1. Eight African elephants; seven on pairs of pythons.
2. A secretary bird, a grey heron, fifteen saddle-bill storks, a giraffe, and a saddle-bill holding an Egyptian sand boa.
3. Eleven lions.
4. Eleven Barbary goats.
5. Twelve Nubian asses.
6. A pariah dog and eleven scimitar oryx.
7. Ten N. African porcupines.
8. A pariah dog and ten aurochs.
9. A star representing a plant. Ten ratels or honey badgers.
10. A carp-like fish and seven scimitar oryx.

Sides of Boss: Four ratels or honey badgers, four Nubian asses, and two stars or plants.

Rows B
1. Seven sacred ibises and a carp like fish.
2. Nine ibexes.
3. Nine lions.
4. Six Barbary goats and a pariah dog.
5. Six Nubian asses.
6. Seven scimitar oryx.
7. Two aurochs and eight jackals (?)
8. Ten aurochs.
9. A scimitar oryx and ten ratels or honey badgers.
10. Nine aurochs.

II
Order *Insectivora*
Hedgehogs Family *Erinaceidae*

ḥnt3 henta Wb. III, 122

ḥntj henty Wb. III, 121

E Hedgehog; F Hérisson; G Igel; A Qunfid, Abu Ghunfis, Abu Gunfod

Nomenclature: The hieroglyphs for hedgehog and porcupine are the same, both meaning spiny.

General description: Large insectivores (head and body length 14-22 cm) with spiny pelage on sides and upper-parts of the head and body, large ears, short tails, and rounded backs (fig.2-1).

Natural history: Hedgehogs can erect their spines with dermal musculature; and by contracting a special circular muscle (*orbicularis panniculi*) around the body and a muscle on the head, they can curl up and become entirely enclosed into a spiny ball.

Food includes insects and larvae, scorpions, snails, young mice, eggs and nestlings of ground-nesting birds, lizards, snakes, carrion, and various fruits.

Hedgehogs are nocturnal and hide during the day in burrows, crevices or any available shelter.

Genera and species in Egypt: Two genera of hedgehogs are known from Egypt. They are distinguishable by the lack of a gap or division in the spines on the forehead in *Hemiechinus* and a gap in the forehead spines in *Paraechinus*.

One or more of the following species may have been pictured in Egyptian art:

2-1 Live example of a desert hedgehog, Paraechinus deserti. *Source: Author.*

Long-eared Hedgehog *Hemiechinus auritus* (Gmelin, 1770)

Description: This is the smallest of Egyptian species. The ears are proportionately larger in comparison with other species. The dorsal spines are white-tipped with buffy subterminal bands and brownish bases. The face and forehead are pale brown, ears white, and underparts and belly white. Feet are whitish to pale brown. There is no gap in the forehead spines.

The common name derives from the length of the ears being longer than the dorsal spines, which are only about 1.5 cm in *Hemiechinus* and 2.7 cm in *Paraechinus*.

Means and extremes of measurements in cms of Egyptian speciments are head and body length 18 (14-20), tail 2.4 (1.5-4), and ear 4 (3.4-4.5).

Habitats: This hedgehog is commonly found in gardens, olive groves, cultivated areas, and the more densely vegetated parts of the Coastal Desert. It is not known to occur in true desert.

Distribution: Northern Sinai Peninsula, northern part of the Eastern Desert, Nile Delta, Nile Valley south to Samalut, El Faiyum, Wadi el Natrun, and the Western Mediterranean Coastal Desert.

Further distribution includes the Libyan Coastal Desert to the west and eastward into Israel, Jordan, Syria and northern parts of the Arabian Peninsula, Cyprus, Asian Turkey, Iraq, Iran, Transcaucasia, southern Russia, and farther east into India and northeastward into Mongolia.

2-2 Two hedgehogs (lower center), a hare (right) with head missing, four Barbary goats, and two tesem hounds (upper and lower right) on white cross-lined pottery from the Early Gerzean period, Diospolis Parva. Source: Petrie (1901b: pl. XIV, 93b).

2-3 An oversized hedgehog (lower center) in a hunting scene in the Tomb of Aba, Dynasty VI, Deir el Gebrawi. Source: Davies (1902 I: pl. XI).
Two scimitar oryx are left, a fox (?) above, and a dorcas gazelle to the right.

2-4 An oversized hedgehog (lower center) in a hunting scene in the Tomb of Aba, Dynasty XXVI, Thebes (Assasif). Source: Davies (1902 I: pl. XXV).
Two beisa oryx are left, a jackal above, and a dorcas gazelle to the right.

Desert Hedgehogs Genus *Paraechinus*

There is some disagreement in the literature regarding the species of *Paraechinus* that occur in Egypt and beyond the borders. The so-called desert hedgehogs are either considered as races belonging to one species, *Paraechinus aethiopicus* (Harrison, 1964 I: 20 ff.; Haltenorth and Diller, 1980: 310; Honacki et al., 1982: 67; and Corbet and Hill, 1991: 28), or as three separate species: *P. aethiopicus* in the southeastern Eastern Desert, *P. deserti* in the northern Western Desert, and *P. dorsalis* in Sinai (Osborn and Helmy, 1980: 57 ff.). Heim de Balsac (1963, quoted by Kowalski and Rzebik-Kowalska, 1991: 49) was of the opinion that the populations from "northern Algeria belonged to *P. deserti*, while those from the southern mountains belonged to *P. aethiopicus*."

This would verify the discontinuous distribution of *P. aethiopicus* apparent in the distribution quoted below from Osborn and Helmy (1980: 68).

Desert Hedgehog *Paraechinus deserti* (Loche, 1858)

Description: The tips of the dorsal spines are pale, the subterminal bands blackish, and basal bands whitish to grayish. The face is brownish anteriorly; forehead whitish, chin and throat white, and belly white with brown patches. Ears, legs, and feet are brownish. There is a gap in the forehead spines.

Means and extremes of measurements in cms of Egyptian specimens are head and body length 21.5 (19–22), tail 2.2 (2–3), and ear 5 (4.5–5.8).

Habitats: Semi-barren desert and vegetated coastal desert; occasionally in gardens.

Distribution: Southwestern margin of the Nile Delta, Western Mediterranean Coastal Desert, and Siwa Oasis.

Further distribution includes scattered areas in Libya, Tunisia, northern Algeria and Morocco.

Ethiopian Hedgehog *Paraechinus aethiopicus* (Ehrenberg, 1833)

Description: The tips of the dorsal spines are light brown; bases blackish-brown. The anterior part of the face; lower lip and chin; large areas on the throat, center of belly, and genital region; legs; and anterior surface of the ears are dark brown. The forehead and most of the throat and belly are white and sometimes the inner part of the ears. There is a gap in the forehead spines.

Means and extremes of measurements in cms are: head and body length 19.6 (17-22), tail 2 (1.5-2.2), and ear 4.4 (4-4.5).

Habitats: Rocky, vegetated valleys and dense stands of vegetation on coastal plains.

Distribution: Southeastern part of the Eastern Desert. Further distribution southward in Africa includes Sudan, Eritrea, and Somalia; and in the west, scattered localities in Libya (Hufnagl, 1972: 29), Azben (Air) in northern Nigeria, and in Algeria, Morocco, and Mauritania. Harrison (1964 I: 23) concluded that races of this species occurred in Sinai, Israel, Jordan, Iraq, and the Arabian Peninsula (see *P. dorsalis* below).

Desert Hedgehog ***Paraechinus dorsalis*** (Anderson and De Winton, 1901)

Description: Specimens from Sinai have blackish spines; face, forehead, belly, and legs blackish; and a white mark on the throat. The spines are divided on the forehead.

Means and extremes of measurements in cms are: head and body length 20 (18-22), tail 2 (1.3-3), and ear 5 (4.4-5.5).

Distribution: Southern Sinai Peninsula and probably eastward into the Arabian Peninsula and several bordering countries.

Ancient Records of Hedgehogs

Prehistoric records: Hedgehog remains, unidentified to species, were found in terminal Paleolithic and Neolithic materials from the Nabta area in the southern Western Desert (Gautier, 1980: 327). No rock drawings of hedgehogs have been found. The oldest known representations are on Early Gerzean pottery (fig. 2-2) from Naqada.

The Dynastic period: The nocturnal habits of the hedgehog may have associated it with the sun and rebirth. When the sun set it came out of its hiding place and at dawn it retreated. Droste zu Hülshoff (1980: 45) suggested that its appearance in desert scenes was probably as a symbol of rebirth.

In many scenes hedgehogs appear to be walking calmly while other animals, especially hares, are wildly leaping about (fig.1-20b). In two of such scenes oversized hedgehogs with spines erected are more or less centrally located (figs 1-18, -21). The latter figure is probably *Paraechinus deserti*, because of the black face. Wilkinson (1878 II: 92 f.) called it a porcupine.

There is a large hedgehog in the Dynasty IV relief from Pepi II (fig.7-61) and two oversized hedgehogs appear in the Dynasty VI and XXVI Tombs of Aba (figs 2-3,-4). The types of animals and the arrangement in these scenes are similar and Davies (1902 I:40) described the latter as having been borrowed from the Dynasty VI prototype.

There are also numerous portrayals of hedgehogs entering or leaving a stylized burrow or shelter (figs 2-5, 7-107,-147, 13-173), often with crickets in their mouths. Hayes (1953 I: 98) interpreted such an action in the Tomb of Re-emkuy as "a hedgehog rooting for insects in what may be an anthill." Hares and jerboas, however, were also shown entering identical structures (figs 5-5, 6-10).

2-5 Two hedgehogs in a hunting scene. One is leaving a burrow with a cricket in its mouth. Tomb of Ptahhetep, Dynasty V, Saqqara. Source: Davies (1901 II: pl. XXII).

2-6 A boat with a hedgehog head on the bow and an unidentifiable head on the stern. Tomb of Pepi-ankh-her-ab, Dynasty V, Meir. Source: Kamal (1915: fig. 3).

2-7 Relief of the head of a hedgehog on the bow of a boat. Tomb of Ti, Dynasty V, Saqqara. Source: Steindorff (1913: pl. 76).

2-8 *Hedgehog carried in an offering procession, Mastaba of Mereruka, Dynasty VI, Saqqara. Source: Author.*

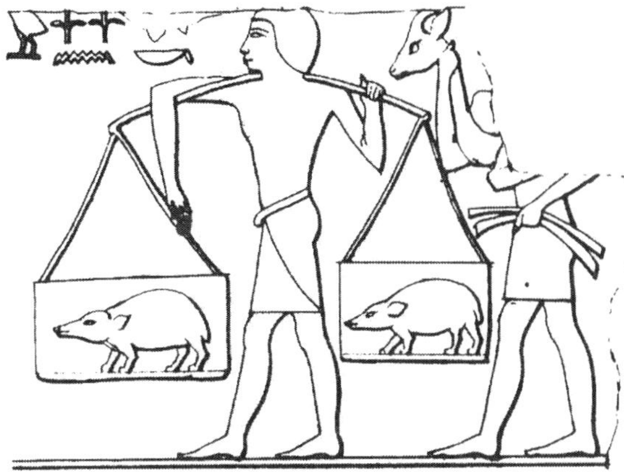

2-9 *Hedgehogs carried in an offering procession, Tomb of Pehenouka, Dynasty V, Saqqara. Source: L.D. II, 36.*

In a partly destroyed hunting scene in the Dynasty V Tomb of Ti, hedgehogs are mating (Epron and Daumas, 1939 I: pl. VI).

Heads in the reversed position appear on the bows and sometimes the sterns of sacred barges and fishing and hunting boats of the Old Kingdom (figs 2-6,-7). Droste zu Hülshoff (1980: 46) explained that this indicated the wind direction, because the hedgehog was capable of predicting the direction of the wind. Therefore, on a ship sailing southward up the Nile, the head always faced into the wind (fig. 2-6).

These figures, like other hedgehog representations, also had an apotropaic function – they averted evil and protected boats and passengers from sand banks, crocodiles, and other dangers (*loc. cit.*).

Junker (1941 V: 72) suggested the possibility that a real hedgehog was originally bound to the prow to dispel the terrors of the river.

Hedgehogs carried in cages were commonly included in offerings (figs 2-8,-9, 7-213). These date mostly to the Old Kingdom, but there are some from the Middle Kingdom (fig. 1-33, 7-218).

Sethe (1937: 27) supposed that because the hedgehog was "so often included among the offerings of food animals in the Old Kingdom, it must have been, like the hyena, a food-animal whose use did not survive."

There is no evidence that hedgehogs were eaten in Egypt. Those carried in offering processions were probably symbolic gifts intended for release in the dwellings of the deceased to eradicate snakes, scorpions, and insects and to ward off evil as were the various amulets and statuettes that were found in tombs and coffins.

Another possibility was that hedgehogs were cherished for their eventual use in 'medicine'. All parts of the animal had some medico-magical value (Droste zu Hülshoff, 1980: 13-17).

Of particular interest are the comments of

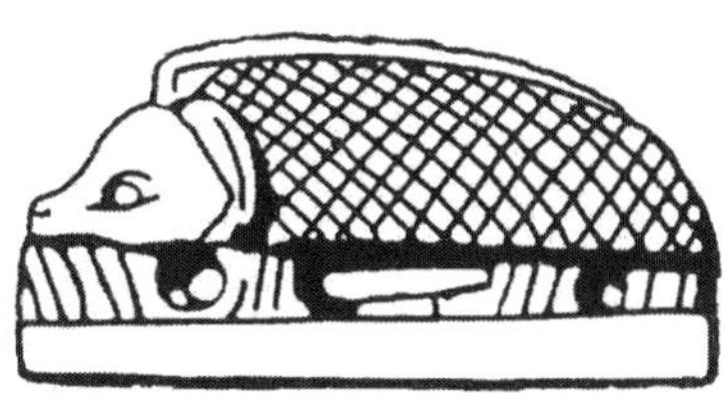

2-10 *(left) Globular flask of black clay in the form of a hedgehog, Greco-Roman. Source: Droste zu Hülshoff (1980: pl. VIII, 84).*
2-11 *(centre) Hedgehog statuette of blue faience from Thebes, Middle Kingdom. Source: Droste zu Hülshoff (1980: pl. XI, 103).*
2-12 *(right) A Middle Kingdom hedgehog seal. Source: Firth (1927a: pl. 36, 220).*

Fakhry (1942: 79): "Its thorny skin is burnt and sniffed by the fever stricken; its grease is useful for ear-ache."

Dried hedgehog skins are sold today in the markets of Cairo to be burned and sniffed for headaches, colds, and fevers.

The fact that hedgehogs attacked and killed snakes and their ability to erect their spines and survive being struck by poisonous snakes certainly put them in a position of high respect.

The further ability of hedgehogs to enclose themselves into a spiny ball and then emerge from this ball when danger passed or upon awakening must have greatly impressed the Egyptians. Perhaps this accounted for the association with rebirth, just as the scarab beetle emerging from a ball of dung was associated with spontaneous creation and regeneration. Hence, the placing of magic amulets of these animals in coffins to ensure resurrection.

From early historical into Greco-Roman time the hedgehog was a popular model for the production of vessels. These varied in style from broad, open vases to globular flasks with a narrow spout and a large loop for a handle (fig. 2-10). Statuettes with large, laterally spread ears probably represented the long-eared hedgehog (fig. 2-11).

Cosmetic vessels, according to Droste zu Hülshoff (1980: 29), may have been prized, because the night vision of the hedgehog might be magically transferred to the user of the contents.

Rattles in the shape of a hedgehog were evidently produced because the sound resembled that of the foraging, tooth-clicking animal.

Hedgehog figures, like those of other animals, were in standing, sitting, and reclining positions. Their bodies were sometimes smooth, but usually ornamented with blunt points or cross-hatched engravings to simulate spines (figs 2-10,-11,-12).

Hedgehog amulets in the shape of scarabs, scarabs with hedgehogs engraved on their backs, and hedgehogs on seals were also produced in large numbers (fig. 2-12).

Further evidence that the hedghog was revered derives from Middle Kingdom faience statuettes, which were green, the symbolic color of fertility and growth; and blue, the symbolic color of divinities.

2-13 The goddess Ab'as with a hedgehog on her head. She is standing behind Ba-neb-Dadu, the ram god of Mendes. Tomb of Ba-n-nentin, Dynasty XXVI, Baharia Oasis. Source: Fakhry (1942: fig. 41).

Dynasty XVIII and Late Period bronzes have also stimulated the belief that the ancient Egyptians really worshipped this animal.

Hedgehogs were not mummified nor considered to be sacred or associated with a god or goddess, except for one example: In the Dynasty XXVI Tomb of Ba-n-nentin in Bahariya Oasis, the goddess Ab'as, mistress of heaven and of gods, is shown with a blue hedgehog on her head (fig. 2-13).

Errors and discrepancies: Many early Egyptologists called hedgehogs porcupines. For example, Newberry (1892 I: 14) called the hedgehog in Figure 13-78, row 4 a porcupine. This was biologically incorrect. Nevertheless, definition no. 2 of hedgehog in the Oxford American Dictionary (1980) is 'the porcupine'.

Paton (1925: 17, fig. 2) referred to a hedgehog in one of the earliest hunt scenes as a 'pig'. Likewise, Darby *et al.* (1977 I: 190, fig. 4.11) alluded to an oversized hedgehog (fig. 2-4) as a "wild boar/hedgehog." Various aspects of these figures, such as position and shape of ears, shape of snout or shortness of snout, and in one the indication of protruding spines on the forehead indicate that the artists conceived hedgehogs.

Shrews Family *Soricidae*

2-14 *Various shrews. Upper left:* Crocidura flavescens; *lower left:* C. nana; *lower right:* Suncus murinus. *Source: Anderson (1902: pl. XXII). Anderson used specific names* olivieri, religiosa, *and* crassicauda.

 *'m'mw* amamu Wb. I, 186

E Shrew, Shrewmouse; F Musaraigne; G Spitzmaus; A Far, Ersa

Nomenclature: Brunner-Traut (1984) translated the hieroglyphic name for shrew as meaning a 'glutton'.

General description: Shrews are small and mouse-size with short, dense, dark gray or brownish fur. They have long, slender, and slightly bilobed snouts (figs 2-14, -16) with long whiskers; very small eyes; small, but conspicuous ears, especially on Egyptian bronzes; relatively short legs; and slender tails with bristly hairs either on the proximal part or along the entire length.

Natural history: Shrews are mainly nocturnal and hide in nests in vegetation, under stones or in rodent burrows. Piles of corn stalks or other farm plants also provide hiding and nesting places. They also inhabit houses.

Food consists mainly of insects and their larvae, other arthropods, and snails. Larger species prey on young mice.

Species found as mummies:

Egyptian Giant Shrew, Giant Musk Shrew
Crocidura flavescens (I. Geoffroy St.-Hilaire, 1827)

Nomenclature: The obsolete synonym, *Crocidura olivieri* Lesson, 1827, was originally applied to mummified specimens of unknown origin.

Mummies of this shrew have also been misnamed *Suncus murinus* Linnaeus, 1776, the Latin name of the house or musk shrew of Near Eastern and Oriental countries. The only specimen of the latter from Egypt was collected in a house at Suez (Anderson, 1902). That species has been cancelled from the list of mummified shrews (Brunner-Traut, 1965: 127).

Another name misapplied to *C. flavescens* in the literature was *Sorex giganteus* Geoffroy, 1831.

Description: Dorsum dark brown and belly grayish. The tail is darker than the body and bristly along the proximal two thirds. This is the largest of Egyptian species of *Crocidura*.

Means and extremes of measurements of Egyptian specimens in cms are head and body length 11.8 (10-14); tail 7 (6-8) and 60 (46-69) percent of head and body length.

Distribution: Known from El Faiyum, various localities in the Delta, and the Nile Valley as far south as Dahshur until Boessneck and von den Driesch (1982: 15, 24 ff., 55 ff.) found undatable remains in a Middle Kingdom grave on Elephantine Island, Aswan.

Shrew remains along with those of two species of mice, some insects, a skink, and feces in a chewed and rotten grave cloth indicated that the animals had penetrated the grave (Boessneck, 1988: 61 f.).

Further distribution includes Sudan and Ethiopia south to South Africa, and West Africa north to Dakkar (Heim de Balsac and Barloy, 1966: 604 ff.).

Prehistoric records: Remains were found in the Neolithic site of Merimde-Benisalama in the southwestern Delta (von den Driesch and Boessneck, 1985: 51 f., tables 26, 27).

The Dynastic period: Mummified specimens of unknown origin were found at Saqqara (Lortet and Gaillard, 1905: 33), Memphis (Heim de Balsac and Mein, 1971: 241), Akmim, and Drah Abou el Neggar (Lortet and Gaillard, 1909). Boesneck (1988: table 9) listed remains from Tell el-Maskhuta near Ismailiya.

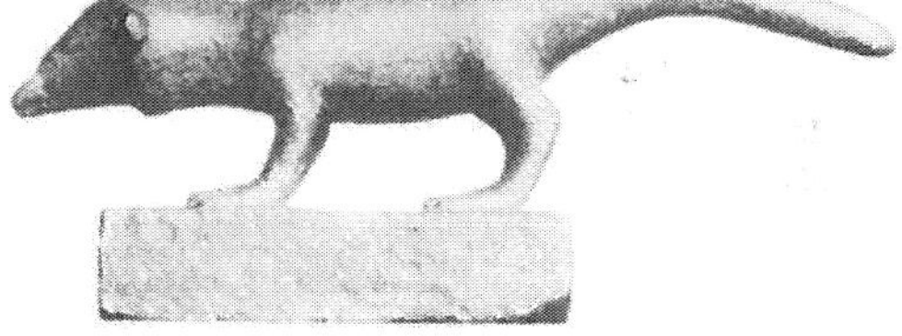

2-15 Wooden sarcophagus with a carving of a shrew on the cover, from Abu Rawash (Ruawash, Roash). Length 11 cm. Source: Gaillard and Daressy (1905: pl. LIX).

2-16 Bronze shrew from Letopolis (Ausim, S. Delta), New Kingdom. Source: Brunner-Traut (1965: fig. 1a).

2-17 Bronze shrew from Letopolis, New Kingdom. Source: Brunner-Traut (1965: fig. 3b).

2-18 Bronze shrew with a short tail. Source: Roeder (1936: fig. 14).

Dwarf Shrew ***Crocidura nana*** **Dobson, 1890**

Nomenclature: This shrew was originally described as *Sorex religiosus* I. Geofroy, 1827, from mummified specimens found in a Theban tomb. Later, comparable live specimens were collected in Giza (Anderson, 1902). Heim de Balsac and Mein (1971: 243) considered the material unidentifiable and applied the name *Crocidura nana* Dobson, 1890. Corbet (1978: 27) concluded that the specific name, *religiosa*, was valid.

Description: A very small shrew with a dull gray dorsum tinged with brown and underside light gray. The tail is bicolored and bristled to the tip.

Averages and extremes of measurements in cms of Egyptian specimens are head and body length 5 (4-6); tail 3 (2-4) and 65 (61-75) percent of head and body length.

Distribution: Known from a few specimens from the southern Delta (Osborn and Helmy, 1980: 78, fig. 28). Further known distribution is in East Africa from Ethiopia south to Zimbabwe (Rhodesia).

The Dynastic period: Mummies of unknown origin were found in tombs at Giza, Saqqara, Akhmim, and Thebes (Lortet and Gaillard, 1905: 36; 1909; Gaillard, 1934). Boesneck (1988: table 9) listed remains from Tell el-Maskhuta near Ismailiya.

Flower's Shrew ***Crocidura floweri*** **Dollman, 1915**

Description: A small, pale cinnamon-brown shrew with a white belly and bicolored tail bristled on the proximal half.

Measuremens from Flower (1932) are head and body length 6-7 cms; tail 5.5-6 and 75 percent of head and body length.

Distribution: This shrew was known only from Baltim and Giza in the Nile Delta and El Faiyum, but recently Goodman (1989) found lower jaws in pellets of the little owl at Wadi el Natroun.

Prehistoric records: Remains of this species of shrew were found in the Prehistoric cave discovered in the South Galala Plateau in the northern part of the Eastern Desert (Hobbs, 1989: 97; Goodman *et al.*, 1992: 83), which indicates that previous distribution was wider than in Dynastic and Recent times. This find also indicates that previously permanent water and dense stands of grasses and reeds existed in this area (*op. cit*, 85) or nearby.

The Dynastic period: Mummified specimens were found at Thebes and one mummified with a bird at Giza (Heim de Balsac and Mein (1971: 238).

Shrews in Pharaonic and Greco-Roman Times

Worship and mummification of shrews began in the New Kingdom, probably at Letopolis (Ausim, near Giza). Plutarch, quoted by Brunner-Traut (1965: 154), wrote that shrews received divine honors from the ancient Egyptians "because they were believed to be blind and because darkness is more ancient than light." The belief may have derived from their becoming active only at night and thereby symbolizing darkness. Brunner-Traut (*op. cit.*, 149) also mentioned that the shrew played the role of guide in the nether world.

Blindness identified the shrew with 'Blind Horus', the form of the god that supposedly appeared when the evil god Seth (Typhon) blinded him.

The shrew was also sacred to the Uraeus or Cobra goddess, Uatchet (Buto of the Greeks), who supposedly took the form of a shrew to help Horus escape when Seth was going to destroy him.

Another possible reason for veneration of shrews suggested by Lortet and Gaillard (1905: 36) and Bodenheimer (1960), may have originated from the refusal of cats to kill and eat shrews. Cats are known to kill shrews, however, but generally avoid them and do not eat them because of their odor.

Herodotus and Diodorus are quoted as having said that sacred shrews were mummified in large numbers and buried in Uraeus' city, Buto (Kom el Fara'in), in the western Delta. No remains of shrews have been reported from that locality. Other findings, however, are listed above.

Shrews were not only mummified, but wooden coffins with carved figures on the lids (fig. 2-15) often held their remains. Keller (1909 I: 16) remarked that the 'giant shrew', although seldom found, was carefully embalmed in gilded sarcophagi with the animal's figure carved on the lid.

Shrew amulets dated to about 1,000 B.C. (Petrie, 1914: 46) and many bronze figures have been found, dating to the Late Dynasties and Ptolemaic period (figs 2-16,-17,-18) and were often engraved on the back with the name of the blind Horus.

Pliny was said to have written that shrew amulets or dead shrews were passed around boils as healing charms (Petrie, *op.cit.*). Brunner-Traut (1965: 145) cited further remarks from the ancients about the noxiousness of shrews: "If a man drinks water in which a shrew has drowned he will become blind in both eyes ... . A pulverized shrew put into any food and eaten will cause a man to swell up and die... In contrast, the powdered head was used for healing wounds and to cure 'sick' ears."

Further discussion of shrews is not possible without including the ichneumon, which was also sacred to the cobra goddess. The ichneumon represented the complimentary figure of the shrew. This important relationship lay in the belief that each morning the blind shrew metamorphosed into the ichneumon, which symbolized the rising sun, Aten (Aton), and also represented the 'seeing side' of Horus (Brunner-Traut, 1965: 133).

Conversely, the ichneumon, which was associated with various sun gods, transformed at sunset into a tiny shrew.

Shrew and ichneumon cults spread from Letopolis in the Delta to Bubastis (Tel Basta), Säis, and Buto; and up the Nile to Memphis, El Faiyum, Heracleopolis Magna (Ihnasya el Madina), Athribis. (Nag Hammadi), Thebes, and Kom Ombo.

Hundreds of shrew and ichneumon bronzes of Ptolemaic origin have been found deposited in tombs from Dynasty III into the Ptolemaic Period. Both must be discussed because there are errors and discrepancies in identification. The characteristics of the stylized bronzes described by Brunner-Traut (1965) are in Table II and can be used in identifying the two types, examples of which are Figures 2-16,-17,-18, 7-137,-138,-139.

Errors and discrepancies: Some authors have confused the bronzes and called many obvious shrews ichneumons. Roeder (1936: 29), for example, referred to a series of shrews (*op. cit.*, figs 12, 13, 14, 15a b, 16, 17) as ichneumons. All of them have typical shrew features and inscriptions, except for 16 and 17, which have recumbent tails.

In his later work, Roeder (1956) repeated errors (*op. cit.*, Plates 54f,g, 55e, and 85c,d), but some of the figures on closer inspection, have combined features. For example, his 54f, an ichneumon that Brentjes (1967c: fig. 17) said could not be interpreted zoologically, has a slender tail base; another ichneumon, 54i, has a smooth body, feet opposite, and posterior rump; 85a, also an ichneumon, has feet opposite and atypical ears; and 85c is typically a shrew except for the mouth. Several obvious shrews have recumbent tails.

Brentjes (1967b: figs 9, 14) also called two bronzes ichneumons, which were obviously shrew-like because of their pointed snouts, raised tails, opposite feet, ruffs on necks, and engravings on their backs.

An example of a combination of characteristics is the 'Ichneumon' discovered by Emery (1971: pl. IX 2) in northern Saqqara (fig. 2-19), which at first glance suggests shrew, because of the long, pointed nose, small eyes, raised tail, and parallel feet. In contrast, the mouth is not shrew-like; the ear is single lobed; legs stout and not bent nor defined on the body; the tail is somewhat thick; and the body is etched.

Some artists were probably unfamiliar with the accepted styles or became careless. Another possibility is that intermediate forms were created deliberately to represent animals in stages of transformation from shrews to ichneumons or vice versa.

Table II Characteristics of bronze shrews and ichneumons

Shrews	*Ichneumons*
Body and legs slender	Body and legs stout
Legs opposite or parallel	Legs in walking position
Belly line rising or straight against thigh	Belly line sloping against thigh
Rump above or posterior to the legs	Rump above the legs
Body smooth except for symbols on the back	Body may be deeply etched to represent coarse hair
Head long; snout elongate, probosis-like; usually divided into two 'tubes'	Head relatively short; snout short, tapering
Lower lip usually prominent	Lower lip not prominent
Eyes in depressions	Eyes on surface or raised
Ears projecting; consisting of two deep lobes (shells)	Ears close lying, single lobed
Neck often with hairy mane	Neck not maned
Tail thin; curved or straight; rarely recumbent	Tail thick, recumbent
Upper parts of fore and hind legs distinct (bent at joints)	Upper parts of hind legs only distinct (not bent at joints)
Toes two to four, seldom five	Toes three to five

2-19 Bronze 'Ichneumon' from N. Saqqara, Dynasty III. Source: Emery (1971: pl. IX, 2).

III
Bats Order *Chiroptera*

E Bat; F Chauve-souris; G Fledermaus, Fledertier; A Wat-Wat

Nomenclature: The ancient Egyptians classified bats together with birds as animals of the air, because both had wings and could fly.

They recognized two major types of bats, however, which today are divided into two suborders. These are represented by hieroglyphs and a few illustrations in Egyptian art.

Description: Bats are the only mammals that actually fly. The wings consist of membranes (patagia) between the greatly elongated digits (fingers), fore- and upper-arms, the body, and the hind legs. There is also a membrane (uropatagium) between the hind legs and tail. In some species this membrane is vestigial and only extends along a small portion of the tail.

Bats are also described as flying mammals with mouse-like bodies; hence, the German name, 'flying mouse'. The wings of bats are hairless, which could account for the French name, 'bald mouse' (Allen, 1940: 10).

Fruit-eating Bats Suborder *Megachiroptera*

Description: As the subordinal name indicates, the bats in this group are large. They are easily separated by their larger body size (head and body length 12-15 cm) from the smaller insectivorous bats, which have head and body lengths less than 10 cm.

One family was represented in Egypt by one genus, of which only one species is extant.

Egyptian Fruit Bat ***Rousettus aegyptiacus*** (Geoffroy, 1810)

 *śḏ3ḫm* zedjakhem Wb. IV, 24

E Fruit Bat, Flying Fox; F Ptérop(od)idés; G Flughund; A Wat-Wat el Fack Ha

Nomenclature: An obsolete synonym is *Pteropus aegyptiacus* Geoffroy, 1810.

Description: The characteristics of this family and the species are a smooth, elongated muzzle; long,

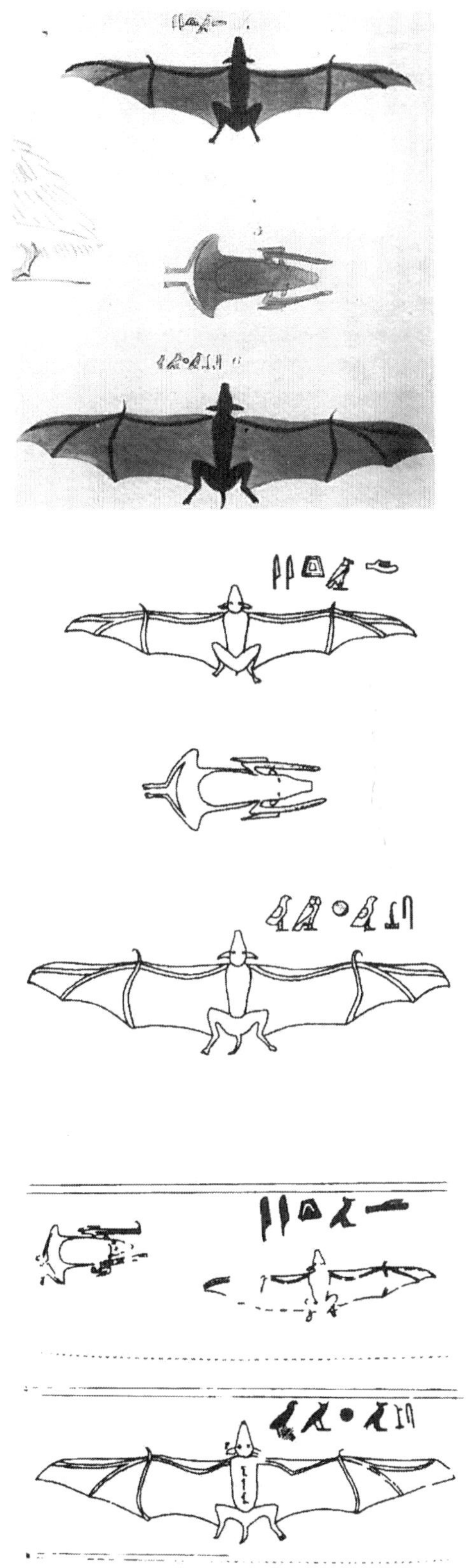

a

b

c

Fig. 3-1a,b,c Bats from the Tomb of Baqt, Dynasty XII, Beni Hasan. Sources: a) Rosellini (1834 II: pl. XIV; b) Champollion (1845 IV: pl. CCCLXXXIV; c) Davies (1949: pl. III).

simple ears that are funnel-shaped at the bases; claws on the index fingers as well as the thumbs; and large eyes. The tail is short (1.6-2 cm), free of and beneath the small interfemoral membrane.

The genus was named *Rousettus* from the reddish color of the fur of the earliest known specimens. The cheek teeth, unlike those of insect-eating bats, have blunt crowns, an adaptation for chewing fruits, flowers, and succulent stems.

Natural history: Fruit bats have large eyes and accurate vision. They use echolocation like other bats, but only in the darkness of tombs, caves, etc. Their signals, which are audible to the human ear, are clicks made with the tongue and sent out of the corners of the mouth. Clicking fruit bats appear to be 'grinning'.

These bats hang wrapped in their wings with their heads tucked inward at right angles to the body; not with the nose pointing downward like other bats.

Large colonies, sometimes numbering into the hundreds, roost in caves, rock crevices, temples, tombs, mosques, and houses, wherever they can hang. Their feces and urine stain walls and columns.

Fruit bats locate food by sight and smell. They feed on various fruits, flowers, soft stems, and nectar. They are the chief pollinators of the silk cotton and sausage trees.

Climbing ability is very good and is aided by the additional claws on the index fingers.

Distribution: Fruit bats occur throughout the Nile Delta and the Nile Valley south to Aswan, Suez Canal area, Wadi el Natroun, Faiyum Oasis, and the vicinity of Mersah Matruh on the Mediterranean coast. Recently, colonies were discovered in Dakhlah Oasis (Churcher, 1991). Eastward, the range includes Yemen, Israel, Jordan, Lebanon, Syria, Cyprus, southern Turkey, Aden, southern Iran, and western India. Southward, the range includes southern Sudan and Eritrea, extends across sub-Saharan Africa, and south to the Cape.

The Dynastic period: The hieroglyphs for 'fruit eating' and 'insect eating' bats were drawn with three bats together with birds in the Dynasty XI Tomb of Baqt (Baget, Baket) at Beni Hasan (fig. 3-1 a,b,c).

All were originally a drab brownish pink, and the one on the right and above with a darker browny-red body (Davies, 1949: 14). On the drawing by Davies in Figure 3-1c, however, 'greenish yel' is printed on the back of the fruit bat on the left.

Anderson (1902: 92) called them 'fruit bats' and others identified them as two fruit bats and a tomb bat, *Taphozous perforatus* (Allen, 1940: 10, fig. 2; Houlihan, 1986: 139).

Allen (1940: 10, fig. 2) said, "the top and bottom pictures probably represent *Rousettus*. The middle shows a bat with wings folded and what appears to be a membrane between the upper sections of the hind legs". There is no tail in his copy (fig. 3-1a), which was from Rosellini (1834: pl. XIV) and said by Allen to be "the oldest known picture of bats."

The copy by Davies (1949) in Figure 3-1 c is more detailed than the others and was drawn to scale. Therefore, the bat with folded wings is comparable in dimensions with the bat on the left (lower in other copies), which shows those two to be fruit bats, *Rousettus aegyptiacus*. The central figure lacks a tail in other copies.

The illustration in Newberry (1894 II: pl. IV) is very small and lacking in details. Recent photos in Houlihan (1986: figs 196-198) that were taken in the tomb show the painting to be in very poor condition.

Further discussion is in the suborder Microchiroptera.

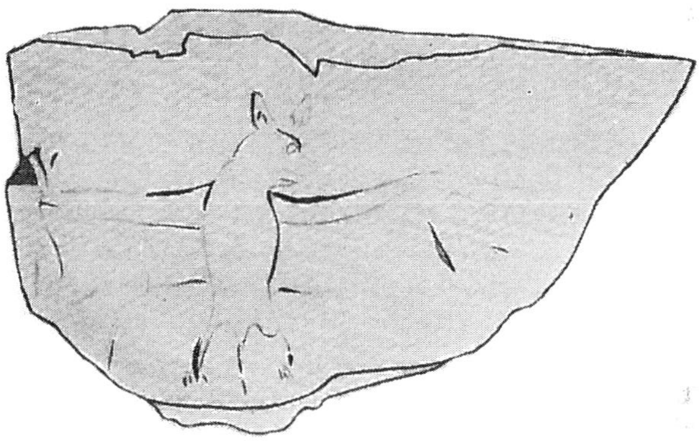

Fig. 3-2 Ostracon of a bat, Rhinopoma sp., *from Deir el Medineh, Dynasty XIX. Source: Vandier d'Abbadie (1936 I: pl. XXXII, 2232).*

Insect-eating Bats Suborder *Microchiroptera*

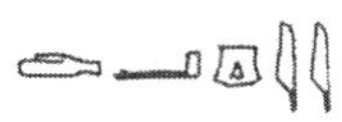 *d'gjj* dagy Wb. IV, 419

F Microchiroptères; G Fledermäuse; A Wat-Wat, Koffash

Description: As the subordinal indicates, the bats in this group are individually smaller than those in the suborder Megachiroptera. Other distinguishing features are claws on the thumbs only, longer tails that are partly or completely enclosed in the interfemoral membrane, and smaller eyes. The ears are not funnel-shaped at the bases and have projections (tragi or antitragi) from the lower medial margins. These were included in one drawing of a bat (fig. 3-2).

The sharply cusped teeth of the insect-eating bats indicate the difference in their diets from that of the fruit-eating bats.

In the suborder Microchiroptera seven families, 12 genera, and 20 species are known to exist in Egypt (Gaisler *et al.*, 1972: 31, table 20; Qumsiya, 1985). All are extralimital.

Two genera can be recognized in Egyptian art: *Taphozous* (fig. 3-1) and *Rhinopoma* (fig. 3-2).

Natural history: The Microchiroptera are specialized in the use of echolocation (bat radar). Various modifications of the ears, and in some species, leaf-like outgrowths on the nose and muzzle are associated with sending high frequency sounds, which these bats use in orientation and to find, pursue, and capture prey in the dark.

In the leaf-nosed bats (families Nycteridae, Rhinolophidae, and Hipposideridae, with the exception of the Rhinopomatidae) signals are emitted through the nose instead of the mouth. The 'leaves' function in amplifying and concentrating the sounds and deflecting them from the ears.

In general, insect-eating bats capture and hold prey in their mouths. Some are capable of scooping insects with one wing while in flight and also to use the interfemoral membrane to catch and hold prey.

The Predynastic period: There is a schist make-up palette of Naqada II origin from El Gebelein (Gabalin) southwest of Luxor that represents a bat with outstretched wings (fig. 3-3). It is perforated for suspension.

A similar artifact, probably of Naqada I origin, from Khozam (Khuzam), northeast of Luxor, was pictured by Tupinier (1984: 297) and other similar museum specimens were also mentioned (*op. cit.*, 298). Petrie (1920: pl. XLIV) published a few line drawings of palettes in the shape of bats.

The Dynastic period: Batrawi (1948: 595) discovered skeletons of the mouse-tailed bat, *Rhinopoma microphyllum*, in the Dynasty IV pyramid of Snefru at Dashur. He said that it was prevalent, almost to the exclusion of any other species in the same locality at that time.

The skeletons were in the mummy case of a barn owl, *Tyto alba*. The bat and the owl, being nocturnal and able to fly, he said, may have represented an offering symbolic of the power of flight at night, which might have been of service to the Ka (soul) of the deceased in its journey through the darkness of the unknown life after death.

Although bats were listed among the mummified mammals by McHargue (1972: 38), dried bats found in tombs may only be bats that have died there (Gaisler *et al.*, 1972: 13).

Dawson (1925) referred to the smaller bat in the Dynasty XI Tomb of Baqt (fig. 3-1a,b,c) as a sheath-tailed bat, genus *Taphozous* in the family Emballonuridae. In these bats half of the tail projects from the middle of the upper surface of the interfemoral membrane. His conclusion appears to be correct, because there is an indication of there having been a short tail.

There is one very realistic drawing of a bat with outstretched wings on a Dynasty XIX ostracon from Deir el-Medineh (Medina), Thebes (fig. 3-2). The head is in profile and has a concavity in the forehead. There is a small vertical projection (leaf) on the nose. The ears are in frontal view and the

Fig. 3-3 A Predynastic makeup palette in the form of a bat with outstretched wings. Provenance: Gebelein in Upper Egypt. Source: Vandier d'Abbadie (1936/37: pl. I).

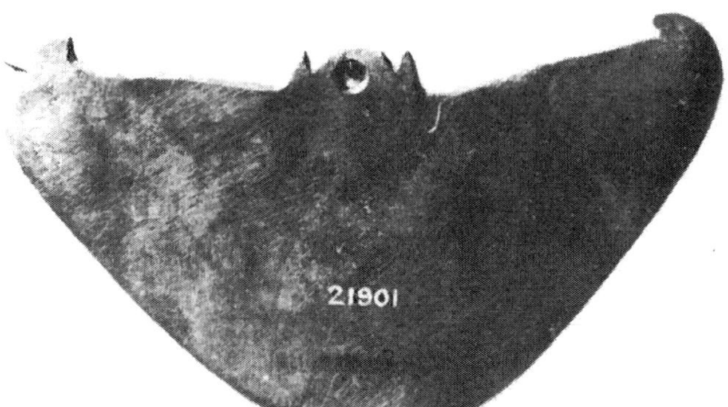

Fig. 3-4 Bat-headed vase covers from a Dynasty XVIII-XIX tomb at Abydos. Source: Peet (1914 II: pl. XXXIV).

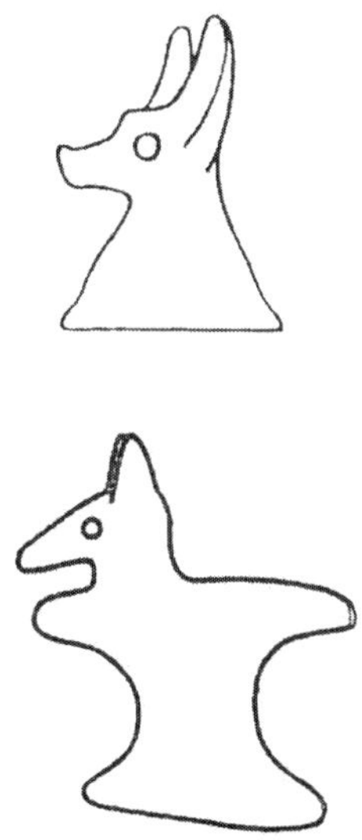

tragi are represented. The tail extends beyond the interfemoral membrane, which is also characteristic of the mouse-tailed (rat-tailed) bats of the genus *Rhinopoma*.

Two of the animal head vase covers from a Dynasty XVIII-XIX tomb at Abydos could represent bats (fig. 3-4). One has shoulder projections that suggest wings. The other has a vertical projection on the nose and a concavity in the forehead similar to the *Rhinopoma sp.* on the ostracon in Figure 3-2. Others with similar ears (Peet, 1914 II: pl. XXXIV) can only be classed as carnivores.

A bronze statuette (fig. 3-5) has been called a bat with its wings wrapped around its body. Price (1893: 341) identified it first as a 'kangaroo', but when zoologists assured him there were no kangaroos in Egypt, he decided it was a bat... "with a sharp-pointed nose, large prick ears, pierced for earrings, full cheeks, and mammae. Its forelegs or arms are broken off at the elbows, but from the attitude of the arms it may be inferred that the hands hung down in front of the body... It is seated on its haunches after the manner of a kangaroo... The tail is brought round on the left side... it appears to have wings folded upon its back, below the shoulders is a division, and the whole of the back, including the wings, arms, legs, and neck is covered with a reticulated pattern, which can be intended for nothing else but wings."

Except for the ears, which are also large in cat figures and pierced for earrings, Prices' (*op. cit.*) description indicates practically no relationship between this figure and a bat.

Although this statuette is not among the illustrations of Langton (1940), there certainly are numerous bronzes with comparable head and ear shapes and with similarly engraved dresses or robes (*op. cit.*, Frontispiece and pl. XVI). Forelegs or arms, and hands (said to be broken off) are not a part of bat anatomy. The tail is not clear in the illustration, but from the description, 'being turned to the left', it could be similar to that of a cat.

The so-called reticulated patterned wings appear to be a robe wrapped around the body.

Numerous authors labeled the statuette 'a bat' without question (Fechheimer, 1922: 124; Vandier d'Abbadie, 1936/37: 120; Roeder, 1956: 384, no. 514; Brentjes, 1971a: 182; and Houlihan, 1986: 139, fig.199). Tupinier (1984: 299) called it a standing bat, but Boessneck (1988: 64) said it was a "bat resembling a sitting cat."

From the description and comparative illustrations of Langton (*loc. cit.*), this statuette was probably intended to represent the cat goddess, Bast (Bastet) with which it should be compared (fig. 7-183). The attitude or beliefs of the ancient Egyptians regarding bats are poorly known. Vandier d'Abbadie (1936/37: 123) assumed that

Fig. 3-5 A seated bronze figure of the cat goddess Bastet, which has been called a 'bat'. Provenance: Benha in the southern Delta, Ptolemaic period. Source: Price (1893: opp. p. 344).

Fig. 3-6 Drawing of an enamelled clay amulet of a stylized bat with folded wings, Dynasty XIX from Luxor. Source: Vandier d'Abbadie (1936/37: fig. 3).

bats were not considered as sacred, but as objects of repulsion.

Nevertheless, bats had some magico-medicinal value. Dawson (1925) in reference to Papyrus Ebers wrote that bat's blood smeared on eyelids after lashes have been pulled, will prevent regrowth. Blood in a man's eyes, however, supposedly caused blindness, but bat urine mixed with some other ingredients was a cure for dimness of sight.

Hanging a bat's head around the neck was supposed to prevent sleep and a bat slit open and bound on the throat was a cure for infection.

Amulets of bats (fig. 3-6) might have been used for the same purposes as the head and body of a bat mentioned above and also to keep away evil spirits.

IV
Primates
Order Primates
Family *Cercopithecidae*

4-1 (left) Limestone statue of a female hamadryas (?) baboon and young from Hierakonpolis, dated to the Protodynastic. Source: Quibell (1900 I: pl. XVIII 1).

4-2 (right) Alabaster statue of a hamadryas baboon dated to early Dynasty I and the reign of Menes (Mendes). Source: Hamann (1944: fig. 53).

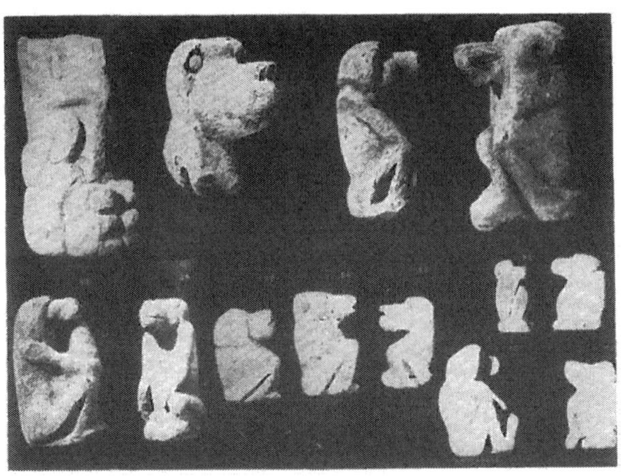

4-3 Glazed figures of hamadryas baboons from Abydos Temple, Dynasty I. Source: Petrie (1903 II: pl. VI).

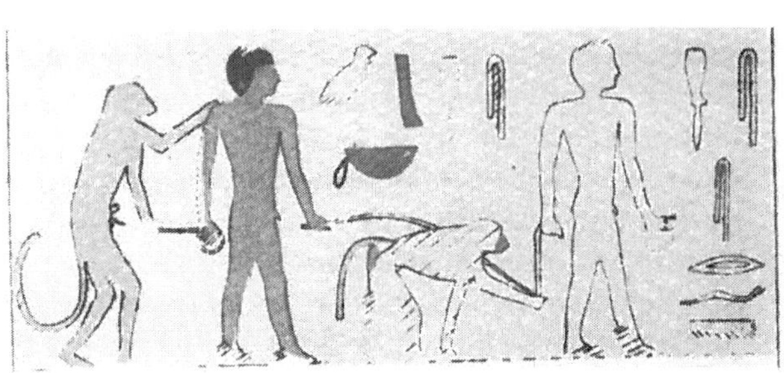

4-4 Hamadryas baboon and patas monkey being led by two young men in the Tomb of Nefermat, Dynasty IV, Medum. Source: Petrie (1892b: pl. XXVII).

Baboons Subfamily *Papiinae*

General description: Baboons are large primates with dog-like heads and long, naked muzzles. The hair on the neck and shoulders is very long in some species and forms a pronounced mane or cape. Tails are relatively short and either arched backwards or bent at an angle above the base, but never touching the ground. The tips are tufted.

Nomenclature: Baboons are commonly called 'apes' and 'cynocephalus' in Egyptological literature. Apes are tailless primates and *Cynocephalus* is an obsolete generic and specific name for baboons.

Hamadryas Baboon ***Papio hamadryas*** (Linnaeus, 1758)

 *iʿn* *ian* Wb. I, 41

E Sacred Baboon; F Hamadryas; G Hamadryas, Mantelpavian, Felsenpavian; A Qerd

Description: This is one of the smaller baboons. Males have a head and body length of 75-95 cm and tail length, 50-65 cm; females, 50-65 and 42-60 cm. Males have a long mane or mantle extending from the head onto the neck, shoulders and back. The ears are hidden in the long hair. The tail curves backwards, but is never angled near the base. The face is reddish and also the large, naked callosities on the buttocks.

Males are ashy grey with a brownish wash; females are yellowish-brown and lack manes.

A notable feature in this species is that the nostrils do not protrude beyond the upper lip as in *P. anubis*. This is not always clearly shown, however, in Egyptian art.

Natural history: Hamadryas baboons live in small troops of one male and several females with young or united in large groups called 'packs'.

They inhabit savanna and semi-desert, preferring rocky areas, especially for sleeping. They are terrestrial, but can climb well and will also use trees for sleeping.

Food is primarily plant life, but some insects and other arthropods are eaten; lizards; eggs and young of ground-nesting birds, and sometimes the newborn young of other mammals.

Distribution: The present distribution is limited to eastern Sudan, Somalia, and Ethiopia in Africa, and the Red Sea Hills in the southwestern Arabian Peninsula.

Prehistoric and Predynastic records: No fossil remains of baboons have been found in Egypt; therefore, there is no definite knowledge of ancient distribution.

The baboon cult apparently began in the Predynastic when the species existed in Egypt. One indication is the limestone statue called 'a monkey and young' (Quibell, 1900 I: 7) from Hierakonpolis (fig. 4-1).

The Dynastic period: Smith (1969: 31) estimated that this baboon became extinct in Egypt by the third millennium B.C. or First Dynasty.

There is an alabaster statue of a hamadryas baboon from the First Dynasty bearing the name of Menes (Mendes), the first king of Egypt (fig. 4-2) .

Many green glaze, ivory, clay, and limestone figurines of baboons were discovered in Dynasty I and later graves and the temple at Abydos (fig. 4-3). There are also some natural flint fragments that were apparently collected because of their similarities to man-made carvings.

Just when the importation of hamadryas baboons and other primates into Egypt began is not definitely known, but it was probably early in the Old Kingdom.

Two illustrations of baboons and monkeys appeared in the Dynasty IV Mastaba of Nefermat and his wife Atet. In Figure 4-4 their two young sons are leading a tame hamadryas baboon and patas monkey and in Figure 4-5 "a very small boy is looking after an ape — who seems to have the better of him — and a monkey in front who cannot resist pulling the bird's tail" (Petrie, 1892b: 27).

An odd combination of animal figures appeared in the Dynasty XII Tomb of Baqt where a man is facing a sitting cat and 'rat' below which are a pair of hamadryas baboons, colored green with red faces and buttocks, and a pair of green monkeys that were not colored. The female monkey carries a young one on her back (fig. 4-6).

Another combination is a wall painting with two monkeys and two baboons followed by the mythical Sag (fig. 4-7).

A baboon shaking hands with a priest who is wearing a leopard skin (fig. 4-8) supposedly represented a hieroglyph for the determinative of the priestly title An-met-f, 'pillar or support of his mother'. Griffith (1896 III: 27) said, "The animal taking part in this function may of course

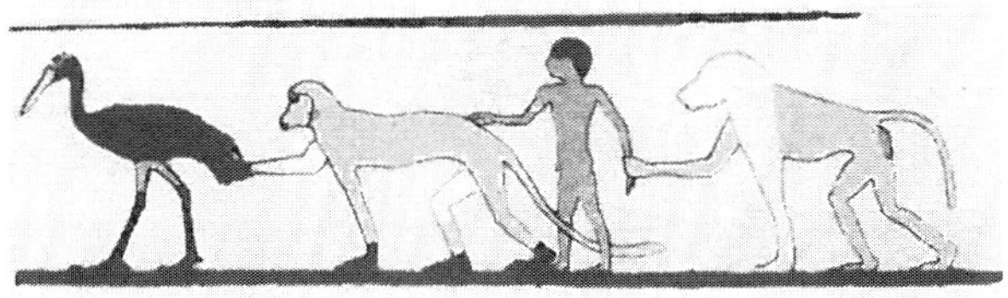

4-5 A small boy with a hamadryas baboon and a green monkey in the Tomb of Nefermat, Dynasty IV, Medum. Source: Petrie (1892b: pl. XXIV).

4-6 A cat and a rat (above). Below (right to left), a pair of hamadryas baboons and a pair of green monkeys. Tomb of Baqt III, Dynasty XII, Beni Hasan. Source: Newberry (1894 II: pl. VI).

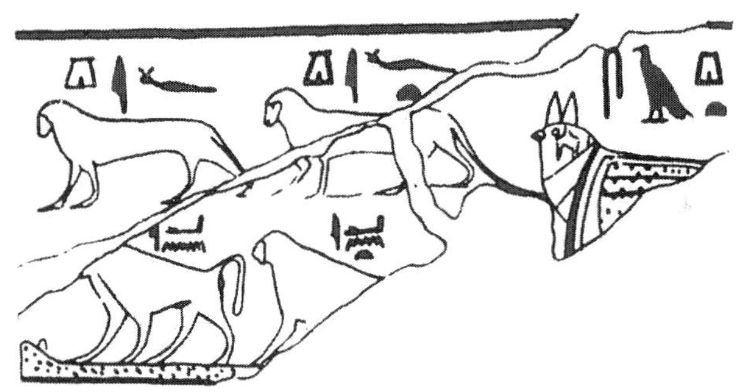

4-7 A pair of green monkeys (above) and a pair of hamadryas baboons. Behind them is the mythical Sag. Tomb of Nehera, Dynasty XII, El Bersheh. Source: Griffith and Newberry (1894 II: pl. X 5).

4-8 (right) A baboon and a priest shaking hands. Tomb of Chnemhotep, Dynasty XII, Beni Hasan. Source: Griffith (1896 III: pl. VI).

4-9 (below) Pets of male hamadryas baboon and patas monkey in the Tomb of Nebemchut, Dynasty IV, Giza. Source: L.D. II, 13.

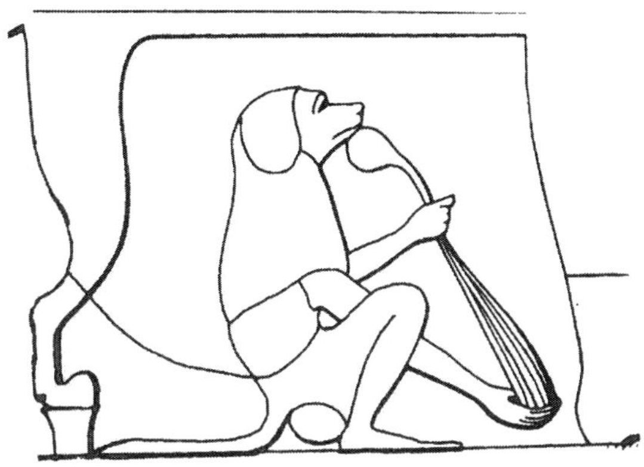

4-10 (above) Hamadryas baboon eating an onion under the throne of Amenemhet, Dynasty XVIII, Abd el Qurnah (Gurnah), Thebes. Source: L.D. III, 19.

4-11 (left) Three dogs and a hamadryas baboon at the feet of Khety, Dynasty XI, Beni Hasan. Source: Newberry (1894 II: pl. XVI).

have been a man or a woman dressed in mask and skin, but the tail contradicts the ape-like character of the rest of the body."

Baboons were generally kept in temples and embalmed. They rarely became pets, because of their aggressive nature. Females were more docile than males and may have occasionally become pets of women with whom they were more tractable (McDermott, 1938: 38 ff.).

An exception appears in a Dynasty IV scene described by Erman (1894: 243) in which Nebemchut and his wife, accompanied by their 'two uncouth long-maned baboons', are inspecting the work of his artisans. The pets are pictured as a male hamadryas baboon and a female (?) patas monkey (fig. 4-9). The baboon's mane is on one side only and its ears are exposed and in the wrong position. The monkey is partly damaged, but the upturned tail and long hind legs indicate a patas monkey.

Of the numerous primates that were shown under chairs or thrones one appears to be a hamadryas baboon eating an onion (fig. 4-10). There is an interesting error in the drawing of what is supposed to be the right arm of the animal.

Another example of a possible pet is the baboon with three dogs at the feet of Khety (fig. 4-11).

From Keimer's (1939b) discussion of the baboon and the dom palm (*Hyphaene thebaica*) we learn that the fruit of this tree, called 'nuts', was a nourishing food. Its importance was emphasized by numerous ostraca and statuettes from Deir el Medineh showing baboons and monkeys with sacks of dom fruit and climbing the trees (*op. cit.*, pls. 18-20).

Another illustration with baboons below a dom palm appeared in Hatshepsut's wall paintings of Punt (fig. 4-12). Here, they are facing a hippopotamus (see *Errors and discrepancies* in the Hippopotamus chapter).

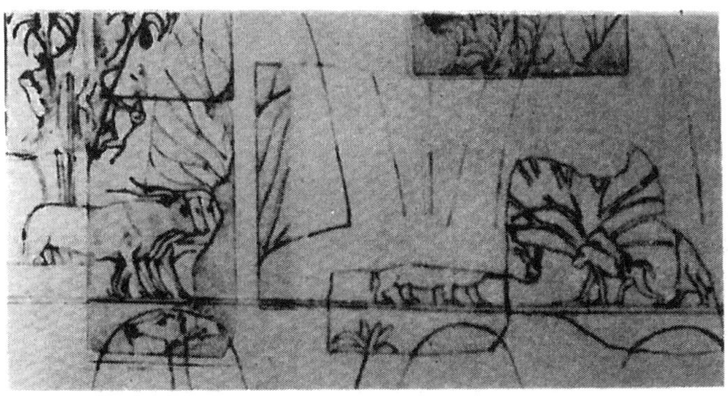

4-12 (above, left) A female baboon with her young on her back in a part of a wall painting of Punt in the Temple of Hatshepsut, Dynasty XVIII, Deir el Bahari, Thebes. Source: Smith (1962: 61). The baboons are facing a hippopotamus. To the left a monkey and a baboon are climbing a dom palm.

4-13 (left) "The oldest representation of the baboon watching the weighing of the heart; he is here called 'Thoth, lord of the words of the god'". (Papyrus Nebseni). Source: Budge (1934: 85).

4-14 The baboon sitting on the beam of the scales. Source: Budge (1926: 230). Anubis is trying to balance the heart of the deceased against the feather, symbol of law or truth. The ibis headed Thoth, scribe of the gods, is noting the result of the trial, and behind him waits the monster Amam (Am-mit), the Devourer. This scene is from the Dynasty XVIII Papyrus of Ani.

The location of Punt is referred to as along the two shores of the Straits of Bab el Mandob at the southern end of the Red Sea and along the coast of N.E. Somalia and southern Arabia. Punt, according to Erman (1894:505), "evidently signified the more tropical coast lands of the Red Sea, the south of Arabia, and the Somali coast".

Thoth in the form of this sacred animal reportedly lived in the tops of dom palms, which became the sacred tree of this god (Keimer, *loc. cit.*).

Throughout the dynasties the baboon was associated with Thoth, the moon god. Thoth was the scribe of the sun god, Ra, and patron of arts, speech, writing, science, wisdom, healing, and magic. A baboon was believed to have taught him the sacred hieroglyphs. All sacred baboons were believed to have been capable of writing.

A sacred bird, the ibis (*Threskionoris aethiopicus*), was also associated with Thoth, and commonly pictured as a man with the head of an ibis. He occurs, together with the baboon, in various pictorial interpretations of the weighing of the heart, the soul of the dead (Budge, 1967: 255 ff.). The purpose of this ceremony in the Hall of Judgement was to check the confession of the deceased that he had not committed any faults or crimes. His heart was weighed against the feather of Maat, symbol of truth and justice.

The hamadryas baboon, lord of the scales, sits beside the scales (fig. 4-13) or on the beam of the scales (fig. 4-14) and reports to Thoth when the pointer of the scales is in the middle of the beam. Anubis steadies the scales and tells Thoth when the two sides balance each other perfectly. Thoth, scribe of the gods, with an ibis head, writes down the result. Amam, the devourer, usually sits near the balance waiting to eat the heart of the deceased who fails to pass this test.

Worship of the sun was a sacred aspect interpreted from the behavior of baboons at dawn and dusk or when the sun reappeared from behind clouds. They were very active and constantly chattering (barking) during these periods. Numerous statues and reliefs, primarily from the Late dynasties or New Kingdom and later, show them standing with forepaws raised representing their greeting and worshipping of the sun (figs 4-15, -16).

4-15 (top) Hamadryas baboons worshipping the sun on the obelisk of Ramses II, Dynasty XIX, Meiamoun, Luxor. Source: Prisse d'Avennes (1847: pl. 24).

4-16 (bottom) Hamadryas baboons greeting the sun in the Temple of Medinet Habu, Ramses III, Dynasty XX, Thebes. Source: Keimer (1953a: pl. X).

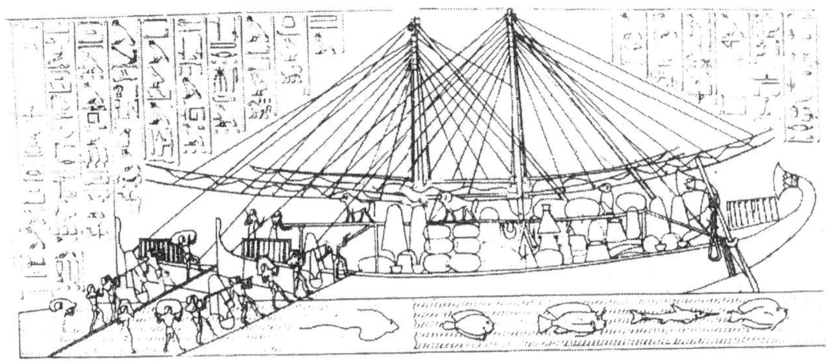

4-17 (top) One of 12 hamadryas baboons painted on the wall of Tutankhamun's Tomb, Dynasty XVIII, Valley of the Kings, Thebes. Source: Edwards (1976b: 44).

4-19 (bottom) Baboons on a bronze axe head from Dynasty XIX-XX. Source: Keimer (1953a: pl. XI 2).

4-18 (top) A baboon dancing in the Tomb of Uarna, Dynasty V, Sheikh Said, S. of Bersheh. Source: Davies (1901b: pl. IV).

4-20 (bottom) Baboons on a ship being loaded at Punt. Temple of Hatshepsut, Dynasty XVIII, Deir el Bahari, Thebes. Source: Naville (1898 III: pl. LXXIV).

Budge's (1904c: 257) explanation of the 'chattering' at sunrise was: "The Egyptians believed that they were the spirits of the dawn which saluted the rising sun and that when the luminary had risen they turned into apes".

On the wall of Tutankhamun's burial chamber 12 hamadryas baboons were painted (fig. 4-17), which were supposed to guard him through the 12 sections (nomes) of the underworld (Tuat) on his first night after death.

Other aspects of baboons that supported their sacredness were their apparently high intelligence and similarity to man. They were capable of understanding some words and would sometimes dance.

Davies (1901b: 13) described a dancing ape [*sic*], "whose faithful imitation of its superiors leaves nothing to be desired". Possibly it was trained for this (fig. 4-18).

In this relation, Caminos (1954: 85) commented that "Posener aptly points out that Cynocephali were taught to read, dance, and play musical instruments".

Except for the scene of dancing, mentioned above, the various illustrations of baboons as field hands, fishermen, servants, musicians, etc., are, in the estimation of McDermott (1938: 12), "pure caricature".

There are some truly artistic reproductions on Middle and New Kingdom bronze axe heads of stylized, symmetrical baboons grasping papyrus stems (fig. 4-19).

The major period of primate importation was the New Kingdom. In the scene of loading ships in Punt, from the Tomb of Queen Hatshepsut, items listed in the inscriptions above the vessels include baboons and monkeys (Naville, 1898 III: 68, pl. LXXIV; Breasted, 1906 II: 109). Only baboons are shown on these ships (fig. 4-20).

In Rekhmire's tomb 'apes' are listed among the taxes that are being brought from Nubia (Breasted, 1906 II: 283, par. 718). Tribute processions in this tomb (figs 4-21,-22) and others include baboons and monkeys that appear to have already been 'tamed'.

In the Dynasty XVIII Tomb of Amunedjeh (Amunezeh) Nubians are bringing a hamadryas baboon and green monkeys as tribute (fig. 4-23).

Without reference to any source of information, MacDonald (1965: 114) said the Egyptians' knowledge of the baboon's wisdom and magical attributes was reason for their "importing thousands of the animals from what is now Ethiopia and the Sudan".

Information on primate mummies is also somewhat confusing from the various comments that have been made and the lack of supporting data. Regarding numbers of specimens,

4-21 (top left) Tribute from Punt in the Tomb of Rekhmire, Dynasty XVIII, Thebes. Source: Davies (1943 II: pl. XVII). Animals from left to right: cheetah, green monkey, Nubian ibex, and hamadryas baboon. The men carry ostrich plumes, ebony logs, an elephant tusk, and a cheetah (?) skin.

4-22 (top right) Tribute from Punt in the Tomb of Rekhmire, Dynasty XVIII, Thebes. Source: Davies (1943 II: pl. XIX). Animals from left to right: green monkey, hamadryas baboon, leopard. The men carry ostrich plumes and eggs, elephant tusks, ebony logs, a hyena dog skin, and a fox skin.

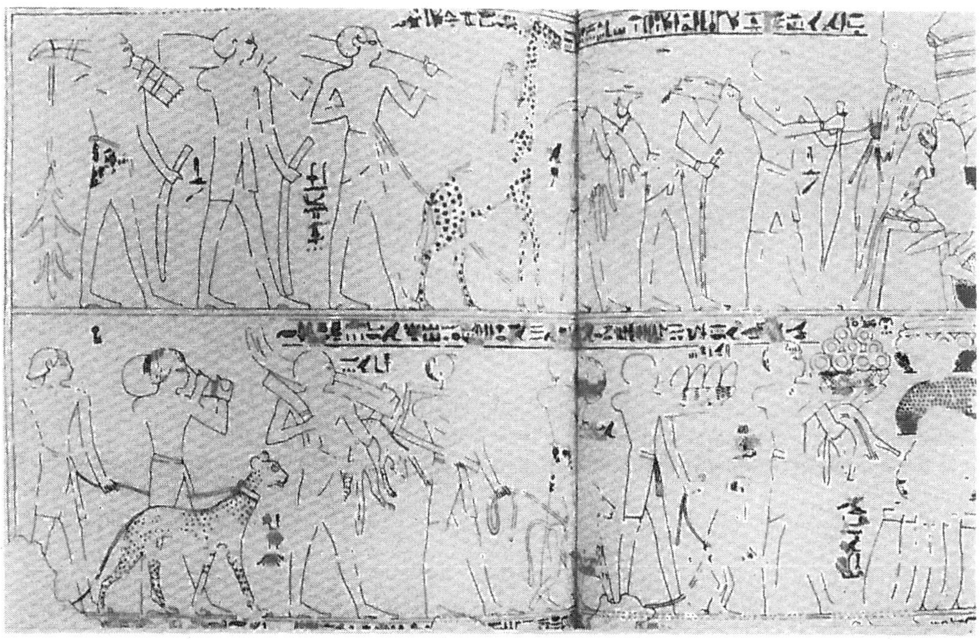

4-23 Nubian tribute in the Tomb of Amunedjeh, Dynasty XVIII, Sheikh Abd el Gurneh, Thebes. Source: Davies (1942: pl. V). Upper row, left to right: Live animals are a giraffe with a green monkey on its neck and a green monkey on a stool. The men carry elephant tusks, ebony logs, wands, fox and leopard or cheetah skins, and giraffe tails. Lower row, left to right: Live animals are a cheetah, a hamadryas baboon, and a green monkey. The men carry elephant tusks, leopard or cheetah skins, ostrich eggs, and various other objects.

MacDonald (*op. cit.*, 114) and L.H. Lovison (*in* Young World/32) stated that thousands of hamadryas baboons had been mummified because they were so highly venerated and respected. Another author (Rabb, 1968: 3), also without data, said "hundreds of thousands of mummified baboons have been found".

Brunner (1969: 560) remarked on the findings of Emery of thousands of mummified ibises at Saqqara that caused the species to come close to extinction and "similar fates befell the cats in Bubastis ... and baboons in Tuna el Gebel".

Boessneck (1988: 142 f.) noted that baboon mummies were by all means much fewer than ibis mummies, for in the Late Period no more baboons of either species were imported and they were no longer kept in temples.

In Tuna el Gebel crouching baboon mummies with hands on their knees were found in niches; others were sitting entombed in wooden coffins. Many of them had skull and skeletal deformities, which Boessneck (*op.cit.*) attributed to improper diets and vitamin deficienies. None were said to be in as good a state as those found by Lortet and Gaillard (1905: 207 ff.; 1909: 1 ff.).

Kessler's (1989: 18 ff.) list of Late Period animal necropolises (cemeteries) includes, for the most part, single remains or mummies of baboons and green monkeys and one location only of a patas monkey. At the site of Tuna el Gebel there were 40 specimens of *Papio anubis* and single specimens of *P. hamadryas* and green monkey, *Cercopithecus aethiops*.

The worship of baboons continued into the Christian era. Much more information on the religious aspects of baboons can be found in McDermott's (1938) review in the 'Ape in Antiquity'.

Anubis Baboon ***Papio anubis*** (Linnaeus, 1758)

 *'nr* *aner* Wb. I, 192

E Black Faced Baboon, Olive Baboon; F Papion anubis, Babouin doguera; G Anubispavian

Nomenclature: The specific name derives from the supposed similarity of this baboon to the god Anubis; probably when he was called the 'dog-headed' god.

The taxonomic status of this species is unsettled and various names have been applied, including *P. cynocephalus anubis* (Lesson, 1824) and *P. doguera* (Pucheron, 1856).

Description: The head and body length of this baboon is about one meter. The mane is slightly developed and does not cover the ears. The color is olive-green to brownish. The face and the callosities on the buttocks are blackish- to purplish-grey. The nostrils protrude beyond the upper lip. The tail is sharply angled at the basal one-third and then turns sharply downwards.

Natural history: Anubis baboons live mainly in savannas. Habits are similar to those described for *P. hamadryas*.

Distribution: The present distribution is across central Africa south of the Sahara, except in the extreme east and west.

Prehistoric and Predynastic records: As with the other primates, there are no early records of distribution in Egypt.

The Dynastic period: Illustrations of the Anubis baboon are rare and the protruding nostrils and angled tail are not clearly represented nor can facial and buttocks coloration always be verified. It was doubtless imported along with the hamadryas baboon, but in only a few illustrations from the New Kingdom can this be confirmed.

In the Dynasty V Tomb of Tepemankh (fig. 4-24) the baboon grasping a man by the leg is referred to as a 'police baboon' catching a thief in the vegetable market. It appears to represent a male Anubis baboon because of the lack of a mantle. There is no indication of its sex, however, but behind it a female is carrying a baby, which suggests they are a pair of *P. anubis*.

The baboons in a fig tree (fig. 4-25) are a dark green color with reddish-brown faces and callosities and without mantles. The one on the lower right is a male as indicated by Davies' (1936: pl.VII) reproduction. Therefore, they probably represent Anubis baboons.

They were called 'monkeys' by Erman (1894:

4-24 (top left) An Anubis baboon grabbing a man by the leg. Tomb of Tepemankh, Dynasty V, Saqqara. Source: Wolf (1957: fig. 201). Behind is a female with young on her back.

4-25 (middle left) Anubis baboons in a fig tree. Tomb of Khnemhotep (Chnemhotep), Dynasty XII, Beni Hasan. Source: L.D. II, 127.

4-26 (bottom left) Male Anubis baboons on a ship being loaded at Punt. Temple of Hatshepsut, Dynasty XVIII, Deir el Bahari, Thebes. Source: Dümichen (1879: between pp. 102-103).

4-27 (top right) Male Anubis baboon in tribute from Punt. Temple of Hatshepsut, Dynasty XVIII, Deir el Bahari, Thebes. Source: Naville (1898 III: pl. LXXVII).

4-28 (bottom right) One of nine Anubis baboons on the wall of the Tomb Chapel of Petosiris, Dynasty XVIII, Tuna Deraw (Deraw) south of Kom Ombo. Source: Lefèbvre (1924: pl. XLII).

199) and said to be helping with the harvest. This seems unlikely, because they appear to be about to eat the figs in their hands.

Houlihan (1997: 34, fig. 2), in reference to this and other figures of primates in fruit trees, concluded that they were not trained as harvesters or fruit pickers.

McDermott (1938: 12) noted that these baboons were probably not the hamadryas, because its sacredness "would prevent its being used for such service, and the fierceness of its nature would make it an unlikely pet".

Anubis baboons are on one of the ships being loaded in the Punt expedition (fig. 4-26) and together with tribute from Punt (fig. 4-27). Although the tails of these drawings are atypical, the ears are visible and the lack of manes on the males is sufficient evidence for their identification.

These baboons were equal in religious status with the hamadryas. The fact that they were also found as mummies and even in greater numbers (Kessler, 1989: 18 ff.) is proof of this.

Boessneck (1988: 142) recorded that only Anubis baboon mummies had been found in the Tuna el Gebel necropolis west of Hermopolis, but Kessler (1989: 19) listed 40 Anubis and one hamadryas. Both species were found at Thebes.

Various other sites where Late Period mummies of 'baboons' were found are Hermopolis Parva (Damanhur in the western Delta), Tanis (Zoan in the eastern Delta), Kom Madinet Gurab near El Lahun southeast of El Faiyum, Mustai in the south central Delta, and some questionable remains at Saqqara.

The nine Anubis baboons in the Tomb Chapel of Petosiris (fig. 4-28) can be compared with the 12 hamadryas baboons in Tutankhamun's tomb (fig. 4-17). They also symbolized protection of the tomb owner during his underworld journey.

Long-tailed Monkeys Subfamily *Cercopithecinae*

Green Monkey ***Cercopithecus aethiops*** (Linnaeus, 1758)

 *gf* gef Wb. V, 158

E Guenon; F Grivet, Vervet; G Grünmeerkatze; A Nesnas

Description: The general color is light grayish- or yellowish-olive, the face and callosities are black, there is a white band across the forehead and the sides of the face are white. Males have head and body lengths of 45-83 cm, tails 55-114 cm. Females are smaller. The long tail is carried above or below the line of the back when the animals are walking and horizontally (or upright) when running or climbing.

Natural history: This monkey lives in troops generally in woodland and savanna, but not in rain forest. The diet is chiefly vegetarian, but invertebrates, eggs, nestling birds, and the young of rodents and hares are also eaten.

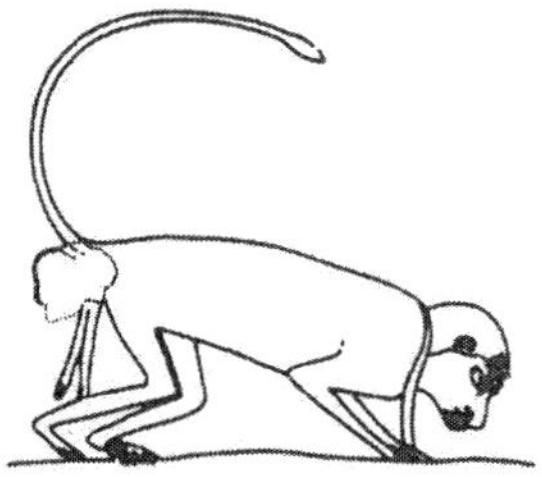

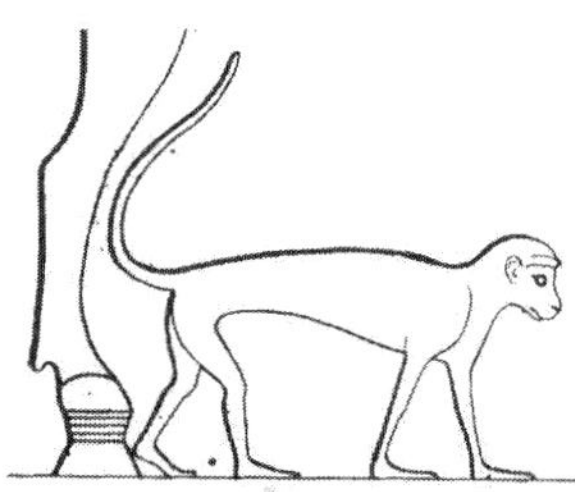

4-29 (left) Monkey giving birth in a hunting scene. Tomb of Ukhotep, Dynasty XII, Meir. Source: Blackman (1915 II : pl. VII).

4-30 (right) Monkey under the throne of Debehen, Dynasty IV, Giza. Source: L.D. II, 36.

4-31 Monkey and three tesem hounds in miniature under the chair of Ptahotep, held on leashes by a servant. Dynasty V, Saqqara. Source: Wreszinski (1936 III: pl. 2).

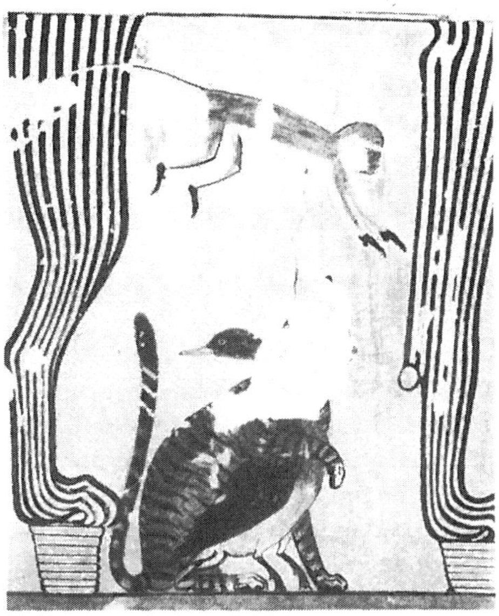

4-32 *Pet animals under Queen Tiy's chair: A leaping green monkey and a cat cuddling a pintail duck. Tomb of Anen (Onen), Dynasty XVIII, Thebes. Source: Davies (1933: fig. 6).*

4-33 *A dwarf leading Mereruka's pet monkey under his sedan chair followed by his three tesem hounds (two are not shown) and another dwarf attendant. Mastaba of Mereruka, Dynasty VI, Saqqara. Source: Duell (1938 II: pl. 158).*

4-34 *Dwarfs leading a green monkey, a leopard, and two tesem hounds. Mastaba of Gemnikai, Dynasty VI, Saqqara. Source: von Bissing (1905: pl. XXIII).*

4-35 *A dwarf carrying a green monkey and a basket of dom nuts. Tomb of 'Ankhm-'Ahor, Dynasty VI, Saqqara. Source: Badawy (1978: fig. 33).*

Distribution: This species is widely distributed in Africa south of the Sahara (Haltenorth and Diller, 1980: 291, 293 f.).

Prehistoric and Predynastic records: Remains and rock drawings of green monkeys are lacking in Egypt.

Bones from Holocene deposits in Dakhla Oasis that were first recognized as "? monkey *Cercopithecus* " by Churcher *et al.* (1997) have been reidentified as *Felis silvestris libyca* (*op.cit.*, p. 3, *corrigenda*).

The Dynastic period: Green monkeys were never considered to have been sacred, but were very popular as pets. One of the earliest examples is in the Dynasty IV Mastaba of Nefermat (fig. 4-5), where a green monkey is accompanied by a small boy and a hamadryas baboon.

Combinations of pairs of monkeys and baboons are common (figs 4-6,-7), possibly as indications of pairing and producing young. There is a Dynasty XII relief of a monkey giving birth (fig.4-29).

Numerous other examples are household pets under the chairs or thrones of their owners, who were usually women (figs 4-30.-31,-32). They were also commonly shown together with hounds on leashes attended by dwarfs or servants (figs 4-31,-33,-34, 7-31). One is pictured on the shoulder of a dwarf (fig. 4-35).

A variety of illustrations of monkeys under chairs, monkeys together with dogs on leashes, and on boats in the Nile from the Old into the New Kingdom were published by Vandier d'Abbadie (1964, 1965, 1966).

There appears to be a pet monkey in the upper left of Figure 4-18.

Monkeys were not only popular as household pets, they were also sent as gifts and objects of trade to various parts of the Mediterranean and to Mesopotamia (McDermott, 1938:14 f.).

Monkeys appeared in dom palms together with hamadryas baboons in Hatshepsut's Temple (fig. 4-12); in two pieces of decorative art in the Tomb of Kenamun, Dynasty XVIII, Thebes (Davies, 1930 I: pls. XIII, XIV); and in a gift of Nubian artistry to Tutankhamun (fig. 13-44) .

Monkey figures as ornamentals were very popular with women and decorated kohl jars, cosmetic spoons (fig, 4-36), and other objects of daily use.

Importation of monkeys from the south, as with other primates, doubtless began in the earliest dynasties, but was not pictured until much later. The examples indicate that they were already tamed (figs 4-21,-22,-23,-37,-38).

Single specimens of mummified green monkeys were listed by Kessler (1989: 18 ff.) from the Late Period animal cemeteries of Thebes,

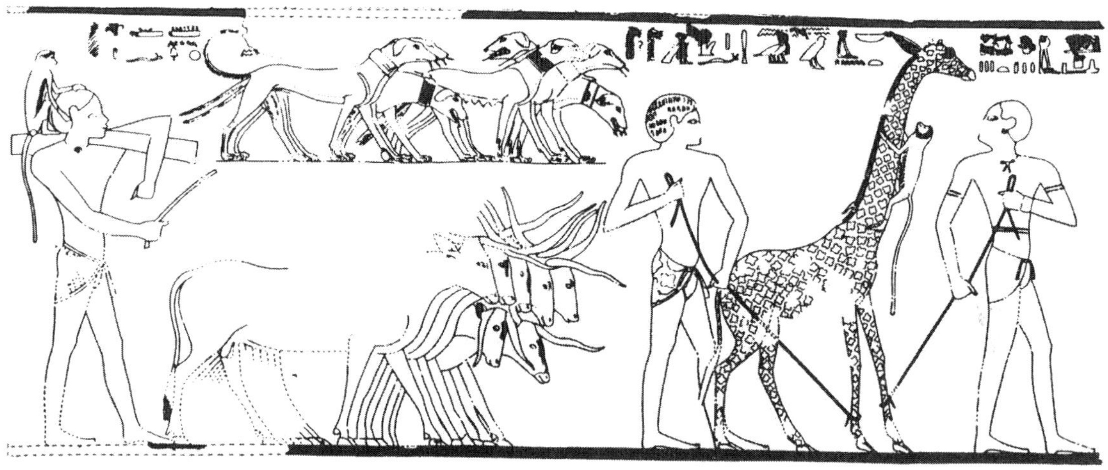

4-36 (top left) A green monkey on a schist cosmetic spoon; probably from the New Kingdom. Source: Keimer (1953a: pl. XII).

4-37 (bottom) Nubian tribute, Tomb of Rekhmire, Dynasty XVIII, Thebes. Source: Davies (1943 II: pl. XX).
Animals from left to right: Green monkey, seven saluki hounds, seven cattle, and a giraffe with a green monkey on its neck.

4-38 (top right) Nubian tribute in the Temple of Ramses II, Dynasty XIX, Beit el Wali south of Aswan. Source: Ricke et al. *(1967: pl. 7). Animals in upper row from left to right: A bull with a bent horn, a beisa oryx, and a lion. The men carry a young dorcas gazelle and cheetah and genet skins. Other tribute including elephant tusks is piled on the right.*
Animals in lower row: Cheetah, ostrich, dorcas gazelle, two saluki hounds, two cattle, a giraffe, and a cheetah. A child carries a green monkey, two men have green monkeys on leashes, one carries a dorcas gazelle, and another has a green monkey on an ebony log and carries a genet (?) skin.

Dendera, at Tuna el Gabal (Hermopolis) W of the Nile NW of Mallawi, Madinet Gurob, and Old Cairo.

Patas Monkey ***Erythrocebus patas*** (Schreber, 1775)

E Red Monkey, Red Huzzar Monkey; F Singe rouge, Patas; G Husarenaffe

Description: A large, tall, and slenderly built monkey with long legs and tail. The head is round and the muzzle short and roundish. The nose is narrow and flat. The back is horizontal. Head and body lengths of males are 60-75 cm, tails 62-74 cm. Females are smaller.

The upper part of the body is brick-red; underparts are whitish. The long tail is carried upwards above the back when the animals are moving. Patas monkeys can run up to 35 mi p.h. (50 km p.h.).

Natural history: Patas monkeys, like other primates, are diurnal and live in bands. Their diet is mainly vegetarian with a minimal amount of animal material, such as insects.

The habitat is high grassy plains, savannas, and open river banks generally near forested or rocky areas. They are apparently capable of surviving for long periods without water, because Mason (1936: 78) shot one north of Wadi Hawar in northwestern Sudan and also found skulls in the area "hundreds of miles from any water".

Distribution: Patas monkeys frequent the southern Sahara and central Africa from the Upper Nile Valley and Atbara west into Senegal and Mauritania.

These monkeys, because of their being capable of surviving without water for long periods, probably existed in what is now desert into the early dynasties.

Predynastic records: Rock drawings of patas monkeys (fig. 4-39) were called 'dogs' by Červíček (1974: 177), except for Figure 4-40 , which was listed as *'Affen'* (*op. cit.*, 169). Although the head of this drawing is 'ape-like', the tail position is comparable with those of the patas monkeys.

Another drawing of patas monkeys (fig. 4-41) was called 'Tiergruppe' by Rhotert (1952: 37).

The Dynastic period: Patas monkeys were probably popular as pets during the dynasties, but reproductions are difficult to distinguish from green monkeys (guenons). The position of the tail cannot always be relied upon as distinguishable.

The tall, light brown monkey in Figure 4-4 probably represents a patas monkey. Vandier d'Abbadie (1964: 152) called it "cercopithe'que *Ruber*." Another patas monkey on the right in Figure 4-9 has an upturned tail and long hind legs.

Kessler (1989: 18 ff.) listed one patas monkey from the Late Period animal necropolis in Dendera.

4-41 Rock drawings of two patas monkeys and unidentifiable animals. The locality is Karkur Tahl, Gebel Uweinat. Source: Rhotert (1952: pl. XIX 3).

4-39 (above left) Rock drawings of patas monkeys, a man with a lasso, and other beasts. The locality is Mamla el Otuani, east bank of the Nile, northeast of Edfu. Source: Červíček (1974: fig. 372). Above left is an aurochs; left to right in the row are a saluki hound (?); a patas monkey, a man with a lasso, a patas monkey, and a gazelle (?).

4-40 (above right) Rock drawings (left to right) of a dromedary camel, an ostrich, aurochs, patas monkey, and aurochs. The locality is Gebel Silsila, east bank of the Nile, north of Kom Ombo. Source: Červíček (1974: fig. 477).

V
Order *Lagomorpha*
Family *Leporidae*

Cape Hare ***Lepus capensis*** Linnaeus, 1758

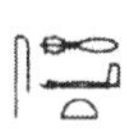 *sḫ't* zekhat Wb. IV, 268

E Brown Hare; F Lièvre du Cap; G Kaphase; A Arnab, Arnab gabaly

Nomenclature: Lepus capensis is synonymous with *L. europaeus* Pallas, 1778, the brown or European hare. Various names that were originally applied as species names, such as *aegyptius, sinaiticus, isabellinus, and rothschildi*, were retained as subspecific. *Lepus vulgaris* used by Keller (1909) is obsolete and not listed in Allen's (1939) checklist.

The common name, rabbit, was used by Darby *et al.* (1977 I: 260-261) and Mercatante (1978:9) in reference to Egyptian hares, but rabbits are not known to have existed in Egypt.

5-1 Hare hieroglyph. Mastaba of Ptahetep, Dynasty V, Saqqara. Source: Davies (1900 I: pl. VI).

Description: Hares are easily recognized by their long ears, which are about one-third the length of the head and body, but exaggerated to one-half or more of the head and body length by Egyptian artists (figs 5-1, 5-8); long, slender hind feet with densely furred soles; and a short tail. Head and body lengths average 40 cm and ears 12.

The pelage is soft and woolly. Dorsal hairs are yellowish to buffy gray with black tips giving the body a somewhat grizzled appearance. There is generally a narrow buffy stripe on the side and flank. The throat and nape are buffy and the nape is sometimes rufous. The tail is black above, white below.

In Egyptian portrayals hares often appear to be striped, but that was apparently a technique to indicate the grizzled or streaked pelage. They were sometimes painted pink (fig. 5-3); red (fig. 5-4), the color of the hare nome sign (fig. 5-8); or yellow (Vandier, 1950: fig. 22).

Natural history: Hares inhabit lower levels of vegetated wadis, patches of desert vegetation, and cultivated areas. They feed on various desert plants, including some saline species; consume fallen acacia blossoms (Osborn and Helmy, 1980: 90); and gnaw the bark of a desert tree (*Moringa peregrina*) known as Yassar (Tregenza, 1958: 83). Hares also have the habit of refection, eating their own feces. Hares are mainly nocturnal; hiding during the day in vegetation, rock crevices, burrows of other animals or hollows scooped out of sand hills.

Distribution: The present distribution in Egypt includes Sinai, the Eastern Desert, Nile Valley, coastal desert west of the Delta, and the northern oases of El Faiyum, Maghra, and Siwa.

Further distribution in Africa extends westward from Egypt and northern Sudan to Morocco and Rio de Oro and south into eastern and southern Africa.

This hare is also widely distributed in Europe, Asia, Asia Minor, and the Arabian Peninsula (Harrison, 1972 III: 338 f.).

Prehistoric records: Skeletal remains of hares dated from the late Pleistocene to recent times have been found along the Nile Valley within the limits of the present range (Gautier, 1976: 352 ff.; von den Driesch and Boessneck, 1985: 50; Churcher, 1972: 44, figs 11, 12). Boessneck (1988: 47) mentioned 'scattered localites' only.

Of special interest are fragments found in the terminal Paleolithic and Neolithic at Nabta Playa and Bir Sahara in the southern part of the Western Desert (Gautier, 1976: 327), and Dakhla Oasis in the central part of the Western Desert (Churcher, 1982:

5-2 Ostracon of a leaping hare and two hartebeests. Dynasty XIX, Deir el Medineh. Source: Brunner-Traut (1956: pl. XL, 127). A saluki hound is biting the penis of a hartebeest.

5-3 A white tesem hound grasping an oversized pink hare. Tomb of Atet, Dynasty III-IV, Medum. Source: Petrie (1892b: pl. XXVII.

5-4 A white tesem hound speckled with red grasping an oversized hare. The hare is red with white underparts and muzzle. Mastaba of Ankhtifi, First Intermediate (Dynasty XI), Moalla. Source: Vandier (1950: fig. 46).

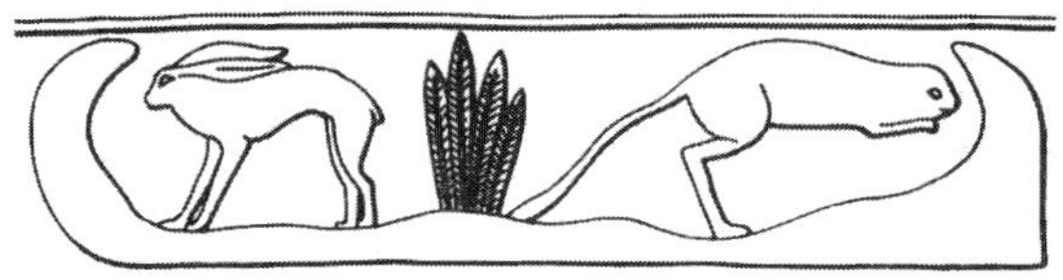

5-5 A hare and a jerboa approaching shelters in a hunting scene in the Causeway of Unas, Dynasty V, Saqqara. Source: Hassan (1938: pl. XCVII A).

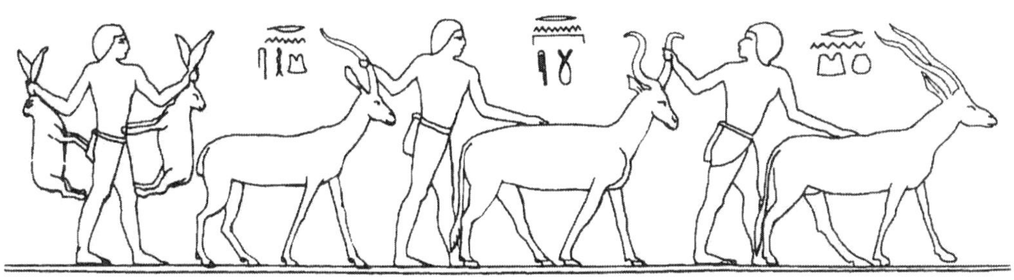

5-6 *Hunting scene (above) and return (below and upper left) with live animals in the Tomb of User. Dynasty XVIII, Thebes. Source: Davies (1913: pl. XXII). In the hunting scene two hares are leaping, several hornless antelopes are pierced with arrows, a saluki hound is subduing a large bovid, and a fox is hiding under a shrub. Various bovids and another canid are partly destroyed. The animals below are (left to right) a dorcas gazelle, a hyena, two hares, an ostrich, a beisa oryx, and two hares. Upper left are an ibex and dorcas gazelle.*

5-7 *(bottom) Two fat hares carried in an offering scene behind a 'stall fed' dorcas gazelle, hartebeest (with hieroglyph for kob), and addax in the Tomb of Manufer, Dynasty V-VI, Saqqara. Source: Rosellini (1834 II: pl. XVIII).*

110, table 1; 1983: 185; and Churcher *et al.*, 1997: 2), which indicate that previously the distribution in Egypt was more extensive.

One rock drawing of a hare from Mamla el Otuani in the Eastern Desert northeast of Edfu (fig. 7-73) was published by Frobenius (1933: pl. 41) and Červíček (1974: fig. 365).

There is a hare along with hedgehogs and other animals on a Gerzean pot (fig. 2-38). A gaming piece carved from limestone in the form of a hare was found in a Naqada grave (Petrie and Quibell, 1896: pl. VI). And a running hare is clearly depicted on the Predynastic Lion Hunt Palette (fig. 1-3).

The Dynastic period: Several rock drawings of hares said to date from the early dynasties have been recorded. Winkler (1938 I: 9; 1939 II: 8, pl. XI) listed one at Site 30 about halfway between Nag' Hamadi and Armant and at Site 68 on the Ghubari Road east of Dakhla Oasis. The latter shows a hare lying behind a hunter armed with a bow and arrows. Another drawing of a hare together with cattle was found near Halfat el Bir in the eastern extremity of Dakhla Oasis (Giddy, 1987: 276, Graffito No. 4b).

The bounding locomotion of frightened hares must have appealed to Egyptian artists, for throughout the dynasties they appear in hunt scenes leaping among the other animals (figs 1-18, -

20b, -21, -29, -30, 5-6, 7-148, 7-29, and Frontispiece). The ears were often shown spread apart rather than in the normal vertical position or laid back.

A leaping hare pictured on a Late Dynasty ostracon (fig. 5-2) was called a fennec by Keimer (1948a: 22). Although the snout is pointed, the ears are certainly more like those of a hare than a fennec. There is a comparable reproduction on Tut's bow case (fig. 13-189).

Hares were also shown pierced by arrows and grasped by hounds (figs 5-3, 5-4), hiding (figs 7-68, 1-18), reclining (fig. 7-63), and entering shelters (fig. 5-5). Hares were carried by their ears (figs 1-18, 5-6) or in cages along with hedgehogs (figs 1-33, 7-215), as prizes of a hunt (7-159a,b) or as offerings.

Two fat hares carried behind a row of bovids that are labelled 'stall fed' (*rn*), indicates that hares may also have been fattened for eating or sacrifice (fig. 5-7). Rosellini (1834 II: pl. XVIII) mistakenly interpreted the scene as 'Return from the hunt'.

In another tomb a live hare is walking, together with a young and an adult hyena, in a procession of stall fed wild animals (fig. 7-153a).

In the Tomb of Rekhmire a hare is included in a pile of dead game (fig. 7-159b). These scenes verify the comment of Darby *et al.* (1977 I: 260 f.) that "there is little doubt that it was eaten".

Aside from being a popular animal of the hunt, the hare was a cult animal as indicated by the amulets of blue and green glaze recorded by Petrie (1914: 44, pl. XXXVIII) and a 'Greek style' bronze of a crouching hare published by Roeder (1956: 500b, pl. 54e). In the British Museum a Dynasty XVIII head rest in the form of a hare with the ears extended laterally suggests that it was also popular as an art form.

The hare was the sign of the 15th Nome, Hermopolis Magna, of Upper Egypt (fig. 5-8), whose patron was the goddess Unnut or Wenenut with the head of a hare. Her male counterpart was Wenenu, who was sometimes identified as a form of Osiris or Ra (Mercatante, 1978: 211).

Although Budge (1904 II: 371) said the hare was worshipped as a diety, probably called Unnu, it was not a sacred animal, only emblematic.

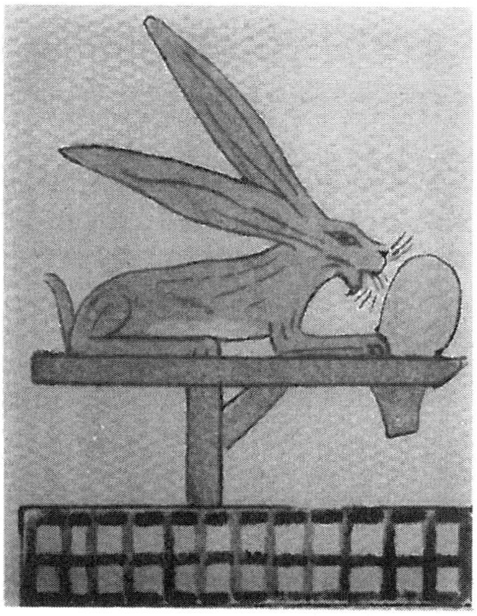

5-8 Hare sign of the 15th Nome, Hermopolis Magna, of Upper Egypt. Source: Griffith (1898a: pl. IX, 175).

Amulets were symbolic of Unnut and also of Osiris, according to Petrie (*op. cit.*), because of the meaning of the figure of the hare as the hieroglyph *wn* (Un), 'being'.

Unnefer, a title applied to Osiris, god of resurrection, has been given several meanings: 'He who is continually happy' (Mercatante, 1978: 205), 'the good being' (Petrie, *op. cit.*), and 'the springer' (Budge, 1904 I: 427). The latter name was applied because Osiris as Ra, the rising sun, 'sprang up like a hare' (Hopfner, 1913: 59).

Errors and discrepancies: Mackenzie (1978: 75) opined that "the hare was identified with a god of the underworld". Hence, the Seth animal in Figure 5-9 might be interpreted as a hare, despite the long neck; although Brunner-Traut (1979: 57) thought the figure derived from a giraffe because of the long neck and small head and the Seth-like ears, which she interpreted as combined ears and horns.

5-9 Ostracon of a hare in the form of the Seth animal. Dynasty XIX, Deir el Medineh (?). Source: Brunner-Traut (1979: pl. XXV, 29).

VI
Rodents Order *Rodentia*

This order contains the largest number of families, genera, and species in the existing Egyptian mammalian fauna and doubtless in ancient times as well. The extant rodent fauna includes six families, 16 genera, and 30 species, 28 of which range far beyond the borders of Egypt.

The following descriptions and discussions include a few species that have been identified from archaelogical remains, mummies, and ancient art. These and some additional species are listed in Boessneck (1988: tables 2 and 9).

Rodents are 'gnawing' mammals and their distinguishing characteristics are the upper and lower pairs of continuously growing, curved incisor teeth and the prominent gap between the incisors and the cheek teeth.

Food is primarily vegetable matter, but some species eat insects and other small animals, carrion, and gnaw bones.

Squirrels Family *Sciuridae*

Striped Ground Squirrel ***Euxerus (Xerus) erythropus*** (E. Geoffroy, 1803)

E Geoffroy's Ground Squirrel, Western Ground Squirrel; F Ecureuil foisseur; G West-Erdhörnchen

Prehistoric record: This species is known from Neolithic remains found in the area of Bir Kiseiba in the southeastern Western Desert (Gautier, 1984).

Distribution: This squirrel lives today in savanna from Mauritania to Ethiopia, Kenya, and Uganda (Dorst and Dandelot, 1970: 27, and Haltenorth and Diller, 1980: 138f., 145). Setzer (1956: 480 f., fig. 4c) recorded a number of localities in Sudan south of the latitude of Khartoum.

The previous existence of this species in Egypt is indicative of there having been a mesic climate in that region.

Mice and Rats Family *Muridae*

 *pnw* penu Wb. I, 508

Nomenclature: 'Mouse' and 'Rat' are the names commonly applied to genera and species of this family, particularly *Mus musculus, Rattus rattus*, and *R. norvegicus*.

Genus ***Mus***
House Mouse ***Mus musculus*** Linnaeus, 1758

F Souris grise; G Hausmaus; A Far, Sisi

Description: The house mouse is a small murid with a gray or brownish dorsum and a white to buffy venter. Four variations occur in Egyptian populations: light brown, dark brown, tawny, and gray. Body size and tail length vary only slightly. The average adult head and body length is 8.4 cm and tail lengths are approximately the same.

Natural history: This mouse lives in all habitats, except dry, barren desert. Burrows are usually under vegetation and consist of several short tunnels leading to a large nest chamber.

Food includes a variety of vegetation from crop plants and stored products to halophytic plants in saline habitats. House mice are generally nocturnal, except for those living in buildings.

Distribution: This species is common in the Nile Delta and Valley, coastal areas, and oases. Distribution in general is worldwide.

Prehistoric records: Neolithic remains of *M. musculus* were listed from Beni-Salama (Merimda) in the S.W. Delta, 15 km west of Ismailiya (von den Driesch and Boessneck, 1985: 60).

The Dynastic period: A mouse held in the mouth of a cat pictured on a Dynasty XIX - XX ostracon (fig. 6-1) probably represents *Mus musculus*.

6-1 Ostracon drawing of a cat holding a mouse in its mouth, Dynasty XIX-XX, Deir el Medineh. Source: Vandier d'Abbadie (1936 I: pl.XXV, fig. 2201).

Boessneck (1988: 63, table 9) listed remains from V-VI Dynasty graves at Elephantine and Middle Kingdom ruins at Tell el Maskhuta in Wadi Tumilat in the eastern Delta.

Genus *Rattus*

Two cosmopolitan species exist in Egypt that were probably introduced originally via ships during the Ptolemaic Period.

House Rat *Rattus rattus* (Linnaeus, 1758)

E Black Rat; F Rat commun, Rat noir; G Hausratte; A Far, Far el Eswed, Gerz el Shona

Description: This rat is brownish in color, with a gray, buff or white belly. The muzzle is sharp or narrow compared with that of *R. norvegicus*. It also differs from the latter in having a shorter head and body length and a thinner tail, which is longer than the head and body length. Also, the tail is not bicolored as it is in *R. norvegicus*.

Head and body length averages 18 cm, tail 22, about 120 percent of the head and body length.

Natural history: This is a commensal species and common in houses and buildings, especially where grain is stored. It inhabits canal banks and cultivated areas, but prefers drier habitats than does *R. norvegicus*.

Distribution: R. rattus lives in the Nile Valley and Delta, Suez Canal area, coastal towns, and a few oases in the Western Desert. Distribution in general is worldwide.

The Ptolemaic period: Bones of *Rattus rattus* were found in the viscera of mummified raptors from Giza and Kom Ombo by Lortet and Gaillard (1905: 39 f.). These were originally recorded as *Mus alexandrinus* Geoffroy, 1864. Skeletal remains of six *R. rattus* were found in the stomach and dung balls in the skeleton of a domestic cat from the Roman Period at Quseir on the Red Sea (Boessneck and von den Driesch, 1983: 211 ff.).

Norway Rat *Rattus norvegicus* (Berkenhout, 1769)

E Brown Rat, Sewer Rat; F Rat surmulot; G Wanderratte; A Far, El Far el Eswed, Gerz el Shona

Description: This rat is dark brown with a gray venter. The tail is thick, bicolored, and shorter than the head and body. Head and body length averages 22 cm; tail 20, and 88 percent of the head and body length.

Natural history: R. norvegicus is also commensal with man and lives in houses and buildings, but generally at lower levels than *R. rattus*, because of humidity. It burrows below buildings and also inhabits stables and chicken houses. In the wild it burrows in canal banks and near water, but also around and under buildings.

Distribution: This rat lives along most of the Nile Valley and Delta, Suez Canal area, Mediterranean coastal towns, a few localities on the Red Sea coast, and a few oases in the Western Desert. As with *R. rattus*, this species is worldwide, because of accidental transportation by man.

Genus *Arvicanthis*

Nile Rat *Arvicanthis niloticus* (Desmarest, 1822)

E Nile Kusu, Kusu Rat, Grass Rat, Field Rat; G Nil-Grasratte, Kusu Grasratte, Mullratte; A Far el Gheiti, Far el Hashayesh

Description: Arvicanthis is a large rodent with pelage speckled black and yellowish dorsally and with a middorsal black stripe. The belly is white. The tail is thin and bicolored; blackish above, yellowish below. Head and body length averages 18 cm and tail 14 cm; slightly more than three-fourths of the head and body length (fig. 6-2).

*6-2 A live specimen of a Nile rat (*Arvicanthis niloticus*) at Abu Rawash, a western suburb of Cairo. Source: Author.*

Natural history: This rat inhabits almost any damp area under vegetative cover or piles of crop wastes. Burrows are shallow and long with many openings. It is active during the night and day and is very damaging to crops.

Distribution: This species is common in the Nile Delta and Valley; El Faiyum, Dakhla, Kharga, and El Maghra Oases; Wadi el Natroun; and banks of

6-3 *Nile rats (?) mating and giving birth in a relief in the Causeway of Unas, Dynasty V, Saqqara. Source: Smith (1965: fig. 179).*

canals extending into the Western Mediterranean Coastal Desert. Further distribution includes northeastern and southern Sudan, much of tropical Africa, and the southwestern corner of Arabia (Yemen) and possibly southern Arabia (Harrison, 1972 III: 456).

Prehistoric records: Neolithic remains were discovered at Elephantine and Benisalama (Boessneck and von den Driesch, 1982: tables 7 and 24; and von den Driesch and Boessneck, 1985: 52 f.).

The Dynastic period: In the Causeway of Unas there is a relief showing 'rats' giving birth. Above them is the hieroglyph *ms'*, signifying birth. Beneath them two pairs of 'rats' appear to be mating and the hieroglyphs indicate that males are over the females (fig. 6-3). Ikram (1991: 55) called these animals '*Mus rattus/Arvicanthis niloticus*'.

Although identification of these figures can only be guessed, they probably represent *A. niloticus*.

Remains of the Nile rat were listed from Elephantine graves of the V-XI Dynasties (Boessneck and von den Driesch, 1982: 26) and undatable remains from the Satet Temple, and Middle Kingdom ruins at Tell el-Maskhuta (Boessneck, 1988: table 9).

The Greek and Roman periods: According to Pliny's Natural History, "... at the time of inundation of the Nile; for the moment that it subsides, little mice are found, the rudiments of which have been formed by the generative powers of the waters and the earth; in one part of the body they are already alive, while in that which is of later formation, they are still composed of earth."

This reference was doubtless to the Nile rat, which Sonnini (1800: 287) referred to later and told a similar story of rats and mice issuing from flooded fields and giving rise to the belief that they were produced from Nile mud and that observers claimed to have seen mice "at the moment of their pretended formation, and when one half of their body was flesh and the other half mud".

He also said that villagers in the neighborhood of Rosetta (Rashid) catch rats for food when flood waters have lowered.

Darby *et al.* (1977 I: 261) stated that there was no evidence that mice were eaten in Ancient Egypt. Several species of rodents, however, are known to be eaten by Bedouins and Fellahin (Klunzinger, 1878, 148; Osborn and Helmy, 1980: 242, 339). This habit might date back into Dynastic times.

Other remarks, but without reference to species, by Darby *et al., op. cit.* were that the fat of mice was used by physicians in ointments and as hair salve and "mixed with the fat of seven other animals... Magicians were even more weird. They fed a sick child or its mother a cooked mouse and had them wear its bones, wrapped in a linen cloth knotted with seven knots".

Smith and Dawson (1924: 161 f.) found remains of skinned 'mice' in the alimentery canals of several children in the Predynastic cemetery of Nag-ed-Der, which were "apparently given as a final medicine to children *in extremis*".

Errors and discrepancies: Petrie (1891: 8) wrote that in the ancient town of Kahun "Rats were as great a plague in the XIIth dynasty as they are at present in Egypt. Nearly every room has its corners tunneled by the rats; and the holes are stuffed up with stones and rubbish to keep them back."

This damage could not have been done by *Rattus sp.*, because of the early date. *Rattus rattus* and *R. norvegicus* were introduced into Egypt via Greek and Roman ships.

Drummond *et al.* (1990: 98) ascribed such damage to the Nile rat (*Arvicanthis*) and said that "unlike, for example, *Rattus rattus*, it is an animal which not infrequently burrows into the walls of houses and other mud structures in and around Egyptian villages...There seems to have been no other rodent in Pharaonic Egypt whose behavior could account for such structural damage."

In contrast with these assumptions, Flower (1932) said that *A. niloticus* was never known to enter houses. And Hoogstraal (1963: 22) remarked that although these animals live in close contact with human structures, they are "seldom if ever encountered inside buildings." Harrison (1972 III: 458) said, "They live near human buildings, but are seldom if ever found inside them..."

Obviously, further information is necessary in order to solve this problem of identification. Another species worthy of investigation is *Nesokia indica*, but very little is known about its burrowing habits or whether or not it inhabited or entered houses.

Genus *Acomys*
Spiny Mouse *Acomys cahirinus* (Desmarest, 1819)

E Cairo or Egyptian Spiny Mouse; F Rat épineux, Souris épineuse; G Stachelmaus; A Abu Shoaka, Far Shoky Masry

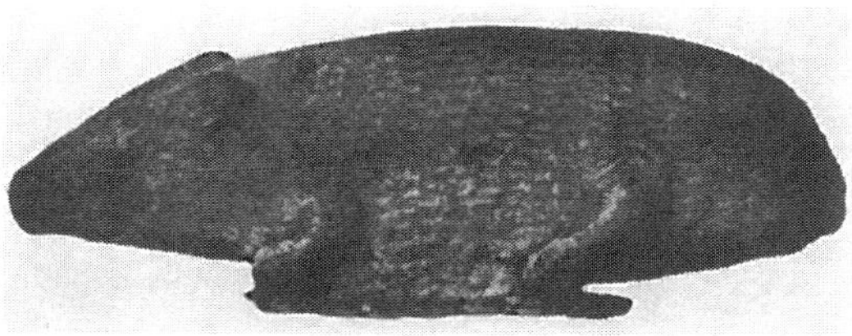

6-4 Bronze statuette of a spiny mouse purchased in Qena, date of origin unknown. Source: Roeder (1936: fig.2).

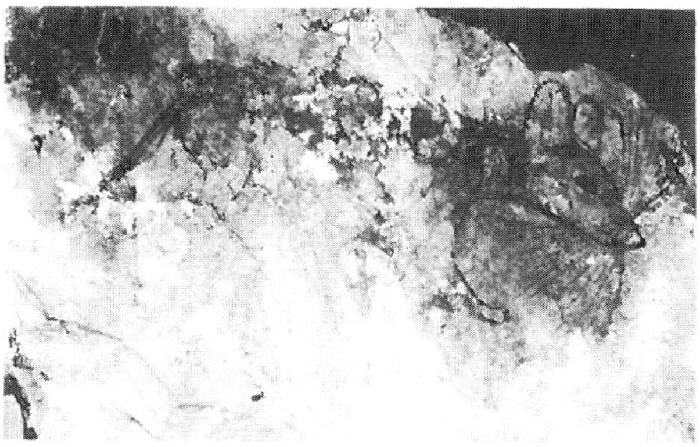

6-5 Ostracon drawing of a spiny mouse from the vicinity of the second Tomb of Senmut, Dynasty XVIII, Deir el Bahari. Source: Metropolitan Museum of Art, N.Y.

Nomenclature: In this work, as in Osborn and Helmy (1980: 293 f.), *Acomys cahirinus* is not considered to be specifically distinct from *A. dimidiatus,* as was designated by Ellerman and Morrison-Scott (1951: 615) and van den Brink (1957: 105). *A. dimidiatus* is, therefore, regarded as a subspecies. Contradictory conclusions have been presented by Setzer (1959: 93 f.) and Harrison (1972 III: 481).

Description: Spiny mice are medium sized murids with spiny dorsal pelage and prominent ears. Tails have broad annulations alternating with short bristles. Head and body length averages 10-11 cm and tail length about the same. Color varies from brownish cinnamon dorsally, with white belly and feet, to overall slate with white toes. The darker (melanistic) individuals are always found within or near human habitations.

Natural history: Acomys cahirinus inhabits rocky areas of the desert, palm groves, and human habitations. In the Nile Valley and Delta it is the commonest of commensal species and called the 'Cairo house mouse'.

Food is a variety of plants and seeds, insects, and snails. Spiny mice living in tombs scavenge the feces of fruit bats (*Rousetus aegyptiacus*) for seeds and also eat the dried flesh and bone marrow of mummies (Osborn and Helmy, 1980: 299).

Distribution: This species is common in the Nile Delta and Valley, much of the Eastern Desert, and in southern Sinai. Scattered populations occur in Bahariya, Farafara, Dakhla, and Kharga Oases, and Gebel Uweinat. Further distribution in Africa extends westward from Egypt to Morocco and southward through Sudan, Ethiopia, Somalia, Kenya, Tanzania, and Zimbabwe, thence west to Nigeria and southern Algeria.

Eastward the range extends through the Arabian Peninsula, southern Asia Minor, including Cyprus and Crete, Palestine, Jordan, southern Iran, and further eastward into western India.

The Dynastic period: The only identifiable figures of spiny mice are a tailless bronze statuette with a hole in the rear for insertion of a tail (fig. 6-4), and a sketch on the verso of an ostracon (fig. 6-5). The latter was referred to as 'an admirable drawing in black ink of a lean, hairy rat with prodigiously long whiskers' (Hayes, 1959 II: 110), but was reinterpreted by Janssen (1990) as being 'clearly a fox' and possibly a 'fennec'.

The head of this figure, particularly the muzzle, is typically rodent-like; the muzzle of a fox is long and very slender (fig. 7-54); that of a fennec, shorter, but more slender (fig. 7-75). The whiskers of a fox are not so abundant nor proportionately as long as on rodents and on this reproduction. Further interpretation from head to tail is as follows:

The mouth with its opening receding the nose is small and rodent-like. The mouth of a fox opens directly below the nose and extends below the eyes, although not always pictured thus in Egyptian art.

The ears resemble those of a rodent rather than a fox, because they lack the pointed appearance of fox ears and are not proportionately broad at the base. From what can be seen of the pelt the hairs appear bristly like those of a spiny mouse (see figs in Kolar, 1960).

The lankiness of the legs might give the impression of a fox, because rodents are rarely portrayed with legs extended.

The tail is slender and possibly hairless; not bushy like that of a fox. It is proportionately short, but perhaps part of it was defaced.

Close examination of the photograph and comparison with reproductions of rodents, foxes, and fennecs (e.g., Grzimeks Tierleben and various references from Janssen, *op. cit.*) indicated that it represented a rodent and quite possibly a spiny mouse (*Acomys cahirinus*).

Three specimens of *Acomys* were found 'mummified' with birds at Tuna (Tuna el Gabal) by Lortet and Gaillard (1905: 38) and some others were found in the intestines of raptors from Thebes.

Remains were also found in Dynasty V-XI graves at Elephantine (Boessneck and von den Driesch, 1982: 26) and in Middle Kingdom ruins at Tell el-Maskhuta in Wadi Tumilat in the eastern Delta (Boessneck, 1988: table 9).

Errors and discrepancies: In the Ibis Cemetery at Abydos, Roman Period 150 A.D., Peet and Loat (1913 III: 41, pl. XX, 34) reported finding bundles containing 20-30 mummies of "shrews (*Acomys cahirinus*), a small insectivorous mammal, not unlike the common mouse in appearance". Further on (*op. cit.*, pp.43 and 45) only the name shrew was used for these mummies.

Whittemore (1914) said that some bundles from Abydos contained the shrew or field mouse and ichneumon.

Peet (1914 II: 63) remarked that in tombs of the Middle Kingdom and Intermediate Period "several skulls of a small rodent (shrew ?)" were found. These were indexed as 'shrew-mice'. One incisor identified as rodent was found in a grain kiln (*op. cit.*, p. 7).

Unfortunately, to the Author's knowledge, this material has not been identified to species. The fact that '20-30' specimens were found in bundles suggests that they were probably mice, perhaps *Acomys cahirinus*, because that species could have been captured in much larger numbers than shrews. Besides, Ancient Egyptians may not have always distinguished mice from sacred shrews.

Genus *Nesokia*
Bandicoot Rat *Nesokia indica* (Gray and Hardwicke, 1832)

F Bandicoot rat d'Inde; G Bandikutratte; A Girdi, Abu Emaya, Abu Afan

Description: This is a large, stocky, rat-like rodent with a pale brown dorsum, buffy venter, white feet, a blunt muzzle, large ears, and tail shorter than the head and body length. Head and body length averages 18 cm and tail 12.

Natural history: This rat lives only in damp soil along the banks of canals, the borders of saline lakes, and in cultivated land and wasteland. Its burrows are a network of corridors half a meter or less below the surface.

Food is vegetable material, mainly fleshy roots, and also various crop plants.

These rats are very aggressive, bite readily, and apparently cannot be tamed (Osborn and Helmy, 980: 313 f.; Lay, 1967: 190).

Distribution: A few populations are scattered in Egypt and isolated in a few areas: El Shallufa near Suez, northwestern margin of the Nile Delta, Wadi el Natroun, El Faiyum, and Bahariya Oasis. Specimens in the British Museum dated 1904 indicate it previously occupied the vicinity of Cairo. Beyond Egypt the range includes northern Saudi Arabia, Israel, eastern Turkey, and Syria eastward through southwestern Asia into Chinese Turkestan (Robinson, 1966).

Prehistoric records: Gautier (1976: 352 f.) reported remains from Upper Paleolithic sites of Idfu and Isna. Fossil jaws were collected from Late Pleistocene sites in Upper Egypt at Khor el Sil near Kom Ombo (Reed *et al.*, 1967; Reed and Turnbull, 1969) and Wadi Halfa in northern Sudan (Robinson, 1966). Neolithic remains from Beni Salama (Merimde-Benisalame) were listed by von den Driesch and Boessneck (1985: table 15).

The relict populations of bandicoot rats in Wadi el Natroun, El Faiyum, and Bahariya Oasis have been explained by Abu Al-Izz (1971) as evidence of wetter climate during the Oligocene and Miocene when there was contact between the Nile Valley and the lakes in the oases and with the Faiyum in the Pleistocene. Subsequent dry periods resulted in isolation (Osborn and Helmy, 1980: 315).

Family *Cricetidae*

This family includes a large number of small to relatively large rodents commonly known as jirds, sand rats, gerbils, and dipodils. Some dictionaries mistakenly describe gerbils as desert rodents with long hind legs for leaping, the proper name for which is jerboa.

The genus *Meriones* appears to have been represented in Egyptian art.

Jirds Genus *Meriones*

E Sand Rat; F Mérion; G Sandratte; A Jird

Description: Jirds are slender to stocky with back and sides yellowish-brown and underparts whitish. Tail length is about that of the head and body, which ranges from 12 to 16 cm. All Egyptian species have a prominent tail brush and relatively large ears (fig. 6-6).

Natural history: Jirds occupy semidesert and true desert. Burrows can be found in hard, barren ground or in mounds under vegetation. Fruits, seeds, and vegetation of various desert plants are the primary food source. Some species occupy barley fields and palm groves.

Distribution: All of the five species in Egypt and Sinai are widely distributed beyond the borders.

Prehistoric records: Meriones crassus is known from the Neolithic remains at Beni Salama (von den Driesch and Boessneck, 1985: table 15).

The Dynastic period: Remains are listed from ruins at Tell el Maskhuta (Boessneck, 1988: table 9). In a Beni Hasan tomb a sitting cat is facing a large rodent (fig. 4-6), which has been referred to as an ichneumon (Brentjes, 1965: fig. 94) and as a Nile rat (Boessneck, 1988: 62; Drummond et. al., 1990: 97) 'from its relatively small ears and the length of its tail'.

A drawing of an earlier date (fig. 6-7) shows that the 'rat' has a tuft on the tip of the tail, which suggests it may have represented a jird of the genus *Meriones*.

Another possible example of a jird is in a scene from Kenamun (fig. 7-68) where Davies (1930: 37) noted that "a half-sketched rat is added to the wealth of animal life, which the desert accommodates".

Errors and discrepancies: Faience figurines of gerbils or jirds similar to those in Figure 6-8 were called 'jerboa mice' by Phillips (1948: fig. 21). Hayes (1953 I: 224, fig. 140) said they had kangaroo-like hind legs and also referred to them as 'jerboa mice'.

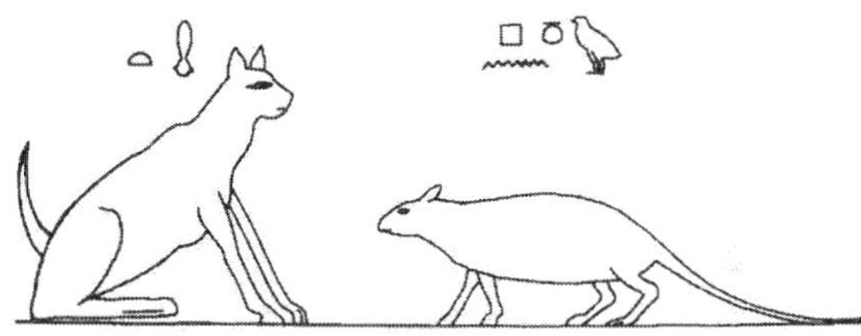

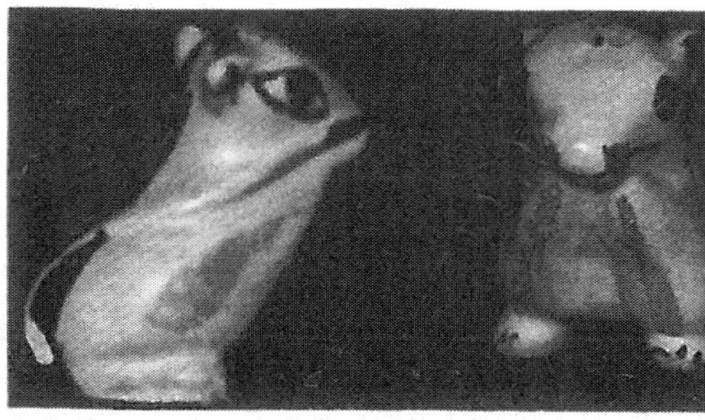

6-6 (top) A live specimen of Shaw's jird, Meriones shawi, *at El Maghra in the Western Desert. Source: Author.*

6-7 (centre) A cat facing a jird, Meriones sp., *in the Tomb of Baqt III, Dynasty XII, Beni Hasan; an earlier representation than that in Figure 4-6. Source: Champollion (1845 IV: pl. CCCCXXVIII). The hieroglyphs above the animals are* miu *(cat) and* pnw *(rat).*

6-8 (bottom) Copies of Egyptian faience gerbils or jirds from a museum gift shop. Source: Author.

Jerboas Family *Dipodidae*

E Desert Rat; F Gerboise; G Springmaus, Wüstenspring maus; A Gerbouh

Nomenclature: The common name, jerboa, is applied to two genera, *Jaculus* and *Allactaga*.

Description: Jerboas are relatively small to large rodents (head and body lengths 10-15 cm) with elongated hind legs, short forelegs, and tails about one and a half times the head and body lengths (fig. 6-9). Tails are tufted and have a subterminal black band and a white tip. Ears are relatively long; much longer in *Allactaga*. The soles of the hind feet are covered with hairs in *Jaculus*, naked in *Allactaga*. Color varies from brownish- to blackish-orange dorsally. Underparts are white.

Natural history: The larger jerboas, *Allactaga tetradactyla* and *Jaculus orientalis*, inhabit salt marsh and semidesert areas. The lesser jerboa, *J. jaculus*, is more specifically a desert animal. All three are

6-9 A live specimen of a lesser jerboa, Jaculus jaculus, *at El Maghra (Moghra) Oasis in the Western Desert. Source: Author.*

nocturnal. All species feed on fruits, seeds, and vegetation.

A jerboa will leave its burrow during the day or night if a car is driven near. The approach of running game probably stimulated the same reaction and could have been the reason for jerboas having appeared in Egyptian hunting scenes.

Distribution: Allactaga tetradactyla is limited to the Western Mediterranean Coastal Desert of Egypt and Libya. *Jaculus orientalis* is distributed in northern and southwestern Sinai and also the Coastal Desert. Beyond Egypt it inhabits coastal desert westward into Morocco. *J. jaculus* occupies much of Sinai and the Eastern and Western Deserts.

Its general distribution includes other North African countries, as well as Sudan and Somalia, and parts of Saudi Arabia, Israel, Jordan, Lebanon, Syria, and Iraq.

Prehistoric and Predynastic records: Two rock drawings of jerboas from the area of the second cataract in Sudanese Nubia were illustrated by Hellstrom and Langballe (1970, Vol. 2: figs 154a, 19; 154b, 7).

Neolithic remains of *J. jaculus* from Beni Salama were listed by von den Driesch and Boessneck (1985: 62 f.).

The Dynastic period: Either species of *Jaculus* could have been represented in Egyptian hunting scenes, but *J. jaculus* being the most common in the desert, was probably the one that was illustrated. Size gives no clue to identification, because most figures were proportionately large (figs 6-10, -11, 1-30, 5-5, 7-27,-39). A jerboa was shown behind the serval in the Dynasty XII Tomb of Chnemhotep (figs 7-186, -188). Drawings of jerboas entering a shelter or burrow (figs 6-10, 7-27, 5-5) appear to have been deviations from nature, because burrows of *J. jaculus* are dug in flat, barren sand or gravel and

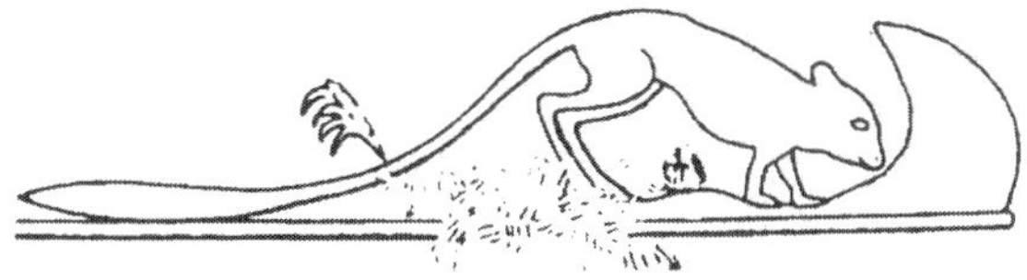

6-10 A jerboa entering a 'burrow' in a hunting scene in the Tomb of Sahure, Dynasty V, Abu Sir. Source: Borchardt (1913 II: pl. 17).

6-11 An oversized jerboa in a hunting scene in the Tomb of Ukh-hotep, Dynasty XII, Meir. Source: Blackman (1915 II: pl. VII).

excavated material is blown away (Osborn and Helmy, 1980: 350).

Remains of *J. jaculus* were found in ruins at Tell el Maskhuta in Wadi Tumilat in the eastern Delta (Boessneck, 1988: table 9).

There is a bronze statuette of a jerboa from Mit Rahina (Memphis) dated to the Ptolemaic (Maspero, 1904: fig 1). It is standing on its hind legs, the forelegs are missing, and the body is badly oxidized.

Errors and discrepancies: Various copies of the jerboa entering a shelter in the Tomb of Ptahetep (figs 7-27, 6-12a,b,c) show some variations in tail shape and length, shape of ears and snout, and the hind legs. Nevertheless, it can be identified as a jerboa.

But, Hartmann (1869: 30) referred to Figure 6-12b as a 'Genettkatze *Viverra genetta* Linn'.

a

b

6-12a,b Variations in copies of the jerboa entering a 'burrow' in the Tomb of Ptahetep, Dynasty V, Saqqara, for comparison with the copy by Davies (fig. 7-27). Sources: a) Paget and Pirie, 1898: pl. XXXII; b) Dümichen, 1869: pl.VIII.

Porcupines Family *Hystricidae*

Crested Porcupine ***Hystrix cristata*** Linnaeus, 1758

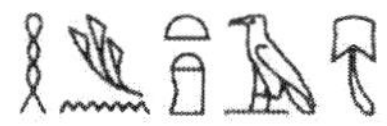 *ḥnt3* henta Wb. III, 122

 *ḥntj* henty Wb. III, 121

E North African Porcupine; F Porc-épic; G Stachelschwein; A Abu Shok taweel, Sayd el leil, Hanhan

Description: A large rodent (head and body length 65-85 and tail 12-17 cm) with coarse pelage and long, round, hollow black and white quills on the head, back, flanks, and tail. The spines on the back are up to 30 cm in length. Spines on the head are whitish, much shorter, and flexible. The tail has short spines not extending beyond those of the back. The swollen naso-frontal region of the head has a prominent rounded profile. The ears are short.

Natural history: Porcupines live in colonies in rocky and brushy habitats. They are nocturnal and hide during the day in burrows or caves. They feed on a variety of green plants, roots and tubers, bark, and various fruits, including the bitter desert gourd (*Colocynthis vulgaris*), and are reported to gnaw bones and eat carrion.

The short spines of the tail produce a rattling noise when the animals move or are suddenly disturbed.

Cats and canids that prey on porcupines are not always successful. Porcupines can erect their spines and dash sideways or rush backward at attackers; then run away leaving them penetrated with quills.

Distribution: At present the porcupine is not known to exist in Egypt. Osborn and Helmy (1980: 358) recorded a kill by a Bedouin in the 1950s in the cliffs north of Salum near the Libyan border.

Bisharin tribesmen described an animal called '*hanhan*' in the Red Sea or Kassala District of northeastern Sudan, which Keimer (1949: 414) interpreted as porcupine. He said they also spoke of a 'mountain of the porcupine'. Mason (1936: 115) mentioned holes and tracks of porcupines in Wadi Hawar, northwestern Sudan.

The present distribution includes Sudan, Ethiopia, Somalia, and Kenya; thence across central Africa and northwest through Mauritania, Algeria, Tunisia and parts of Libya.

This porcupine is also known from southern Italy and Sicily. Many zoologists consider it to have been introduced there from Africa by the Romans (Hanák, 1977: 132).

Quills found by Wassif (1954) in northeastern Sinai may have been of *H. indica*, which is known from scattered localities in the Arabian Peninsula and Asia Minor and eastward into India and Ceylon (Harrison, 1972 III: 405).

6-13 Lion and porcupine on the ivory handle of a Late Gerzean flint knife. Source: Asselberghs (1961: pl. XXXVI, fig. 51).

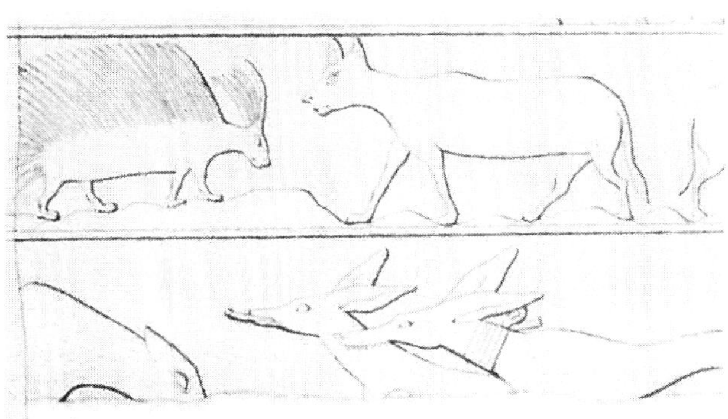

6-14 (top) Porcupine with quills raised facing a jungle cat. Tomb of Pehenouka, Dynasty V, Saqqara. Source: Keimer (1949: fig. 7). Below is a partly destroyed figure of a tesem hound attacking a fox.

6-15 (bottom) Copy of the scene above. Source: L.D. II, 46.

Prehistoric records: Fossil material of *Hystrix* sp. was discovered in the terminal Paleolithic and Neolithic site at Nabta Playa in the southeastern Western Desert (Gautier, 1980: 327 f., Table A 4.3). No rock drawings have been found.

Three ivory knife handles of prehistoric vintage bear figures of porcupines. One was originally called a hedgehog by Petrie (1902b: 17). Capart (1905: 71) said, "A fragment of a similar specimen in the Berlin Museum proves, however, that this animal is a species of antelope." He based his opinion on the long, slender, exaggerated head crest, which he interpreted as horns.

The 'similar specimen' (fig. 6-13), as well as the first, were correctly renamed porcupines by Petrie (1920: 12).

Both of these handles, however, have intertwined snakes on the reverse sides, which indicate Mesopotamian origin (Asselberghs, 1961: 276). Therefore, the porcupines probably represent the Asian species, *H. indica.*

On a third carving from the Naqada III site of Abu Zaidan (fig. 1-7), the porcupines in row A7 were originally described by Gaillard (*in* de Morgan, 1909: 274) as striped hyenas. Bénédite (1918: 229) called them 'Undetermined quadrupeds: horns, dorsal mane, tail in the form of a bowl'.

Keimer (1949: 411) chose to call them spotted hyenas, arguing that the figures complied with nature, because hyenas could raise the hairs of the back and tail.

Churcher (1984: 159) compared these figures with the African crested porcupine on the bases of "frontal tufts of long quills, a strong dorsal patch of quills, a short and horizontally directed tail with quills, short legs, a large head held low on the body, small ears and a large, short muzzle".

The Dynastic period: The only representation of a porcupine from Pharaonic times is in the Dynasty V Tomb of Pehenouka (Penhuika) at Saqqara (figs 6-14,-15). With head lowered and spines raised it faces a marsh cat (*Felis chaus*). Keimer (1949: 397 ff.) likened the figure to the work of a modern artist.

The crested porcupine most certainly existed in the margins of the Nile Valley and adjacent hills and valleys, and also rocky and vegetated areas of the Eastern and Western Deserts and coastal areas, well into the early dynasties. It was probably eaten by local tribesmen and the quills were no doubt used as decoratives. They may also have been used by the Egyptians as pens.

Errors and discrepancies: Besides the erroneous identifications mentioned above, a common error in the older literature was to call the hedgehog a porcupine (see Hedghog chapter).

VII
Order *Carnivora*
Family *Canidae*

Golden Jackal ***Canis aureus*** Linneaus, 1758

 *wnš* wenesh Wb. I, 324

E Common Jackal, Wolf Jackal; F Chacal commun; G Goldschakal; A Diib, Abu Soliman

Nomenclature: The Egyptian race of jackal was named *C. a. lupaster* (Hemprich and Ehrenberg, 1833) because of its large size and wolf-like appearance. The attempt by Ferguson (1981) to prove that it is a wolf (*C. lupus*) and not a jackal was not convincing.

The Arabic name, Diib, which is applied to the wolf (*Canis lupus)* and the jackal, probably caused confusion for early explorers.

Some obsolete species names for jackals are *C. variegatus, C. sacer, and C. doederleini.*

Description: Jackals are dog- or wolf-like in general appearance; having relatively long legs, long ears with rounded tips, but a relatively short tail reaching to or slightly below the hocks. This is not clearly shown in many drawings.

There is a dorsal mane of long, yellowish, black-tipped hairs extending from the crown to the tail base and laterally onto the shoulders and hips. The sides are yellowish with a scattering of black- and white-tipped hairs. Agouti hairs on the hips give an appearance of broken stripes. The chin is grayish and the throat and belly whitish. The legs are buffy to reddish on the outer sides; whitish to yellowish on the inner sides. The crown is reddish or grizzled with yellow and black. Ears are reddish behind and buffy on the inner sides. The brush-like tail is blackish dorsally, yellowish below, and has a black tip.

There is a slight, but noticeable frontal elevation. The snout is relatively long and stout (figs 7-1,-2).

Averages and extremes of measurements in cm are: Shoulder height about 40-50; head and body length 87 (82-92); tail 31 (29-34), 36 (34-40) percent of head and body length. Ears, 11 (10-12) are slightly longer than those of the fox, but proportionately shorter, 62 (57-64) %, than the length of the head.

Natural history: Jackals are nocturnal and crepuscular. Dens are in natural caves, crevices, and tombs. They will sometimes run out of their dens during the day when approached by a vehicle.

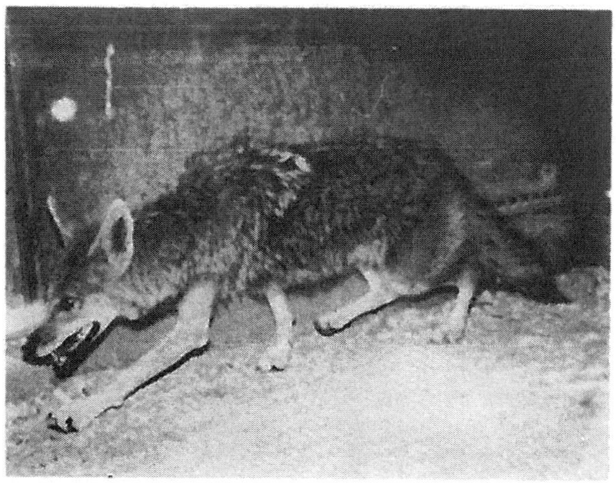

*7-1 Egyptian jackal (*Canis lupaster*) from Brehm's Tierleben, Ed. 4, Vol. 12. Source: Antonius (1922: fig. 47).*

7-2 A captive subadult jackal from Siwa Oasis. Source: Author.

The diet includes a variety of fruits in season as well as corn (maize), watermelons, and pumpkins. Jackals prey on various small mammals and hares and also raid farms for chickens. They kill sheep and goats; especially the young. Fish are eaten where available. Jackals also scavenge human rubbish dumps and eat carrion. Remains of insects and snails have been found in the stomachs of specimens collected in the semi-desert (Osborn and Helmy, 1980: 370). Jackals are known to hunt in packs in Libya (Hufnagl, 1972: 36), but there are no definite reports of this behavior from Egypt.

Distribution: Jackals inhabit the Nile Delta and Valley and bordering deserts, Western Mediterranean Coastal Desert, and some of the oases in the Western Desert. Distribution in Sinai is poorly known, but is probably limited to the coastal regions.

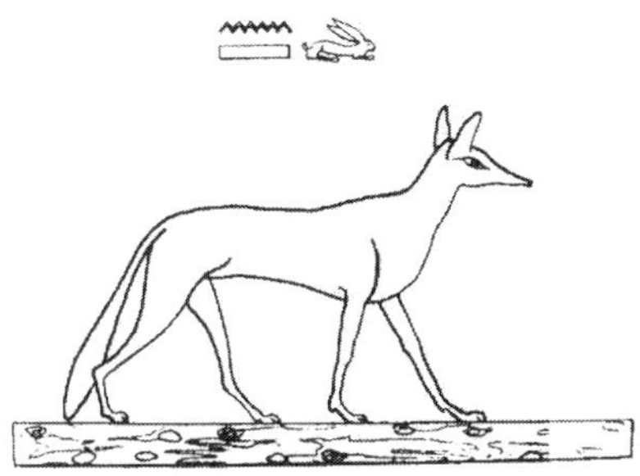

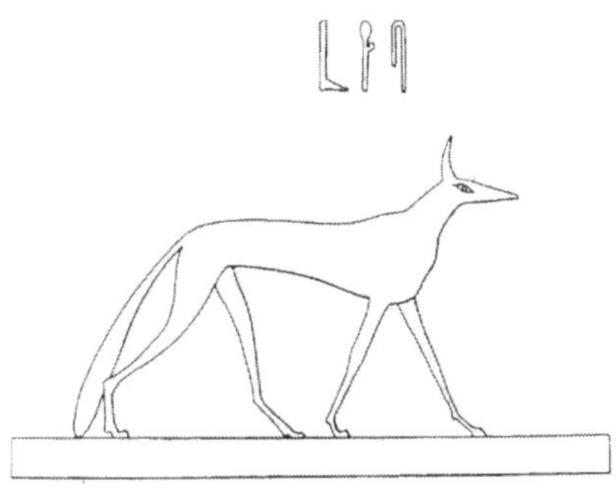

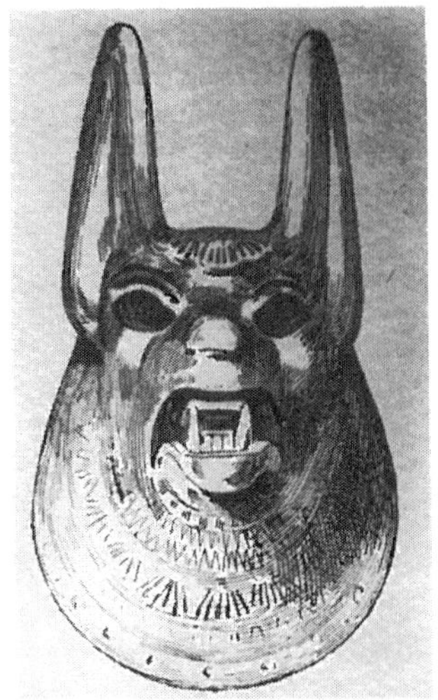

7-3 (top left) Drawing of a jackal from the Tomb of Baqt, Dynasty XII, Beni Hasan (fig. 1-29). Source: Champollion (1845 IV: pl. CCCLXXXIV).

7-4 (bottom left) Drawing of a fox from the Tomb of Baqt, Dynasty XII, Beni Hasan (fig. 1-29). Source: Champollion (1845 IV: pl. CCCLXXXIV).

7-5 (centre) A Roman bronze statue of a jackal, probably meant to represent Anubis. Dated to about 600 B.C. (?) in the Dokki Agricultural Museum, Cairo. Source: Author.

7-6 (right) A 'talking statue' or head of a jackal dated to Dynasty XIX-XX. Source: Keller (1909 I: fig. 5).

Further distribution southward in Africa includes Sudan, Ethiopia, Somalia, and Kenya; and westward, Libya to Morocco and Rio de Oro, thence south to Senegal.

Jackals are extant in the Eastern Mediterranean countries, northern Saudi Arabia, southeastern Europe, and Asia Minor; and eastward into western Russia and India.

Prehistoric and Predynastic records: Late Pleistocene remains were found in Wadi Halfa, northern Sudan (Reed and Turnbull, 1969: 55). A lower jaw was found in Late Paleolithic-Neolithic deposits at Bir Tarfawi in the southern Western Desert (Gautier, 1980: 320). Churcher (1982: table 1) listed Neolithic remains from Dakhla Oasis and von den Driesch and Boessneck (1985: 44) from Beni Salama (Merimda).

No rock drawings of jackals have been identified from Egypt, but a few were published by Hellström (1970 I: 2,N) from Sudanese Nubia.

Jackals were identified on two Predynastic ivory knife handles: the Brooklyn (Abu Zaidan) handle (fig. 1-7; table I, row B7) and the Pitt Rivers handle (fig. 1-8, row 5). The four animals in the third row on the reverse of the Davies ivory comb (fig. 1-10), are hyenas (see Hyena chapter).

The Dynastic period: A few figures in Dynastic hunting scenes can be identified as jackals, but some remain questionable. Several that were called jackals are clearly foxes (see Fox chapter).

The two jackals and two foxes in the Tomb of Baqt (fig. 1-29) are identified by the hieroglyphs *wenesh* for jackal (fig. 7-3) and *zab* for fox (fig. 7-4). These figures show the jackal to be slightly larger than the fox and not as slender, as indicated by the belly lines and the legs; to have a thicker muzzle and a more prominent frontal stop (projection); and broader and less pointed ears, which appear to be, and are, proportionately shorter than the length of the head. Tail lengths and shapes, however, were not accurately drawn and show almost no differences. These drawings can be compared with Figures 7-1,-2, and 7-54.

Jackal and fox were also identified in the Tomb of Antefoker (fig. 7-38).

In the Late Dynastic Tomb of Amenemhat (fig. 1-18, reg. 2) a jackal is leaping beside an ibex. In the Tomb of Neferhotep (fig. 1-24, reg. 3) a jackal is attacked by a saluki hound.

Another jackal, identifiable by the short, slender tail, is above the oversized hedgehog in Figure 2-4.

Artistic reproductions of jackals are rare. The bronze statue of a jackal from the Roman Period in Figure 7-5 was probably intended to represent the Anubis god.

Errors and discrepancies: Schweinfurth's (1874: 633) list of carnivores in Kharga Oasis included the 'wolf-dog' (*Canis lupaster*) and the 'more numerous' jackal (*C. aureus*).

References to wolf or wolf-dog in Egypt are doubtless to truly feral dogs that live in packs.

There are many recent stories about the sighting of 'wolves' and feral dogs that validate this assumption.

Other assumptions that all figures of canine gods represented the jackal, dog, or wolf are without substantial evidence and are discussed in a following sub-chapter, Canine Gods.

The Dynasty XIX-XX bronze head of a jackal or Anubis with a moveable lower jaw (fig. 7-6) has been called a bat by Keller (1909 I: 12) and others.

Domestic Dog ***Canis familiaris*** Linnaeus, 1758

 *ṯsm* tjesem Wb. V, 409

E Hound; F Chien, Chien de Chasse; G Hund, Jagdhund; A Kalb Beity

Nomenclature: The ancient determinative, a figure of the curl-tailed, prick-eared tesem is apparently used without reference to a distinct breed, 'but rather means 'hound', *i.e.* hunting dog' (Fischer, 1980: 77).

In notes from a dictionary: The use of the name 'hound' varies according to varieties of dogs and is often applied to any dog. The more practical use is in reference to breeds of dogs trained to pursue game.

Ancestry: The ancestors of Near Eastern, African, and Egyptian dogs were bred from tamed wolves (*Canis lupus pallipes*) some 8-10,000 years B.C. in southwestern Asia (Lawrence, 1967; Clutton-Brock, 1987: 34).

Some authors (Carrington, 1972: 72) have assumed that there was also 'some admixture from the jackal'.

Further support of the ancestral wolf presented by Brewer *et al.* (1994; 110 ff.) included some morphological and genetic characteristics that are lacking in jackals.

Two characteristics, prick ears and cocked tails, are indicative of the earliest dogs. Prick ears are typical of the wolf and other wild canids, but the cocked tail developed in tame young wolves raised in captivity (Epstein, 1971 I: 52).

Hundreds and hundreds of years elapsed before men were able successfully and selectively to reproduce definite types or breeds without variation.

Prehistoric records: The earliest known remains of dogs in Egypt have a wolf-like appearance. They are from the Badarian site of Beni Salama (Merimda) in the southwestern Delta and dated to 4,800 B.C. (Epstein, 1971 I: 53; von den Driesch and Boessneck (1985: table 2). Later records are known from the Gerzean of Maadi and Heliopolis (Moustafa, 1952, 1955). These dogs are doubtless of the pariah type.

Brewer *et al.* (1994: 116) recognized three types of prick-eared dogs in rock drawings: A large, stout form pictured with early hunters; a smaller and stockier dog with a straight tail; and a slender greyhound type.

Herein the largest form is referred to as a 'Pariah' and is a stout type with prick ears, and tails varying from straight to partly curled. The short, stocky, prick-eared type with a more or less straight tail can also be called a 'Pariah'. Similar dogs have also been called 'Pomeranians'. (Epstein, 1971 I: 53 f.).

7-7 Rock drawing of a hunt scene with pariah dogs and tesem-like hounds and scimitar oryx. Autochthonous Mountain Dwellers(?),Wadi Hamra, Gilf el Kebir. Source: Rhotert (1952:pl. XXVII, 3).

7-8 Rock drawing of a hunt scene with pariah dogs, ibex, and ostrich. Magal Abu Agag east of Aswan. Source: Červíček (1974: fig. 313).

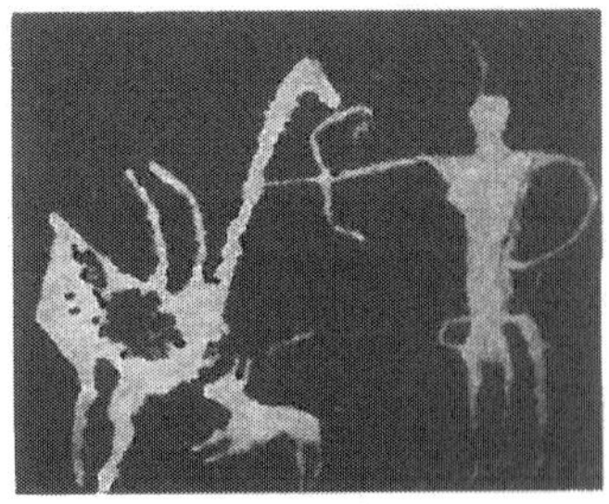

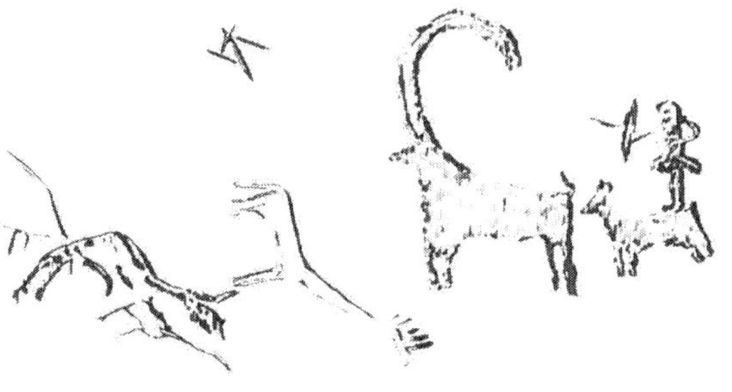

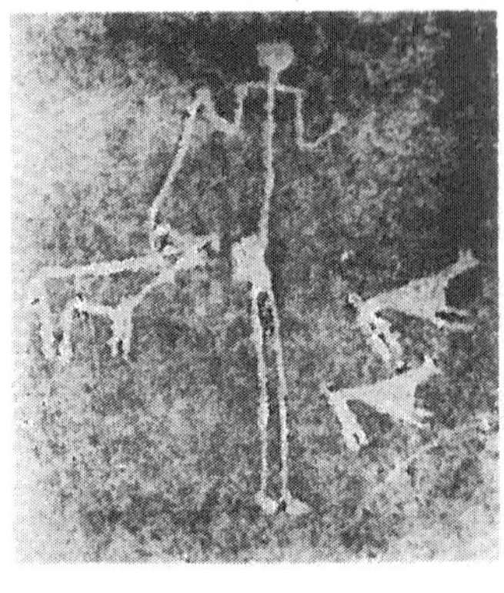

7-9 (top row left) Rock drawing of a herding scene including men and several long-horned cattle, a Barbary goat (lower left), a pariah dog (upper left), and a tesem hound ? (left) behind a cow. Autochthonous Mountain Dwellers: Uweinat Cattle Breeders, Karkur Tahl, Gebel Uweinat. Source: Winkler (1939 II: pl. XXXVIII, 1).

7-10 (top row right) Rock drawing of a hunt scene showing a hunter with a bow, an ass, a gazelle, a giraffe, a pariah dog, a lion, and ostriches. Autochthonous Mountain Dwellers, Qena-Quseir Road, north side. Source: Winkler (1938 I: pl. XIX, 3).

7-11 (2nd row left) Rock drawing of a hunt scene showing pariah dogs: one facing an ass (upper left); one behind a (?) gazelle (lower right); another dog (?) in the centre. Early Nile Valley Dwellers, Wadi Gash 50 km. east of Qus. Source: Winkler (1938 I: pl. XII, 2).

7-12 (2nd row right) Rock drawing of two pariah dogs and a scimitar oryx. Autochthonous Mountain Dwellers (?), Karkur Tahl, Gebel Uweinat. Source: Rhotert (1952: pl. XII, 8).

7-13 (3rd row centre) Rock drawing of a pariah dog behind a gazelle(?). Garf (Gerf) Hussein, west bank of the Nile 95 km south of Aswan. Source: Červíček (1974: fig. 228).

7-14 (3rd row right) Rock drawing of a hunter shooting an ostrich with an arrow. Below is a short, stocky pariah dog. Eastern Invaders, Wadi Abu Wasil, Eastern Desert, 85 km. S.E. of Qift. Source:Winkler (1938 I: pl. XXIII, 3).

7-15 (4th row left) Rock drawings of a giraffe from the Epi-Paleolithic and an ibex, pariah dog, and hunter from the Neolithic/Late Pre-dynastic Eastern Desert, Qift-Quseir road, south of the 59.8 km mark. Source: Redford and Redford (1989: fig. 10, p. 13).

7-16 (4th row centre) Painting on a Naqada I pot of a hunter leading four tesems. Source: Scharff (1928: pl. XXVII, 4).

7-17 (4th row right) Rock drawing of two tesems, a man, and a Barbary goat by Early Nile Valley Dwellers, west bank of the Nile about 5 km north of Aswan. Source: Winkler (1939 II: pl. XII, 1).

Although 'Pariah' is a name given in the Dynasties to stray (feral) dogs or interbred races of dogs without a home, it is applicable to unnamed early varieties, which were the transitional stage in development between wolves and domestic dogs.

The greyhound type, which is referred to as a 'Tesem', has a slender head and body, long legs, pricked ears, and cocked or curled tail.

Illustrations of dogs appear in the rock drawings of Autochthonous Mountain Dwellers (figs 7-7,-9, -10) who were contemporaneous with the Badarian period; of Earliest Hunters (fig. 13-31); and of Early Nile Valley Dwellers (figs 1-1, 7-11,-17). Some of these appear to be forerunners of the tesem type with cocked and curled tails, long legs, and slender heads and bodies (figs 7-7,-17, 13-165,-167). One slender figure has a long, S-shaped tail (fig. 13-82).

There are also stouter types with elongated or slightly curved tails, which were probably variants of the pariah (figs 7-8 to 7-15, 13-103, 13-168) and a few drawings with very short and cocked tails (figs 7-15, 12-3, 13-28).

The pariah dog behind the giraffe in Figure 13-28 may give the impression of being a young giraffe, but the cocked tail is not a giraffe characteristic, and "A newborn baby giraffe is as tall as a tall man" (Knault, *et al.*, 1971: 309).

The leaping dogs with extended tails in Figure 1-22 are probably pariahs. The three stout dogs with ears not shown in the ibex hunt in the Hierakonpolis tomb (fig. 13-171) have also been called pariahs (Brewer *et al.*, 1994: 116).

Distinct examples of the pariah with stout bodies were carved on the Carnarvon ivory knife handle, the Davis ivory comb, and the Gebel Araq and Gebel el Tarif knife handles (figs 1-9 to 1-12). Similar dogs with short tails are in a Predynastic, probably Amratian (Naqada I), etching on an ostrich eggshell (fig. 13-87) and in various rock drawings (figs 7-15, 12-3, 13-28,-31,-167). The Gebels Araq and Tarif handles are of Mesopotamian origin, but the dogs are comparable with those imported into Egypt.

Epstein (1971 I: 165) said that the dogs on the Gebel el Araq handle "can hardly be designated as greyhounds ... rather their sturdy bodies, prick ears and shallow stop suggest a generalized form within the type range of some pariah types ... the sickle tail, verging on the ring tail, may have been the forerunner of the Tesem's coiled up tail".

A Prehistoric flint figure of a dog (fig. 1-6e) was said by Petrie (1920: 10) to be the "usual Egyptian cur". Other forms of the tail could have been made from flint, although similar short, upright tails have appeared in drawings as noted above.

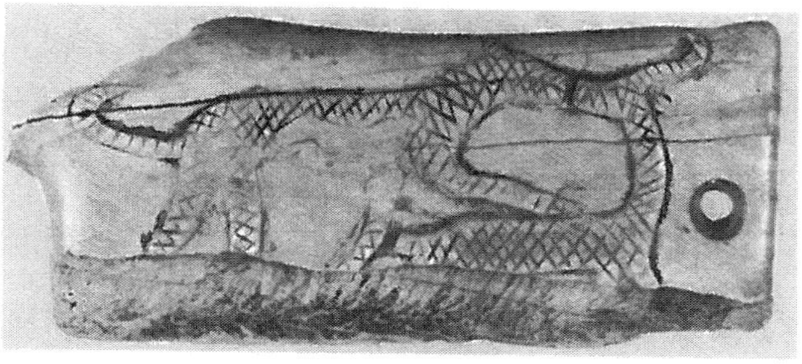

7-18 A saluki attacking a gazelle on an ivory knife handle dated to the Naqada period. Source: Petrie (1920: pl. XLVIII, 6).

Two types of hunting dogs or hounds, commonly called 'greyhounds', were imported into the Nile Valley and can be recognized in some rock drawings and early artifacts. They were used in hunting and as guards and were also popular as pets.

These were:

1) The tesem (tjesem, tešem, thesemu, tzmu), a slender, prick-eared curl-tailed hound. The earliest recorded representation of tesems is a painting on a Naqada I pot of a hunter leading four on leashes (fig. 7-16). There are also tesems on white cross-lined red pots from the Early Gerzean (Naqada II) in Figures 2-2, 13-170, and -210. The tesems in the latter figure have balls on the tips of their ears, doubtless an art form.

The earliest clearly defined rock drawing of tesems with tightly curled tails (fig. 7-17) can also be dated to Naqada II.

The obvious curled tails of the dogs on the Brooklyn knife handle (fig. 1-7, table 1: rows A6, A8, B4) identify them as tesems, although the heads and bodies are more like those of pariahs. True conformation, however, would be difficult to carve correctly in such small figures.

2) The saluki (seluki, slughi) is lop-eared and has a curved or saber tail, sometimes in the cocked position. Early records are on a Naqada knife handle (fig. 7-18), the obverse of the Hierakonpolis palette (fig. 1- 2a), and the lop-eared hounds on the Pitt Rivers knife handle (fig. 1-8, ends of rows 3 and 6, boss side; possibly the left animal, row 6 (reverse). An earlier representation may be the saber-tailed, pointed-nosed animal behind the patas monkey in a 4th millenium B.C. rock drawing fig. 4-39).

Predynastic representations of another dog, the mastiff, a sturdy dog with a short, massive muzzle, relatively long tail, and lop-ears have been found in Hierakonpolis. These consist of a partly damaged figurine (fig. 7-19) and a recent restoration (fig. 7-20); some ivory heads (fig. 7-21); and a scepter head with a row of mastiffs and lions (fig. 7-22). The 'circular interlocking' of these

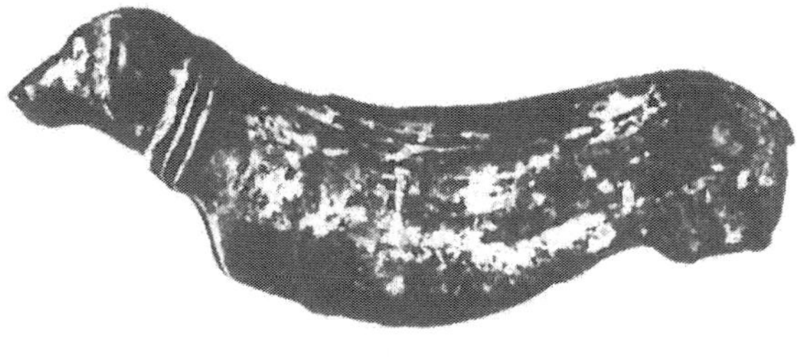

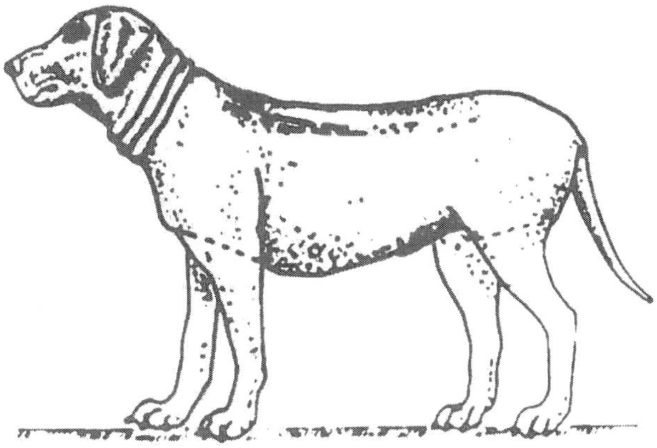

7-19 *A damaged Predynastic figurine of a mastiff from Hierakonpolis. Source: Boessneck (1988: fig. 139).*

7-20 *Reconstruction of the mastiff in Figure 7-19. Source: Churcher (1993a: fig. 1b).*

7-21 *(top) Predynastic ivory head of a mastiff from Hierakonpolis. Source: Quibell (1900 I: pl. XII, 7).*

7-22 *(centre) A row of mastiffs and lions on a Predynastic ivory scepter head from Hierakonpolis. Source: Quibell (1900 I: pl. XIX, 6).*

7-23 *(bottom) Predynastic ivory statuettes of mastiffs from Abu el Melek (Malak) west of the Nile 20 km north of Beni Suef. Source: Möllers and Scharff (1926: pl. 39).*

figures was said to be typical of Mesopotamian style (Epstein, 1971 I: 71). Likewise, the manes extending along the bellies of the lions indicate the Asian race.

A series of ivory statuettes of mastiffs dated to the Predynastic was found at Abu Sir el Melek (Malak) 20 km north of Beni Suef (fig. 7-23).

The Dynastic period: Dogs or hounds in Dynastic reproductions can be separated into those listed above and a few more types or breeds.

Tesem: Tesems have long slender muzzles, prick-ears, tightly curled tails, and slender bodies. Color varies from light tan to yellowish or greyish to blotched brown or black on white.

'Basenji' is a name applied to similar curl-tailed hounds in other parts of Africa.

Tesem hounds of the Dynasties were first depicted attacking dorcas gazelles on a Dynasty I steatite gaming disc (fig. 7-24). Two Dynastic rock drawings also clearly illustrate the curled tails of this hound (figs 7-25,-26).

Tesems were pictured into the Middle Kingdom in hunting scenes attacking foxes (figs 6-14,-15, 7-59,-60,-63) and hares (figs 5-3,-4) and chasing and subduing other game (figs 1-29, 7-27,-28,-29). In the Dynasty VI Mastaba of Mereruka at Saqqara (Duell,

7-24 *Tesems attacking dorcas gazelles on a steatite gaming disc from the Tomb of Hemaka (?), Dynasty I, Saqqara. Source: Emery (1938: frontispiece).*

1938 II: pls 24, 25) eight tesems are attacking one ibex and single hounds are attacking another ibex and a scimitar oryx.

Tesems were also pictured as pets (fig. 7-30); sometimes on leashes with primates and other tame animals (figs 4-33,-34) or under the chairs or thrones of their owners (figs 4-31, 7-31). In the latter figure the servants who are leading the animals were dwarfed to fit below the chair.

The tesem under the chair in Figure 7-32 was named 'The Created One' (*Wb.* I: 139). It was mistakenly called an 'orycteropus' by Hartmann (1864: 28).

The leash of the tesem shown under Mentuherkhepeshef's chair (fig. 7-33) is held by his mother's pet monkey.

These hounds were obviously bred in the early dynasties of Egypt, because they are shown with a puppy in the Dynasty V Tomb of Ptahetep (figs 7-27, 7-162) and a female is suckling three puppies in the Dynasty V Tomb of Zau (fig. 7-34). A young curl-tailed tesem that has been called a 'piglet' (see below) is in the Dynasty VI Tomb of Kagemni (fig. 7-35).

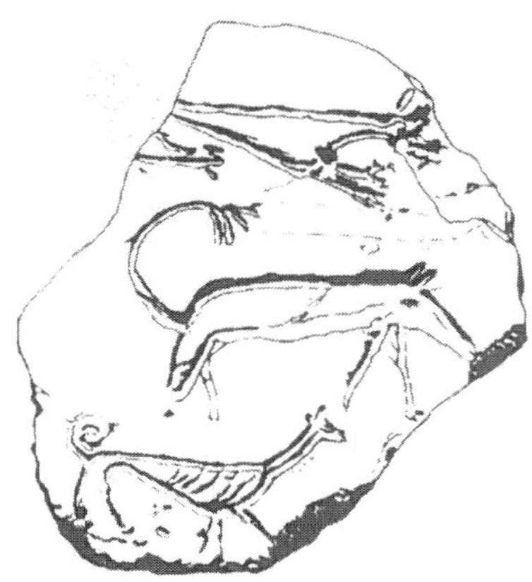

7-25 (top) Two tesems and a pig engraved on a slab of sandstone from Dakhla Oasis and dated 'earlier than 3,000 B.C. or Old Kingdom Dynasty V or VI'. Source: Churcher (1993a: fig. 15).

7-26 (bottom) Rock drawings of two tesems at the site of Berber, s.w. of Aswan, and dated to Dynasty VI. Source: Schweinfurth (1912: fig. 23).

7-27 Hunting scene, Tomb of Ptahhetep, Dynasty V, Saqqara. Source: Davies (1900 I: pl. XXII). Animals in the upper register are (left to right) a tesem restraining two young striped hyenas, a tesem subduing a scimitar oryx, a gazelle suckling its young, a tesem attacking an ibex, leopards mating, and red foxes mating. Animals in the lower register are two tesems on leashes, a tesem puppy, a deficating aurochs bull grasped by a lion, a tesem downing a gazelle, a tesem subduing a scimitar oryx; and a hartebeest and two aurochs, one of which is held by a man with a bola. The inserts above are a crouched dorcas gazelle, an ichneumon, a jerboa entering a shelter, and two hedgehogs, one of which is leaving a shelter with a cricket (?) in its mouth.

7-28 A hunting scene dominated by tesems. Tomb Chapel of Senbi's son Ukh-hot(e)p, Dynasty XII, Meir. Source: Blackman (1915 II: pl. VIII). Tesems are subduing various animals that are pierced with arrows: red fox, gazelle, hare, scimitar oryx, and ibex. On the upper right a red fox sniffs at the foal of an ass. On the lower right are a giraffe and a striped hyena behind an injured (?) deer.

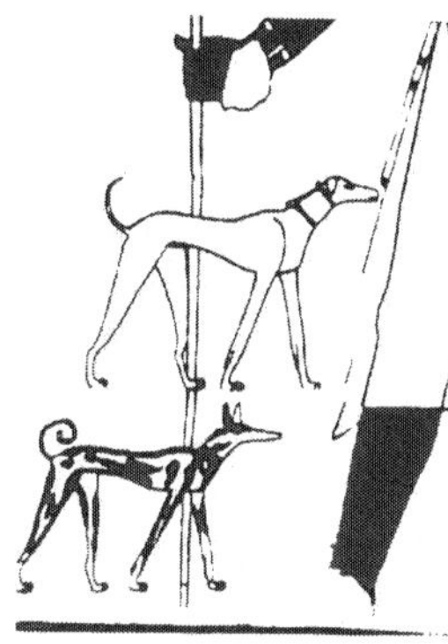

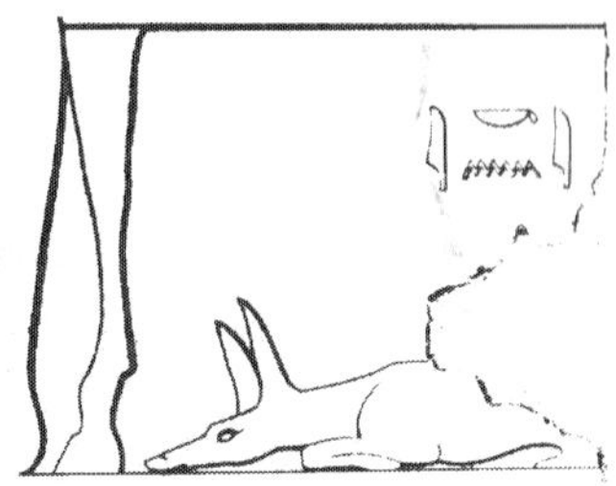

7-29 (top) Bowmen shooting and hounds attacking wild game in an enclosure. Tomb Chapel of Ukhotep's son Senbi, Dynasty XII, Meir. Source: Blackman (1914 I: pl. VI). The animals in the upper left are a tesem attacking a bovid (probably a gazelle), and three more tesems. To the right of the destroyed section are three gazelles, three hartebeests, an ass giving birth, a gazelle on its back, a hare, and an aurochs. Below, left, a greyhound is grabbing the neck of an ibex pierced by an arrow; farther right leopards are mating and a dorcas gazelle suckles its young. In the next row a saluki grabs the neck of a dorcas gazelle; two ibex are pierced with arrows, and also one of three scimitar oryx, which are proceeded by a calf; and a lion grabs an aurochs bull by the nose. Next, a saluki runs into the scene; below, a hare leaps over a hedgehog; a greyhound subdues an ibex pierced by an arrow; a hyena paws at an arrow in its mouth; another greyhound attacks a Barbary goat; a saluki attacks a hartebeest; and to the right one of two galloping hartebeests is pierced by an arrow.

7-30 (bottom left) A saluki (above) and a tesem with the tomb owner Amenem-het, Dynasty XII, Beni Hasan. Source: Newberry (1893 I: pl.XIII).

7-31 (bottom centre) A tesem and a monkey led under the sedan chair of Queen Ti, Dynasty V, Saqqara. Source: Steindorff (1913: pl. 132).

7-32 (bottom right) A tesem under a chair in Tomb 16, Dynasty V, Pyramids of Giza. Source: L.D. II, 52.

The tightly curled tail of the tesem type also appeared on various other kinds of dogs pictured in the Old and Middle Kingdoms (figs 4-11, 7-52,-53); see below in *Various dogs*.

Hilzheimer (1932: 418) remarked that "According to Egyptian ideas this curly tail must certainly have formed a sign of good breeding, for it is always carefully represented in all works of art, often to an exaggerated degree. Obviously the Egyptians were especially proud of this characteristic, quite unnatural in a greyhound, who needs a long tail to guide himself; it must, therefore, have been extremely difficult to obtain by breeding."

Boessneck (1988: 84) noted, however, that curled tails were not identifiable as yet in buried remains of dogs.

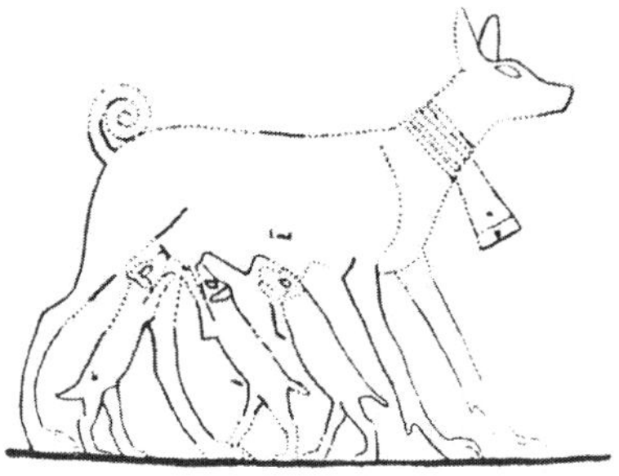

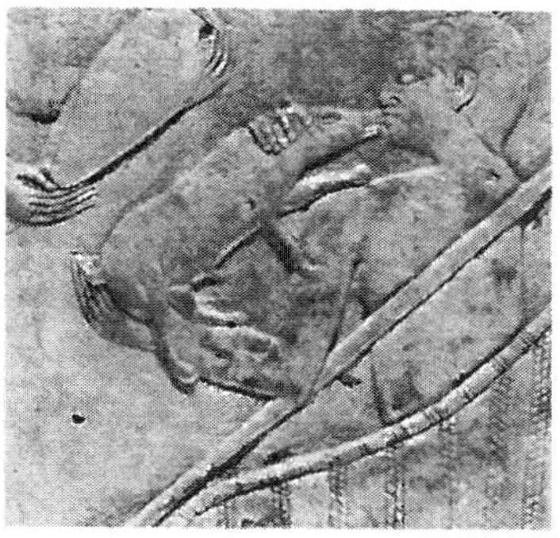

7-33 (above) A tesem under the chair of Mentuherkhepeshef, Dynasty XVIII, Thebes. His mother's pet monkey holds its leash. Source: Davies (1913: pl. IV).

7-34 (top centre) A female tesem suckling puppies under the chair of Zau, Dynasty VI, Deir el Gebrawi. Source: Davies (1902 II: pl. XV).

7-35 (top right) A man mouth feeding milk to a tesem puppy in the Tomb of Kagemni (Mastaba of Gemnikai), Dynasty VI, Saqqara. Source: M. Zemina. Above, an adult tesem is drinking milk from a bowl.

7-36 (bottom left) Three tesems with thick, curled tails on a limestone fragment from the First Intermediate Period, Dynasty XI, Koptos (Coptos, Qift). To the right of the owner is a small hieroglyphic tesem. Source: Stewart (1979 II: pl. 10.1).

7-37 (bottom right) A typical tesem standing on a boat on a fragment of a limestone relief from the First Intermediate Period, Koptos. Source: Stewart (1979 II: pl.22, fig.8).

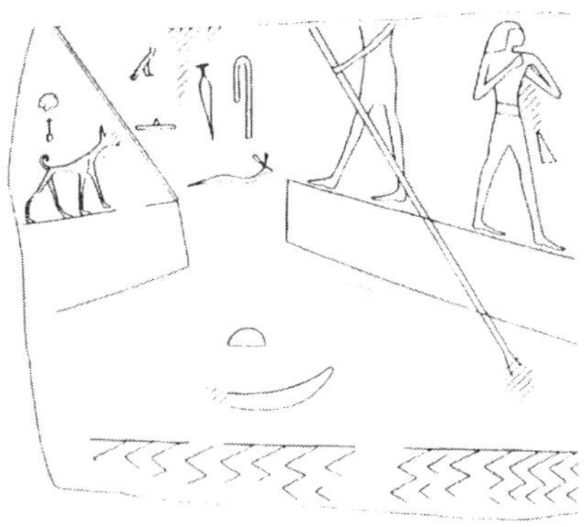

There are some variations in works of art depicting not only the curled tail of the tesem, but also some other characteristics of this type of greyhound. Three rather sturdy prick-eared hounds have thick, but tightly curled tails and heavy snouts (fig. 7-36). They were described as being in 'crude raised relief' (Stewart, 1979 II: 12). The smaller 'incised' figure in front of the tomb owner is normal in conformation, but probably represents the determinative for tesem (hound). Another tesem of similar style standing on a boat (fig. 7-37) was named *Tp-nfr* (Tep-nefer), Beautiful Head.

The relief in the tomb of Kagemni of a man mouth-feeding a young hound (fig. 7-35), which looks somewhat like a piglet, has aroused some interesting comments.

First of all, Firth and Gunn (1926 I: 21, 114) referred to 'boys feeding a puppy' and 'a man giving to a young dog, from his mouth, some fluid, probably milk, of which a jar is being held forward by another man'.

Janssen and Janssen (1989: fig. 27) titled their figure of the scene, 'A swineherd weans a suckling piglet using milk placed on his tongue...' Their illustration of the animal, said to be 'from the mastaba of Kagemni', has hoofs instead of paws in contrast with photographs of the original relief (fig. 7-35; Firth and Gunn, 1926 II: pl. 52; Darby *et al.*, 1977 I: fig. 4.4; Brewer *et al.*, 1994: fig. 7.15).

The figure was obviously intended to represent a young curl-tailed, lop-eared tesem, and the ear appears to be hanging.

Brewer *et al.* (1994: 96) remarked that "the blunt, tapering face of the young animal, coupled with the distinctive fat abdomen and short curly tail would apparently disqualify it as the pup of the slim saluki, but not rule out the possibility that it is the pup of another variety of canine or hyena."

Obviously the puppy is of a variety of canine. The tail is curled and the abdomen is fat as in the tesem puppy in Figure 7-162. The prominent penis is comparable with that of the tesem puppy in Figure 7-27, which also has a fat abdomen, but the ear and tail are not clearly depicted.

The tesem puppies in Figure 7-34 are lop-eared and have short and straight tails.

In reference to the tesems in Figure 7-27, Paget and Pirie (1898: 28) called them 'large greyhounds' and the puppy and the deficating bull a 'cow and her calf'. Davies (1900; 10) called the tesems '*slughis*' and the puppy 'a small dog of a peculiar type'.

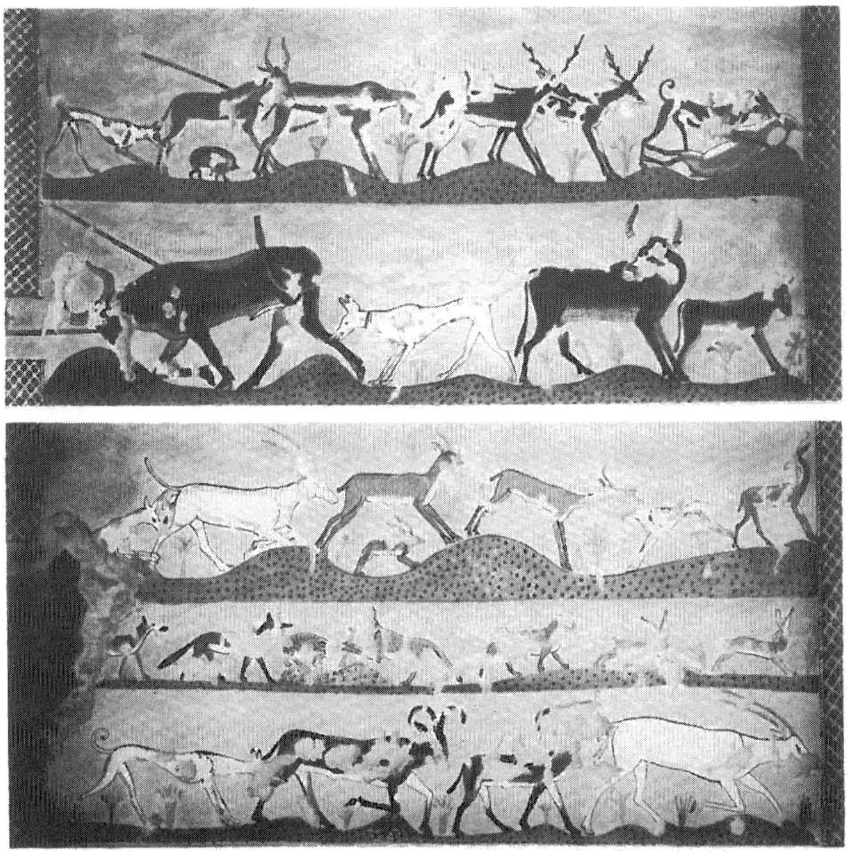

7-38 Netted animals in the Tomb of Antefoker, Dynasty XII, Sheikh Abd el Kurneh, Thebes. Source: Davies and Gardiner (1920: frontispiece). Animals in registers are left to right:

Register 1: Greyhound grasping leg of one of two hartebeests, a hedgehog, two dama deer, and a tesem (?) subduing a dorcas gazelle.

Register 2: Aurochs bull, greyhound, aurochs cow and calf.

Register 3: Greyhound (?), scimitar oryx, hare, two dorcas gazelles, greyhound, and dorcas gazelle.

Register 4: Jackal, red fox, unidentifiable animal (hedgehog ?), jackal (?) with an arrow in its mouth, a wild cat, and two hares.

Register 5: Tesem hound (?), two Barbary goats, and a scimitar oryx foaling.

7-39 (left) A saluki hound and a jerboa left of Registers 1,2 in the hunting scene, Tomb of Chnemhotep, Dynasty XII, Beni Hasan (fig. 1-30). Source: Newberry (1893 I: pl. XXX).

7-40 (bottom) Two greyhounds and a saluki left of register 4 in Figure 1-30. Source: Newberry (1893 I: pl. XXX).

Another erroneous conclusion was made by the Egyptian specialists at the Dokki Museum, Cairo, who considered the tesem feeding from a bowl in the upper portion of the relief in the Tomb of Kagemni (fig. 7-35) to be an antelope, 'because dogs are not known to have been portrayed eating from bowls, whereas wild desert game including ibex, antelope, and other forms were frequently depicted in this manner' (Darby *et al.*,1979 I: 207, fn. 11).

Greyhound: The name greyhound can be applied specifically to another thin, prick-eared hound with a saber tail, which appeared to vary in coloration in the same way as the tesem from light greyish or yellowish to blotched brown or black on white.

In the Dynasty XII Tomb of Antefoker (fig. 7-38) two of the prick-eared hounds have partly curled tails and three have saber-tails. These illustrations give the impression of a transition from the curled tail of the tesem to the saber-tail of the greyhound.

Greyhounds were not common in Pharaonic art and appeared in only a few more Dynasty XII hunting scenes (figs 1-30, -32, 7-29). The two greyhounds and a saluki in Figure 7-40 were not shown in Figure 1-30.

7-41 Saluki hounds attacking Nubians in a battle scene on Tutankhamun's Painted Box, Dynasty XVIII, Thebes. Source: Davies and Gardiner (1962: pl. II).

7-42 Tutankhamun's gold dagger sheath, Dynasty XVIII, Thebes. Source: Edwards (1976b: no. 36). The obverse is covered with a feather pattern and the head of a fox (Anubis) on the tip. On the reverse an ibex is attacked by a lion; a saluki on the back of a calf bites its tail; another ibex is attacked by a cheetah and a lion; a saluki is biting a bull; and a calf is running below.

7-43 A saluki chasing bustards or ostriches on Tutankhamun's ostrich feather fan base. Dynasty XVIII. Source: Metropolitan Museum of Art, N.Y.

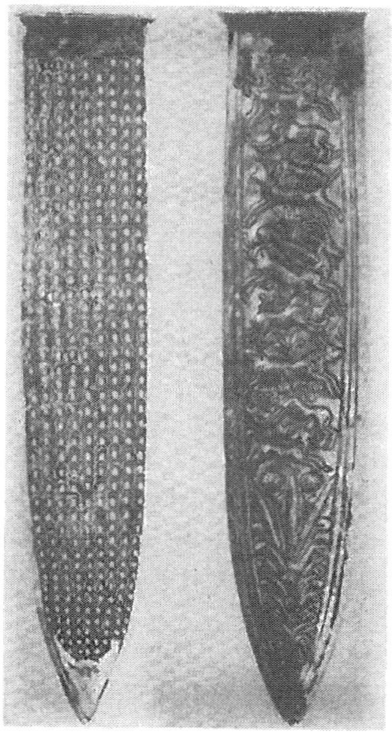

Saluki: Salukis have a shorter and heavier muzzle than tesems and greyhounds. They are lop-eared and saber-tailed. Color varies from black and tan, to yellowish, cream or white, and also blotched brown or black on white. Some varieties have fringes of long hair on ears, hips, and tail.

Although lop-eared, saber-tailed salukis were pictured on some Predynastic artifacts, they appeared at least once in the Old Kingdom, but were commonly illustrated in the Middle and New Kingdoms.

Salukis appear in several Middle Kingdom hunting scenes together with 'greyhounds' and tesems (figs 7-29,-30).

In Figure 7-39 there is a saluki and a jerboa and another saluki is in Figure 7-40.

Salukis dominate several New Kingdom hunting scenes (figs 1-18,-21,-23,-24) where they are attacking or capturing various game animals.

In the Dynasty XVIII Tomb of Rekhmire (fig. 7-148) a saluki is grabbing the foreleg of a hyena. Other salukis in the scene, which are not included in this copy, are attacking an ostrich, a bubal, and an arrow-pierced gazelle. In another scene from this tomb there is a saluki with a row of men who are bringing live trophies of a hunt (fig. 7-159a).

In the fragmented hunting scene in the Dynasty XVIII Tomb of User (fig. 5-6) a saluki is subduing a dorcas gazelle. And in the complicated scene in the Dynasty XVIII Tomb of Kenamun a saluki is subduing an ibex (fig. 13-177).

In Figure 13-111 a black and white saluki faces a hyena that has an arrow in its mouth and below right another hound that is grabbing the penis of an aurochs appears to have erect ears, but the tail is not clear.

Many of the treasures from the Tomb of Tutankhamun are decorated with salukis. In the hunt scenes on the painted box salukis are attacking hartebeests (fig. 12-6, reg.6) and lions (fig. 7-206), and in the battle scene (fig. 7-41) his salukis are

7-44 (top) A saluki under a chair in a relief from the Dynasty XI Temple at Koptos. Source: Stewart (1979 II: pl. 19.2).

7-45 (2nd row) A saluki under the chair of User. Dynasty XVIII, Thebes. Source: Davies (1913: pl. XXVIII).

7-46 (3rd row) A saluki and two short-legged dogs with prick ears and hanging tails. Tomb of Chnemhotep, Dynasty XII, Beni Hasan. Source: Newberry (1893 I: pl. XXX).

7-47 (bottom) Salukis in tribute from Nubia in the Tomb of Amenmose, Dynasty XVIII, Sheikh Abd el Kurneh, Thebes. Source: Davies and Davies (1940: pl. XXIV).

'pulling and tearing at the defeated foe' (Carter, 1927 II: 17 f.).

Two salukis are attacking game on the gold dagger sheath (fig. 7-42) and one is chasing bustards or ostriches (Reed and Osborn, 1978: 275; Osborn, 1985: 160) on the ostrich feather fan base (fig. 7-43). Lions and salukis are pictured attacking aurochsen, an ibex, and a gazelle on the alabaster salve jar (fig. 7-216b). Tut was also shown on an ostracon accompanied by his pet saluki when spearing a lion (fig. 7-205).

Pet salukis were pictured with their owners (7-44,-45), sometimes together with other hounds or dogs (figs 7-30,-46).

Salukis were included in tribute from Nubia together with monkeys, various animal skins, ostrich feathers, and ivory (figs 4-37, -38, 7-47).

This dog has been called 'the Egyptian greyhound', but its inclusion in these tribute scenes indicate that it was also bred beyond Egypt's ancient borders.

There are some pictures on Dynasty XIX-XX ostraca of salukis chasing a hyena (fig. 7-169) and a caricature of salukis and hyenas in 'dispute' (fig. 7-170). Another saluki on an ostracon is biting the penis of a hartebeest (fig. 5-2).

***Pariah**:* Pariah dogs can be generally described as having broad heads, erect and pointed ears (pendulous in young), and short to long cocked or pendant tails, which are often bushy. Color varies and they may be brownish, tawny, yellowish or greyish, and sometimes black or white. The blotched dogs in Figure 4-11 below the baboon could also be pariahs.

Schweinfurth (1912) published some Middle Kingdom rock drawings of pariahs that show some variations in length and curvature of tails (figs 7-48,-49). In the Dynastic rock drawings in Wadi Hammamat a hunter and two pariahs are behind an ibex (fig. 13-103).

The heavy-bodied dog with an upright tail in the Dynasty XI Tomb of Khety (fig. 7-50) with tan back and ears, grey flanks, and white venter was named a 'pariah or shenzi dog' by Churcher (1993: fig. 1, c). The ball-shaped tip on the tail in Churcher's figure appears to be an artist's error.

Another good example of a pariah (in outline) is in the offering procession in the Tomb of Baqt I, Beni Hasan (fig. 7-135).

***Mastiff**:* Mastiffs are powerfully built with large heads, short muzzles, lop-ears, and hanging tails. The pelage is short, brownish or fawn-colored, and streaked or spotted.

According to Epstein (1971 I: 71) mastiffs can be traced into the period of the First Dynasty when

"They probably accompanied nomadic foreign tribes thither, and soon became extinct for lack of further stock". He said they were not known again until the 'later period'. Reference was made to a wall painting in the Tomb of Redmera (Dynasty XVIII?) at Thebes with a mastiff among eight dogs in an Asian tribute (op. cit., 72).

In a Dynasty VI offering scene a lop-eared, curl-tailed dog described as a 'heavy jawed dog of the saluki breed' (Badawy, 1978: 26) shows some other features that indicate it might represent a mastiff (fig. 7-51). These are the thick head, the stoutness of the body and limbs, and the thick tail, which make it similar to the mastiff on a 'Babylonian relief, 2200 B.C.' (Epstein, 1971 I: 171, fig. 182).

In the Dynasty XVIII hunt scene in the Tomb of Neferhotep (fig.1- 24) the large, lop-eared canid on the left of Register 3 has been called a hyena with pendant ears (Keimer, 1940: 54), but it probably represents a mastiff.

"Among 38 skulls of dog mummies from Abydos, Thebes, and Asyut in the Vienna Museum of Natural History, one cranium ... resembles a mastif skull" (Epstein, 1971 I: 73).

Various dogs: In addition to the hounds, pariahs, and mastiffs that were discussed above, there are illustrations of pet dogs of smaller height with pricked ears and curled, cocked, or hanging tails (figs 4-11 and 7-46). The majority of these are short-legged (brachymely), two of which are in the Dynasty VI Mastaba of Mereruka (fig. 7-52), and one in the El Bersheh Tomb of Tehutihetep (fig. 7-53). The latter was named Ankhu, 'The Living One'.

The upper dogs in Figures 4-11 and 7-50 appear to be variations of the tesem type.

Dwarfed and deformed skulls, called 'pomeranian', have been found on mummified dogs from Abydos, Thebes, and Asyut (Epstein, 1971 I: 57).

Dog cemeteries: Dog burial dates to the Predynastic. Dogs were not worshipped nor considered as sacred at that time nor during the Dynasties, but great numbers found in graves support the conclusion that they were greatly respected for their close attachment to man. Pet, guard, and hunting dogs that were buried with their masters, mistresses, or caretakers were doubtless preparations for continuation of friendship or service in the afterlife.

Masses of mummified dogs dated to the Greco-Roman Period have been found in the Abydos and other dog hypogea. Peet (1914 II: 101) said that in some chambers at Abydos there were layers of dogs from eight to ten feet deep, 'so that in

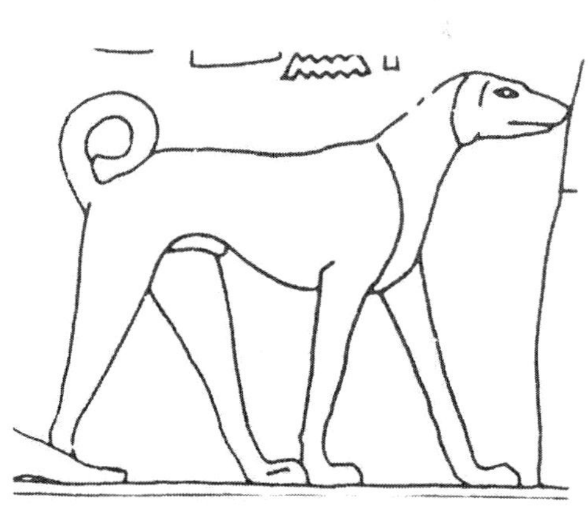

7-48 (top) Pariah dogs in a Middle Kingdom ibex hunt on a sandstone block in Wadi Abu Agag, N.E. of Aswan. Source: Schweinfurth (1912: fig. 1).

7-49 (2nd row) A pariah dog with an S-shaped tail, men, and an 'antelope' with young in a Middle Kingdom rock drawing near Aswan. Source: Schweinfurth (1912: fig. 4).

7-50 (3rd row) Three pet dogs in the Tomb of Khety, Dynasty XI, Beni Hasan. Source: Newberry (1894 II: pl.XIV).

7-51 (bottom) A mastiff (?) in an offering scene. Tomb of 'Ankhm-'Ahor, Dynasty VI, Saqqara. Source: Badawy (1978: fig. 34).

the whole hypogeum there must be some tens of thousands'.

During this time dogs were mummified and interred for another reason – because they were identified with the 'jackal' gods, Anubis and Wepwawet.

The sacredness of the dog was also indicated by the remarks of Herodotus and Strabo, "that when a dog died in an Egyptian house the family shaved the whole of their bodies."

Medical uses: Darby *et al.* (1977 I: 251 f.) and Brewer *et al.* (1994: 135, f.n. 362) have summarized the medical uses of dogs: The legs and dung of a dog and the hoof of an ass together with some other ingredients were used for external applications for relief of pain in the limbs, for infections, eczema, and a remedy for baldness. Genital (menstrual) blood of a bitch was used for hair removal and the genitals to prevent whitening of hair. For rabies the liver of a mad dog roasted and eaten was supposed to protect the bitten from the fear of water. The tooth of the dog that did the biting was put into a bag and tied to the arm of the victim.

7-52 (left) Curl-tailed, short-legged dogs on leashes in the Mastaba of Mereruka, Dynasty VI, Saqqara. Source: Duell (1938 II: pl. 168).

7-53 (below) A short-legged dog in the Tomb of Tehuti-hetep, Dynasty XII, El Bersheh. Source: Newberry (1892 I: pl. XXIX).

Red Fox ***Vulpes vulpes*** (Linnaeus, 1758)

 *š3b* zab Wb. III, 420

E Nile Fox; F Renard fauve; G Rotfuchs; A Taalab, Abu Hussein, Taalab el Nil, El Taalab el Ahmar

Nomenclature: The Egyptian race of the red fox is *Vulpes vulpes aegyptiaca (*Sonnini, 1816). Obsolete synonyms are *Canis niloticus* Desmarest, 1820; *Canis anubis* Hemprich and Ehrenberg, 1833; and *Canis vulpecula* Hemprich and Ehrenberg, 1833.

Description: Red foxes are slender with relatively short legs; long, pointed muzzles; long, bluntly pointed ears; and long, bushy tails reaching to the ground (fig. 7-54). The tail hairs are 'short on the proximal two inches and then become quite suddenly elongated and maintain an approximately even length throughout the brush' (Harrison, 1968 II: 206).

The body is reddish to reddish-brown dorsally, grizzled gray and yellowish on the sides, and brownish or blackish on the throat and belly.

7-54 A tethered red fox. Source: Happold (1967: pl. VI).

During molt foxes may appear to be almost black because of their dark underfur. Hence, a specimen in molt was mistakenly called *Canis anubis* by Hemprich and Ehrenberg (1833), because Anubis was commonly portrayed as a black animal.

The ears are pale on the inner sides and brownish to black on the backs. The tail is reddish or brownish above and paler below, with a prominent white tip. Sometimes there is a faint black ring above the white tip.

The forehead is almost flat in profile.

The pupils of the eyes of foxes in this genus are elliptical and vertical in bright light, but this feature never appeared in Egyptian art.

The shoulder height is about 36 cm, head and body length 60 (55-65), tail 37 (30-40), and 62 (58-72) percent of the head and body length. The ears are proportionately long, 9-11 cm, and about 74 (69-84) percent of the head length.

Natural history: This fox is not strictly nocturnal and may often be seen during the day outside of a burrow or tomb. Foxes will often run out of dens during the day when approached by a vehicle or even by a man on foot. Dens are usually dug in hillsides beneath rocks, but foxes also burrow in palm groves and beneath man-made structures. Ruins, tombs, and quarries are also commonly inhabited.

Red foxes eat a variety of fruits, insects, rodents, birds, eggs, domestic fowl, dead fish, and other waste from fishermen, and probably carrion. They are also scavengers of human dumps.

Distribution: Red foxes are limited in distribution by availability of fresh water. The present distribution in Egypt is the Nile Valley and margins of the Delta; El Faiyum, Kharga, and Dakhla Oases; and northern parts of the Mediterranean Coastal Desert, Eastern Desert, and Sinai Peninsula.

Beyond Egypt the red fox occurs in northern Sudan, and in coastal Africa north of the desert westward into Morocco. It is widely distributed throughout Arabia, Asia Minor, northern and southwestern Asia, and all of Europe except for the extreme north.

Prehistoric records: Skeletal remains of red fox are known from the Neolithic site of Beni Salama (Merimda) (von den Driesch and Boessneck, 1985: 44 f.) and the Late Pleistocene of Wadi Halfa (Reed and Turnbull, 1969).

A rock drawing of an animal with a long tail and ears (fig. 7-55) which was not identified by Červíček (1974: 260), could represent a fox.

The long-tailed, long-eared figure playing a flute on the Predynastic Oxford or Hunting Dogs Palette (fig. 1-2b) was originally referred to as a

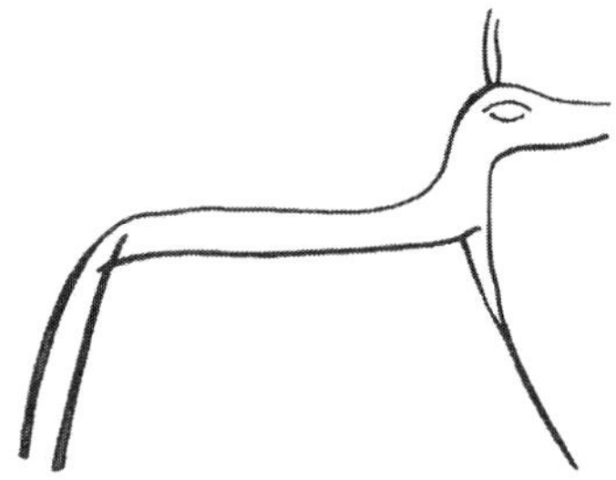

7-55 (left) Rock drawing of a red fox at Kanais, Wadi Mia, 45 km east of Edfu (Idfu). Source: Červíček (1974: fig. 260).

7-56 (right) A red fox (above) and an ichneumon on white lined prehistoric pottery. Source: Petrie (1920: pl. XVIII, 67).

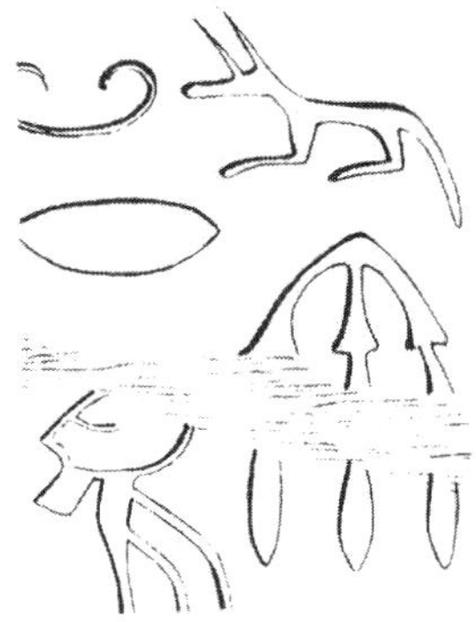

7-57 Symbol (left) of three fox skins on the tablet of Aha-Men, Dynasty I, Abydos. Source: Petrie (1901a II: pl. XI,1).

7-58 (right) Relief of three fox skins. Source: Daressy (1903: fig. 2).

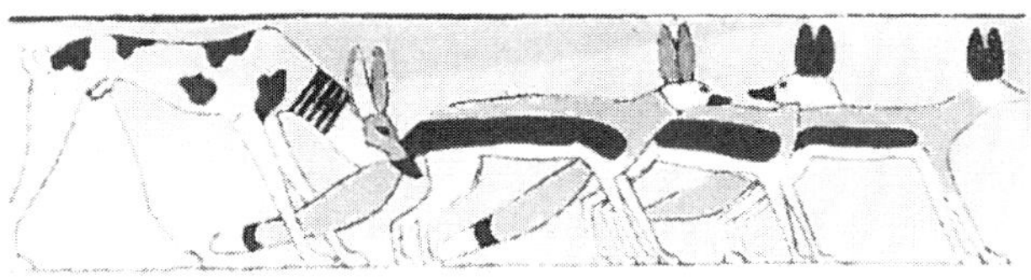

7-59 Red foxes in a hunting scene, Tomb of Nefermaat, Dynasty III, Medum (Meidum). Source: Petrie (1892b: pl. VIII). A tesem hound is holding one fox by the base of its tail.

7-60 Red foxes in a hunting scene, Tomb of Rahotep, Dynasty III, Medum (Meidum). Source: Petrie (1892b: pl. IX). A tesem hound is holding one fox by the base of its tail. Below are a ratel (?), two dorcas gazelles and an ibex.

7-61 Two red foxes (lower left) walking in a hunting scene. Tomb of Pepi II, Dynasty IV, Saqqara. Source: Jequier (1938: pl. 43).
Other animals in the lower row are (left to right) Barbary goat, hyena with young, two hartebeests and young, and above them a young dorcas gazelle (?) crouched and eating. In the upper row are (left to right) a hedgehog, four scimitar oryx and two young, two dorcas gazelles, and two ibex.

7-62 Red foxes mating in a hunting scene, Tomb of Ptahotep, Dynasty V, Saqqara. Source: Davies (1901 II: pl. XXII).

7-63 A red fox with an extremely broad tail, grasped by a tesem hound, in a hunting scene. Tomb of Re'-em-kuy (Re'emka), Dynasty V-VI, Memphis. Source: Hayes (1953 I: fig. 56).
Other animals are: above, on inserts, a reclining hare and gazelle. To the right another tesem hound grasps the hind leg of one of three dorcas gazelles.

7-64 A series of animals in the Causeway of Unas, Dynasty V, Saqqara, include (left to right) a wild cat (?), an ibex, a fox, and a bear. Source: Keimer (1956: fig. 5).

7-65 (left) A red fox in the Tomb of Tehuti-hetep, Dynasty XII, El Bersheh. Source: Newberry (1892 I: pl.XX). Behind the fox is the hieroglyphic name for a pool of wild fowl on the left.

7-66 (right) A red fox sniffing at or about to grasp the foal of an ass in a hunting scene, Tomb of Ukh-hotep, Dynasty XII, Meir. Source: Blackman (1915 II: pl. VIII).

man in jackal disguise, but Legge (1909: 303) thought it might be an ape or monkey. Later, Vandier (1952 I: 582) and Smith (1969: 312) referred to it as a fox disguise and the latter noted "... it is suggested that it may be a decoy".

Two foxes are running on the Hunters Palette (fig. 1-3). The tail lengths and slenderness of the bodies indicate that the figures represent foxes. Fox tails hang from the hunters' waists.

Another long-tailed, long-eared animal on a piece of pottery (fig. 7-56) was called a 'deer' by Capart (1905: 111) and a 'jackal' by Petrie (1920: 15), but the logical design of the artist is a fox.

The Dynastic period: Below the fox or Anubis crouched on a Dynasty I tablet of Aha-Men there is a partly destroyed symbol (fig. 7-57), which is comparable with that of the three fox skins tied together (fig. 7-58). The hieroglyphic representation of these figures is *(ms')*, 'the fan', which signifies birth (Borchardt, 1907a: 75 f.).

Emery (1938: 36, pl. 18) mentioned that the absence of tops on the green drawings in the Tomb of Hemaka, Dynasty I, Saqqara, made identification difficult. His reproduction is similar to the one in Figure 7-57.

The complete symbol also appears between the names of two Libyan striped weasels that are giving birth in the Dynasty V Tomb of Ne-user-re (fig. 7-102) and in the relief by Daressy (fig. 7-58), and a drawing by Borchardt (1907a: fig. 2).

Störk (1977a: 348) commented that the connection of the fox with Hathor, as well as the fox pelts of the hieroglyph *ms'*, also showed a widespread relationship in Egypt between the fox, eroticism, and fertility.

Although Störk (*op. cit.*) remarked that foxes were seldom pictured in Dynastic art, representations are fairly common. Most of these have been called jackals, despite their pointed muzzles, proportionately long ears, slender bodies, and long, bushy tails.

The earliest and most obvious foxes, first described as 'jackals' (Petrie, 1892b: 25), are in the Dynasty III Tomb of Nefermaat at Meidum (fig. 7-59). Although the body markings are a bit abstract, the tails are typical as well as other features. The original colors were black, reddish-pink, and white.

A similar group appears in the Tomb of Rahotep (fig. 7-60). Two of these have tails shorter than normal, but there should be no doubt that all of them were intended to represent foxes.

Two foxes walking in the relief of a hunting scene in the Dynasty IV Tomb of Pepi II (fig. 7-61) are easily identified by the long, thick tail; slender bodies and legs; and shape of heads and ears.

In the Dynasty V hunting scene in the Tomb of Ptahhetep foxes are mating (fig. 7-62). They were

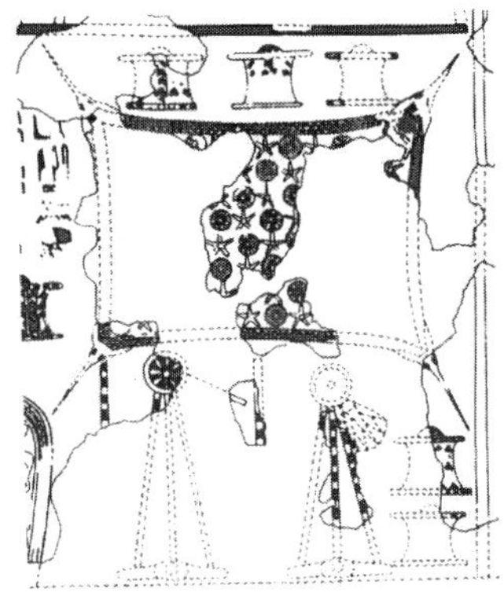

7-67 Exaggerated red fox heads on the corners of a red horse cloth from the Tomb of Kenamun, Dynasty XI, Thebes. Source: Davies (1930 I: pl. XXII).

7-68 A red fox biting the foal of an ass. Tomb of Kenamun, Dynasty XI, Thebes. Source: Davies (1930 I: pl. XLVIII). Additional animals are ostriches, hyenas, a rodent, hare, calf, hartebeest, gazelle (?), and to the left the tail of a hound and the rear of an ibex (fig. 1-15).

7-69 A red fox hiding in a hunting scene, Tomb of User, Dynasty XVIII, Thebes. Source: Davies (1913: pl. XXII).

originally named 'jackals' by Paget and Pirie (1898: 28) and Davies (1900: 28). Note what appear to be wattles on their throats. Keimer (1955b: 10) said foam was dribbling from the mouths of the "wild dogs (*Canis lupaster*)" that were in "a spasm of sexual joy". Vandier (1964 IV: 796), without referring to the wattles, called the figures 'foxes'. Most authors have called the figures 'jackals' (Hartmann, 1869: 30).

In another Dynasty V hunting scene (fig. 7-63) a fox grasped by a tesem hound has an extremely broad tail. Hayes (1953 I: 98) referred to it as a 'desert fox', probably because of the location of the scene. The size of this animal, however, in comparison with the dog indicates that it is a red fox.

A fox also appears among the many mammals in the causeway of Unas (fig. 7-64) and in the Tomb of Antefoker (fig. 7-38).

There is a partly obliterated fox in the Dynasty VI tomb of Aba. The long, slender snout; long mouth; and the shape of the hind leg indicate a canid, although the ears are shaped like those of a hare (fig. 2-3).

In the Dynasty XII Tomb of Tehutihetep at El Bersheh a canid called a 'jackal' (fig. 7-65) by Newberry (1892 I: 14) is distinctly a fox. Another canid that is facing the ostriches in Figure 13-78, row 5 was also called a jackal by Newberry *(op. cit.)*.

In a Dynasty XII hunting scene from the Tomb of Ukh-hotep (fig. 7-66) a fox is sniffing at or about to grab the foal of a wild ass. Behind it a tesem hound grasps the throat of a fox (fig. 7-28).

A fragment of a similar scene of a fox grabbing a foal is in the Dynasty XVIII Tomb of Mentuherkhepeshef (Davies, 1913: pl. XIII).

Comparison between foxes and jackals in the Dynasty XII Tomb of Baqt (fig. 1-29), together with hieroglyphs, are presented in the jackal chapter (figs 7-3,-4). These can be compared with Figures 7-1,-2, and 7-54.

In the Dynasty XVIII Tomb of Rekhmire a fox appears in a pile of dead game (fig. 7-159b) and live trophies of the hunt being carried toward the pile include a fox trussed on a pole (fig. 7-159a). Surely foxes were not eaten, but hunted for sport and for their skins. Some tribute scenes show Nubians carrying red fox skins (figs 4-22,-23).

Long-eared heads on a red horse cloth (fig. 7-67) and a royal loin cloth were called 'fennecs' by Davies (1930 I: 31), who remarked that "The snout is inordinately long and pointed."

Since the fennec was rarely shown in Egyptian art, it is quite probable that these decorations were stylized red fox or Anubis heads.

Fox heads also appear on ivory wands (fig. 1-14) and Tut's gold dagger sheath (fig. 7-42), which was called a 'jackal's head' (Carter, 1927 II: pl. LXXXVIII, 132).

Errors and discrepancies: Errors in identification of foxes is apparent in Egyptological literature. Likewise, there are some discrepencies in copies of original drawings. This is obvious in animals in the Tomb of Chnemhotep, Dynasty XII, Beni Hasan (figs 1-30,-31). In the fourth row, the third animal from the right appears to be a fox sniffing at the foal of an oryx. In Newberry's reproduction (fig. 1-30) the tail is long and fox-like and the body is slender. In L.D. (fig. 1-31) the tail is relatively short and slender, but with a tufted tip, and the body is stout. In the third row the fourth animal from the right has a fox-like tail in Newberry (fig. 1-31), but a genet-like tail in L.D. (fig. 1-31). There are similar differences between the fifth animals in row three.

Davies (1930 I: 37) referred to the animals in the Tomb of Kenamun (fig. 7-68) as hyenas or jackals scuttling in and out of their burrows and the one grabbing the foal of an ass as a jackal. Judging from the slender head and snout, the body shape, and the long, bushy tail, this animal is a fox. Others with striped tails may be hyenas. Further discussion of this scene is in the Hyena chapter.

A fox hiding in the hunt scene in the Tomb of User (fig. 7-69) was called a 'fennec'; and others on an ostracon (fig. 7-70) and a salve container (fig. 7-71), 'jackals'.

7-70 A red fox in a 'sniffing' position on an ostracon, Dynasty XIX, Deir el Medina. Source: Brunner-Traut (1956: pl. XXIX, 129).

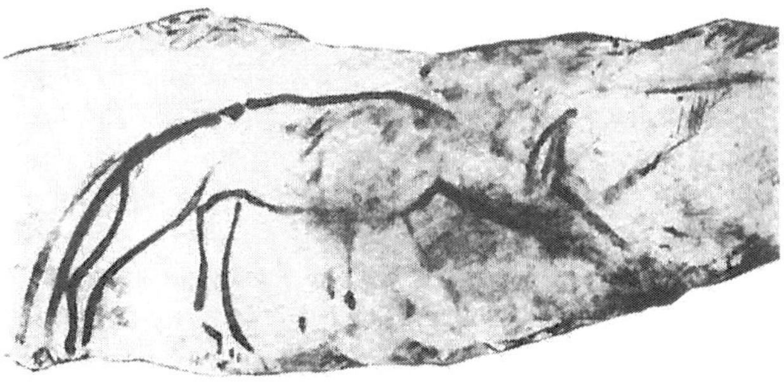

7-71 Red fox and a fish decorating a wooden salve container dated to the New Kingdom. Source: Fechheimer (1922: fig. 144).

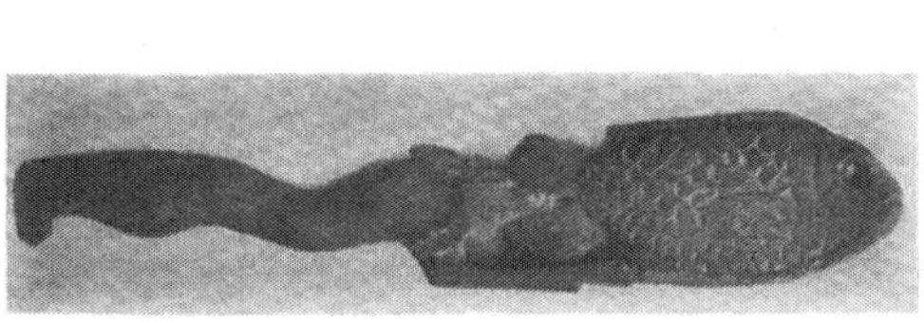

Rueppell's Fox *Vulpes rueppelli* (Schinz, 1825)

E Sand Fox, Desert Fox; F Renard famélique, Renard du desert; G Sandfuchs, Rüppellfuchs; A Taaleb, Abu Hussein

Nomenclature: An obsolete synonym used in earlier literature is *V. famelicus* Cretzschmar, 1826. Fennec is sometimes used, mistakenly, as a common name.

Description: Rueppell's fox is almost a miniature of the red fox, but the color is paler, the belly is whitish rather than brown or blackish, and the white tip on the tail is much shorter (fig. 7-72).

Shoulder height of males is about 26 cm, head and body length 46 (42-52), tail 34 (29-38), and 74 (66-84) percent of the head and body length. Females are slightly smaller.

Natural history: Rueppell's fox, like the red fox, is not strictly nocturnal. Its food habits are similar, except for the larger mammals, although it may prey on lambs (Osborn and Helmy, 1980: 387).

This fox is much more widely distributed in Egypt than the red fox. Being more adapted to the desert, it is often found in waterless areas.

Von den Driesch and Boessneck (1985: 45) said the sand fox was common in the rooms of ancient sites.

Distribution: Rueppell's fox occurs throughout most of the Western and Eastern Deserts and the Sinai Peninsula. Eastward its range extends through the Arabian Peninsula and into Iran and Afghanistan. In North African deserts the range extends south into Sudan, Somaliland, and Zaire and west through Libya into southern Algeria (Harrison, 1968 II: 215).

Prehistoric records: Bones of this fox together with those of the red fox were found at the Neolithic site of Beni Salama (von den Driesch and Boessneck, 1985: 45). One bone identified as *V. rueppelli* (?) was found in Early or Middle Paleolithic deposits at Bir Tarfawi in the southern Western Desert (Gautier, 1980: 320).

7-72 An adult Rueppell's fox taken from a live trap. Source: Osborn and Helmy (1980: fig. 116).

A rock drawing of a fox that was called a fennec by Červíček (1974: 174) is doubtless a Rueppell's fox because of its size in comparison with the hare beside it (fig. 7-73). Fennecs are not larger than hares.

The Dynastic period: Ruppell's fox remains were listed from an Old Kingdom tomb in Dakhla Oasis (Churcher, 1982: table 1).

The fox robbing a nest in a papyrus swamp in the Tomb of Senbi (fig. 7-74) was overlooked by Brentjes (1967b), who had called most of the genets

7-73 (left) Rock drawings of a Rueppell's fox and a hare at Mamla el Otuani on the east bank of the Nile northeast of Edfu (Idfu). Source: Červíček (1974: fig. 365).

7-74 (right) A Rueppell's (?) fox robbing a nest in a papyrus swamp. Tomb of Senbi, Dynasty XII, Meir. Source: Blackman (1914 I: pl. II).

that were climbing papyrus stems, little foxes. Which species is represented is not definite, but it could represent *V. rueppelli*.

According to Brentjes (*op. cit.*, 15), who had called the genets either *V. rueppelli* or *V. pallida*, the latter lived along the banks of the Nile and entered water. Whether it lived in Egypt is not known. Its present northern limit is south of the Sahara.

The two foxes in the lower right of the hunt scene in Figure 1-18 are small enough to represent the Rueppell's fox. Comparison of size with the hare in this scene is useless, because it is obviously enlarged.

A skull identified as *V. famelica* (=*V. rueppelli*) was found in a Roman cemetery near Rifeh (Petrie, 1907: 29).

Fennec ***Fennecus zerda*** (Zimmermann, 1780)

E Fennec Fox; F Fennec; G Wüstenfuchs, Fennek; A Fennek, Taalab el fannak

Nomenclature: "*Fenek* is an Arabic word for a small fox ... *zerda* (Arab) derived from *zardawa*, a fennec" (Gotch, 1979: 160).

An obsolete synonym is *Canis zerda* Zimmermann, 1780. As a common name, Abyssinian fennec has been mistakenly used.

Description: Fennecs are small, pale foxes with long, broad ears (fig. 7-75). The long, silky pelage is whitish in juveniles, but buff colored in adults with a pale reddish dorsal stripe. The brush-shaped tail is tipped with black and slightly more than one-half the head and body length. Long hairs of the feet cover the pads. The nose is short, slender, and pointed.

The shoulder height is 19-21 cm, head and body length 36 (34-38), tail 20 (18-23) and 55 (52-64) percent of the head and body length.

Natural history: Fennecs live mainly in sandy areas of the desert, but usuallly near vegetation, under which they dig burrows. Von den Driesch and Boessneck (1985: 45) wrote that it was not surprising to find that fennecs dug burrows under houses on the desert margins of the Delta near Beni Salama.

This species appears to be entirely independent of water (Osborn and Helmy, 1980: 394).

Food is small rodents, birds, reptiles, insects, and some plant material.

Distribution: In Egypt fennecs occur in northern Sinai and and in the Western Desert south of the Mediterranean Coastal Desert. Beyond Egypt the range extends westward across Libya and into Morocco; southward through Sudan into Zaire. The fennec is rare in the Arabian Peninsula and known from only a single museum specimen from Kuwait (Harrison, 1968 II: 220).

Prehistoric records: Skull fragments were found at the Neolithic site of Beni Salama (Merimda) on the western margins of the southern Delta (von den Driesch and Boessneck, 1985: 45).

The Dynastic period: Fennec remains were listed from an Old Kingdom tomb in Dakhla Oasis (Churcher, 1982: table 1).

Errors and discrepancies: Droste zu Hülshoff (1980: 82) referred to a hare and a 'fennec' being carried by the third man behind the caged lion and leopard in the Dynasty V Tomb of Ptahetep (fig. 7-213). There is no indication of a tail. The ears, although short, are not broad at the base. It can only be identified as a young hare.

Sharpe and Bonomi (1864: 5, fig. 3) identified the fennec with Set (Seth) and said: "The square-eared dog was the Abyssinian fennec ...; and by the side of it is the hieroglyphic copied from it by the Egyptian sculptor" (fig. 7-76).

Although these drawings are good, except for

7-75 (left) Young fennecs in a den in Wadi Muwellih south of El Faiyum. Source: Author.

7-76 (right) The fennec together with the Set animal. Source: Sharpe and Bonomi (1864: fig. 3).

the feet of the fennec, there is no similarity between them. The fact that the fennec lives in the desert must have been the only reason for their assumption.

Reference was made to hieroglyphic drawings of Seth on the sarcophagus of Oimenepthah I, late Dynasty XVIII, Thebes (*op. cit.*, pl. 19, figs 77-79), but none are comparable with the Seth drawing in Figure 7-76.

Appendix
Canine Gods

Canine gods, who were recognized from an early period, are Khenty-Imentiu (Khenti-Amentiu), Duamutef (Tuamutef), Wepwawet (Upuaut), and Anubis (Anpu, Inpu).

Khenty-Imentiu or 'Head of the Westerners' (i.e. of the dead) was a local god of Abydos during the Old to Middle Kingdoms who eventually became identified with Osiris, god of the dead and resurrection. His determinative animal was shown crouched, like that of Anubis (fig. 7-77).

Wepwawet or 'Opener of the Ways' was worshipped at Lycopolis (Assiut, Asyut) and emblematically guided divine boats and souls of the dead through the desert to the Kingdom of Osiris. He was thought to originally have been a war god and leader of armies (Emery, 1961: 127). Later he became associated with Anubis and was often pictured in the Hall of Judgement as a man with a canid head leading the deceased toward the scales where Anubis, god of the dead, balanced the heart against the feather of Maat (fig. 4-14), the symbol of truth, justice, and righteousness.

The determinative of Wepwawet is a canine figure standing on a nome standard (fig. 7-78) and is very similar to the crouched representation of Anubis (fig. 7-77). The two gods were often

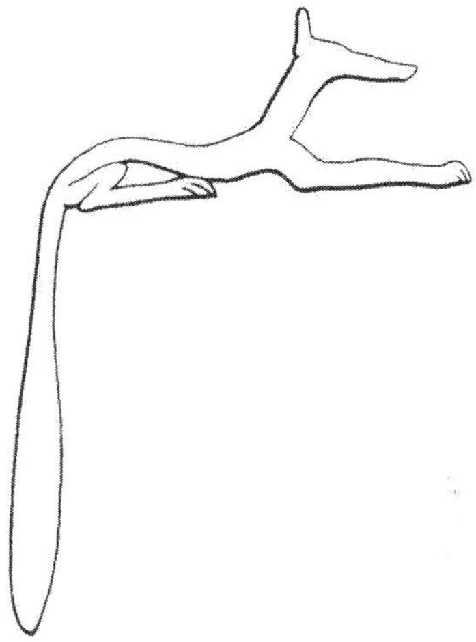

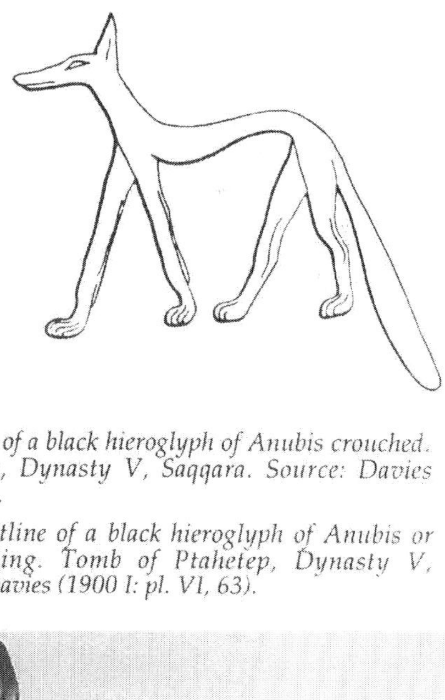

7-77 (top) Outline of a black hieroglyph of Anubis crouched. Tomb of Ptahetep, Dynasty V, Saqqara. Source: Davies (1900 I: pl. VI, 61).

7-78 (bottom) Outline of a black hieroglyph of Anubis or Wepwawet standing. Tomb of Ptahetep, Dynasty V, Saqqara. Source: Davies (1900 I: pl. VI, 63).

7-79 Black wooden statue of Anubis on the shrine, Tomb of Tutankhamun, Dynasty XVIII, Thebes. Source: the Ashmolean Museum, Oxford.

7-80 Wooden statue in the Lyon Museum of a crouched Anubis representing a jackal or dog. Source: Lortet and Gaillard (1909 II: fig. 208).

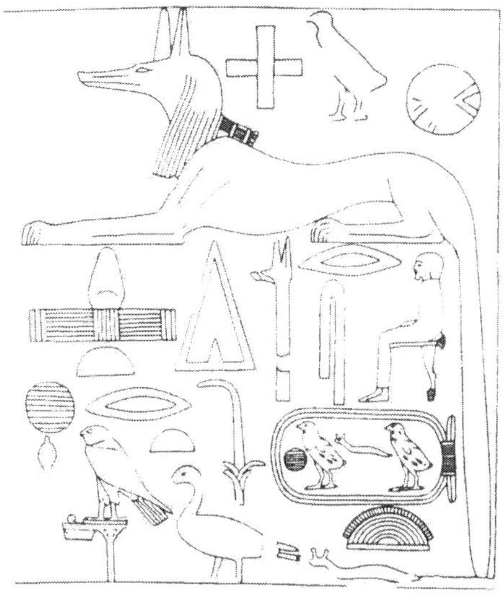

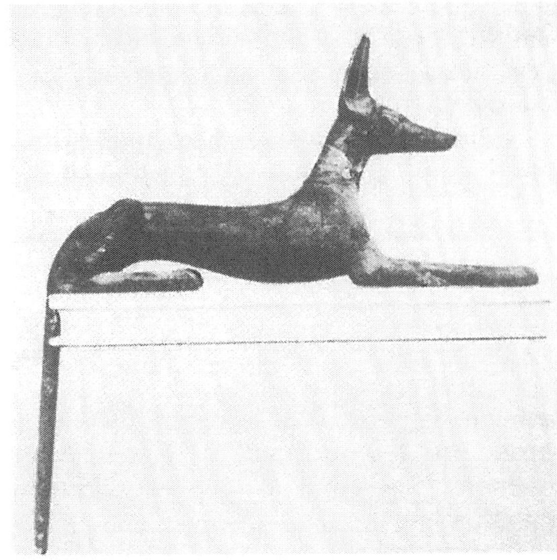

7-81 (top left) Wooden statue of a crouched fox labelled 'Anubis' dated to the New Kingdom, in the Dokki Agriculture Museum, Cairo. Source: Author.

7-82 (top right) Black wooden statue of Anubis from the New Kingdom in the Berlin Museum. Source: Brunner-Traut (1981: fig. 57b).

7-83 (left) Drawing of Anubis wearing a wig from a relief in the Chapel of Khafkhufu I, Dynasty V, Giza. Source: Simpson (1978: fig. 25).
Below is a scepter with the head of Anubis.

combined in their functions.

Anubis is represented as a black animal, the color of the dead and embalming resin, crouched on a shrine or pedestal (fig. 7-79) or as a human with an Anubis head (fig. 4-14). His chief sanctuary was Cynopolis (El Qeis), but he was worshipped throughout Egypt as god of the dead, guardian of tombs, the overseer of embalming, and one of the judges of the dead.

During embalming ceremonies priests identified themselves with Anubis by wearing masks.

Several other canine-headed gods were known who were representative of Anubis, but they were either known for a limited time or were of little importance. For example, Duamutef (Tuamutef) was a canine-headed son of Osiris and Isis,who guarded the stomach of the deceased. Further information on Anubis and other gods is in Erman (1894), Bissing (1905), Budge (1926), Kees (1941), and Mercatante (1978).

There is confusion as to which canine – wolf, dog, jackal, or fox – represented these gods (Meyer, 1904: 97 f.; Peet, 1914 II: 109 f.).

There is also confusion as to which animal is represented in many of the drawings, paintings, and statues. The discordant characters of the Anubis statue in Figure 7-80 were partly clarified by Lortet and Gaillard (1909: 292).

The head is like that of a dog or jackal, but the ears are fox-like. The tail, although bushy, is relatively short like that of a jackal. The black color is typical of Anubis statues and paintings, although black canines were rarely seen in Egypt.

A Roman bronze in the Dokki Agriculture Museum, Cairo (fig. 7-5) can be recognized as representing a jackal in all characters. A wooden Anubis in this museum (fig. 7-81) is, in comparison, a typical fox.

Brunner-Traut (1981: fig. 57b) called another fox-like Anubis (fig. 7-82), "The truly genuine wolf-jackal, the great black devil (*Canis lupaster*)".

Other fox-like representations of Anubis with exaggeratedly stylized tails are in Figures 7-79 and 7-83.

Numerous authors have expressed their opinions and often more than one kind of canid was suggested. Usually the determinations of the Greeks and Romans were the most influential, mainly because they associated the Wolf City, Lycopolis (Asyut), and Wepwawet, with the wolf (jackal *sic.*); and the Dog City, Cynopolis (El Qeis) SW of Beni Mazar, and Anubis, with the dog.

Wilkinson (1878 III: 159, 279) accused the Greeks and Romans of erroneously calling Anubis a dog instead of a jackal, because "The jackal is the invariable emblem of Anubis." He also listed the fox (*op. cit.*, 258), along with the dog, wolf, and jackal as sacred, possibly at Lycopolis.

7-84 (above) A jackal- or dog-headed statue of a seated man. Source: Lortet and Gaillard (1905: fig. 119).

7-85 (top right) Hieroglyph of Anubis from the Tomb of Ramses IX, Dynasty XX, Thebes. Source: Guilmant (1907: pl. LXVII).

7-86 (bottom right) Hieroglyph of Anubis from the Tomb of the Vizier Ramose, reign of Amenophis, Dynasty XVIII, Thebes. Source: Davies (1941: pl. XLII).

The worship of the wolf at Lycopolis was questioned by Denon (1803 II:2), who said it was an animal not found in Egypt and was confused by the Greeks and Romans, "who at that time paid little attention to natural history."

Meyer (1904: 99 f.) noted that the Greeks recognized only two sacred canines and he concluded that Anubis and Khenty-Imentu were dog gods and Wepwawet a wolf god.

Emery (1961: 127) referred to Wepwawet as a wolf and Montet (1964: 174), without comment, said that the wolf represented the God Upuaut and the dog was identified with Anubis.

According to Flower (1932), "No real wolf occurs in Egypt; all 'wolves' sent as such to the Giza Zoological Garden and Museum were specimens of the Greater Jackal." (See comments under Jackal in *Nomenclature*).

The dangerous packs of wolf-dogs reported by Schweinfurth (1874: 633) were doubtless feral dogs. Wolf-dog was also a name commonly applied to large dogs by other Egyptologists. Kamal (1916: 67), for example, referred to wolf-dog mummies found together with humans.

Klunzinger (1878: 147) mentioned, "The half-wild jackal-like dog, which, like the jackal, was once sacred, and at Lycopolis was embalmed in multitudes."

Erman (1894: 23) was apparently not deceived by the Greeks and Romans and called the 12th Nome, which lay on the eastern bank, 'his Mountain' and likewise, Asyut on the opposite bank of the Nile, as the chief seat of worship of Anubis, the jackal-headed god of the dead.

The jackal was assumed to have been the symbol of Wepwawet because it was a 'desert animal', familiar with all the terrain, living in the desert, but never far from an oasis (Ayrton *et al.*, 1904 III: 8; Cobern, 1913: 1048 f.). And because of its tracks in the desert showing the travelers the 'way', it was called 'the path finder' or 'opener of the ways', for it guided souls to the Kingdom of Osiris (Caulfield, 1902: 15).

The jackal was also said to have become the totemic animal of Anubis because it was 'the one that prowls through the cemeteries at night eating the offerings from the tombs' (Ayrton *et al.*, 1904 III: 9).

Peet's (1914 II: 110) interpretation was: "Anubis is usually called the jackal god and it has been suggested that his connection with burial is due to the fact that the jackal is a haunter of spots where anything is buried. This evidence is insufficient." He also referred to the jackal as a desert animal and guide of the souls (*op. cit.*, 105, 108).

Reports of jackals prowling about tombs are commonly mentioned in the literature and Petrie was quoted (Spence, 1915: 104) as saying, "The guides to the Egyptian tombs are the jackal trails." Spence (*op. cit.*) added that association of the jackal with the burial ground could account for his becoming the mummifier.

The jackal was also identified with death because it was a nocturnal animal, an eater of carrion, and a carrier of rabies, and its bite could be fatal. Another 'fact' was its habit of sitting on tombs. It was said, therefore, to be 'death personified' (Murray, 1937 II: 4).

A remark by Carter (1933 III: 41 f.) shifts attention to another factor: "...when one takes into account the qualities of the domesticated canine family – devotion to its master, knowledge and defence of his property, attachment to him until death – it may be the reason why those ancients selected this jackal-dog as the vigilant watcher over their dead."

Other authors have commented on the identification of Anubis, but few have given any evidence in support of their conclusions.

Keimer (1948a: 22) said that the jackal, *Canis lupaster*, was a true prototype of the God Anubis. Westendorf (1968: 214) said, "Strictly speaking, Anubis was a dog, as zoologists have proved to the Egyptologists, but the jackal that they come to prefer is apparently ineradicable." Mackenzie (1978: 75), without further comment, said, "Anubis was the jackal."

A few comments were published that suggest the possibility of the fox (*Vulpes vulpes aegyptiaca*) having been the original symbol of the Anubis clan.

Wilkinson (1878 III: 258) listed the fox as sacred to Anubis at Lycopolis (Asyut).

Bissing (1898: 410), when discussing identification of hieroglyphs and the jackal, 'symbol of various gods of the dead', inserted the comment: "I am told that it is more nearly a fox."

Lortet and Gaillard (1905: 250), upon finding dog bones in a statue with a head that looks like a dog or jackal (fig. 7-84), said that they had expected to find fox bones. They also commented (*op. cit.*, preface p. IV f.) that all Egyptologists formerly stated that Anubis may be a jackal and it was accepted by the whole Egyptological world since the time of Champollion that Anubis is a jackal. The zoologists, however, seem to say it would be a fox. They added that if a mummified animal is lacking wrappings it is a dog. This last remark was not clarified.

Two black figures of Anubis were outlined and analyzed by Davies (1900 I:18f.). The standing animal (fig. 7-78) was given a hieroglyph meaning 'wise' (not *wnš*, 'jackal') and the recumbent (fig. 7-77) was designated as the word sign for *Yup'w*, Anubis. He remarked: "It is among the nonmythical animals in Beni Hasan II, pl. IV" (fig. 1-29). "In spite of its black colour and exclusively slender proportions, the evidence seems to identify it with the *Canis niloticus* or Egyptian fox, and with no other Egyptian animal now extant can it be identified."

These statements have never been challenged nor even discussed, but there is more evidence favoring Davies' conclusion.

The Beni Hasan animals referred to by Davies (*op. cit.*) are identified by the hieroglyphs *wnš* for jackal and *zab* for fox (figs 1-29, 7-3,-4). These figures show the fox to be slightly smaller and slenderer than the jackal, as indicated by the belly lines and the legs; having a slenderer muzzle and less prominent frontal projection (stop); and narrower and more pointed ears, which appear to be longer in relation to the head length. Tail lengths and shape, however, show no differences.

In most of the drawings and statuettes of Anubis the tail is very long, but slender (figs 7-79,-82,-83), and certainly suggestive of a fox.

Prior to reading the comments by Westendorf (1968), Lortet and Gaillard (1905), and Davies (1901 I:18 f.), Osborn and Helmy (1980: 367) said: "In 1965 we searched many of the Gebel Durunka tombs, but found only fox (*Vulpes vulpes*) remains along with mummified humans. We are inclined to believe that Anubis was a fox rather than a jackal, because all (most, *sic.*) of the statuary and hieroglyphs of Anubis are of an animal with the tail of a fox." The 'search' was superficial, however, because they were not permitted to disturb or remove any remains from the tombs and only allowed to trap mice, through the kindness of the guards.

7-87 Hieroglyph of Anubis or Wepwawet from the Mastaba of Qar, reign of Pepi II, Dynasty VI, Giza. Source: Simpson (1976a II: fig. 20).

7-88 Anubis figures drawing the sacred bark on the funerary papyrus of Hirweben, Dynasty XXI, Deir el Bahari. Source: Piankoff (1949: pl. VIII).

Correct identification of the mummified canids in these tombs SSW of Asyut is certainly a necessity.

Many of the remarks cited above concerning the jackal could also be applied to the fox. Red foxes use abandoned tombs as den sites (Osborn and Helmy, 1980: 378) and they can often be seen during the day sitting in the shade of the entrances (Author, pers. obs.). Food habits of foxes are similar to those of jackals and they might also eat offerings from the tombs. Thus, the fox can be interpreted as a haunter of burial grounds as well as the jackal.

It is no more of a desert animal than the jackal, however, and the 'tracks in the desert' referred to above by Caulfield (1902: 15) could be tracks of the Rueppell's fox, which is often found in waterless areas.

The stylization established by the ancient Egyptians of certain features, such as the shallowness or absence of the frontal stop; the long and slender snout; shape, length and pointedness of the ears; length and shape of the tail, which is sometimes too thin; slenderness of the body, particularly the abdomen; and the slender legs, identify the majority of representations as foxes. Emphasis of fox characteristics can be easily recognized by comparing photos of a live fox (fig. 7-7) and jackals (figs 7-1,-2) with the various figures listed above and a series of Anubis hieroglyphs (figs 7-85, -86,-87).

The staff in Figure 7-83, which was shown in a series of hieroglyphs, was described by Griffith (1898a: 58 f.) as a "symbolic staff with canine head; color blue probably for earlier black...it seems...to denote canine powers of free, swift movement, intelligence."

One of the most obvious illustrations of Anubis as a fox is that of the four black foxes towing the sacred bark (fig. 7-88).

Folk tales of the cunningness of the fox date far back into Assyrian and Sumerian history (Brentjes, 1965: 15 f., Aynard, 1972: 65). Thus, it is surprising that this aspect of the fox was not presented in ancient Egyptian beliefs.

Sacred animals were supposedly not hunted. Foxes, however, were pictured being attacked by hounds in various hunting scenes (figs 7-59,-60,-63), and in trophies of the hunt (fig. 7-15a,b). Jackals were also hunted (fig. 1-24).

Perhaps only the black fox, a fox in molt, was considered sacred. Recall that a specimen of a molting fox was called '*Canis anubis*'. (See comments in *Nomenclature* and *Description* in the Red Fox chapter).

Hyena Dog *Lycaon pictus* (Temminck, 1820)

E Hunting Dog, Wild Dog, Spotted Wild Dog, Cape Hunting Dog; F Cynhyène, Chien-Hyène, Lycaon, Loup peint, Chein chasseur; G Hyänenhund; A Kelab el Barrary

Nomenclature: An obsolete name used by various authors (Hartmann, 1869; Schweinfurth, 1874; Anderson. 1902) was *Canis pictus.* The valid name, *Lycaon pictus*, translates to 'painted wolf' (Gotch, 1979: 161).

Dorst (1970: 102) called these canids 'the wolves of Africa'.

The use of the name 'hunting dog' can be confusing, because dogs (hounds) used in hunting are also called 'hunting dogs' and the name is applied in the literature to both animals on slate palettes and in various illustrations.

Description: Hyena dogs are very large, slender, and dog-like with level backs; large heads; large, broad, rounded ears; long, thin legs; and long, slightly bushy tails reaching to or slightly below the hocks. The rudimentary fifth toes on the feet are absent, although present on most other canids.

The coloration of the body and legs is piebald brown, black, yellow, and white. The tail is yellowish at the base with black blotches and a white tip. The bushiness of the tail is more pronounced on the distal half.

Measurements are shoulder height 70-75 cm, head and body length 80-108 cm, and tail 30-40 cm.

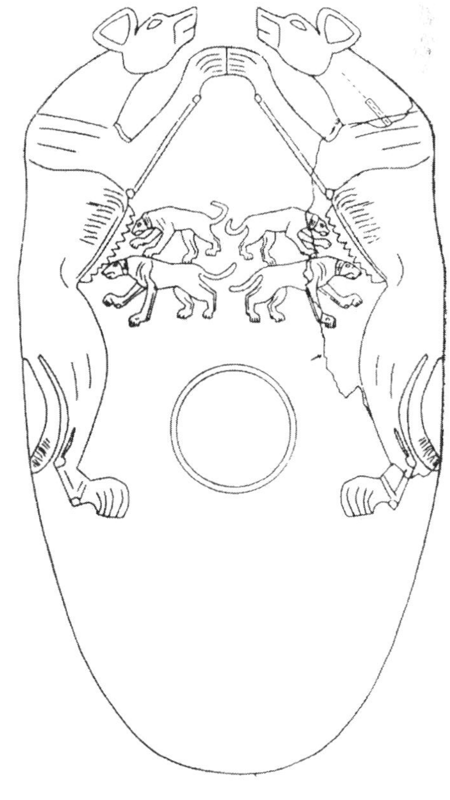

*7-89 Female hyena dogs (*Lycaon pictus*) on a palette nursing puppies. A reconstruction by Fischer (1958) dated to the Late Predynastic. Source: Asselberghs (1961: fig. 25).*

Natural history: Hyena dogs are diurnal and live and hunt in packs. Their prey is mainly gazelles and various antelopes and often the foals of larger species, such as wildebeest and zebras. Small mammals are also hunted.

The habitats are open or wooded savannah and mountain areas.

Distribution: The last recorded sighting of a hyena dog in Egypt was south of Kharga Oasis by Schweinfurth (1874: 633) in 1874. This was probably a stray animal that had come up the Darb el Arba'in camel road from Sudan. In 1935, Mason (1936: 128 ff.) killed several 'wild hunting dogs' from a pack of 14 that he chased in Wadi Hawar, northwestern Sudan. Setzer (1956: 552) listed a museum specimen from Bir el Girud in the Gebel Elba area of southeastern Egypt.

The general distribution, according to Dorst (1970: 101) and Haltenorth and Diller (1980: 177), extends from northern Sudan westward south of the Sahara and most of eastern and south-central Africa.

Prehistoric records: There are two slate cosmetic palettes from the third millenium with hyena dogs as the dominant animals (figs 1-2,-5). Various fragments of palettes from the Late Gerzean to Dynasty I showing hyena dogs were published by Asselberghs (1961: figs 133, 134, 142, 170).

A badly damaged palette from El Munagat in the eastern Delta that was reconstructed by Fischer (1958: 73, figs 13, 20) shows two female hyena dogs in the same position as those on the Oxford Palette and suckling lop-eared young (fig. 7-89).

Thus, it is quite evident that this beast existed at least in Lower and Middle Egypt into the late Predynastic (Brentjes, 1967d: 172 f.).

7-90 (top) A hyena dog in the Tomb of Uk-hotep, Dynasty XII, Meir. Source: Blackman (1915 II: pl. VII).

7-91 (bottom) Hyena dog (left) and leopard skins in Nubian tribute in the Tomb of Rekhmire, Dynasty XVIII, Thebes. Source: Davies (1943 II: pl. XVIII).

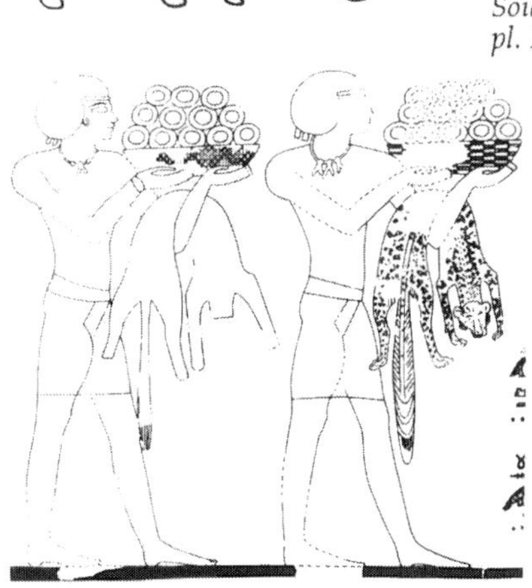

There is no question as to the identification of these figures, although they have been called 'jackals' (Legge, 1909: 303) and 'hyenas' (Westendorf, 1968: 19).

Typical features are the slender bodies; large, round ears; and large heads. The tails are much too long, but the etching on the tips indicates that the tails represent those of hyena dogs.

Judging from the numerous artifacts this animal was probably a cult animal in the late Predynastic and early Dynastic periods. This opinion was fostered by Brentjes (1971b: 338 ff.) who suggested that the hyena dog was the prototype of the god Seth.

The Dynastic period: One reproduction of a hyena dog is in the Dynasty XII Tomb of Ukh-hotep (fig. 7-90). The features are unmistakable, although some confusion was indicated by Blackman (1915 II: 19) who listed it as an okapi, but said later in a footnote (*op. cit.*, 40), "Mr. Henry Balfour is inclined to think that the animal on Pl. VII is not, as we have suggested, an okapi, but a hunting-dog, *Lycaon pictus* (Northern variety)."

During the New Kingdom pelts of hyena dogs were brought as tribute by Nubians (figs 7-91,-92). They were described as being 'white with red blotches' (Davies and Davies, 1940: 135). The pelts have typical hyena dog tails, but the heads and feet were removed. Similar blotched 'skirts' are shown worn by some of the tribute bearers (fig. 7-92).

Errors and discrepancies: Keller (1909 I: 89) wrote that the hyena dog was trained in Egypt long before the cheetah during Dynasties IV and V for hunting gazelles and antelopes and referred to the hyenas in Figures 7-160,-162 as examples and also to the Theban hunting scene (fig. 1-21), none of which show any indication of this activity.

Bodenheimer (1960: 122) repeated this error, but designated the Third Millenium B.C. as the time when this animal was used for hunting and that it was replaced by the dog. Brentjes (1966a: 312 f.) suggested that these conclusions were based on erroneous interpretations of 'Jaghund-Darstellungen' (representations of hunting hounds).

7-92 Leopard (?) and hyena dog skins in Nubian tribute. The latter have black blotches and lack heads. Tomb of Amenmose III, Dynasty XVIII, Thebes. Source: Davies and Davies (1940: pl. XXIV).

Bears Family *Ursidae*

Brown Bear ***Ursus arctos*** Linnaeus, 1758

htmt hetemet Wb. III, 198

E Brown Bear; F Ours brun; G Braunbär

Description: Bears are stocky with heavy limbs; short, broad, plantigrade feet with long claws; large rounded rumps; very short tails; and large, dog-like heads with erect, rounded ears. The Syrian race is pale yellowish or grayish-white.

The shoulder height is about 82 cm, head and body length 155, tail 35, and ear 10 (Harrison, 1968 II: table 17; and other sources).

Natural history: Bears tend to be solitary in habit. Their diet is omnivorous and includes fruits and vegetables, insects and other invertebrates, small and sometimes large vertebrates (including domestic animals), honey, fish, and carrion.

Distribution: Bears formerly inhabited the coastal mountains of the Eastern Mediterranean. The present range may include the mountains of Syria, Iraq, Iran, and Asia Minor.

General distribution also includes much of Asia, Eastern and Western Europe, and North America.

Fossil remains date the existence of bears in northwestern Africa from the Pleistocene into the Holocene, but all reports of bears having existed there in the Prehistoric or later are without any substantial evidence (Kowalski and Rzebik-Kowalska, 1991: 25, 29, 301 f.).

Bears were never native to Egypt although numerous representations from there were dated from the Predynastic into Roman times.

Prehistoric records: Neolithic amulets and a green slate or schist figure that were identified as bears (Budge, 1922: 281 f.; 1930: 118) are no longer on display in the British Museum collection. Keimer (1956: 336) was doubtful of the identification of these figures and commented that the tail of the schist bear was long.

There is the rear of a bear (?) on the boss side of the Carnarvon ivory knife handle (fig. 1-9). An easily identified bear appears on the late Gerzean knife handle from Gebel el Tarif (fig. 1-12), which was probably an early import from Mesopotamia (Asselberghs, 1961: 276).

The Dynastic period: A sitting bear from Abydos dated prior to Dynasty IV was described by Petrie (1903 II: 24, pl.II) as "a young bear, with a short, curly tail; the attitude and character of the animal

7-95 Syrian elephant and tusks and a bear in a tribute scene in the Tomb of Rekhmire, Dynasty XVIII, Thebes. Source: Keimer (1956: fig. 6).

7-93 (top) Bears in the remains of a scene of Syrian booty brought to Egypt by Sahure, Dynasty V, Abu Sir. Source: Keimer (1956: fig. 4).

7-94 (right) A bear and cub of clay from Abydos, Dynasty XII or XIII. Source: Garstang (1901: pl. IV, E 251).

7-96 A bear on a leash in part of a Syrian tribute scene from the Tomb of Amunedjeh, Dynasty XVIII, Thebes. Source: Davies and Davies (1941: pl. XIII).

7-97 A small bear on a leash (?) in a Syrian tribute scene. Tomb of Ann'a (Annena, Ineni), Dynasty XVIII, Western or Luxor Temple (?), Thebes. Source: Müller (1906: pl. 8).

7-98 Wooden carving of a bear from the New Kingdom. Source: Eggebrecht (1987: fig. 93).

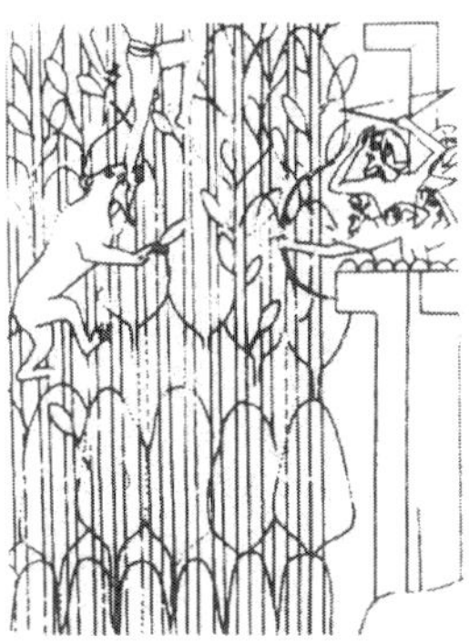

7-99 A bear attacking a man in the Battle of Satuna, Dynasty XIX, Luxor Temple. Source: Smith (1965: 219).

are well given". Keimer (1956) questioned the determination of this figure as well as that of a bear and cub, which is mentioned below, but it is difficult to identify these figures with any other beasts.

Seal amulets dated to Dynasties IV-XI, and probably of Egyptian origin, included a bear that Brunton (1937: 108, pl. LX, 6) called 'a quadruped (pig or bear?)', but the ears and snout are short and the feet are bear-like. Three tethered bears and a jar are all that remain of a portrayal of the booty that King Sahure brought from Syria (fig. 7-93). The bears were painted dark yellow and are easily recognized.

In the Dynasty V causeway of Unas (fig. 7-64) a bear was included in the procession of animals the king had apparently hunted at home and abroad (Keimer, 1956: 337). The round rump, short tail, and plantigrade feet identify a bear.

A Middle Kingdom clay model (fig. 7-94) was described by Garstang (1901: 6) as "The rough pottery figure resembling a bear and cub."

Live bears in Syrian tribute scenes undoubtedly represented tame bears, which would have been of special attraction to the Egyptians. If live bears were brought to Egypt, no remains or burials have been found, despite the remarks of Herodotus that the Egyptians buried bears, which were rare, and the bodies were found in a couched position (Keimer, 1955a: 455).

Some 1300 years after Sahure's picture of live bears, a yellowish-brown isabelline bear on a leash together with an elephant was shown in the Dynasy XVIII tomb of Rekhmire (fig. 7-95). Another bear on a leash, said by Davies and Davies (1941: 97) to have been the same color and done by the same artist as the above, is from the Dynasty XVIII tomb of Amunezeh (Amunedjeh), a contemporary of Rekhmire (fig. 7-96).

The blue color of the small bear in the Dynasty XVIII tomb of Ann'a (Annena) was said by Müller (1906: pl. 8) to have evidently represented gray or light black (fig. 7-97).

A very accurate wood carving (fig. 7-98), 5.9 cm high, was dated to the New Kingdom by Eggebrecht *et al.* (1987: 176), who remarked that being an exotic animal it was designed for the amusement of adults and children.

A well-known scene is the Dynasty XIX battle of Satuna in Luxor Temple (fig. 7-99). A Syrian who was attempting to flee the battle was treed by a bear which then grasped his ankle. The man has managed to draw his dagger and a nearby soldier in the tower of the castle that is under siege is shown about to shoot an arrow at the bear (Burchardt, 1914; Posener, 1944; Keimer, 1956: 340).

Numerous statues in clay and stone, as well as reliefs and paintings from the Greco-Roman into the Christian era were also included in Keimer's (1956: figs 12-25) discussion.

Errors and discrepancies: Bodenheimer (1960: 45) stated that "on Egyptian monuments the Syrian as well as the Abyssinian bear appear among the tribute animals". Of course he gave no evidence for such an imaginative remark, nor did he refer to Hartmann (1864: 21), who had written that the occurrence of the bear in Abyssinia was unlikely.

Two Ramessid ostraca from Deir el Medina that Vandier d'Abbadie (1937 I: 48) called 'hyenas' (fig. 7-100) were correctly described as bears by Keimer (1956: 340) on the bases of the rounded ears, head shape, and plantigrade feet. The striping on one shows little resemblance to the stripes of a hyena and was probably the artist's attempt to depict the grizzled or shaggy pelage.

7-100 A bear on a Ramessid ostracon, Dynasty XIX-XX, Deir el Medineh. Source: Vandier d'Abbadie (1937 I:pl. XXXI).

Family *Mustelidae*

Libyan Striped Weasel ***Poecilictis libyca*** (Hemprich and Ehrenberg, 1833)

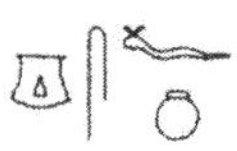 *gsfnw* gezefenu Wb. V, 206

E Striped Weasel; F Zorille de Libye; G Streifenwiesel; A Abu menten, Ersa Mekhatata, Shefshefa

Nomenclature: There is confusion among the names applied to this taxon. It was originally in the genus *Mustela* (true weasels); then *Ictonyx*, with which, as Corbet (1978: 174) suggested, "it should probably be reunited." It differs from the latter chiefly by having more swollen bullae (swelling in the skull beneath the ear opening), less clearly defined striping on the back, and long hair on the feet covering the soles and toe pads.

Keimer (1939: 37; 1942a: 15 ff.) used the name *Ictonyx libyca* and it was also the name given by Anderson (1902).

Description: This is a shaggy, long-haired, bushy-tailed, black and white weasel. A white band circles the black head between the eyes and ears. The back is white (sometimes yellowish) with four to five irregular black stripes produced by black underhairs; tail black and white above, black below; legs and feet black; palms and soles covered with hair. The legs are proportionately short.

Head and body lengths of adults are 25-28 cm and tails 16-19 (Osborn and Helmy, 1980: table 48).

Natural history: Libyan striped weasels live in sparsely vegetated semi-desert where they dig shallow burrows. They are nocturnal and prey on

7-101 (top) A striped weasel from the Causeway of Unas, Dynasty V, Saqqara. Source: Keimer (1942a: fig. 13).

7-102 (bottom) Striped weasels from the Sun Temple of Ne-user-re, Dynasty V, Abu Gurob (Gurab, Gharab, Gharob) north of Saqqara. Source: Keimer (1942a: fig. 10).

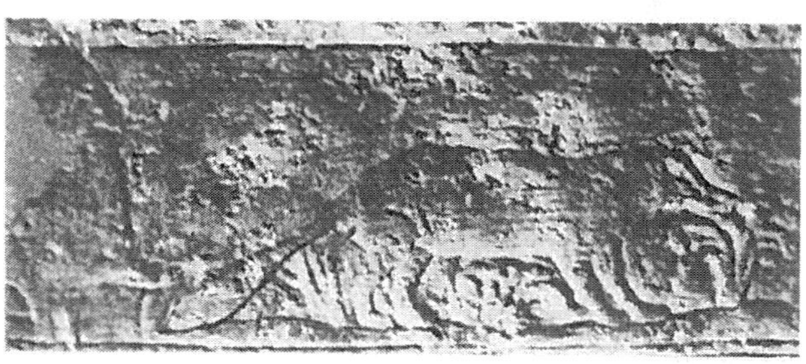

7-103 A striped weasel from the Sun Temple of Ne-user-re, Dynasty V, Abu Gurob north of Saqqara. Source: Wildung (1984: fig. 11).

7-104 A fragment of a striped weasel from the Tomb of Rahotep, Dynasty IV, Meidum. Source: Aufrère (1985: fig. 9).

insects and larvae; rodents; reptiles; and ground-nesting birds and their eggs and young. Anal scent glands produce and can spray a strongly maladorous liquid. Bristling hair and erection of the tail are warning signs to an aggressor.

Distribution: In Egypt this species is known only from the western margin of the Nile delta, Western Mediterranean Coastal Desert, Wadi el Natroun, El Maghra Oasis, and tracks reported from the Gebel Uweinat area in the southwest corner bordering Libya (Osborn and Helmy, 1980: 396 f.). Beyond Egypt it is circum-Saharan in distribution including the coastal semi-desert west into Morocco; thence in northern parts of Mauretania, Mali, Nigeria, Chad, and Sudan (various sources).

Reports on the occurrence of this species in Asian Turkey were erroneous (Ellerman and Morrison-Scott, 1951: 267).

Prehistoric records: Skull and skeletal remains were described from Neolithic deposits at Beni Salama (von den Driesch and Boessneck, 1985: 46 ff.).

The Dynastic period: Two representations described by Keimer (1942a: 15 ff.) are a relief in the Causeway of Unas (fig. 7-101) and a pair giving birth in the Temple of Ne-User-Re (fig. 7-102). Above each of the latter is the hieroglyph for *gs'fn-w* and between is the hieroglyph *ms'* associated with birth. Another relief fragment (fig. 7-103) from the Temple of Ne-User-Re shows the same features as the above, a bushy tail with a slender base and ears not extending above the head. Above it the name can be recognized from remnants of the hieroglyph. A fragment of a sketch from the Tomb of Rahotep (fig. 7-104) is probably of a libyan striped weasel.

Errors and discrepancies: Brentjes (1966b: 280) suggested that the animals shown in Figure 7-102 could be musk shrews (*Suncus*) or ichneumons (*Herpestes*) and said that those pictured in Wreszinski (1936 III: 84) had whitish-yellow pelts. This coloration is a normal variation (Dorst, 1970: 104; Haltenorth and Diller, 1980: pl. 31, 6).

Although the animals in Figure 7-102 appear to be giving birth to fully developed young and are standing, this may have been an inaccurate observation. Brentjes (*op. cit.*) said that these animals normally lie down to give birth and Flower (1932: 404) described the newborn as 'pink, hairless and helpless'.

Zoril *Ictonyx striatus* (Perry, 1810)

E Striped Polecat, Zorilla; F Zorille commun; G Zorilla, Streifeniltis, Band-Iltis; A Abu Afene

Description: Pelage shaggy. Back with three black and four white stripes; all of completely black or white hairs. Head black with white marking on snout and an incomplete white band between the eyes and ears. Upper and lower base of the tail are black, distal hairs have white tips and black bases. Belly, legs, and feet are black. Soles of feet and toe pads are bare. The legs are proportionately short.

Head and body lengths of adults are 30-38 cm and tails 22-30 (Haltenorth and Diller, 1980: 182).

Natural history: This species lives in bush savanna, forest, and mountains. In feeding habits and behavior it is similar to *Poecilictis libyca*.

Distribution: In Egypt this species is known only from the southeastern corner. It occurs across sub-Saharan Africa from Sudan to Mauretania and in Eastern Africa, except for northern Somalia; thence south to the Cape including Angola and Namibia, but not in the rain forest.

This species was probably not represented in Dynastic art.

Ratel *Mellivora capensis* (Schreber, 1776)

E Honey Badger; F Ratel, Blaireau mangeur (friand) de miel; G Ratel, Honigdachs; A Abu Keem, Abu Djaga, Abu Kaab (father of the claws)

Nomenclature: Mellivora ratelus and *M. ratel*, the names used by Keimer (1939a: 40), were previously applied to the Asian race, *M. capensis indica* Kerr, 1792 (Ellerman and Morrison-Scott, 1951: 268).

The generic name derives from '*mel* (L), genetive *mellis*, honey and *voro* (L) I devour; a reference to its favourite food...' Gotch (1979: 169).

Description: The ratel is heavily built with a large head, small rounded ears, relatively short legs, plantigrade feet, very long claws on the forefeet, and a short bushy tail, often held upright (Dorst, 1970: 106). The legs and lower parts of the body, most of the head, and distal part of the tail are to black. The entire back from the crown of the head

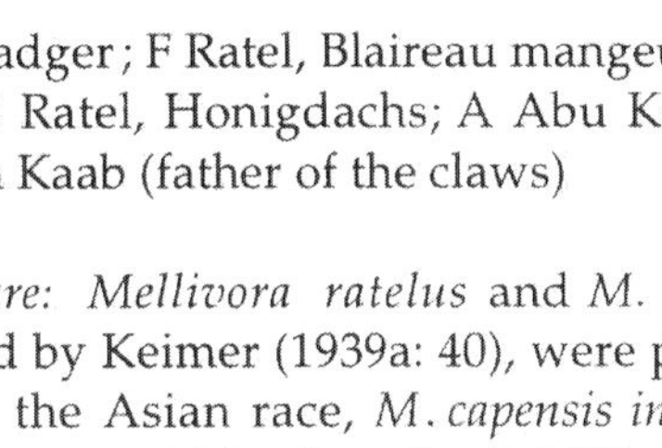

7-105 Rock drawing of a ratel in Gebel Aigat west of Abrak, southeastern Eastern Desert. Source: Červíček (1974: 170, fig. 60).

to the middle of the tail is grayish- or brownish-white with a white margin.

The head and body length is 65-75 cm., tail 18-25 (about 30% of head and body length), and shoulder height 23-38.

Natural history: Ratels are mainly nocturnal and hide during the day in their burrows. Their digging ability helps them capture lizards, rodents, and hares. They also eat various insects and larvae, fish, tortoises, ground nesting birds and their eggs and young, carrion, and some roots and fruits. Ratels are particularly fond of bees and honey and are able to climb trees to obtain these delights. From this habit the common name, honey badger, was derived.

Ratels live in various environments from semi-desert to forest and mountains.

Distribution: Ratels live throughout much of Sudan as far north as Suakin (Setzer, 1956: 554) and most of Africa south of the Sahara and in the northwestern countries: Senegal, western Mauritania, Western Sahara, and southern Morocco. It is considered to be extinct in Egypt, although an animal thought to have been a ratel was killed near Port Said in 1870 (Keimer, 1948a: 386 fn. 1).

Ratels also occur in the Arabian Peninsula, the Negev, Iran, southern Russian Turkmenia, Afghanistan, and India (Harrison, 1968 II: 247).

Prehistoric records: Gautier (1976: 372) listed a 'badger (?)' from the terminal Paleolithic in El Faiyum.

Rock drawings from Wadi Aigat (fig. 7-105) and Khor Abagag were listed by Červíček (1974: 170).

Rows of ratels occur on both sides of the Naqada III ivory knife handle from Abu Zaidan (fig. 1-7), rows A9 and B9, and on the boss at the level of row B6 (Churcher, 1984: 160, 164, 165, fig. 35). The actual size of the figures, less than one cm, certainly limited the ability of the artist(s) to show correctly all of each animal's features. Head shapes and positions, tail shapes and positions, heavy bodies, short legs, and plantigrade feet conform, especially in numbers 8, 9, and 10 in row A9, with natural features (Churcher, *op. cit.*, 165).

Previous names suggested for the ratels on the Abu Zaidan handle were wild boar (?) by de Morgan (1909: 276), hippopotamus or wild boar (Bénédite, 1918: 229), ichneumon (Vandier, 1952 I: 544), and hippopotamus (Asselberghs, 1961: 275).

Boessneck (1988: 29 f.) thought that the diagnosis 'hippopotamus' was highly doubtful and that the figures more clearly represented swine, but

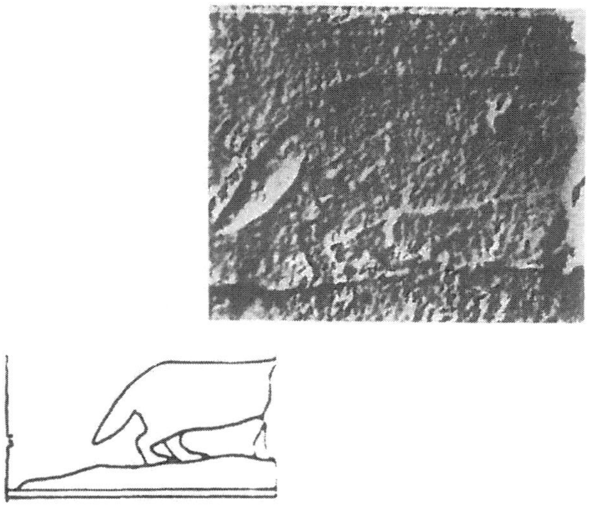

7-106 (top) Relief of a ratel from the Temple of Sahure, Dynasty V, Saqqara and a drawing of the figure below it. Source: Keimer (1942a: figs 7 and 8).

7-107 (bottom) A ratel in the Temple of Rathures, Dynasty V, Abu Sir. Source: von Bissing (1956: pl. XXIIIb). Behind the ratel a hedgehog is entering a shelter; before it is a resting gazelle.

might be determined as warthogs. He added, however, that whether warthogs came so far north in 4-3,000 B.C. is an unanswered question.

None of these figures have the elongate heads nor slender tails that are typical of wild pigs; features that any artist would certainly have been capable of reproducing.

Rows of similar carvings appear on the fifth or lower rows on both sides of the Davis ivory comb (fig. 1-10). The badly damaged Pitt-Rivers knife handle apparently had a lower row of ratels on either side, also (fig. 1-8).

The ratels on the Davis comb and the Pitt-Rivers handle were called hippos or pigs by Bénédite (1918: 229), hippos ? or hyenas ? by Asselberghs (1961: 99), and wild pigs by Hayes (1953 I: 27).

The Dynastic period: A partly destroyed relief in the Dynasty V Temple of Sahure (figs 7-106a,b) was recognized as a ratel by Keimer (1942a: 11 f.) and Brentjes (1967b: 314). The partially destroyed animal in the lower part of Figure 7-60 could also be a ratel.

Another figure that could have been intended as a ratel is in the Dynasty V tomb of Rathures (fig. 7-107). It has been called an ichneumon (von Bissing, 1956: 337, in reference to Anderson, 1902), and a zoril (Droste zu Hülshoff, 1980: 56 and Aufrère, 1985: 28).

Otter Genus *Lutra*

F Loutre; G Otter

Description: Otters are slender and sinuous with sharply tapering tails that are thick and muscular at the base. The head is broad with a flattened crown and a short, blunt muzzle. Ears are small and rounded; slightly projecting above the fur. The eyes are small. Whiskers are numerous, long, and tactile.

The pelage is short and very dense with a fine, waterproof underfur. Coloration varies between species, but they are generally grayish to dark brown with buffy to yellowish underparts.

The legs are short and stout and the feet broad with five long, webbed, and sharply clawed toes.

Natural history: Otters are adapted to an aquatic life, but are also quite agile on land. They nest near water in available shelters or dig burrows with underwater entrances.

Being mainly noctural in habit, otters are not easily observed in nature.

The food of otters is mainly fish, but they also eat shellfish, crayfish, frogs, eggs, nestling birds, small rodents, and insects.

Genera and species in Egypt: Two species may have lived in Egypt into the Late or Greco-Roman Periods.

Spotted-necked Otter ***Lutra maculicollis*** Lichtenstein, 1835

F La Loutre à cou tacheté; G Fleckenhalsotter

Description: Upper parts of the body, head, legs, and tail are light chestnut to dark brown. Chin, throat, chest, and most of belly whitish to orange with irregular brown spots.

The head and body length is 60-65 cm and tail 35-40 cm (Haltenorth and Diller, 1980: 184).

Distribution: Africa south of the Sahara, except Somalia, a broad strip of East Africa, and most of South Africa (for details see Haltenorth and Diller, 1980: 184).

Common Otter ***Lutra lutra*** (Linnaeus, 1758)

F Loutre d'Europe; G Fischotter

Description: Upper parts of the body, head, legs, and tail are dark to yellowish brown, chin and throat grayish white, belly light brown to yellowish. The head and body length is 60-95 cm and tail 25-55 cm (Haltenorth and Diller, 1980: 185).

The slightly longer hair on the throat gives the appearance of a ruff, especially when wet. This is exaggerated on some Egyptian bronzes (fig. 7-108).

Distribution: Morocco (from the coast to the Atlas Mts.) and northern Algeria; most of Europe and Asia; Asia Minor; and the larger rivers of northern Arabia, Jordan, and Palestine (Harrison, 1968 II: 251 f.).

Records and Artifacts of Otters

Prehistoric record: Part of a lower jaw was found in a site called Catfish Cave near Korosko (Kurusku) and dated 7060 - 120 B.P. (Reed, 1966b: 38). The bone was identified as 'probably of *Lutra maculicollis*', because '...the present range of this species, which extends into the drainage of the White Nile in Sudan (Setzer, 1956: 555), is the closest to Egypt of any of the African otters'.

The Dynastic period: A very realistic otter is pictured eating a fish in the Dynasty VI Mastaba of Mereruka (fig. 7-109). Its features, with the exception of the very short space between the eye and the ear, are typical of an otter.

The animal is shown sqatting on the surface of the water as though it were on the shore.

Positive determination of the species of the Mereruka otter is uncertain, because, except for spotting on the neck of one species, external differences are limited (Boessneck, 1988: 51).

7-108 Bronze of a common otter with a throat patch and a uraeus and sun disc on its head. Source: Roeder (1936: fig. 4, no. 10).

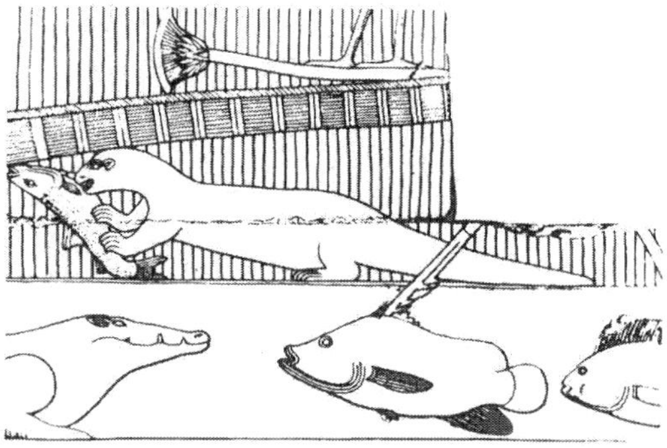

7-109 Otter eating a fish (Mugil sp.) *in the Mastaba of Mereruka, Dynasty VI, Saqqara. Source: Duell (1938 II: pl.128.*

7-110 Otters in the Nile with fish in their mouths. Roman period mosaic. Source: Keimer (1955a: fig. 7).

Greco-Roman period: Herodotus was quoted by Waddel (1939: 190) as having written that "otters are said not to be found in the Nile." Nevertheless, Herodotus referred to the otter as a sacred animal. Keimer's (1955a: 460) comment on this was that Herodotus had confused the ichneumon with the otter.

Through interpretations of the Physiologus (dated 200 B.C.) Brunner-Traut (1968: 42) verified that the otter not only lived in ancient Egypt, but was also a sacred animal, since it was incorporated into the cult of Uto.

According to the accounts of Diodorus and Strabo the otter was disappearing from Egypt around the end of Pharaonic times and was replaced in its religious status by the ichneumon.

Further verification of the otter in Egypt is a 193-211 A.D. Roman mosaic that portrays the Nile in flood and includes, among other animals, two otters (*enhydris* or water animals) with fish in their mouths (fig. 7-110).

In museums throughout the world there are bronze statuettes of otters that have been labelled 'ichneumons' (Roeder, 1936, 1956). All of these 'aufgerichtete' or up-standing figures pictured by Roeder (*op. cit.*) were renamed 'otters' by Brunner-Traut (1968: 44). This characteristic ability of the otter to stand upright for long periods with paws upraised (figs 7-108, 7-111 to 7-116) and several other basic differences appear in the bronzes indicating that they are otters and not ichneumons. Of course ichneumons can also stand upright, but only for a minute or so.

The whitish-gray zone of longer hair on the throat and neck of the otter, which is prominent on a wet animal, is indicated on some bronzes either as a specially engraved area or a throat patch (fig. 7-108).

Male sex organs are prominent on most otter figures, but absent on ichneumons.

The fore and hind feet of the otter are broad and have five clawed, functional toes that are webbed. Webs are not always indicated on

7-111 Bronze of a common otter with a uraeus and sun disc on its head. Source: Roeder (1936: fig. 3, no. 8).

7-112 Bronze of a common otter with a sun disc on horns on its head. Source: Roeder (1936: fig. 5, no. 11).

7-113 Bronze of a common otter with a ureaus, a sun disc, and horns on its head. Source: Roeder (1936: fig. 6, no. 12).

7-114 (left) Bronze of a common otter standing on its hind feet and supported by its tail. There is a ureaus and a sun disc on its head. Source: Emery (1971: pl. VIII, 6).

7-115 (centre) Bronze of a common otter with a ureaus on its head in frontal and lateral view. Source: H. Satzinger, Kunsthistorische Museum, Vienna.

7-116 (right) Bronze of a common otter with a ureaus and sun disc on its head. Source: H. Satzinger, Kunsthistorische Museum, Vienna.

statuary, although the fore paws of the otter in Figure 7-108 were shown in a drawing (Roeder, 1956: 378, fig. 534) with webs between the five fingers.

Ichneumons have narrow feet with four functional toes and short claws. The hind toes are partly webbed. The legs of the otter are short and stout; ichneumons have longer and slenderer legs. Comparisons between the legs and feet of the upstanding bronze otters can be made with the reliefs in the Tomb of Idut and Mastaba of Mereruka (figs 7-129 and 7-134).

The otter has a shorter and blunter snout than the ichneumon and its eyes are therefore closer to its nostrils.

All of these features are not correctly shown on all figures, but by making comparisons the two animals can usually be distinguished.

Bronze statuettes of otters are always standing upright with the forepaws raised as though in adoration. Head ornaments usually include the Uraeus or divine cobra of the goddess Buto (fig. 7-115) and the sun disc, symbol of Aten (figs 7-108,-111,-114,-116); or the sun disc supported on the horns of Hathor, the cow goddess (fig.7-112) plus the Ureaus (fig. 7-113).

Upstanding otter bronzes are resting on their haunches, but there is one that is actually standing on its hind feet with the tail extended posteriorly for support (fig. 7-114). It was called an ichneumon by Emery (1971: pl. VIII, 6), but it is quite similar to the otter in Figure 7-108, except the throat patch is lacking.

The otter was incorporated into the cult of Uto at Buto in Lower Egypt and Nekhebet at El Kab in Upper Egypt. Nekhebet was 'sometimes represented as a vulture, sometimes as a snake' (Erman, 1894: 20).

The otter, like the ichneumon, was included in mythology. Its enemy in water was the crocodile, whereas the ichneumon's enemy on land was the snake. A charming story, which has also been told about the ichneumon, probably because of the confusion in identification in ancient times, describes the otter's technique of killing crocodiles:

The otter covers itself with mud for camouflage and watches for a crocodile to crawl out on a sand bank to sleep. When the basking crocodile opens its mouth, the otter dashes down its throat. The crocodile's jaws snap shut, but too late to catch the swift otter, which eats through the monster's intestines and body wall and escapes unscathed, leaving the crocodile in its death throes.

Errors and discrepancies: In two treatises (Hinton and Dunn, 1967: 90, fig.16; Dücher, 1972: 171) bronze statuettes of otters with throat patches were pictured as examples of ichneumons.

Surprisingly, the otter in the Mastaba of Mereruka (fig. 7-109) was once called a crocodile (Daressy, 1898: 554). Houlihan (1996: 49, pl.1) called this obvious otter an 'Egyptian Mongoose'.

Datings and provenances of most of the statuettes discussed above have not been found.

Family *Viverridae*

Common Genet *Genetta genetta* (Linnaeus,1758)

E Small-spotted Genet; F Genette vulgaire, Genette commune; G Gemeine, Europaische, Kleinfleck Ginsterkatze; A Gharneet, El Zabaad, Zooraiga

Nomenclature: Genetta dongolona, the name used by Anderson (1902: 188) and Macramallah (1935: 16, 42), is an obsolete synonym of *G. genetta.*

7-117 (left) Small-spotted genet, Genetta genetta. Source: Anderson (1902: pl. XXVI).

7-118 (right) Genet on the right and ichneumon climbing papyrus stems to raid bird nests. Tomb of Senezm-ib, called Inti, Dynasty V, Giza. Source: L.D. II 77.

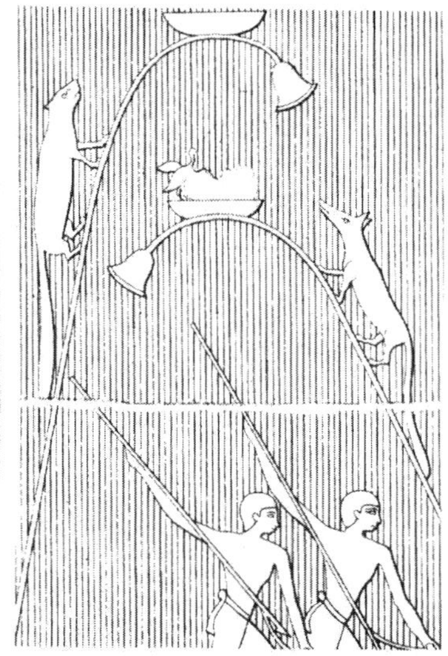

7-119 Genet approaching nestling pied kingfishers. Tomb of Ti, Dynasty V, Saqqara. Source: Douglas J. Brewer.

Description: Genets are elongate, slender-bodied, and catlike with proportionately short legs, and semi-retractile claws.

Averages and extremes of measurements in cms are: Head and body length 45 (40-53); tail 38 (35-52), 85 (66-98) percent of head and body length.

The head is small with a long, slender snout. Ears are longer than broad and prominent. The fur is short and light gray; sometimes with a buffy or brownish tinge. There is a black crest on the back from shoulders to base of tail and rows of roundish to elongate black spots on the back and sides. The slender tail has 8-10 black rings and usually a pale tip (fig. 7-117).

Anal scent glands produce a strong, musky odor.

Natural history: Genets are nocturnal hunters and prey upon hares, rodents, birds, lizards, bird and reptile eggs, frogs, fish, crayfish, mussels, water snails, insects and their larvae (Michaelis, 1972: 66).

Habitats include vegetated slopes of wadis, parkland and savanna; preferably near water.

Genets are expert climbers (Hanák, 1977: 74) and are also reported to be able to swim well (Panouse, 1957: 90).

Distribution: The present distribution in Egypt is based on a few specimens from the most southwestern and southeastern parts of the Eastern Desert (Osborn and Helmy, 1980: 411 ff.) and a sight record from Bir Abraq about 200 km southeast of Aswan (I. Helmy, 1981, pers. com.).

This genet had previously been listed as extinct in Egypt (Hilzheimer, 1913: 182; Bodenheimer, 1960: 122; Brentjes, 1967c: 304; and Störk, 1977c: 598).

The range includes much of Sudan and the savanna and parkland of Africa south of the Sahara; also northwestern Africa and southwestern Europe;

7-120 Fowling scene in the Tomb of Pepionkh, Dynasty VI, Meir. His wife is pointing at a genet climbing a papyrus stem. Source: Blackman (1924 IV: pl. VII).

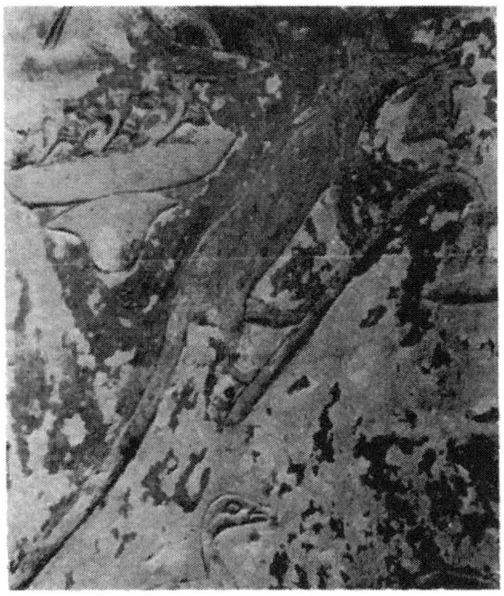

7-121 Genet with a duckling in its mouth. Mastaba of Idut, Dynasty V, Saqqara. Source: Author.

7-122 Drawings of genet (above) and ichneumon in the Mastaba of Idut, Dynasty V, Saqqara. Source: Macramallah (1935: pl. VII).

7-123 (above) Genet (right) and ichneumon (left) in the Tomb of Akhethetep, Dynasty V, Saqqara. Source: Davies (1901a: pl. XIV).

7-124 Genet about to raid the nest of a kingfisher and being attacked by the parent bird. Tomb of Sahure II, Dynasty V, Saqqara. Source: Borchardt (1913: pl. 74).

Palestine and parts of the Arabian Peninsula: Aden and Yemen.

Prehistoric records: No rock drawings of genets have been discovered.

Remains of this genet found in a cave in the South Galala Plateau in the northern part of the Eastern Desert (Hobbs, 1989: 97; Goodman *et al*, 1992) indicate that previous distribution was much wider than in Dynastic and later times.

The Dynastic period: Numerous depictions of genets appear in Dynasties IV to VI where they were pictured in swamp scenes climbing papyrus stems, along with ichneumons, to raid bird nests. Many were in unpainted relief (fig. 7-118); the most striking example being in the Tomb of Ti (fig. 7-119).

There is little doubt that genets could clamber through the thickets, but their graceful ascending of single, curving stems upon which bowl-shaped nests are balanced, were figments of imagination (figs 7-118,-119,-120).

Genets in the Tombs of Idut and Mehu (fig. 7-121) were painted dark gray with black markings. They slightly resemble foxes, but, as Macramallah (1935: 42) said of the figure in Idut's tomb, "in comparing the scene with other representations of the same class one is not deceived by our identification. The tail is very heavy, the gray pelage is striped with black, the tail is ringed in the same color."

Outlines of the genet and an ichneumon are clarified in Figure 7-122, and another fox-like genet is shown in Figure 7-123.

A swamp scene in a Middle Kingdom tomb at Beni Hasan includes genets, an ichneumon, and a cat (fig. 1-27).

The Egyptian style of portrayal was to combine genets with ichneumons in swamp scenes; therefore, any resemblance of genets to foxes was accidental.

Other examples of fox-like genets are in the Dynasty VI Mastaba of Tesen at Giza (Hassan, 1944: fig. 123) and the Dynasty V Tomb of Sahure at Saqqara (fig. 7-124).

For a true representation of a fox in the papyrus see Figure 7-74.

Among animals in the so-called 'desert hunt scenes', genets are rarely pictured. There is one of a genet hiding in a shelter (fig. 7-125) in the Dynasty XVIII Tomb of Rekhmire, which Janssen (1990: 47) called 'a fox-like animal'.

Another may be the long-tailed animal in the upper left of the Beni Hasan hunt scene (figs 1-30,-31).

Nubians in the Dynasty XVIII Tomb of Huy at Thebes have genet tails tied to their upper arms and

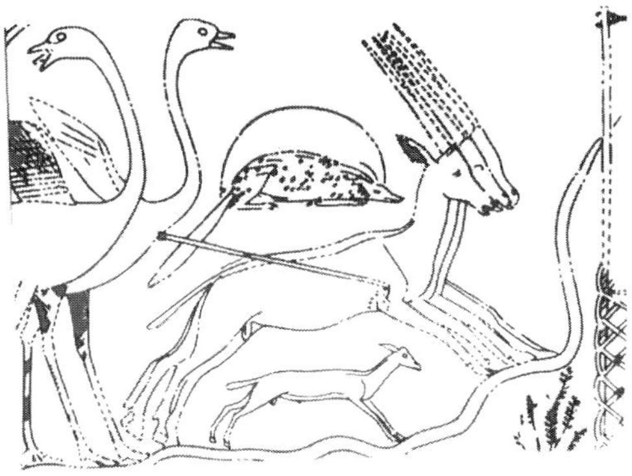

7-125 (above) Genet hiding in a shelter. Tomb of Rekhmire, Dynasty XVIII, Thebes. Source: Davies (1943 II: pl. XLIII). This part of the scene includes two ostriches and three beisa oryx with one young.

7-126 (top right) Suppliant people from the north and south in alternate positions. The people from the south are wearing genet tails on their waists and elbows. Tomb of Meyryre, (no.226) Dynasty XVIII, Sheikh Abd el Kurneh (Gurneh), Thebes. Source: Davies and Davies (1933b: pl. XLI).

7-127 (bottom right) Genet giving birth. Tomb of Idut, Dynasty V, Saqqara. Source: Macramallah (1935: pl. XXVI).

elbows. They are probably tails of *G. tigrina*, because of the black tips, although they were previously called 'cat's (?) tails' (Davies and Gardiner, 1926: pl. XXVIII). In another scene, Nubians are wearing genet tails on their waists and elbows (fig. 7-126).

On a fragment of a marsh scene (fig. 7-127) a genet is giving birth while standing on a papyrus stem. The long ears and snout of the fetus are unmistakably genet, according to Egptian stylization. Figure 7-128 , which was called a zoril by Wildung (1984), does not have a tail like that animal. The fetus has a long snout, but the ears are not erect, which is probably normal for the newly born.

Genets are reported to be easily tamed and they may have been the original 'cats' of Egypt (Panouse, 1957: 90), despite their strong, musky odor. But the odor of tame genets, according to Quitzow (1961), is not unpleasant.

Pinney (1964: 37) also said that the Egyptians had domesticated the genet, but gave no evidence. Gotch (1979: 170) suggested that the Abyssian genet, *G. abyssinica*, which inhabits Ethiopia and Sennar, "can be tamed and was probably the original 'cat' of ancient Egypt."

Kingdon (1977 IIIA: 143) wrote that the common genet was kept by Egyptians and is still kept by Berbers of Northwest Africa as a rat and snake exterminator. He thought that possibly the cat took over because of the better smell, but it seemed "more likely that the common cat was not only better at killing rats, but also able to kill genets."

The hostility of the genet toward snakes and possibly its resemblance to cats have encouraged some authors (Kees, 1941: 33; and Brentjes, 1967b: 305) to consider it as being a cult animal associated with the Goddess Mafdet. A genet with upturned tail climbing a papyrus stem (fig. 7-120) is suggestive of the snake-killing goddess climbing a 'guillotine' (fig. 7-211).

Vandier (1952 I: 851) even considered the details of the Mafdet figure sufficient to indicate it was almost certainly a genet.

The numerous illustrations of genets in papyrus verify their existence in the Nile Valley during the dynasties. There is no explanation, however, for their disappearance in later times. Perhaps competition with cats was a factor. Lack of genets beyond the Nile Valley was doubtless a result of climatic change and disappearance of forests or parkland.

No mummies or skeletal remains, except from the Galala cave (Goodman *et al*, 1992: 86), are known from Egypt. We have no evidence, therefore, that species other than *G. genetta* inhabited Egypt.

Errors and discrepancies: Various names have been applied to genets in the Old Kingdom marsh scenes, such as cat-like animals (Kees, 1941; 33); mustelopardus or weasel panther (Keller, 1909 I: 157); weasel (Erman, 1894=1971: 236, and Lefebure, 1903: 191 f.); civet-cat (Anderson, 1902: 188 and Malek, 1979: 619); genet-cat (Davies, 1902 I: 13-14; II: 22); and ichneumon or mongoose by Blackman (1924 IV: 28, 45, figs VII, XVII) and Hassan (1944 V: 267, fig. 123).

Harpur (1987) made no distinction between genets and ichneumons and apparently considered all of the long-tailed climbers to be genets (see also

Ichneumon chapter) even though her illustrations included numerous excellent reproductions distinguishing both animals.

Some authors have called genets foxes, probably because of the raised heads, upright ears, and thickened tails. Examples are Murray (1937: 26) and Brentjes (1967a: 117) in reference to the Tomb of Ti (fig. 7-119). Brentjes also erred in referring to the genet in the Tomb of Achti-hetep-hrai (Wreszinski, 1923: pl. 106) as a fox. One author (Bourriau, 1988: 18, fig.7) called a nest-robbing genet a 'jackal (?)' and said that "Various authors have called it a fox, an ichneumon and jackal."

Comparison of these examples with that of Idut (fig. 7-121) should eliminate any questions regarding identity.

7-128 Genet giving birth. Temple of Ne-user-re, Dynasty V, Saqqara. Source: Wildung (1984: fig. 12).

Ichneumon *Herpestes ichneumon* (Linneaus, 1758)

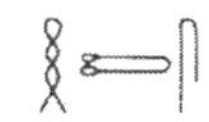 *ḥtš* hetjez Wb.III, 204

E Mongoose, Egyptian Mongoose, Pharaoh's Cat or Rat; F Mangouste ichneumon; G Eigentliches Ichneumon, Manguste, Pharaonenratte; A Nims, El Nims el Masry

Nomenclature: The Latinized name has a direct origin from the Greco-Roman period: '*herpestes* (Gr) a creeper; an illusion to its stalking habits; *ikhneumon* (Gr) the tracker' (Gotch, 1979: 174).

In Allen's (1939) Checklist an obsolete synonym is *Ichneumon pharaon* Lacepède, 1801. *Mungos* was another generic name used by earlier authors (Ellerman and Morrison-Scott, 1951: 293).

Prosper Alpin (1581-1584: 443) wrote that in Egypt there lived a species of wild rat, *Mus pharaonis*, which the indigenous called *rat de Pharaon* and that formerly the ancients called *ichneumon* or a searcher for rats.

Description: Ichneumons are slender-bodied and weasel-like with relatively short legs. The head is elongated and narrow, but thick in profile with a tapering, but not sharply pointed snout. Ears are short and rounded, broader than long, and not projecting above the head (figs 7-129,-130). Many Egyptian reproductions, however, have prominent ears (figs 7-118, -138, -141 to -144).

The pelage is long and coarse, grizzled blackish-brown and cream, giving the animal the appearance of being larger than its actual size. An excited ichneumon with bristling hair and arched back can appear to be twice its actual size.

The tail is long and slender and tapering in outline from the lengthy hairs on the base (fig. 7-131). The shape is not always accurately shown in Egyptian art nor in recent copies (figs 7-118,-144). It is the color of the body, but with a black tuft at the tip. The tuft is rarely shown in Egyptian art or in modern illustrations. An exception is the drawing in Figure 7-132.

There are four functional toes on all feet; the first toes being vestigial. Averages and extremes of measurements of Egyptian specimens in cms are head and body length 56 (54-60); tail 43 (36-46) and 77 (66-82) percent of the head and body length (Osborn and Helmy, 1980: table 51).

Natural history: Ichneumons are diurnal and crepuscular and hide in burrows or crevices during the night.

7-129 Ichneumon climbing papyrus. Tomb of Idut, Dynasty V, Saqqara. Source: Author.

7-130 Copy of a relief of an ichneumon climbing papyrus. Tomb of Ti, Dynasty V, Saqqara. Source: Murray (1937: pl. II).

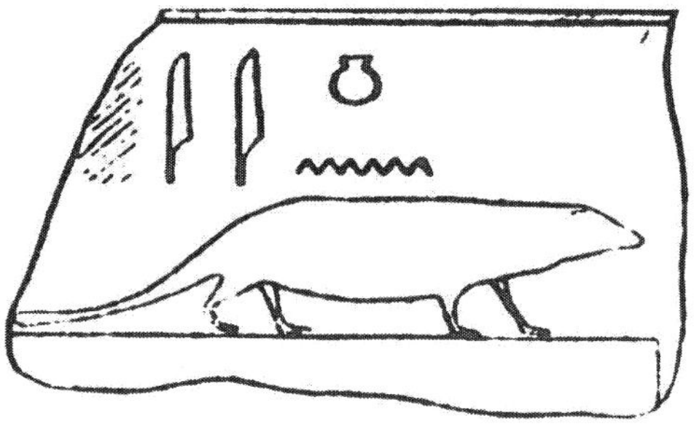

7-131 (left) Ichneumon with a duckling in its mouth. Part of a bird hunting scene in the Tomb of Methethi, Dynasty V, Saqqara. Source: Kaplony (1976: no. 1).

7-132 (centre) Ichneumon as an emblem of Atum on the wall of the Hall of Nekhthoreb at Bubastis (Tell Basta), Dynasty XXX. Source: Naville (1891: pl. XLVf).

7-133 (right) Photo of the ichneumon portrayed in the marsh scene in Figure 1-27. Source: Douglas J. Brewer.

Families are sometimes seen slithering in single file across roads or through vegetation; verifying their Latin name.

They were said to be entirely terrestrial by Dorst (1970: 121), but Michaelis (1972: 15) and Haltenorth and Diller (1980: 202) regarded them as 'moderate climbers'. Rensch and Dücker (1959: 188) described a caged ichneumon that climbed readily and quickly time after time and would jump down from a height of two meters and immediately climb again.

The depictions of ichneumons climbing papyrus stems and robbing nests (figs 7-118, 7-131, 1-27) could, therefore, have been based on observations of wild animals and not tame ones that were released or controlled, as some authors (Montet, 1968: 118) have suggested.

Ichneumons readily enter water and swim well. Hence, their appearance in papyrus thickets.

Prey animals are rodents; birds and their eggs and young; reptiles and their eggs, including those of the crocodile; fish; crayfish; mussels; water snails; and insects and their larvae (Osborn and Helmy, 1980: 422).

In the Late Dynastic Period, after the introduction of domestic fowl, the ichneumon's habit of eating poultry eggs gave it a bad reputation among farmers and keepers of birds.

Wild ichneumons are extremely vicious, but the young are easily tamed. They may have become house pets before cats.

They are very alert and agile; particularly when attacking snakes. An ichneumon can predict and dodge the strike of a snake, then catch its head before it can strike again. Erection of the long, stiff

7-134 An oversized ichneumon held by the tail in a fowling scene. Another ichneumon (upper left) with a nestling bird in its mouth walks down a papyrus stem. Mastaba of Mereruka, Dynasty VI, Saqqara. Source: Wreszinski (1936 III: 107). Crocodiles and hippopotamuses are in the water below.

7-135 Ichneumon on a leash and a pariah dog. Tomb of Baqt I, Dynasty XII, Beni Hassan. Source: Newberry (1893: II: pl. XXX).

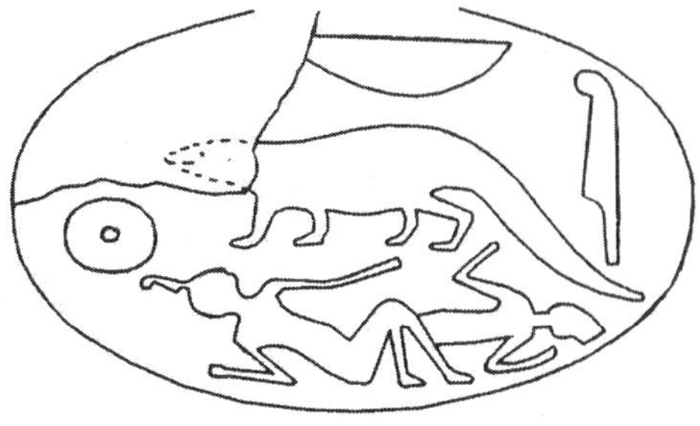

7-136 Seal impression of an ichneumon representing Amenhotep III of Dynasty XVIII as being victorious over his enemies. Source: Brunner-Traut (1965: 143).

hair provides some protection in case of a mistake. In addition, ichneumons are supposed to have a partial immunity to snake poison; about 10 times that of other animals their size (Hinton and Dunn, 1967: 17).

The habitats of ichneumons today are cultivated fields and vegetated canal banks in Lower Egypt. Human habitations and villages are also occupied. Previously, as indicated in Dynastic portrayals, they probably hunted in papyrus swamps, a habitat that no longer exists in Egypt, and also frequented the vegetated semi-desert.

Haltenorth and Diller (1980: 202) listed the habitats in Africa as forests, moist and dry savanna, steppe, and semi-desert, mountains to 2,000 m, and a preference for areas near water.

Distribution: In Egypt the ichneumon occurs throughout the Nile Delta and most of the Valley; El Faiyum; and parts of the Mediterranean Coastal Desert where it was seen in the vicinity of an irrigation canal (Osborn and Helmy, 1980: 421).

The distribution beyond Egypt includes most of Africa from Sudan south and west; also Morocco, Algeria, and formerly Libya (Hufnagl, 1972: 40); Spain; Portugal; Dalmatia; Turkey; Syria; Lebanon; Palestine; and Jordan.

Prehistoric records: Skull fragments of H. ichneumon were discovered in the Neolithic horizon at Nabta Playa in the southeastern Sahara (Gautier, 1980: 330).

No rock drawings of ichneumons have been discovered. Petrie (1920: 15) identified a figure on Predynastic white cross-lined pottery as an ichneumon with pelage raised (fig. 7-56). There seems to be no other plausible identity.

The Dynastic period: During the IVth to VIth dynasties ichneumons were repeatedly depicted in marsh scenes climbing papyrus stems together with genets and raiding bird nests (figs 7-118,-123,-124). Their climbing ability as well as that of genets, however, was very stylized and unnatural in Egyptian illustrations.

In the Dynasty XI Tomb of Chnemhotep at Beni Hasan the bicolored animal shown perched in the papyrus is probably an ichneumon (fig. 1-27). The same scene in L.D. II,130 is in color. The black-spotted genets are pale bluish on the back and the ichneumon is black and white. A recent photo (fig. 7-133) does not indicate the color contrast between the upper and lower parts of the ichneumon and 'Color slides show the animal to be brown' (Brewer, pers. com.). For further comparisons see Brewer and Friedman (1989: figs 2.5a,b; pl. II).

These scenes appear to be symbolic in the sense that these animals are frightening the birds into the air for the pleasure of the tomb owners and their families and friends.

Two scenes give the impression that ichneumons were tamed in the Old to Middle Kingdoms: the oversized animal held by the tail (fig. 7-134) and one on a leash (fig. 7-135). Comments on these depictions were that they

7-137 (top) Bronze figure of an ichneumon on a coffin. Source: Brunner-Traut (1965; fig. 4b).

7-138 (bottom) Bronze coffin for young ichneumons that are represented. Dated to about 560 B.C. Source: Brunner-Traut (1965: fig. 2a).

7-139 Bronze ichneumon on a coffin. Source: Roeder (1936: fig. 11).

7-140 Bronze figure of an ichneumon with some features resembling a bronze shrew. Source: Roeder (1936: fig. 10).

represented pets used to frighten birds or were trained for hunting and retrieving (Lauer, 1976: 56 f.). Neither assumption has been confirmed.

A symbiotic relationship developed between the ichneumon and man. Although some were undoubtedly tamed as indicated in Figures 7-134,-135, their importance was in their elimination of rats, mice, and snakes.

Tame ichneumons may have become votive offerings because skulls have been found mixed with cat mummies in the Dynasty XX cat cemetery at Bubastis. Naville (1891: 55) remarked, "As we know that the ichneumon was an emblem of Tum (Tem), there is nothing extraordinary in the fact that these animals should be mixed with the cats which represented Bast and Mahes."

A mummy and a large number of skulls were found at Dendereh (Petrie, 1900: 59) and skulls were also found in the Ibis Cemetery of the Roman Period at Abydos (Whittemore, 1914).

Ichneumons were kept in temples and fed Nile fish and bread soaked in milk (Diodorus note in Darby *et al.*, 1977 I: 503). The hundreds of mummies from the Late Dynastic Period and Greco- Roman times were undoubtedly temple animals (Boessneck, 1953: 31).

Despite the possibility that the animals reproduced in these foster homes, they have only been considered as tamed animals; not domesticated nor bred under human control (Zeuner, 1963: 404; Boessneck, 1988: 50).

Bonnet (1952: 321) said the ichneumon became a sacred animal in the Late Dynastic Period and the first cult began in the XXIInd Dynasty. Its status developed out of both practical and mythological aspects — its ability to kill rats and snakes, immunity to snake poison, destruction of crocodile eggs, and the belief that it was reborn each day from a shrew.

The ichneumon along with the shrew (see Shrew chapter) was sacred in many cities. In Letopolis it represented the complimentary figure of Buto, the shrew goddess. At Heliopolis it served Atum (Tem) one of the oldest of the creation gods and a form of the sun god, the evening or setting sun. Atum, it was believed, could take the form of an ichneumon, which served Atum as a snake killer and bore the title of *cd*, the tracker (Brunner-Traut, 1965: 157).

Carrington (1972: 88f.) noted that some gods and goddesses had several animals sacred to them. Uto (Buto) of Lower Egypt he said, "was believed at different times to inhabit both the snake and its arch-enemy the mongoose."

The association of the ichneumon with various solar gods, Ra (Re), Horus, Atum (Tem, Tum), Osiris, is understandable when we read the interpretation of Erman (1894: 44) that they "were all different conceptions of the sun god, either as a giver of life, or as a disperser of darkness, or as a being dying today but rising again on the morrow."

Still more god-animal confusion concerning the ichneumon was revealed by Bothmer (1949: 120 ff.). Bronze statuettes of the seated lion-headed goddess from the Late Dynastic Period were found not to represent Sekmet, but *W3dt* (Wadjet, Uatchet, or Buto of the Greeks) and to contain mummified remains of ichneumons. Some of these figures were inscribed with *W3dt*, signifying the Uraeus or cobra goddess.

7-141 (top) The determinative for Hethes. Source: Murray (1937 II: pl. I).

7-142 (bottom) Relief of the determinative for Hethes. Compare with Figure I-13. Source: Keimer (1939: pl. 17d).

Another odd relationship is exemplified in a seal impression (fig. 7-136) on which an ichneumon is illustrated representing *Nebmare* (the first name of Amenhotep III, Dynasty XVIII) victorious over his enemies. Hayes (1951: 167) commented, "Strange as the identification of the victorious king with this animal may seem ... the form on two examples of this seal impression is certainly an ichneumon."

Amulets and bronze figures of ichneumons are well-known. The latter served as sacred gifts and covers for mummy cases (figs 7-137,-138). They were produced, along with shrew figures, in large numbers during the Late Dynastic and Greco-Roman Periods.

Major features of the bronzes were discussed in some detail in the Shrew chapter and summarized in Table II because of some problems in distinguishing one from the other and since each animal was believed to have been a transformation of the other.

Examples are in Figures 7-137,-138,-139. In Figure 7-140 the body shape, head, legs, and tail are typical of the ichneumon, but the body is not etched, the legs are in parallel position, and the ear is bilobed.

Some farfetched stories about the ichneumon were related by the classical writers of the Greco-Roman Period (Herodotus, Aristotle, and Diodorus Siculus). Although supposedly immune to snake poison, the ichneumon was said to have rolled in mud several times and allowed each layer to dry and form a protective shield, before embarking on a snake hunt.

Regarding its eating of crocodile eggs, Diodorus (notation in Budge, 1904a II: 370) declared that "the ichneumon only broke the eggs for the purpose of rendering a service to man, and it derived no benefit from its act. Were it not for the ichneumon, crocodiles would have become so numerous that no one could approach the Nile."

Prosper Alpin (1581-1584: 445) told a story about the ichneumon's technique of killing crocodiles by leaping down their throats. The same tale was also told about the otter (see Otter chapter).

Errors and discrepancies: Egyptian artists did not always emphasize the physical features that distinguish ichneumons. The tails are often too thin at the base or the ears project above the head (figs 7-122,-118), which have caused writers unfamiliar with thefauna to call them rats, weasels, and genets.

Firth (1927a: 107) referred to the ichneumon in the marsh scene of Idut (fig. 7-129) as an "otter (or ichneumon)," Harpur (1987: 198) called the obvious ichneumons in Figures 7-131 and 7-134 'genets', and Simpson (1980: 21, fig. 30, pl. XLIVa) gave an ichneumon the name 'marsh cat'. Although the figure has a genet-like tail, the small ears and rounded snout are more like those of an ichneumon.

The determinative in Figure 7-141 was referred to by Murray (1905 I: 42) as "A little quadruped called *Hethes*. Prof. Sethe translated it as a rat or mouse,... I think that it is a mongoose or ichneumon."

This was doubtless the intended animal, as the hieroglyph indicates, although the head shape is not like that of an ichneumon.

Keimer (1939) published a photo of the relief of the determinative (fig. 7-142) and said that *Hts'* was the nickname for Seker-kha-bau *(H'j-b3 w skr)*, but thought the figure represented *Ictonyx libyca (=Poecilictis libyca)*.

The drawing of the ichneumon in the hunt scene of Ptah-hetep (fig. 7-143) that is creeping along with its head down has ears projecting slightly above the head and a uniformly thick tail, about three quarters the length of the head and body, the same as in the photographs of the relief (Davies, 1901a II: pl. XXV; Wreszinski, 1936 III: pl. 14).

A very similar copy (Griffith, 1898: 28, pl. XXXII) was called an 'ichneumon or large rat'.

Aufrère (1985: fig.8) named the drawing from Davies (fig. 7-143) *Poecilictis libyca* because of the short ears, the tail being the length of the body, and the flat feet. Compare this with Figures 7-142 and 7-101.

Another reproduction (fig. 7-144), however, shows the tail with a very slender base and the ears prominent. Nevertheless, it was called an 'ichneumon (*Herpestes Pharaonis* Geoffr.)' by Hartmann (1869: 30).

In an interesting discussion of 'Pharaoh's Rat' by Cooney (1965) the cover illustration and figures, which he labelled 'Standing Ichneumon', are shrew bronzes.

7-143 (left) Ichneumon in the hunting scene of Ptah-hetep, Dynasty V, Saqqara. Source: Davies (1900 I: pl. XXII).

7-144 (right) Ichneumon in the hunting scene of Ptah-hetep. Source: Dümichen (1869: pl. VIII).

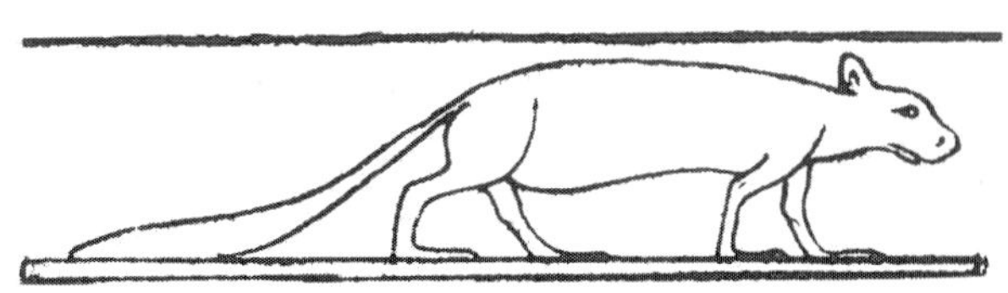

Family *Hyaenidae*

Striped Hyena ***Hyaena hyaena*** (Linnaeus, 1758)

ḥtt hetjet Wb. III, 203

F Hyène rayée; G Streifenhyäne; A Dubbah, Dab, Dab Mekhatat

Nomenclature: The name *Hyaena striata* Zimmermann, 1777, used in much of the older literature (Anderson, 1902: 200; Wreszinski, 1923 I: 26c) is now obsolete.

Description: Striped hyenas are easily recognized by the transverse brownish or blackish stripes on the neck, body, and legs on a whitish or pale buff body color; a large black area on the upper throat; and a blackish muzzle. The ears are large and pointed. The erectile mane, with black-tipped hairs up to 25 cm, extends from the nape to the tail. The tail is relatively short and bushy. The shoulders are much higher than the hips, resulting in a distinctly sloping back. The head is very large and the jaws are massive (fig.7-145).

Shoulder height is 65-80 cm, head and body length 102-108, tail 29-35 and 28-32 percent of the head and body length, and ears 14.5-15.5 cm.

Natural history: Striped hyenas are strictly nocturnal and hide during the day in caves, rock crevices, and ancient tombs and temples (Belzoni, 1821: 383 and Murray's *Handbook for Travelers in Lower and Upper Egypt*, 1891).

They are carrion eaters and their powerful jaws and teeth enable them to crush the bones of larger mammals. Tooth marks often enable archaeologists to recognize hyena-chewed bones.

Food is often dragged or carried to denning areas where bone middens accumulate. Osborn (1968: 14) shot a hyena that was carrying the carcass of another that had been killed the night before.

Hyenas are described as being shy, but during the night they are known to enter camps and to search villages for food. They will attack living prey when very hungry. Hobbs (1989: 33) was told by Bedouins of the Kushmaan clan in the northern Eastern Desert that in the winter time hyenas 'prey almost exclusively on sheep'.

Although there are many stories about hyenas attacking humans, none have been substantiated.

The habitats are semidesert areas bordering the Nile Valley, oases, and coastal regions.

Distribution: The striped hyena continues to inhabit the Sinai Peninsula and parts of the Eastern and

7-145 A cadaver of a striped hyena in Wadi Allaqi east of the Nile in Upper Egypt. Source: Author.

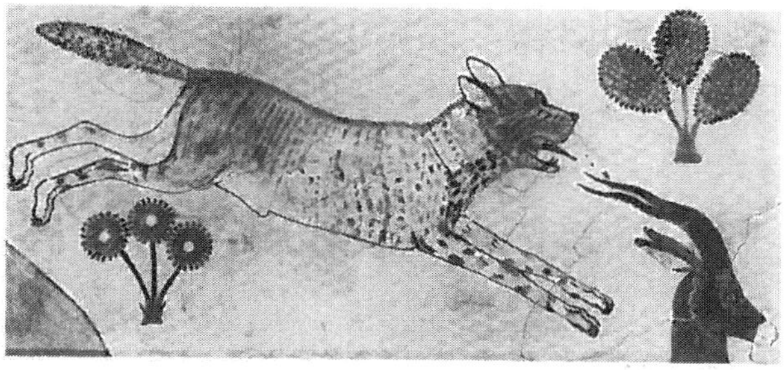

7-146 A leaping hyena in part of a hunting scene in the Tomb of Antef, Dynasty XVIII, Thebes. Source: Säve-Söderbergh (1957 I: pl. XVII). The animal on the right is a hartebeest.

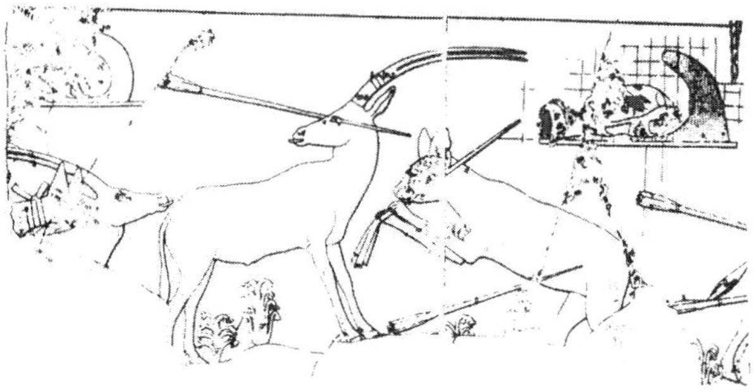

7-147 Hyena pawing at an arrow in its mouth in a hunting scene in the Tomb of Sahure, Dynasty V, Abu Sir. Source: Borchardt (1913 II: pl. 17). On the left are two scimitar oryx. One is seized by a tesem hound. Above, a hedgehog and another animal are entering shelters.

7-148 Hyenas in a hunting scene in the Tomb of Rekhmire, Dynasty XVIII, Thebes. Source: Davies (1943 II: pl. XLIII). One hyena is biting at an arrow in its chest. Behind it another hyena pierced by arrows is grasped by a saluki hound. Above is a leaping hare.

7-149 Hand feeding a hyena in the Mastaba of Mereruka, Dynasty VI, Saqqara. Source: Author.

7-150 Hand feeding hyenas and cattle in the Mastaba of Kagemni (Gemnikai), Dynasty VI, Saqqara. Source: von Bissing (1905 I: pl. XI).

7-151 Hyena led in an offering scene in the Tomb of Nekawra, Dynasty V, Giza. Source: L.D. II, 15.

7-152 Hyena being driven in an offering scene in the Tomb of Kafra-ankh, Dynasty V, Giza. Source: L.D. II, 11.

Western Deserts, particularly the areas bordering the Nile Valley south of Cairo to Nubia (Osborn and Helmy, 1980: 429). Further distribution includes most of North Africa, the Arabian Peninsula, Asia Minor, and much of Asia eastward into India (Harrison, 1968 II: 279).

Prehistoric records: Remains of striped hyenas are known from only a few localities in Egypt: Late Pleistocene deposits of Kom Ombo (Churcher, 1972: 44) and Neolithic at Beni Salama (von den Driesch and Boessneck, 1985: 46).

A rock drawing from Abu Agag northeast of Aswan, dated to the Predynastic, was pictured by Schweinfurth (1912: fig. 3, 6). Those listed by Červíček (1974: figs 31, 244, and 391) are questionable.

In reference to the Predynastic Pitt-Rivers ivory knife handle from Sohag (fig.1-8), Murray (1905: 29 f.) called the animals in the fifth rows hyenas, because it was supposedly a sacrificial knife. The latest identification of those figures was '?jackals' by Churcher (1984:167). One animal on the boss side, however, has a sloping back. Row B3 on the Davis Ivory comb (fig. 1-10), although called jackals by Churcher (*op. cit.*), were referred to as hyenas by various authors (Bénédite, 1918: 229; Paton, 1925: 23; and Asselberghs, 1961: 99). Hayes (1953 I: 27) called them 'hyena or hyena dog'.

This is the only row of figures in comparison with the other ivories (figs 1-7a row 5,1-7b row 7; 1-8a row 5, 1-8b row 5) that have sloping backs and marks across the snouts, which probably delineate the black muzzles of hyenas.

Despite the apparently accurate description of jackals by Churcher (*op. cit.*, 163) for Row B 7 on the Brooklyn knife handle (fig. 1-7), these and other figures that were called jackals are questionable.

The reason for adding this remark is that jackals were not commonly pictured on other Predynastic artifacts or in tomb decorations. Also, errors were sometimes made in engraving animal figures of such small dimensions (less than one cm); *e.g.*, note the long tails on some of the ibex in Row B2, Figure 1-7.

On the Dynasty I mace handle from Seyala (fig. 1-13) there is one animal that can be identified as a hyena, despite its strange markings and non-sloping back. The blunt snout, pointed ears, and relatively short tail indicate a hyena.

On the basis of the above-mentioned data the four animals in Figure 1-10, third row, opposite the row of a dog and three lions, can be called hyenas.

The Dynastic period: Striped hyenas were commonly pictured in hunt scenes leaping amongst or above the other game (figs 7-146, 1-18), attacked by dogs, and pierced by arrows (figs 1-21,-24, 7-147,-148, 13-112. The hyena biting or clawing at an arrow in its

7-153 (top left) Hyenas and other 'stable fed' animals in the Offering Chapel of Sekhem-ankh-ptah, Dynasty V, Saqqara. Source: Simpson (1976b: pl. D). The animals are being led behind a scribe (not shown). Upper half of the procession (left to right): Ibex with beard obliterated (above it is the hieroglyph for Barbary goat); hyena; young hyena and hare (above on a separate ground line); dama deer; and hartebeest. Lower half: Dorcas gazelle, addax, scimitar oryx, and ibex.

7-154 (top right) Female hyena with young in an offering scene in the Tomb of Sahure, Dynasty V, Saqqara. Source: Borchardt (1913 II: pl. 56). Behind them is a young hartebeest.

7-155 (bottom right) Young hyena carried in an offering procession in the Tomb of Sekhemka, Dynasty V, Saqqara. Source: Murray (1905 I: pl. VII). Animals (left to right) are goose, young hyena, dorcas gazelle, and crane.

7-156 (bottom left) Young hyena carried in an offering procession in the Mastaba of Khafkhufu, Dynasty V-VI, Giza. Source: Simpson (1978: fig. 33). Animals (left to right) are dorcas gazelle, young hyena, calf, dorcas gazelle, crane, and two ducks.

a

b

7-157 (above) A food offering list from the Tomb of Seshathotep, Dynasty V, Giza. Source: Junker (1934 II: fig. 33). Heads of animals (left to right) are hyena, dorcas gazelle, scimitar oryx, four different cattle, and various water birds.

7-158 (top right) A partly obliterated dwarfed hyena in an offering procession in the Mastaba of Ptahhetep II, Dynasty V, Saqqara. Source: Murray (1905 I: pl. X). The dwarfed animals (left to right) are a calf, a calf replacing the hyena, and an ox.

7-159a,b (bottom right) Trophies of a hunt, live and dead game. Tomb of Rekhmire, Dynasty XVIII, Thebes. Source: Davies (1943 II: pl. XLIV).
a) Live trophies (left to right): A beardless ibex, hyena, fox, dorcas gazelle and hare, dorcas gazelle, beisa oryx, hartebeest, ibex, and hare. A saluki hound is below the hyena.
b) A guided ibex leading the procession and a pile of dead game. From the top down these are: Hartebeest, Soemmering's gazelle (?), hare, dorcas gazelle, ibex, fox, beisa oryx, and aurochs.

7-160 (top) A tesem hound and two young hyenas witnessing the suppression of a scimitar oryx by another hound in a hunt scene in the Tomb of Ptah-hetep, Dynasty V, Saqqara. Source: Davies (1900 I: pl. XXII).

7-161 (bottom) The same scene as in Figure 7-160 with some variations. Source: Dümichen (1869: pl. 8).

7-162 Part of a scene called 'Return from the hunt.' Hyenas and tesem hounds on leashes with young are behind various animals in cages, which are shown in Figure 7-218 from the Tomb of Ptah-hetep, Dynasty V, Saqqara. Source: Paget and Pirie (1898: pl. XXXIII).

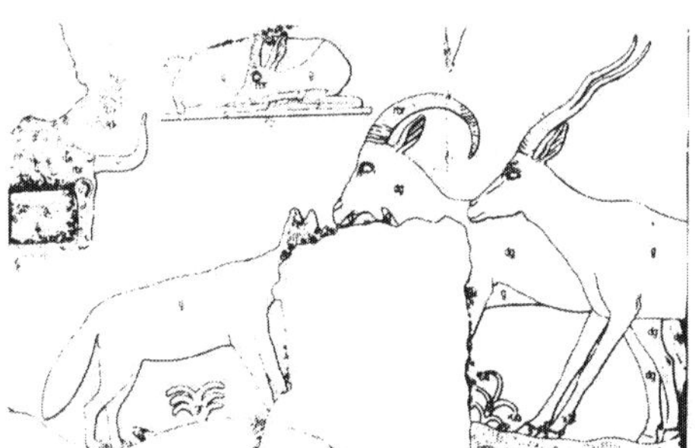

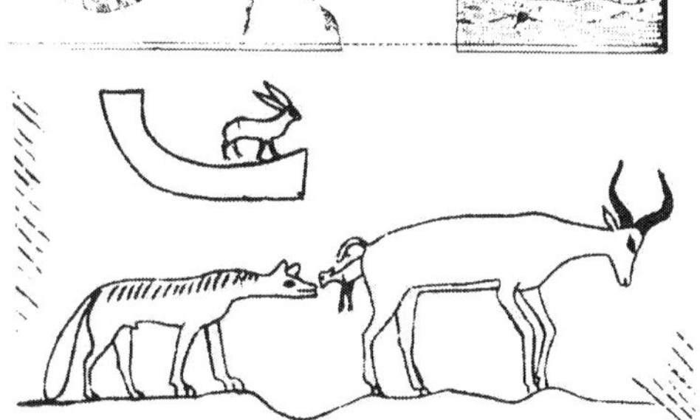

7-163 (top) Hyena facing a Barbary goat in part of a hunting scene from the Tomb of Sahure, Dynasty V, Abu Sir. Source: Borchardt (1913 II: pl. 17). Other animals are an aurochs (left), addax (right), and dorcas gazelle (above).

7-164 (bottom) Hyena sniffing at the foal of a hartebeest in part of a hunting scene from the Tomb of Baqt II, Dynasty XII, Beni Hasan. Source: Newberry (1894 II: pl. XXXV).

mouth, neck or chest, which first appeared in the Dynasty V Tomb of Sahure (fig. 7-147), became a popular theme in numerous Old, Middle, and New Kingdom tombs (Smith, 1946b: 179).

Besides being hunted for sport, hyenas were captured and tamed in the Old Kingdom and included in the food sacrifices for the dead and their *kas* and in offerings to noblemen.

Reliefs in the Mastabas of Mereruka (fig. 7-149) and Kagemni (fig. 7-150) show them being fed along with other semi-domesticated animals. They were staked while awaiting feeding, then placed on their backs either with legs tied or held by an attendant while another man 'force fed' them with quantities of flesh and roasted (?) ducks or geese. Note that the hieroglyph for *rn* appears above the hyena on the left in Figure 7-150, which Paton (1925: 23) called a 'stable reared (female) hyena'.

Keimer (1955b: 18 f.) observed that in the Gemnikai (Kagemni) scene (fig. 7-150) hyenas were foaming at their mouths and the saliva looked like beards on the standing animals. They were probably salivating in anticipation for the taste of food. This is an interesting feature for ancient artists to have illustrated.

Despite the many examples of hyenas being fattened, they were never included in butchering scenes (Montet, 1910: 43 f.), although they were tethered with other food animals and led or driven in offering processions (figs 7-151,-152,-153, 13-93).

Sometimes females were accompanied with young (fig. 7-154); an indication, but not proof of captive breeding. In numerous scenes young hyenas are carried together with other live offerings (figs 7-155,-156). Regarding such scenes, Clark (1971: 62) said, "Young hyenas make devoted, though somewhat repulsive pets and there would have been no special problem involved in keeping them."

The heads of a hyena, various bovids, and waterfowl were pictured in a Dynasty V offering list (fig. 7-157) that Junker (1953: 237) interpreted as numbering thousands of 'young' hyenas and other food animals. In reference to Junker's statement, Boessneck (1988: 44) translated *rn* as meaning 'fattened' rather than 'young' hyenas.

Dwarfed striped hyenas led by peasants bringing offerings appear in Old Kingdom tombs (Dunham and Simpson, 1974 I: fig. 4). In Figure 7-158 a woman has a calf on a leash, but there are traces of the tail, hind leg, and ear of a hyena. Murray (1905: 29) suggested that this figure dated the period when the keeping of hyenas for food was going out of fashion.

Similar scenes appear in the Dynasty VI Saqqara Tombs of Nefer-sekhem-ptah and `Ankhm-`ahor (Capart, 1907 I: 48; II: pls. LX, LXI, LXII) in which hyenas were replaced by a gazelle or a calf, although the hyena was retained in the Tomb of Nefer-seshem-ptah (*op. cit.*, pl. LXXXII).

As to the eating of hyena flesh, Anderson (1902) wrote that it was eaten by poor people and he found "that the flesh taken from the head was not at all bad," and Quibell (1932: 482) said, "The meat was very sweet".

In contrast, Montet (1910: 43) opined, "We have with some repugnance to think that the Egyptians ate that horrible animal; the matter is nevertheless certain". He concluded that following the fattening of hyenas in Dynasty VI, the Egyptians stopped providing even the dead with such an unappetizing meat.

Despite this assumption, the presentation of hyenas continued, although they were only shown being brought alive from hunts tied on poles (fig. 5-6). In Figure 7-159a the hyena and other trophies, including several bovids, are being carried or led by hand toward the pile of dead game shown in Figure 7-159b where a scribe is recording the catch.

Another contrast in interpretations is that of hand feeding. Some authors have assumed that instead of being fattened for eating and in preparation for offerings, hyenas were prepared for hunts by feeding before by hand to remove any temptation to eat the prey (Gaillard, 1912: 343 ff.; Lauer, 1976: 61 f.). There is no evidence, however, that hyenas were trained and used for hunting, but remarks, often quoting Gaillard (*op. cit.*), that hyenas were probably trained for hunting in the Old Kingdom have been made by numerous authors (Boessneck, 1953: 30; Montet, 1964: 115; Zeuner, 1963: 422; Vandier, 1964 IV: 797; Červíček, 1974: 148, 177 f.; Janssen and Janssen, 1989:53 f.).

A contradiction by Fischer (1980: 78) was: "The hyena... was domesticated for food in the O.K., but was not used for any other purpose."

A controversial scene in this respect is in the Dynasty V Mastaba of Ptah-hetep, where two young and apparently tame hyenas, accompanied by a hound, are witnessing the subduing of an oryx by another hound (figs 7-160, -161). The hyenas appear to be restrained by the tesem hound, which has a paw on the shoulder of one and is holding the ear of the other one in its jaws, which in return is licking the dog's throat. This feature was not shown in Dümichen's drawing (fig. 7-161), but it is quite clear in Davies' photograph (1901a II: pl. XXV) and drawing (fig. 7-160).

Hartmann (1869: 28f.) considered these animals and likewise those in the return from the hunt (fig. 7-162) to be *Lycaon*, hyena-dogs.

Thus, Paget and Pirie (1898: 28 f.) concluded that the 'hyenas' in the scenes from Ptahetep were 'wild dogs of the desert, *kelb es samakh*, *Canis pictus* (?), one of which was caught by a slughi'. And

7-165 (top) Tomb owner, Amenemheb, facing an excited hyena, Dynasty XVIII, Thebes. Source: Wreszinski (1923 I: pl. 21).

7-166 (bottom) Animals pierced with arrows on Tutankhamun's bow case are a striped hyena, dorcas gazelle, Nubian ibex, beisa oryx, and a tumbling aurochs. Tomb of Tutankhamun, Dynasty XVIII, Valley of the Kings, Thebes. Source: Fox (1951: pl. 52).

7-167 Amulet of a hyena from Harageh southwest of Gebel Abu Sir, New Kingdom. Source: Engelbach (1923: pl. XXI).

Griffith (1900: 10) also referred to a greyhound attacking two wild hyenas or hyena dogs.

Keller (1909 I: 89) referred to the hyenas as examples of hunting dogs used in hunting.

Vandier (1964 IV: 797) described 'two domesticated hyenas trained for the chase, at the same time they appear to be happy with the dog', and Lauer (1976: 61f.) said: "two hyenas appear, in fact, to be ready for action."

In Figure 7-162 two leashed hyenas and one young are walking together with four leashed hounds and a lop-eared pup behind an assortment of captured and caged animals. These hyenas also appear to be tamed and certainly were not being brought directly from the wild, although that is the impression the artist apparently wanted to give.

7-168 (left) Ostracon of a striped hyena (above) and a fox (below) from Deir el Medineh, Dynasty XIX-XX. Source: Brunner-Traut (1956: pl.XL).

7-169 (top right) Striped hyena attacked by saluki hounds on a Dynasty XIX-XX ostracon from Deir el Medineh. Source: Vandier d'Abbadie (1936: pl. XXVI, 2211).

7-170 (bottom right) Hyenas and saluki hounds in dispute on a Dynasty XIX-XX ostracon from Deir el Medineh. Source: Vandier d'Abbadie (1946 III: pl. XCIV, 2726).

Even though hyenas were pictured in hunt scenes facing or leaping above bovids, an attack was never depicted. In Figure 7-146, as in many other scenes where one animal appears to be leaping directly above another, it may be to one side or the other, because complex hunting scenes were not drawn in perspective. Besides, if animals were attacking, they were shown in contact with their prey, except for some of the dogs that were released for chasing and subduing the game.

In the Tomb of Sahure a hyena faces a Barbary goat (fig. 7-163) and another hyena with an arrow in its mouth faces an oryx (fig. 7-147), which is also pierced by an arrow. Although there is no indication of an attack in either depiction, the hyenas were described as chasing the game and the one with an arrow in its mouth as bounding at the head of the oryx.

Hilzheimer (1913: 175 f.) concluded that these scenes confirmed without a doubt that the hyena was used to hunt large game in the desert.

In Figures 7-164 and 1-30 (Register 3), hyenas appear to be only sniffing at the foals of a hartebeest and gazelle. The hyena behind the deer (figs 7-28, 13-42) was mistakenly called a 'jackal, *Canis lupercus*' by Blackman (1915 II: 20). Although it has a pointed snout, the shortness of the ears, the tail shape, and the heavy body are more typical of a hyena than a jackal.

The only illustration of an aggressive hyena is in the Tomb of Amenemheb (fig. 7-165) showing the owner with a club in his hand facing a huge female. Wreszinski (1923 I: pl. 21) suggested she had just born her young (indicated by the large mammaries) and in consequence was bolder than such a cowardly animal shows itself to be when face to face with a man.

Smith (1965: 161) said this was an imaginative scene from the tomb owner's experiences in Syria.

Well into the New Kingdom hyenas were favored animals and symbolic of the hunt (fig. 7-148). Spectacular chases including hyenas appear in the Dynasty XVIII Tombs of Userhet (Wreszinski, 1923 I: 26a; Westendorf, 1968: 122) and Amenemhet (fig. 1-18); and on Tutankhamun's painted box (fig. 12-6) and bow case (fig. 7-166), where a highly stylized hyena has an arrow in its muzzle.

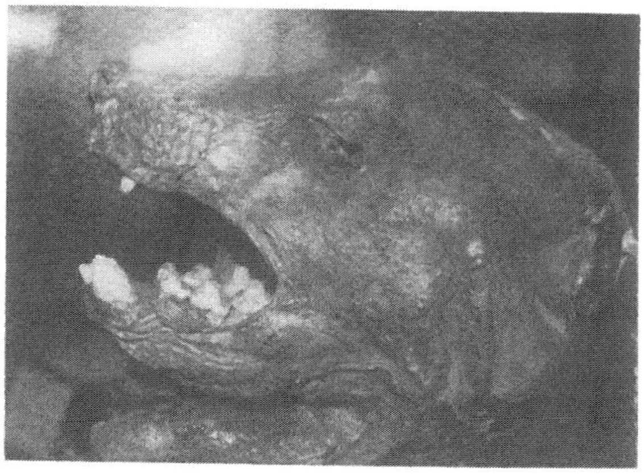

7-171 *Mummified head of a striped hyena in the Dokki Agricultural Museum, Cairo. Source: Author.*

7-172 *Striped hyenas without stripes; three adults and one immature (right), and a lop-eared young (left). Tomb of Fetekta, Dynasty V, Saqqara pyramids south of Abu Sir. Source: L.D. II, 96. Inserts: A canid (?). Separate ground line: an ibex with a misplaced beard, two Soemmering's gazelles, and three dorcas gazelles.*

An amulet from Harageh, Dynasty XI-XVI appears to be a male hyena (fig. 7-167). It may have symbolized some of the medicinal values aftributed to its flesh, such as a cure from rheumatism, and the apotropaic powers of its eyes and teeth.

Striped hyenas also appear on several ostraca from Dynasty XIX-XX (figs 7-168, -169, -170). Figure 7-169 is the most realistic regarding markings and proportions.

A few Dynastic remains have been found. Boessneck (1981b: 67) reported on a skull found in the Dynasty XVIII Tomb of Haremheb at Thebes. In the Dokki Agriculture Museum there are two undated mummified heads from Gebelein (fig. 7-171).

Errors and discrepancies: Brentjes (1966a: 310) concluded that all animals previously called hyenas in fattening and offering scenes, those in the tomb of Ptah-hetep, and on ostraca, were aardwolves (*Proteles cristatus*), because of the long, bushy tails and the presence of manes. Striped hyenas, he said, could only be identified in hunt scenes, except for two cases: the large striped hyena facing Amenemheb (fig. 7-165), and the one biting a newborn foal in the Tomb of Kenamun (fig. 7-68), which is, however, a fox.

One cannot help questioning Brentjes' decisions, because striped hyenas also have prominent manes. Their tails are bushy, but not as much so nor as long as those of aardwolves. Egyptian artists, however, had a habit of depicting tails disproportionately. The presence or absence of manes was another inconsistency of the artists. The large, white hyenas with tails and manes fringed with black in the Tomb of Fetekta (fig. 7-172) and those being fed in the Tomb of Gemnikai (Kagemni) (fig. 7-150), are the only representations prior to Dynasty XVIII with manes and tail hairs indicated.

The large proportions of most of the figures in question, particularly the massive heads and large muzzles, contrast with the small heads and slender muzzles of aardwolves. The shoulder height of aardwolves is only about one-half to three-quarters that of hyenas and weight is about one-quarter to one-third. Brentjes (1966a: 311) assumed that the large sizes and proportions were of no consequence. He described the hyena in the Tomb of Nefer (fig. 13-93) as an aardwolf, because of its small head, slender feet, and long tail. There is a close similarity, however, between this figure and the striped hyena opposite page 189 in Grzimek's Tierleben (1962, Vol. 12, Säugetiere 3).

Brentjes (*op. cit.*) also said that the lop-eared animals in the Mastaba of Mereruka (fig. 7-173) were aardwolves in a state of excitement. Boessneck (1988: 44 f.) noted that very young hyenas, like young hounds, also have lop-ears. He referred to the above examples and Figure 7-162. Lop-eared young hyenas also appear in Figures 7-172,-173.

The lop-ears on the large young and the adult hyena in Figure 7-173 may have been an artist's error.

There is a confusing remark by Brentjes (*op.cit.*, 311) about a rope in the mouth of the animal in

7-173 *Lop-eared young hyenas and mother awaiting feeding. Mastaba of Mereruka, Dynasty VI, Saqqara. Source: Duell (1938 II: pl. 153).*

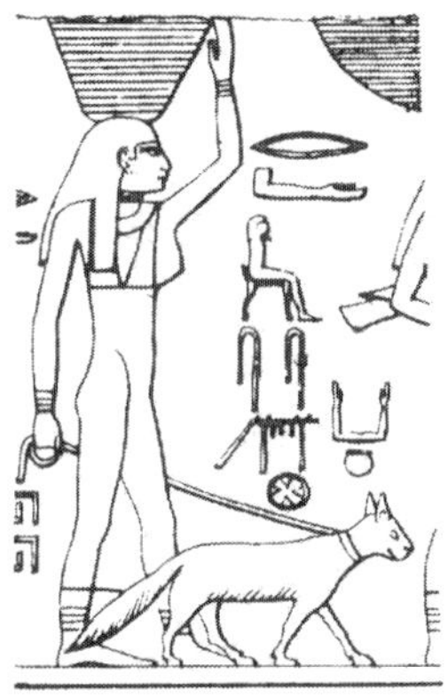

7-174 (top left) Hyena hanging in a bush in a hunt scene in the Tomb of Userhat, Dynasty XVIII, Luxor. Source: Pijoan (1977: fig. 135).

7-175 (right) A leashed hyena in an offering procession in the Tomb of Ra-shepses, Dynasty V, Saqqara. Source:. L.D. II, 61b.

7-176 (bottom left) Rock paintings of a spotted hyena and a giraffe in Karkur Tahl, Gebel Uweinat. Source: Rhotert (1952: pl. XXII, 5).

Figure 7-150. He said it could not be a hyena, because its teeth would have sliced the rope. His interpretation appears to be in error, because the rope passes through the mouth just behind the canines where there is a gap (fig. 7-171), which would prevent the premolars from cutting it.

Boessneck (1981b: 72) considered Brentjes' (*op. cit.*, 310 f.) statement that aardwolves rather than hyenas were force-fed and fattened (figs 7-149,-150) to be absurd, and said later (Boessneck, 1988: 44 f.) that because of their food habits the animals had to be striped hyenas.

Aardwolves have very small teeth and eat mainly termites and insects; therefore they would be unable to masticate bony fowl and chunks of meat. Thus, there can be no doubt that the fattened animals were striped hyenas.

Another error of Brentjes (1966a: 311) was the identification of striped and brushy tailed animals on an ostracon in figure 7-168 as aardwolves. Comparison of the striped animal with others in this chapter should remove any doubt of its identity. The slenderness of the body and the bushy tail of the animal below suggests a fox.

In Figure 7-169 there is an unmistakable hyena with a black throat patch. Two hyenas are also represented in a satirical depiction of a dispute with two dogs in which a small dog is apparently the arbitrator (figure 7-170).

In the Dynasty XVIII Tomb of Kenamun (fig. 7-68) the carnivore grabbing the foal of an ass, which Brentjes (*op. cit.*, 310) called a striped hyena, appears to have too small a head for a hyena and the shape of the body is not comparable. The short mane is also not a decisive feature. What one might call stripes could be lines depicting grizzled fur.

Smith (1965: 157) referred to all similar animals in Figure 7-68 as 'hyenas popping out of their holes', but the only animal that could be identified as a hyena is crouched above the ibex. It is much larger than the others and has a proportionately shorter tail.

Another interesting comment by Brentjes (*op. cit.*, 312) is in reference to what he calls an aardwolf in an offering scene. The animal is a hyena and he called the young hyena above it a 'bat-eared fox'. Presumably, he was not referring to the hare (fig. 7-153).

One more problem is the hyena-like animal hanging helplessly in a bush in the hunt scene of Userhat (fig. 7-174). Wreszinski (1923 I: pl. 26a) called it a 'jackal' (*Canis aureus*) and Pijoan (1977: fig. 135), a 'dying fox'.

The color is much darker, however, than other hyenas that are shown (Wreszinski, *op. cit.*, pl. 21). There is practically no indication of striping on this animal, but the prominent forehead is characteristic of the hyena.

Keller (1909 I: 82, fig. 28b) called an animal in an offering scene from the Tomb of Ra-shepses (fig. 7-175), 'Karakal, ägyptisch'. It lacks ear tufts, however, and has a tail much too long and thick for a caracal. Keimer (1948b: 372, 382) considered Keller (*op. cit.*) to have been incorrect in his decisions on cats. The animal is probably a striped hyena.

Aardwolf *Proteles cristatus* (Sparrman, 1783)

F Protèle, Loup fouisseur; G Erdwolf, Zibethyäne; A Deeb, Deeb ardy, Osbar

Description: Aardwolves are Hyena-like, but considerably smaller and slenderer and with fewer stripes on the body and legs. The mane is longer and more conspicuous and the tail is proportionately longer and bushier than that of the striped hyena. The muzzle is black, but the large, black throat patch, which is conspicuous on the striped hyena, is lacking. The head is small and the muzzle is slender. The teeth of this animal are small and peg-like.

The head and body length is 65-80 cm, tail length 20-30, and shoulder height 45-50 (Haltenorth and Diller, 1980: 216).

Natural history: Aardwolves are strictly nocturnal. Their food is primarily termites and insect larvae; perhaps bird eggs, small vertebrates, and some carrion.

Distribution: Two specimens were reported from south- eastern Egypt (Osborn and Helmy, 1980: 432) and I. Helmy (pers. com.) saw one in Wadi Dom on the Gulf of Suez in 1983 and near Gebel Hamra Dom in southeastern Egypt in 1984.

Further distribution continues from northeastern Sudan southward in Tanzania. There is a break in the distribution from there to the South African countries.

Prehistoric records: No remains and no rock drawings are known from Egypt.

The Dynastic period: Although Brentjes (1966a) attempted to establish this species instead of the striped hyena as the animal that was tamed and fattened by the ancient Egyptians, his explanations are not conclusive. See *Errors and Discrepancies* in the Striped Hyena chapter above.

Spotted Hyena *Crocuta crocuta* (Erxleben, 1777)

F Hyène tachetée; G Fleckenhyäne, Höhlenhyäne, Tüpfelhyäne; A Dab Menakat

Description: A large hyena with sloping back, very large head, and short, rounded ears. The pelage is short, body color buff to dull gray; face, muzzle, and lower legs dark brown. The body and upper legs are irregularly marked with round black spots. There is a short mane on the neck and shoulders. The tail is short with a black, bushy tip, and often carried upturned.

The head and body length is 120-180 cm, tail length 25-30, and shoulder height 70-90 (Haltenorth and Diller, 1980: 219).

Natural history: The spotted hyena is mainly, but not strictly nocturnal. It is a scavenger, but preys on gazelles and larger animals.

Distribution: "Africa south of Sahara (in E. from N. Sudan) except in closed forest" (Haltenorth and Diller, 1980:219).

Prehistoric records: Remains of both spotted and striped hyena dated to the Late Pleistocene are known from Kom Ombo (Churcher, 1972: 44, table 5) and spotted hyena from Paleolithic remains at Helwan (Gautier, 1984: 43 f.). Churcher (1974: 373) noted that the spotted hyena had disappeared from the Near East and North Africa in the Neolithic and was replaced by the striped hyena.

A rock drawing with upward curving tail near Berber, southwest of Aswan might represent a spotted hyena (Schweinfurth, 1912: 654, fig. 21) and also a rock painting in Karkur Tahl, Gebel Uweinat (fig. 7-176).

Family *Felidae*

Wild Cat ***Felis silvestris*** Schreber, 1777
[and **Domestic Cat** ***Felis catus*** Linnaeus, 1758]

 *mjjt* miit Wb. II, 42 (wild)

 *mjw* miu Wb. II, 42 (domestic)

E African Wild Cat, Kaffir Cat; F Chat sauvage d'Afrique; G Falbkatze; A Qut Gebeli

Nomenclature: The specific name derives from '*silva* (L) a wood, hence *silvestris* (L) belonging to the woods' (Gotch, 1979: 76).

The Egyptian race of *F. silvestris* was originally considered to be a separate species, *Felis libyca* Forster, 1780. Various other obsolete synonyms, such as *F. ocreata (ochreata), F. maniculata, F. bubastis, and F. vereata* have been misapplied to this cat by zoologists as well as Egyptologists.

Description: The wild cat is very similar to the domestic cat, but with slightly longer legs and tail.

7-177 A short-tailed, fat cat under its mistress' chair on a stela from Koptos, Dynasty XI. Source: Stewart (1979 II: pl. 19, 1).

There is a black dorsal line; the back is buff grizzled with black and white or yellow; the sides and outer sides of legs are paler; throat, chest, belly, and inside of legs are white. Pale brown spots on the belly and sides change to faint vertical lines on the shoulders and flanks. There are stripes on the legs and broken stripes on the feet. The tail is two-thirds to three-quarters of the length of the body, blackish above at the base, and with four to five black distal stripes, (not clearly shown in drawings) and a black tip. The ears are bluntly pointed and without tufts; whitish on the inner side, reddish on the back.

Head and body length of Egyptian specimens average 45 cm; tail 29 cm and 64 percent of the head and body length (Osborn and Helmy, 1980: 441, table 53). Haltenorth and Diller (1980: 229) listed shoulder ht. as 30-36 cm.

Natural history: Wild cats are mainly nocturnal in habit and hide during the day in trees, dense vegetation or rock shelters. Their food is hares, rodents, reptiles, birds, fish, and probably the young of gazelles. They are said to also eat insects and fruits (Dorst 1970: 136).

The habitats are vegetated margins of the Nile Valley and Delta; oases; Western Mediterranean and Sinai coastal deserts, including barley fields; and rocky areas in these regions.

Distribution: This species has a very wide distribution in Africa and is absent only from the Sahara Desert and the tropical rain forest. It inhabits all of Europe, Asia Minor, much of Arabia , and Asia including southern Russia and China.

7-178 (top) A cat tied to the leg of its mistress' chair and looking back at a bowl of food. Tomb of May, Dynasty XVIII, Thebes. Source: Davies and Gardiner (1936 I: pl. XXVII).

7-179 (bottom) A cat eating a fish under the chair of the wife of Nakht. Tomb of Nakht, Dynasty XVIII, Thebes. Source: Phillips (1948: fig. 24).

7-180 Enlargement of the wild cat in Figure 1-27 seated on a papyrus stem. Tomb of Chnemhotep, Dynasty XI, Beni Hasan. Source: Griffith (1900: pl. V).

Prehistoric records: There are no rock drawings of wild cats. Remains have been found in the Neolithic site of Merimde-Benisalama in the western Delta (von den Driesch and Boessneck, 1985: 46) and beyond the present distribution, Gautier (1980: 330) discovered bone fragments at the Neolithic site of Nabta Playa in the southeastern Western Desert. Bone fragments are also known from the Holocene Bashendi site in Dakhla Oasis (Churcher *et al.*, 1997: 3).

There is evidence of man's familiarity with wild cats from their having been occasionally interred in human graves in the Predynastic period (Baldwin, 1975: 431), 'but there is no evidence that these were domesticated'.

The Dynastic period: Hilzheimer (1928: 272) said there was no artistic evidence of cats prior to Dynasties V and VI. The earliest representation, according to Baldwin (1975: 432), is a fat cat under a chair (fig. 7-177). It was wrongly described as a dog by Petrie (1896: 12).

Further illustrations of tame cats under chairs appeared in Dynasty XVIII (figs 4-32, 7-178,-179).

Although Keimer (1948b: 348) referred to the cat in the Dynasty XII hunting scene of Antefoker (fig. 7-38) as a 'lynx', it is probably a wild cat, judging from the short ears, relatively short legs, stout body, and slender tail.

Meanwhile, other cats that were doubtless tame were depicted in a number of Middle and New Kingdom fowling scenes (figs 1-27, 7-180,-181,-182). These cats were supposedly released by their masters to frighten birds into the air for the advantage of the hunter. Normally, wild cats did not enter these aquatic habitats.

In the Middle Kingdom Tomb of Chnemhotep (figs 1-27, 7-180) a long-tailed, pale cat with obscure markings is perched in the papyrus. Two genets and an ichneumon are climbing toward bird nests.

Boessneck (1988: 85) was dubious about the scene and said that a cat in the papyrus should be a swamp cat, *Felis chaus*, not the wild cat, and there was no indication that it was a pet cat.

Griffith (1900 IV: 2) had remarked: "...Dr. Anderson thinks the present example really figures a domestic cat. In New Kingdom pictures tame cats are often shown accompanying the sportsman; but this animal seems to be independent of him. Still, it must be remembered that the tame cat is apt to stray and hunt for itself."

7-181 Cats in papyrus in a fishing and fowling scene in the Tomb of Menna (Menena), Dynasty XVIII, Thebes. Source: Davies and Gardiner (1936 II: pl. LIV).

7-182 A cat in a portion of the fowling scene in the Tomb of Nebamun, Dynasty XVIII, Thebes. Source: Davies and Gardiner (1936 II: pl. LXVI).

The posture of this cat is typical of many later illustrations and figurines. The tail curls between the flank and thigh and then turns upward. In most figures the tail is curled on the right side (Langton and Langton, 1940: 6).

The upper animal in Figure 7-181 is obviously a wild cat from the stripes on the body, the long tail, and the blunt nose. It was called a fox by Brentjes (1967b). The lower animal is of the same build, but has rounded ears and a pointed nose. It has been called a genet, but certainly shows no resemblance, except for the pointed nose. It was probably meant to represent a young wild cat.

The most spectacular and well-known of these scenes is from the Dynasty XVIII Tomb of Nebamun (fig. 7-182). Here, the artist appears to have attempted to produce all possible evidence that the tame wild cat was serving its master by flushing the birds and retrieving those that were struck down by his boomerangs. This is also the concensus of Egyptologists from this imaginative depiction of a cat balanced precariously on two bent papyrus stems while grasping birds in its fore and hind claws and holding a duck by the wing with its mouth.

An interpretation by Janssen and Janssen (1989: 17) was: "The role of the cat appears to have been to flush out the roosting birds, its penetrating scent causing them to flutter and thus provide an easy prey for the fowler's throwstick. Cats were never trained to retrieve the stunned birds, since that goes against their nature."

There are no pictures of cats bringing birds to the hands of their masters.

Although there are numerous illustrations indicating that cats were tamed, at least by the Middle Kingdom, full domestication probably did not occur until Dynasty XVIII in the New Kingdom (Carrington, 1972: 78; Clutton-Brock, 1981; 111) or as late as Dynasty XXI (Baldwin, 1975: 437).

Baldwin's (1975: 443) hypothesis in summary was that cats were domesticated in ancient Egypt because they had been prepared for it by a long period of loose association with man; and they were believed to have been the manifestions of two major dieties, Bast and Ra.

Janssen and Janssen (1989: 16), however, considered the Dynasty XI illustration of the fat cat under a chair (fig. 7-177) to be proof of full domestication.

Relationship with man in agricultural areas is thought to have begun in early times because of the cat's ability to catch and kill rodents (*op. cit.*). Reminders of this are the tense cat facing a large rodent (figs 4-6, 6-7), probably a jird of the genus *Meriones*; and a cat with a mouse in its mouth (fig. 6-1).

Perhaps later, as Boessneck (1988: 86) suggested, it was not so much the ability of cats to kill rats, but their desirability as household pets, just as in modern cities, that promoted their domestication.

When true domestication began it was doubtless strongly influenced by the already established worship of cats, which was indicated by small cat and cat-headed 'protective' amulets from Dynasties V-VI (Langton and Langton, 1940: 2). Further indications are the amulets of cat families, which may have been symbols of fecundity 'to insure more children in the future or protection of children in being' (Langton, 1936: 120); especially the cat goddess Bast (figs 7-183, 3-5). Bast (Bastet) was the protector of pregnant women as well as the goddess of joy. Her counterpart was the lioness goddess Sekhmet, who represented 'the fierce destructive power of the sun' (Mercatante, 1978: 20). In the very late dynasties, Bastet was converted into a lioness goddess (fig. 7-210).

Large bronzes, such as Figure 7-184 were 'used for home worship, for guarding house walls and field boundaries, or as offerings' (Langton and Langton, 1940: 5).

There are several characteristics of the cat that could have incited its divinization. Langton and Langton (1940: 1) said, "...the cat possesses, to the highest degree, that quality of aloofness which is so

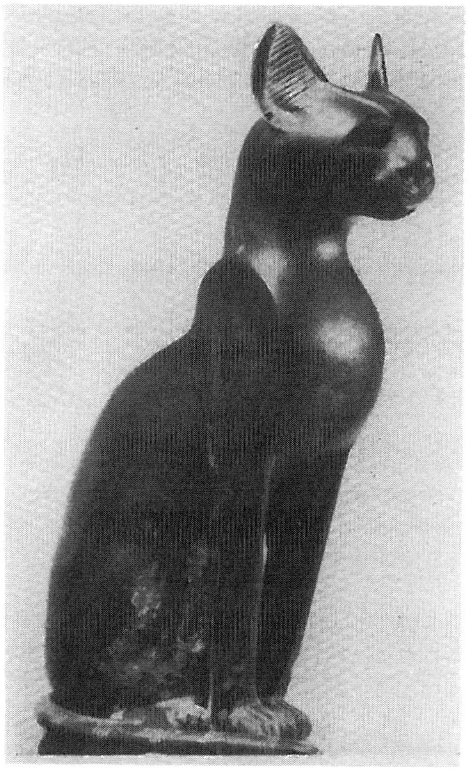

7-183 *The goddess Bast with four cats at her feet; no date and provenance given. Source: Budge (1904c: 153).*

7-184 *A bronze statuette of a cat dated to 700 B.C., provenance not given. The height is 27 cm. Source: Boessneck (1988: pl.142).*

suggestive of divinity and which to early minds must have been notably impressive." Added by one of Langtons' readers there is the following penciled footnote: "Likewise, ability to see in the dark may have been seen as a divine quality."

Eye shine was another reason for its reverence, because of the belief that its eyes reflected the sun even at night when it was hidden from man.

The ability of the cat to kill snakes was also important. 'The divine cat was the destroyer of evil symbolized as a snake' (Murray, 1937: 7).

This has been pictured (fig. 7-185) and described as 'The cat (Ra) killing the serpent of darkness (Apep) symbolic of the triumph of Law, Order and Goodness over Chaos, Wrong, and Evil' (Budge, 1930: 145). This cat was also called Mau and considered an equivalent of the sun god Ra. It is a typical wild cat with slightly pointed ears and stripes on the body and legs. It appears to have no connection with Maftet (Mafdet), the mythical snake killing lynx goddess (Müller, 1923: 107).

A popular story that emphasizes the Ancient Egyptians' love of cats was told by Diodorus, the Sicilian who visited Egypt in the first century B.C. He described how a Roman soldier in Alexandria killed a cat and was immediately seized by a mob of people and executed. To kill a cat at that time was a crime.

Herodotus in Dynasty XXVI wrote that when a house caught fire the only desire of the owners was to save their cats, not their property.

When a cat died a natural death the owners shaved their eyebrows and upon death of a dog, their entire bodies were shaved.

Dead cats were buried or mummified and although Bubastis was the city of the cat goddess Bastet, cats were rarely mummified there, 'while it was the rule in other cemeteries like Beni-Hassan' (Naville, 1891: 54).

Several acres between Tell Basta (the site of ancient Bubastis) and Zagazig were honeycombed with pits beside which were heaps of white bones of cats. One pit was said to have contained over 720 cubic feet of cat bones. The love of cats is also emphasized from the buried and mummified cats that were dug up at Bubastis, Giza, Beni Hasan, and other places during the late 1800s and early 1900s from which an estimated 19 tons were shipped to England for making fertilizer (Morrison-Scott, 1952).

7-185 *The sacred cat (Ra) killing the snake of darkness (Apep, Apophis). No date and provenance given. Source: Budge (1930: 145).*

Of those specimens examined by zoologists almost all were of the wild cat, *Felis silvestris*. In a series of 192 skulls from Giza dating from 600-200 B.C., there were three jungle cats, *Felis chaus* (Morrison-Scott, 1952: 863), seven ichneumons, three jackals, and one fox (Petrie, 1907: 29).

Jungle Cat *Felis chaus* Güldenstädt, 1776

E Swamp Cat; F Chat de marais; G Rohrkatze, Sumpfluchs; A Qut Barri (m), Qutta Barria (f), Qut el Mostankaat, Qut el Ahrash, Qut tefa, Tafawa

Nomenclature: The common name jungle cat derives from the habitats of this cat, which were tall, dense papyrus and reed beds, and jungles of tamarisk and reeds along rivers.

Description: This cat is similar to *F. silvestris*, but has longer legs, a shorter tail that doesn't reach the hocks and has three instead of five rings above the tip. The color is paler and markings less distinct, except on the hind legs. Cheek stripes are lacking and there are black ear tufts.

Head and body lengths of adult Egyptian specimens are 67 (60-76) cm; tail 25 (21-28) and 38 (34-44) percent of head and body length (Osborn and Helmy, 1980: table 53). Shoulder ht. from Haltenorth and Diller (1980: 230) is 40-48 cm.

Natural history: F. chaus climbs and swims well and inhabits marshy areas, reed beds, low cultivated areas, and fields of beans, sugar cane, and barley; and other thick cover.

Despite its common name 'swamp cat', *F. chaus* coexists with *F. silvestris* in the Western Mediterranean Coastal Desert and the oases.

Food includes fish, which it either scavenges or steals from fisherman. Whether or not it catches live fish is not known. The diet also includes reptiles, amphibians, rodents, hares, birds, and eggs. Farmers and Bedouins say it preys on lambs.

Unlike most other carnivores, this cat is often active during the day.

Distribution: In Egypt *F. chaus* has been found in the Nile Delta, Nile Valley south to Aswan; El Faiyum, Farafra and Dakhla Oases; and the Western Mediterranean Coastal Desert. Beyond Egypt the range includes northern parts of the Arabian Peninsula, southeastern Turkey, Iran, Iraq, and eastward into most of southern Asia.

Prehistoric and Predynastic records: No fossil remains of this cat have been identified and no rock drawings or other illustrations are known.

The Dynastic period: There are only a few representations of the jungle cat from Pharaonic times. One is in the Dynasty V tomb of Pehenouka (Penhuika) at Saqqara, which is facing a porcupine (figs 6-14,-15). Another is probably the short-tailed cat in the Dynasty XVIII Tomb of Neferhotep (fig. 1-24, register 1).

Three specimens of *F. chaus* were found among a sample of 192 skulls from Late Dynastic burials from Giza (Morrison-Scott, 1952: 863).

Serval *Felis serval* Schreber,1776

F Serval, Chat-tigre; G Servalkatze

Nomenclature: Leptailurus Svertzov, 1858, is a subgeneric name sometimes used in place of *Felis* as in Haltenorth and Diller (1980: 226).

Description: The serval is a sturdily built and rather long-legged cat about the size of the caracal with a comparatively smaller head; larger ears that are broad at the base and relatively long and pointed. The tail is about one third of the head and body length, although much longer in copies of Egyptian drawings (figs 1-30, 7-186, -187, -188).

The color is yellowish-buff marked with rows of black spots; stripes above and at the corners of the eyes. Backs of the ears are black. The underside is whitish to buffy and also spotted. The tail has five to seven black rings and is with or without a black tip.

Measurements are shoulder height 45-55 cm, head and body length 65-90, and tail 25-35.

Natural history: Servals are solitary in habit and occupy old burrows, rock crevices, bushes, etc. in steppe, bushland, forest, marshy areas along rivers, and also live in high mountains.

Prey includes various rodents, hares, and occasionally smaller hoofed mammals; birds up to the size of guinea fowl; lizards; fish; and some insects.

They are not strictly nocturnal and are active during the cooler periods of the day.

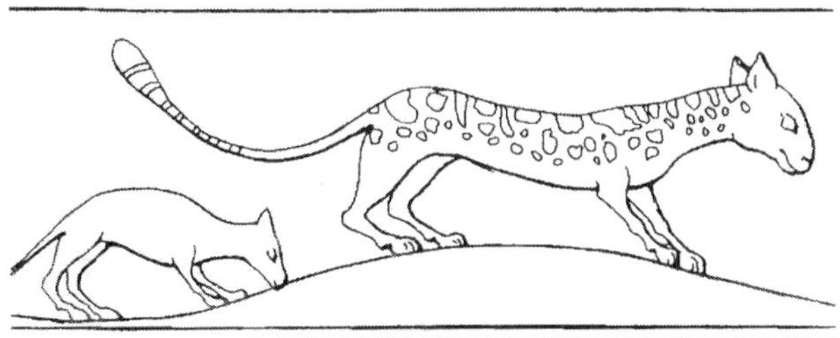

7-186 Copy of the serval in the Tomb of Chnemhotep, Dynasty XII, Beni Hasan (fig. 1-30). Source: L.D II, 131 dated to 1849-1859.

7-187 Copy of the serval in the Tomb of Chnemhotep, Dynasty XII, Beni Hasan (fig. 1-30) by Howard Carter dated to 1892- 1893. Source: The Metropolitan Museum of Art, N.Y.

Distribution: This cat once inhabited most of Africa, but today it occurs in Constantine, NE Algeria and south of the Sahara, except for tropical rain forest. In Sudan it lives as far north as Khartoum (Störk, 1980: 367).

Prehistoric records: There are no fossil remains and no rock drawings of servals in Egypt.

The Dynastic period: An outline of a serval appears in the Dynasty XII Tomb of Chnemhotep at Beni Hasan (fig. 1-30, reg. 1). Detailed copies of the original show considerable variation: The one by Lepsius (fig. 7-186) has an odd conformation and is of no use for proper identification. Carter's and Davies' copies (figs7-187,-188) are comparable. In both copies there are exceptionally long tails, but the same error was made with caracal drawings (figs 7-192,-193). The black rings on the tails are one less than listed by Haltenorth and Diller (1980: 226) and one is without the black tip. Head markings, stripes above and at the corner of the eye are typical as are the large ears that are long and broad at the base.

Davies (1933: 26) referred to his copy (fig. 7-188) as 'a cat of some sort'. Boessneck (1988: fig. 33) and Brentjes (1967c: 305, fig. 3) called it a genet.

7-188 Copy of the serval in the Tomb of Chnemhotep, Dynasty XII, Beni Hasan (fig. 1-30) by N. de G. Davies in 1932. Source: Davies (1933: fig. 7). Behind the cat is a jerboa, which is clearer than the one in fig. 7-186.

Errors and discrepancies: Boessneck (1988:165, note 3) said that the often quoted, solitary occurrence of servals under the masses of cat mummies from the New Kingdom still has to be confirmed.

Petrie (1906:148: figs 153, 154) referred to figurines of cats and cats on painted tiles (fig. 7-189a,b) 'as serval cats and cheetahs'. Most of these, however, are like the usual cat figures with the tails curving around from the inside of the thigh and too long for servals. The ears are too small and narrow for servals and the striping style of markings is also comparable with those of *Felis silvestris* (figs 7-178,-181,-182).

In Figure 7-189, numbers 6 and 8 represent cheetahs. The head on number 10 is serval-like and the ears are broad.

Zeuner (1963: 391) also listed, without a figure, a painted tile of Dynasty XVIII date from Serabit el-Khadim (S.W. Sinai) and said it showed a serval cat, an imported species.

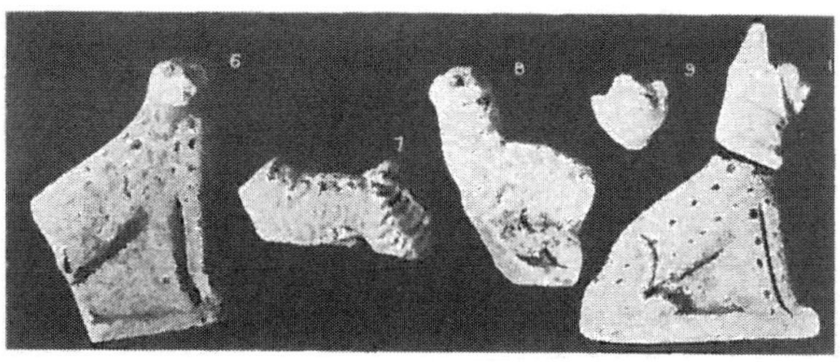

7-189 Glazed figurines and plaques of cats on painted tiles from Serabit el-Khadem, Dynasty XII, Sinai. Source: Petrie (1906: figs 153, 154).

Caracal *Caracal caracal* (Schreber, 1776)

jnb ineb Wb. I, 94

E African Lynx; F Caracal; G Wüstenluchs; A Umm Rishat

Nomenclature: An obsolete synonym is *Felis caracal* Schreber, 1776.

Description: This cat is of medium size, long-limbed, short-tailed, and with long ear tufts. The body color is almost uniform from light sandy to dark reddish-brown. The belly is paler and with faint spots. There are black stripes from the forehead to the eyes and nose. The ears are elongate with long black tufts on the tips. The backs of the ears are blackish; the inner sides and margins are whitish. Black individuals sometimes occur.

The tail is relatively short, one-half to one-third of the head and body length. The pads of the feet are partly covered with fur.

Measurements of head and body length are 65-90 cm; tail 20-30, and shoulder ht. 40-50 (Haltenorth and Diller, 1980: 225).

Natural history: Caracals live solitarily in savanna, plains, and semi-desert, and in rocky and mountainous country. They are primarily nocturnal and prey on birds, reptiles, and mammals ranging in size from rodents to gazelles. There is a report of one having killed a Barbary goat in the southern part of the Eastern Desert in 1981 (I. Helmy, pers. com.). They also prey on domestic animals. Caracals are excellent climbers and will hide in trees, if available, during the day.

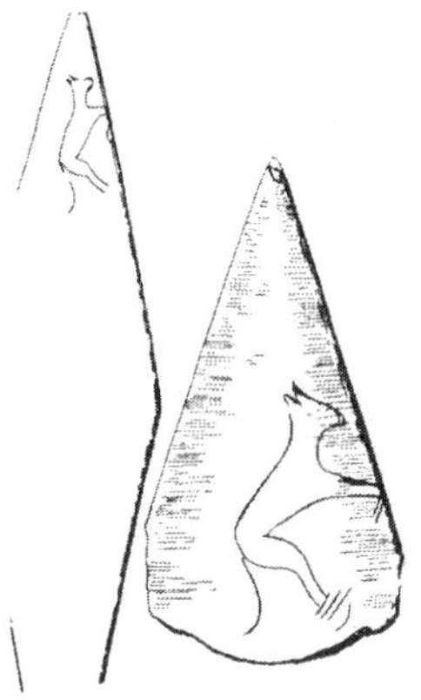

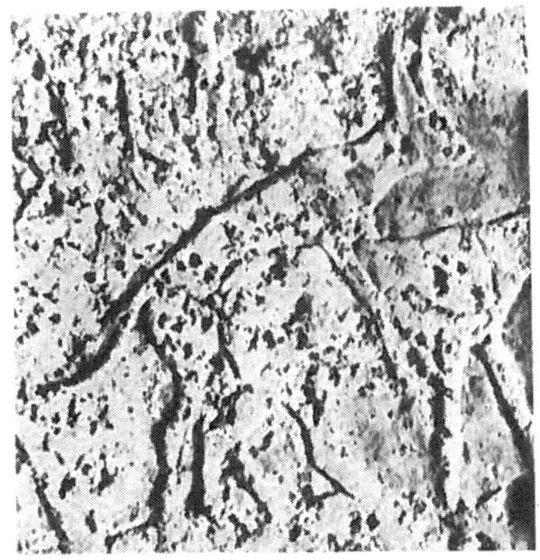

7-190 (left) Graffiti of caracals on Predynastic schist palettes from Beit -Allam. Source: de Morgan (1897 : figs 510, 511).

7-191 (right) Relief of caracals mating in the Mastaba of Issi-mr-ntr, Dynasty V-VI, Giza. Source: Keimer (1948b: pl.I).

7-192 Caracals from the Tomb of Chnemhotep, Dynasty XII, Beni Hasan. Source: Champollion (1845 IV: pl. CCCXCIII).

Distribution: In Egypt the caracal is known from scattered localities in the Eastern Desert and Sinai. It may be nearing extinction.

Beyond Egypt this cat inhabits much of Africa south of the Sahara, except for the rain forest; parts of northern Libya, Tunisia (?), Algeria, and Morocco; the Arabian Peninsula; and Asia Minor eastward into India.

Prehistoric records: Fossil remains and rock drawings of caracals are not known from Egypt.

There are two examples of caracals inscribed on Predynastic slate palettes (fig. 7-190).

The Dynastic period: Caracals mating in the relief in the Dynasty V-VI Mastaba of Issi-mr-ntr at Giza are easily recognized by the long ears and relatively short cylindrical tail (fig. 7-191).

Two caracals in the Dynasty XII Tomb of Chnemhotep at Beni Hasan (figs 1-30,-31, register 3) were originally painted brownish-red and with ear tufts. The color appears to have been correct, but the tails are too long and too thick and the posture of the standing figure is somewhat unnatural. Hartmann (1864: 11), however, described them as true to nature.

Champollion's (1845 IV: pl.CCCXCIII) copies show some slight variations from the originals (fig. 7-192a,b). Davies (1933: 26) copied the standing caracal and remarked: "The artist has not been able to achieve much grace of action. It is a stuffed specimen, badly set up."

An almost identical copy was published by Keimer (fig. 7-193).

7-193 Standing caracal, Tomb of Chnemhotep, Dynasty XII, Beni Hasan. Source: Keimer (1948b: pl. VIII).

The caracal was assumed to have been sacred and was called Maftet (Mercatante, 1978: 90). Budge (1904 II: 363) referred to it as having a benevolent disposition and said it was supposed to have protected mummies from snakes.

There are no illustrations of the caracal as Maftet, but one cat that was called Maftet is a lioness (fig. 7-211).

Errors and discrepancies: Kingdon's (1977 IIIA: 337 f., 339) references to caracals having been 'embalmed' is without confirmation and his illustration of a bronze cat is apparently *F. silvestris*. The only similarity with the caracal is the somewhat short tail, which may have been broken.

The animal called 'Lynx' by Keimer (1948b: 384, fig.5) is probably the wild cat (*F. silvestris*) shown in Figure 7-38, register 4.

Budge (1934: 82) said the lynx was often mentioned in religious texts as Maftet. On page 83 (*op. cit.*) there are two illustrations of a cat killing a snake with a knife. Neither can be identified as lynx, even though the ears are pointed. (See Figure 7-185).

Large Cats

Lion ***Panthera leo*** (Linnaeus, 1758)
[African Lion and **Asian Lion]**

 *m33j* may Wb. II, 11

F Lion; G Löwe; A Asad Afriiky

Nomenclature: An obsolete synonym is *Felis leo* Linnaeus, 1758.

Description: The lion is the largest African cat, having a shoulder height of 75-112 cm, head and body length 145-200 and tail 67-102. The head is large and broad, ears short and round, legs relatively long and stout, tail long and tufted. The pelage is short, but the male has a dark, shaggy mane on the head, neck, and chest. The general color is yellowish to light brown and paler on the chin, breast, and belly.

Lions have a 'short dark vertical stripe over the inner corner of the eye' (Haltenorth and Diller, 1980: 221), which is sometimes shown in Egyptian figures and is exagerated on the cat on the lid of Tutankhamun's ungent jar (fig. 7-216a).

On early Egyptian artifacts the mane extends over the shoulders and along the belly as on the Barbary and Asian lions.

Natural history: Lions are nocturnal in habit and occupy open country ranging through semi-desert, savanna, and mountains, but not in dense forest, except for the extinct Barbary lion. They prey upon medium to large mammals and will eat smaller prey if necessary. They can survive for long periods without water.

Distribution: Lions no longer exist in Egypt and are limited in Africa mainly to savanna south of the

7-194 Long-maned granite lion in the Berlin Museum. Late Pre- or early dynastic (about 3,000 B.C.). Source: Hamann (1944: 56, fig. 54).

7-195 Reconstruction of the ancient Egyptian lion. Source: Hemmer (1963: fig. 3).

7-196 Rock drawing of a lion at Gebel Silsila east bank of the Nile north of Kom Ombo. Source: Červíček (1974: fig. 476).

7-197 Man dompting two lions in a Hierakonpolis wall painting of Gerzean (Predynastic) vintage. Source: Quibell and Green (1902 II: pl. LXXVI).

7-198 Lion chasing a bull on the Pre- or Proto-dynastic Min statue, Koptos. Source: Petrie (1896: pl. III, 4).

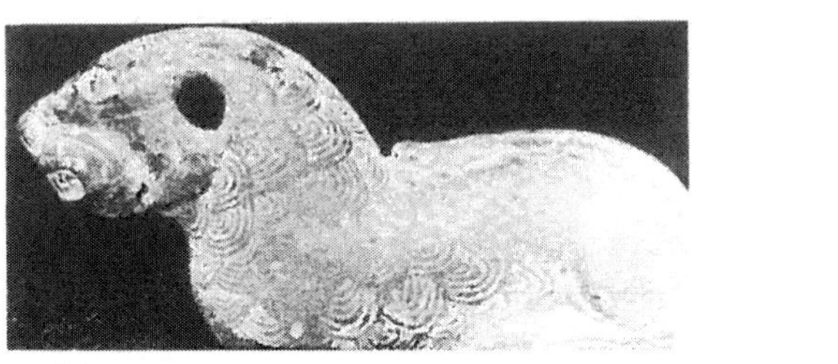

7-199 Ivory gaming piece of a lion with an extensive mane from beside the Tomb of King Djer (Zer-Ta), Dynasty I, Abydos. Source: Petrie (1901a II: pl. VI, 4).

Sahara. They are extinct in Europe and Asia, except in a reserve in N.W. India.

Original distribution in Egypt probably included most of the Western and Eastern Deserts and Sinai during the subpluvial.

The question of whether or not the long-maned lions on Predynastic and early Dynastic palettes and ivory knife handles represented only the Asian race is a difficult one to answer. Some of these artifacts show definite Mesopotamian style and therefore cannot be considered as true reproductions of Egyptian fauna. For example, the Gebel el Arak and Gebel el Tarif knife handles (figs 1-11,-12) are typically Mesopotamian as was mentioned in the introduction. The interlocking row of mastiffs and long-maned Asian lions on a Predynastic ivory scepter (fig. 7-22) are also Mesopotamian. But, on the Dynasty I gold mace handle (fig. 1-13), even though the style is Mesopotamian, some of the animals are definitely Egyptian.

Long-maned lions doubtless originated in Africa and were among the North African cats and other mammals that migrated out of Africa into Asia during the Pliocene-Pleistocene transition (Colbert, 1973: 274). They probably inhabited all of North Africa until climatic changes favored the more desert adapted short-maned race. Remnants of the long-maned lion existed in the forested mountains of Morocco and Algeria until exterminated by hunters in the early 1900s (Kowalski and Rzebik-Kowalska, 1991: 163).

Except for a granite statue (fig. 7-194) dated to the Late Predynastic or Early Dynastic period, all lion figures dated beyond the second dynasty have short manes. Following a thorough search of Egyptian artifacts and paintings, Hemmer (1963, 123 f.) concluded that the belly-maned (long-maned) lions of ancient Egypt were an 'artistic connection' and that the prevailing conception of a continuous range of long-maned lions in North Africa and the Near East could not be supported. He also published a reconstruction of the ancient Egyptian lion (fig. 7-195).

There are no lion mummies and a lack of skeletal material, which would either support or contradict Hemmer's conclusions.

Prehistoric records: Very few fossil remains of lions have been found. Von den Driesch and Boessneck (1985: 45) listed two burned bones from the Neolithic site of Beni Salama (Merimda).

The Predynastic period: Rock drawings of lions are not common and only a few were pictured by Winkler (1938, 1939) and Červíček (1974). Some examples are in Figures 13-36, -107, and 7-196. The latter is a rare example of an early illustration of a very short mane. The act of attack is a common theme in lion portrayals in predynastic and dynastic art (*op. cit.*, 179).

Lions that are called Asian type, because their manes extend over the shoulders and along the belly, appear on a few predynastic palettes and ivory knife handles (figs 1-2b,-3,-4a,-5a,-9,-11,-12,-13, and 6-13). The manes on the two Hierakonpolis lions in Figure 7-197 are not clear, but appear to be short despite the similarity between this figure and one on the Gebel el Arak knife handle (fig. 1-11).

In Figures 1-7 and 1-8 manes are not indicated; one lion in Figure 1-9 has a long mane; and neck fringes are shown in Figure 1-10. The lion in Figure 6-13 has a belly mane and there are intertwined snakes on the reverse side of the handle, which indicates a Mesopotamian origin.

A relief on the pre- or proto-dynastic statue of Min (fig. 7-198), which has been called a 'hyena chasing a bull' (Petrie, 1896: 8; Bissing, 1905 I:36; Paton, 1925: 23), has short, round ears, a short muzzle, and stout legs and represents a lion. This appears to have been the earliest representation of a theme that often appeared during the dynasties – a lion chasing or attacking a bull or cow. Sometimes other animals, such as gazelle, ibex, and oryx were substituted.

The Dynastic period: Illustrations and figures of lions with extensive manes continued into the early dynasties (figs 1-13, 7-199,-200), but in later artifacts, reliefs, statues, and paintings manes were absent or limited to the head, neck, and chest.

Other illustrations of the above-mentioned lion and bull antagonism appeared in hunt scenes in the Dynasty V Tomb of Ptahetep (fig. 7-27), Dynasty VI Mastaba of Mereruka (Duell, 1938 I: pls. 24, 25), and Dynasty XII Chapel of Senbi (fig. 7-29). The same theme was also carved on a Dynasty XVIII military axe head (fig. 7-201), the original of which was well illustrated by Steindorff (1926: fig. 50).

Erman (1894: 242) interpreted the Ptahetep illustration as the result of the lion having been baited with a live bull.

Wilkinson (1878 II: 87 f.) remarked that lions had been "trained expressly for the chase, like the cheetah or hunting leopard of India; but there is no appearance of the leopard or the panther having been employed for this purpose, and the lion was always the animal they preferred."

In these hunting scenes (figs 7-27,-29) the Pharaoh's lion may simply have been released like his hunting dogs and the aurochs was assumed to have been its natural prey.

In a hunting scene in Beni Hasan (fig. 1-29), a lioness is subduing an ibex. Wilkinson (1878 II: no. 351) said that the inscription reads '*Net'er nerau'*, overthrowing the dorcas goat'. His copy (fig. 7-202)

7-200 Obverse of the Libyan or Towns palette, Late Gerzean, Dynasty I, Abydos. Source: Asselberghs (1961: pl.XCII, 164). A long-maned lion and other symbolic animals are destroying fortified enclosures in Upper Egypt.

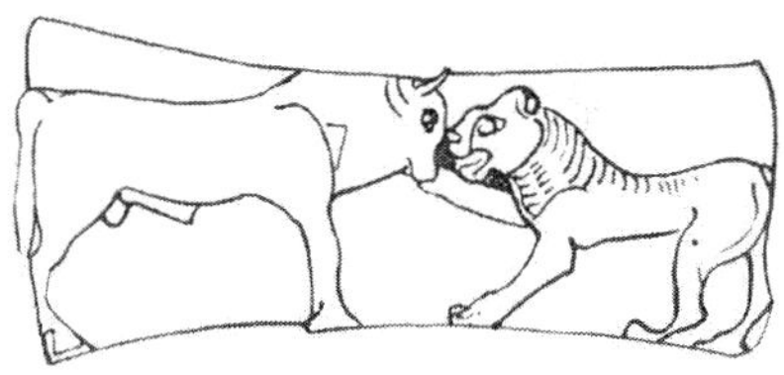

7-201 Bronze axe head from Dynasty XVIII with a lion attacking a bull. Source: Vandier d'Abbadie (1946 III: fig. 24).

7-202 A lion subduing an ibex in the Tomb of Baqt, Dynasty XII, Beni Hasan (see Figure 1-29). Source: Wilkinson (1878 II: no. 351).

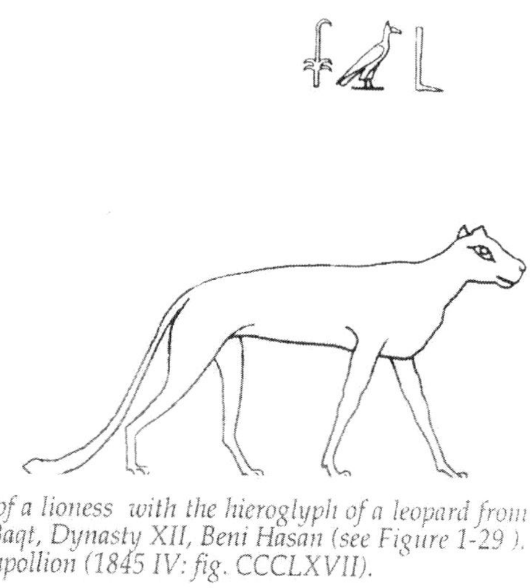

7-203 Copy of a lioness with the hieroglyph of a leopard from the Tomb of Baqt, Dynasty XII, Beni Hasan (see Figure 1-29). Source: Champollion (1845 IV: fig. CCCLXVII).

7-204 A lioness knocking down a hartebeest. Tomb of Amenemhet, Dynasty XII, Beni Hasan. Source: Newberry (1893 II: pl. XIII).

7-205 Tutankhamun, accompanied by his hound, spearing a lion. Ostracon from the Valley of the Kings, Dynasty XVIII, Thebes. Source: Phillips (1948: fig. 34).

is somewhat different from that in Figure 1-29. There are two other lionesses further right that are walking. These are misidentified (left to right) by hieroglyphs for cheetah and leopard. The 'leopard' was pictured in a simple line drawing without body markings in Figure 7-203 where it looks more like a leopard than a lioness, despite the hieroglyph.

As already mentioned, a theme of lion attacking other beasts was popular among dynastic artists.

In a badly damaged scene in the Tomb of Zau, Dynasty V, Deir el Gebrawi, a lion is grabbing a gazelle by the nose (Davies, 1902 II: pl.XV). In the Dynasty XII Tomb of Chnemhotep (fig. 1-30) a lion is attacking an oryx.

Decorations on Tutankhamun's ungent jar (fig. 7-216a,b) and gold dagger sheath (fig. 7-42) include lions attacking aurochs and an ibex.

In the Tomb of Chnemhotep (fig. 1-30) a short-maned lion only walks with other beasts.

In another Beni Hasan scene a lioness is knocking down a hartebeest (figs 1-32, 7-204). Although the animal resembles a lioness, the tail is not tufted and there are indications of distal striping as in the leopard, but there are no body markings. This figure is comparable with that of the lioness on the ungent jar (fig. 7-216a,b).

The hunting of lions was a privilege of the pharaohs and others of high rank. Their killing of lions single-handed was proof of their virility (Carrington, 1972: 74), as in the drawing showing Tutankhamun spearing a lion (fig. 7-205). One of the most spectacular and imaginative portrayals is that of Tutankhamun in his chariot killing one lion after another with arrows (fig. 7-206).

There are numerous stories of Egyptian kings killing large numbers of lions. Brunner (1969: 561) related the killing of 'five wild lions in one single instance' by Tuthmosis III and of Amenophis III having killed 110 savage lions during the first 10 years of his reign.

Tame lions were kept by some pharaohs including Ramses II, III, and VI (Bissing, 1914: pl.54B) and Tutankhamun (Carter, 1927 II: T1). They were sometimes pictured running beside the kings in their chariots and were called 'battle lions' (fig. 7-207), which supposedly frightened the enemy and knocked down any who dared to approach the chariot. On Tutankhamun's golden shrine his pet lion is shown accompanying him during recreation (fig. 7-208).

The lion cult, one of the oldest in Egypt, was centered at Leontopolis in the southeastern Delta south of Shibin Kantar where sacred lions were probably kept.

7-206 Tutankhamun hunting lions in his chariot. Source: Davies and Gardiner (1962: pl. IV).

7-207 A pet lion running beside the chariot horse of Ramses II, Dynasty XIX, Beit el Wali. Source: Wreszinski (1935 II: 181).

The remains of seven captive lion cubs were found around the Dynasty I Tomb of Hor Aha at Umm el Qab near Abydos (Boessneck, 1988: 32). These and the worship of lion gods and goddesses at that early time indicate the feelings of the Egyptians toward this beast.

Various gods and goddesses that were associated with lions included Tefnut, Mut, Aker, Pakheth, Sekhmet, Tefnet, Bastet, the sun gods Ra and Horus, and others (Budge, 1904a; Müller, 1923; Mackenzie, 1978; Mercatante, 1978).

Tefnut and Sekhmet were women with heads of lionesses 'surmounted by either a sun disk or the Uraeus or both' (Mercatante, 1978: 142, 184). Either may have been represented on the Kom Ombo Temple (fig. 7-209).

Budge (1904a I: 446) remarked that "Bastet's identification with a lioness probably belongs to a comparatively late period" and the head of the goddess was usually surmounted by a Uraeus, the divine snake (fig. 7-210).

The cat climbing a guillotine in Figure 7-211 has been said to represent Mafdet, the lynx goddess (Budge, 1934: 82; Müller, 1923: 107); a genet (Kees, 1941: 33; Vandier, 1952 I: 851); a wild cat, leopard, and cheetah (Bonnet, 1952, 434); and a lioness (Petrie, 1901 II: 25; Mercer, 1949: 216). After some debate as to the possibility of it being a mongoose, Gardiner (1938: 89 f.) decided that Mafdet was really a cat goddess.

The cat in Figure 7-211 certainly represents a lioness from the tuft on the long tail and the short, rounded ears. Figures of lions range in size from gaming pieces (fig. 7-199), small amulets (Petrie, 1914: figs 219, 221), and statuettes (fig. 7-212) to huge life-like statues and reliefs (fig. 7-213), and sphinxes (Schweitzer, 1948). Lions were carved on thrones and chairs (fig. 7-214), statues guarded palaces and tombs, and carved heads of lions protected the pharaohs in their sleep.

One of the beds or biers found in Tutankhamun's Tomb was decorated with the carved wooden head of a lion (fig. 7-215), which was correctly identified by Schweitzer (1948: 48) and Fox (1951; 18). Desroches-Noblecourt (1963: 302) and Westendorf (1968: 147) called it a 'cheetah', probably because of the artistic blue lacrimal lines. The lion is the logical animal, because of its long association with kings and the belief in its being a guardian of sleep (Montet, 1964: 297).

The lion ungent jar (fig. 7-216 a,b) among Tutankhamun's treasures is also of particular interest. According to Gilbert et al. (1976: cat. no. 16), it 'may have been intended to suggest the king's lion-like character'.

There is no indication of a mane on the figure carved on the lid of the jar, however, which indicates that it represents a lioness. Just what this

7-208 Tutankhamun, accompanied by his queen and lion cub, shooting wild ducks. Source: Carter (1927 II: pl. I, B).

7-209 The goddess Tefnut or Sekhmet on the Ptolemaic Temple of Kom Ombo. Source: M. Zemina.

7-210 The goddess Bastet. Source: Budge (1904a I: 444).

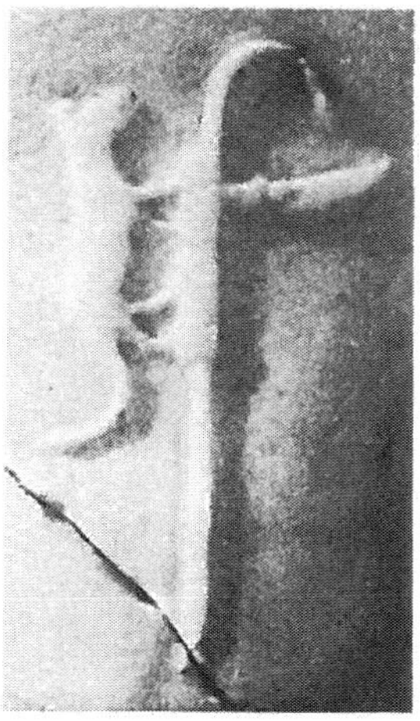

7-211 A lioness climbing a 'guillotine'. Source: Petrie (1901aII: pl.VII, 7)

7-212 Red pottery statuette of a lion from the Dynasty I Temple of Hierakonpolis. Source: Quibell and Green (1902 II: pl. XLV).

7-216 a,b Lion ungent jar of alabaster from the Tomb of Tutankhamun, Dynasty XVIII, Thebes. Source: the Ashmolean Museum, Oxford. A recumbent lioness decorates the lid. Below, on the jar lions are attacking aurochs and salukis attack an aurochs and a gazelle.

7-213 Life-sized relief of a lion at the Temple of Hatshepsut, Dynasty XVIII, Deir el Bahari. Source: Schweitzer (1948: pl. VI, 1).

7-217 Part of an Asian tribute scene in the Tomb of Huy, Dynasty XVIII, N of Medinet Habu, Thebes. Source: Davies and Gardiner (1926: pl. XIX). The animal figures in the upper row include the head of a lamb on a jar, a short-maned lion, and a horse. Below, there is a bovid head on a jar and a leopard pelt.

7-214 A lion carved on the sedan chair of Sesheshet, mother of Mereruka, Mastaba of Mereruka, Dynasty VI, Saqqara. Source: Schweitzer (1948: pl. VI, 4).

signifies is not clear.

The tail has two black distal stripes above the black tip (fig. 7-216a).

Distal stripes are also present on the tails of male lions decorating Tutankhamun's head rest (Edwards, 1976a: cat. no. 48, pl. 29; 1976b: cat. no. 37). These marks are characteristic of leopards.

There are prominent vertical marks above the eyes, which are also exaggerated on other species - cheetah (fig. 7-230) and black leopard (fig. 7-226).

Lions were occasionally portrayed in tribute processions. In the Asian tribute scene in the Tomb of Huy (fig. 7-217) the short-maned lion on a leash appears to be of the Egyptian race. It is probably an artist's error.

Nubians were shown in the Dynasty XIX Temple of Ramses bringing a tame lion along with other animals (figs 1-26, 4-38).

A lion and a leopard in cages appear in a return from the hunt pictured in the Tomb of

7-215 Lion's head on a couch from the Tomb of Tutankhamun, Dynasty XVIII, Thebes. Source: Cairo Museum by M. Zemina.

Ptahetep (fig.7-218) along with various other animals.

As with other wild beasts, lions were sometimes shown mating (fig. 7-219) and giving birth. On the latter, Hassan (1955: 138) when listing the animals in the Dynasty IV-V Causeway of Unas at Saqqara, added: "The artist slipped up badly; he has represented a full maned male lion - giving birth to a cub!" Unfortunately, he neglected to publish this picture.

Errors and discrepancies: A few errors were mentioned above.

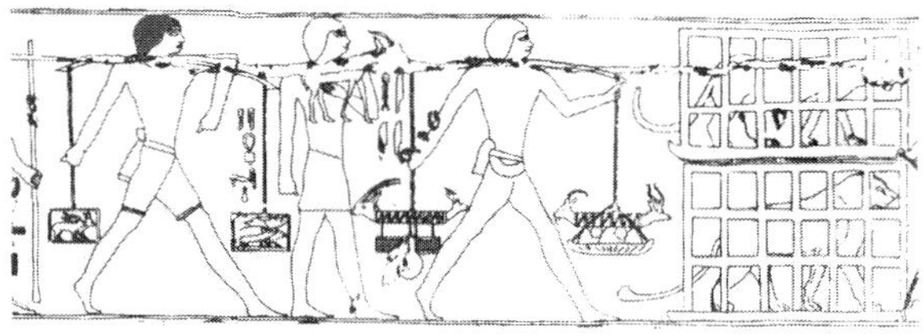

7-218 (top right) Caged lion and leopard in the return from a hunt. Tomb of Ptah-hetep, Dynasty V, Saqqara. Source: Paget and Pirie (1898: pl. XXXIII). Four men (not shown) are pulling the two cages. Behind the cages the first man is carrying what appear to be a bound bubal, ibex, gazelle, and oryx. The second man carries a young ibex (?), and the third, two cages containing hedge-hogs and hares.

7-219 Lions mating in the Tomb Chapel of Ukhotep's son Senbi, Dynasty XII, Meir. Source Blackman (1915 II: pl. VII)

Leopard *Panthera pardus* (Linnaeus, 1758)

 *3bjj* abi Wb. I, 7

 *b3-šm'* bashema Wb. I, 4-5

E Panther; F Panthère d'Afrique; G Leopard; A Nemoura, Nimr

Nomenclature: An obsolete synonym is *Felis pardus* Linnaeus, 1758.

Description: Leopards are large, sturdily built cats with a long tail, muzzle of median length, and short, roundish ears.

The body and legs vary in color from pale yellow and yellowish-gray to darker shades. Underside is white to whitish gray or yellowish white. The head, neck, and underside are covered with solid black spots. Over the rest of the body there are rosettes (broken spots). These patterns are not always so distinctive as in Figure 4-22. Sometimes the cheetah, which has solid spots, is also depicted with rosettes (fig. 1-32).

Another feature that is generally distinctive is the position of the head. Leopards are usually shown with their heads lowered (figs 4-22, 7-221–223), while cheetahs have their heads raised (figs 4-21,-23), with some exceptions (figs 4-38, 1-30,-32).

The tail is spotted, except for several black distal rings and a black tip. The ears are black on the back with a white spot. There is a black blotch on the lower throat.

There are no distinctive facial markings, except those shown artistically on the black panther upon which King Tutankhamun is shown standing (fig. 7-226) and on some artificial heads on robes (fig. 7-225). Measurements are shoulder height 50-70 cm, head and body length 130-190, and tail 70-100.

Natural history: Leopards are solitary in habit and may be active day and night. They inhabit all kinds of environments from desert to rain forest and high mountains. They are good climbers and can swim well. Prey includes a variety of reptiles, birds, and mammals, including the young of predators.

Distribution: Leopards probably inhabited most of Egypt during Pharaonic time. Recent distribution included oases of the Western Desert, the Mediterranean Coastal Desert, the Eastern Desert, and Sinai. Today it is on the verge of extinction and may survive only in the southeastern part of the Eastern Desert and possibly southern Sinai (Osborn and Helmy, 1980; 451 ff.).

Beyond Egypt the range includes parts of Algeria and Morocco; most of Africa south of the Sahara; the Arabian Peninsula; and Asia Minor eastward into southern and northern Asia.

Prehistoric records: Remains of leopard were reported by Boessneck (1988: table 5) from the Chalcolithic (Copper Age) in Maadi near Cairo. Goodman et al. (1992: 84) identified remains of 20 leopards from a cave in the South Galala Plateau of the Eastern Desert, which were dated to the

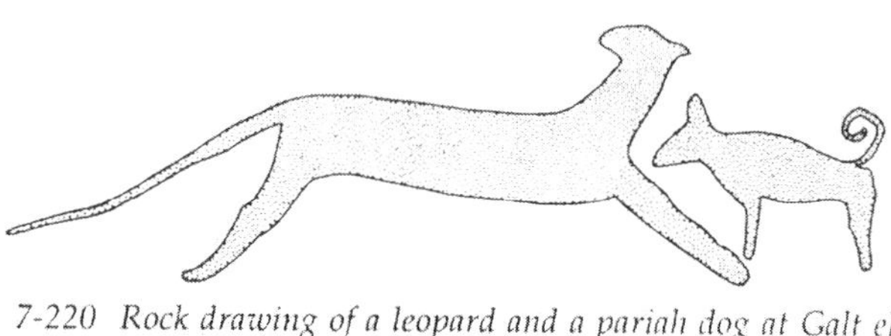

7-220 Rock drawing of a leopard and a pariah dog at Galt el Aguz, 30 km northwest of Gebel Abraq in the southern Eastern Desert. Source: Červíček (1974: fig. 184).

7-221 A tame leopard in the Tomb of Nefermat, Dynasty III, Medum. Source: Petrie (1892b: pl. XVII).

7-222 A leopard with the hieroglyph for cheetah in the Tomb of Baqt III, Dynasty XII, Beni Hasan. Source: Champollion (1845 IV :pl. CCCLXXXII).

7-223 A leopard behind a beisa oryx in the Tomb of Khety, Dynasty XI, Beni Hasan. Source: Newberry (1894 II: pl. XIII).

7-224 A leopard attacking a male ibex on Tutankhamun's ornate chest. Source: Reed and Osborn (1978: fig. 14).

Epipaleolithic and also the Predynastic and Intermediate Periods (7,000 to 3,000 B.C.).

The Predynastic period: Rock drawings of leopard and cheetah are difficult to distinguish. Probably the best example of a leopard is from Červíček (1974) in Figure 7-220.

A leopard can be identified on the Predynastic ivory knife handle from Gebel el Tarif (fig. 1-12). Leopards are also represented on ivory carvings from Hierakonpolis (Quibell, 1900 I: pl. XIII) and the Hierakonpolis palette (fig. 1-2b).

The Dynastic period: The earliest Dynastic representation of a leopard is the stylized carving on the Dynasty I mace handle (fig. 1-13). Another early depiction is the apparently tame leopard in the Dynasty III Tomb of Nefermat (fig. 7-221). Although most of the spots appear to be solid on this figure and the tail has a white tip, as in the cheetah, the head is large and held down, the body and limbs are stout, and there is a distinctive black leopard mark on the throat, but no stripe from the eye to the mouth as on the cheetah.

Brentjes (1965; 84, fig. 86) called the animal a cheetah (gepard) on a line and referred to Wreszinski 1923 I: pl.396. But it is apparently free and the man behind it holds only sticks in his hands.

A leopard and a lion in cages are included in the return from a hunt in the Dynasty V tomb of Ptahetep (fig. 7- 218).

In a Dynasty V-VI relief a tame leopard is being led by dwarfs along with dogs and a monkey (fig. 4-34). The posture and body shape of this cat are typical of a leopard.

Leopards and cheetahs appear in several Beni Hasan hunting scenes, but identification is difficult.

In the Tomb of Baqt (fig. 1-29) the 12th animal from the left is a leopard with its large head lowered. The spots on the body are cheetah-like, but continue onto the underside. The legs are slender, but the body is stout like that of a leopard. The hieroglyph, however, is for the cheetah. A copy by Champollion (fig. 7-222) has irregular spots and can be identified as a leopard.

In the Tomb of Khety, another cat with minute spots, but heavily built and with its head lowered obviously represents a leopard (fig. 7-223).

Leopards are shown mating in the Dynasty V Tomb of Ptahetep (fig. 7-27) and also in the Dynasty XII Tomb Chapel of Senbi (fig. 7-29).

Training of leopards for hunting is not evident and illustrations of them attacking other animals are rare. A leopard is attacking a male ibex on Tutankhamun's ornate chest (fig. 7-224). Hobbs (1980: 99, f.n. 82) suggested that the cat attacking a spotted bull on this chest was also a leopard. No clear pictures of this have been published.

7-225 (left) A priest wearing an imitation leopard skin robe. Dynasty XII, Beni Hasan. Source: Griffith, ed. (1900 IV: pl.XIV). The artificial head has marks below the eyes like a cheetah.

7-226 (right) Tutankhamun standing on the back of a black leopard (panther). Source: Gilbert et al.*(1976: pl. 21). Marks above and below the eyes of the leopard are an artistic addition.*

Brunner (1969: 561) apparently assumed that such figures represented animals trained especially for hunting.

A tame leopard and probably a pelt were brought into Egypt in tribute from Punt (fig. 4-22) and there is an easily identified pelt in tribute from Asia (fig. 7-217).

Leopard skins decorate the table in the Nubian gift to Tutankhamun in Figure 13-44.

Leopard skins, real and artificial, were worn by priests and pharaohs as symbols of status on festive occasions and at sacrifices. The artificial skin worn by a priest in Figure 7-225 has leopard markings and a tail suggestive of a leopard, except for its shortness. The artificial head has cheetah-like marks below the eyes. Some 'skins' were decorated with stars as Erman (1894: 297) noted on the figure of the high priest of Heliopolis at a funeral sacrifice.

The goddess of literature and the library, Sefkhet-Aabut (Seshat, Shesheta), who was closely associated with Thoth, the god of wisdom, was also shown wearing a 'panther-skin garment' (Mercatante, 1978: 140).

Carter (1923 I: 113) discovered an imitation leopard skin priestly robe with decorations of gold and silver stars in the Tomb of Tutankhamun. Another questionable representation of a leopard skin is on Tutankhamun's folding stool (Reed and Osborn, 1978: 282, fig. 15).

The so-called leopard head that was found attached to a real skin in Tutankhamun's Tomb (fig. 7-229) quite obviously represents a cheetah head from the lacrimal marks below the eyes and the smallness of the muzzle. The exaggerated marks above the eyes are apparently an artist's conception as in Figure 7-226.

Regarding the statuette of Tutankhamun standing on the back of a black leopard (fig. 7-226), Gilbert et al. (1976: pl. 21) wrote that it "seems to have been connected with incidents in the passage of the king through the underworld. The leopard is black, the color of darkness, but it would have been inappropriate to depict the king in black because he was associated with the sun god who brought a brief spell of light to the underworld as he passed through it each night."

Errors and discrepancies: No additional errors and discrepancies can be added to this chapter.

Cheetah ***Acinonyx jubatus*** (Schreber, 1776)

 *b3* ba Wb. I, 414

 *b3-mh* bameh Wb. I, 415

E Hunting Leopard; F Guépard; G Gepard; A Fahd, El Fahd el Sayad

Nomenclature: An obsolete synonym is *Felis jubata* Schreber, 1776.

Description: Cheetahs are long-tailed, long-legged, slender bodied cats with a short muzzle and short, roundish ears. There is a short mane on the neck and shoulders. The body and legs are light yellow to pale buff or grayish-white and covered with

7-227. Two collared cheetahs in a tribute scene from Punt in the Dynasty XVIII Hatshepsut Temple at Deir el Bahari. Source: Naville (1898 III: pl. XXX).

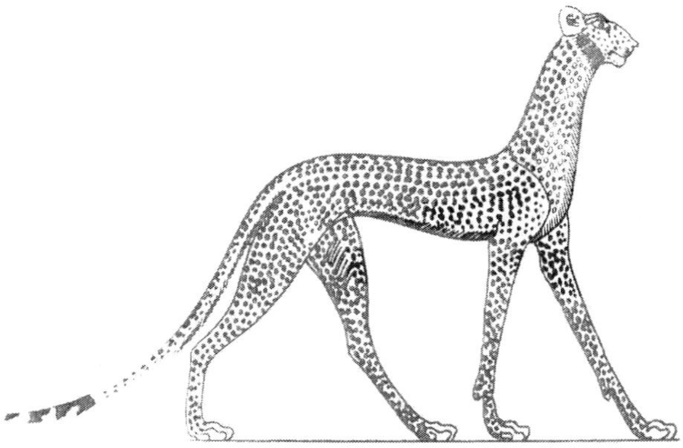

7-228. A copy of the cheetah in the tribute scene from Punt in the Dynasty XVIII Tomb of Rekhmire II, Thebes (see Figure 4-21). Source: Champollion (1845 IV: pl. CCCCXXVIII).

brownish to black solid spots. The belly is white. The tail is spotted, except for a few black distal rings and a white tuft on the tip. There is a curved black lacrimal stripe from the eye to the corner of the mouth, which is not shown on all figures. Small marks also appear above the eyes as are shown in the drawings of cheetah heads by Kingdon (1977 III A: 107) with marks above and below the eyes.

The ears are yellowish, black at the base.

Measurements are shoulder height 75-85 cm, head and body length 110-140, and tail 65-80.

Natural history: Cheetahs live mainly in semi-desert, savanna, and open bush country; never in forest. They are chiefly diurnal in habit. The prey is a variety of mammals from hares to antelopes and the young of large mammals; also domestic stock.

Prey is generally selected from a vantage point, stalked to a distance of about a 100 meters, and then pursued for some distance at a speed of up to 80 km per hour. The prey is knocked down or tripped with a forepaw or pulled down with the large dew claw and then grabbed by the throat.

Cheetahs reputedly tame very easily.

Distribution: Cheetahs are known to have lived in the northern Sinai Peninsula and the northern half of the Western Desert. Beyond Egypt the range in Africa includes scattered localities in Algeria and Morocco, the broad strip of savanna and steppe south of the Sahara, and in East Africa south to South Africa. Eastward the range includes parts of Saudi Arabia, Iran, southern Russia, and parts of India.

The cheetah is extinct in a large part of its former range and probably extinct in Egypt, judging from the last reports by Hoogstraal *et al.* (1966-1967).

Prehistoric records: Fossil remains of cheetahs are not known from Egypt.

Predynastic records: Rock drawings of cheetahs in Červíček (1974) and Winkler (1938 I) are questionable.

The Dynastic period: The earliest Dynastic representations of cheetahs appear in the Middle Kingdom tombs of Beni Hasan. In the Tomb of Chnemhotep (fig. 1-30, reg. 1), a cheetah appears to be sniffing at a hedgehog. It has a cheetah-like build and a long neck in Figure 1-30, but broken spots and a large head in Figure 1-31.

In the Tomb of Amenemhet (fig. 1-32) another cheetah with a long neck and head down and broken spots is similar to the one in figure 1-30.

Illustrations of cheetahs attacking animals are rare and there is no evidence of their having been trained for hunting. Two cheetahs attacking an oryx were drawn on a New Kingdom ostracon from Deir el Medineh (fig. 13-100) and a cheetah and a long-maned lion are attacking an ibex on Tutankhamun's gold dagger sheath (fig. 7-42). In an enlargement in Edwards (1976b: cat. no.36) lacrimal stripes are clearly visible on the cheetah. This scene could be imaginative, because cheetahs and ibexes are not known to have inhabited the same environments.

Whether or not cheetahs were tamed in Egypt is not known, but there are various New Kingdom illustrations of collared cheetahs and cheetahs on leashes in tribute scenes. Two collared cheetahs from Punt are easily identified in the Temple of Deir el Bahari (fig. 7-227).

Live cheetahs and pelts (?) are pictured in tribute scenes from Punt in the Dynasty XVIII Tomb of Rekhmire (fig. 4-21), in Nubian tribute in the Dynasty XVIII Tomb of Amunedjeh (fig. 4-23), and the Dynasty XIX Temple of Ramses II (fig. 4-38). In the latter figure the heads of the cheetahs are lowered. The bodies are without markings because this is a copy of a relief.

There is a comparable copy by Champollion (fig. 7-228) of the cheetah in Figure 4-21. Lacrimal lines are lacking in both figures and there are some obvious differences in size and arrangement of spots.

Despite the lack of any indication or evidence that cheetahs were trained for hunting in Egypt, numerous authors have published statements or quotations favoring this supposition: Phillips (1955), Zeuner (1963: 418), Brentjes (1965: 84), Hyams (1972: 52), Osborn (1977: 15), Clutton-Brock (1981: 176), and Janssen and Janssen (1989: 55).

An imaginative comment by Bodenheimer (1960: 40) was that "The cheetah (*Acinonyx jubatus*) was known and used as a hunting leopard by the old Assyrians and Egyptians. In Egypt it replaced the hyena dog (*Lycaon pictus*), which held this place throughout the third millenium B.C. as an animal for hunting antelopes and gazelles."

Störk (1977b: 530) remarked that the use of cheetahs as trained hunting animals has been assumed, but without definite proof.

Errors and discrepancies: A cheetah head of wood overlaid with gold (fig. 7-229), which was called a leopard's head and said to have belonged to a real leopard skin (Gilbert *et al.*,1976: 104) was found among the treasures of Tutankhamun. The general shape of the head is clearly more like that of a cheetah than a leopard. Likewise, the lacrimal marks below the eyes are typical of the cheetah. The marks above the eyes are an artistic addition as they are also on the head of the black leopard in Figure 7-226.

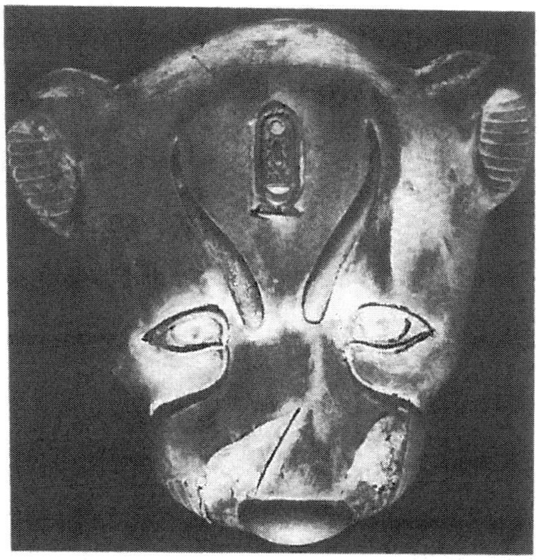

7-229. A cheetah head of wood overlaid with gold from the Tomb of Tutankhamun, Dynasty XVIII, Valley of the Kings, Thebes. Source: Gilbert et al. *(1976: pl. 3).*

VIII
Order *Tubulidentata*
Family *Orycteropodidae*

Aardvark *Orycteropus afer* (Pallas, 1766)

E Ant Bear, Earth Pig; F Cochon de Terre, Fourmilier, Oryctérope; G Erdferkel; A Abu Zelaaf

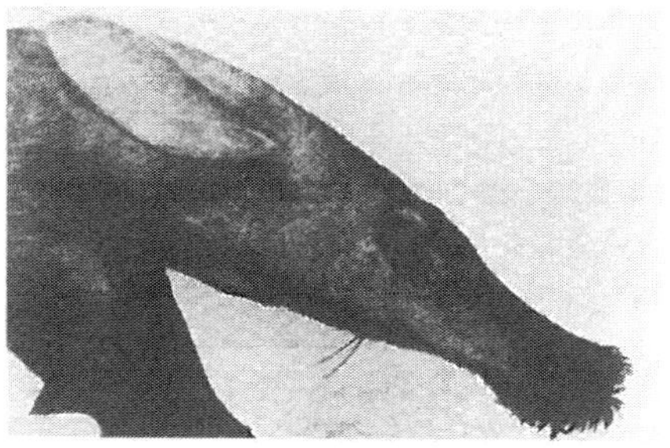

8-1 Predynastic vase from Aulad Yahlya near Girga. Source: Needler (1984: 60, pl. XVIII).

8-2 Copies of three aardvarks painted on a Predynastic vase in Figure 8-1. Source: Keimer (1944b: figs 1, 2, 3).

8-3 The lowered head of a live aardvark. Source: Keimer (1944b: fig.5).

Nomenclature: The common name aardwark is derived from the Afrikaans for 'earth pig' (Gotch, 1979: 188)

An obsolete Latin synonym is *Orycteropus aethiopicus.*

Description: The aardvark has a somewhat pig-like shape, except the snout and ears are longer and the tail is relatively long, very thick at the base and tapers to a thin tip.

The thick, pinkish-gray skin is sparsely haired and the tail is naked. Tufts of hair surround the large nostrils. There are four large claws on the front feet, five on the hind feet. Foreclaws are used for digging. The teeth are tubular in shape. The long, extensible, and sticky tongue is used for obtaining food.

Measurements are head and body length, 120-140 cm; tail, 45-60; and shoulder height, 60-65.

Natural history: This animal is strictly nocturnal in habit and spends the day in lengthy burrows alone or in small groups.

Food is mainly termites and other insects. Haltenorth and Diller (1980: 133) mentioned that soft wild cucumbers were also eaten.

The habitats range from dry savanna to rain forest, depending on the food supply.

Distribution: Aardvarks are distributed throughout Africa south of the Sahara.

Prehistoric records: No remains of aardvarks have been found in northeastern Africa.

Kowalski and Rzebik-Kowalska (1991: 19, 21, 25, 31) listed fossil remains from the Magreb (Morocco) dating to the Middle Miocene and the Holocene, and Neolithic rock drawings in the Tassili n'Ajjers Mts. of S. Algeria.

The only definite evidence of the aardvark having existed in Ancient Egypt is the representations on a Naqada III jar, dated to about 3,200-3,000 B.C., from Aulad Yahlya near Nag ed-Deir north of Girga, which is decorated with snakes and three long-tailed and long, blunt-nosed animals (fig. 8-1).

Needler (1984: 209 f.) concluded that these figures did not suggest a burrowing animal and listed the otter (*Lutra* sp.) as the only possibility, primarily because of the lack of ears.

Copies of these three aardvarks (fig. 8-2) were published by Keimer (1944b). They are comparable with modern drawings of aardvarks except for the lack of visible ears and the smallness of the feet and claws (Haltenorth and Diller, 1980: pl. 25, 7; Dorst, 1970: fig. 7).

The lowered head of the live aardvark in Figure 8-3 with ears laid back indicates why the ears may not have been visible in Figure 8-1. Another feature that is characteristic of the aardvark is the small tuft of long hairs on the throat, which is clearly indicated in Figure 8-3.

Keimer (1944b: 1 ff.), in comparing the paintings with modern pictures of the species, concluded that all features were typical of *Orycteropus* except for the small feet and five instead of four toes on the front feet. He assumed that the ears could have been in a flattened position as they sometimes are when the animals have their heads down. Aside from these discrepancies, other characteristic features are the arched backs; shape and position of tails, except for a defect in the tip on Figure 8-2,1; and the tubular and blunt snouts, one of which is a bit thick.

Other Predynastic artifacts analyzed by Keimer (*op. cit.*, figs 11, 12), which had been called aardvarks, were either unidentifiable or could not be distinguished from pigs or wild boars.

If this beast did exist in Egypt, it probably disappeared in the Predynastic along with other migrants due to climatic change.

IX
Order *Pholidota*
Pangolins Family *Manidae*

Temminck's Ground Pangolin *Manis temmincki* (Smuts, 1832)

E Cape Pangolin; F Pangolin de Temminck; G Steppenschuppentier

Description: The upper part of the body and both sides of the tail are covered with large, brown, broadly rounded, overlapping scales. The face and underside of the body are whitish-gray and almost naked except around the eyes, bases of ears, and the cheeks.

There are five long claws on all feet; the middle three of the forefeet being especially long.

These animals lack teeth and have a long, extensile tongue.

Head and body length is 50-60 cm; tail, 40-50.

Natural history: Pangolins are solitary and nocturnal in habit, spending the day in burrows.

Food is ants and termites dug out of dung heaps, rotten wood, and nests.

The habitat is dry steppe and bush country, particularly in areas of light sandy soil.

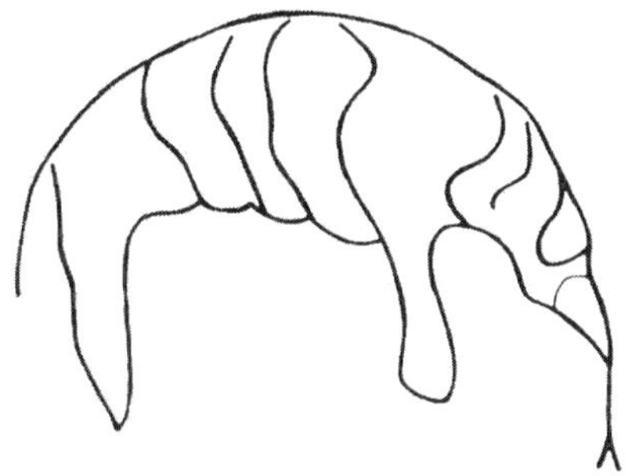

9-1 Rock drawing of Manis temmincki *from El Hagandia. Source: Červíček (1974: fig. 123).*

Distribution: This pangolin exists in southern and western Sudan, Ethiopia and Somalia south through eastern and southwestern Africa. It probably existed earlier in Upper Egypt and migrated southward in the Predynastic.

Prehistoric records: One rock drawing is known from the site of El Hagandia on the west side of the Nile north of El Silwa Bahari (fig. 9-1).

X
Order *Proboscidea*
Elephants Family *Elephantidae*

African Elephant ***Loxodonta africana*** (Blumenbach, 1797)
[and
Asian Elephant ***Elephas maximus*** (Linnaeus, 1758)]

 *3bw* abu Wb. I, 7

F Eléphant d'Afrique; G Afrikanischer Grosselefant; A Feel Afriecky

Description: Elephants are the largest living land mammals. The nose is in the form of a long, flexible 'trunk'. The upper incisor teeth are long, continuously growing 'tusks'. Further description of this well-known beast is hardly necessary, except for a few characteristics that distinguish the African from the Asian elephant.

The African elephant is larger and has much larger ears, longer tusks, and is sway-backed, whereas in the Asian species the back arches upward. The forehead of the African species is lower and the crown of the head is without the two 'bumps' that are characteristic of the Asian species. There are two 'fingers' on the tip of the trunk of the African, but only one on that of the Asian elephant.

Natural history: Elephants live in herds led by an old female. Old bulls generally leave the herds and become solitary.

They are active during most of the day, except in the warmer hours. Daily drinking of water is necessary and if enough water is available, elephants bathe each day and then have a mud or a dust bath, which is a protection against parasites.

Food includes a variety of vegetation: leaves, buds, flowers, and fruits of trees and shrubs, and various grasses and small plants. All food is gathered and put into the mouth with the trunk.

Distribution: This species formerly lived throughout Africa except for deserts. Today it is extinct north of 13 degrees N. latitude and "south of the southern tropic except for isolated pockets" (Haltenorth and Diller, 1980: 125).

The elephant lived all over Egypt during the Paleolithic and Neolithic as late as the Aeneolithic (Chalcolithic) period (4,000 B.C.).

During the Predynastic it was gradually pushed out of Lower and Middle Egypt into Upper Egypt south of Qena-Quseir. Butzer (1959:26) estimated this to have occurred about 2,600 B.C., and therefore earlier than the second subpluvial, which supports the conclusion that man was responsible for driving the elephant south into Upper Egypt. It lived in this region during the Old Kingdom and no later.

10-1 Rock drawings of an elephant (left), ibex and pariah dog, and a scimitar oryx, dated to the Epi-Paleolithic. Location: S of the 59.8 km mark on the Qift-Quseir Road in the Eastern Desert. Source: Redford and Redford (1989: fig. 12).

10-2 Rock drawing of a hunting scene north of the 60.5 km mark on the Qift-Quseir Road. Source: Redford and Redford (1989: fig. 13).
The figures in the upper row (left to right) are: an undated aurochs (?); two elephants dated to the Neolithic, between which is a scimitar oryx dated to the Late Predynastic; a camel dated to the Roman Period; and a scimitar oryx dated to the Late Predynastic.
Lower left are three men driving animals with a net, then a Barbary goat, an unidentifiable animal, two men linking arms, and a dog (?) dated to the Epi-Paleolithic.

10-3 (top left) Elephant rock drawing at Kanais, 45 km E of Idfu (Edfu). Source: Červíček (1974: fig. 252).

10-4 (top right) Rock drawing of two elephants and two wild asses at Chor es-Salam W of the Nile, S of El Hosh. Source: Červíček (1974: fig. 85).

10-5 (bottom left) Elephant rock drawing at Gebel el Dakar in Wadi Abu Subeira E of the Nile and 10 km N of Aswan. Source: Červíček (1974: fig. 505).

10-6 (bottom centre) Elephant rock drawing at Kanais, 45 km E of Idfu (Edfu). Source: Červíček (1974: fig. 253).

10-7 (bottom right) Elephant rock drawing at Gerf (Garf) Hussein, W of the Nile and about 90 km S of Aswan. Source: Červíček (1974: fig. 229).

Although the destruction of agriculture by elephants and their competition with livestock may have been the main reason for their early disappearance, we cannot overlook the comment of Needler (1984: 357) that "An insatiable demand for ivory by the expanding elite doubtless contributed to the elephant's disappearance from Egypt during the Early Dynastic period."

Darby *et al.* (1977: 259) said it is evident that elephants were of no significant importance as a source of food in ancient times.

The elephant first became extinct in Egypt and then in the central Sahara about 2,000 B.C. (Butzer, 1959: 43). Lack of food, shade, and water forced it to continue retreating southward into the limits known today.

Prehistoric records: Neolithic remains of elephants have been found in Dakhla Oasis (Churcher, 1980: 387 f.; 1981: table I; 1982: table I; Churcher *et al.*, 1997) and the Faiyum (Caton-Thompson and Gardner, 1934 I: 72, 84, 89). A concave base arrowhead was found amongst the bones of one animal (*op. cit.*, 72). A molar fragment together with pottery was found in Karkur Ibrahim, Gebel Uweinat and Neolithic remains in Wadi Baqt (Bakht), Gilf el-Kebir by Gautier (1980: 341 f.), who said that elephants may have been very uncommon visitors to the region. He also said: "In fact, their remains may even be manuports" (imports by man).

Several rock drawings in the vicinity of the Qift-Quseir Road in the middle part of the Eastern Desert (figs 10-1,-2) were dated to Epi-Paleolithic by Redford and Redford (1989: figs 9, 12, 13 and 14). One of these (fig. 10-1) was said to be similar to a style found in Nubia (Säve-Söderberg, 1970: corpus G: 2, 8, 32).

The Predynastic period: McArdle (1982: 15) reported elephant bone fragments in surface remains of a Predynastic animal graveyard at Hierakonpolis.

Additional rock drawings from the Qift-Quseir Road were dated to the Late Predynastic by Redford and Redford (*loc.cit.*, figs 44, 45).

Many rock drawings of elephants occur along the eastern and western margins of the Nile Valley, the Eastern Desert, and a few localities in the Western Desert. A variety of styles were depicted, but most of the drawings are easily identified (fig. 1-1).

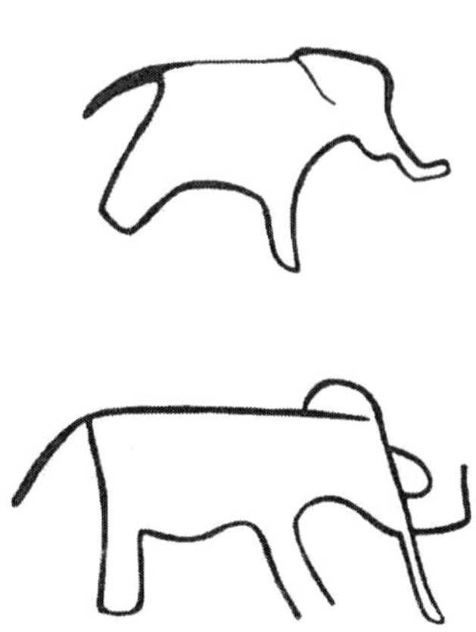

10-8 Rock drawings of two elephants in Wadi el Sharab at the junction with Wadi Mia, 24 km NE of Idfu (Edfu). Source Červíček (1974: fig. 466).

Some drawings are comparable with modern graphic art (fig. 10-3) and a variety of styles were pictured (figs 10-4 to -9). Those with odd 'butterfly wing' ears and the zig-zag mark on the body (figs 10-10 to -14, 13-208) are datable, as Winkler (1939 II: 33) noted, "...with pots and palettes of the Amration Period. We may therefore conclude that the Earliest Hunters lived before and at the time of the Amrations."

A few pottery figures (figs 10-15,-16,-17) and an elephant incised on a slate palette (fig. 10-18) illustrate Winkler's *(op. cit.)* remark.

Another similar rock drawing with one ear up and one down (fig. 10-19) stimulated an odd figure title from Dunbar (1941: pl. XX, fig. 97): 'What is it? A wild boar? A pig eating a fish? An aardvark?'

Lucas and Harris (1962: 32 f.) noted that carvings of ivory objects from both elephant and hippo tusks began in the Neolithic and onwards into the Dynasties.

Váhala (in press) wrote that "Ivory was used to make arrow, spear, and harpoon heads; wands; handles for knives, fans, and whips; mace heads; throw sticks (boomerangs); scoops, spoons, and shallow dishes; disks and figurines for games; articles of jewelry, such as bracelets, anklets, rings, pendants, combs, hairpins, and earings. Very few scarabs and sealing cylinders were preserved, but many tablets, boxes, various sticks, canes, furniture legs, and inlays, etc. have been found. Several carved tusks with a head at the tip (usually bearded), or with other decorations, have also been discovered. Most ivory objects have been found in Upper Egypt south of Asyut; only a few are known north of there."

Not all articles have been identified as to the source of ivory, elephant or hippo, but large objects with a width or diameter of more than six cm were doubtless carved from elephant tusks, as has been noted by Churcher (1984:153), who also remarked that the radii of curvature in hippo tusks are too small to give the straight grain observable in the longer ivory knife handles.

Among the ivory handles (figs 1-7,-8,-9,-11,-12) and the Davis ivory comb (fig. 1-10), probably only the Brooklyn and Pitt Rivers handles (figs 1-7,-8) and the ivory comb (fig. 1-10) are of elephant ivory.

The most interesting figures on these artifacts and also on a Dynasty I gold mace handle (fig. 1-13) are the elephants trampling on snakes. The accuracy of the carving on the Carnarvon handle was described by Bénédite (1918: 234, fig. 2), who pointed out how well some features of the African elephant were depicted: the sloping brow, size of the ears and furrows indicating flexibility, the anatomy of the legs, and the prominence of the iliac bone near the rump (fig. 10-20). The latter is not clear, however, in this copy.

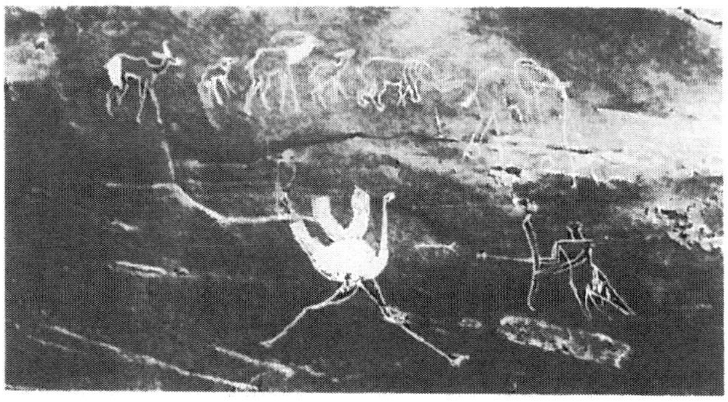

10-9 (top) Rock drawings from the west side of the Nile opposite Silwah by Autochthonous Mountain Dwellers. The row of animals (right to left) includes an elephant, black rhinoceros (?), young oryx, adult scimitar oryx, young oryx, and dorcas gazelle. Below, a man releases an arrow at a running ostrich. Another man with arms raised stands to the left of the ostrich. Source: Winkler (1938 I: pl. XX, 1).

10-10 (bottom left) Rock drawings of an elephant with 'butterfly wing' ears and zig-zag marking on the body; a man, and an ostrich at Kanais. Source: Červíček (1974: fig. 282).

10-11 (bottom right) Rock drawings of two elephants with 'butterfly wing' ears, a boat, and a man at El Hagandia E of the Nile and seven km. N of Silwa. Source: Červíček (1974: fig. 109).

The symbolism of these figures is not known, but they may have been intended to provide the owner with protection from snakes. Montet (1968: fig. 2) remarked that the animosity between these animals was mentioned by the Greek and Roman historians.

Besides elephants being carved in ivory, there is a variety of figurines in pottery (figs 10-21,-22,-23) and in the form of slate palettes.

Another Predynastic theme was reliefs of elephants and other animals standing on what appear to be mountains (figs 10-24,-25).

"The elephant clan, as can be seen from Gerzean vases, founded the town of Iebo, Elephantine, on the island of the same name" (Montet, 1968: 173 f.). The ensign was sometimes shown on figures of boats (fig. 10-26).

An elephant god doubtlessly existed in the Predynastic as indicated from the statuette of a man with the head of an elephant (fig. 10-27), which was discovered by Vercoutter (1959/1960) in a temple in Sudan (Gerster, 1964: 99).

The Dynastic period: During the dynasties elephant tusks were brought by Nubians to the Island of

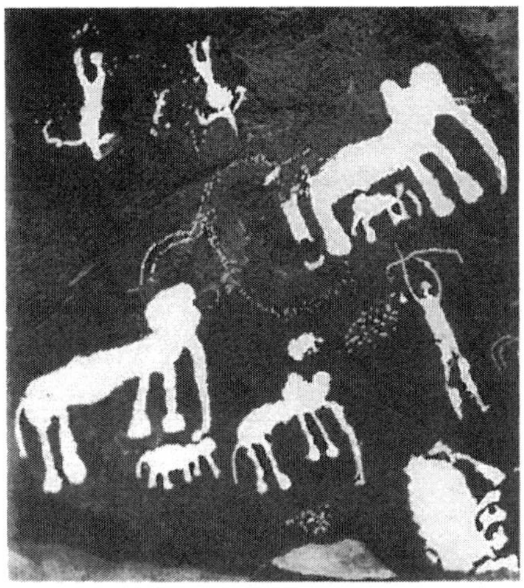

10-12 (left) Rock drawing by Earliest Hunters of elephants with young in a hunting scene at Wadi Atwani, N of the western part of the Qift-Quseir Road. Source: Winkler (1938 I: pl.XXVII, 3).

10-13 (top centre) Rock drawing of a feather decorated man shooting an elephant in Wadi Menih, a southern tributary of Wadi Hammamat SE of Qift (Koptos). Source: Winkler (1937: fig. 14).

10-14 (top right)Rock drawing by Earliest Hunters of an elephant with zig-zag markings on the body. Location: Ghubari Road between Kharga and Dakhla Oases. Source: Winkler (1939 II: pl. LVII, 2).

10-15 (bottom right) Elephants and bulls on Predynastic polished red pottery from El Mahasnah, nine km W of Girga (Girgeh). Source: Scharff (1928: fig. 5).

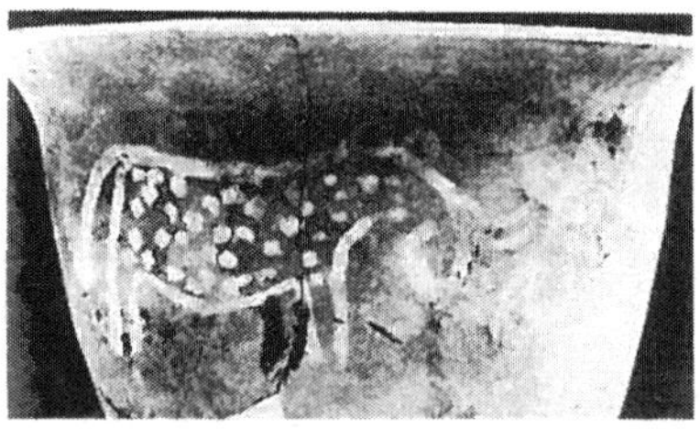

10-16 Elephant on a polished red pottery bowl, Predynastic grave at El Mahasnah. Source: Ayrton and Loat (1911: pl. XIV, 3).

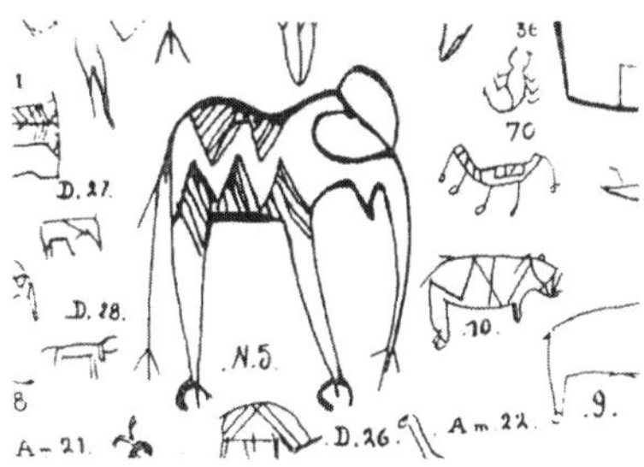

10-17 Elephant with decorative zig-zag markings and other animal etchings from Predynastic pottery. Source: Capart (1905: fig. 111).

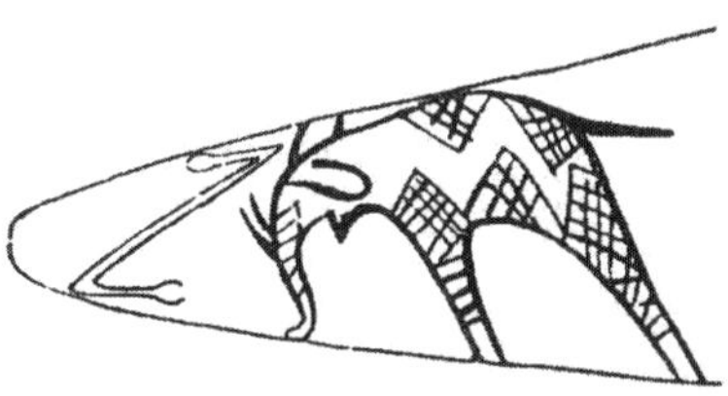

10-18 Elephant with zig-zag markings incised on a Predynastic slate palette from Diospolis Parva SE of Nag Hamadi (Hiw). Source: Petrie (1901 b: pl. XII).

10-19 Rock drawing of an elephant with 'butterfly wing' ears at El Malki N of Korosko (Kurusku). Source: Dunbar (1941: pl. XX, fig. 97).

Elephantine opposite Aswan (Syene) and traded for Egyptian products. The Town of Abu (Ivory Town) on the island was the importation point for trading. It was also the capital of the first province (nome) of Egypt.

Budge (1904 II: 365) said the island was called Elephantine because it resembled the animal in shape "... just as ... Khartoum was called 'elephant's trunk' on account of its resemblance to that part of the body." Later, Budge (1934:83) suggested that the ivory market was the origin of the name of the island.

Váhala (1970) was of the opinion that the name derived from elephant herds having lived there.

Mercatante (1978: 42) said that the island was called Elephantine because the rocks looked like elephants or because it was a depot for ivory trade.

The earliest and most logical conclusion regarding the origin of the name was by Platt (1908) who said that the hieroglyphic for Elephantine meant not the island, "but the 'District of the Elephant Rocks', or Elephant Hills, so-called from their resemblance to the animal" (fig. 10-28) and the granite rocks south of the island (fig 10-29).

There are a few figures that are dated to the Dynastic period. The carving in the Dynasty V Causeway of Unas (fig. 10-30) represents the hieroglyphic determinative for the description of red granite having been brought from Elephantine to build the Pyramid of Unas. The general shape of the figure, however, is very rhinoceros-like.

Another hieroglyph on the kiosk of Senusret, Dynasty VI, at Karnak (fig. 10-31), was said by

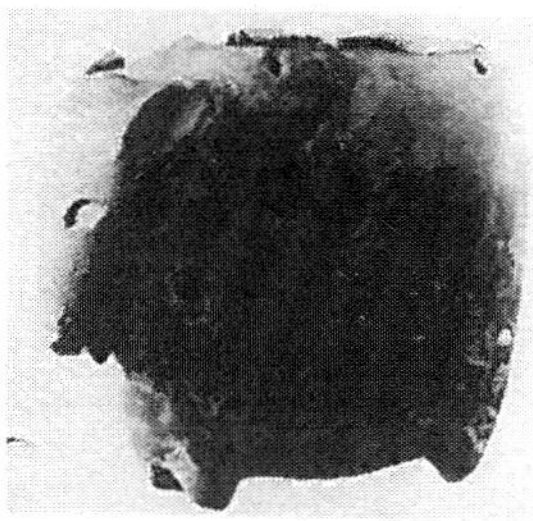

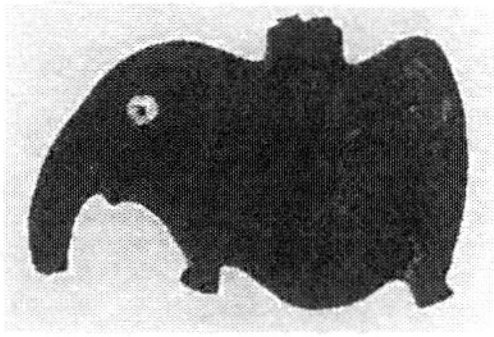

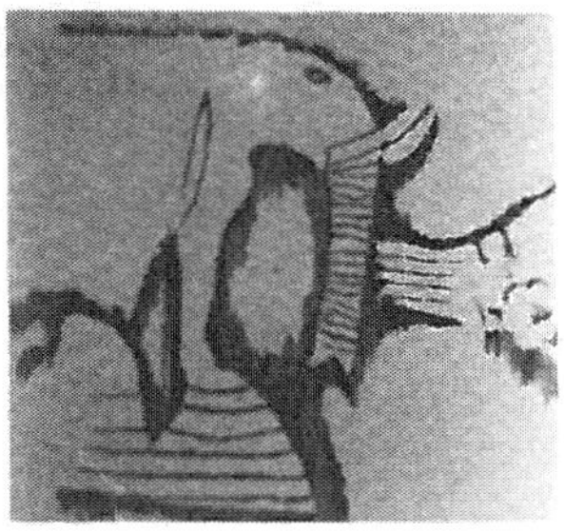

10-20 (top left) Elephant trampling on snakes from the side without boss of the Carnarvon ivory knife handle (fig. 1-9). Source: Bénédite (1918: fig. 2).

10-21 (top centre) Molded elephant on the rim of a Predynastic pot. Source: Scharff (1928: pl. XXVII).

10-22 (top right) Late Predynastic or Early Dynastic pink limestone vase in the shape of an elephant. The lower part of the trunk is broken off. Source: Aldred (1965: ill. 12).

10-23 (bottom left) A cosmetic palette in the shape of an elephant, Naqada I period. Source: Asselberghs (1961: pl. LVI, fig. 99).

10-24 (bottom centre) Ivory carvings of elephants standing on hills, Hierakonpolis, "Dynasty O". Source: Quibell (1900 I: pl. XVI).

10-25 (bottom right) Part of a relief of an elephant standing on a hill on the Min statue, Early Dynasty I, Koptos. Source: Petrie (1896: pl. III, 4).

Fairman (1943: 284) to be "presumably a nisbe {adjective, *sic*} derived from *hw* 'elephant tusk.'" This, like Figure 10-30, also has a rhino-like body.

In several Dynasty XVIII tomb paintings elephant tusks are brought as tribute from Nubia and Punt. Tusks were carried by men (figs 7-21,-22,-23) or shown in piles as in Figure 7-38 and in Davies and Gardiner (1926: pls. XXIII, XXIV).

Syrian tribute to Rekhmire included an Asian elephant and tusks along with a tame bear (fig. 7-95).

Newberry (1944: 75) retold the Dynasty XVIII story related by Amenehab the lieutenant commander who accompanied Tuthmosis III when

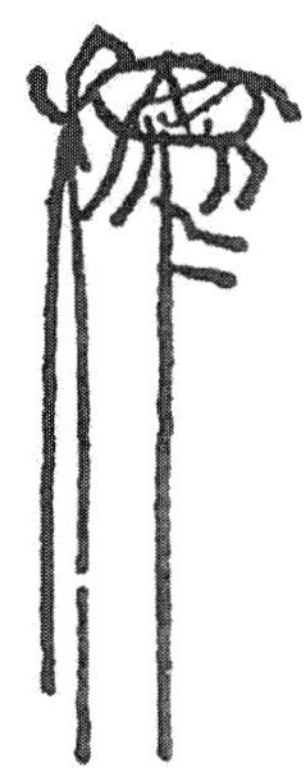

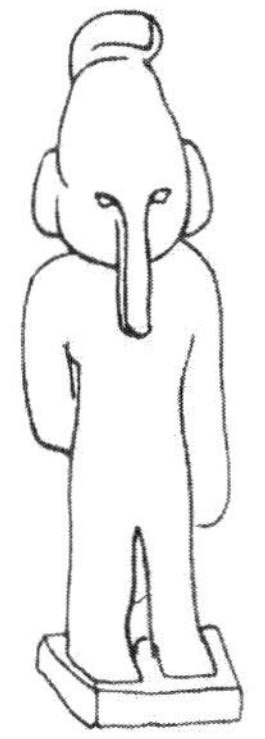

10-26 (left above) Ensign of the Elephant Clan on Predynastic pottery. Source: Montet (1968: fig. 8).

10-27 (right above) Drawing of a statuette of a Predynastic elephant god from temple ruins in Wad Ban Naqa (Naga), Sudan, 155 km N.E. of Khartoum. Source: Gerster (1964: 99, fig. 18).

10-28 (right) 'Elephant Hills' on the south of Elephantine Island. Source: Unknown.

10-29 (left) Granite rocks south of Elephantine Island. Source: Author.

10-30 (above) Elephant hieroglyph in the Causeway of Unas denoting the source of red granite from Elephantine for the Pyramid of Unas, Dynasty V, Saqqara. Source: Author.

hunting a herd of 120 elephants in Niy (Mesopotamia). The largest among them threatened the Pharaoh and Amenehab cut of its dirt *(drt)*, 'hand', and saved Tuthmosis' life, for which he received a gift of gold and raiments. *Drt* was apparently the earliest name for the elephant's trunk.

Errors and discrepancies: Rosen (1994) said the Asian elephant in the Tomb of Rekhmire (fig. 7-95) "... was more like a reconstruction of a living mammoth than an immature elephant."

Obviously the lengths of the tusks indicate a mature elephant. But, as Davies (1935) had previously remarked, the artist kept animals small lest they overpower his procession, but the lengths of the tusks show that he was thinking of an adult elephant.

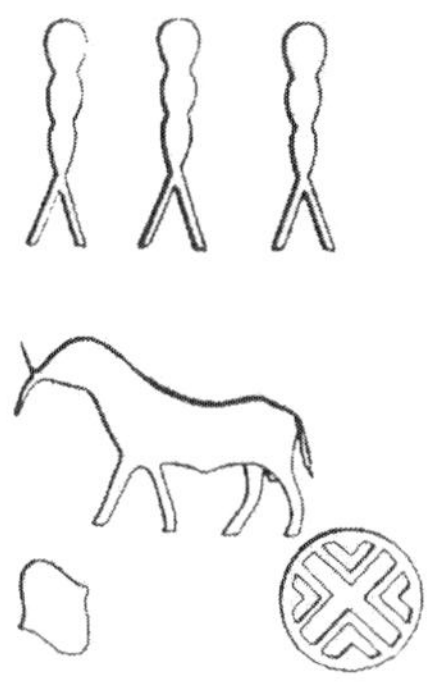

10-31 Elephant hieroglyph on the Kiosk of Senusret, Dynasty VI, Karnak. Source: Fairman (1943: fig. 55).

XI
Order *Hyracoidea*
Family *Procaviidae*

Hyrax ***Procavia capensis*** (Pallas, 1766)

E Coney, Cape Dassie, Rock Dassie, Cape Rock Hyrax, Daman; F Daman de rocher; G Klippschliefer, Wüstenschliefer; A Wabar, Buar, Kalidob, Wabar el Kab

Description: Hyraxes are short-eared and tailless with rabbit-like bodies. The fur is short and grayish to yellowish-brown.

The head and body length is about 40 cm.

Natural history: This animal lives in colonies in cliffs and rock falls and usually in the vicinity of acacia trees. White, bleached urine streaks on rocks are a sign of its presence.

Hyraxes are diurnal and nocturnal, but feed mainly at night. Acacia leaves and pods are staple food, but a variety of plants are eaten.

They are especially adapted to climbing due to glandular cohesive foot pads and almost opposable inner hind toes.

This is the nearest living relative of the elephant.

Distribution: In Egypt distribution is limited to southern Sinai and the Eastern Desert. Further distribution in Africa includes Libya, Algeria, Tibesti, Azbine, Sudan, Ethiopia, and Somalia southwards to South Africa and westwards to Senegal.

This species also occurs in Israel, Lebanon, Syria, and the western and southern Arabian Peninsula (Harrison, 1968 II: 316 f.).

The cutting of acacia trees to produce charcoal and hunting by Bedouins drastically reduced hyrax populations in Sinai and the Eastern Desert (Osborn and Helmy, 1980: 465 f.).

Prehistoric records: Late Paleolithic remains of a hyrax were reported from Wadi Halfa by Gautier (1984: 46 f.). One rock drawing of a hyrax is known from Upper Egypt (fig. 11-1) in Khor Abagag, southeast of Aswan, an area that was once well populated with hyraxes. It was called a 'honey badger' by Červíček (1974: 170).

Lower jaws of a hyrax were found in a site called 'Catfish Cave' near Korosko in Nubia (Reed, 1966b: 40).

The Dynastic period: No illustrations of hyrax have been found in Dynastic art. The Ancient Egyptians must have known the animal, however, because lower jaws were found at Elephantine in Dynasty III-IV Satet temples and in the Dynasty VI cemetery (Boessneck, 1988: 39 f.).

Errors and discrepancies: The lamb's head on a jar (fig. 11-2) in a Dynasty XVIII Syrian tribute scene (fig. 7-217) was erroneously called a 'hyrax' by Gaillard (*in* Montet, 1937: 106). Despite the woolly appearance, long ears, general shape of the head, and the indication of a horn developing above the ear, he said that the short muzzle and the slightly projecting ear remind one of the hyrax.

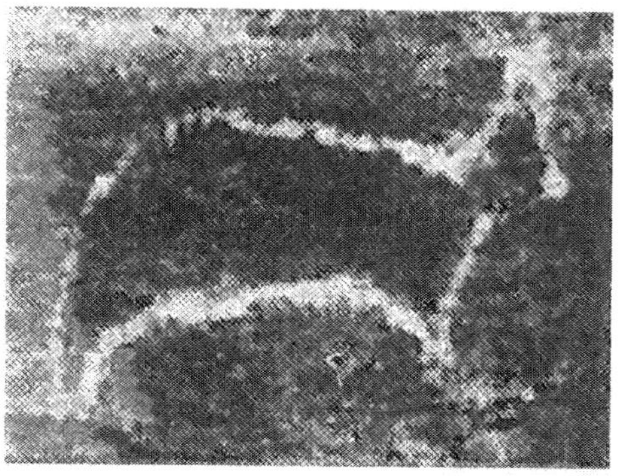

11-1 Rock drawing of a hyrax in Khor Abagag southeast of Aswan. Source: von der Esch (1943: opposite p. 145).

11-2 Head of a lamb, which was called a hyrax, on Syrian pottery in a tribute scene, Tomb of Huy, Dynasty XVIII, Thebes. Source: L.D. III, 116.

XII
Order *Perissodactyla*
Equids Family *Equidae*

Equids are medium to large size horse-like hoofed animals, characterised by the reduction of the number of toes to one. All of them are sociable grass and herbage feeders, living in open habitats (savannahs, steppes, semi-deserts, and sometimes even deserts). They inhabit East, Middle, and Near Eastern Asia, and Southeastern and South Africa.
Recent Equidae are taxonomically treated within one genus, *Equus*, and according to Volf (1977: 137) split into three subgenera: *Equus* (horse), *Asinus* (ass), and *Hippotigris* (zebra). These subgenera are presented by Haltenorth and Diller (1980: 109) on a generic level as g. *Equus*, g. *Asinus*, and g. *Hippotigris*. One more genus, *Hemionus* (onagers), is listed by these authors for the Asian asses, otherwise treated only as a species, *Equus hemionus*, with several subspecies (Volf, *loc. cit.*)

Wild Ass ***Equus asinus africanus*** (Fitzinger, 1857)

 '3 aa Wb. I, 165

E Wild Donkey, Nubian Ass; F Ane sauvage de l'Afrique; G Afrikanischer Wildesel; A Homar el Wadi, Homar Beri, Homar Gabaly

Nomenclature: Equus asinus asinus (Linnaeus, 1758) was the name given to the domestic donkey, and *E. a. africanus* (Fitzinger, 1857) to the northeast African wild ass or Nubian wild ass (see Gotch, 1979: 197). The Nubian ass is considered to have been the ancestor of the domestic donkey.

Note that Dorst (1970:159) used the Latin name *Equus (Asinus) asinus* L.; Haltenorth and Diller (1980: 159), *Asinus africanus* (Fitzinger, 1857); and Gotch (1979: 197), *Equus africanus*.

Description: Wild ass are slender and horse-like with large heads and long ears. The back and sides are pale gray with a reddish tint; legs are paler; the eye ring, muzzle, underside of lower jaw, and venter are white. There is a short mane on the neck. The tail is long and tufted and extends slightly below the hocks. There is a prominent black shoulder stripe or cross (fig. 12-1). In the Nubian race there are no stripes on the head, neck or legs as there are in the Somalian race.

Shoulder height is 115-125 cm.

Natural history: Wild asses live in small herds and occupy arid, remote wadis and plains with xerophytic vegetation (Ziccardi, 1970) and are capable of traversing rocky terrain (Floyer, 1887: 671). They normally drink water daily, but can survive two or three days without water. Like other semidesert animals, they spend most of the day in shade and are active in late afternoon, night, and early morning.

Distribution: Equus asinus africanus according to Churcher (1971: 373 f.) entered Egypt from Sinai during Paleolithic and eventually replaced *E. burchelii*, and occupied all of North Africa during the Late Pleistocene. Today they are limited to southeastern parts of Egypt and northeastern Sudan, Eritrea, Somalia, and possibly northern Chad. Individuals are only occasionally seen in the southeastern desert of Egypt. The latest records are Wadi Allaqi in 1974 and Wadi Diib in 1981 (I. Helmy, pers. com.). Further data on 'recent' sightings are in Osborn and Helmy (1980: 472 ff.).

Prehistoric and Predynastic records: There are numerous sites in Egypt where wild ass remains, especially teeth, have been found. Gautier (1980:

12-1 (left) A semi-domesticated wild ass belonging to the Ababda Bedouin tribe of the southern Eastern Desert (Nubia). Gebel Qattar, about 48 km west-southwest of Hurghada, is in the background. Source: Author.

12-2 (right) Rock drawing of a wild ass at Kanais (El Kanäyis) in Wadi Mia 45 km east of Edfu (Idfu). Source: Červíček (1974): fig.255).

12-3 (left) Rock drawing by Eastern Invaders of a boat, wild asses, men, and a pariah dog. Location: Wadi Abu Wasilin the Eastern Desertabout 95 km southeast of Qus. Source: Winkler (1938 I: pl. XXIII, 1).

12-4 (right) Rock drawing by Autochthonous Mountain Dwellers of wild asses caught in the nooses on spiked wheel traps. Two hunters are included in the scene. Location: Wadi Abu Wasil in the Eastern Desert about 95 km southeast of Qus. Source: Winkler (1938 I: pl. XVIII, 2).

320 f., 341) recognized wild ass fragments from several sites in the southern and southwestern Western Desert, dated to the Middle Paleolithic at Bir Tarfawi and Bir Sahara and the Neolithic in Wadi Bakht (Baqt) in Gilf el Kebir. Late Paleolithic remains in shoreline deposits have also been found in Faiyum (Butzer and Hanson, 1968).

Churcher's (1983: 181; 1986: 420) findings from Early Neolithic sites in Dakhla Oasis included teeth and other remains.

Reed and Turnbull (1969: 55) assigned equid material in the Late Pleistocene sites in Nubia (Kom Ombo and Wadi Halfa) to the Nubian ass, *Equus asinus*. This included Gaillard's (1934) find of a tooth he had referred to as '*Equus caballus*'.

Churcher (1972: 48 ff., table 5; 1974: 367, 373, table 1) also catalogued remains from several sites of Late Pleistocene deposits in the vicinity of Kom Ombo: Oasis Depression, Gebel Silsila, and the Sebil area.

Wendt and Reed (1966: 41 f.) listed a phalanx (toe bone) from the Paleolithic site of Wadi Or (Mor) south of Abu Simbel in Nubia.

Bronze and Copper Age remains of wild ass from Maadi and Elephantine were recorded by Boessneck and von den Driesch (1982: 22).

Rock drawings of wild ass in Egypt and Nubia date to Late Prehistoric time (Červíček, 1974: 172).

A clear example of a wild ass (fig. 12-2) is of interest because of its similarity, except for the longer neck, with the ass on the comb in Figure 12-8.

12-5 Hunting scene in the Tomb of Mentuherkh-hepeshef, Dynasty XVIII, Thebes. A jackal or fox is grabbing the foal of a wild ass. In front of the ass are three dorcas gazelles. Source: Davies (1913: pl. XII).

A load carrying ass was also described by Winkler (1938 I: pl. XVI,1) in an Early Nile Valley Dwellers rock drawing, which suggests early taming of this animal. The figure is not clear, however.

In two early Predynastic rock drawings (figs 12-3,-4) the wild asses were referred to by Nibbi (1979: 152) as domestic donkeys. Those in Figure 12-3 he said were towing the boat, but there is no evidence for this in the drawing. Those in Figure 12-4 he described as domestic donkeys tethered to a post in the ground. The correct interpretation, however, would be as Winkler (1938 I: 21) has noted: They are wild asses caught with what are called 'spiked wheel traps'. Above the wheel is a loop or snare through which the animal can put its foot. The spiked wheel prevents the loop from falling off the animal's foot. The other end of the rope is attached to a peg or a log or stone drag.

Another interesting error by Nibbi (*op. cit.*, 151) is his description of the man in jackal or fox disguise on the Hierakonpolis palette (fig. 1-2,b) as a 'man imitating a wild ass'.

In a drawing of a hunting scene (fig. 7-11) by Early Nile Valley Dwellers (Pre- to Early Dynastic) an ass is faced by a pariah dog in the upper left.

Rows A 5 and B 5 on the Predynastic ivory knife handle from Abu Zaidan (Zeidan) (fig. 1-7, Table I) were identified as wild ass.

The Dynastic period: Churcher (1981: 200, table 1; 1982: table 1) listed wild ass remains from the Old Kingdom in Dakhla Oasis.

In the Dynasty XII Tomb of Ukh-hotep (fig. 7-28) and duplicate (fig. 7-66) a fox is sniffing at the foal of a wild ass. Another wild ass is shown foaling on another panel in the tomb (fig. 7-29). There are similar scenes in the Dynasty XVIII Tombs of Mentuherkh-hepeshef and Kenamun (figs 12-5 and 7-68) where a jackal or fox is grabbing the

12-6 *Hunting scene called 'The Desert Hunt' on Tutankhamun's painted box. Source: Davies and Gardiner (1962: pl. III). Tutankhamun in his chariot is not shown in the photo. The animals are left to right:*
Reg. 1. Three dorcas gazelles and three bubals.
Reg. 2. Dorcas gazelle, bubal, and young bubal.
Reg. 3. Bubal pierced with three arrows, four wild asses (two are without shoulder stripes), and an arrow-pierced bubal on its back.
Reg. 4. Dorcas gazelle, bubal, and a striped hyena.
Reg. 5. An arrow pierced bubal, two ostriches, and a somersaulting arrow-pierced bubal.
Reg. 6. Two salukis subduing arrow-pierced bubals and a third saluki grabbing the neck of the last of five arrow- pierced bubals.

foal. The shoulder stripes on these asses are shown only on Figure 7-68.

Although there are numerous scenes of wild ass being hunted, Clark (1971: 57) noted that they were not shown among the animals hunted in Beni Hasan scenes.

Later hunting scenes show Tutankhamun and Ramses III and his helper in their chariots chasing and shooting wild asses and various other animals (figs 12-6 and frontispiece). Two of the asses in Figure 12-6 have shoulder stripes, but none of them in the Frontispiece.

Domestic Ass *Equus asinus asinus* (Linnaeus, 1758)

'3-ḥmt aa-hemet Wb. I, 165

E Donkey; F Ane, Baudet; G Esel; A Homar, Homar Beity, Atan (female)

Nomenclature: Equus asinus asinus Linnaeus (1758) is the accepted Latin name for the domestic donkey.

Description: Domestic asses are paler in color than wild asses and white varieties are common. The shoulder stripe, which appears on early domestic forms, 'is lacking in Middle Kingdom and later donkeys' (Brewer *et al.*, 1994: 100). An exception is in the Dynasty XII tomb in Figure 12-10.

Ancestry: Evidence that the wild ass was the progenitor of the domestic ass was clarified by Brewer *et al.*(1994: 99) who noted that the chromosome number was the same in both races and 'that crosses between these two forms produce fertile offspring'. Crosses between other forms can produce living offspring, but they are not fertile.

Natural history: The donkey from earliest times was much more than a farm or draft animal and was a hardy and adaptable beast of burden, fulfilling most of the functions that were performed later by the camel (Carrington, 1972: 70). Several of such activities are referred to below.

Prehistoric and Predynastic records: The earliest representation of the domestic donkey is on the

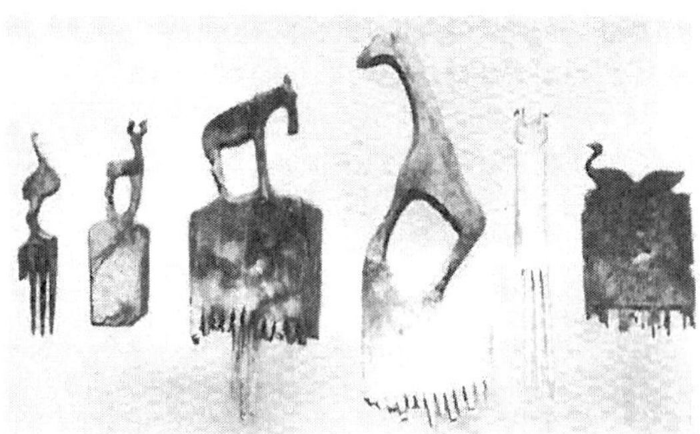

12-7 (left) Reverse of the Predynastic Libyan or Towns Palette from Abydos (Early Gerzean, Nagada II), with rows of domestic cattle, donkeys, and screw-horned sheep. Source: Asselberghs (1961: pl. XCII, 165).

12-8 (right) Predynastic ivory combs with handles of ostrich, bubal, ass, giraffe, birds, and geese. Provenances were not listed. Source: Hayes (1953 I: fig. 12).

reverse of the Libyan or Towns Palette (fig. 12-7). They are pictured together with domestic cattle and screw-horned sheep, and said to have represented booty from Libya and to be dated to the late 4,000 B.C. (Boessneck, 1988: fig. 12). This palette was also called the Tehenu Palette after the land of the Libyans beyond the oases of the Western Desert.

Although the donkey was estimated to have been domesticated in the Nile Valley (Zeuner, 1963: 376) in the Early Gerzean period (3,600 B.C.), Zeuner (*op. cit.*) remarked that Antonius (1922) thought it was first domesticated in Libya and that the practice spread to Egypt. This theory could be attributed to the data on the Libyan Palette.

The donkeys on this palette have very large shoulder markings, which Nibbi (1979: 148) said were broader than true markings and the donkeys were wearing their forward harness.

The markings appear to be no more than an artist's exaggeration when compared with the shoulder marks on the cattle above.

The handles of Predynastic ivory combs (fig. 12-8) include an ass, which was called "the strange okapi" by Hayes (1953 I: 20). 'A small ivory donkey' (Ayrton and Loat, 1911: pl. XII, 2) from the Predynastic cemetery at El Mahasna is comparable with the one in Figure 12-8.

Despite the general acceptance of Egypt or Libya having been the areas of original domestication of the donkey, Uerpmann (1987: 141 f.) in reference to bones found at Uruk (Iraq) by Boessneck, von den Driesh, and Steger (1984), and dated to the end of the 4th millenium B.C., said that the evidence from Mesopotamia was better at the present state of research.

The Dynastic period: There are a few examples of domesticated donkeys in Dynasty I graves. The earliest were three young donkeys in a grave at Abusir (Boessneck *et al.*, 1992: 2). Three donkeys were also found in a Dynasty I grave at Turkhan, west bank, 37 miles south of Cairo. They were referred to as "favourite animals buried with the master", because of the careful mode of burial (Petrie, 1914: 6).

The donkey never became commonly used as a riding animal, but a seat called a palanquin or sedan chair fitted between two donkeys was popular with the upper class (fig. 12-9).

Uerpman (1987: 141 f., fig. 62) presented a similar scene (reproduced from Zeuner, 1967, and dated Dynasty V). He considered it "The oldest clear evidence for the use of the donkey in Egypt ..." and he continued: "The Predynastic people of southern Mesopotamia and the Nile Valley may both have domesticated this animal, the evidence from Mesopotamia being better at the present state of research".

12-9 Nianchnum riding in a palanquin (sedan chair) between two donkeys, Dynasty V, Saqqara. Source: Moussa and Altenmüller (1977: pl. 42).

Scenes of donkeys trampling grain in place of the usual oxen appear in various tombs including the Dynasty V Tomb of Ti (fig. 1-17) and the Dynasty XII Tomb of Tehutihetep (fig. 12-10). Note that in some of these figures the shoulder stripes are still present.

In the Dynasty V Tomb of Akhet-hetep a donkey carries sheaves of grain represented by the pyramidal figures on its back (fig. 12-11). In another Dynasty V tomb (fig. 13-154) a donkey is carrying a basket full of young gazelles from the desert.

Donkeys were also used to carry stones from quarries to building sites and supplies for workmen as well as for the Pharaoh's armies.

The importance of this domesticated beast can be realized by the numbers that were kept in droves. For example Epstein (1971 II: 393) noted that in the Dynasty IV Tomb of Khaf-Re-Ank at Giza a scribe recorded 760 asses among his master's

12-10 (top) Six donkeys trampling grain in the Tomb of Tehutihetep, Dynasty XII, El Bersheh. Source: Newberry (1892 I: pl. XXXI).

12-11 (bottom) A donkey in an agriculture scene carrying sheaves of grain. Tomb of Akhet-hetep, Dynasty V, Saqqara. Source: Davies (1901a: pl. VII).

herds of over 5,000 animals and in other tombs of the same period over 1,000 asses belonged to individual owners. Erman (1894: 473) mentioned that 50 oxen and 200 donkeys carried supplies for 350 men working in the quarries of Wadi Hammamat.

Other comments that emphasized the donkey's importance were made by Nibbi (1979: 168), "that the well-treated ass may continue to work until his twenty-fifth year," and Janssen and Janssen (1989: 37), that "the animal could work up to its fortieth year or even longer". Neither authors gave citations.

Decorative figures of donkeys appeared on Predynastic combs (fig. 12-8), cosmetic palettes (Darby *et al.*, 1977: 235), and pottery (fig. 12-12).

Various parts of the donkey (Darby *et al.*, 1977: 236), as with many other animals, were used medicinally, such as fat, liver, blood, bone-marrow, and gonads. Donkey milk also had medicinal use (*op. cit.*, 580, 764), and was given to children and adults.

Although Darby *et al.* (1977: 235) said that the flesh of the donkey was not eaten, the scenes of wild ass being hunted (figs 12-6 and frontispiece) suggest an opposite opinion. Of course the skins were doubtless used for making leather, but the flesh is edible. This may have been a reason for the ass having been a sacrificial animal (Erman, 1894: 509).

Despite the practical uses of the donkey and its importance in the Egyptian economy, in later times it became associated with the evil god Seth (Budge, 1904a II: 397).

Darby *et al.* (1977 I: 235) remarked that the donkey eventually became the 'supreme scapegoat' and that its image was destroyed in magic rituals.

12-12 A male ass outlined on a Middle Kingdom pot from cemetery 118, at El Allaqi. Source: Firth (1927b: fig. 6,3).

Domestic Horse ***Equus caballus*** (Linnaeus, 1758)

[hieroglyphs] *ššmt* *zezemet* Wb. IV, 276

E Horse; F Cheval; G Pferd, Ross; A Housan, Faras, Moher

Nomenclature: The Latin name *caballus* means 'a pack horse, a nag' (Gotch, 1979: 196).

12-13 A horse (above) and hinnies (below) pulling chariots in the Tomb of Nebamun, Dynasty XVIII, Thebes. Source: Brewer et al. *(1994: fig. 8.3).*

Description: Horses of ancient times were very similar to the Arabian horse of today. Shoulder height was about 135 cm and bodies were slender. A good example is in Figure 12-13. There is a forelock and a prominent mane. Tail hairs are very long and begin at the base in comparison with the mule and donkey that have long hairs only on the distal half of the tail. The dominant colors of horses were brown and reddish-brown; gray or white, pale yellow, black and dappled were also portrayed (Boessneck, 1988: 81).

Natural history: The Egyptian horse, like its immediate ancestor, was bred and used as a swift animal to pull chariots; and there are also numerous examples of it being ridden.

Predynastic records: A single tooth from Pleistocene (Sebilian) deposits on the Kom Ombo plain that was determined to be from *Equus caballus* by Gaillard (1934) was classified later as being *E. asinus* (Reed and Turnbull, 1969; Churcher, 1972: 50).

The Dynastic period: The earliest known skeletal remains of the horse in Egypt are from the fortress of Buhen at the second cataract of the Nile in what is now Sudanese Nubia. When this building was first destroyed in 1675 B.C. a horse was killed and covered with debris. The burial of the horse was

12-14 (top left) Rock drawing of a man riding a horse dated to the Middle Kingdom (?). Wadi Naam north of Bir Abrak in the southeastern Eastern Desert. Source: Červíček (1974: fig. 99).

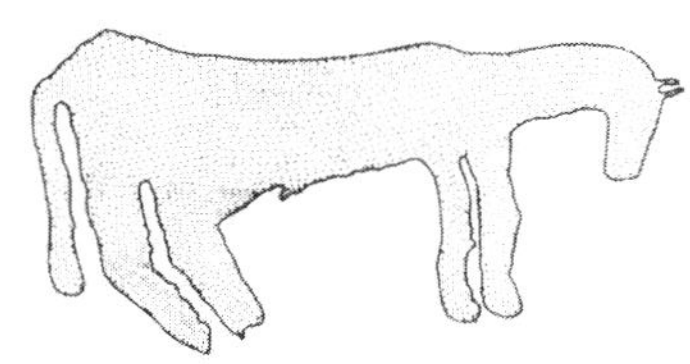

12-15 (top right) Rock drawing of a horse dated to the New Kingdom or later. El Hosh on the west bank of the Nile south of Edfu (Idfu). Source: Červíček (1974: fig. 154).

12-16 (bottom left) Rock drawing of a horse feeding from a manger dated to the New Kingdom or later. El Hosh on the west bank of the Nile south of Edfu (Idfu). Source: Červíček (1974: fig. 142).

12-17 (bottom right) Rock drawings of riders on horses armed with lances and swords, dated to X Group (250–600 A.D.). Aswan. Source: Červíček (1974: fig. 67).

found by Emery (1965: 107). The animal was identified later as being 19 years old (Clutton-Brock, 1974: 89 f.). There is no further evidence of the horse in the Nile Valley until Dynasty XVIII, when another horse, 5-6 years old, and in its own coffin, was found in the Tomb of Senmut, 1430-1400 B.C., at Thebes (Clutton-Brock, 1974: 93 f.).

The Buhen record serves to predate the numerous rock drawings of horses along both banks of the Nile River and in the southeastern desert that were published by Červíček (1974). A few of these are in Figs 12-14 to -17. An interesting feature of these drawings is that in most of them the animals are ridden.

Re-introduction of the horse began during the Hyksos invasion of Egypt (ca. 1730 B.C.) some 2-3,000 years after its domestication in Asia. Large numbers of horses were imported and the Egyptians probably "based their handling practices on the established skills of the Hyksos and other Asiatics" (Brewer, *et al.*, 1994: 101).

Horses continued to be imported into Egypt during Dynasty XVIII following the overthrow of the Hyksos. Syrians brought horses as tribute (fig. 12-18) and Egyptian pharaohs captured booty, such as that of Tuthmosis III from Megiddo, Syria, numbering "2041 horses, 191 young animals, both male and female, six stallions, and a number of foals" (Brewer, *et al.*, 1994: 102).

Illustrations of horses drawing chariots are numerous in New Kingdom battle and hunting scenes (figs 7-206,-207, 12-6, and frontispiece). The postures of the latter were called the 'flying gallop' (see more in Introduction, figs 1-18,-23). Baikie (1932: 610) described this posture as "a rocking horse action from which the Egyptian artists could never get away in the render of a horse".

In the Tomb of Nebamun (fig. 12-13) a horse and hinnies are shown pulling chariots. A hinny is the offspring of a female donkey and a male horse (stallion). A mule is the offspring of a male donkey and a female horse (mare).

Nibbi (1979: 167) commented that the mule and the hinny were not common in ancient Egypt because of difficulties in breeding and their lack of interfertility.

The riding of horses became popular in the New Kingdom, especially with a small, but important, branch of 'mounted scouts' in the Egyptian army (Schulmann, 1957). They were much more adaptable than horse drawn chariots; being able to move more rapidly in rough terrain.

Saddles were not produced in those days, but saddle cloths apparently helped to keep the riders in a good position.

Schulmann's illustrations (*op. cit.*, figs 1 to 7) and descriptions clearly indicate the popularity of horse-riding in the New Kingdom. These included Phillip's wooden statuette of a horse ridden by its young groom (fig. 12-19); a relief; various ostraca and statuettes; a horse and rider on a bronze battle axe and the handle of a bronze razor. Galloping horses also decorated other toilet implements (Janssen and Janssen, 1989: figs 32, 33) and a charioteer's whip handle (fig. 12-20).

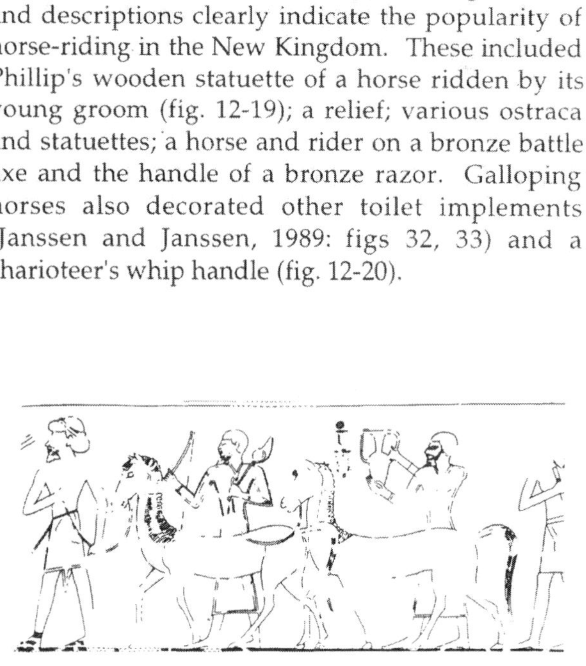

12-18 Horses in Syrian tribute in the Tomb of Amunedjeh, Dynasty XVIII, Thebes. Source: Davies and Davies (1941: pl.XIII).

12-19 A painted wooden statuette of a horse being ridden by its young groom from early Dynasty XVIII at Sohag. Source: Phillips (1948: fig. 38).

12-20 A charioteers' whip handle in the shape of a horse carved from ivory and painted. Dynasty XVIII, Thebes. Source: Phillips (1948: fig. 39).

Phillips (1948: fig. 38) remarked that the statuette is one of the earliest reproductions of the horse in Egypt. Schulman (1957: 266) and Rommelaere (1991: 48) said the white lines respresented either piebald patterns or artistic decorations. The latter is more probable.

Zebras

Zebras were apparently unknown to Ancient Egyptians as no artistic depictions were found.

Palaeozoological research, however, revealed the existence of the following species of this group in the territory of Egypt.

Burchell's Zebra *Equus burchelli* (Gray, 1824)

F Zèbre de steppe; G Steppenzebra

Nomenclature: Dorst and Dandelot (1969: 162) listed this zebra as *Equus (Hippotigris) burchelli* Gray; and Haltenorth and Diller (1980: 113) as *Hippotigris (Quagga) quagga* (Gmelin, 1788).

Distribution: According to Churcher (1974: 374) "the absence of zebras from Sinai or Palestine for the Pleistocene suggests that *E. burchelli* was the original equid inhabitant of north eastern Africa." Replacement in northern Africa by *Equus asinus* was already mentioned above (see *Natural history* in Wild Ass). The present distribution is the eastern and south eastern part of Africa south of the Sahara.

Prehistoric records: Although Churcher (1982: table 1) listed this species from Dakhla Oasis in Late Neolithic sites, his later finds (Churcher, 1983: fig. 2; 1986b: 420) indicated that *E. burchelli* was no longer part of the Neolithic fauna of Dakhla Oasis.

Grevy's Zebra *Equus grevyi* (Oustalet, 1882)

F Zèbre de Grévy; G Grevyzebra

Nomenclature: Dorst and Dandelot (1969: 159) list it as *Equus (Dolichohippus) grevyi* Oustalet, and Haltenorth and Diller (1980: 112) as *Hippotigris (Dolichohippus) grevyi* (Oustalet, 1882).

Distribution: This zebra lives in arid areas of southern Ethiopia, northern Kenya, and southwestern Somalia (Churcher, 1993b: 1 f., fig. 5).

Prehistoric records: Remains dated to the early Neolithic have been collected in two localities in Dakhla Oasis by Churcher (1983: 179; 1986a: 1; 1986b: 415 ff., 420; 1993b: 2).

[Cape Zebra *Equus capensis*]

Fragmentary Quarternary remains from Dakhla Oasis have been tentatively identified as the extinct Cape zebra, *E. capensis* (Churcher *et al.*, 1997).

Rhinoceroses
Family *Rhinocerotidae*

 *jrb3* irba Wb I, 115

General description: African rhinos are large, thick-skinned, and hairless, except for fringes on the ear tips and tassled tails. The ears are long and tubular; tails of medium length. The feet have five hoofed toes. There are usually two horns on the upper nose; the front one being the longest (fig. 12-21).

The 'horns' do not have a core and sheath, but are solid masses of keratin, a substance like that of fingernails, which is formed from skin cells (Ryder, 1962).

Two species occurred in Ancient Egypt, but both disappeared in the Late Predynastic or Early Dynastic.

Black Rhinoceros *Diceros bicornis* (Linnaeus, 1758)

F Rhinocéros noir; G Nashorn, Spitzmaulnashorn; A Khartteet Eswed, Karkadan

12-21 Rock drawing by Autochthonous Mountain Dwellers of a black rhinoceros at Site 35 between Hosh and Wadi Sab'er Rigal on the west bank of the Nile opposite Silwa Bahari, about 27 km N of Kom Ombo. Source: Winkler (1938 I: pl. XXI).

Nomenclature: The name derives from *di-* (dis, Gr) two; *keras* (Gr) a horn; *bi-* from *bis* (L) twice, two; *cornu* (L), genitive *cornus*, the horn of an animal; so here it is first in Greek for the genus, and then in Latin for the species; a 'two-horned two-horn' (Gotch, 1979: 199 f.).

Description: The black rhino is grey. There is no hump on the neck. The upper lip is narrow and has a prehensile projection; an adaptation for browsing.

Natural history: Black rhinos inhabit mainly bushland and open forest, although they may be found in savanna with little cover and in dense forest.

Gautier (1980: 321) commented that although both species of rhinoceros may occur together, the browsing black rhino generally occurs in lusher vegetation, which may account for the black rhino having lived along the Nile and the white rhino in the Western Desert.

Black rhinos are active during early morning and late evening, but remain in shade or in mud wallows during the heat of the day. They normally drink every day, but in the dry season can survive

12-22 Rock drawing of a black rhinoceros in a hunting scene near Abrak in the southern Eastern Desert. Source: Cervíček (1974: fig. 23).

without water for several days. Foliage of numerous flowering plants, shrubs, and trees is browsed, but grass is rarely eaten.

These rhinos are generally solitary, except for mating pairs, females with young, small groups of immature animals, and gatherings of both sexes of various ages in mud wallows.

Distribution: The present distribution is in scattered areas south of the Sahara in central, southeastern, and southwestern Africa and a large area including southern Sudan, and Ethiopia southward into Mozambique (Haltenorth and Diller, 1980: 115 f.).

This rhinoceros has not been reduced by poaching as severely as the white rhinoceros, probably because it is more difficult to hunt.

Prehistoric and Predynastic records: Rock drawings of black rhinos are known from several localities in the Eastern Desert (figs 12-21,-22). Fossil records are rare.

Further notes on black rhinos are in the *Dynastic period* in the white rhinoceros section.

White Rhinoceros *Ceratotherium simum* (Burchell, 1817)

E Square-lipped Rhinoceros; F Rhinocéros blanc; G Nashorn, Breitmaulnashorn; A Khartteet Abyad

Nomenclature: The name apparently derives from *kerato* (Gr) horn *therion* (Gr) beast and *simum* (L) snub-nosed or flat-nosed.

Description: The white rhino is not white, but a lighter grey than the black rhino. There is a prominent nuchal hump on the neck, and the head is usually carried low. Other features are similar to those of the black rhino, except the front horn is usually very long, the body is larger, and the upper lip is very broad, an adaptation for grazing (plucking grass).

Natural history: White rhinos require shrubby areas for shelter and trees for shade, and grassy plains for

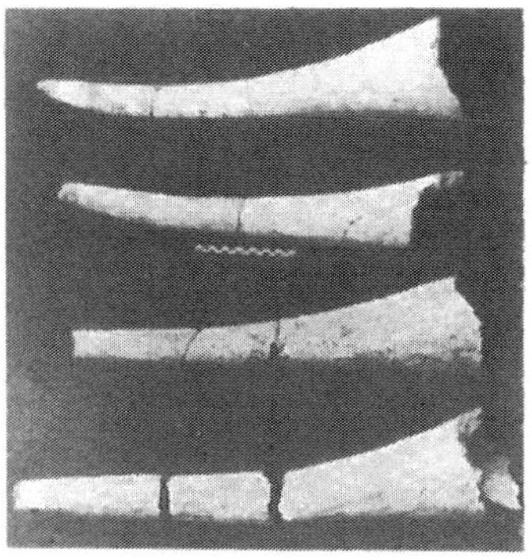

12-23 Pottery horns of white (?) rhinoceroses in the Mastaba of Hor-Aha, Dynasty I, Saqqara. Source: Emery (1939: pl. 17,B).

12-24 Bone and rawhide carvings of rhinos from the Middle Kingdom site of Kerma in southern Nubia. Source: Hilzheimer (1931: figs. 1,2).

grazing. Otherwise, their habits are similar to those of the black rhino, although they can survive for longer periods without drinking water.

Distribution: The present distribution of this species is limited to scattered localities in the southern half of Africa (Haltenorth and Diller, 1980: 118 f.). There are recent records from southern Sudan (Setzer, 1956: 570). Migration south of the Sahara was doubtless induced by the desertification that began in the Late Predynastic to early Dynastic after 3,000 B.C.

Prehistoric records: The distribution of this species in ancient times from west of the Nile valley across

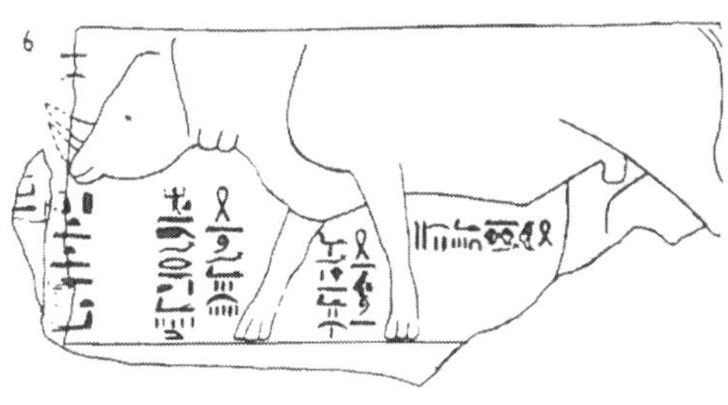

12-25 Drawing of a sunken relief of a white rhinoceros on the Dynasty XVIII pylon of Tutmosis III, in the Temple of Armant (Hermonthis), west bank of the Nile, about 16 km S.W. of Luxor. Source: Mond and Myers (1940: pl. XCIII, 6).

12-26 Drawing of a fantastic beast in the Tomb of Baqt, Dynasty XI, Beni Hasan. Source: Keimer (1948c: fig. 4).

North Africa is verified by a few archeological records. Churcher (1980: 388) found tooth fragments of *Ceratotherium simum* (?) in a Neolithic site in Dakhla Oasis. Gautier (1980: 321, table A 4.2) listed remains of white rhino from Upper Pleistocene (Terminal Paleolithic and Neolithic) at Bir Tarfawi and Bir Sahara in the southern Western Desert. Regarding north-western Africa, Kowalski and Rzebik-Kowalska (1991: 30) said that the fauna of the Acheulian Culture (Lower Paleolithic) in the Erg Tihoudaine on the edge of the Tassili n'Ajjers Mts. contained remains of *C. simum* and that fossil records were recorded in the Magreb from Pliocene to Holocene (*op. cit.*, 24, table III). Hufnagl (1972: 17 f.) listed rhinos from Miocene to Recent in Libya.

The Dynastic period: Various illustrations and artifacts of black and white rhinos appeared in the Dynasties. Not all of them can be unmistakenly identified to species; therefore, both 'species' are included in this and the following subdivisions.

In the Dynasty I Mastaba of Hor-Aha at Saqqara a number of pottery rhinoceros horns were found. These were imperishable imitations along with offerings of meat, vegetables, and bread (fig. 12-23).

Rhinoceros horns were believed to have strong magical powers and for that reason the King was given these lasting and destruction-resisting imitations in his grave.

Rhinoceros horns were and continue to be important in folk medicine in Egypt and other parts of Africa and also in Asia. They are supposed to be a strong aphrodisiac when ground into a powder.

Powdered horn mixed with water and drunk is still believed by Bedouins of the Kushmaan Clan of the Maaza Tribe in the Eastern Desert to be "an excellent treatment for scorpion stings and snake bites, although few people have owned or tried this remedy" (Hobbs, 1989: 63).

Middle Kingdom bone and rawhide carvings of white and black rhinos (fig. 12-24, left and right) from Kerma in southern Nubia (Sudan), although partly damaged, are recognizable.

On the Dynasty XVIII pylon of Tuthmosis III in the Temple of Armant (Hermonthis) on the west bank of the Nile, about 16 km S.W. of Luxor, there is a sunken relief depicting a white (?) rhinoceros (fig. 12-25). Tuthmosis III reportedly killed the beast in the vicinity of Miu in the southern desert region of Nubia.

A number of measurements are inscribed below the figure. These were translated into inches by Mond and Myers (1940: 204) and said to be comparable with the measurements from black and white rhinos. Measurements listed were length of limbs; height of forleg from the ground;

circumference of the foot, and of the back leg; size of horn, and girth.

Further remarks and dating of rhinoceros figures are in the *Errors and discrepancies*.

Greco-Roman times: During the three centuries when rhinos appeared in Rome they were thought to have been imported through Egypt from west of the Nile in Sudan.

Keimer (1948c:50) wrote that information on rhinoceros importation to Egypt (Alexandria) and to Rome proved that importations were from Asia as well as Africa.

Errors and discrepancies: Various reproductions show that the Ancient Egyptian artists could not clearly distinguish rhinoceroses from elephants nor from hippopotamuses.

A good example is the 'fantastic beast' with a single horn in the Dynasty XI Tomb of Baqt in Beni Hasan (fig. 12-26), which is labelled *3bw*, elephant. It was called an 'elephant' by Hilzheimer (1926: fig. 3) and a 'fantastic animal (Elephant-Rhinoceros)' by Keimer (1948c: 52, fig. 4).

Davies (1933a: 26) said that the single horn brought it nearer to the rhinoceros and ..."At a time when knowledge of both animals could come only from second-hand reports of visitants to the far south, their characteristics could easily be confused."

Four horns labelled elephant ivory that are pictured in the Dynasty XVIII Temple of Deir el Bahari and that were called rhinoceros horns by Naville (1898 III: 14, pl. LXXVIII), are probably elephant tusks. Keimer (1948c: 52, fn. 1), said this was absolute proof that the Ancient Egyptians also gave the name *3bw* to the horns of the rhino.

The horned animal in a relief of the hieroglyph for rhinoceros (fig. 12-27) was described by Hilzheimer (1926: 167, fig. 25) as being wrongly interpreted as a rhinoceros: ..."It carries a horn-like structure on the forehead, but otherwise has not the slightest resemblance to a rhinoceros and the animal will probably with error be interpreted as a rhinoceros." Keimer (1948c: 50) said that the artist who designed the animal had certainly never observed a rhino nor an elephant and the determinative was a fantastic beast.

Although the position of the horn is incorrect, this figure could only be interpreted as a rhino despite the long snout, which is no longer than those on the rhinos in Figures 12-21,-22.

The entire figure is comparable with the hieroglyph *jrb3* for rhinoceros in Wb. I, 115, 4.

In a painting of the hieroglyph (fig. 13-27) the 'horn' on the rhinoceros protrudes from the lower jaw like the tusk of a hippopotamus or an elephant. Despite this error, the nuchal hump and other features of the head and body indicate that it represents the determinative for the rhinoceros hieroglyph.

(See also *Errors and discrepancies* in the Hippopotamus chapter).

12-27 A relief of the rhinoceros hieroglyph in the Dynasty V Temple of Ne-User-re, Abu Gurab, N.N.W. of Saqqara. Source: Hilzheimer (1926: fig. 25).

XIII
Order *Artiodactyla*
Pigs
Family *Suidae*

Wild Boar *Sus scrofa* Linnaeus, 1758
[and **Domestic Pig** *Sus scrofa domestica*]

 *š3j* shay Wb. IV, 405

E Wild Hog; F Sanglier; G Wildschwein; A Hanzir

13-1 (above) Wild boar in a trap carved on an ancient club from Gebelein (Gabalin). Source: Keimer (1937; fig.1).

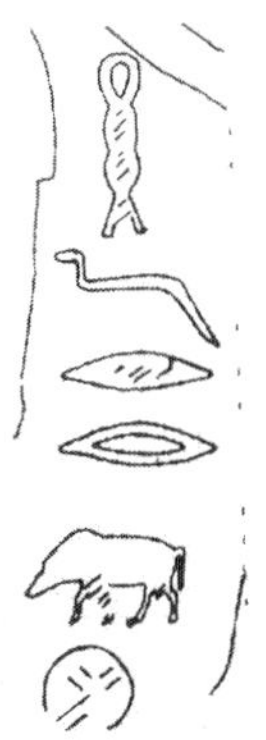

13-2 (right) Hieroglyph in relief meaning 'Boar bane' from the Tomb of Nefermat, Dynasty III, Medum. Source: Petrie (1892b: pl. XXI).

Description: Wild boars are large and sturdily built with a hump over the shoulders. Limbs are relatively short and slender. Toes are four, but only two are functional. The tail has a bushy tip, is not curled, and reaches the hocks. The ears are densely haired, prominent, and pointed. The muzzle is elongated and narrow, with a flattened, naked nose pad. The pelage is bristly and shaggy. Color is yellowish mixed with dark greyish-brown. Limbs, muzzle, backs of ears, and tail tuft are darker. The young have linear yellowish-buff stripes on a dark brown body color.

Canine teeth are continuously growing; those of the upper jaw form upward and outward curving tusks, which are much larger in males than females.

Measurements in cm are: Shoulder height 70-90, head and body length 110-113, and tail 15-21.

Natural history: Wild boars inhabit woodlands, savanna, and swamps. Water is essential for drinking and bathing, especially in mud. Periods of activity vary throughout the day.

Food consists of various fallen fruits and numerous roots and tubers that are rooted out of the ground with the snout.

Distribution: Wild boars continue to exist in Western and Eastern Europe (now extinct in Great Britain), parts of Western Russia, the Middle East, and much of Asia (Harrison, 1968 II: 375); North Africa in the northernmost parts of Morocco, Algeria, Tunisia, and Libya (Haltenorth and Diller, 1980: 31); but is extinct in Egypt. In northern Sudan feral pigs exist in the wild (Setzer, 1956: 570).

Until the early 1900s wild boar lived in the reed beds and swamps of El Moghra Oasis, Wadi el Natroun, El Faiyum, the Nile Delta, Giza, and other parts of Lower and Middle Egypt.

Either the long continued ravaging of swine in agricultural lands or the Muslim abhorence inspired a government campaign in 1846 to exterminate the wild boar in the Delta (Lower Egypt). An estimated 860 were killed (Epstein, 1971 II: 326).

The wild boar continued to exist in Egypt until its final extermination in Wadi el Natroun in the early 1900s (Strekalovsky, 1949; Russell, 1951: 19).

Prehistoric records: Uerpmann (1987: 72) remarked that the wild boar expanded from the Levant into Africa during the Upper Pleistocene, but there is no proof from faunal remains for the existence of Pleistocene wild boars in Northeast Africa (*op. cit.*, 42 fn. 4).

Rock drawings of swine are apparently rare. One was found by Churcher (1993) on a sandstone slab in Dakhla Oasis (fig. 7-25) and dated to the late Neolithic or Old Kingdom.

According to Brewer *et al.* (1994: 95) taming and domestication of wild boars began in the Predynastic when settled agricultural communities were being established.

In contrast, Churcher (1974: 375) wrote: "Zeuner (1963) states that pigs were common in Egypt from the Neolithic into early dynastic times, and that the pig was introduced into Egypt after 10,000 B.C. This agrees with the absence of the pig [in deposits, *sic*] at Kom Ombo or Wadi Halfa." Churcher concluded that pigs, considered native by various authors, "may be feral descendants of the Neolithic domestic stock".

The following comments indicate that there is uncertainty as to just when true domestication began: "Capturing and domestication ... was customary up to recent times" (Boettger, 1958: 21) and "Wild swine, if captured when young, can be

13-3 (top left) Faience amulet in the form of a domestic pig. Source: Keimer (1937: fig. 7).

13-4 (top right) Pigs on sealings from the Tomb of King Aza-Merpaba, Dynasty I, Abydos. Source: Petrie (1900 I: pl. XXVI).

13-5 (bottom) Partially domesticated (?) pigs in a swamp in the Tomb of Khety, Dynasty XII, Beni Hasan. Source: Davies (1933: fig. 6).

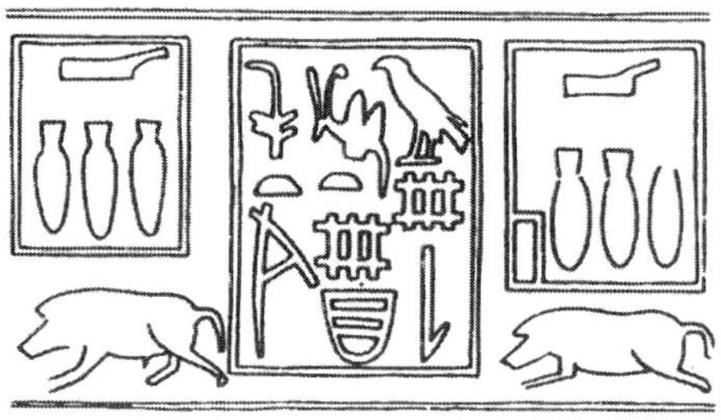

tamed and domesticated very easily" (Bökönyi 1974: 207).

Among the artifacts depicting wild boars is a carving of a boar in a trap (fig. 13-1) and hieroglyphs in relief that translate to a name meaning 'Boar bane' (fig. 13-2). Newberry (1928) said it was a place name, 'pig-bane'. Note that the tails in these reproductions are not curled.

Keimer (1937: 155) remarked that numerous amulets from the Predynastic or Old Kingdom in the form of a pig were generally in the shape of the domestic pig (fig. 13-3).

The Dynastic period: On some Dynasty I sealings (fig. 13-4) pigs are shown with tails like wild boars, but with rather stout bodies. Although the curled tail is indicative of domestic pigs, there are drawings that look like wild boars, but have curled tails (fig. 13-5).

Illustrations of fat, domestic pigs from the Greco-Roman and Roman periods do not appear to have curled tails, although they are otherwise typical of domestic pigs (figs 13-6,-7).

History and domestication of pigs is treated at length in another volume in this series as well as a discussion of the debatable subject of pork avoidance (Brewer *et al.*, 1994: 93-97). Therefore, only a limited amount of information was presented herein.

Wart Hog ***Phacochoerus aethiopicus*** (Pallas, 1767)

F Phacochère; G Warzenschwein

Nomenclature: The Latinized name derives from *phakos* (Gr) a mole or wart, *khoiros* (Gr) a pig or hog, and *aethiopicus* a name often used to indicate Africa as a whole (Gotch, 1979: 204).

Description: Below the eyes and on the cheeks there are large wart-like glandular swellings. The head is large and pig-like. The tail is long and thin with a terminal tuft and carried upright when the animal is moving. The skin is gray and sparsely haired, except for a prominent yellowish to brown mane on the neck, shoulders, and back. The upper tusks curve outward, upward, and inward, forming a

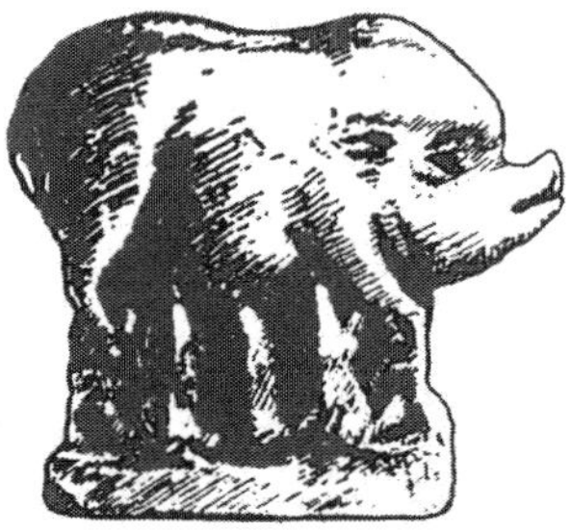

13-6 Baked clay molding of a domestic sow with young from the Roman Period at Faiyum. Source: Keimer (1937: fig. 6).

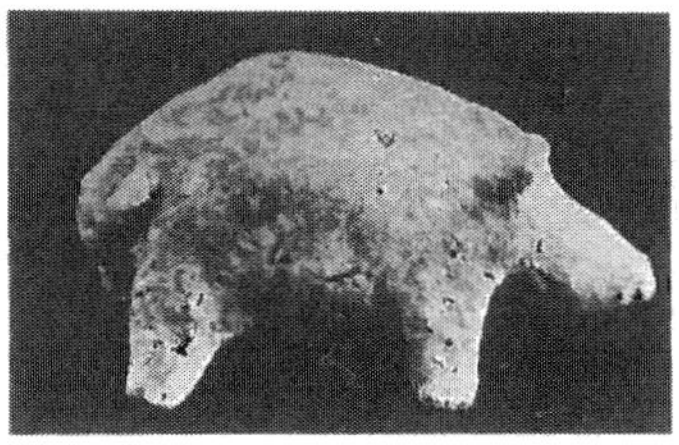

13-7 Baked clay molding of a domestic pig from the Greco-Roman Period at Faiyum. Source: Keimer (1937: pl. IIIa).

semi-circle. The lower tusks wear against the bases and become sharp cutting weapons.

Measurements in cm are: Head and body length 105-150, tail length 35-50, and shoulder height 55-85. Females are smaller than males.

Natural history: Wart hogs are generally active in mornings and afternoons. Food is principally short grass, fallen fruits, and green bark. During drought bulbs, tubers, and roots are dug out with the snout and tusks.

The preferred habitat is treeless open savannas, especially where water is available for drinking and wallowing.

Wart hogs live in family groups and larger herds. They are preyed upon by leopards and lions.

Distribution: Wart hogs occupy much of Africa south of the Sahara.

Prehistoric and Predynastic records: Gautier (1980: 321 f.) found mandible and tooth fragments from the late Quaternary at Bir Sahara. Haynes (1980: 368) found tooth fragments at Barqat el Shab Playa dated to the pre-Neolithic age of the Quaternary. These sites are about 300km west of Abu Simbel.

Churcher *et al.* (1997) included the wart hog in a list of fragmentary mammal remains from Dakhla Oasis dated to the Quaternary.

Errors and discrepancies: The wart hog was mistakenly associated with the mythical Set (Seth) animal (Jensen, 1934: 7).

Hippopotamuses
Family *Hippopotamidae*

Hippopotamus ***Hippopotamus amphibius*** Linnaeus, 1758

 *dbj* deby Wb. V, 433

E Hippo; F Hippopotame, Hippopotame amphibius; G Flusspferd, Grossflusspferd, Nilpferd; A Barnik, Sayed Eshta

Nomenclature: The name derives from *hippos* (Gr) a horse and *potamos* (Gr) a river (Gotch, 1979: 204).

Description: A very large, heavily built amphibius mammal with short, stout legs, four toes, and a short tail. The brownish-gray skin is nearly naked except for bristles on the muzzle and tail.

The male is larger than the female and has more massive forequarters and jowl (Kingdon, 1977 III: 209). A slight protuberance between the ears also distinguishes the bull from the cow (Meissner, 1963: 140).

Natural history: Hippos are splendidly adapted for their amphibious life and can lie in the water with only ears, eyes, and nostrils protruding. When submerging, ears and nostrils close flap-like. Hippos can then sink and walk and feed for periods of up to six minutes. Hippos spend the day on banks of lakes or streams or in the water. They forage at night on aquatic plants, grasses, other vegetation, and fallen fruits; often many kilometers from the shore. The only enemies, besides man, are lions, crocodiles, and possibly hyenas, which prey upon the young.

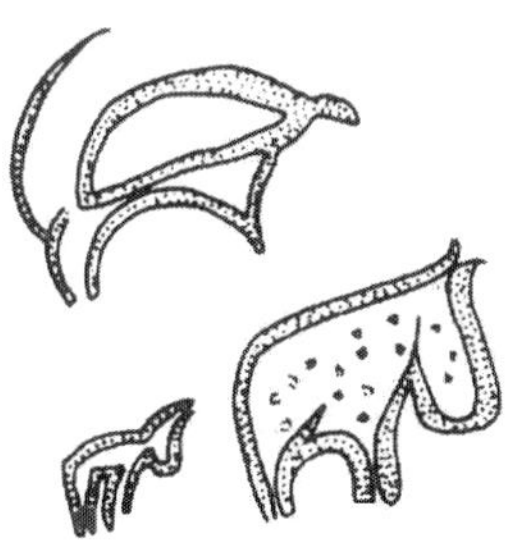

13-8 Rock drawing of a hippopotamus and young at Kanais in Wadi Mia, 45 km east of Idfu. Source: Červíček (1974: fig. 270). The animal above cannot be identified.

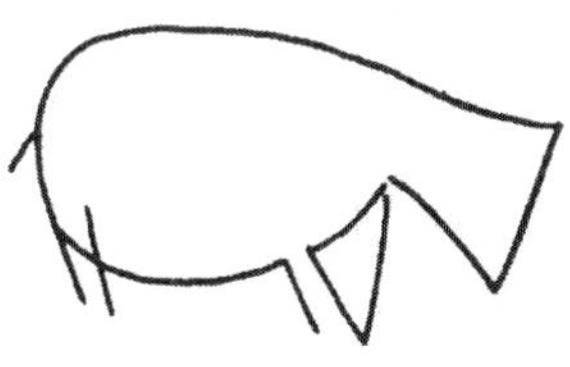

13-9 Rock drawing of a hippopotamus at El Hagandia, east of the Nile north of Šilwa Bahari. Source: Červíček (1974: fig. 129).

Distribution: In Egypt hippos were originally distributed throughout the Nile Delta, in the Faiyum, and along the Nile wherever the shores were suitable and the current was not too rapid.

Previous distribution beyond Egypt included parts of north Africa and coastal localities in the Eastern Mediterranean, at least into the early Pleistocene (Kowalski and Rzebik-Kowalska, 1991: 30 f.; Uerpmann, 1987: 46).

The present distribution includes most of Africa south of the Sahara. In the Nile River the northern limit in Setzer's (1956: 571) records was Khartoum. Kock (1970a: fig. 3b) noted a questionable sighting in the area of Berber north of Khartoum for 1965, but listed the northern limits for 1960 at Gebelein on the White Nile south of Khartoum.

Despite severe hunting pressure for centuries, hippos are known to have existed in Egypt into the early 1800s (Kock *op. cit.).*

Prehistoric records: Numerous sites that contained hippo remains occur along the banks of the Nile from Giza to Wadi Halfa were listed and mapped by Uerpmann (1987: 46, table 7, fig. 15). Most of these sites were discussed by Churcher (1972: 53 ff.). At Neolithic Beni Salama (Merimda) in the southwest Delta, Baumgartel (1960 II: 138) discovered leg bones (tibia) having been used as steps into subterranean huts. At Faiyum a skeleton was found with a concave-base arrowhead between its ribs (Caton-Thompson and Gardner, 1934: 84).

13-10 (top) Hippopotamuses on Predynastic white cross-linea ware. Provenance Naqada or Abydos. Source: Scharff (1928: fig. 1). Note the protruding tusks.

13-11 (bottom) Hippopotamuses on a Prehistoric white-lined vase from Naqada. Source: Petrie (1920: pl. XVIII, 72).

13-12 *A long-haired hunter has speared a hippo standing in a pond with its young. Another speared hippo is on the other side of the pond. This was a white decoration on the inside of a polished red pottery bowl from Predynastic cemetery B at Abydos. Source: Ayrton and Loat (1911: pl. XXVII, 13).*

13-13 *A predynastic cosmetic palette with a man in a boat harpooning a hippo. Source: Asselberghs (1961: pl. XLVI, 70). Another hippo is shown (left) and a hyena (?) attacking a gazelle.*

Churcher *et al.* (1997) listed hippopotamus remains from several Pleistocene and Holocene/Neolithic sites in Dakhla Oasis. Hippos have a habit of walking long distances at night and in rainy weather. Thus, they may have reached Dakhla Oasis via small lakes that existed in the Pleistocene savanna (Churcher, pers. com.).

Some additional sites are Abassiya (Massoulard, 1949: 6) and Maadi (Boessneck, 1988: table 5) near Cairo; and Hierakonpolis (McArdle, 1982, 120).

The Predynastic period: Hippos in Predynastic rock art are easily identified (figs 1-1, 13-8) even though some were very stylized (fig. 13-9). They were commonly pictured on pottery with various body designs (figs 13-10,-11). Hunting scenes appeared on pottery (fig. 13-12) and on a schist palette (fig. 13-13), where a man harpooning a hippo from a boat is very similar to Dynastic portrayals in tombs.

Hippo hunting in those early times was probably mainly for skins and meat, although the tusks were also used for carving.

A late Predynastic piece of unique artwork is the flint hippo from Hierakonpolis (fig. 1-6a).

The oldest representation of the female hippo goddess Taurt is a dual form on a Pre- or Protodynastic comb made of breccia (fig. 13-14) and described by Seligman (1916: 53) as 'the highly stylized form and conventional position in which she is habitually represented in later times'.

The cult of the goddess Taurt was established in the Predynastic (*op. cit.*). She was worshipped as the overseer of pregnancy and childbirth, a belief that probably developed from observations of female hippos protecting their young.

13-14 *The goddess Taurt on a Pre- or Protodynastic comb. Source: Seligman (1916: 53).*

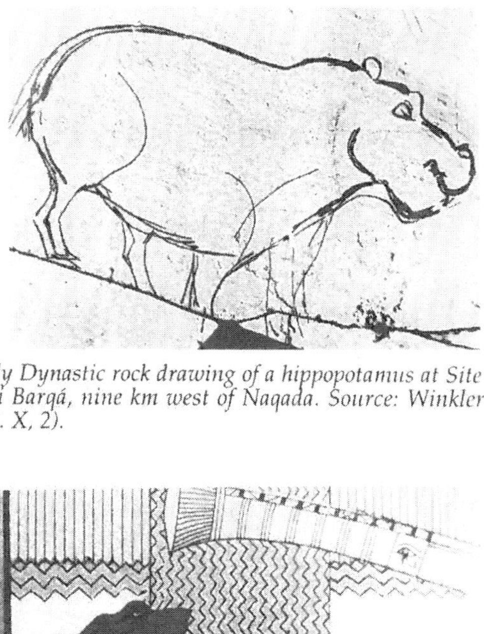

13-15 *Early Dynastic rock drawing of a hippopotamus at Site 45 in Wadi Barqá, nine km west of Naqada. Source: Winkler (1939 II: pl. X, 2).*

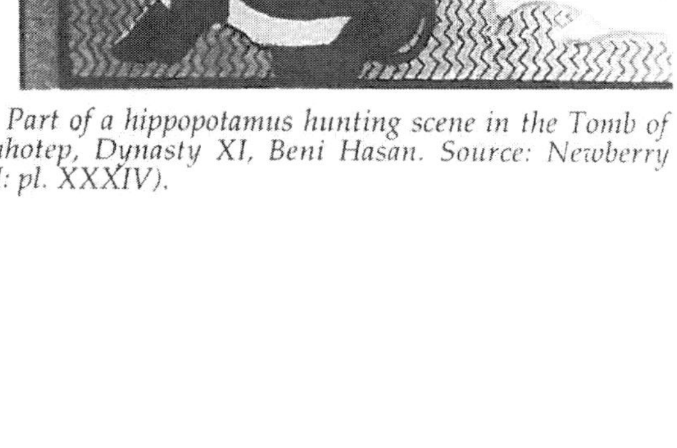

13-16 *Part of a hippopotamus hunting scene in the Tomb of Chnemhotep, Dynasty XI, Beni Hasan. Source: Newberry (1893 I: pl. XXXIV).*

13-17 Part of a hippopotamus hunting scene in the Mastaba of Mereruka, Dynasty VI, Saqqara. Source: M. Zemina. Above are two oversized locusts.

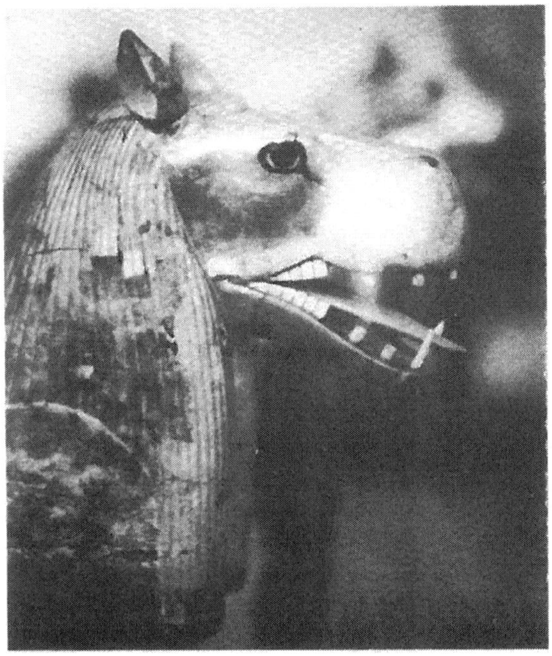

13-18 Head of Taurt on a couch from the Tomb oj Tutankhamun, Dynasty XVIII, Thebes, in the Cairo Museum. Source: M. Zemina.

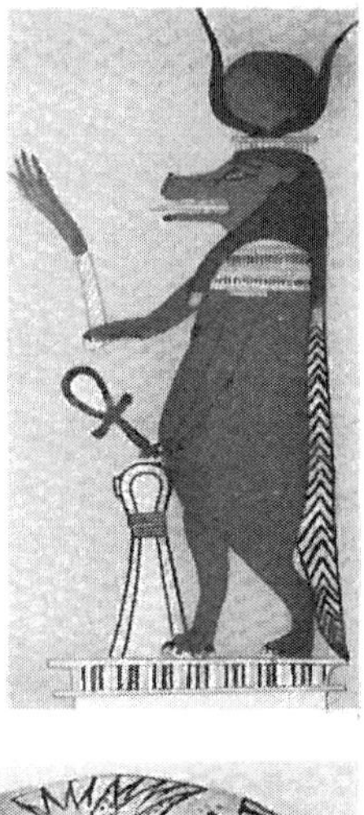

13-19 (left) Taurt standing upright with right 'hand' on the Sa. Greenstone statuette, Dynasty XX, Karnak, Thebes. Source: Heise (1947: pl. XXXII).

13-20 (right) Taurt with sun disc and horns on her head and a torch and Ankh in her 'hands'. Source: Budge (1904a II: opposite p. 30).

13-21 Blue faience statuette of a female hippo from the Tomb of Soneb, Dynasty XII, Mir. Source: Hayes (1953 I; fig. 142).

The Dynastic period: There is a very realistic rock drawing of a hippopotamus dated to Dynastic time in Figure 13-15. The legs, however, are too slender.

During Dynasty V-VI the hippo appeared in fowling scenes in the marshes and as an object of the hunt (figs. 1-26,-27). A popular art style showed them with open mouths and heads reversed (figs. 1-27,-28, 13-16). In early illustrations the tomb owner was shown directing his servants who were doing the harpooning. By the time of the New Kingdom (fig. 1-28) the king was shown as the harpooner (Säve-Söderbergh, 1953: 12 ff., 15 f.).

The method of harpooning was to first pierce the nostrils with the first harpoon so the animal would be unable to submerge (figs. 1-27, 13-17) and further spearing would be possible.

The harpoon was a shaft with a detachable point that was connected to a line with a float at the other end. If the hippo submerged it could be followed and speared again upon emerging. When the animal was exhausted from bleeding or was dead it could be dragged ashore either with the ropes on the harpoons or with a lasso over its head.

Because of the hippo's destructive habits of eating and trampling crops it became symbolic of the enemies of the king and to kill it meant that he had conquered all the evil powers that were against him. In the Late period the hippo became incorporated into a Seth animal and the hunting of it , according to Plutarch, supposedly evoked the memory of the struggle between Horus and Seth (Davies and Gardiner, 1915: 30).

Throughout the Dynasties the male hippo was hunted by noblemen and peasants killed it to protect their crops as well as to obtain its various products: skin, flesh, fat for making hair grow, and ivory for carving.

Darby *et al.* (1977 I: 256) commented: "The question of whether the Ancient Egyptians ate this animal as do some of southern Sudanese tribes today, must, however, be left open."

Althought the male hippo was persecuted as a symbol of evil, the female was worshipped as the goddess Taurt, overseer of pregnancy and childbirth.

In the New Kingdom carved hippopotamus heads decorated bed frames (fig. 13-18); probably as protective symbols. Of particular interest is a bottle in the shape of Taurt that was used to suckle babies (Ghalioungui and El Dawakhly, 1965: 30).

Mond and Myers (1937: 42) reasoned that female hippos may have been kept in shallow pools, tamed by feeding, and used to drive away crocodiles. Säve-Söderbergh (1953: 17) considered these conclusions to be fanciful and impossible.

Figures of Taurt are standing upright, have large, sagging breasts, a swollen abdomen, and one hand on a Sa. The Sa, a symbol of protection, is a

13-22 A votive stela with Taurt and Mut from Deir el Medineh, Dynasty XIX-XX. Source: Hayes (1959 II: fig. 242).

13-23 Hippopotamus in a sycamore (fig) tree. Source: Vandier d'Abbadie (1937 II: fig. 31).

stylization of the papyrus life preserver that was worn by river travelers (fig. 13-19). Taurt was identified with Hathor and sometimes wore a disk and horns on her head. She may also be holding a torch in her right hand and in her left, which rests on the Sa, holding the Ankh or symbol of life (fig. 13-20).

Various spellings of Taurt's name are Taueret, Taweret, Thoueris, and Thoeris. Other names applied to the 'Mother Goddess' were Apet, Ipet, Opet, Reret, and Rertu.

Mercatante (1978: 183) noted that the literal translation of her name was 'the great [fat] one'. Säve-Söderbergh (1953: 48) said that her name, 'the White One', was in harmony with the character of goodness, "white being very often a colour symbolizing something good, costly and powerful". In contrast, the evil male hippopotamus was painted red.

There are several scenes depicting an annual 'Feast of the White Hippopotamus' (*op. cit.*, figs 12, 13), but texts explaining the occasion are lacking (*op. cit.*, 49). Likewise, there are references to a celebration of the hunt of the red hippopotamus or the day of 'harpooning the hippopotamus'.

Much more can be learned about this divinity, as well as the evil male, in Säve-Söderbergh's (1953) well-documented exposition.

Besides the Taurt figurines of bronze and various other materials, numerous statuettes of ordinary hippos have been found (Petrie, 1914: pl.

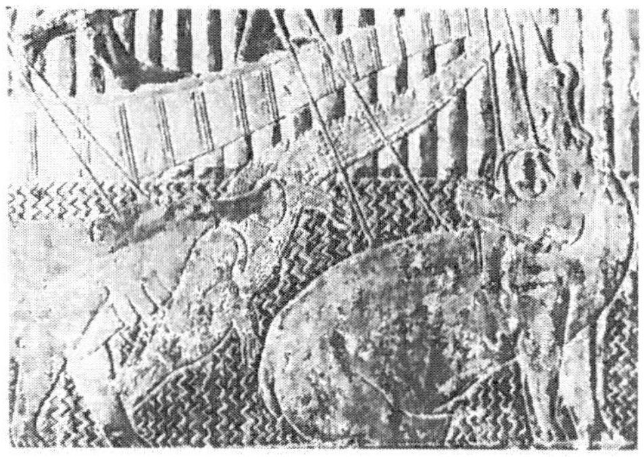

13-25 Part of a hippotomus hunting scene in the Tomb of Ti, Dynasty V, Saqqara. Source: Wild (1953 II: pl. LXXXV). The hippo on the left has a crocodile in its jaws and its recurved tusk is shown having pierced the animal's body.

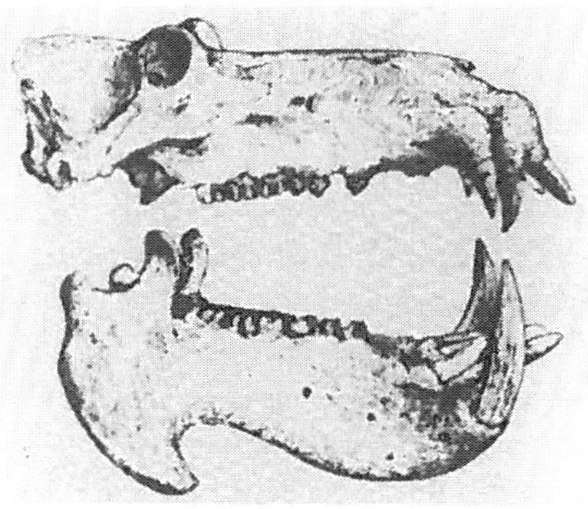

13-26 A hippopotamus skull. Source: Sclater (1900: 266).

13-27 Painting of the rhinoceros hieroglyph above the head of an elephant (?) in the Solar Sanctuary (Sun Temple) of Ne-User-Re, Dynasty V, Abu Gurab, N.N.W. of Saqqara. Source: Edel and Wenig (1974: pl. D).

XL). As Darby *et al.* (1977 I: 257) remarked in reference to a faience statuette (fig. 13-21), "These may not have been cult objects, however, but 'charms' to ward off the destructive effects of these creatures."

Two great mother goddesses, Taurt and Mut, are pictured on a votive stela from Deir el Medineh (fig. 13-22). The disks and horns on their heads associate them with Isis and Hathor.

Hayes (1959 II: 386) said that although the acacia tree behind Ipet (Taurt) seemed vague, her assimilation with Isis and Hathor "helps to explain Ipet's appearance as a tree goddess".

An ostracon of a hippo in a tree (fig. 13-23) was

13-24 A crocodile about to grasp the foal of a hippopotamus. Tomb of Idut, Dynasty VI, Saqqara. Source: Author.

13-28 Rock drawing of a giraffe followed by a pariah dog in Wadi Sharab 25 km northeast of Edfu (Idfu). Source: Červíček (1974: fig. 468).

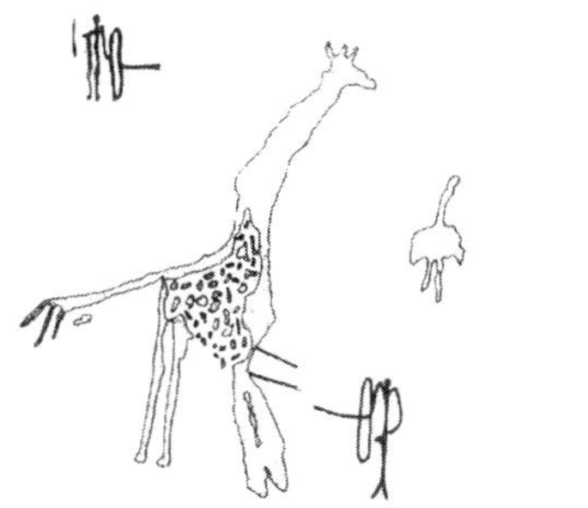

13-29 Rock drawing of a giraffe in a hunting scene at El Hosh, west bank of the Nile River opposite Silwa. Source: Červíček (1974: fig. 151).

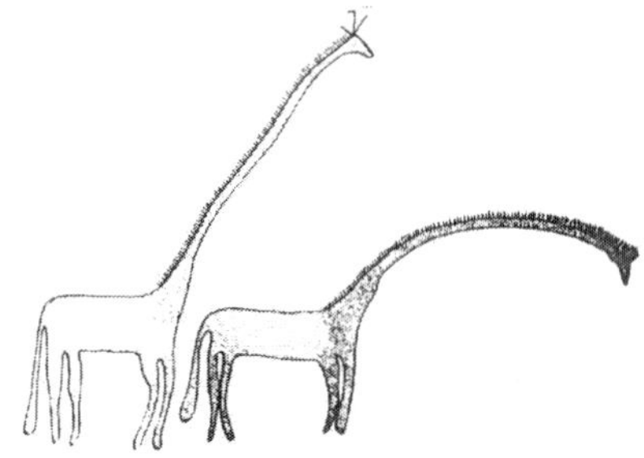

13-30 Rock drawings of giraffes in Chor (Wadi) es-Salaam west of the Nile and south of El Hosh. Source: Červíček (1974: fig. 77).

referred to as 'satirical' (Vandier d'Abbadie, 1937 II: 63 f.), but there may be a connection, because some trees were sacred to Horus, Ra, Hathor, Isis, and Mut, who supposedly lived in trees (Mercatante, 1978: 195).

Errors and discrepancies: There are some scenes where a crocodile is grasping or about to grasp the foal of a hippo (figs 7-134, 13-24). Likewise, there are others of crocodiles in the jaws of hippopotamuses (figs 7-134, 13-25). Similar scenes might have been observed in nature by the Egyptians, as Váhala (in press) remarked, "but not necessarily by the artists themselves." Thus, some aspects of these figures are not realistic.

For example, hippos give birth away from the herd on land in trampled grass nests or in shallow water; therefore, an attack on a foal from the rear in the depths of water that are pictured and in the company of other hippos is unlikely. Hippos may have attacked and bitten crocodiles in protecting their young, but they could not have opened their mouths widely enough to insert such long, recurved lower canine tusks into the body of a crocodile as are shown in Figures 7-134 and 13-25.

The upper and lower canine teeth grow continuously. The lower teeth are longer than the upper ones, but do not develop into long, recurved tusks. The reason for this is wear from occlusion of upper and lower teeth (fig. 13-26). Hippo incisors are also continuously growing and both types of teeth become very sharp from occlusion.

The tusked animals in Figure 13-27 were referred to by Hilzheimer (1931: 42) as rhinoceroses, but he assumed that the artist had never seen the animal. Bissing (1956: 36 f.) identified them as elephants or 'water elephants', because elephants love water and the fish and duck behind the lower animal's head indicated an aquatic situation.

The tusks on these creations are comparable with those pictured on hippopotamuses biting crocodiles (figs 7-134, 13-25). The colors in Plate D of Edel and Wenig (1974) are reddish-brown, representing the male hippo (fig. 13-27). The artist may have intended to represent hippos, but another figure similar to the one intended for the determinative and with a horn on the forehead instead of the falsely protruding tusk, was obviously supposed to represent a rhinoceros (fig. 12-27).

Another animal is shown on a fragment of a wall decoration of scenes from the Land of Punt, Deir el Bahari, at Thebes. Naville (1898 III: pl. LXX, 13 f.) remarked, that it looked like a hippopotamus "... But as it is seen walking on land, and not near the water as is generally the case in Egyptian sculptures, it is possible that the artist intended to represent the rhinoceros".

Smith (1965: 138, fig. 174) referred to a mother ape with her young on her back confronting a rhinoceros, a rarely depicted animal.

His restoration of the scene includes the head of the animal (fig. 4-12). The curved tusk appearing to be on the nose does not look like a rhino horn. Other hippo characters in the picture are the thick muzzle, the projection on the forehead, and the shortness of the legs. The only rhino-like character is the long tail.

Giraffes Family *Giraffidae*

Giraffe ***Giraffa camelopardalis*** (Linnaeus, 1758)

 *m'm'* mama Wb. II, 58

 *śr* zer Wb. IV, 189

F Giraffe; G Giraffe; A Zirafa, Zarafah

Nomenclature: The generic name derives from the African native name *Zirafa;* the specific name from the Greek description of a camel with the pelt of a leopard.

Description: This long-necked, long-legged animal with a sloping back and long, tufted tail hardly requires a description except to mention the characteristic short frontal horns covered with skin and short hair and a third projection on the forehead. The color pattern of the body consists of chestnut brown patches of irregular shapes separated by a network of light buff lines.

Shoulder height is 270-330 cm.

Distribution: The giraffe was known to have lived in Egypt as far north as the latitude of Memphis. It was more common west of the Nile because of the flat terrain. According to the findings of Váhala (in press) the giraffe was driven southward by man when it began eating his trees, bushes, etc., which it was forced to do because of progressive desertification and scarcity of food east and west of the Nile Valley. His conclusions are based mainly on Butzer's (1976: 26 f.) data on the increasing dessication after the Late Predynastic (3,000 B.C.) when the estimated annual rainfall of 50 mm decreased. The present distribution is south of the Sahara in dry, open bush and acacia steppe.

Prehistoric and Predynastic records: Giraffe remains dated to the Late Neolithic were listed by Uerpmann (1987: 145) from sites in Gilf Kebir in southwestern Egypt.

The clearly defined giraffe (fig. 7-15) from a site near the 59.8 km mark on the Qift-Quseir road was dated to the Epi-Paleolithic by Redford and Redford (1989: fig. 10).

There is a rather poor reproduction of a giraffe with a long body (fig. 13-83) in Wadi Abu Qwei north of the Qift-Quseir road that was dated to the 'Epi-Paleolithic (?)' by Redford and Redford (op. cit., 18, fig. 25).

Giraffe hunting was pictured in Predynastic times (figs 13-29 to -36). The skins were probably highly valued. The wiry tail hairs were doubtless used in stringing beads as in later periods. The meat may have been eaten, although in later times '...there is no evidence to support a claim that they were eaten' (Darby *et al.*, 1977 I: 259).

The giraffe followed by a pariah dog (fig. 13-28) is similar in style to those on Predynastic white cross-lined pottery (fig. 13-37). Contrariwise, Petrie (1920: 16) said, "On 73, the larger animal must be the African goat by the wattles on the throat."

Additional pottery designs that include giraffes are in Figures 13-38,-39, and -40.

Giraffes were carved on Predynastic slate palettes (figs 1-2b,-4b,-5b), ivory knife handles (figs 1-7,-9), and combs (figs 1-10, 12-8). On several of these artifacts a single giraffe was carved in rows of saddle-billed storks (figs 1-7,-9,-10 and probably in the missing part of Figure 1-8). The reason for this association is yet to be discovered.

13-31 Rock drawings by Earliest Hunters of giraffes, scimitar oryx, a pariah dog (far right), and men with lassos in Wadi Saab er Rigal northwest of El Hosh. Source: Winkler (1939 II: pl. LI, 1).

13-32 Rock drawings of giraffes at Gebel Silsila north of Kom Ombo. Source: Červíček (1974: fig. 475).

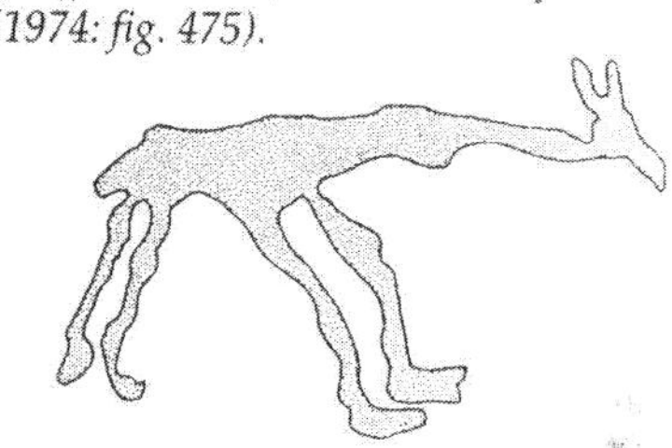

13-33 Rock drawing of a giraffe at Maria North on the west bank of the Nile in Upper Egypt south of the Tropic of cancer. Source: Červíček (1974: fig. 408).

13-34 Rock drawings by Earliest Hunters of lassoed giraffes and hunters near the Ghubari Road west of Kharga Oasis. Source: Winkler (1939 II: pl. LIV, 1).

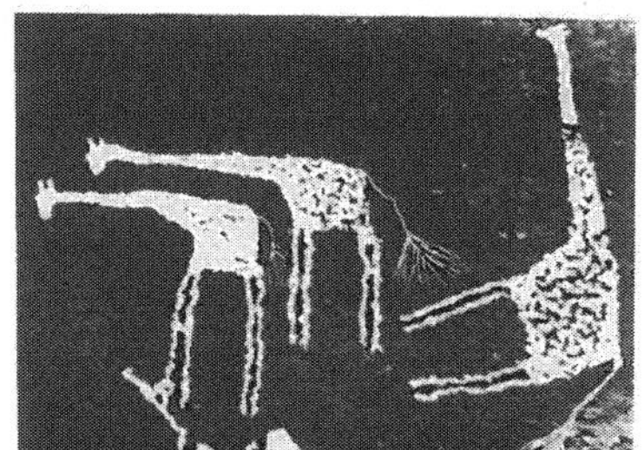

13-35 Rock drawings by Earliest Hunters of three giraffes and a hunter with a lasso on the west bank of the Nile River northwest of El Hosh. Source: Winkler (1939 II: pl. LI,2).

13-36 Rock drawings of giraffes and a lion (left) by Autochthonous Mountain Dwellers at Gebel Uweinat. Source: Winkler (1939 II: pl. XXXI, 1).

13-37 Giraffes, a Barbary goat, and an ibex on Predynastic white cross-lined pottery, locality uncertain. Source: Petrie (1920: pl. XVIII, 73).

13-41 A hunting scene in the causeway of Unas, Dynasty V Saqqara. Source: Hassan (1955: pl. XIII, 1). Animals from lef to right are: Soemmering's gazelle, bubal hartebeest ?, dorca gazelle ?, Soemmering's gazelle, and mating scimitar ory Below are a hare and a dwarfed giraffe.

13-38 Giraffes, snakes, scorpions, and a man on Predynastic pottery. Source: Scharff (1931, fig. 58).

13-39 Three giraffes and a row of oryx, possibly an ibex to the left, on Predynastic decorated pottery from Abu Sir el Meleq. Source: Möllers and Scharff (1926: fig. 8).

13-40 Figures of giraffes and a hartebeest on Late Prehistoric pottery from Qustul, Upper Egypt. Source: Williams (1980: 15).

The Dynastic period: A very clear representation appears on the Dynasty I mace handle from Seyala in Nubia (fig.1-13). Numerous ivory combs from the early dynasties were decorated with figures of giraffes (fig. 12-8). Otherwise, Dynastic depictions of giraffes were rare. A giraffe of the same size as a hare was included in the Dynasty V relief of the hunt scene in the causeway of Unas at Saqqara (fig. 13-41). Several other alien animals appear there and probably the giraffe does not represent an extant species. The giraffe in the hunt scene from the Dynasty XII Tomb of Ukhotep (figs 7-28, 13-42) was also supplementary.

In the XVIIIth Dynasty giraffes were being brought from Nubia as tribute and may have been kept in private gardens of the nobility. Perhaps the frontal of a male giraffe found by Boessneck and von den Driesch (1987) in a palace enclosure near Qantir in the Eastern Delta, dated to Dynasty XIX-XX, was from a 'garden pet'.

The best known tribute giraffe is in the Tomb of Rekhmire (fig. 4-37). The markings of the animal are well illustrated, except for the error of Egyptian artists in showing the legs spotted below the 'knees'. Dawson (1927) said the Egyptians knew only the northern races with the legs unmarked and white below the 'knees' and the median horn well-developed in males. In another Dynasty XVIII tribute the markings are black spots instead of irregular patches (fig. 4-23). To the right of this figure is the hieroglyph *mmy* or *mmj* for giraffe. In the Tomb of Huy (fig. 13-43) the giraffe has only a few spots on the neck.

Some of the gift bearers carry giraffe tails (figs 4-22,-23), which were presented to noblemen for fly whisks (Davies and Gardiner, 1926: 24 f., pl. XXVIII).

A piece of Nubian art included in the tributes brought to Tutankhamun by Huy (fig. 13-44) was a table covered with leopard skins and woven material and a representation of a Nubian landscape: dom palms with boys and monkeys in the branches, a thatched hut, men in postures of reverence, and two men with giraffes on leashes. This piece of artistry was also pictured by Davies and Gardiner (*op.cit.*, pls. XXIII and XXVI).

Worth noting here are the heights of the giraffes compared with the men in Figure 13-44. Live giraffes in tribute scenes are only slightly taller than their attendants and therefore were young animals (Spinage, 1968: 35). This observation may

13-42 (left) Relief of part of the hunting scene in Figure 7-28 showing the giraffe, striped hyena, and dama deer in the Tomb Chapel of Senbi's son Ukh-hotep, Dynasty XII, Meir. Source: Blackman (1915 II: pl. XXXII, 1).

13-43 (right) A giraffe in Nubian tribute in the Tomb of Huy, Dynasty XVIII, Thebes. Source: Davies and Gardiner (1926: pl. XXVII).

be correct, because the horns always appear short as in young giraffes.

A few more giraffes were pictured in the late dynasties: A giraffe was among the animals in the representation of the Puntite village in the Temple of Queen Hatshepsut at Deir el Bahari (fig. 4-12); a tribute giraffe in the Dynasty XIX Temple of Ramses II at Beit el Wali (fig. 4-38); and on a partly damaged ostracon from Deir el Medina (fig. 13-45).

The extraordinary silhouette of the giraffe was used in the hieroglyph for the verb 'to foretell' (Janssen and Janssen, 1989: 55).

Okapi ***Okapia johnstoni*** (Sclater, 1901)

E Forest Giraffe; F Okapi; G Okapi

Nomenclature: "Okapi is a native name used by pygmies in the Semliki Forest area of Zaire" (Gotch, 1979: 211 f.).

Description: The general color is dark chestnut with conspicuous stripes on the upper parts of the legs; lower legs are white. Ears are proportionately larger than on asses and giraffes. Horns are short, sloping backward and covered with pelage as in the giraffe. The tail is rather short, not reaching the hocks, and with a small terminal tuft.

Shoulder height is 150-165 cm.

Distribution: The okapi was first discovered in Zaire in 1900 by H.J. Johnston, explorer and author. Known distribution is only in Zaire in dense rain forest. There is no evidence that this species occurred in Egypt or was known by the ancient Egyptians or Nubians.

Various authors who considered the okapi to have been the true Seth animal in Egyptian mythology, gave the impression that it formerly existed in Egypt.

The final word by Te Velde (1984: 909) regarding the Seth animal was "... it seems to be a fabulous animal (Fabeltiere) supposed to live in the desert just like the griffin".

13-44 Giraffes in a piece of Nubian artistry presented as tribute to King Tutankhamun via Huy, Viceroy of Nubia, Dynasty XVIII, Thebes. Source: Erman (1887: 663).

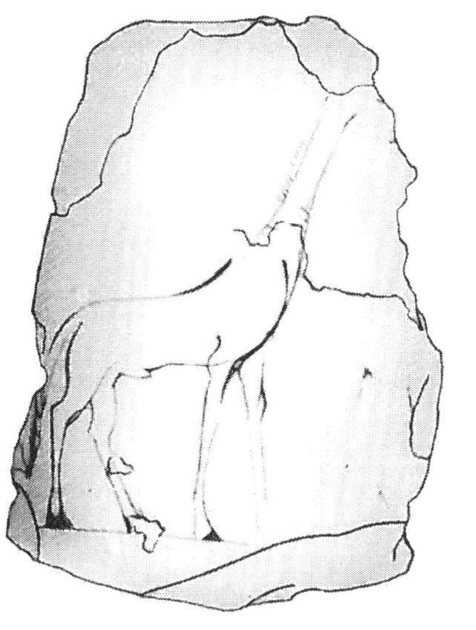

13-45 A giraffe on an ostracon from Deir el Medinah, Dynasty XIX. Source: Vandier d'Abbadie (1937 II: pl. XXXI, 2233.

Family *Cervidae*

Dama Deer ***Dama mesopotamica*** **Brooke, 1875**

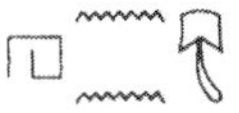 *hnn* henen Wb. II, 495

E Fallow Deer; F Daim; G Damhirsch

Nomenclature: Two known forms, *dama* and *mesopotamica*, were considered as species by Ellerman and Morrison-Scott (1951) and Haltenorth (1959, 1961a,b, 1963), and subspecies by Harrison (1968) and Corbet (1978). An obsolete name that was applied to the ancient Egyptian fallow deer is *Dama schaeferi* Hilzheimer, 1927.

Description: The color is yellowish-brown (fallow) with white spots. The belly is white and the tail is white and partially black on the upper side of the base.

13-46 (above) Antlers of Dama mesopotamica *from Iran in the Stuttgart Museum. Source: Haltenorth (1959: fig. 11e).*

13-47 (right) Predynastic relief of the head of a dama deer on a Min statue from Koptos. Source: Petrie (1896: pl. III, 1).

The antlers (deciduous horns) are present on males only. Brow tines are short and the area of the beams above are expanded or flattened and generally bear one inner and two anterior points. The upper parts of the antlers usually have three points and are rarely flattened (palmate). There is considerable variation in shape (fig. 13-46).

Males have a very long penis, which is shown in most Egyptian illustrations.

Shoulder height is 95-105 cm and lower than the height of the hips. The tail is 15-16 cm with a terminal tuft of 14.5 cm, which makes it appear very long.

Natural history: The habits of recent dama deer were summarized by Lay (1967: 236) and Harrison (1968 II: 368) who said the species lived in dense jungles of tamarisk and poplar bordering rivers in SW Iran. Food consists mostly of browse.

Dama deer pass the day in dense vegetation and are only seen near the edge of cover in early morning and late evening.

Distribution: This species formerly ranged through Asia Minor to Iran, the eastern Mediterranean, Arabian Peninsula, Sinai, and NE Africa. Recent distribution was recorded from river banks in southwestern Iran (Lay, 1967:236). The "war between Iraq and Iran may have wiped out the last wild representatives of this species" (Uerpmann, 1987: 58).

According to Hilzheimer (1913: 170 f.) dama deer from southwest Asia crossed the Isthmus of Suez into Egypt during the Pleistocene diluvium and became established in the Nile Delta, wandered westward to Tripolitania, and from there southward to Tassili n'Addjar. The species is said to have extended its range through Lower and Upper Egypt and Nubia into southeastern Abyssinia (Joleaud, 1935: 13-14, 44-46; Haltenorth, 1959: 14). During that period the Sahara desert did not exist, but was steppe and heavily wooded along the river banks and coastal regions.

Support of the theory of migration is evidenced by the numerous Pleistocene remains of Mesopotamian fallow deer in Palestine indicating the presence of a large population, which could have been the origin for migrations into Egypt (Bate, 1937: 210). Although very few Pleistocene remains of deer have been found in Egypt (see below under *Prehistoric records*), several other large mammal species: ass, pig, wild cattle, Barbary goat, ibex, and hyena are known to have migrated from Asia during the period indicated (Churcher, 1974: 372 ff., 379 f.).

Prehistoric records: Quaternary (Pleistocene) fossils (teeth) of dama deer have been recorded from Gau (Qaw el Kebir) south of El Badari and from Wadi Halfa (Joleaud, 1935; Haltenorth, 1959: 15).

13-48 Rock drawings (left to right) of an ostrich ?, a man on a donkey, dama deer, (?), giraffes, and aurochs in Wadi Sabah Regala of Gebel Silsila, east bank of Nile N of Kom Ombo. Source: Petrie (1892a: fig. 57).

13-49 Predynastic rock drawing of a dama deer by 'Federschmuck-leute' in Wadi Menih in the southern tributaries of Wadi Hammamat, Eastern Desert. Source: Winkler (1937: fig. 13).

Predynastic records: Representations on Predynastic artifacts include the Hunters Palette (fig. 1-3) and two ivory knife handles: Pitt Rivers, row 2 (fig. 1-8) and the Carnavon handle, boss side (fig. 1-9). The Gebel el Arak (fig. 1-11) and the Gebel Tarif (fig. 1-12) handles also have deer carvings, but they appear to have been of Mesopotamian origin.

Of the two deer on the Carnarvon handle (fig. 1-9) the one on the left was named red deer (*Cervus barbarus*) by Bénédite (1918: 11 f.), because of the prominent frontal projections that he called brow tines. These structures, which do not arise from the bases of the antlers, could be a mistake by the artist. Otherwise, the antlers are comparable with those of a dama deer. The deer on the right clearly represents a dama deer.

This handle, like the Gebel el Arak and Gebel Tarif handles, may have been of Mesopotamian origin or carved by a Mesopotamian immigrant, because a bear is represented above the deer.

A relief of the head of a dama deer (fig. 13-47) on the Min statue from Koptos has four tines on each antler and appears to be staked on the long projection from the mouth (Petrie, 1896: 7).

There are a few rock drawings that appear to represent dama deer. Figure 13-48 was classed as Protohistoric by Joleaud (1935: 29) and the drawing by 'Federschmuckleute' (fig. 13-49) is probably Predynastic. Another crude example is undated (fig. 13-50).

Dama deer doubtless existed in the wild in Predynastic Egypt, but in very limited numbers.

The Dynastic period: A dama deer is one of the spotted animals on a Dynasty I mace handle (fig. 1-13). It was called an axis deer by Bénédite (1918: 14), which was incorrect, because the axis deer was southeast Asian in distribution.

Firth (1927b: 207) referred it to the "antlered deer, now extinct in Egypt, but still found in Algeria and Tunis".

Judging from the small number of published illustrations, deer were rare in ancient Egypt. Dawson (1934) published 15; Keimer (1934b), 25; Haltenorth (1959), 15; and Butzer (1977 II: 1220), said he counted 33 from over 1,000 wild animal figures that he examined.

The few reproductions herein serve mainly to illustrate the antler variations and to show that dama deer appeared in offering and hunting scenes from the IVth into the XVIIIth Dynasty when they reportedly became extinct in Egypt.

In offering scenes dama deer stags are usually shown being led by their antlers (figs 7-153, 13-51,-52,-53) with the exception of a dwarfed deer on a leash in the Dynasty VI Tomb of Kagemni (Gemnikai), Saqqara (von Bissing, 1905 I: pl.XXV, 5; Haltenorth, 1959: fig. 8, 11).

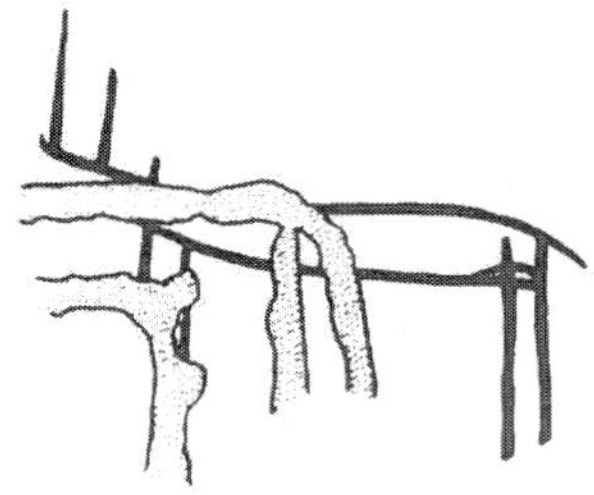

13-50 Undated rock drawing of a dama deer at Sharab 25 km N.E. of Edfu in Wadi Mia, Eastern Desert. Source: Červíček (1974: fig. 457).

13-51 A reddish-brown stag in an offering scene. Tomb of Atet, Dynasty IV, Medum. Source: Petrie (1892 b: pl. XXVII).

13-52 A stag of reduced size in an offering scene. Tomb of Meho, Dynasty V-VI, Saqqara. Source: Author.

13-53 A stag in an offering scene. Tomb of Ti, Dynasty V, Saqqara. Source: Wild (1966 III: pl. CXLII B).

13-54 A stag in a hunting scene. Tomb of Sahure, Dynasty V, Abusir. Source: Borchardt (1913 II: pl. 17).

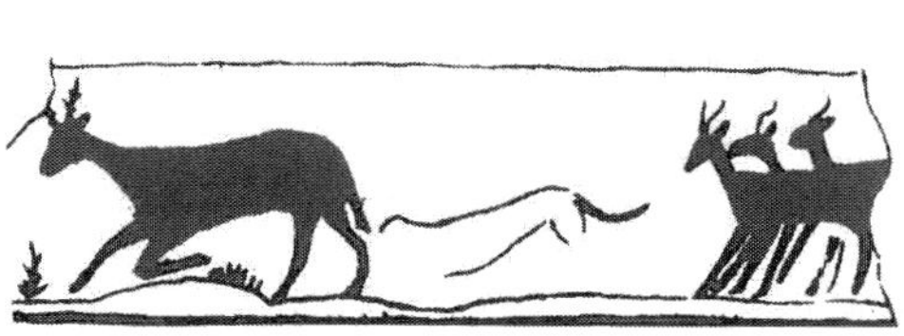

13-55 A stag attacked by a hound. Tomb of Nehera, Dynasty XII, El Bersheh. Source: Griffith and Newberry (1894 II: pl. XI). To the right are three dorcas gazelles.

13-56 (left) Head of a stag with a single antler on a fragment of a hunting scene. Tomb of Akhanekt, Dynasty XII, El Bersheh. Source: Griffith and Newberry (1894 II: pl. XVI).

13-57 (below) Stags in a hunting scene. Tomb of Antefoker, Dynasty XII, Thebes. Source: Davies and Gardiner (1920: pl. VI).

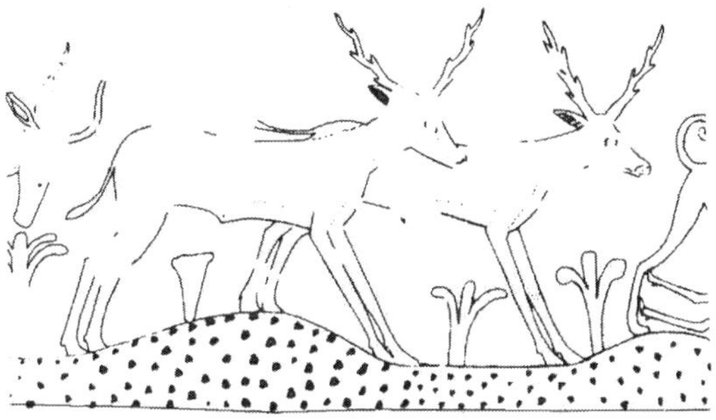

In one offering scene (fig. 7-153) a dama deer and various other animals are labelled *rn*, which indicates that deer were sometimes semi-domesticated.

Dama deer stags were most frequently pictured in hunting scenes together with a variety of desert and semi-desert species (figs 1-29, 7-28, 13-42,-54 to -60).

Hassan (1944: 530; 1955: 138) listed the stag among the animals being hunted in the Dynasty V Causeway of Unas, Saqqara, but did not illustrate it.

Two females are included in the Tombs of Khety and Baqt (Newberry, 1894 II: pls. XIII, XXXV). Another female occurs together with a stag in Figure 13-59. The fawn of this pair is mistakenly shown suckling the antlered one.

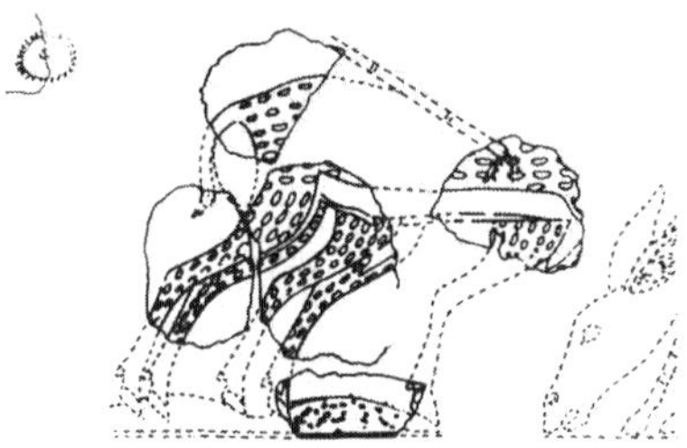

13-58 Fragments of two dama deer in a hunting scene. Tomb of Antef, Dynasty XVIII, Thebes. Source: Säve-Söderberg (1957 I: pl. XVI).

13-59 Male and female deer in a hunting scene. Tomb of Puyemre, Dynasty XVIII, Thebes. Source: Davies (1922: pl. VII). On the left a hound is subduing a dorcas gazelle. Below are an ostrich and two hares.

Various authors have commented on the inability of ancient artists to accurately reproduce the antlers. As with many other horned beasts, however, the heads of the deer were shown in profile and the antlers in frontal view. One exception is in the Tomb of Puyemre (fig. 13-59) where the antlers are in profile and show a distal palmation. This feature is not characteristic of all *Dama mesopotamica*, because there is a great deal of variation in the shape of this part of the antlers, which can be seen in Figure 13-46 and in Keimer (1934b: fig. 32) and Haltenorth (1959: figs 10, 11).

Dawson (1934: 137) and Allen (1939: 467) were convinced that fallow deer never existed in Egypt as part of the natural fauna, but were probably introduced. Various other authors recognized it as a part of the wild fauna, but always uncommon (Joleaud, 1935: 43, 44; Keimer, 1934b: 301; Haltenorth, 1959: 14; and Boessneck, 1988: 39, 58).

There are no depictions of this species being brought as tribute from Asia before Dynasty XVIII as there are of elephants, bears, zebu, and Arabian oryx.

Antler fragments of dama deer have been found from the New Kingdom at Deir el-Medineh, Thebes (Keimer, 1934b: 274) and Qau el-Kebir (Dawson, 1934: 143 f.n.). Boessneck (1988: 58) listed bones of captive dama deer from a palace in an ancient city near Tell el-Daba in the eastern Delta.

Following the Dynasty XVIII extinction of the dama deer in Egypt, however, there is a record of a deer having been imported from Syria during the reign of Tuthmosis III (Davies, 1922 I: 46; L.D. III, 31a).

The reasons for extinction of dama deer in the wild could easily be attributed to overhunting and loss of habitat due to desertification. Why deer were not maintained and bred in enclosures as they appear to have been in earlier times (fig. 7-153) is an unanswerable question.

The last illustrations of dama deer appeared in the Greek Tomb of Petosiris (fig. 13-61).

A few medicinal notes summarized by Darby *et al.* (1977: 239) included the use of stag horn as an external application to cure headaches and "binding the hide of this agile animal to gouty legs". Bénédite (1918: 12 f.n. 2) wrote: 1) that deer horn was included in a fumigant to expel an affection from the body of the sufferer, and 2) the horn pounded with incense and another substance and mixed together with a sweet beer is employed against the affection which "weakens all the members in summer and in winter".

Errors and discrepancies: Various errors were included in the text above. But, in regard to identification, Houlihan (1987: 241) finalized a review of the evidence for existence of red or dama deer in ancient Egypt with the statement: "Only further archaeological and zooarchaeological findings can hope to answer more firmly our questions about the deer".

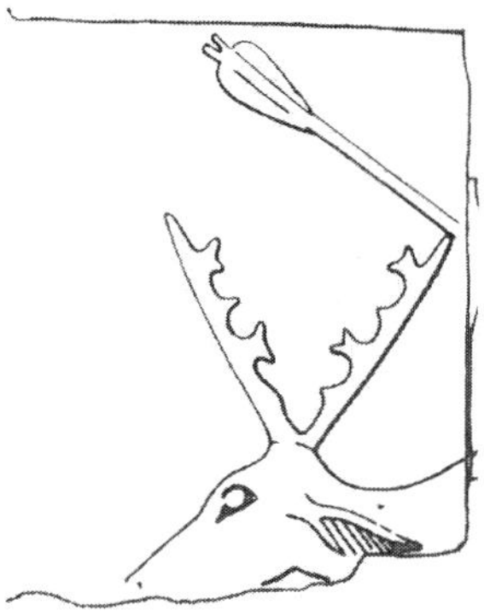

13-60 (left) A stag's head in a fragment of a hunting scene. Tomb of Mentuherkhepshef (Menthirkhopshef), Dynasty XVIII, Thebes. Source: Davies (1913: pl. XII).

13-61 (right) A dama deer stag with a beard in an offering scene in the Greek Tomb of Petosiris at Tuna el Gebel (Hermopolis-West), Ptolemaic Period. Source: Lefebvre (1924 III: pl. XLIX).

Camels Family *Camelidae*

Dromedary Camel *Camelus dromedarius* Linnaeus, 1758

E Single-humped Camel; F Chameau de Dromedaire; G Dromedar; A Gamal (Jamal), Baarour, Nakah (Nagah)

Description: Camels differ from other ungulates in having one or two fatty humps on their backs. The hooves are not functional because the toe bones are imbedded in broad cutaneous pads on which the animals walk; an adaptation to sandy terrain. Camels are longer necked and longer legged than most other ungulates and the knees are exposed on the hind legs.

The ears are relatively small. The lips are thick and somewhat hanging.

The teeth of camels also differ from other ruminants in the presence of upper incisors and the third incisors being developed like canine tusks. True canines are also present, but the first premolars are also canine-like and separated from the others by a gap (diastema). For further details see Clutton-Brock (1987).

Dromedaries have one hump. The pelage is relatively short and the color is light or pale brown in summer and darker in winter. There are short dorsal and ventral manes on the neck and a crown of long hair on the hump.

Natural history: Camels do not need to drink water when green forage is available. During summer they need to drink only every fifth day. Females and males can drink up to 120 or 150 liters of water, respectively, in one draught (Cloudsley-Thompson, 1977: 103).

Water is not stored in the hump nor in the stomach, but in the tissues.

Prehistoric records: Remains of wild C. dromedarius were found in a Holocene site on the southern slope of the Gilf el Kebir in southwestern Egypt. Remains of the now extinct *C. thomasi* were found in a Middle Paleolithic site at Bir Sahara, east of the Gilf el Kebir and in an Upper Paleolithic site at Wadi Halfa in northern Sudan (Uerpmann, 1987: fig. 18). Fragmentary remains of *Camelus cf. thomasi* were also found in Pleistocene deposits near Dakhla Oasis (Churcher, *et al.* 1997b).

How late these species remained in Egypt is

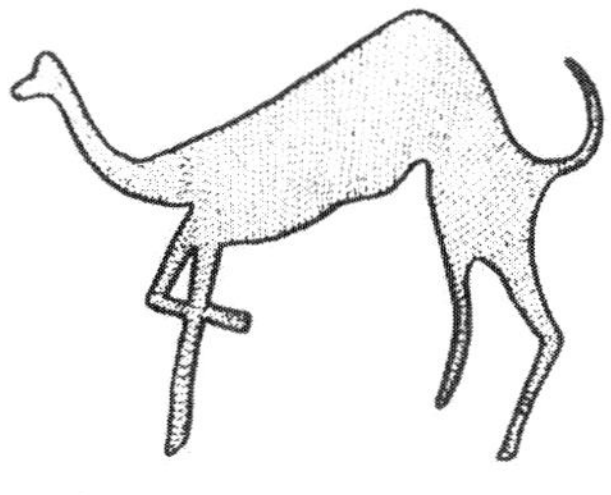

13-62 Pre- or early historic rock drawing of a camel from Kanais in Wadi Mia 45 km east of Edfu (Idfu). Source: Červíček (1974: fig. 256).

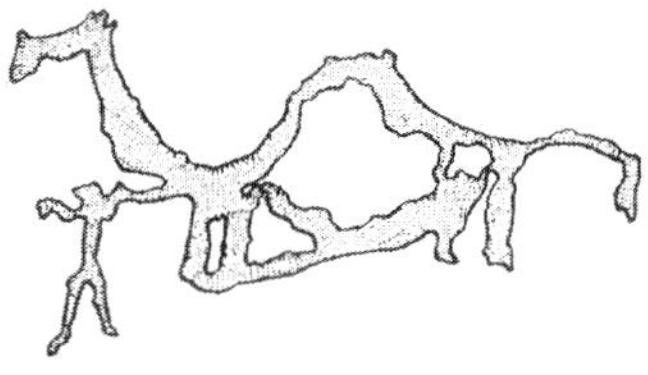

13-63 Pre- or early historic rock drawing of a man and a camel from Magal Hodein in Wadi Naam, southeastern Eastern Desert. Source: Červíček (1974: fig. 321).

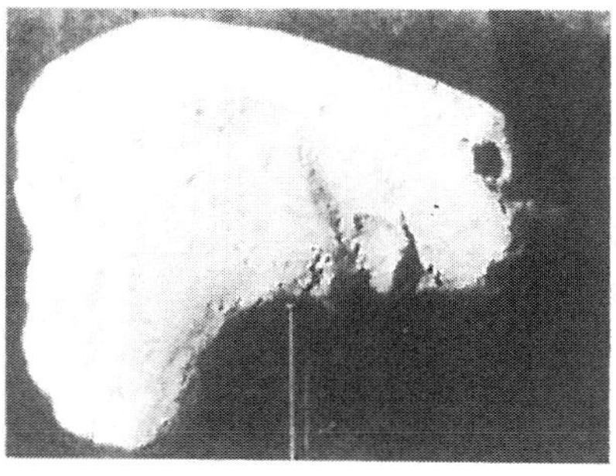

13-64 A terracotta head of a camel from Hierakonpolis dated to Dynasty I. Source: Quibell and Green (1902 II: pl. LXII, 2).

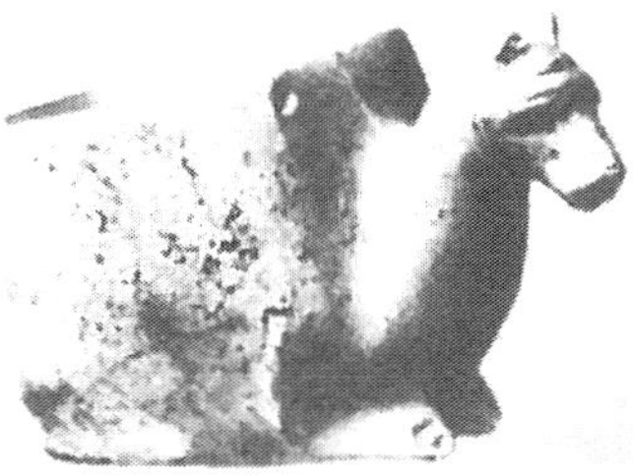

13-65 A limestone figurine of a kneeling camel with a tank on its back (form of an ointment jar) from a Dynasty I tomb at Abusir-el-Meleq, dated to about 3,000 B.C. Source: Möllers and Scharff (1926: pl. 24, 209).

13-66 Rock drawing of a camel led by a man in Wadi Abu Agag north of Aswan, dated to Dynasty VI. Source: Schweinfurth (1912: fig. 2).

13-67 Rock drawings by Blemyans of camels and horses in Wadi Abu Wasil, tributary of Wadi Menih, dated to the 1st Millenium, B.C. Source: Winkler (1938 I: pl. II, 2).

unknown, but in Uerpmann's (1987: 52) opinion probably no Post- Pleistocene wild camels existed. Neither of these species were domesticated from wild stock in North Africa.

Sometime later in Predynastic or early Dynastic times, domesticated *C. dromedarius* was brought into Egypt from Arabia where it was originally domesticated (Epstein, 1971 II: 571 f.).

There is evidence for the presence of the camel as a domesticate from the remains found together with a human in a Dynasty I cemetery at Helwan (Brewer, *et al.*, 1994: 104, fig. 8.4)), which was discovered by Saad (1951: 38) who said it could possibly be interpreted as 'the burial of an animal servant with its master'.

13-68 Arab rock drawing of a caravan of camels with riders south of the Qift-Quseir road in Wadi Abu Qwei. Source: Redford and Redford (1989: fig. 24).

There are also some earlier records from the Prehistoric and Predynastic periods, such as the rock drawings from Onib in Wadi Allaqi, Nubia of some camels that are ridden (Parker and Burkitt, 1932). Drawings of camels from Kanais in Wadi Mia 45 km east of Idfu and Magal Hodein in Wadi Naam in the southeastern Eastern Desert also indicate the presence of camels in the pre- and early historical periods (figs 13-62,-63).

Keimer (1929) described a terracotta tablet with a man on a camel being led by another man, which was found in a Predynastic cemetery north of Gurna.

Dynastic period: Several terracotta camel heads listed by Epstein (1971 II: 559) included the Dynasty I figurine from Hierakonpolis (fig. 13-64), which was previously called a 'donkey' (Quibell and Green, 1902 II: 49).

Zeuner (1963: 350) said that the limestone receptacle for ointment found at Abu Sir-el-Meleq in a Dynasty I cemetery (fig. 13-65) puts domestication back into the fourth millenium B.C.

A rock drawing near Aswan (fig. 13-66) is linked with the hieratic figures (not shown) to the left with Dynasty VI. Schweinfurth (1912) assumed from this figure that domestic dromedaries were known in Egypt before 2250 B.C.

These figurines and other data on remains do not support the survival and domestication of the camel until the introduction of the domesticated species from Arabia.

The camel seems to have disappeared from Egypt in the Old Kingdom (Hobbs, 1980: 25). Later, camels were introduced via Blemyans in the south as is indicated by a rock drawing (fig. 13-67) from southern Upper Egypt dated to the first Millennium.

"The first millennium B.C. was marked by a new motif: representations of horsemen and camel riders ... The camel nomads populated the eastern Desert towards the end of that millennium" (Červíček, 1974: 204). Theories on introduction of camels also range in time from the Middle Kingdom (3rd Millenium B.C.) to the Roman Period and later.

Under Ptolemy Philadelphus (285-247 B.C.) trade routes were established across the Eastern Desert (Brewer *et al.*, 1994: 105). Camels were the important carriers of trade goods.

A series of rock drawings along the Qift-Quseir Road that follows Wadi Hammamat in the central Eastern Desert (Redford and Redford, 1989) show a number of dromedary camels in Arab (fig. 13-68) and Roman style (fig. 13-69). One figure (*loc. cit.*, 26, fig. 41) was said to be a "Depiction of a Bactrian dromedary. Obviously drawn by someone who had been to Persia or farther east as only the one-humped Arabian camels are known in Egypt" (fig. 13-70). The Bactrian or two-humped camel was not known to have existed in Ancient Egypt, nor in later times.

By the beginning of the Roman Period the dromedary camel attained its modern position in Egypt.

A comment on the camel by Darby *et al.* (1977 I: 254) is worth inserting here: "... the history of the camel in Ancient Egypt is as perplexing as is that of the horse."

There are other sources of interesting information on history and origin of the African camel (Epstein, 1971 II: 558 ff.).

Errors and discrepancies: A three foot long twisted cord said to have been made of camel hair was found in a rubbish slope of a Dynasty III-IV gypsum works of Umm-es-Sawan in the Faiyum (Caton-Thompson, 1934: 21; Caton-Thompson and Gardner, 1934: 119, 123). A careful microscopic study of hair and comparison with hairs of ox, sheep, goat, horse, ass, and man was made under normal and polarized light.

Caton-Thompson (*op. cit.*) refered to this find as proof for the existence of the camel in the early Old Kingdom.

The cord was identified later as being made of sheep hair (Midant-Reynes and Braunstein-Sylvestre, 1977: 347).

13-69 A rock drawing of a Dromedary camel and an ibex in Wadi Abu Qwei dated to the Roman Period or later. Source: Redford and Redford (1989: fig. 21).

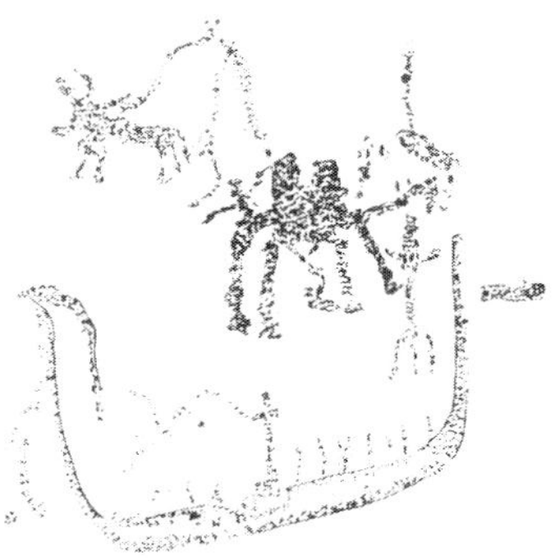

13-70 Persian rock drawing of a 'Bactrian dromedary' in Wadi Abu Qwei south of the Qift-Quseir road. Source: Redford and Redford (1989: fig. 41).

Bovids Family *Bovidae*
Subfamily *Tragelaphinae*

Giant Eland ***Tragelaphus (Taurotragus) oryx*** (Pallas 1766)

F Elan(d) de Derby; G Elenantilope, Reisen-elenantilope

Nomenclature: The nomenclature of this species and various races is not clearly defined as can be seen in comparing Setzer (1956: 573), Dorst and Dandelot (1969: 186 f.), Gotch (1979: 216), Haltenorth and Diller (1980: 65 f.), and Honacki et al. (1982: 343).

Description: Elands are large, slender bovids with a small hump on the shoulders, and a small dewlap (fold of skin) under the throat. Horns occur in both sexes, but are larger in males. They are diverging and have a "close screw-like spiral" (Dorst and Dandelot, 1970: 186).

Colors are greyish to reddish-brown with transverse body stripes. The short tail tuft reaches almost to the hocks. Measurements are: Shoulder height 130-180 cm, head and body length 210-270, tail 50-90. Males are considerably larger than females.

Natural history: Elands are browsers and grazers. With green food available they can survive for weeks without drinking water.

Distribution: The present range is south of the Sahara in Sudan and Ethiopia, in part of West Africa, and the northern part of Zaire, except for deserts and dense forest.

Prehistoric and Predynastic records: Gautier (in Wendorf, 1968) listed possibly eland in the Quaternary fauna of Nubia. Later he found (Gautier, 1980: 324) bones of what he considered to be *Taurotragus derbyanus* or giant eland at the Quaternary site of Bir Tarfawi in the southern Western Desert. His decision was based on the large size of the fossils and the present distribution of this species and *T. oryx*.

The Dynastic period: An eland is recognizable on the Dynasty I mace handle from Seiyala (fig. 1-13); the only representation known from historic time.

Sitatunga ***Tragelaphus spekei*** (Sclater, 1863)

F Sitatunga, Guib d'eau; G Sitatunga, Wasserkudu, Sumpfbock

Nomenclature: An obsolete synonym is *Limnotragus spekei*.

Description: Only males have horns, which have one and a half spiral twists and two keels. The uniform body color varies from dark to light brown, yellowish or grizzled- grey, with six to eight transverse body stripes. Shoulder height is 75-125 cm. Males are larger than females.

Natural history: Sitatungas are nocturnal and diurnal, depending upon disturbances in habitat. They are strictly confined to swampy areas, swim and dive very well, and may remain submerged with only nostrils exposed. They browse on semi-aquatic vegetation.

Distribution: Sitatungas occupy Upper Nile swamps in southern Sudan and Ethiopia, Lake Chad to the west, and the Togo area in Gambia. Southward, the range includes much of the west-central part of Africa.

Prehistoric and Predynastic records: Wassif (1976: 97) reported archeological finds from northern Egypt.

Subfamily *Hippotraginae*

Addax ***Addax nasomaculatus*** (Blainville, 1816)

nwdw nudju Wb. II, 226

E Addax Antelope, Screwhorned Antelope, Mendes Antelope; F Addax au nez tacheté; G Mendes-antilope; A Abu Meha, Abu Akash, Bagar el Wahsh (Wild Cow)

Nomenclature: Obsolete synonyms are *Antilope addax* and *A. suturosa*.

"*Addax* (L) a wild animal with crooked horns, derived from an African word, *nasus* (L) the nose, *macula* (L) a spot, a mark , *-atus* (L) suffix meaning provided with; this refers to the brown [or white?, *sic*] patches on the nose" (Gotch, 1979: 217).

Description: Addax are very distinct in having long, slender, spirally twisted horns that slope backward. There are 2½ to 3 twists in male and 1½ to 2 twists in female horns (fig. 13-71). Male horns are 100-125 cm long and female, 95-110 cm. There are prominent rings ⅔ to ¾ of the length.

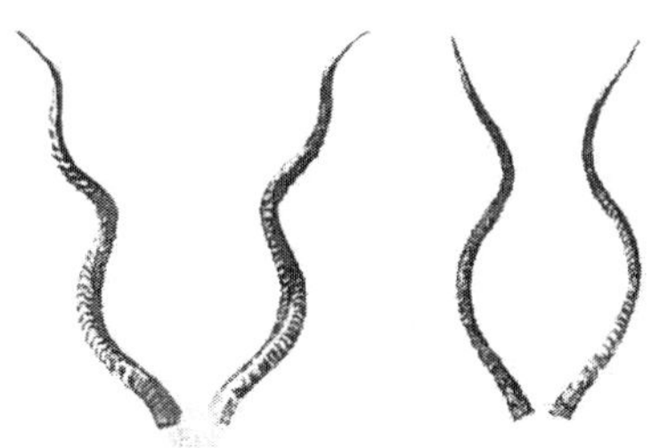

13-71 Addax horns in frontal view (male left, female right). Source: Sclater and Thomas (1894-1900: figs 95, 96).

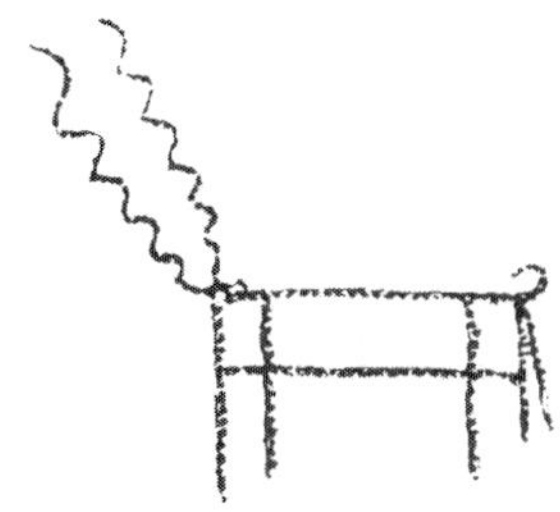

13-72 Rock drawing of an addax from Wadi Abu Agag in the Eastern Desert. Source: Schweinfurth (1912: fig. 16).

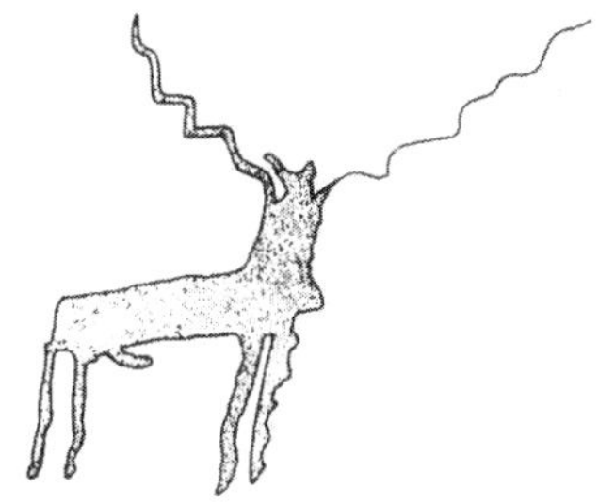

13-73 Rock drawing of an addax from the west bank of the Nile in the southern Mariya district north of El Dakka. Source: Červiček (1974: fig. 416).

The twists are easily recognized in most Egyptian representations although the horns were usually shown in lateral view (figs 1-16, 7-153,-163, 13-74), except in Figure 13-78, row 4) and in two rock drawings (figs 13-72,-73).

Color varies from white to grayish-white in spring and summer to brownish-gray in winter. The rump, tail (except for the black tuft), underparts, and limbs are white. The head is darker than the body and has a white X-like mark across the muzzle and cheeks in front of the eyes, from which the name *nasomaculatus* was derived. There is a conspicuous brownish to blackish mat of hair on the forehead. Long hair below the ears and on the throat and neck simulate a mane.

Natural history: Addax are true desert animals and herds migrate with availability of pasture. They can survive without drinking water if green food is available.

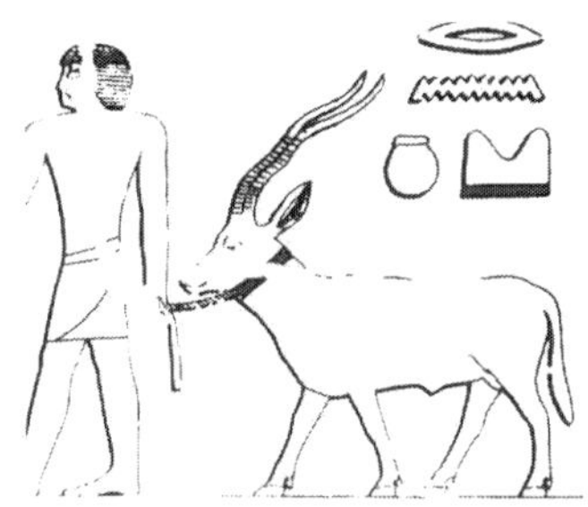

13-74 Addax in an offering procession, Tomb of Akhetep, Dynasty V, Saqqara. Source: Davies (1901a: pl. XIX).

13-75 Addax and gazelle with young in an offering procession in the Tomb of Ti, Dynasty V, Saqqara. Source: Steindorff (1913 : pl. 128).

These antelopes are stockier and shorter legged than other members of this group and cannot run as rapidly; therefore, addax are more easily hunted and have been exterminated over most of their previous range and are in danger of extinction (Tate, 1971: 83 f.).

Addax are easily tamed in captivity as indicated in Figures 13-74,-75,-76.

Distribution: Previous distribution probably included all of the vegetated regions of the Eastern and Western Deserts of Egypt and the whole of the Sahara. Today small herds survive in a few scattered localities in Mauretania, Niger, and Chad (Haltenorth and Diller, 1980: 68).

The species became extinct in Egypt in the early 1900s (Flower, 1932), probably because it was easily run down and shot as a pastime for foreign soldiers.

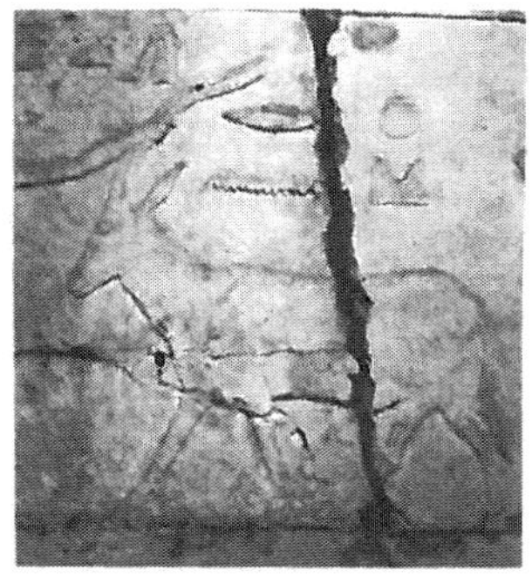

13-76 Addax led in an offering procession, Tomb of Idout, Dynasty VI, Saqqara. Source: Author.

13-77 A dwarfed addax in an offering procession, Tomb of Idout, Dynasty VI, Saqqara. Source: Macramallah (1935: pl. XII). Other dwarfed animals in the procession, which were not copied, are a calf, an ibex, and a gazelle.

Prehistoric records: Uerpman (1987: fig. 36, table 16) listed two sites in southwestern Egypt where identifiable remains have been found, Wadi Bakht in the Gilf Kebir (Late Neolithic) and site K 2 (Holocene) a few km to the north. Remains were also found at the well-known site of Wadi Shaw (Early Neolithic-Bronze Age) in northwestern Sudan.

The Predynastic period: A few rock drawings called

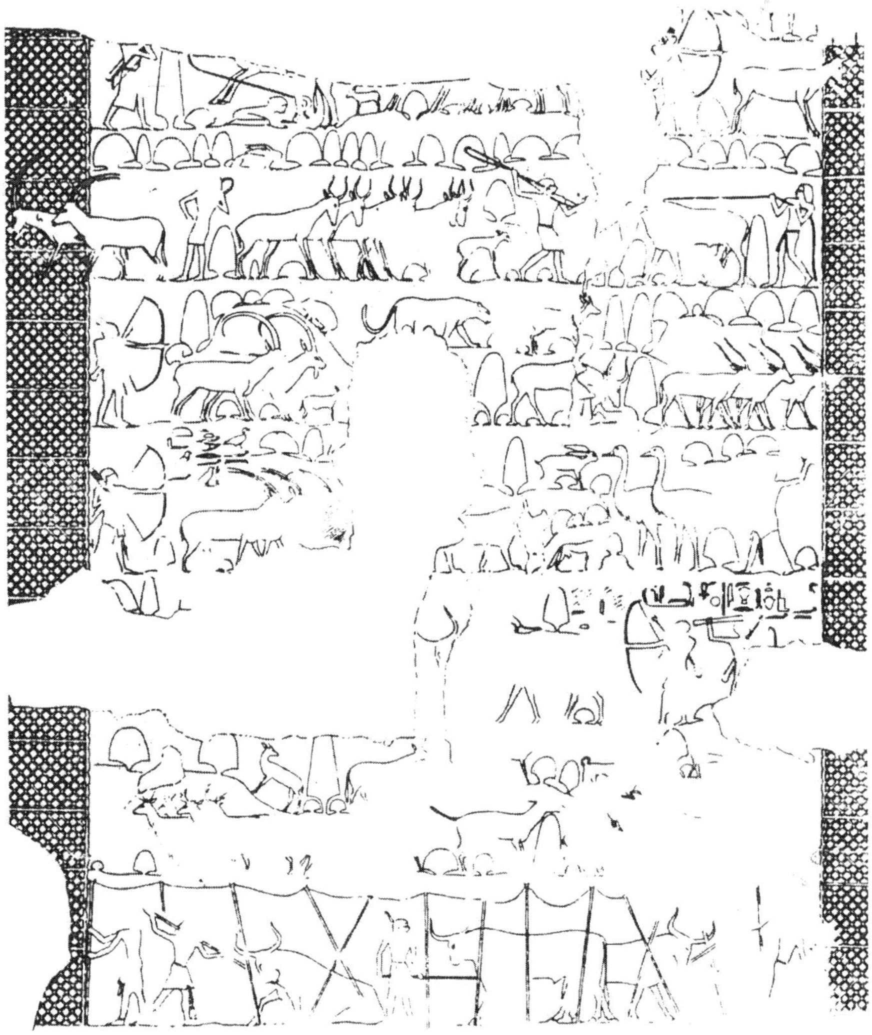

13-78 A hunting scene from the Tomb of Tehutihetep, Dynasty XI, El Bersheh (Barsha). Source: Newberry (1892 I: 14. pl. VII). One or two upper rows were destroyed. In the existing rows the animals are listed left to right as follows:
Row 1: A man advances toward an aurochs (note the long tail) with calf. The animal is apparently caught by a bola or lasso and another man is attempting to tie the rope to a peg. The legs of numerous animals are to the right and on the far right an archer is about to release an arrow at a hartebeest.
Row 2. A hare is hiding in a row of bushes.
Row 3. Two scimitar oryx and a man pulling at a bola that has been destroyed; six hartebeests and a calf; a man about to throw a lasso at an aurochs, which is already caught by another man.
Row 4. An archer shooting at one of two ibex with a calf. Above them a hedgehog climbs a hillock and next is a lioness following a dorcas gazelle. Below are a hartebeest with calf and three female addax with horns in frontal view.
Row 5. An archer is shooting at one of three scimitar oryx. Beyond the damaged portion is a lion, a hare, a fox ?, and two ostriches being driven.
Row 6. To the right are the remnants of an archer shooting at an aurochs, above the fore-legs of which are the hind-legs and tail of a jerboa (?).
Row 7. The heads of four deer, a gazelle, two other bovids, and the rear of a curl-tailed hound.
Row 8. The partly damaged bovid is not clear.
Row 9. Men are setting posts for nets and driving back what appear to be domestic oxen.

Mendesantilope were published by Červiček (1974: figs 150, 171, 416), which were from the west bank near El Hosh; Galt el Aguz in the Eastern Desert, northwest of Gebel Abrak; and the west bank in the southern Mariya district north of El Dakka. The latter (fig. 13-73) was crudely drawn with exaggerated horn curvatures.

Drawings with similar horns were published by Schweinfurth (1912: figs 15 and 16) from Wadi Abu Agag in the Eastern Desert, northeast of Aswan (fig. 13-72).

None of the 'antilope' drawings referred to by Winkler (1938, 1939) can be called addax.

The Dynastic period: In the Old Kingdom the addax was pictured among other bovids being 'stall fed' (fig. 1-16) and there are numerous illustrations of addax being led in offering scenes in Dynasty V-VI tombs (figs 7-153, 13-74 to 76). There is a dwarfed addax in an offering procession in one tomb (fig. 13-77) and in another an addax and a gazelle are accompanied by young (fig. 13-75).

Addax appeared in at least two hunting scenes (figs 7-163 and 13-78, row 4). Those in the latter are unique, because the horns are shown in frontal view, whereas in all other Dynastic depictions the horns are in lateral view.

Errors and discrepancies: In a scene from the Tomb of Ti there are two 'antelopes' labelled with the hieroglyph *(nudu)* for addax. The male on the left (fig. 13-79) is obviously a hartebeest, judging from the shape of the horns in frontal view. There is a slight similarity between the horns of hartebeests in frontal view (figs 1-16, 13-78, rows 1, 3, 4, and 13-79) and those of female addax (figs 13-71 and 13-78, row 4), but the hieroglyphic identification in Fig. 13-79 is quite obviously erroneous.

13-79 A male hartebeest and a female addax with the hieroglyphs for addax in the Dynasty V Tomb of Ti, Saqqara. Source: Epron and Daumas (1939 I: pl. XXIV).

Oryx Genus *Oryx*

 *m3ḥḏ* mahedj Wb. II, 11

(All species of oryx were identified by the same hieroglyph.)

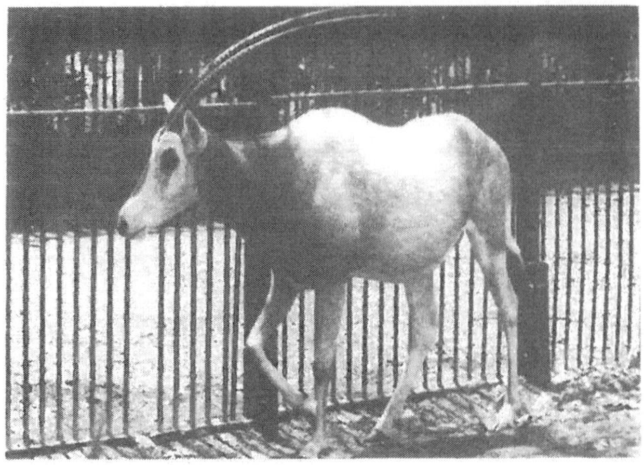

13-80 Scimitar oryx, O. dammah, *in Giza Zoological Garden, Cairo. Source: Author.*

Nomenclature: An obsolete synonym for *Oryx* is *Antilope,* but oryx are commonly referred to as antelopes or antilopes.

Some authors, following the classification of Haltenorth (1963), consider all oryx to be conspecific, and group them under *Oryx gazella* (Linnaeus, 1758), whereby the given species names are subspecific (Haltenorth and Diller, 1980: 67). Herein, the earlier system of recognizing separate species is followed (Dorst, 1970: 201 f.).

General description: Oryx are large antelopes with a shoulder hump; long, slender, straight to slightly curved or strongly curved horns, about one meter or more in length; and long tails with dark tufts reaching below the hocks.

Coloration is pale with a black pattern on the head, body, and legs, excepting one species, *Oryx dammah.* There is a short, erect mane on the nape and throat.

Shoulder heights average about one meter.

13-81 Rock drawings of oryx east of Dakhla Oasis. Source: Winkler (1939 II: pl. XLI, 1). Upper left two figures are beisa oryx. The third figure is questionable. Lower row, two possible scimitar oryx, third without horns. Winkler's site 67, Ghubari Road. Dated to Early Oasis Dwellers.

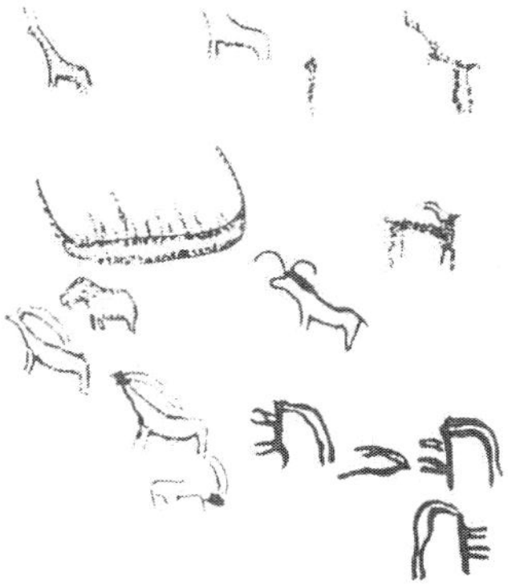

13-82 *(left) Rock drawings of elephant (above), hound, scimitar oryx and young. Lower right, beisa oryx and two unidentifiable figures. El Hosh, west bank of Nile, Upper Egypt. Source: Winkler (1938 I: pl. XXVII, 2).*

13-83 *(right) Rock drawings on the Qift-Quseir road about 300 m east of Wadi Abu Qwei. Source: Redford and Redford (1989 fig. 43). A gerenuk and a giraffe above the boat and a hippopotamus below the boat are dated to the Late Predynastic/Early Dynastic. Three scimitar oryx below the hippopotamus are dated to the Neolithic. A Barbary goat on the lower right of the boat is dated to the late Predynastic. A gazelle farther right is dated to Late Predynastic/Early Dynastic. On the lower right are three ibex drawn vertically and dated to the Neolithic.*

Natural history: Oryx live in small herds of 10 to 12 or more depending on size of the population. Old males are sometimes solitary. Steppe, savanna, and semidesert are inhabited, but never forest or mountain areas. Food is grasses, shrubs, and a variety of other vegetation. Oryx drink water when available, but can survive for weeks without it.

A comment on oryx behavior by Harrison (1968 II: 349) is applicable to all species: "Unapproachable and wild by nature and unquestionably dangerous when wounded, it is strange that the Oryx is easily tamed, becoming remarkedly docile in captivity."

The semi-domestication (taming) of oryx by the ancient Egyptians is well documented in their tomb decorations. They kept two species, scimitar oryx (*O. dammah*) and beisa oryx (*O. beisa*), in captivity.

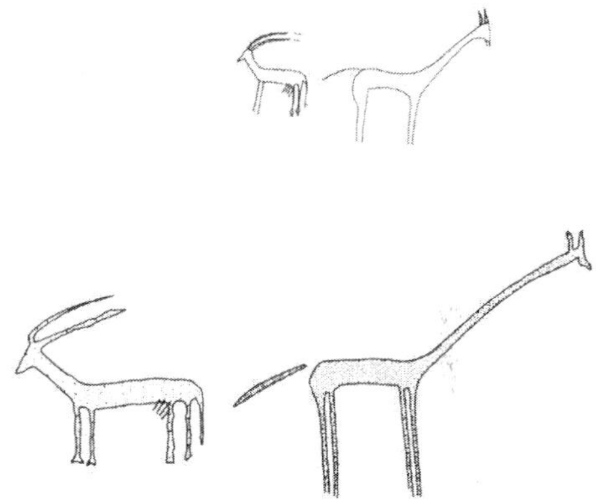

13-84 A scimitar oryx (above) and beisa oryx (below) together with giraffes. Magal Abu Hagag 22.5 km east of Aswan. Source: Červíček (1974: figs 297, 298).

13-85 Scimitar oryx (lower left and right) and beisa oryx (left) together with a wild cow, seven ostriches, and several unidentifiable zoomorphs. Galt el-Aguz 30 km northwest of Gebel Abrak, Eastern Desert. Source: Červíček (1974: fig. 209).

Scimitar Oryx ***Oryx dammah*** (Cretzschmar, 1826)

E Scimitar-horned Oryx, Sabre Oryx, White Oryx; F Oryx algazelle; G Säbelantilope; A Maha, Abu Herab (Father of Spears)

Nomenclature: The common name, white oryx, is also given to the Arabian oryx and this has caused confusion as to which species was described or pictured in Egyptian literature. Herein, therefore, the name scimitar oryx will be used for the species *O. dammah.*

This species has also been called *O. algazel* (Oken, 1816) and *O. tao* (Smith, 1827).

Description: The scimitar oryx, as the name indicates, has long, slender, and curving horns (fig. 13-80), which measure 80-125 cm. The body color is white, washed with reddish- brown on the neck, shoulders, back, upper base of the tail, lower part of the body, and flanks. The head is white with large grayish or brownish patches on the nose and forehead that may or may not connect with the stripes passing through the eyes from the bases of the ears or horns. The legs are whitish; brownish on the foreparts.

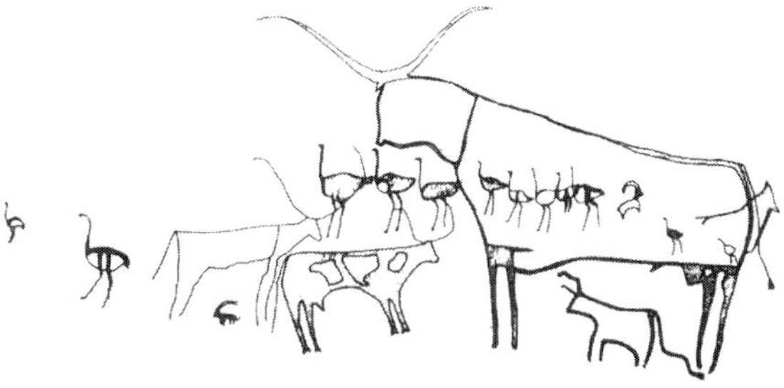

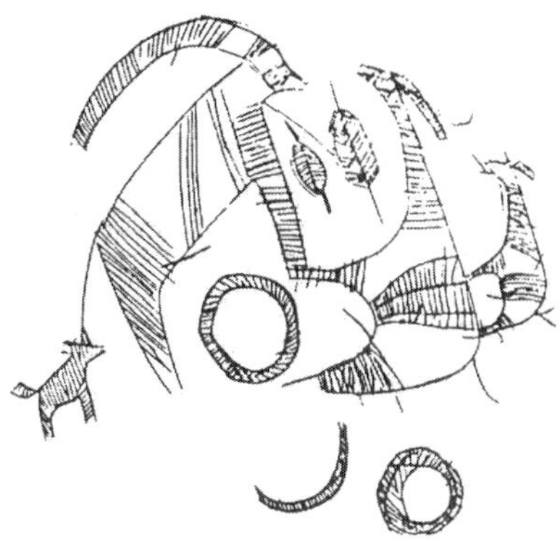

13-86 (left) Scimitar oryx (lower left) below a wild cow, ibex (upper right) behind the row of ostriches, and several wild cattle. El-Beida in Wadi Naam north of Gebel Abrak, Eastern Desert. Source: Červíček (1974: fig. 106a).

13-87 (right) A Predynastic etching on an ostrich eggshell of a scimitar oryx followed by a pariah dog. To the right are two long-necked gazelles (?). Source: Kantor (1948: fig. 1).

13-88 A Predynastic ivory carving of two ibex (above) and a scimitar (?) oryx (below) from Hierakonpolis. Note the shoulder markings that indicate Mesopotamian style. Source: Quibell (1900 I: pl. XII, 8).

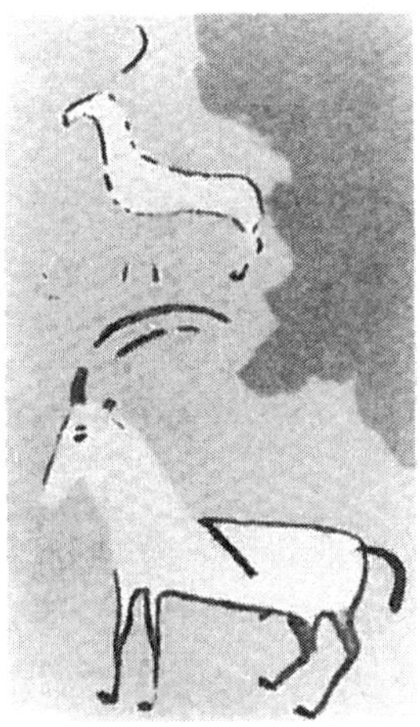

13-89 A gazelle (above) and a scimitar oryx in the wall painting of the Hierakonpolis tomb. Source: Quibell and Green (1902 II: pl. LXXVII).

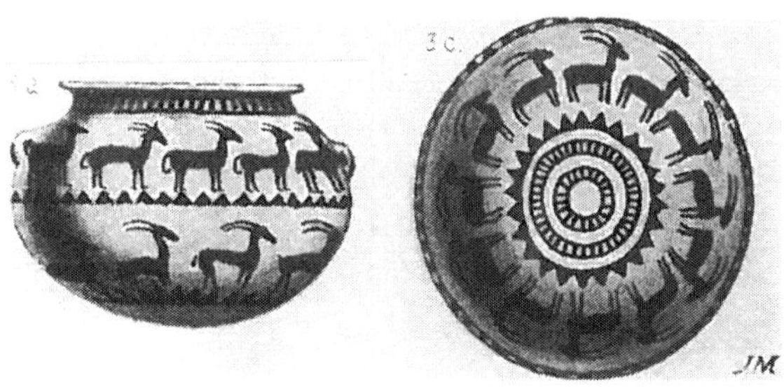

13-90 Oryx figures on prehistoric pottery from Abydos. Source: De Morgan (1896: pl. V, 3a,3c).

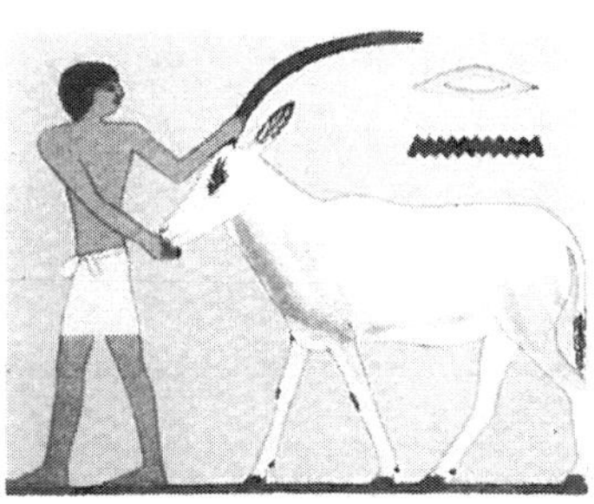

13-91 Scimitar oryx as offering in the Mastaba of Rahotep, Dynasty III or IV, Medum. Source: Petrie (1892b: pl. XI).

Distribution: A little over 150 years ago *O. dammah* lived throughout the vegetated parts of the Western Desert of Egypt (Kock, 1970b: 28) and the western Sahara. No specimens exist from the Eastern Desert (Osborn and Helmy, 1980: 480), although rock drawings are fairly common (see below).

Today the range is limited to a sub-Saharan strip between Air and Ennedi (Dorst and Dandelot, 1970: 223; Haltenorth and Diller, 1980: 66,67).

Small herds migrate northward and southward depending upon rainfall. Occasionally strays are found far beyond the known limits. In 1975 one oryx was seen near the Siwa road 130 km SSW of Mersa Matruh and tracks in 1980 near Ras el Qattar (aprox. 29° 59' N, 27° 18' E) on the western margin of the Qattara Depression (I. Helmy, pers. com.).

The reason for the reduction in range was not climatic change, as with many African species formerly found in Egypt, but excessive slaughtering, especially by military personnel.

Prehistoric and Predynastic records: Remains of this oryx are rare and skeletal bones are difficult or impossible to identify to species (Uerpmann, 1987: 83). No sites are listed from Egypt, but remains dated from 8,000-1,200 B.C. were found in Wadi Shaw, northwestern Sudan (*op. cit.*, fig. 36).

Rock drawings in the Western Desert (figs 13-81, 7-7) and the west bank of the Nile (fig. 13-82) verify the former distribution of this species, but drawings along the eastern borders of the Nile Valley cannot be considered reliable distribution records for the Eastern Desert. Drawings of oryx with curved and straight horns in remote areas of the Eastern Desert, however, indicate that both *Oryx dammah* and *O. beisa* (see below) could have penetrated this region. The broad wadis and coastal plains of the southern two thirds of the Eastern Desert would have provided suitable habitats for these species.

Drawings of oryx with curved horns dated to the Epi- Paleolithic, Neolithic, Late Predynastic,

Early Dynastic, and Roman periods from sites along the middle of the Qift-Quseir road were published by Redford and Redford (1989: figs 12, 13, 14, 43, 49, 50, 56, 59). Although these examples were called 'gazelles' and 'antelopes', the horn shapes suggest *O. dammah* (figs 10-1,-2, 13-83).

Červíček's (1974) rock drawings from the Eastern Desert also include a few curved-horned oryx. One from the site in the vicinity of Magal Abu Agag, which is about 22.5 km east of the Nile (fig. 13-84), is of particular interest because of the straight-horned oryx below and the adjoining giraffes. One set of drawings is possibly a poor copy of the other.

Additional sites are Galt el Aguz, 30 km northwest of Gebel Abrak (fig. 13-85), and El Beida in Wadi Naam north of Gebel Abrak (fig. 13-86), which is about 190 km east of the Nile. The horns of the latter figure are like those of some ibex drawings, but the tail is long enough for an oryx. Additional examples listed by Červíček are questionable.

A scimitar oryx and other animals are etched on an ostrich eggshell (fig. 13-87). The oryx was called an 'ibex' by Kantor (1948: fig. 1), but the tail is long and tufted like that of an oryx, the animal lacks a beard, and the horn curvature is more like that of an oryx.

Ivory carvings from the Gerzean Period that portray scimitar oryx include the Brooklyn or Abu Zaidan knife handle (fig. 1-7, rows A6 and B6 and a displaced figure in row B9), the Pitt Rivers handle (fig. 1-8, 2nd row on the boss side), the Carnarvon handle (fig. 1-9, lower left on the boss side), and the Davis ivory comb (fig. 1-10, 4th row on side A).

An oryx with slightly curving horns on an ivory carving from Hierakonpolis (fig. 13-88) could be either *O. dammah* or *O. beisa*. There are very clear paintings of scimitar oryx on the wall of the Hierakonpolis tomb (fig. 13-89).

Two fragments of Late Gerzean palettes surmounted by two confronting oryx were pictured by Asselberghs (1961: figs 131, 132, 135, 136). The intact horns on the first pair identify them as scimitar oryx. The second, as indicated by Needler's (1984: fig. 41) reconstruction, also represents this species.

Oryx figures on pottery from Abydos (fig. 13-90) have horns varying in shape from straight to strongly curved and tails of normal length, short or absent. The general impression, however, is that the scimitar oryx was the model animal.

The Dynastic period: The first known reproduction from the dynasties is on a Dynasty I gold mace handle (fig. 1-13). The stylized patterns are in the same position as the reddish-brown areas on the neck, chest, and flank (fig. 13-80).

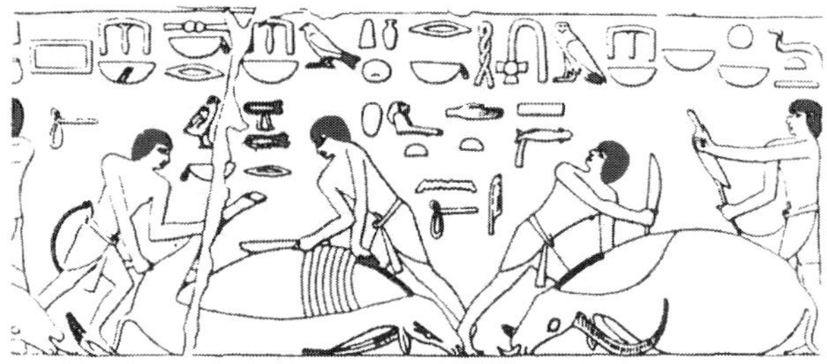

13-92 Butchering of cattle, scimitar oryx, and ibex in the Tomb of Idut, Dynasty VI, Saqqara. Source: Macramallah (1935: pl. XX).

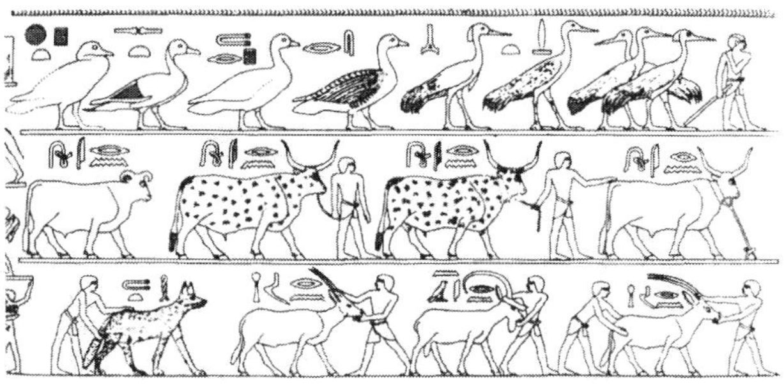

13-93 Offering scene, Tomb of Nefer, early Dynasty VI, Giza. Source: Junker (1943: fig. 16). Row 1: Ducks, geese, and cranes. Row 2: Four oxen. Row 3: Striped hyena, beisa oryx, ibex, scimitar oryx. Note that the hyena lacks the hieroglyph for rn (ren, stall fed).

13-94 A lassoed aurochs and two oryx in the Tomb of Baqt I, Dynasty XII, Beni Hasan. Source: Newberry (1894 II: pl. XXIX).

13-95 Scimitar oryx with young. Tomb of Khety, Dynasty XI, Beni Hasan. Source: Newberry (1894 II: pl. XIV).

Throughout the dynasties scimitar-and straight-horned oryx were pictured in hunt, booty, tribute, and offering scenes and as decorative objects.

Darby *et al.* (1977: 235) remarked that the oryx "...was deemed a valued offering to be made by kings to the gods..." and provided numerous references in support of this statement.

Figure 13-91 is one of the earliest examples of a scimitar oryx in an offering scene.

An excellent relief of scimitar oryx is in the Dynasty IV Tomb of Pepi II (fig. 7-61).

13-96 Feeding scimitar oryx in the Tomb of Chnumhotep, Dynasty XII, Beni Hasan. Source: Newberry (1893 I: pl. XXVII).

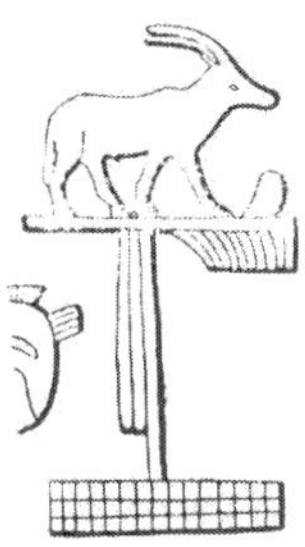

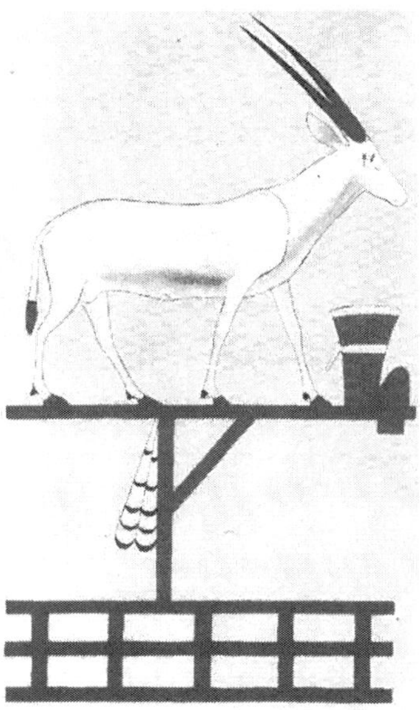

13-97 (left) Oryx, symbol of Nome XVI of Upper Egypt with straight horns. Source: Griffith (1896 III: frontispiece).

13-98 (above) Oryx, emblematic of Nome XVI of Upper Egypt with curved horns. Tomb of Snefru, Dynasty IV-V, Dashur. Source: Fakhry (1961 II: fig. 16).

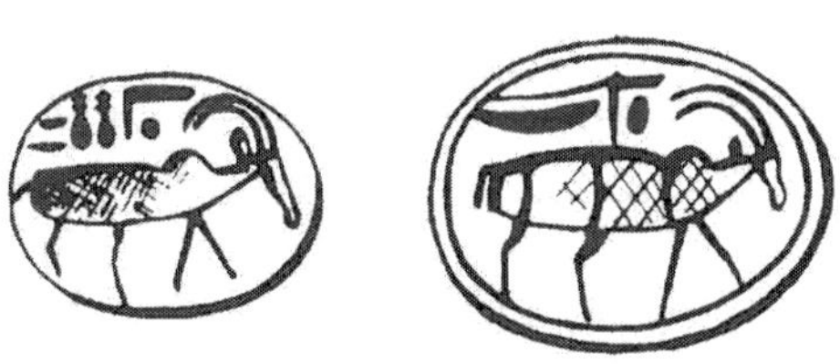

13-99 Scarabs of scimitar oryx from the Late Middle Kingdom ruins of Kuban, Nubia. Source: Firth (1927b: pl. 35).

The thirteen adults and one young that were included in the 'Great Hunt Scene' from the Dynasty V Tomb of Sahure (Borchardt, 1913: pl. 17) are obviously scimitar oryx (fig. 7-147). Another clear depiction of a scimitar oryx is in Figure 7-153.

The slight curvatures of the horns of oryx in the feeding and butchering scenes in the Mastaba of Mereruka and Tomb of Idut (figs 1-16 and 13-92) might suggest they are *O. beisa,* but comparisons with the offering scene from the Tomb of Nefer in which both scimitar- and straight-horned oryx are depicted (fig. 13-93), should remove any doubt.

A dwarfed scimitar oryx was included in the offering scene in the Dynasty V Tomb of Ptah-hetep (fig. 1-25).

Identification of oryx in various Beni Hasan panels is difficult; particularly when comparing drawings in Newberry (1893 I: pl. XXX) with those in L. D. II, 129 and 131. Beisa oryx appear to be correct for Figures 1-30,-31. The second oryx from the right, which is giving birth, has slightly curving horns, but less curved in Figure 1-30. In Figure 1-32 there is a beisa oryx in the lower row and outside the fence in the second row (left) and the lower row (right). The mating oryx in Figure 1-29 (upper row, left) have horns almost straight and likewise those in the lower row (right).

In another comparison the horns are slightly curved in Newberry (fig. 1-35), but distinctly curved in L. D. (fig. 1-36).

Further confusion appears where one of a pair of supposed oryx has a doubly bent horn and the other has horns curved near the tips (fig. 13-94). In Figure 13-95, however, the species is recognizable.

In all of the above examples there are no facial or body markings, but curvature of horns in some individuals shows that both species, *O. dammah* and *O. beisa* were recognized.

Further illustrations suggest that *O. dammah* was the dominant species in Beni Hasan illustrations. The oryx being hand fed in Figure 13-96 have slightly curved horns, indistinct marks through the eyes, and body shading similar to Figure 13-80, but some artist forgot to darken the tail tip.

A similar painting of the emblematic oryx of the XVIth Nome of Upper Egypt (fig. 13-97) has a comparable color pattern plus a black tip on the tail, but the horns are straight. This figure, like the others described above, was doubtless intended to represent the scimitar oryx, but the artist made one obvious mistake.

Griffith (1896: 4) remarked: "The animal is slightly conventionalized, and it is impossible to say whether the figure represents *Oryx beisa* or *O. leucoryx*. It is of the male sex. The horns are very slightly curved; horns, hoofs, fetlocks and the tip of the tail are black, the rest of the body is white with buff under the neck, chest and belly; the eye is defaced and indistinct."

Drawings of this nome emblem that were published by Montet (1961 II: 156) show some variations in horn shape. The relief in the Dynasty

IV-V Tomb of Snefru, as indicated, has markedly curved horns that could only represent *O. dammah* (fig. 13-98).

The figures of scimitar oryx on two Late Middle Kingdom scarabs are easily identified (fig. 13-99). The exaggerated shoulder humps are rarely shown in other figures.

An oryx attacked by two cheetahs (fig. 13-100) was identified by Osborn (1988: 71) as *O. dammah* even though the 'horns are almost straight, which at first implies *O. beisa*, but there is a lack of distinct markings on the body, legs, and head, except around and in front of the eye'. The horns could have been 'so rendered, because of the position of the head'.

This could be another rare example of perspective that appeared in a rock drawing (fig. 13-107, below) where an oryx has its head turned and horns in frontal view.

In the Dynasty VI Tomb of Aba at Deir el Gebrawi there is a hunt scene showing scimitar oryx (fig. 2-3) and in a similar scene from a Dynasty XXVI tomb at Assasif, Thebes (fig. 2-4) of an owner by the same name, the oryx have straight horns. Davies (1902 I: 36) referred to the latter reproduction as 'direct borrowing'.

Errors and discrepancies: Confusion regarding species of oryx that were depicted in ancient Egyptian art can be traced to early authors who were totally unfamiliar with the characteristics of the species.

For example, Hilzheimer (*in* Borchardt, 1913 II: 168 f.) referred to photographs of oryx with curved horns and dark areas around their necks and chests (*op. cit.*, fig. 26) and also the obvious curved-horned oryx in the hunt scene of Sahure, as 'Oryx leucoryx Pallas. Säbelantilope'. Paton (1925: 12) repeated Hizheimer's error.

The German common name Säbelantelope translates to sabre or scimitar-shaped in English; therefore, the correct common name was used by these authors together with the incorrect Latin name.

Hilzheimer (1926; 152) also called the oryx being hand fed (fig. 13-96) and the one representing the nome sign (fig. 13-97) as *O. gazella* (= *O. beisa*), because of their straight or relatively straight horns. These figures have other features, however, which indicate that they represent *O. dammah.*

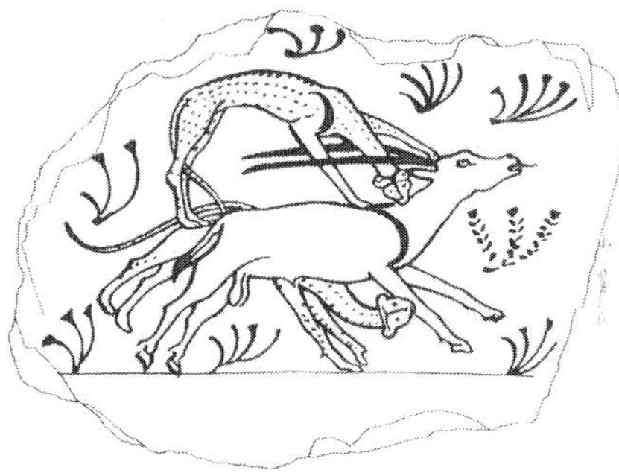

13-100 A scimitar oryx attacked by two cheetahs. Ostracon from Deir el Medina, Dynasty XIX. Source: Náprstek Museum. Prague.

Beisa Oryx ***Oryx beisa*** (Ruppell, 1835)

E East African Oryx; F Oryx beisa; G Eritrea Spiessbock; A Abu Herab

Description: The horns in this species are 65-110 cm, straight or almost straight, slenderer and sometimes longer in females than males. The body is light yellowish brown; underside grayish-white. The head is white with a black triangular patch on the muzzle between the nose and eyes joined by a narrow strip with the black area between the horns. Black stripes from the bases of the ears through the eyes join a black throat stripe that extends to the chest. Ear tips are black. There is a black spinal stripe from the head to the base of the tail. The tail tuft is also black. There are black flank stripes. The buttocks is white and the legs are white except for the narrow black rings above the 'knees' of the forelegs. Although all these characteristics are not depicted in Figure 13-101, particularly the black tail tip, it is recognizable as a beisa oryx.

Distribution: This species formerly occupied the Red Sea coastal region of Somalia, Eritrea, Ethiopia, Sudan, and probably the southeastern part of Egypt and most of the Western Desert, if the drawings with straight horns are correct (figs 13-81,-82,-84,-

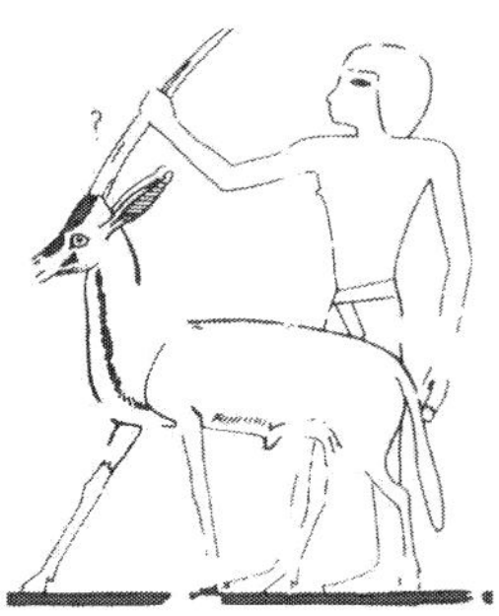

13-101 (left) Beisa oryx in offering scene. Tomb of User, Dynasty XVIII, Thebes. Source: Davies (1913: pl. XXII).

13-102 (right) Rock painting of an oryx hunt in Karkur Tahl, Uweinat. Lower left, beisa oryx; upper right, questionable. Source: Almasy (1936: pl. IV).

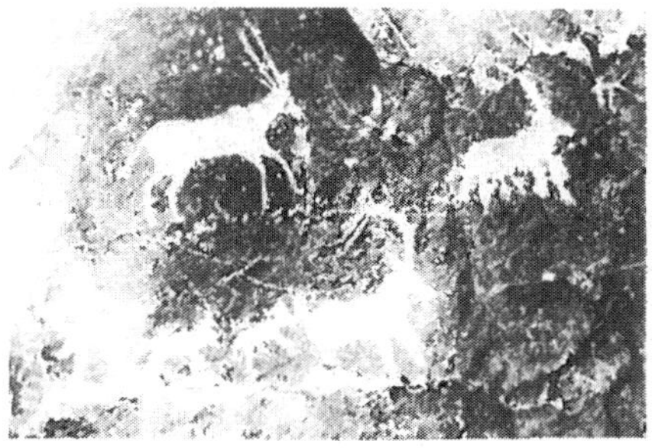

13-103 Rock drawings of two beisa oryx (above) and an ibex followed by two pariah dogs and a hunter. Wadi Hammamat, Eastern Desert. Source: Goyon (1957: pl. XLVI).

13-104 Rock drawings of a long-horned cow and a beisa oryx. Wadi Aigat, west of Gebel Abrak, Eastern Desert. Source: Červíček (1974: fig. 59).

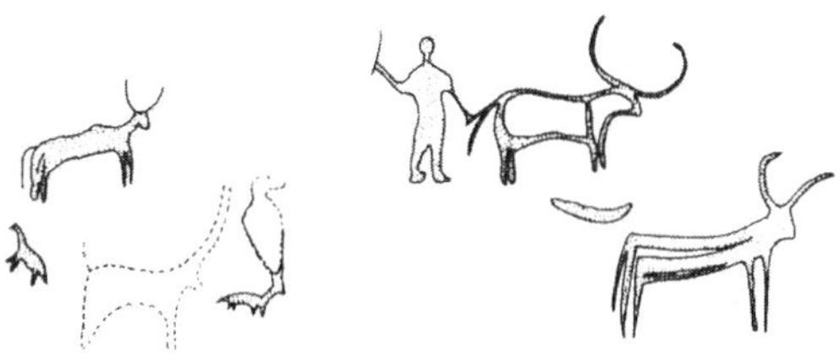

13-105 Rock drawings of beisa oryx, addax (?), and cattle plus an unidentifiable animal. Galt el Aguz northwest of Gebel Abrak in the Eastern Desert. Source: Červíček (1974: fig. 171).

13-106 (left) Rock drawing of a beisa oryx at Bir Kanais in Wadi Mia 45 km east of Edfu (Idfu). Source: Červíček (1974: fig. 273).

13-107 (right) Rock drawing of a beisa oryx attacked by a lion (?). Wadi Abu Subeira east of the Nile 10 km north of Aswan. Source: Červíček (1974: fig. 510).

13-108 Rock drawings of two beisa oryx (center) and one (lower left) dated to the Dynastic period. Two other oryx-like figures in the center and the dog (?) on the right are not dated. Qift-Quseir road near Qasr el Banat. Source: Redford and Redford (1989: fig. 3).

85). Today it is found in the Red Sea coastal region of Ethiopia beside Eritrea and Somalia, south to about 6 degrees North Latitude (Haltenorth and Diller (1980: 67).

Predynastic records: Drawings of straight-horned oryx in the Eastern Desert are numerous (figs 13-84,-85, 13-103 to -108). The one shown in Figure 13-88 is questionable.

A rare sight in rock art is the oryx in Figure 13-107 with its head and horns in frontal view.

Two straight-horned examples, one with tail raised (fig. 13-108) at the Qasar el Banat site on the Qift-Quseir road were dated to Pharaonic times and described as being "skillfully drawn in Dynastic Nile Valley fashion" (Redford and Redford, 1989: 10).

Beisa oryx appear on both sides of the ancient Hierakonpolis palette (fig. 1-2a,b) and there are glazed clay figures from Hierakonpolis (fig. 13-110).

The Dynastic period: Although Beisa oryx do not appear in early Dynastic hunt or feeding scenes, one is pictured with other 'stall fed' animals, including a scimitar oryx, in a Dynasty VI offering (fig. 13-93).

Beisa oryx are pictured along with scimitar oryx in Dynasty XII Beni Hasan hunts (figs 1-29 to 1-32) but, as was mentioned above, it is difficult to segregate them.

Tribute from Nubia in Dynasties XVIII and XIX included beisa oryx (figs 1-26, 13-111).

Several Dynasty XVIII hunt scenes as well as the trophies of the hunts include this oryx (figs 1-24, 7-125, 13-112,-114). In the upper part of the Dynasty XX hunt of Ramses III part of the game are beisa oryx (frontispiece).

The head of a beisa oryx decorates one end of the magical boat of Seker, death god (fig. 13-113), but no reason is given for this animal having been chosen (Mercatante, 1978: 141).

Hilzheimer (1926: 151 f.) postulated that in ancient Egypt the straight-horned oryx was not the African *O. beisa*, but the Asian *O. leucoryx*. He also said this was the first animal to penetrate Africa from Asia. Kock (1970b: 34) apparently agreed with these conclusions, but added that in a favorable climatic period the relict species *O. beisa* could have come still farther north.

A more logical conclusion can be based on the fact that straight-horned as well as scimitar-horned oryx were often illustrated in rock art in Eastern and Western desert localities (figs 13-84,-85, 13-102 to -109), which indicate residence there for a long period of time. In addition, there are other similarities, besides horn shape, that indicate a close relationship between *O. beisa* and *O. leucoryx*.

Herds of what are now known as beisa oryx must have penetrated Asia in very early times and eventually the Isthmus of Suez became the east-west barrier and the isolated '*O. beisa*' evolved into a distinct species known today as *O. leucoryx*.

The sizes of individual animals in northern populations of '*O. beisa*' in the Eastern Desert may have been relatively smaller than their present day southern relatives. Here we might have another example repudiating Bergmann's Rule that individuals in northern populations of a species average larger in size than their southern relatives.

Errors and discrepancies: Hilzheimer (1926: 1152) listed the beisa oryx on the reverse of the Hierakonpolis palette as a 'Säbelantelope'. There is a very slight curvature in the horns, but this can be seen in other depictions of the species (figs 13-101,-104,-105,-108).

Boessneck in his caption for the offering scene from Junker 1943 (Boessneck 1988: fig. 47) correctly named the animals (fig. 13-93), except for the straight-horned oryx, which he called a 'young Säbelantilope'.

A bovid with very long and straight horns, a short tail, and a very large penis (fig. 13-114) was referred to as Loder's gazelle (Boeser, 1911a: pl. XIII) and Dünengazelle (Boessneck, 1953: 30; 1981a: 32). These conclusions are questionable for several reasons: This gazelle (*G. leptoceros*) was not represented elsewhere in early Egyptian art, except possibly in Figure 1-33. The horns are too long and straight for a Loder's gazelle; the large penis is typical of oryx (fig. 1-26), not gazelles; and the head

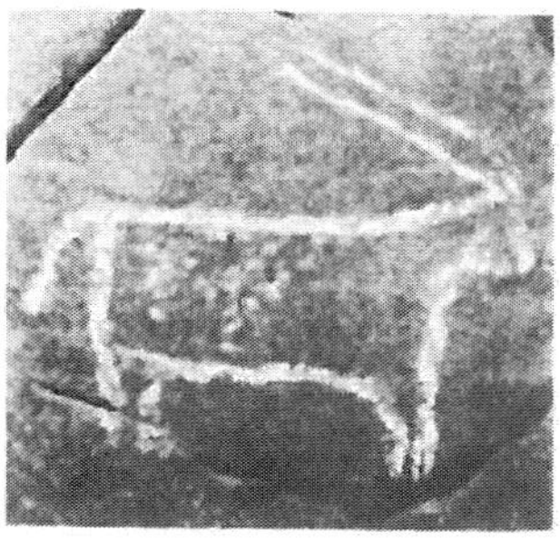

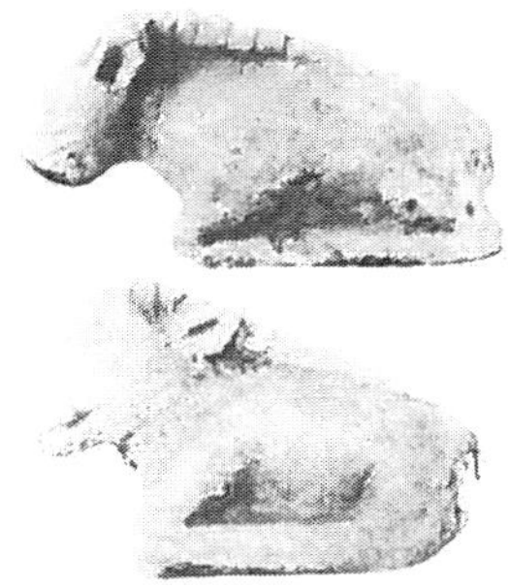

13-109 (left) Rock drawing of a beisa oryx in Karkur Tahl, Gebel Uweinat. Source: Rhotert (1952: pl. XII, 10).

13-110 (right) Predynastic glazed clay figurines of beisa oryx from Hierakonpolis. Source: Quibell (1900 I: pl. XXII, 13, 17).

13-111 Two beisa oryx in tribute from Nubia. Tomb of Huya, Dynasty XVIII, El Amarna. Source: Davies (1905 III: pl. XV).

is proportionately longer than that of a gazelle. The only gazelle-like feature is the short tail.

A comparison can be made with two similar animals in sacrificial scenes (figs 13-115,-116), which, despite their short tails, are otherwise also oryx-like.

The black spinal stripe and tail in Figure 13-115 are also indicative of the beisa oryx, but the

13-112 (left) Part of a hunt scene in the Tomb of Ineni, Dynasty XVIII, Thebes. Source: Davies and Gardiner (1936 I: pl. XXI). Upper right: Hare and beisa oryx. Center: A saluki, a hyena with an arrow in its mouth, and two hartebeest. Lower right: A hartebeest grasped by a hound.

13-113 (centre) Head of beisa oryx on the magical boat of Seker (Sokar), Dynasty XVIII, Kurnah. Source: Davies and Gardiner (1948: pl. VII).

13-114 (right) Part of an offering procession in the Tomb of Meri Meri, Dynasty XVIII, Mit Rahina (Memphis). Source: Boeser (1911a: pl. XIII). Left to right are a bull, a young ibex being carried, and a beisa oryx.

  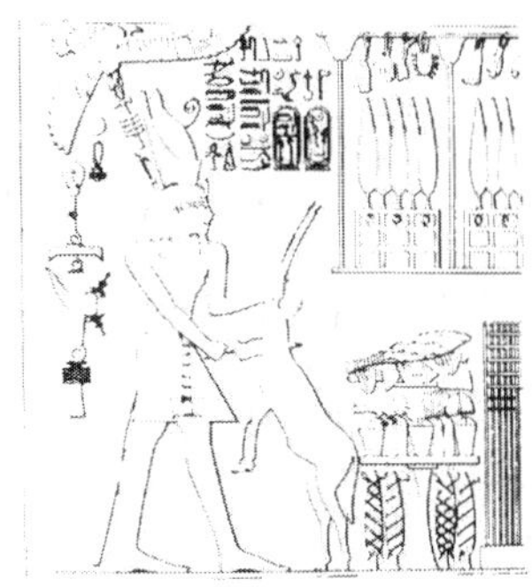

13-115 *(left) The king sacrificing a beisa oryx in the Tomb of Ramses IX, Dynasty XX, Thebes. Source: Guillmant (1907: pl. XXVII).*

13-116 *(centre) The king sacrificing a beisa oryx in the Ptolemaic Temple of Hathor, Dendera. Source: Mariette (1871 III: 71d).*

13-117 *(right) King Amenophis III sacrificing a beisa oryx, Temple of Luxor, Dynasty XVIII. Source: Gayet (1894: pl. XVI, fig. 50).*

shoulder stripe is erroneous.

Egyptian artists surely would not have exaggerated the shorter and spreading horns of the Loder's gazelle to such an extent. The only feature in this series of figures that indicates a gazelle is the short tail, which could simply be artists' errors.

Another example that was being sacrificed and called 'a gazelle, symbol of impurity' (Gayet, 1894: 49), has slightly curved horns and the long tail of an oryx (fig. 13-117).

Arabian Oryx ***Oryx leucoryx*** (Pallas, 1777)

E White Oryx; F Oryx leucoryx; G Arabische Spiessbock, Weiss Oryx; A Abu Herab, Mahah Araby

Description: This species is the smallest of the three described herein. Horn length is 48-71 cm. The body color is whitish and the head markings are similar to those of *O. beisa*, except for a black nose and no connections between the muzzle patch and that between the horn bases. A striking difference is the dark brown coloration of the fronts of the legs and the white pasterns. The tail tuft is dark brown. There are faint flank stripes on some individuals. The ears and mane are white.

13-118 Part of a Syrian tribute scene with an Arabian oryx and a humped zebu, Tombs of Sheikh Abd el Gurna (Gurneh), No.119, Dynasty XVIII, Thebes. Source: Wreszinski (1923 I: 340).

This species is obviously closely related to *O. beisa*.

Distribution: Formerly the distribution included the Arabian Peninsula, Sinai, Palestine, Jordan, Syria, and Iraq (Harrison, 1968 II: 346). Today the species is extinct, except for a few small herds in southeastern Arabia. It survived in Sinai and lower Palestine until about 1800 (Talbot, 1960).

Prehistoric records: The straight-horned oryx on the Gebel el Tarif knife handle (fig. 1-12) could represent *O. leucoryx*, because various other animals on this artifact represent Asian species and artistic techniques (see Introduction).

The Dynastic period: An example of *O. leucoryx* appeared in a Dynasty XVIII, Syrian tribute scene (fig. 13-118). Facial markings are obliterated, but the black legs are sufficient identification marks.

Bones found beneath the waste from a mine dated to the Second Intermediate Period (or Early Dynasty XVIII) on Gebel Zeit north of Hurghada in the coastal mountains bordering the Gulf of Suez were identified as *O. gazella leucoryx* by Boessneck (1988: 37) and Boessneck and von den Driesch (Boessneck, pers. com.). Proof of their determination is yet to come.

Roan Antelope ***Hippotragus equinus*** (Desmarest, 1804)

E Horse Antelope, Maned Antelope; F Hippotrague, Antilope chevaline ou rouanne; G Pferdeantilope; A Abu Uruf or Abu 'Ruf (Father of the Mane)

Description: These are large, horse-like antelopes with high shoulders and thick necks. The blackish scimitar-shaped horns, short in proportion to body size, arise from a prominence above the eyes at an obtuse angle with the plane of the face, and curve sharply backward. The tail is black with a long tassel reaching the hocks. The body color is dark to pale reddish brown; underside white. There is a

13-119a,b (left) Rock drawings called roan antelopes: a) El Kagug, east bank of the Nile, four km N of Gebel el Silsila, b) Mamla-el-Otuani, east bank of the Nile N of Edfu (Idfu). Source: Červíček (1974: figs 238, 406).

13-120 (right) Horns of various roan antelopes. Source: Keimer (1943b: fig. 6).

a

b

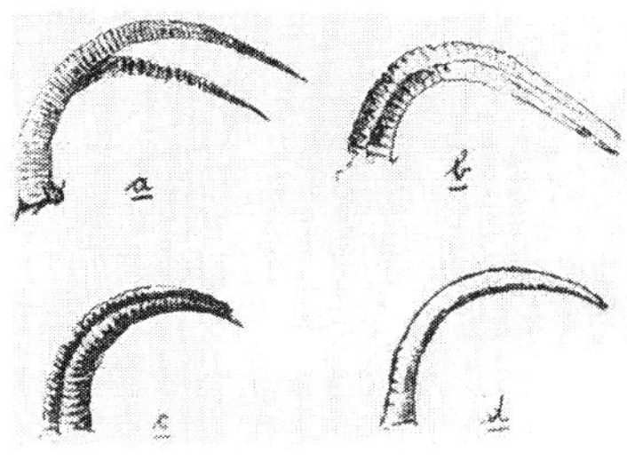

blackish mane from crown to shoulders and a strip of long, dark hair on the lower neck and the chest. The face is black with white stripes in front of the eyes from the horn bases to the cheeks; muffle, chin, and throat are white. Ears are long, slender, and slightly curved with pointed and tufted tips. There are blackish patches above the 'knees' on the forelegs.

Shoulder height is 150-160 cm in males, 140-150 in females.

13-121 A relief of a roan antelope (right) giving birth, followed by a hartebeest that is also foaling. Causeway of Unas, Dynasty V, Saqqara. Source: Keimer (1943b: fig. 2a).

Natural history: Roan antelopes are chiefly grazers, but some foliage is browsed. They inhabit grasslands and sparsely wooded areas in the vicinity of water. In ancient Egypt they probably lived in the oases and suitable areas along the Nile.

Distribution: The present distribution is Africa south of the Sahara. Northeastern limits are western Ethiopia and southern Sudan.

Prehistoric records: Remains of roan antelope are unknown from Prehistoric and Predynastic times.

Rock drawings in Figure 13-119a,b, called horse (roan) antelopes by Červíček (1974: 169) are not clearly separable from ibex as to horn shape and the tails are also shorter than on roan antelopes. In these drawings the horns are distinctly enlarged, quite different from those in Figures 13-120 and 13-121, and more like those of ibex. The only similarity with roan antelopes is the enlarged animal in Figure 13-119b, which has a thick neck. The three ibex in Figure 13-186 were also called horse antelopes (Červíček, 1974: 169, fig. 246).

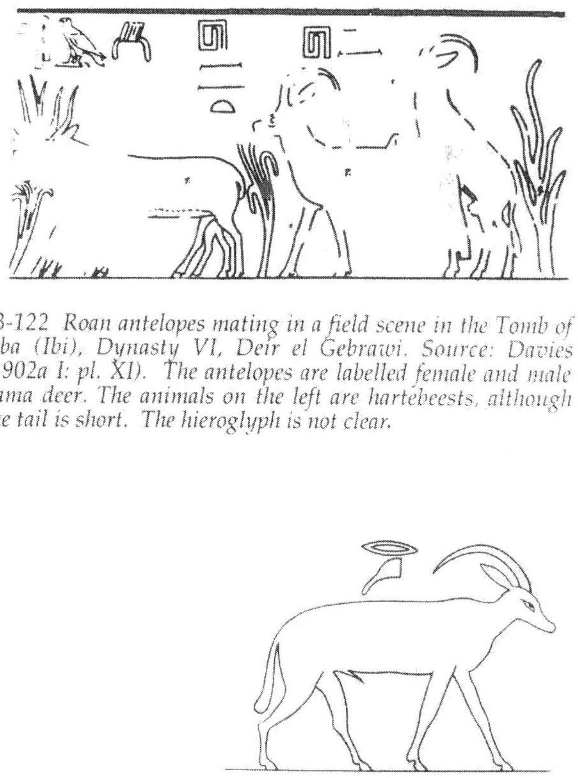

13-122 Roan antelopes mating in a field scene in the Tomb of Aba (Ibi), Dynasty VI, Deir el Gebrawi. Source: Davies (1902a I: pl. XI). The antelopes are labelled female and male dama deer. The animals on the left are hartebeests, although the tail is short. The hieroglyph is not clear.

The Dynastic period: There is very little data on this species. It probably retreated southward during the Middle Kingdom.

The earliest Dynastic reproduction is in the Dynasty V Causeway of Unas (fig. 13-121). A drawing of this scene is in Hartebeest chapter (fig. 13-137).

13-123 Roan antelope from the Dynasty XII Tomb of Baqt, Beni Hassan. Source: Champollion (1845 IV: CCCCXXVIII).

Later illustrations are: The Dynasty VI mating antelopes that are labelled male and female dama deer (fig. 13-122). These were called 'ibex' by Davies (1902a: 17), Keimer (1934b: 292), and Dawson (1934: 140 f.n.), but the long tails, horn shapes and positions, and the thick necks indicate they are roan antelopes. Two more roan antelopes appear in a Dynasty XII hunting scene in the Beni Hasan Tomb of Baqt (fig. 1-29). These are labelled with hieroglyphs for male and female ibex. Athough the necks are slender, the long tails, horn shapes, slender heads, and lack of a beard on the male indicate they are roan antelopes. A copy of one of these by Champollion (1845) is in Figure 13-123 to which he added a part of the hieroglyph for male ibex, *ni3w* nia.

Another copy (fig. 13-124) was compared with an ibex and referred to by Jequier (1922: 112) as "L'Amait, some kind of an ibex".

Bones of roan antelope together with remains of elephant, hartebeest, and lion dated to the Dynasty XIX-XX (Ramessid period) were found at Tel el Daba near the ruins of Qantir Palace in the eastern Delta (Boessneck and von den Driesch, 1982: 140). These were probably palace animals and the roan antelope and elephant were late imports from Upper Nubia or Sudan.

Errors and discrepancies: These were included in the above paragraphs.

13-124 A female ibex with young (left) from the Tomb of Ti, Saqqara (Steindorff, 1913: pl.128) and a roan antelope (right) from the Tomb of Baqt, Beni Hasan (Champollion, 1845 IV: pl. CCCCXXVIII). Source: Jequier, 1922: figs 73 and 74).

Subfamily *Reduncinae*

Kob *Kobus (Adenota) kob* (Erxleben, 1777)

šš shez Wb. IV, 539

ḏbnw djebenu Wb. V, 568

E Puku; F Cobe de Buffon, Puku; G Grasantilope

Description: The horns develop only in males and are "lyre-like and S-shaped in outline from the base upwards, 10-15 rings" (Haltenorth and Diller, 1980:

13-125 (top) Kobs on a Gerzean (Predynastic) clay box from El Amra (Abydos). Source: Aldred (1965: 27, ill. 13).

13-126 (bottom) Three kobs and two gazelles (?) caught in a leg trap in the Predynastic wall painting in Hierakonpolis. Source: Quibell and Green (1902 II: pl. LXXVI). Above are a scimitar-horned oryx and a gazelle, to the right a man appears to be slaughtering an aurochs, below is a lassoed hartebeest, and left a man is dompting two lions.

73). Color varies from yellowish- to dark reddish-brown on the upper body and legs; undersides are whitish.

Head and body lengths are 125-180 cm, tail 18-40, and shoulder height 70-105. Females are smaller than males.

Natural history: Kobs are grazers and occupy grassy plains and savanna in large herds. They also feed on aquatic plants. Water is a daily necessity.

Distribution: The range is south of the Sahara in Sudan, Senegal, Gambia, S.W. Ethiopia, and Zambia, and westward into N.W. Nigeria.

This species, as with others, probably withdrew from Egypt prior to 3,000 B.C.

Prehistoric and Predynastic records: Wendorf (1968 I: 87) reported Late Pleistocene remains from southern Egypt.

Drawings appear on a clay box from the Gerzean Period (fig. 13-125). Although the horns show no bending other than the forward curvature of the tips, the only possible models appear to have been kobs. They certainly do not represent kudu as was stated by Aldred (1965: 27, fig. 13).

These figures were also called 'ibex' by Capart (1905: 132). Glanville (1926: 75-76, pl. XVIII) said they were neither oryx nor ibex, but kudu.

Three similar animals are shown caught in a leg trap in the Hierakonpolis wall painting (fig. 13-126).

Animals with similar horns, but longer tails in a rock drawing from Galt el Aguz (fig. 13-127) were simply referred to by Červíček (1974: 43, fig. 203) as 'antilopes'.

13-127 Rock drawings of kobs and ostriches from Galt el Aguz in S.E. Egypt, 10-15 km N.W. of Gebel Abraq. Source: Červíček (1974: fig. 203).

Nile Lechwe ***Kobus (Hydrotragus) megaceros*** (Fitzinger, 1855)

E Mrs. Gray's Lechwe; F Cobe de Mrs. Gray, Cobe Lechwe; G Weissnacken Moorantilope, Litschi-Moorantilope, Frau Grays Moorantilope

Nomenclature: An obsolete synonym is *Onotragus megaceros.*

Description: Only males have horns, which are lyre-like and S-shaped in outline. The color is reddish- or blackish- brown and there is a white nape stripe and shoulder saddle patch, which are lacking in females.

Measurements in cm of head and body length average 165 in males, 135 in females; tail length 50 and 45; shoulder height 100-105 and 80-85. Horn length varies from 45-87.

Natural history: Lechwe are active mainly in the morning, evening, and night; avoiding the sun during the day. They live in very large herds and their habitat, swamps and marshes, give protection from predators. Food is grass and aquatic plants.

Distribution: This species is now limited to the Upper Nile swamps in southern Sudan and southwestern Ethiopia. It probably migrated southward from Egypt prior to 3,000 B.C.

Prehistoric and Predynastic records: Wassif (1976: 97) reported archeological finds in northern Egypt.

Subfamily *Alcelaphinae*

Hartebeest ***Alcelaphus buselaphus*** (Pallas, 1766)

 *šš3w* shezau Wb. II, 487 (male)

 *hbn* heben Wb. IV, 543 (female)

E Bubal, Bubal Hartebeest; F Bubale; G Kuh-antilope; A Begra el Ouash

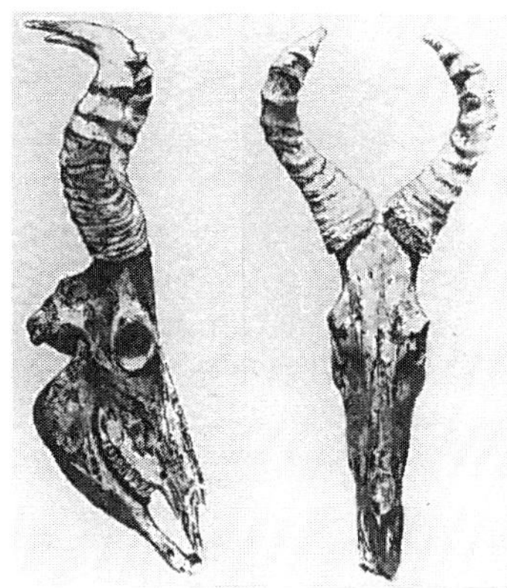

13-128 Lateral and frontal views of a hartebeest skull from Saqqara. Source: Lortet and Gaillard (1905: fig. 41).

13-129 Hartebeests on part of the Predynastic great stone mace from Hierakonpolis. Source: Quibell and Green (1902 II: pl. XXVI, B).

13-130 Rock drawing of a man lassoing a hartebeest. Location: El Kagug east bank of the Nile 4 km north of Gebel el Silsila. Source: Červíček (1974: fig. 236).

13-131 (top left) A stall fed hartebeest in the Mastaba of Mereruka, Dynasty VI, Saqqara. Source: Author. However, it is labelled with the hieroglyph for kob.

13-132 (top right) A hartebeest in an offering procession in the Tomb of Akhethetep, Dynasty V, Saqqara. Source: Davies (1901a II: pl.XIX). It is labelled with a shortened hieroglyph for hartebeest (bubal in Hartmann, 1864:23).

13-133 (bottom left) A hartebeest in an offering procession in the Tomb of Ptahhetep, Dynasty V, Sakkara. Source: Davies (1900 I: pl.XXIV).

13-134 (bottom right) A hartebeest (left) with elongated horns and two aurochs, one of which is lassoed, in a hunting scene in the Tomb of Ptahhetep, Dynasty V, Saqqara. Source: Davies (1900 I: pl.XXII). Above are two hedgehogs; one with a cricket (?) in its mouth.

Nomenclature: Hartebeest is a combination of 'hart' (male deer) and 'beast'. Derivations of the Latinized names are *alke* (Gr) the elk, *elaphos* (Gr) a deer, and *bous* (Gr) a bullock or cow (Gotch, 1979: 220).

Bubalis is an obsolete generic name (Allen, 1939: 470 f.).

Description: The horns are shorter than the head; arising behind the eyes from a large frontal pedicle; the bases are fused, U-shaped in frontal view, and diverging posteriorly in line with the facial (fronto-nasal) plane, then bending forward and again sharply backward and sometimes upward (fig. 13-128). Variations that appeared in Egyptian art are referred to below.

The head is long and narrow with a straight facial region. The ears are long and slender. The tail tuft reaches almost to the hocks, but the length is variable in Egyptian art.

The color is almost uniform light yellowish- to dark reddish-brown. The underparts and buttocks are paler. Facial markings are faint, except for a prominent lacrimal spot.

Females have slenderer horns and paler coloration than males.

Head and body lengths are 175-245cm, tail 45-70, and shoulder height 120-145. Females are slightly smaller than males.

Natural history: Hartebeests inhabit grasslands and wooded savannas, but never forests. They are capable of surviving for several days without water. Daily periods of activity are mornings and late afternoons. They tend to live in harem troops and males defend territories.

Distribution: This species once ranged throughout North Africa from Morocco to Egypt and eastward into northern Arabia and Palestine (Haltenorth and Diller, 1980: 83; Uerpmann, 1987: 87). It was exterminated in Egypt about 1850 and Arabia and Palestine about 1900 (Haltenorth and Diller, 1980: 83); in Egypt probably by intensive hunting. The northern limits of the present distribution are south of the Sahara from Gambia eastward into southern Sudan and southwestern Ethiopia. Populations survive southward through eastern Africa into the southern states.

Prehistoric and Predynastic records: Remains of hartebeests have been found in numerous localities, which were tabulated by Uerpmann (1987: table 17a), from the Late Paleolithic into the Late Predynastic. Sites listed are Wadi Kubbaniya west of Aswan, Elkab (east bank of the Nile opposite Hierakonpolis), Kom Ombo, Idfu, Isna, El Faiyum, and Tell ed-Dab'a (eastern Delta). Questionable records are from Qantir (Uerpmann, *op. cit.*, 154, catalog site no. 133).

Additional Early and Late Neolithic remains were listed by Churcher (1980: 388; 1981: 195, 197, table 1; 1982: 109, 110, table 1; 1983: 186; 1986a: 2,3; 1991a: 179) from various sites in Dakhla Oasis.

Sharp curvatures of the horns in frontal view and lengths shorter than the head was the style that began in the Predynastic (figs 1-2a,b;-3;-6b;-9; 12-6, 13-129). There is a broad horn base on the forehead. Rock drawings in Červíček (1974) are not clear, but one that can be identified correctly (fig. 13-130) has horns that are longer than the head and similar in outline to various Dynastic figures.

The Dynastic period: Old Kingdom remains were found in the area of Sheikh Mubaris tombs in Dakhla Oasis by Churcher (1981: table 1).

In some Old and Middle Kingdom art the horns are narrowly curved and longer than the head and with the outward terminal curvatures sharply defined (figs 1-16,-19, 13-131,-132). In others the horn bases are fused (figs 7-164, 13-112), but normal shapes also continue into the late Dynasties (figs 13-133,-134,-135). Keimer (1943a: 264) considered these variations to have been examples that were recognized by the Egyptian artists.

A striking difference in the two styles appears in the Dynasty XVIII Tomb of Ineni (fig. 13-112).

Two hartebeests (fig. 1-21, no. 19) that are similar to the lower hartebeest grasped by a hound in Figure 13-112 were called 'wild oxen' by Wilkinson (1878 II: 92).

Hartebeests were commonly pictured in field and hunting scenes (figs 13-122,-134,-135), trophies of the hunt (figs 7-159a,b) and offerings (fig. 7-153). One illustration verifies its status as one of the semi-domesticated, 'stall fed' wild animals (figs 1-16, 13-131).

Hartebeests were also shown giving birth in hunting scenes (figs 7-164, 13-121,-136).

Errors and discrepancies: In the Tomb of Ti (fig. 13-79) a male hartebeest is labelled with the hieroglyph *nudu* for addax.

In Figure 13-137 , the copy of a bovid labelled hartebeest, from the Dynasty XII Tomb of Baqt (fig. 1-29), has the horns of an addax.

13-135 (top right) Hartebeests in a partly destroyed hunting scene in the Tomb of Amenemhet, Dynasty XVIII, Thebes. Source: Davies and Gardiner (1915: pl. IX).

13-136 (bottom left) A hartebeest (left) and a roan antelope (?) giving birth in the Causeway of Unas, Dynasty V, Saqqara. Source: Keimer (1943b: fig. 2b).

13-137 (bottom right) A copy of a hartebeest with addax-like horns from the Tomb of Baqt (see fig. 1-29). Source: Champollion (1845 IV: pl. CCCCXXVIII).

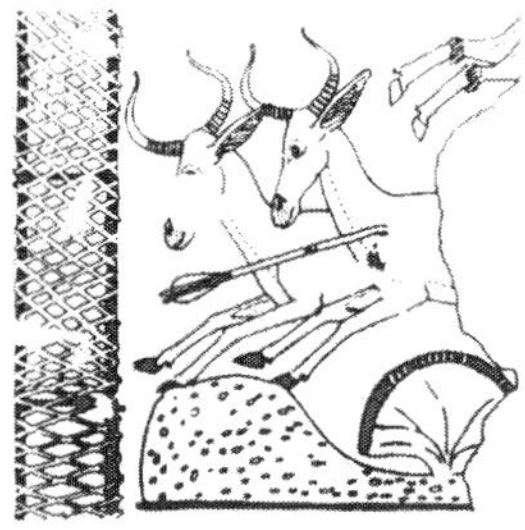

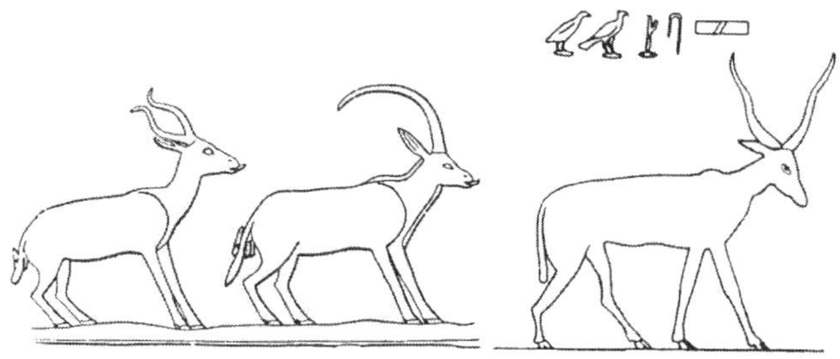

In Figure 13-131 the hartebeest is labelled with the hieroglyph for kob.

Further errors in hartebeests are obvious in Paton (1925: 14, E 21b).

Blue Wildebeest ***Connochaetes taurinus*** (Burchell, 1824)

E Brindled Gnu; F Gnou à queu noire, Gnou bleu; G Weissbartgnu, Streifengnu

Description: Wildebeests are cattle-sized, but with higher shoulders (129-140 cm), tails with a long tassel reaching belc w the hocks, long manes on the shoulders and lower necks, and vertical stripes on the body. The horns are curved slightly downward at the base; then upward, forward, and inward.

Natural history: Large herds of wildebeests are annual migrants in plains seeking palatable grass in the dry season. Although they can survive for several days without drinking water, they were probably pushed out of Egypt during the dry period dated to 3,000 B.C.

Distribution: The distribution is now south of the Equator in S. and S.E. Africa.

Prehistoric and Predynastic records: There are no known archeological remains of wildebeests in Egypt. The only representation is a carving on the reverse of the Hierakonpolis palette (fig. 1-2b), which Quibell and Green (1902 II: 41) referred to as 'a wild ox (?)'. Asselberghs (1961: pl. LXXI, fig. 128) said it had been called 'buffalo and ur'.

Subfamily *Antilopinae*

Gerenuk ***Litocranius walleri*** (Brooke, 1879)

E Giraffe-Gazelle, Waller's Gazelle; F Gazelle de Waller, Gazelle-Giraffe; G Giraffengazelle

Nomenclature: "Gerenuk is from the Somali *garanug*, a long-necked gazelle... The Latin name derives from *lithos* (Gr) stone, *kranion* (Gr) the upper part of

13-138 A man leading a gerenuk in a rock drawing by Autochthonous Mountain Dwellers. Location: Site 36, Wadi Sab' er-Rigal, west bank of the Nile opposite El Hosh. Source: Winkler (1939 II: pl. XVIII, 1). The horns are in frontal view.

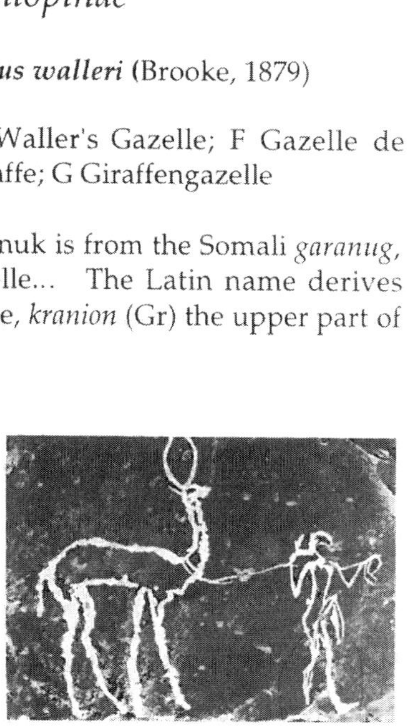

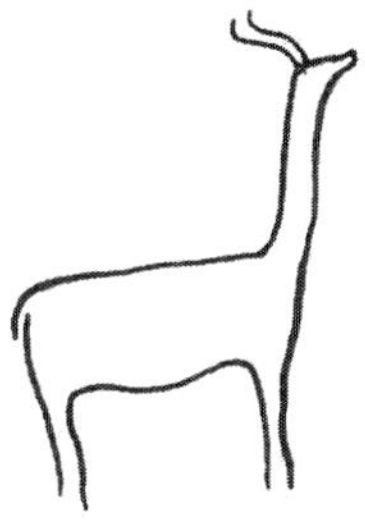

13-139 Rock drawing of a gerenuk with a short tail. Location: El Hagandia east of the Nile north of Silwa Bahari. Source: Červíček (1974: fig. 116). The tail is too short, but other features are comparable with the gerenuk.

13-140 Rock drawing of a gerenuk at Tomas (Tumas), south of the Nile curvature, by El-Derr (El-Diwan). Source: Červíček (1974: pl. 14, photo 28).

the skull, which is almost solid bone at the base of the horns" (Gotch, 1979: 222).

Description: A tall gazelle with an exceptionally long neck and long legs; tail with a black tuft, but not reaching the hocks, and in comparison with gazelles and the dibatag, not held upright. The horns are relatively short, strongly S-shaped in profile, with tips curved forward and inward. The color is reddish-brown, but darker on the back. The rump is the color of the sides. The belly and inner sides of the legs are white. There are whitish areas around the eyes and the bases of the ears. The female is similar to the male, but hornless.

Measurements in cm are shoulder height 90-105, head and body length 140-160, tail 23-35. Males are slightly larger than females.

Natural history: Gerenuks are browsers and can reach foliage, flowers, and fruit with their long necks or by standing erect on their hind legs. They live in sandy and stony steppes where very little free water is available.

Distribution: The present range includes eastern Eritrea and Ethiopia and most of Somalia southward into Kenya and northeastern Tanzania.

Prehistoric and Predynastic records: Previous distribution into the Predynastic period in Egypt is indicated by numerous rock drawings. A very long list was published by Červíček (1987), but there are some errors in identification. A few easily identified figures are 13-138,-139,-140, and 13-83, which is north of the Qift-Quseir road about 300 m east of Wadi Abu Qwei and dated to late Predynastic/Early Dynastic.

Dibatag *Ammodorcas clarkei* (Thomas, 1891)

E Clarke's Gazelle; F Dibatag; G Dibatag, Lamagazelle

Nomenclature: "Dibatag is derived from the Somali words, *dabu* = tall and *tag* = erect" (Dorst,1970: 234). The Latin name derives from *ammos* (Gr) sand, a sandy place and *dorkas* (Gr) a gazelle (Gotch, 1979: 222).

Description: A slender gazelle with a long neck and legs, but not so long as in the gerenuk. The long, thin, black tail reaches the hocks and is held upright or forward when the animal is excited. The horns are relatively long, extending backward and curving forward with tips only slightly diverging. General coloration is cinnamon brown; belly, inside of legs, and rump patch are white. There are white rings around the eyes and white stripes from the bases of the horns to the muzzle. The female is similar to the male, but hornless.

Measurements in cm are shoulder height 80-85, head and body length 152-168, tail 30-36.

Natural history: Dibatags are grazers as well as browsers and eat a variety of vegetation. They also stand upright to reach leaves, etc. They can survive for long periods without water. The habitats are grassy plains and open shrub areas.

Distribution: The present distribution is limited to Eastern Ethiopia and northern Somalia.

This is another species that probably retreated southward in the Late Predynastic period.

Prehistoric and Predynastic records: There are rock drawings of two dibatags on the west bank of the Nile north of Aswan (fig. 13-141).

The Dynastic period: Keimer (1942b: 180) identified the animal ahead of the ostrich in the Beit el Wali offering procession (fig. 13-142) as a gerenuk. The animal is quite small in comparison with the men and may represent a dibatag.

13-141 (left) Rock drawings by Earliest Hunters of two dibatags. Above is an ibex attacked by a pariah dog. Location: Site 53 west bank of the Nile, about 5 km north of Aswan. Source: Winkler (1939 II: pl. LVIII, 1). The long, raised tails are typical of the dibatag.

13-142 (right) Dibatag in a relief of an offering procession in the Dynasty XIX Beit el Wali Temple south of the Aswan High Dam. Source: Roeder (1968: pl. 34).

Gazelle Genus *Gazella*

gḥś gehez Wb. V, 191

All species of gazelles are identified by the same hieroglyph, gehez, except for the Soemmering's gazelle (fig. 13-161).

Nomenclature: An obsolete generic synonym for *Gazella*, as with *Oryx*, is *Antilope*. Gazelles are sometimes referred to as antelopes, which has caused confusion, especially in reference to the gazelle goddess, Anukis, and as a Seth (Typhon) animal.

General description: Gazelles are small antelopes lacking a shoulder hump. Horns are relatively short and curving, except for Loder's gazelle. Tails are relatively short, except for Soemmering's gazelle.

Coloration is pale to light brown or reddish-brown. Most species have a contrastingly darker flank stripe and distinct facial markings.

Natural history: Gazelles may live in pairs or in small family groups, also in small to large herds depending upon the grazing conditions. They inhabit desert, semidesert, steppe, savanna, and sometimes cultivated land.

Dorcas Gazelle ***Gazella dorcas*** (Linnaeus, 1758)

F Gazelle dorcas; G Dorkasgazelle; A Afri, Ghazal, Ghazal Nuby

Description: Male horns are semi-lyrate in frontal view with tips curving anteriorly and inwardly. In lateral view the horns are strongly curved backward and forward. Prominent annulations extend along the greater length of the horns.

Female horns are shorter, slenderer, and straighter than male horns and annulations are much less developed (fig. 13-143a,b).

Horns are distinctive in most Egyptian reproductions, being pictured singly in lateral view and usually exaggerated in length (figs 13-144,-146).

The body color is light reddish-brown dorsally; the sides are paler and bordered with the same color as the back. The head, neck, and legs, are pale. The throat, neck, chest, belly, inner sides of the legs and the small rump patch are white. The tail is short and black Facial markings are distinct and include a reddish central band from the base of the horns, either becoming paler toward the nostrils

13-144 (left) Dorcas gazelle in an offering scene in the Tomb of Idut, Dynasty V, Saqqara. Source: Author.

13-145 (right) Dorcas gazelle in an offering scene in Tomb 15, Dynasty V, Saqqara. Source: L.D. II, 45.

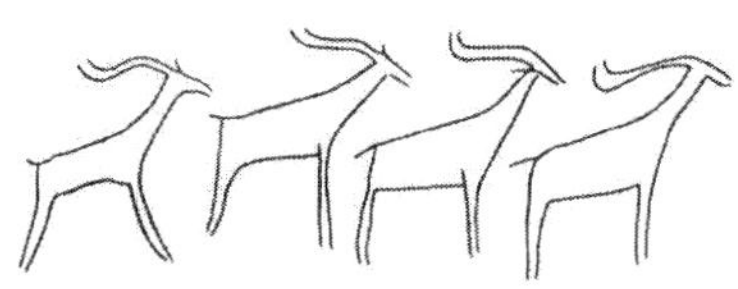

13-146 Rock drawings of dorcas gazelles near El Hagandia north of Silwa Bahari. Source: Červíček (1974: fig. 135).

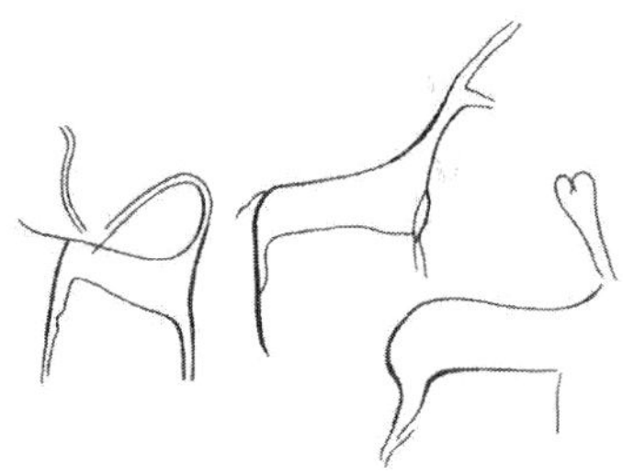

13-147 Rock drawings of dorcas (left), Loder's? (center), and Soemmering's gazelles (right). Location: Hagandia north of Silwa Bahari. Source: Červíček (1974: fig. 136).

13-148 Ivory gazelle heads from wands dated to Dynasty I. Source: Petrie (1907: pl. IV).

b

13-143a,b Dorcas gazelles in Giza Zoo a) two males, b) a female and two young; male in the background. Source: Author.

a

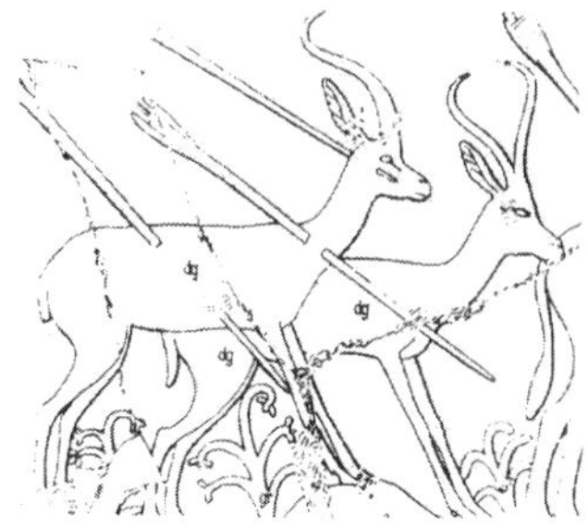

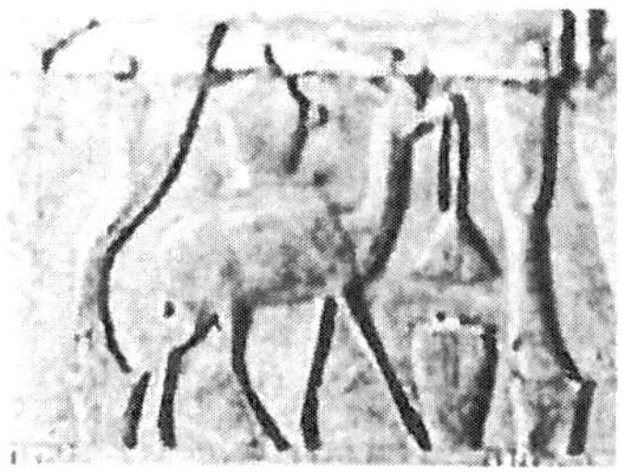

13-149 (top left) Dwarfed animals in an offering scene in the Tomb of Ptah-hetep, Dynasty V, Saqqara. Source: Paget and Pirie (1898: pl. XXXVIII). Animals are (left to right) scimitar oryx, dorcas gazelle, ibex, and a bull. The men carry ducks and geese of normal size.

13-150 (top centre) Dorcas gazelles in a hunting scene in the Tomb of Sahure, Dynasty V, Saqqara. Source: Borchardt (1913: pl. 17).

13-151 (top right) Dorcas and Soemmering's gazelles in a hunting scene in the Tomb of Sahure, Dynasty V, Saqqara. Source: Borchardt (1913: pl. 17).

13-152 (bottom left) Pet dorcas gazelle under the chair of Pabasa (Paebpasa, Pbes) in the 'Asasif at Thebes. Dynasty XXVI. Source: White (1920 II: fig. 13).

13-153 (bottom centre) A Bedouin's hand on a baby gazelle whose mother was 'dancing' 20 or 30 meters away. Photographed in an unnamed wadi 12 km west of Karkur (Wadi) Murr in the southern part of Gebel Uweinat. Source: Author (1967).

13-154 (bottom right) Young gazelles in a basket on a donkey's back. Tomb of Nianchchnum and Chnumhotep, Causeway of Unas, Dynasty V, Saqqara. Source: Moussa and Altenmüller (1977: fig. 13).

or with a blackish nose spot. There are white lateral facial stripes from the horns to the muzzle and dark stripes below from the eyes to the mouth.

Shoulder height of males is 55-65 cm; females are smaller. This is one of the smallest members of the genus.

Natural history: Dorcas gazelles live in pairs and in small herds in semi-desert and vegetated wadis. Where sufficient vegetation is available they survive for long periods without water. Shade from trees and cliffs is an important factor in their survival.

Feeding times are evening and morning and often during the night, especially where crops are accessible.

Distribution: Dorcas gazelles range over much of the northern, eastern, and southwestern part of the Western Desert; northern parts and the southern two-thirds of the Eastern Desert; and northern Sinai. The range extends west of Egypt to the Atlantic, but known localities are scattered. It also includes northern Sudan and parts of northern Ethiopia and Chad. Eastward, beyond Sinai, the range includes parts of Palestine and Arabia.

Hunting and shooting from vehicles has eliminated gazelles from the more suitable habitats; particularly the vegetated coastal deserts.

Prehistoric and Predynastic records: From the archeological sites listed by Uerpmann (1987: 96, table 19, fig. 44) along the Nile Valley and in the desert to the west, "No differences can yet be seen between the ancient and the present range of *G. dorcas* in Northeast Africa". Rock drawings of gazelles are common, but identification to species is often difficult. A few drawings from various localities indicate that rock artists exaggerated the horns (figs 13-146,-147).

A variety of dorcas gazelles also appeared in predynastic art including the Hierakonpolis Palette (fig. 1-2a,b), Hunters Palette (fig. 1-3), and row 2 on the boss side of the Pitt Rivers ivory knife handle (fig. 1-8). Except for the latter, the horns on these gazelles are accurately reproduced.

The Dynastic period: Dorcas gazelles were among the most popular of wild animals in Pharaonic times. Beginning with Dynasty I there are ivory gazelle-head wands (fig. 13-148) that Petrie (1907: 6) found in a grave and said they "were doubtless used by a dancer for marking time, as in the scene of Deshashah." Dancing girls were shown in the tomb of Anta, Dynasty V, Deshasha, holding 'curved wooden sticks ending in the head of a gazelle' (Petrie, 1897: 8, pl. XII). Other early illustrations are in the Dynasty IV Tomb of Fetekta (fig. 7-172).

A dorcas gazelle was among the picketed, 'stall fed' (*rn*) bovids pictured in the Dynasty VI Mastaba of Mereruka (fig. 1-16) and became semi-domesticated in the Old Kingdom as indicated by its frequent appearance in offering scenes (figs 4-38, 7-153,-155 to -157); often in dwarfed form (figs 1-25, 13-149). In some of these scenes females are accompanied by young, which were probably born in captivity.

This gazelle was also a popular animal of the hunt and there are many hunting scenes with one or more (figs 1-18, -21,-24,-29,-32, 13-150,-151). Likewise, they also appeared as trophies of the hunt (fig. 7-159a,b).

Dorcas gazelles were often pictured as pets (fig. 13-152). Young gazelles are easily captured, because the mother will leave her young when approached and prance about some distance away. The young can be found near where the female was first seen, lying under a shrub or sprawled out on the sand (fig. 13-153), and can be picked up and carried away. Jarvis (1933: 204) wrote a similar description: "Natural fear of a female gazelle for her offspring, which is lying hidden under a scrub bush, causes her to dance around in a circle about a hundred yards away from the approaching stranger...ten minutes' search is all that is needed to find the fawn."

This may explain the probable source of the basket full of small gazelles on the back of a donkey in Figure 13-154.

Errors and discrepancies: In the Tomb of Pehenuka (fig. 13-155) an animal labelled *ghs'* has the head and body and long ears of a dorcas gazelle, but the horn is comparable with those of a young or female ibex.

Fakhry (1973; 183) identified the animals in Figure 13-156 as foxes eating grapes. The heads are fox-like, but the short tails and hoof-like feet indicate gazelles. The absence of horns suggests young animals (see fig. 13-143b).

13-155 A gazelle-like animal with ibex horns in the Tomb of Pehenuka, Dynasty V, Saqqara. Source: L.D. II, 46.

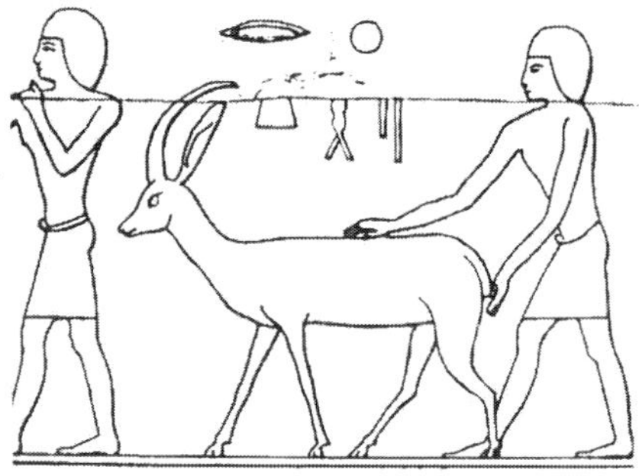

13-156 Hornless gazelles eating grapes (?) in the Tomb of the Crocodile, Late Ptolemaic Early Roman Period, Siwa. Source: Fakhry (1973: fig. 65).

Slender-horned Gazelle *Gazella leptoceros* (F. Cuvier, 1842)

E Loder's Gazelle, Rhim Gazelle, White Gazelle, Sand Gazelle; F Gazelle leptocère, Rhim; G Dünengazelle; A Reem, Ghazal Abiad, Ghazal Arial

Nomenclature: The specific name derives from the Greek *lepto* (thin) and *cera* or *kero* (horn).

Description: Male horns are long, slightly recurving, and gradually diverging from the bases. The smooth tips, one- fourth or more of the horn lengths, curve slightly outward and forward. Annulations are conspicuous on male horns (fig. 13-157). Female horns are shorter, straighter, thinner, and have less conspicuous annulations.

The body color is very pale yellowish to buffy brown dorsally with whitish sides and slightly darker side stripes. The head is whitish with indistinct facial markings. The throat, chest, belly, legs, and rump are white. The short tail is brownish to blackish.

Shoulder height in males is 65-75 cm; females are slightly smaller.

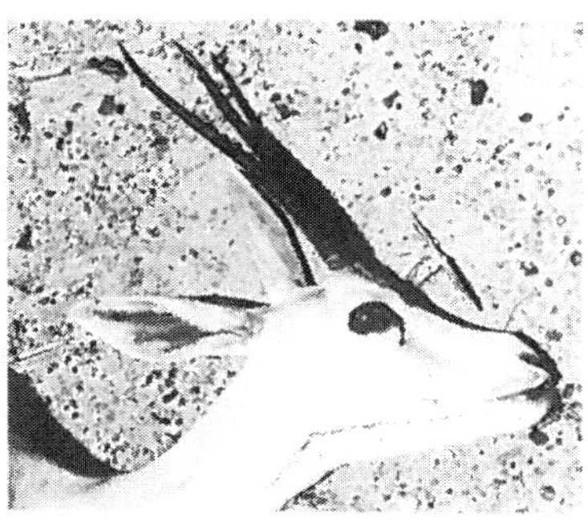

13-157 (left) Head of a Loder's gazelle killed in 1966 in Wadi Mishigeiga south of El Faiyum. Source: Author.

13-158 (right) Soemmering's gazelle in Giza Zoo. Source: Author.

Natural history: This gazelle has been called a 'sand gazelle', because it is generally found in sandy desert and between dunes. It also occurs on hard, stony desert (serir) interspersed with patches of sand. Generally, acacia trees provide shade in such areas. Otherwise, the gazelles will scrape pits in sand mounds under shrubs to obtain shade.

The water requirements of this gazelle are apparently much less than for other species.

The habits are similar to those of the dorcas gazelle and feeding times are early morning and late afternoons or at night. This gazelle lives singly or in small herds.

Distribution: The slender-horned gazelle occurs in Egypt in the northern part of the Western Desert south of the vegetated Mediterranean Coastal Desert and possibly in the vicinity of Gebel Uweinat. It may also occur in northwestern Sudan and is known from Libya, Tunisia, and Algeria (Osborn and Helmy, 1980: 487).

This species may be on the verge of extinction from indiscriminate hunting.

Prehistoric and Predynastic records: Two records have been published from archeological sites at Kom Ombo (Churcher, 1972: 120, 172) and Dakhla Oasis (Churcher, 1982: table 1), but both were listed as questionable (Uerpmann, 1987: 101). The gazelle in the center of Figure 13-147 probably represents a Loder's gazelle.

The Dynastic period: One drawing that could represent a slender-horned gazelle is in a Beni Hasan tomb (fig. 1-33), which is referred to again in *Errors and discrepancies.*

Another appears in the relief of a hunting scene in the Dynasty XVIII Tomb of Amenemhet (fig. 1-18, register 1).

Errors and discrepancies: A straight-horned gazelle, which appears to be *G. leptoceros* is depicted in Figure 1-33. The same animal in a L.D. reproduction of this Beni Hasan scene (fig. 1-34) has the long, curved horns of an ibex, but lacks a beard.

Some antelopes with long, straight horns and short tails that have been called 'gazelles' can only be determined as oryx (see *Errors and discrepancies* in Oryx chapter).

Red-fronted Gazelle *Gazella rufifrons* Gray, 1846

E Heuglin's Gazelle; F Gazelle à front roux, Gazelle corinne; G Rotstirngazelle

Description: Male horns are weakly to strongly lyre-shaped in frontal view; somewhat S-shaped in lateral view with tips curving forward and inward. Female horns are smaller, smoother, and more curved.

The body, neck, head, and outside of legs are sandy to reddish-brown. The side stripe is brownish to blackish. Throat, chest, belly, inside of legs, and rump are white. The tail is black. Facial markings are distinct as in *G. dorcas.*

Shoulder height in males is 68-72 cm; females are slightly smaller.

Natural history: The habits of this gazelle are similar to those of the dorcas gazelle.

Distribution: This gazelle is now limited to the semi-desert strip along the southern margin of the Sahara from Eritrea west to Senegambia.

Prehistoric and Predynastic records: This species may have ranged into Egypt during the Upper Pleistocene, but Uerpmann (1987: 103 ff., table 22) considered the evidence not clear enough to be certain. He listed the findings of Gautier (1976, and 1980 a,b) from Idfu and Isna on the Nile, Bir Tarfawi and Nabta Playa in the southern Western Desert, and Wadi Kubbaniya west of Aswan. The gazelle being leapt on by a hound on the obverse of the Hierakonpolis palette (fig. 1-2a) might represent a red-fronted gazelle.

The Dynastic period: Churcher (1983:185) said that *G. rufifrons* ? was recently extant in the oases.

Dama Gazelle *Gazella dama* (Pallas, 1766)

E Addra, Mohr, Red-necked Gazelle; F Gazelle Dama; G Damagazelle

Nomenclature: This species is sometimes included in the subgenus *Nanger*, which was also used as a generic name.

Description: Male horns are lyre-shaped, but turning backward with the tips turning upward and inward. Female horns are similar, but shorter and thinner.

Coloration of the body and legs, except for a chestnut area (saddle) on the back, varies from dark to light yellowish-brown to almost white. The neck is reddish-brown with a white spot on the front; the head is white, except for the reddish-brown frontal mark.

This is one of the largest gazelles with a shoulder height of 90-120cm.

Natural history: G. dama occupies a variety of habitats from bush and grassland to semidesert and desert. It can live for long periods without water.

Regular migrations are made northward into the Sahara in the rainy season. Wandering herds may associate with dorcas gazelles.

Distribution: This species apparently occurs in scattered areas from northern Sudan westward into southern Morocco.

Part of a skeleton from dried, unfossilized remains found in the Great Sand Sea of the Western Desert is probably the most northern record of the species (Uerpmann, 1987; 104, figs 48, 49). Churcher (1983: 185) had previously remarked that *G. dama*? was recently extant in the oases.

Prehistoric and Predynastic records: Fossilized remains from the Upper Pleistocene at Bir Tarfawi and Nabta Playa in the southwestern part of the Western Desert (Gautier, 1980: 323, 332) indicate that the previous range extended into Egypt.

Soemmering's Gazelle ***Gazella soemmeringi*** (Cretzschmar, 1826)

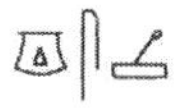 *gś3* geza Wb. V, 204

F Gazelle de Soemmering; G Sömmeringgazelle

Description: Male horns are lyre-shaped, with tips turning strongly outward and inward, and lying backward below the level of the frontal plane of the head. Females have smaller and less curved horns.

Color of the head, upper body, and outside of legs varies from pale to dark cinamon or light cinamon to maize yellow. The lower part of the head, throat, and neck, belly, inside of legs, rump patch, and base of tail are white. Facial markings are distinct. The rump patch is large and extends above the tail and has lateral projections onto the flanks (figs 13-158,-159,-160). The tail is longer than in other Egyptian gazelles, although that is not always indicated.

Shoulder height is 85-92 cm.

Natural history: G. soemmeringi lives in small to large herds in open bush savanna with acacia and in thinly wooded grass steppe. Otherwise, its behavior and activities are similar to those of other gazelles.

Distribution: The northern limits of distribution extend from northeastern Sudan at Berber to the Red Sea at Suakin. Southern limits extend from Sennar on the Blue Nile into the southeastern border of Ethiopia.

13-159 Soemmering's gazelle in an offering scene in the Tomb of Idut, Dynasty V, Saqqara. Source: Author.

13-160 Soemmering's gazelle with white rump patch (left) in an offering scene in the Tomb of Ptah-hetep, Dynasty V, Saqqara. Source: Paget and Pirie (1898: pl.XXXIII). To the right is a hartebeest.

13-161 Copies of dorcas gazelle and Soemmering's gazelle with hieroglyphs from the Tomb of Idut, Dynasty V, Saqqara. Source: Macramallah (1935: pl. XXVIII).

Prehistoric records: No fossils have been recorded from Egypt, probably because of the difficulty in recognizing post-cranial bones.

One rock drawing can be recognized as representing this species (fig. 13-147).

The Dynastic period: Boessneck and von den Driesch (1982: 89, fig. 21) identified foot bones of Soemmering's gazelle in some Old Kingdom remains at Elephantine.

Soemmering's gazelles appear in Old Kingdom hunting and offering scenes. They can be recognized by the horns in frontal view with tips turned inward (figs 13-151,-212) and indications of the extension of the white rump patch (fig. 13-160).

The earliest representation is in the Dynasty IV Tomb of Fetekta (fig. 7-172). Additional portrayals are in the Dynasty V hunting scene in the Tomb of Sahure (fig. 13-151), the offering scene in the Tomb of Idut (fig. 13-159), and the hunting scene in the Dynasty V Causeway of Unas (fig. 13-41). In Dynasty VI a dwarfed Soemmering's gazelle appears in another offering procession in the mastaba of Gem-ni-kai (Bissing 1911: pl. XXXIII).

Errors and discrepancies: Various authors (Hartmann, 1869:28f.; Bissing, 1905: 36; Hilzheimer, 1913: 176; Macramallah, 1935: 40; Keimer, 1943b: 102; Moussa and Altenmüller, 1977: 162, pl. 85, row 2) referred to illustrations of *G. soemmeringi* as *G. isabella*, which is a race of *G. dorcas* in the Blue Nile region of eastern Sudan and northern Ethiopia. These errors are understandable, because the horns of

G. dorcas isabella in frontal view are similar to those of *G. soemmeringi* in the Egyptian reliefs. For a comparison see Uerpmann (1987: fig. 45c).

Darby *et al.* (1977 I: fig. 5.10) referred to their copy of Soemmering's gazelle from the Tomb of Idut (fig. 13-161) as a 'bubal or hartebeest'. The tail on this figure is as long as that of a hartebeest.

Persian Gazelle ***Gazella subgutturosa*** (Güldenstaedt, 1780)

E Goitered Gazelle; F Gazelle Goitre; G Kropf-gazelle

Description: This species is about as large as the dorcas gazelle, but with a stouter build. Coloration is similar, but facial and body markings are lacking. Females are hornless, or with horns variably developed. There is a goiter-like swelling on the throat of males in the breeding season.

Distribution: Arabian Peninsula and S.E. Asia Minor eastward into Afghanistan, Baluchistan, Chinese Turkestan, Mongolia, and Northern Tibet.

The Dynastic period: Several examples of imported female goitered gazelles appear in Egyptian tomb decorations dated to the Eighteenth Dynasty: One is in the so-called Botanical Garden of Tuthmosis III in Karnak (fig. 13-162); another, which is questionable, is in a hunting scene (fig. 1-18 register 2); and a third is in an offering scene in Tell el Amarna (fig. 13-163).

13-162 Female Persian gazelle in The Botanical Garden of Tuthmosis III, Dynasty XVIII, Karnak. Source: Eggebrecht (1984: 389).

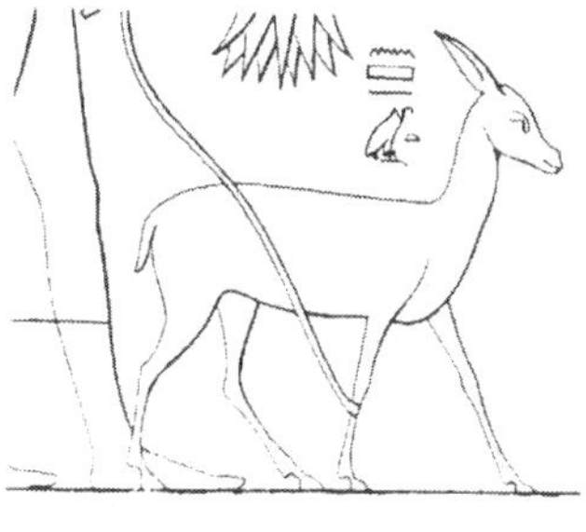

13-163 Persian gazelle in an offering scene on a tomb wall at Tell el Amarna, Dynasty XVIII. Source: Prisse d'Avennes (1847: pl. XV, 5).

Subfamily *Caprineae*

Ibex ***Capra ibex*** (Linnaeus, 1758)

Nubian Ibex ***Capra ibex nubiana*** (F. Cuvier, 1825)

 *nj3w* niau Wb. II, 202

 *jm3t* imat Wb. I, 280

 *nr3w* nerau Wb. II,280

E Slender-horned Ibex; F Bouquetin de la Nubie; G Nubischer Steinbock; A Taytal, Beden, Kebsh el Gebel

Nomenclature: Various Latinized specific names have been applied to this ibex, including *sinaiticus, sinaitica, beden,* and *nubiana* (Hartmann, 1869; Keller, 1909; Hilzheimer, 1913; Paton, 1925; and others). In Allen's (1939) Checklist, Beden is only a common name. An odd, undocumented remark by Darby *et al.* (1977: 230) was that ibex were 'often called Nubian goats (*Ovis lervis*)'.

13-164 Head of a Nubian ibex killed in 1965 near Qusur el Banat in Wadi Rad Ayia (Rawd Ayiad), Eastern Desert. Note the anterior keels between the bosses on the horns. Source: Author.

Description: Male ibex have long, curving, and gradually diverging horns, usually described as scimitar- shaped, with radii diminishing toward the tips. The horns in this race are narrow with the anterior surfaces flattened and bearing regularly arranged transverse bosses three quarters or more along the entire length. There are small, but distinct keels on the anterior margins between the bosses (fig. 13-164). Female horns are much shorter and lack bosses and keels, but are conspicuously annulated. Beards are present on males and older females. Short tails with a brush-like tuft of stiff, black hairs are another distinguishing feature.

The general body color is brownish grizzled with white. The belly, inner sides and backs of legs, 'knees', and pasterns are white. The muzzle, chin, and front part of the legs (except 'knees' and pasterns) are black. There is a faint mark between the eye and mouth (fig. 13-164).

Shoulder height in males is 75-90 cm; females are smaller.

Natural history: Ibex inhabit rocky wadis, cliffs, plateaus, and mountains. They live in small herds led by adult males. Old males are often solitary. Ibex feed during the night and cooler hours of the day; often descending to lower levels. Although they eat a great variety of plants, ibex cannot survive without water and will, if possible, take shelter from the sun in the vicinity of water.

Distribution: Capra ibex was a mid-Pleistocene migrant from Asia into Africa. It continues to exist in the Arabian Peninsula as well as the mountains of Asia and southern Europe, where other species and subspecies have also been described (Ellerman and Morrison-Scott, 1951: 404 ff.).

This ibex, known today as *C. i. nubiana*, populated the plateaus and mountains of Syria; the western parts of the Arabian Peninsula, and higher regions of the south and southeast; Sinai; eastern parts of Egypt and Sudan; Eritrea; and northern Ethiopia, where an isolated population recognized as *C. i. walie* persists in the higher mountains.

There is no substantial evidence verifying the supposition that ibex crossed the Nile River and populated the higher regions of the Western Desert (Kock, 1971: 34, fig. 2). Ibex have not been identified from the Caprini remains in Cyrenaican caves (McBurney, 1967: 18, 39); Hufnagl (1972) did not mention ibex in Libya; and no fossil or other records were listed from Algeria by Kowalski and Rzebik-Kowalska (1991: 39, 102), except for an unsuccessful introduction from Italy in 1979.

Despite these and further negative reports below in Prehistoric records, Haltenorth and Diller (1980: 104) said that the ibex, "in the early Stone Age in N. Africa existed westward to the Atlas Lands."

One puzzling illustration is an isolated rock drawing from Col de Tarit, Ahnet in southern Algeria, which was recorded as 'Ga: gravures anciennes', by Monod (1938: 131, 156, fig. 83). Further discussion below certainly does not support identification of this drawing as that of a wild ibex; perhaps it was a primitive goat.

Prehistoric records: "Archaeological records of *Capra nubiana* (*sic*) are quite rare", according to Uerpmann (1987: 120), because of "the lack of archaeozoological studies and difficulty in distinguishing bones of ibex from other

13-165 Rock drawing of a boat, giraffe, ibex, and a tesem hound. Below (right) are a bovid (?) and a dog (?). Location: one and a half km W of the Nile opposite Gebel Silsila. Source: Červíček (1986: fig.331, photo 38).

13-166 Rock drawing of an ibex head on a boat. Site: Chor es Salaam, west bank S of El Hosh. Source: Červíček (1974: fig.73).

13-167 Rock drawing of ibex and a pariah or a tesem hound in Wadi Hammamat, Eastern Desert. Source: Goyon (1957: pl. XLVII).

13-168 Rock drawings of ibex and pariah dogs near Toshka, Lower Nubia, east bank. Source: Dunbar (1941: pl.IV, 16).

13-169 Ibex with stylized snouts on predynastic painted pottery from Naqada. Source: Petrie and Quibell (1896: pl. LXVII, 16).

13-170 Ibex (left), Barbary goat (right) and dogs on white cross-lined pottery from Naqada. Source: Petrie and Quibell (1896: pl. XXIX, 19).

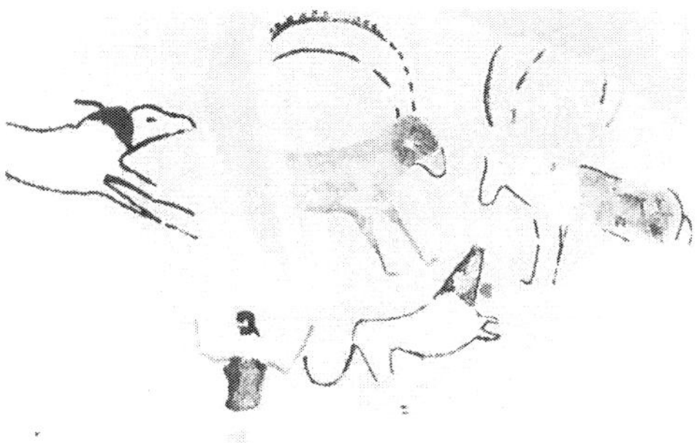

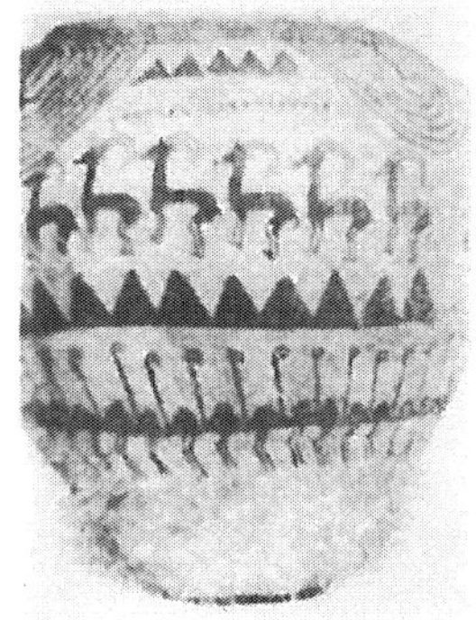

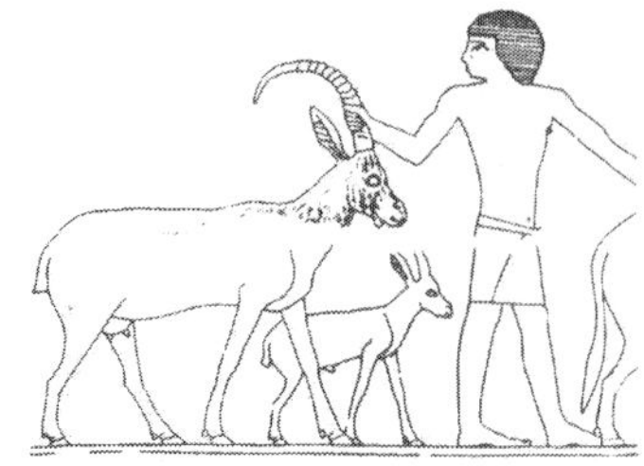

13-171 (top left) Two ibex, two pariah dogs, and a man on the Hierakonpolis painted wall. Source: Quibell and Green (1902 II: pl. LXXVII).

13-172 (top centre) Ibex and flamingos on predynastic pottery from Abydos. Source: Vandier (1952 I : fig. 240).

13-173 (bottom left) Part of a hunting scene in the Tomb of Re'-em-kuy (Re'emka), Dynasty V-VI, Memphis. Source: Hayes (1953 I: fig. 56). One of three male ibex is lassoed. Above left is a hedgehog.

13-174 (top right) A female ibex with young in offering procession. Tomb of Ti, Dynasty V, Saqqara. Source: Wild (1966 III: pl. CLXV).

13-175 (bottom right) Male ibex in offering scene. Tomb of Rahotep, Dynasty IV, Medum, S of Gerza. Source: Petrie (1892b: pl. XIV).

members of the goat family". He listed two sites from Sinai, including one that was questionable, and questionable remains from Dakhla Oasis reported by Churcher (1983: fig. 2).

Although Churcher (1982: table 1) recorded *C. ibex* from Neolithic and Old Kingdom sites in Dakhla Oasis, he had previously remarked, "The question also arises as to whether ...the ibex may not be domestic goat. Such decisions cannot be attempted until extensive cranial materials have been recovered" (Churcher, 1981: 210).

Winkler (1938 I, 1939 II) listed many sites of ibex drawings that are short distances west of the Nile, but only a few pictures were published (e.g. fig. 13-141). Červíček (1986) listed several more from the photo files (fig. 13-165).

These drawings, however, may be no more indicative of previous distribution than the drawing of a boat with an ibex head on the bow at Chor es Salaam south of El Hosh (fig. 13-166).

If ibex did cross the Nile they might not have wandered beyond the bordering cliffs because of the lack of water, vegetation, and shelter.

Winkler (1939 II: 7) also listed a number of sites along the Ghubari Road east of Dakhla Oasis where ibex supposedly occurred. The bovids in his single published photograph (fig. 13-81) are scimitar-horned and beisa oryx.

Červíček (1986: 59, 67) mentioned unpublished caprid and ibex drawings at sites 66 and 69 on the Ghubari Road that were in the Winkler photo collection.

Although Winkler (1939 II: 10) referred to drawings of 'ibex' from Karkur Tahl, Gebel Uweinat, there are no ibex in his figures. Drawings from that area which Rhotert (1952: 32) called antelopes and ibex are Barbary goats (fig. 1-22).

Hayes (1964: 228) and Wendorf and Schild (1980: 237) referred to ibex drawings in these areas and mistakenly credited Winkler (1939 II). Wendorf and Schild also credited McHugh (1971), but McHugh (pers. com.) said that he had not seen ibex drawings in any of these areas (see also McHugh, 1971; 1975) and that Van Noten (1978) had not found ibex in Gebel Uweinat drawings, but noted the frequency of oryx.

Rock drawings of ibex dated from the Neolithic into Roman times (figs 7-15, 13-103,-167,-168,-208) occur throughout much of the Eastern Desert. Horn shape and length vary considerably. Both horns are depicted and sometimes diverging slightly. Bosses are not shown and beards are often lacking, but the tails are usually short and upright. Ibex are commonly drawn being followed or held at bay by dogs and approached by a hunter armed with a bow and arrow.

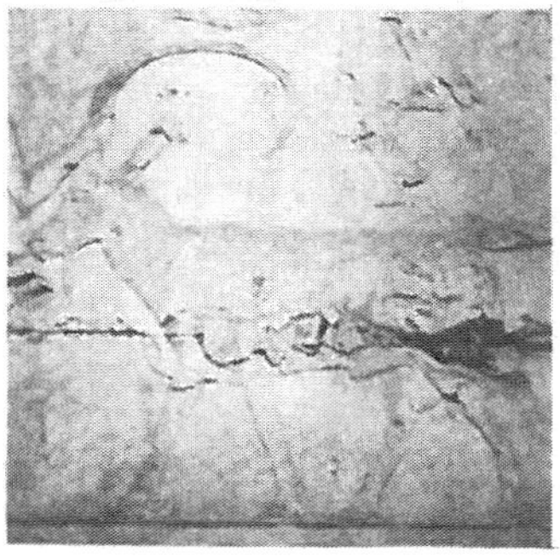

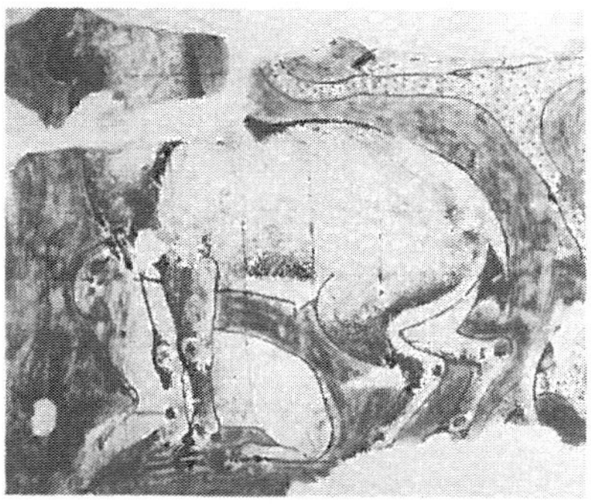

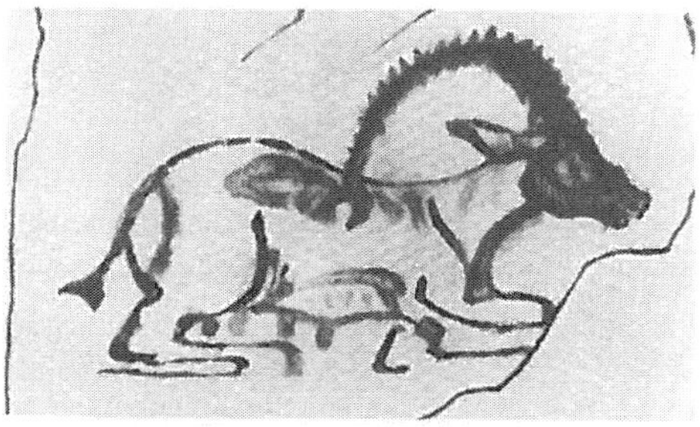

13-176 (top left) Male ibex in offering scene. Tomb of Idut, Dynasty VI, Saqqara. Source: Author.

13-177 (top centre) Ibex being held by a saluki hound in the Tomb of Kenamun, Dynasty XI, Thebes. Source: Davies (1930 I: pl. XLVIII).

13-178 (top right) A chair decorated with an ibex. Tomb of Iouiya and Tiouiya, Dynasty XVIII, Biban el Moluk. Source: Davis (1907: pl. XXXV).

13-179 (bottom left) Ibex on a fragment of a bowl. Temple of Tuthmosis III, Dynasty XVIII, Gurneh. Source: Weigall (1906: 137, fig.10).

13-180 (bottom centre) Ibex with piebald coloration on an ostracon from Deir el Medina (Medineh), Dynasty XIX-XX. Source: Vandier d'Abbadie (1936 I: pl. XXIV, 2193).
Note the exaggerated tuft on the tail and the rump patch.

13-181 (bottom right) Ibex head with hook-shaped horns on the bow of Queen Hatshepsut's boat, Dynasty XVIII, Deir el Bahari. Source: Mariette (1877: pl. 12). The beard is lacking, but is present on the identical head on the stern.

Both horns were pictured on ibex painted on predynastic pottery (figs 1-15, 13-169), although the shape was variable. Sometimes strongly defined bosses appeared on Gerzean pottery (fig. 13-170) and the same stylization occurs in the Hierakonpolis wall paintings (fig. 13-171).

The colors of the latter are imaginative - red and white and black and white. Beards and tails are lacking on many figures and identification must be based on the horns.

Ibex often appear together with flamingos and rows of triangles as a pottery motif (fig. 13-172). The triangles in these motifs, depending on the position, could represent either conical mud nests of the flamingos or the mountainous habitat of the ibex, but a contrast between the Delta and the mountainous desert may possibly be the intended theme (Petrie, 1920: 16 f.; Boessneck, 1988: 27 f.). Another possible reason for the combinations is that the artists simply pictured what they saw in the Naqada area - rows of flamingos standing near the shores of the river, rows of ibex that came to the shores to drink, and a mountainous background.

Other Predynastic representations were discussed and illustrated in the introductory pages (figs 1-7,-11,-12,-15). Very realistic ibex with horns in close parallel, perhaps a carry over from Mesopotamian influence, appear on both sides of the Hunting Dogs Palette (fig. 1-2a,b) and on an ivory carving from Hierakonpolis (fig. 13-88). Ibex figures were also produced in flint by the pressure flaking technique (fig. 1-6 c).

The Dynastic period: Ibex were commonly pictured throughout the dynasties in scenes of hunting (figs 1-11,-18,-21,-29, 13-173) and trophies of a hunt (figs 7-159a,b), offering (figs 13-174,-175), fattening (fig. 1-16), and butchery (fig. 13-92). They were also popular as decorative motifs (figs 13-178,-184).

They are one of the few stall fed animals that were shown with young (fig. 13-174). In Wild's (1966: pl. CLXV) copy of this badly damaged relief there are remnants of a beard on the female and the two teats on the udder; part of the horn on the kid and an indication of a beard. The illustration does not confirm, but is indicative of captive breeding of this species.

In the paintings and reliefs of the early dynasties ibexes are easily identified from the style of showing the horns singly in profile, long and recurving, with diminishing radii toward the tips (figs 13-173,-175,-176). Bosses were rarely shown. Beards were sometimes lacking and tails were often too long (figs 1-29 to -32). Color and markings

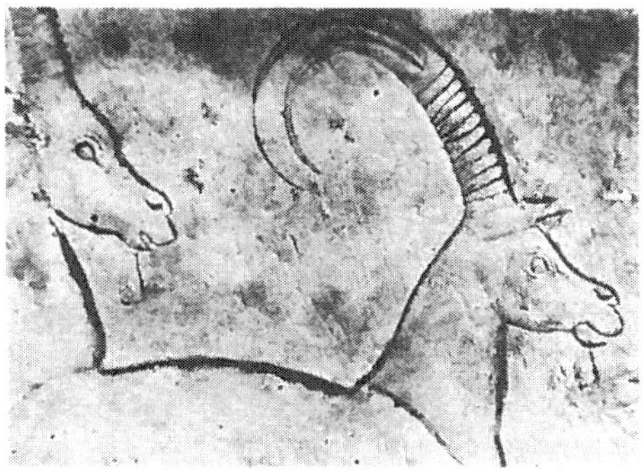

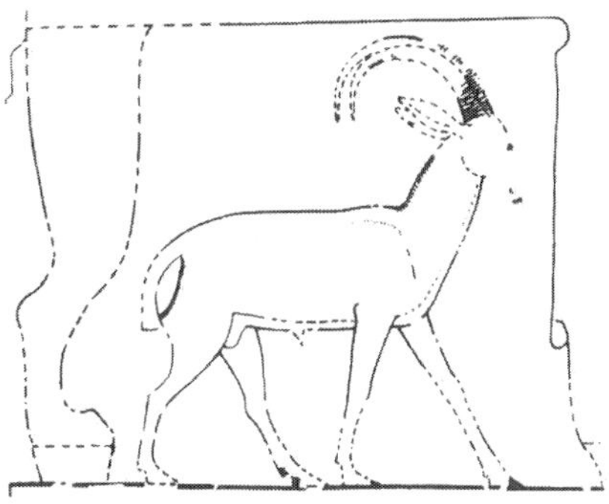

13-182 (top) Ibex with stylized, hook-shaped horns carved on a manger at Tell el 'Amarna, Dynasty XVIII. Source: Newton (1924: pl. XXX).

13-183 (bottom) A pet ibex under the chair of a Dynasty XVIII tomb owner in Thebes. Source: Säve-Söderbergh (1957: pl. VIII).

were not always consistent. Figure 13-175, for example, is green with black horns. A good example of coloration, however, is the mottled gray animal in the Tomb of Kenamun (fig. 13-177).

Keimer (1953a: 127. pl. XVI 1,2) drew attention to a pair of ibex from the Dynasty VI Tomb of Mehu with very slender bodies and long legs. Such exaggeration also appears in some Beni Hasan scenes in which almost all of the animals are thin and long-legged (figs 1-29,-30). The ibex can be identified only by their backward curving, sickle-shaped horns. On the ibex to the right in Figure 1-30 the horns are thicker and there is an indication of bosses, suggesting it is a male.

In the copy of L.D. (fig. 1-31) all the animals have shorter legs. The ibex have double horns in

13-184 Ibex heads on a vase from the Tomb of Meryen Ptah, Dynasty XIX in Wadi Biban el Moluk, Western Thebes. Source: Hayes (1959 II: fig. 221).

parallel in the hook-shaped form and the tails are longer.

Another comparison between ibex figures in Beni Hasan was also described in the Introduction (figs 1-35,-36). Two variants that appeared on ibex in New Kingdom art were piebald coloration and 'hook-shaped' horns. Keimer (1953a: 129; pl.XIX) listed a number of examples of coloration including Tutankhamun's bow case (fig. 13-189); a decorated chair (fig. 13-178); a make-up spoon on which the long-tailed ibex had been called an oryx; a pottery figure that Weigall (1906: 137) had called a gazelle (fig. 13-179); and an ostracon (fig. 13-180). The reason for these colorations is not clear, but they may have been confusions with goats or possibly they were offspring from goat-ibex matings.

The hook-shaped horn style with vertical or almost vertical bases and, in most examples, prominent pedicels, was probably a Syrian import (Osborn, 1987). Among the many examples are the ibex in the 'flying gallop' pose in the hunt scene from Amenemhet (fig. 1-18, register 2), the bow and stern of Queen Hatshepsut's boat (fig. 13-181), and the carvings on a manger at Tell el 'Amarna (fig. 13-182). Further remarks and illustrations are given in the following section on *Capra aegagrus.*

An ibex with normal horns under the chair of an unidentified Dynasty XVIII tomb owner suggests that this animal may have occasionally been tamed. The drawing appears to be of a subadult male (fig. 13-183).

In the Late Dynasties ibex were commonly represented on vases, many of which were of Syrian origin as indicated by the style. One example from a Dynasty XIX tomb (fig. 13-184) was probably of Egyptian origin and was described by Hayes (1953 II: fig. 221) as having "...handles in the form of the slim-horned Nubian ibex, which was probably fitted at one time with ears of silver or gold."

Additional artifacts from the Late Dynasties include a variety of ibex figures on ring molds from Tell el 'Amarna (fig. 13-185). Petrie (1894: 29) noted that "the style of 187- 194 is hardly Egyptian, but they were made at Tell el Amarna." He also commented, "The prevalence of the ibex type, 187-194, is strange, as the animal does not seem to have ever been very common in Egypt; perhaps it was a lucky sign to wear, as it is marked *nefer* on 193."

This remark by Petrie regarding the prevalence of the ibex is also 'strange', because it is one of the most common animals in tomb decorations. In reference to *nefer*, however, Faulkner's (1962: 151) translation verifies Petrie's suggestion, because *nfr* means being 'happy, well, good'.

The ibex was not generally recognized as a sacred animal, although Kuhlman (1983: 7) said it was associated with Min, the god of fertility, and

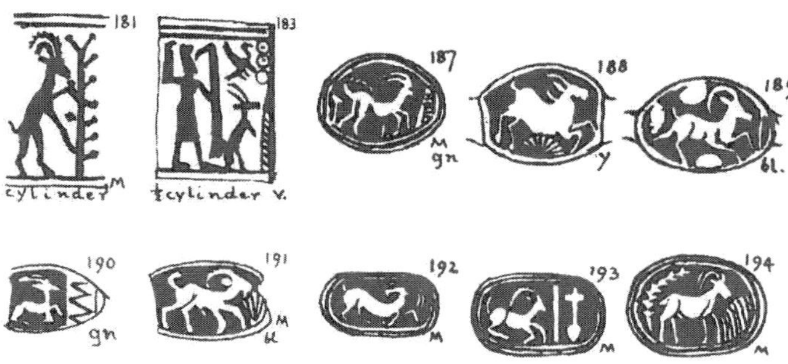

13-185 (left) Ibex figures on ring molds from Tell el 'Amarna, Dynasty XVIII. Source: Petrie (1894: pl.XVI).

13-186 (right) Rock drawing from Kagug-Schibeika, east bank of the Nile 4 km N of Gebel Silsila, dating uncertain. Source: Červíček (1974: fig. 246). The central figure is an ibex, as indicated by the beard, and also the upper left. Upper right is probably an ibex, as indicated by bosses on the horns. Lower right is an aurochs.

was kept in a special enclosure at Akhmim, the sacred city of Min.

There may have been confusion, however, between the ibex and the sacred goat and ram. Besides, there are no ibex mummies in the animal town of Akhmim.

Almost every part of the body of the ibex was considered as having some beneficial or healing property (Ziswiller, 1967: 14). The bezoar, a concretion found in the stomach, was reputedly effective against fainting, melancholy, jaundice, hemorroids, hemorrhagic diarrhea, pestilence, cancer, etc. The blood was a cure for gall stones; the heel bone for splenic diseases; and the droppings for anaemia and consumption and to ensure rejuvination. The heart was eaten for strength.

Errors and discrepancies: A misnamed ibex is at the end of the row of animals being led in the Tomb of Sekhem-Ankh-Ptah (fig. 7-153). Simpson (1976b: 11) referred to the animal as a 'young sheep', because of the hieroglyph *rn ib3w* meaning 'stall fed Barbary sheep' [*sic*, goat]. But the horn is definitely ibex.

To the left of the hunt scene of Amenemhet (fig. 1-18) a young ibex (note the beard) with the horn reversed is carried on a man's shoulders.

In the Dynasty XIX Tomb of Meri-meri (fig. 13-114) a young ibex recognizable by its short horns, short tail, and indistinct beard, is carried in an offering procession. It was mistakenly called a 'Barbary sheep' by Boessneck (1981a: 32).

Červíček (1974: fig. 246) called all horned animals depicted in Figure 13-186 'antelopes'. The central figure with the beard is an ibex, and also the upper left. The upper right is an ibex, as indicated by bosses on the horns. Lower right is an aurochs.

Syrian Ibex or **Wild Goat** *Capra aegagrus* Erxleben, 1777

E Bezoar; F Chèvre véritable; G Bezoarziege

Nomenclature: The name Bezoar derives from the concretion found in the stomach of this ibex, which was once used as a poison antidote and a remedy for many diseases.

C. aegagrus is the recognized ancestor of the domestic goat.

Description: The horn curvature is similar to that of *C. ibex* and the horns are much larger in males than females. They are bilaterally compressed with a sharp anterior keel on which widely spaced longitudinal bosses develop with age; the first appearing at about age three. Conspicuous depressions occur around the horns at these positions. Variations in art are noted below.

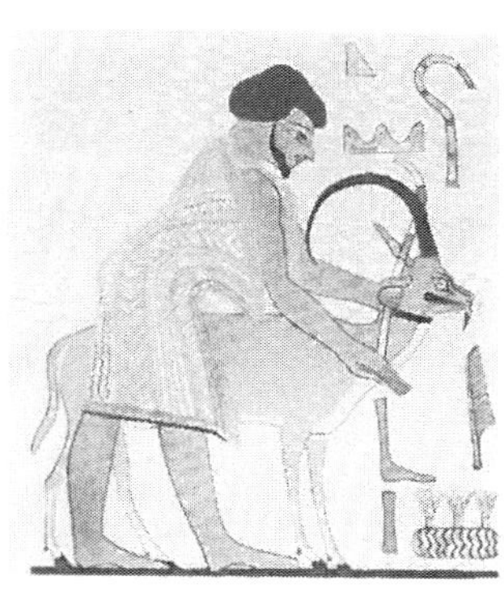

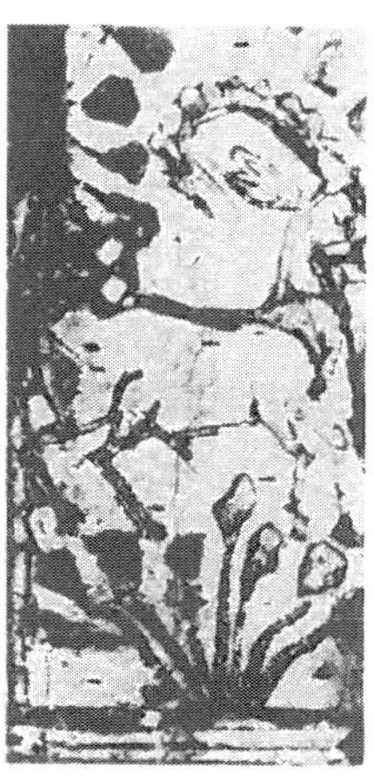

13-187 (left) Syrian ibex in Asian tribute scene, Tomb of Khnumhotep, Dynasty XII, Beni Hasan. Source: Newberry (1893 I: pl.XXXI).

13-188 (right) Syrian style of ibex on Tutankhamun's decorated bow, Dynasty XVIII. Source: Edwards (1976b: catalogue No. 49).

13-189 Syrian style of ibex on Tutankhamun's bow case, Dynasty XVIII. Source: Carter (1933 III: pl. XXIX A).

The body color is brownish gray in winter; yellowish to reddish brown in summer. The belly, inner sides and backs of the legs, 'knees', and pasterns are whitish. Fronts of legs are rusty brown.

Males have a black spinal crest, black shoulder stripes extending from the withers to the blackish chest, and a black beard and tail. The muzzle and cheeks are grayish. The face is reddish brown and there are pale, whitish marks above the eyes.

Young animals and females have a dark brown area on the forehead and muzzle, a dark stripe from the eye to the mouth, and a pale yellow gray stripe between. At what age the stripes disappear in males is not known.

13-190 Syrian ibex head on Tutankhamun's alabaster boat, Dynasty XVIII. Source: Fox (1951: pl. 72).

13-191 Bronze head of a Syrian ibex in Persian style, but said to be an Egyptian production, from Tel el-Maskhuta near Ismailiya in the Eastern Delta and dated to Dynasty XXVII. Source: Bothmer and Keith (1974:74-75).

Distribution: Wild goats still exist in the Aegean Islands and southern Asia Minor; perhaps in Syria, northern Iraq, and the Caucasus eastward through Iran to Sind and Afghanistan and possibly Oman in the southeastern Arab Republic (Harrison, 1968 II: 338). This species was not part of the Egyptian fauna.

Prehistoric records: Various prehistoric artifacts have been found that are obviously of Mesopotamian motif. The ibex on the ivory knife handle from Gebel el Tarif (fig. 1-12) has the horns carved in parallel position with several series of transverse grooves, which was a standard technique of depicting the horns of *C. aegagrus*. Another ibex is on the Gebel Arak handle (fig. 1-11). Although the horns are without grooves on this figure, there are other aspects that indicate its source is Asian, such as the carnivore attacking from the rear (Asselberghs, 1961: 276) and the extensive manes on the lions.

The Dynastic period: In a tribute scene in Beni Hasan, an Asian of the Aamu tribe is bringing a reddish brown ibex (fig. 13-187). The ibex is a female *C. aegagrus* as indicated by the slender, annulated horn, facial markings, and small beard. The horn is much too long for a female, however, and the tail is twice normal length. The facial mark below the eye should extend from the eye to the mouth and the upper stripe is an erroneous division of the band on the forehead and muzzle. The white muzzle and chest are also fictitious.

Illustrations of this animal by Champollion (1845 IV: pl. CCCLXI) and Rosellini (1834 II: pl. XXVI) do not show leg or facial markings, except for a short black line before the eye. In L.D. II, 133 the leg markings are also lacking.

Additional figures of *C. aegagrus* appeared in the Tomb of Tutankhamun: Adult males with large, longitudinal bosses on their horns on the decorated bow (fig. 13-188) and bow case (fig. 13-189); young animals represented by the alabaster 'bleating ibex' (Osborn, 1987: pl. XIX, 1) and the heads on the model boat (fig. 13-190), which have markings on the front of their heads and stripes below the eyes. These alabaster figures have hook-shaped horns carved from bent wood with vertical bases on prominent pedicels, which indicate Syrian or Mesopotamian style (Osborn, 1987). Another example is on Tutankhamun's wooden chest (fig. 7-224).

A Persian period bronze head on a handle from Tell el Maskhuta in the eastern Delta (fig. 13-191), which might have been of Egyptian origin, is another example of imported stylization.

Domestic Goat *Capra hircus* Linnaeus, 1758

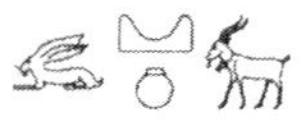 *wnḏw* wenedju Wb. I, 326

F Chèvre; G Ziegen; A Maez beity

Nomenclature: A variety of names have been applied to domestic goats: *Hircus mambricus, H. thebaicus,* and *H. reversus.*

Description: The horns on the earliest domestic goats brought into Egypt varied from the ancestral scimitar shape to a vertical screw-horn shape (fig. 13-192) and twisted horns (figs 13-193,-194,-195). The crescent or scimitar- shape (figs 13-204,-205) did not reappear until the Late period.

The ears in Predynastic figures were upright, hanging in Old Kingdom reproductions, but upright in the Middle and Late Kingdom. The beard on males was a common feature, but not shown in most early figures.

Natural history: Domestic goats, like their ancestors, are adapted to living in highlands and browsing on shrubs and trees (fig. 13-202) and eating various fruits, rather than grazing, which is the habit of sheep.

Prehistoric and Predynastic records: The ancestor of the domestic goat was *Capra aegagrus*. The earliest domestication of goats was in S.W. Asia about the same time or a little later than domestication of sheep. The earliest estimated dates were 9th Millenium B.C. (Final Paleolithic) in Iraq and 7th Millenium B.C. in Jericho-Jarmo north of the Dead Sea (Bökönyi, 1974).

Brewer *et al.* (1994: 90) said that these early dates were disputable, but most scholars agree that by 6,000 B.C. domestic goats and sheep had become well established.

Domestic goats and sheep were herded from Asia across Sinai and the northern coast of Egypt into the mountains of Cyrenaica and up the Nile Valley about 5,000 B.C. (Reed, 1969: 372). At that early date, of course, climate and vegetation would have been very favorable for such an activity.

There are Neolithic remains (5th Millenium B.C.) in the Haua Fteah cave in Cyrenaica and in the Faiyum (Epstein, 1971 II: 223).

Schaller (1977: 23) and Zeuner (1963) have stated that domestic goats with twisted horns did not begin to replace scimitar-shaped horns in the Eastern Mediterranean until about 4,000 B.C.

The earliest illustrations of twisted horned (screw-horn) goats, together with screw-horn

13-192 A screw-horn goat with vertical horns (lower left) and horizontal screw-horn, long-tailed sheep on Predynastic Naqada II pottery from Abydos. Source: Petrie (1902 I: pl. L).

13-193 A troop of twisted-horn goats and a row of flamingos on Predynastic pottery from Abydos. Source: De Morgan (1896: pl. X).

13-194 A row of twisted-horn goats with raised ears followed by a herder with a stick on Predynastic Naqada pottery from Abydos. Source: Naville (1914: pl. V, E 340).

sheep, decorate various examples of Predynastic pottery (fig. 13-192).

Bones of dwarf goats were found in Gerzean middens at Toukh, on the west bank of the Nile between Nagada and Ballas opposite Qift and described as *Hircus reversus* (Lortet and Gaillard, 1905: 280 ff., fig. 152; Epstein, 1971 II: 222).

The Dynastic period: A Dynasty I figure of a 'dwarf' goat was described by Epstein (1971 II: 223) on the great mace head of Narmer from Hierakonpolis (fig. 13-196). Schweinfurth (1912: 647 f.) wrote that an Old or Middle Kingdom rock drawing of a goat southwest of Aswan (fig. 13-197) with scimitar-shaped horns, erect ears, a convex facial profile, and the absence of a beard was comparable with the dwarf goats from Toukh (Lortet and Gaillard, *op. cit.*).

Another rock drawing of similar style, except for the concave facial profile, could also be a dwarf (fig. 13-198). Scimitar-shaped horns and erect ears are also documented in Figure 13-200.

13-195 Twisted-horn goats with lop-ears on a Dynasty I ivory chain from Hierakonpolis. Source: Epstein (1971 II: fig. 325).

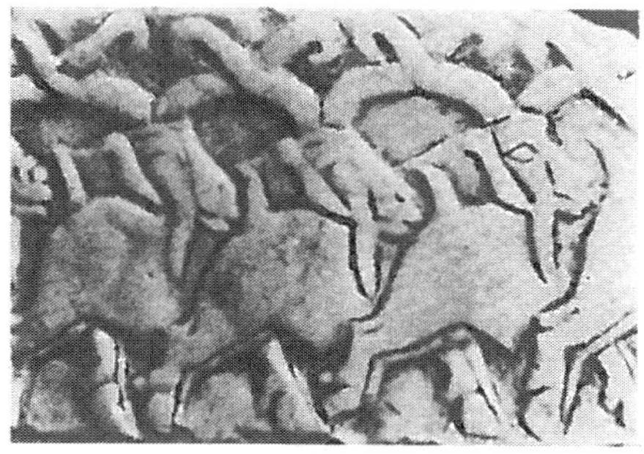

13-196 (left) A dwarf goat with crescent-shaped horns on the Dynasty I great mace head of Narmer from Hierakonpolis. Source: Quibell (1900 I: pl. XXVI, B).

13-197 (centre) A rock drawing of a dwarf (?) goat from the Old or Middle Kingdom southwest of Aswan. Source: Schweinfurth (1912: fig. 11).

13-198 (right) A rock drawing of a young or dwarf goat with short, straight horns. Location: Kanais in wadi Mia, 45 km east of Edfu (Idfu). Source: Červíček (1974: fig. 249).

13-199 A rock drawing of a herd of twisted-horn goats and two herdsmen. The ears are not shown and were probably lopping. Above left is a long-horned ox. Location: Magal Hodein, Eastern Desert, southeast of Gebel Abraq. Source: Červíček (1974: fig. 346).

13-200 A rock drawing of domestic goats with scimitar horns and erect ears. Location: Mamla-el-Otuani, east bank of the Nile, north of Edfu (Idfu). Source: Červíček (1974: fig. 362).

Twisted horn, lop-eared goats continued to be pictured in the Dynasties (figs 13-199,-201). Goats with slightly twisted horns and erect ears were pictured in a Dynasty VII scene from Sawiet el Meitim (fig. 13-202). Dwarf goats with erect ears and crescent horns (fig. 13-197) were probably imported from the south (Schweinfurth, 1912: 647).

Four crouched goats with twisted horns were shown being hand fed in the Dynasty VI Mastaba of Mereruka. These were lop-eared, although the ears were not shown on two examples (fig. 13-201) and the beard is missing on another.

The sharply twisted horns were replaced by slightly twisted horns (fig. 13-203) and later, in the New Kingdom, the horns were again crescent-shaped and the ears were erect. Coloration varied from brown to whitish and piebald (figs 13-204,-205).

Errors and discrepancies: The various twisted-horn goats on Predynastic pottery have been called 'gazelle, antelope, kudu, and addax' (Vandier, 1952 I: fig. 555; Engelbach, 1923: 7; Capart, 1905: 117; de Morgan, 1896; and Petrie, 1902 I: 23). De Morgan (1926 II: fig. 68) also referred to the screw-horn goats being hand-fed in the Mastaba of Mereruka (fig. 13-201) as 'antelopes'.

The crescent horned ibexes on the reverse of the Hierakonpolis Palette (fig. 1-2b) and on the Gebel el Araq ivory knife handle (fig. 1-12) were called 'dwarf goats' by Epstein (1971 II: 223).

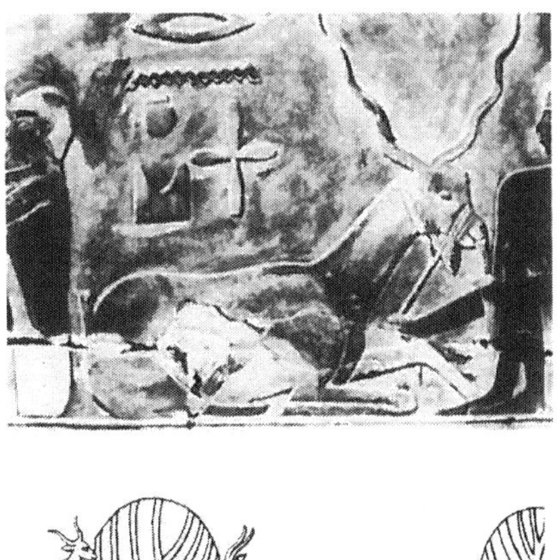

13-201 (top left) One of four lop-eared, twisted-horn goats being hand-fed in the Mastaba of Mereruka, Dynasty VI, Saqqara. Source: Duell (1938 II: pl. 152).

13-202 (bottom left) Goats browsing trees in the Dynasty VII Tomb of Nj-ankh-Pepi at Sawijet el-Meitin on the east bank of the Nile north of Beni Hasan. Source: L.D. II, 111 b.

13-203 (right) Lop-eared, twisted-horn goats being hand-fed in the Tomb of Khnemhotep, Dynasty XII, Beni Hasan. Source: Newberry (1893 I: pl. XXX).

13-204 (top) Goats with erect ears and crescent horns in the Tomb of Huy, Dynasty XVIII, Thebes. Source: Davies and Gardiner (1926: pl. VIII).

13-205 (right) Goats with erect ears and crescent horns in the Tomb of Apy, Dynasty XIX, Thebes. Source: Davies (1927: pl. XXXIV).

Barbary Goat ***Ammotragus lervia*** (Pallas, 1777)

 *jbw* ibu Wb. I, 62

E Barbary Sheep; Maned, Ruffled, and Aproned Sheep; Aoudad, Audad; Arui; F Mouflon à manchettes, Aoudad; G Mähnenschaf, Mähnenspringer; A Arui, Aoudad, Kebsh el Gebel, Waddan

Nomenclature: The original zoological name, *Antilope lervia,* was applied by Pallas to a specimen from Algeria. The species name, *lervia,* was probably taken from a local Berber name, 'Lerwee', referring to its pale color. Later it was considered to be a goat-like sheep and was called *Ovis tragelaphus* (*tragus* Gr goat, *elaphus* Gr a deer or antelope). Within the next century or so the generic name was shifted to *Ammotragus* (*ammos* Gr sand, *tragus* Gr goat); then back to *Ovis* and again to *Ammotragus lervia* (see Harper, 1940; Ellerman and Morrison-Scott, 1951: 409).

Recent authors (Ansell, 1971; Corbet, 1978; Cloudsley- Thompson, 1984) reshuffled the names and decided the genus should be *Capra* (Gr goat), but Gray and Simpson (1980) said it should be *Hemitragus* (Gr half-goat). Finally, the current generic name is *Ammotragus.*

Description: The body color is light brown; paler on the underparts and pasterns. The most distinctive feature is the mane of long, pale hairs extending from the throat to the chest, dividing and continuing onto the forelegs, and covering the 'knees' and lower legs in mature animals like an apron. There is also a short mane on the base of the neck and the shoulders. The tail is thickly haired on the distal half and the tuft sometimes reaches the hocks.

The annulated horns arise along the facial plane with bases very thick and close together and somewhat quadrangular in cross-section, but becoming rounded as they curve backward, outward, and inward in a semicircle. There are weak keels on the front surfaces (fig. 13-206).

13-206 Barbary goats in the Giza Zoological Garden, Cairo. Source: Author.

The shoulder height of males is about one meter. Females are smaller and lighter colored with shorter manes and horns less developed.

Barbary goats lack certain characteristics that are typical of sheep, such as preorbital glands and complimentary cavities in the skull, and glands on the feet. The tail is flattened in cross-section and bare on the underside at the base instead of being rounded and hairy (Hilzheimer, 1936:195).

Although the horns look a little like sheep horns, they are not spiralled nor twisted and do not curve forward.

Differences between the postcranial skeletons of Barbary goats and those of domestic sheep and goats were described and illustrated by Gabler (1985).

13-207 Rock drawings of Barbary goats in Wadi el Hol, Western Desert. Note indications of manes. Other animals are not identifiable. Source: Winkler (1938 I: pl. XXX, 2).

13-208 (left) Rock drawings of Barbary goats, ibex (left), and elephants (below) near Toshka (Tushka), Lower Nubia, east bank of the Nile. Source: Dunbar (1941: pl. IV, 15).

13-209 (right) Rock drawing of a Barbary goat in Khor (Wadi) Zurqan southeast of El Derr, Nubia. Source: Redrawn from Almagro Basch and Almagro Gorbea (1968: fig. 104).

13-210 Hunt scene with Barbary goat and pariah dogs on red, white cross-lined pottery from Naqada. Source: Petrie and Quibell (1896, pl.XXIX, 95).

13-211 Barbary goats, twisted-horn goats, and a hippopotamus in Gerzean pottery marks. Source: Petrie (1901 b: pl. XX).

Research in biochemistry, chromosome analyses, etc., have shown that goats and sheep have a common ancestry, but that Barbary 'sheep', despite the retention of the common name, are more closely related to goats (Dalimier, 1954; Petzch, 1958; Boettger, 1958; Schmitt, 1963; Zeuner, 1963: 155, Benirschke and Kumomato, 1980).

Captive Barbary goats have been crossed with domestic goats and the offspring recrossed with ibex. Attempts to breed them with sheep have not been successful (Ansell, 1971).

At least two 'goaty' characteristics are recognizable by anyone: Barbary goats stand on their hind legs to browse trees and during the mating season males smell exactly like goats, because they have 'goaty' glands at the bases of their tails.

Natural history: Barbary goats are mountain dwellers. They live solitarily or in small herds spending the day in the shade of cliffs and boulders with some individuals acting as sentries. When immobile they are almost invisible because their color blends with the rocky background. They feed at night on mountain vegetation or in valleys.

This goat is the most desert-adapted of all large mammals. It does not require water daily and can survive for weeks on the moisture in vegetation. It will drink and even swim where enough water is available.

Wariness, together with its climbing and leaping abilities, make this animal difficult for predators to capture. Conversely, these features posed a special challenge to human hunters.

Distribution and status: The Barbary goat is assumed to have been one of the mid-Pleistocene migrants, along with the ibex, that crossed the Sinai-Suez land bridge from Asia into Africa. Both species invaded approximately the same areas of plateaus and mountains east of the Nile in Egypt and Lower Nubia. The ibex continued southward along the Red Sea Mountains and penetrated Ethiopia. The Barbary goat spread through Upper Nubia and crossed the Nile, probably in several places, because it was known from cliffs bordering the Nile Valley, some plateaus and mountains in the Western Desert, and similar terrain in Northwestern Sudan. It also spread throughout the more rugged sections of Libya and all major mountain massifs of the Western Sahara north of the 15th parallel (Kock, 1971: 29 ff.; Fiorenza, 1972; Gray and Simpson, 1980; Osborn and Helmy, 1980: 521 ff.). It did not migrate southward as did most large mammals during the Neolithic subpluvial, but remained on the waterless heights.

Pleistocene remains have been found near Kom Ombo (Reed *et al.*, 1967; Churcher, 1972: 121); questionably from Wadi Halfa (Reed and Turnbull, 1969); and in northern Cyrenaica, Libya, east of Benghazi (Bate, 1955). In discussing the Faiyum A Neolithic, Hayes (1964: 219) said, "The scanty remains of sheep or goat found may belong to wild species, such as the Ammotragus."

No fossils, no archaeological remains, no records of this species are known from east of Suez. A few animals probably survive in parts of the Eastern Desert and in Gebel Uweinat (S.W. Egypt and S.E. Libya), but the species is undoubtedly on the verge of extinction in Egypt. Even in Tregenza's (1958: 101) time it was said to be 'rarer than the little white clouds that floated over the plateaus in summer'.

13-212 (top left) Barbary goat and Soemmering's gazelle in an offering procession, Tomb of Ti, Dynasty V, Saqqara. Source: Wild (1966 III: pl. CLXVI).

13-213 (top right) Dwarfed ibex, Barbary goat, and calf in part of an offering scene in the Mastaba of Gemni-kai (Kagemni), Dynasty VI, Saqqara. Source: von Bissing (1911 II: pl. XXXI). As mentioned in the Introduction, most of the paired animals in the entire scene are shown with only two hind legs.

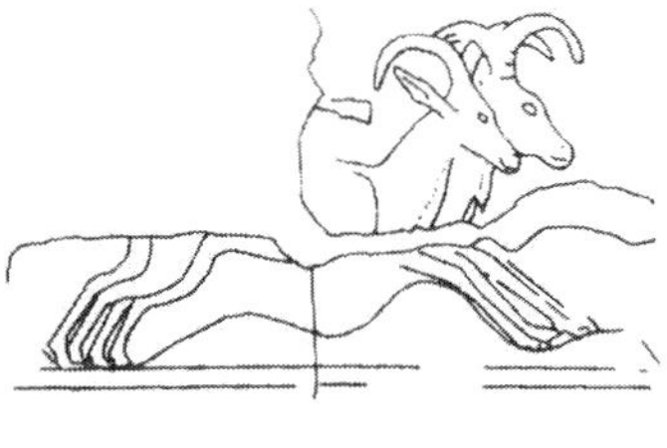

13-214 (right) Two Barbary goats running side by side in a fragment of a hunting scene from the Tomb of Mentuherkh-hepeshef, Dynasty XVIII, Thebes. Source: Davies (1913: pl. XII). The horns of the animals appear to be interlocked.

Prehistoric and Predynastic records: The actual distribution of the Barbary goat in Egypt extended far beyond the records left by prehistoric rock artists. These records are from the Eastern Desert (Winkler, 1938: pl. XIV, W. Gash), Western Desert (fig. 13-207), and the borders of the Nile Valley in the Aswan area (fig. 7-17) and Nubia (fig. 13-208). A few drawings are known from Gebel Uweinat (fig. 1-22).

Drawings are easily recognized by the curved horns in frontal view (figs 1-15, 13-207 to -212) even though the manes may not be indicated and the tails are too short or too long.

Barbary goats were often depicted in hunting scenes together with men and dogs as in the action scene (fig. 1-22), in which Rhotert (1952: 32) mistakenly called them 'ibex or antelope'. The horns on these figures are in the traditional style of frontal view and the extended tails are of normal length. Extension of the tails is typical of Barbary goats in a state of stress.

This animal has also been depicted in very simplistic styles that would vie with the logo techniques of modern graphic artists (fig. 13-209). Almagro Basch and Almagro Gorbea (1968: fig. 104) referred to it as an 'antilope'. Similar figures were published by Piatrowski (1964: fig.4) from the west Nile bank between Gerf Hussein and Kozemna, and by Winkler (1938 I: pl. XIV) from Wadi Gash.

A very realistic figure was reproduced from flint by the Neolithic pressure flaking technique (fig. 1-6d).

Barbary goats are among the few animals pictured on red, white-lined pottery of the Amration and early Gerzean Periods (figs 2-2, 13-210). Although stylized, the horns on these pottery figures are distinct.

The mane, which is also a definitive characteristic, was apparently an alluring ornament for Gerzean potters (fig. 13-211). Pottery marks were another way of expressing variation in artistry (Petrie and Quibell, 1896: pl. LI; Petrie, 1901b: pls. XIV, XX).

Ivory handles of flint knives from the late Gerzean were decorated with rows of animals that included Barbary goats (fig. 1-7,-8) .

On the Oxford Palette from Hierakonpolis (fig. 1-2b) there is a maneless Barbary goat with its head in the reversed position, a pose that became common in Dynastic art.

Two small palettes resembling Barbary goats were also discovered in prehistoric cemeteries. Both have the horns in profile. One has the mane indicated by a row of short incisions below the head (Baumgartel, 1960: pl. VI 6) and was said to have come from Naqada. The other has a long neck and a well-carved pendant mane (Quibell and Green, 1902: pl. LXIV).

The Dynastic period: Barbary goats were not so commonly portrayed in Dynastic art as were most other ungulates. They appear only in reliefs and paintings on the walls of tombs.

Although much of Dynastic art was strictly standardized, there are considerable variations in tail lengths and manes of Barbary goats; the manes often beginning in the form of a beard (fig. 13-212).

The horns, with a few exceptions, were depicted in frontal view. A single horn in profile appears on one animal in the Dynasty V hunt scene of Sahure (fig. 7-163). Unnatural thinness of the horns was common (fig. 7-38, reg. 5) and horns were often depicted unnaturally with bases united and vertical (figs 7-61, 13-212,-214).

Dwarfed Barbary goats appear in offering processions in the Tomb of Ankhm-Ahor, Dynasty VI, Saqqara (Badawy, 1978: fig. 40), and Mastaba of Gemni-kai (Kagemni), Dynasty VI, Saqqara (von

Bissing, 1911: pl. XXXI). In the latter (fig. 13-213) they are bearded like an ibex.

Barbary goats led by a hand on a horn (fig. 13-212) certainly indicates that they were semi-domesticated like other 'small cattle'. They were never shown with young, however, as were ibex, hartebeest, gazelles, and hyenas, which is surprising, because present-day records from zoos indicate they are one of the most abundant and prolific of captive animals (Crandall, 1964: 704).

Although this animal was not sacred, skeletons and a mummy were found at Giza (Gaillard and Daressy, 1905: pls. X, XI; Lortet and Gaillard, 1905: fig. 56).

There are apparently no renderings of Barbary goats after Dynasty XII until Dynasty XVIII. In a hunting scene in the Dynasty XVIII Tomb of Mentuherkh-hepeshef two short-maned Barbary goats are running side by side (fig. 13-214).

The Barbary goat was apparently important as a food animal since it was shown in hunting (fig. 1-29, 7-61) and offering scenes (figs 13-212,-213). Other than that it seems to have been of no further use to the Egyptians, except as Cloudsley-Thompson (1984: 278) remarked, until recently skins were made into tents of noble nomads.

Errors and discrepancies: Lortet and Gaillard (1905: 92) commented that during the late 1800s and early 1900s some naturalists thought the Ram of Mendes resembled the Barbary goat and also regarded it as the parent race of the early Egyptian sheep of the Naqadian Period and all North African sheep.

Budge (1922: 247) stated that the Barbary goat "became the emblem of the God Khnemu" (Khnum, Chnum), the ram-headed god of creation and fertility; originally the Nile god. Comparisons of configurations of the heads of the Barbary goat and ram god show great dissimilarities (figs 13-212,-214,-221, -222). Barbary goat horns curve backward, the facial profile is concave, and ears are erect. Ram god horns are horizontal (twisted) or ammon-shaped, the facial profile is convex, and ears are hanging (or not depicted).

The sources of these erroneous ideas are difficult to trace, but there are some 'rams' on ostraca from Deir el Medina that indicate confusion between true ram gods and Barbary goats (figs 13-215,-216). The latter figure was called a 'skilly drawing of a billy goat' by Brunner-Traut (1979: 59). These figures have manes on throats, chests, and forelegs, as well as hairy hind legs. The tails vary in length. The beards would be symbolic of a sacred animal.

Domestic Sheep ***Ovis aries*** Linnaeus, 1758

sr ser Wb. III, 414

F Mouton; G Das Hausschaf; A Ghanam beity

Nomenclature: Races of domestic sheep in Egypt have been identified as *O. aries longipes (O. longipes palaeoaegyptiacus), and O. a. platyura (O. platyura aegyptiaca).* [Other spellings: *palaeoaegyptius, -ticus; platyra, -tya, -tura.*]

The ancestral sheep was said to have been *O. orientalis* Gmelin 1774, but Gotch (1979: 226) wrote that the actual ancestry of the domestic sheep is uncertain.

Description: Unlike the wild sheep, which have very short tails, 3-4 cm in length, the domestic sheep have long tails reaching to or below the hocks, which in later times became very thick (fat). Although the ears were upright in the earliest domestic sheep (fig.13-192), they became pendant in the Pre- or Early Dynastic period. Horns were

13-215 'Adoration of the Buck', Deir el Medinah, Late Dynasty XX. Source: Brunner-Traut (1956: 79, pl. XXIX, no. 78).

13-216 Drawing of a 'ram' on an ostracon, Deir el Medinah, Dynasty XX. Source: Brunner-Traut (1979: pl. XXVII, 31).

13-217 (left) Corkscrew-horned (horizontal-horned) rams and ewes trampling grain seed in the Tomb of Urarna (Werirni) Dynasty V, Sheikh Said, Thebes. Source: Davies (1901b: pl. XVI).

13-218 (right) Sheep trampling grain seed in the Tomb of Ti, Dynasty VI, Saqqara. Source: Wild (1953 II: pl. LXXIX).

horizontal and broadly twisted in early forms and were replaced later by the ammon-shaped horns. Males had manes extending to the chest. Color varied from white to brown to piebald (figs 13-217,-218,-219).

Natural history: Domestic sheep, like their ancestors, are grazing animals and inhabit uplands. They are not as good climbers as goats and live at lower levels.

Prehistoric and Predynastic records: Domestication of sheep took place in S.W Asia in the 9th to 7th Millenium B.C. or a little later in Iraq and north of the Dead Sea, or about the same time as goats.

Hilzheimer's (1936:195) comments on origins of domestic sheep give the impression that the Asian wild sheep (*Ovis orientalis*) with a short tail, 3-4 cm in length, was the ancestor of domestic sheep.

Butzer (1964:420) said that *O. aries* was probably mainly descended from the urial (*O. orientalis*) although other species may have contributed to certain breeds of domestic sheep. Brewer *et al.* (1994:91), who quote from Clutton-Brock (1987:53), concluded that the short-tailed Asiatic mouflon was 'probably the ancestor of the Early Egyptian domestic forms'.

Domestic sheep were herded across Sinai and the northern coast of Egypt about 5,000 B.C., as was mentioned above under Domestic Goat. Wild sheep never existed in North Africa (Hilzheimer, 1936: 195).

There are, according to Epstein (1971 II: 56), 5th Millenium sheep remains in the Haua Fteah cave in Cyrenaica and in the Late 5th Millenium in the Faiyum A deposits. Lortet and Gailard (1905: 9) reported remains in Merimda Beni Salama (W. Delta), Maadi, Abydos, Armant (S.E. of Luxor), and Toukh between Naqada and Ballas.

The earliest illustration, on the reverse of the Libyan Palette (fig. 12-7), is the row of screw-horn (horizontal-horn) sheep with long, thin tails and the ears in the lateral and backward position as in wild sheep. These are males with manes. They were

13-219 Sheep trampling grain seed in the Tomb of Tehutihetep, Dynasty XII, El Bersheh. Source: Newberry (1892 I: pl. XXV).

13-220 Screw-horn sheep (Ovis longipes palaeoaegyptiacus) *and ammon-horned sheep* (O. platyura aegyptiaca) *being driven together in the Tomb of Khnemhotep, Dynasty XII, Beni Hasan. Source: Newberry (1893 I: pl. XXV)*

13-221 New Kingdom rock drawings of ammon-horned Ovis platyura aegyptiaca *rams at Kagug-Shibeika, east bank of the Nile, 4 km north of Gebel Silsila. Source: Červíček (1974: figs. 242, 243).*

called *Ovis longipes palaeoaegyptiacus* by Keimer (1938:219) and are comparable with the sheep on the Naqada II pottery from Abydos (fig. 13-192).

The Dynastic period: During the Early Dynasties herds of domestic (hair-) sheep (*O. longipes palaeoegyptiacus)* were often used in agriculture to trample seed into cultivated soil (figs 13-217,-218,-219). These sheep had lop-ears and varied in color from white to brown and piebald.

13-222 *(left) The Ram of Mendes (Ba-neb-Tet). Source: Budge (1934: 76).*

13-223 *(right) The Ancient Egyptian hair sheep with a false beard, Dynasty XII, Beni Hasan; probably a representation of the God Khnum. Source: Zeuner (1963: fig. 7: 12).*

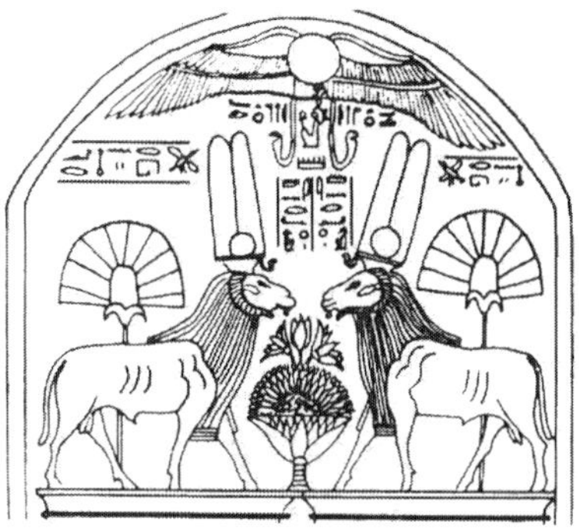

13-224 *Sacred rams on a New Kingdom stele from Deir el Medinah. Source: Nagel (1938: fig. 174).*

13-225 *The sacred Egyptian ammon-horned ram of the New Kingdom wearing a crown of horizontal horns, cobras, and other divine features. Source: Zeuner (1963: fig. 7: 17).*

They were also called long-haired sheep, because of the lack of wool.

In Dynasty XII another race called *O. platyura aegyptiaca* (*O. aries platyura*) was imported into Egypt. It was shown together with the horizontal horned sheep (fig. 13-220), which it later replaced. The horns in this race were ammon-shaped: very thick at the bases and curved backward, downward, and forward. It was represented in a New Kingdom rock drawing (fig. 13-221).

This race of sheep later developed a fat tail, which is common on the Egyptian sheep in modern time. It was also known as the wool sheep and its wool production was apparently the main reason for its replacing the hair sheep.

Incidentally, there is a picture in Budge (1934: 76) showing a statue of the Ram of Mendes with horizontal twisted horns and a fat tail (fig. 13-222).

The sacred ram: The ram-headed God of fertility, creation, and the Nile, Khnum (Khnemu) was originally worshipped on Elephantine Island (Mercatante, 1978: 85 f.). His origin dates to the Predynastic period and, until the XIIth Dynasty, he bore the horizontal horns of *O. longipes palaeoaegyptiacus* (fig. 13-223). Later, these horns were replaced by the ammon-shaped horns of *O. p. aegyptiaca* (fig.13-224). Both types of horns were also shown on some figures (fig. 13-225). The beard, which the Greeks and Romans assumed to identify the god as a goat and not a ram, can only be correctly interpreted as being 'intended to indicate superior status' (Zeuner, 1963: fig. 7:17), just as the false beards on the illustrations of pharaohs had a meaning of divinity. Further complications in the meanings of ram or 'he goat' were discussed by Naville (1894: 19 f.).

Subfamily *Bovinae*

Aurochs or **Wild Cow** ***Bos primigenius*** Bojanus, 1827
[and **Domestic Cow** ***Bos taurus*** Linnaeus 1758]

 *k3* ka Wb. V, 94

 *jw3* iwa Wb. I, 49

E Longhorn Cattle, Urus (*pl.* Uruses); F Aurochs, Boeuf; G Aurochs, Ur

Nomenclature: Bos (L) an ox; *primigenius* (L) original, primitive (Gotch, 1979: 228). Urus derives from the Greek *ouras*, wild ox. The North African race was named *B. p. opisthonomous* Duerst, 1900.

13-226 *A rock drawing of a longhorn aurochs from Karkur Tahl, Gebel Uweinat. Source: Rhotert (1952; pl. XIX).*

Description: These cattle had horns that were relatively long and lyre-shaped, light colored with dark tips. Heads were short and broad; ears normal, but with long hairs on the tips. Color patterns were similar to those of recent cattle. Some were uniformly black or dark red with a pale or whitish saddle mark and underside. Some were spotted or brindled (Epstein, 1971: 221 ff.). Similar types were pictured in hunting scenes in various tombs throughout the dynasties (figs Frontispiece, 1-18, -24, -30, -32, 7-29, -38 reg. 2).

Shoulder height of this breed was approximately 145 cm and body length 170.

Natural history: Cattle are primarily grazers, but early races were also browsers and inhabited forest and scrub growth as well as grassland. Ancient drawings and reliefs also pictured them in marshland (lower half of the Frontispiece). *B. primigenius* could live in fairly dry conditions, but the need for water every second day would have limited its range (Uerpmann, 1987: 72).

Distribution: This species probably expanded from the Levant into Africa during the Upper Pleistocene (Uerpmann *op. cit.*) where it spread up the Nile Valley and westward along the Mediterranean and into much of the Sahara, which at that time was pasture in what is now desert.

Prehistoric and Predynastic records: Domestication began in Neolithic encampments in Lower Egypt and in Badarian farming villages in Upper Egypt in the second half of the 5th millenium B.C. (Epstein, 1971 I: 213). Faiyum encampments date to 4440-4150 B.C. (Childe, 1958).

Archeological remains that can be identified as wild cattle are rare. A few positive records are from the Faiyum (Caton-Thompson and Gardner, 1934: 34), Kom Ombo (Churcher, 1972: 74, 88), and El Kab (Gautier, 1978).

An example of a typical longhorn aurochs is a rock drawing in Gebel Uweinat in S.W. Egypt (fig. 13-226). Long horns are clearly shown on one animal in the row of domestic cattle on the reverse of the damaged Predynastic Libyan Palette (fig. 12-7). Similarly, typical long and lyre-shaped horns have been depicted on aurochs on Predynastic red pottery (fig. 10-15).

Varying lengths and shapes of horns are well documented in drawings published by Červíček (1974: e.g. figs 10, 25, 346, 347, 352) from the southern Eastern Desert and many other localities.

Variations in horn length are discussed in Brewer *et al.* (1994: 82 ff.) in context with the varying habitat. Thus, breeding wild longhorns in well watered areas, such as the Nile valley, Delta, and possibly oases, may result in the appearance of considerably shorter horned domestic shorthorn cattle.

13-227 Shorthorn cattle on prehistoric white lined pottery from Naqada. Source Petrie (1920: fig. XVIII, 70).

Shorthorn cattle were brought into Egypt from Asia in the 3rd millenium B.C. and were doubtless admixed with the existing stock.

On prehistoric white-line pottery from Naqada (fig. 13- 227) shorthorn cattle are depicted .

The third breed, hornless, developed much later, in the Old Kingdom.

Cattle were not only important for their flesh, milk, and hides, but also in medicine. Milk and blood and various organs had specific medicinal uses. Fat, 'ox grease', was used, e.g. for burns (Darby *et al.*, 1977: 156-160).

Cattle were used, as were goats, sheep, donkeys, and pigs, to tread grain seeds into the soil. They also pulled plows.

The sacred bull Apis was kept from the Predynastic period at Memphis as the living incarnation of the craft god Ptah, who fashioned the world. After death he became associated with Osiris, god of the dead and resurrection.

The bull's movements in the courtyard of the temple were carefully watched and interpreted as predictions of the future.

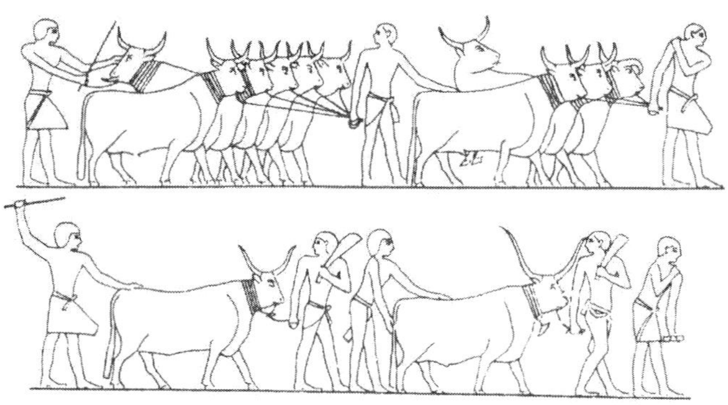

13-228 Shorthorn and longhorn cattle in the tomb of Ptahhetep, Dynasty V, Saqqara. Source Davies (1900 I: pl. XXI).

13-229 Piebald longhorn cows drawing a plow. Tomb of Sennedjem, Deir el Medina, Thebes, Dynasty XIX. Source: Westendorf (1968: 190).

At age 25 years the sacred bull was ceremonially killed, mummified and entombed in the Temple of Memphis. The calf that was chosen to replace the aged bull was identified by a scarab-like lump under its tongue, a colored patch on the tongue and forehead, white marks on its neck and rump that resembled hawk's wings, and a saddle patch on its back.

The cow goddess Hathor, one of the oldest known goddesses, was worshipped all over Egypt. She symbolized the great mother or cosmic goddess, goddess of joy and love. She supposedly nourished the living with her milk and supplied the dead in Tuat, the underworld, with food. Her main temple was at Dendera.

Further data on Apis and Hathor are in Lurker (1974), Darby *et al.* (1977 I) and Mercatante (1978).

The Dynastic period: According to Epstein (1971: 235) the wild aurochs probably became extinct in Egypt in the 14th century B.C. The exact date of extinction in the wild is difficult to establish, but the reason for extinction was probably not only hunting. The main reason 'may have been constant absorption of young and females into domestic herds and the loss of its genetic identity through the lack of reproductive isolation from domestic livestock' (Uerpmann, 1987: 72).

Shorthorn cattle gradually dominated the longhorn breed (fig. 13-228) as more were brought into Egypt by pharaohs following military operations and by Asiatic emigrants (Mason, 1984: 12).

An interesting comment by Bénédite (1918: 8) on the longhorn was: "This animal, which appears not to have survived in Egypt after the Old Kingdom, is thought to have been replaced for the purpose of big game hunting by domestic oxen restored to the wild state or rendered wild."

This could have been the source of 'wild cattle' hunted by Ramses III (Frontispiece). Other interpretations, however, are that the hunt in Dynasty XX took place not in Egypt, but during one of the pharaoh's campaigns in Asia (Boettger, 1958: 58).

Another interesting fact is that in a Dynasty XIX tomb longhorn cows are depicted drawing a plow (fig. 13-229).

Churcher (1982: table 1) listed *Bos taurus* remains from Roman sites in Dakhla Oasis.

Further discussion of Egyptian cattle is in another volume in this series by Brewer *et al.* (1994: 77-90).

Zebu ***Bos indicus*** Linnaeus, 1758

E Brahma; F Zébu; G Buckelrind

Nomenclature: The name zebu was introduced by Buffon who heard it at the Paris fair of 1752.

Epstein (1971 I: 197) wrote that the name was "probably derived from the Tibetan zeu, zeba = the hump of a zebu or camel, according to Webster's International Dictionary, 1919, p. 2368."

Description: Zebus are distinguished by the prominent cervico-thoracic hump, a long face, horns of short and normal lengths, a small brow ridge, drooping ears, a dewlap, and slender legs. The majority of skeletons are evident by bifid processes of the dorsal vertebrate from the seventh on.

Color varies from white to gray and black, and piebald.

Distribution: The zebu originated in India and spread into other Asian countries. It is now only a domestic form.

13-230 Piebald domestic zebu cattle in a Syrian tribute scene in the Dynasty XVIII Tomb of Kenamun, Thebes. Source: Davies (1963: pl.XV).

The Dynastic period: A few zebus were first introduced into Egypt during Dynasty XII from the Somali coast (Epstein, 1971 I: 555). They were pictured in some Middle Kingdom wall paintings such as the Dynasty XII Tomb of Chnemhotep at Beni Hasan (Newberry, 1893 II: pl. XXX).

Later imports came directly from Syria (fig. 13-118, -230) in the New Kingdom. There are also two Dynasty XVIII figurines: an ivory carving on a knife handle and a 4 cm high bronze weight (Zeuner, 1963: figs 8: 39a,b), and some drawings from destroyed wall figures at Thebes (Hornblower, 1927: pl. LV, 2; figs 1,2). Zebus became popular in the Late Dynasties and were interbred with Egyptian cattle.

Cape Buffalo ***Syncerus caffer*** (Sparrman, 1779)

E African Buffalo; F Buffle d'Afrique; G Kaffernbüffel

Distribution: Dorst and Dandelot (1969: 105,107) indicated that the present distribution was over much of Africa south of the Sahara and in a variety of habitats.

Prehistoric records: Late Pleistocene bovine remains from Kom Ombo sites that were referred to as *Syncerus caffer* were considered to be questionable by Churcher (1972: 88 f.). Fragmentary remains from various Early and Late Neolithic sites in Dakhla Oasis have been identified as *S. caffer* (Churcher, 1982: 110 f., table 1; 1983: 179; 1986a: 2). In a summary, Churcher *et al.* (1997: 17) mentioned "African buffalo (? *Pelorovis* or *Syncerus*)" and included it in "taxa so far tentatively identified in Mid-Pleistocene fauna from Dakhleh Oasis."

Extinct Giant Buffalo ***Homoiocerus vignardi (antiquus)***

E Long-horned African Buffalo

Distribution: Ancient distribution of this species probably included most of Africa.

Prehistoric records: Gautier (1981: 322 f.) recorded Middle Paleolithic remains from Bir Sahara and Bir Tarfawi in the southern Western Desert. Churcher (1972: 87 f., figs 28,29; 1974: table 1,377) tentatively identified an astraguli and two molars from the Late Pleistocene Plain of Kom Ombo as *H. vignardi*.

XIV Order *Odontocela*

Dolphins Family *Delphinidae*

Common Dolphin ***Delphinus delphis*** Linnaeus, 1758

 *ḥ3t-mḥjt* hat-mehit Wb. III, 21

F Dauphin commun; G Delphin (Gemeiner)

Description: This is one of the smaller dolphins. Total length is 1.8 to 2.6 meters. Color is dark brown or black above, belly is white, and there are grey, yellow, and white wavy stripes on the sides. The 'beak' is small and narrow.

Distribution: This species is common in the Mediterranean Sea and is almost worldwide.

The Dynastic period: The dolphin goddess, Hat-Mehit, was depicted as a woman with a fish-like head and venerated locally only in Lower Egypt since the Old Kingdom.

Budge (1904e: 142) referred to Hat-Mehit as "a local fish goddess who was widely worshipped in the Delta." Later, Budge (1934: 77) called her a 'dolphin goddess'. Figure 14–1 is more fish-like than the hieroglyph. This is understandable, because the Ancient Egyptians classified the dolphin as a fish.

Hat-Mehit was the badge of the XVIth or Dolphin Nome of Lower Egypt. The capital was Tell el Rub (Mendes) southeast of El Mansoura in the east central Delta. She became the consort of the ram god Ba-neb-Tet (Mendes in Greek, also Ba-neb-djet, Ba-neb-Tatau, Ba-neb-Tettu, Banedbdetet).

14–1 The Dolphin goddess Hat-Mehit with a fish (?) on her head. Source: Budge (1904: 142; 1934: 77).

Summary

Although it is not customary in monographs of this kind, the authors made the following numerical summarization of their results.

Out of the total of 117 mammals listed herein, zoological descriptions for 106 were included and 89 were **identified** from ancient Egyptian art and artifacts either on specific and subspecific, or only on generic levels.

About 52 taxa out of this list are still **extant** in Egypt and 43 are **extinct**. The present status of 10 taxa is not definitely known (aardwolf, Barbary goat, caracal, cheetah, dama, red fronted and slender-horned gazelles, leopard, porcupine, and scimitar oryx). The remaining 12 listed taxa were shown only in tribute scenes or named in literature.

Archeological remains of 60 taxa were listed, 10 of which were recorded as being known only as fossils.

The Egyptians **tamed** about 26 taxa, including a few carnivores: cheetah, genet, ichneumon, leopard, lion, striped hyena, and wild cat. Eight taxa were **semi-domesticated** (hand or stall fed), and many more shown in offering scenes in close contacts with men (either on leashes, led by their horns, or pushed along with hands on their bodies).

Various tamed animals were also brought from other countries as **tribute** (Anubis and hamadryas baboons, bear, cheetah, Asian elephant, Persian gazelle, giraffe, horse, Syrian ibex, green and patas monkeys, leopard, lion, saluki, Arabian and beisa oryx, and zebu).

A variety of **domesticates** were **imported** and continued to be bred in Egypt: Dogs, sheep and goats, short horned cattle and zebu, dromedary camel, horse, and donkey (?).

Among **indigenous domesticates** were cat, pig, donkey, and some breeds of cattle.

Some 20 mammals were **venerated** including those worshipped as gods or goddesses, kept in temples, used as emblematic animals, or being only animals of respect.

Many taxa were **mummified**, because of their association with dieties or their close relationship with man.

Chronology

Based on data tabled in Aldred (1965: 12), Hobbs (1980: ix), and Strouhal (1989: 315). Lower and upper limits of oscillations of dynastic datings are according Beckerat (LÄ, Band I, 270); data marked + are given astronomicaly. Author's additions and changes are in parentheses.

Period	Date B.C.	Culture	
Pleistocene Epoch			
Holocene Epoch			
Early Paleolithic	250,000—30,000		
Late Paleolithic	30,000 —5,000		
PREHISTORIC		**Lower Egypt**	**Upper Egypt**
Neolithic	c. 5000	Faiyum	Tasian
Aeneolithic	c. 4000	Merimda	Badarian
(Chalcolithic)		(Autochthonous Mt. Dwellers)	
		(Earliest Hunters)	
PREDYNASTIC			
Early			Amratian
	(3900 —3650)	(Naqada I)	(Early Nile Valley Dwellers)
Middle	c.3600		Early Gerzean
		(Naqada II)	
		(Early Nile Valley Dwellers)	
		(Eastern Invaders, E. Desert)	
Late	c. 3400	Late Gerzean	Late Gerzean
	(3200 —3100)	(Naqada III)	
HISTORIC (DYNASTIC)			
Archaic (Protodynastic, Early Dynastic) Period			
Dynasty I	3050/2960 —2860/2780		
Dynasty II	2860/2780 —2695/2640		
Old Kingdom			
Dynasty III	2695/2640 —2630/2575		
Dynasty IV	2630/2575 —2505/2460		
Dynasty V	2505/2460 —2345/2310		
Dynasty VI	2345/2310 —2190/2115		
1st Intermediate Period			
Dynasty VII -X	2190/2115 — +2134		
Middle Kingdom			
Dynasty XI	+2134 —1991		
Dynasty XII	1991 —1785		
2nd Intermediate Period			
Dynasty XIII-XVII	1785 — +1560/1551		
Hyksos Rule	1730 —1570		
New Kingdom			
Dynasty XVIII	+1560/1551 — +1320/1306		
Dynasty XIX	+1320/1306 —1200/1185		
Dynasty XX	1200/1185 —1085/1070		
Late Dynastic Period			
Dynasty XXI-XXXI	1085/1070 —332		
GRECO-ROMAN PERIOD			
Ptolemaic (Greek)	332 —30		
Roman Period	30 —395 A.D.		

Abbreviations

A.J.A.	American Journal of Archeology, Baltimore and Norwood.
A.M.N.H.	Annals and Magazine of Natural History, London.
A.S.A.E.	Annales du Service des Antiquités de l'Égypte, Le Caire.
B.I.E.	Bull. de l'Institut d'Égypt, Cairo.
B.I.F.A.O.	Bulletin de l'Institut français d'archéologie orientale du Caire, Cairo.
B.M.M.A.	Bulletin of the Metropolitan Museum of Art, N.Y.
G.M.	Göttinger Miszellen, Göttingen.
H.Ä.B.	Hildesheimer Ägyptologische Beiträge, Hidlesheim.
J.A.R.C.E .	Journal of the American Research Center in Egypt, Boston.
J.E.A.	The Journal of Egyptian Archeology, London.
J.N.E.S.	The Journal of Near Eastern Studies, Chicago.
J.S.S.E.A.	The Journal of the Society for the Study of Egyptian Antiquities, Toronto.
L.Ä.	Lexikon der Ägyptologie, Wiesbaden.
L.D.	Lepsius' Denkmäler. Re: Lepsius, 1897-1913.
M.Ä.S.	Mitteilungen aus der ägyptischen Sammlung. Staatliche Museen zu Berlin, Berlin.
M.D.A.I.K.	Mitteilungen des Deutschen archäologischen Institutes, Abtailung Kairo. Berlin, Wiesbaden.
M.I.F.A.O.	Mémoires de l'Institut français d'archéologie orientale du Caire, Cairo.
N.A.W.G.	Nachrichten von der Akademie der Wissenschaften, Göttingen.
N.Y.	New York
P.S.B.A.	Proceedings of the Society of Biblical Archeology, London.
Wb	Wörterbuch. Re: Erman and Grapow, 1926-31, 1950.
Z.Ä.S.	Zeitschrift für ägyptische Sprache und Altertumskunde. Leipzig, Berlin and Leipzig.
Z.S.	Zeitschrift für Säugetierkunde, Berlin.

Bibliography

Abu Al-Izz 1971 Abu Al-Izz, M.A., *Landforms of Egypt*. Cairo.

Aldred 1965 Aldred, C., *Egypt to the End of the Old Kingdom*. N.Y.

Allen 1939 Allen, G. M., 'A Checklist of African mammals'. *Bull. Mus. Comp. Zool.*, 83:1-763.

Allen 1940 —————, *Bats*. Cambridge, Mass.

Almagro Basch and Almagro Gorbea 1968. Almagro Basch, M. and Almagro Gorbea M., *Estudios de Arte Rupestre Nubio*. Madrid.

Almasy 1936 Almasy de, L. E., *Récentes Explorations dans le Désert Libyque (1932-1936)*. Le Caire.

Alpin 1581-1584 Alpin, P., *Histoire Naturelle de l'Égypte. Livre III*. (Transl. by R. de Fenoyl and S. Sauneron), 1979. Le Caire.

Anderson 1902 Anderson, J., *Zoology of Egypt: Mammalia*. (Revised and completed by W.E. de Winton). London.

Andrews 1987 Andrews, C.A.R., *Catalogue of Egyptian Antiquities in the British Museum VI, Jewelery I*. London.

Ansell 1971 Ansell, W.F.H., *Order Artiodactyla*. In: Meester J. and Setzer H.W., (eds.), *The Mammals of Africa: an Identification Manual*, Part 15. Washington D.C.

Antonius 1922 Antonius, O., *Grundzüge einer Stammesgeschichte der Haustiere*. Jena.

Asselberghs 1961 Asselberghs, H., *Chaos en Beheersing: Documenten uit aeneolithisch Egypte*. Leiden.

Aufrère 1985 Aufrère, S., 'Études de lexicologie et d'histoire naturelle VII. De nouvelles representations de zorilles de Libye *Poecilictis libyca* Lataste'. *B.I.F.A.O.*, 85:23-32.

Aynard 1972 Aynard, J.M., *Animals in Mesopotamia*. Chapt. 3 In: Houghton, Brodrick A, (ed.), *Animals in Archaeology*. N.Y.

Ayrton et al. 1904 Ayrton, E.R., Currelly, C.T. and Weigall A.E.P., *Abydos. Part III*. London.

Ayrton and Loat 1911 Ayrton, E.R. and Loat, W.L.S., *Pre-dynastic Cemetery at El Mahasna*. London.

Badawy 1978 Badawy, A., *The Tomb of Nyhetep-Ptah at Giza and the Tomb of 'Ankhm-'Ahor at Saqqara*. Berkeley.

Baikie 1932 Baikie, J., *Egyptian Antiquities in the Nile Valley*. London.

Baldwin 1975 Baldwin, J.A., 'Notes and speculations on the domestication of the cat in Egypt'. *Anthropos*, 70:428-448.

Bate 1937 Bate, D.M.A., *Palaeontology: The Fossil Fauna of the Wady el Mughara Caves. Part II* In: Garrod, D.A.E. and Bate, D.M.A., *The Stone Age of Mount Carmel*. Oxford.

Bate 1955 ————— *Vertebrate faunas of Quaternary deposits in Cyrenaica*, app.A, pp.274-291. In: McBurney, C.B.M. and Hey, R.W., *Prehistory and Pleistocene Geology in Cyrenaican Libya*. Cambridge.

Batrawi 1948 Batrawi, A., 'A small mummy from the pyramid of Dashur'. *A.S.A.E.*, 48:585-598.

Baumgartel 1955 Baumgartel, E.J., *The Cultures of Prehistoric Egypt I*. (Rev. ed.). London.

Baumgartel 1960 —————, *The Cultures of Prehistoric Egypt III*. London.

Beckerath 1975 Beckerath, J. von, 'Chronologie'. *L.Ä.* Band I:270, 967-971.

Belzoni 1821 Belzoni, G., *Narrative of the Operations and Recent Discoveries in Egypt and Nubia*. London.

Bénédite 1918 Bénédite, G., The Carnarvon ivory'. *J.E.A.*, 5:1-15, 225-241.

Benirschke and Kumomato 1980 Benirschke, K., and Kumomato, A., 'The chromosomes of the Nilgiri tahr'. *Intern. Zoo. Yr.Bk.*, 20:274-275.

Bissing 1898 Bissing, F. de, 'Les origines de l'Égypte'. *Anthropologie*, IX:408-417.

Bissing1905 Bissing, F.W. von, *Die Mastaba des Gem-ni-kai. Vol. I*. Berlin.

Bissing 1911 —————, *Die Mastaba des Gem-ni-kai. Vol. II*. Berlin.

Bissing 1914 ——————, *Denkmäler Ägyptischer Sculptur*. München.
Bissing 1956 ——————, 'La chambre des trois saisons du Sanctuaire Solaire du Roi Rathoures (V c Dynastie) à Abousir'. *A.S.A.E.*, 53:319-338.
Bissing and Kees 1923 Bissing, F.W. von and Kees, H., *Das Re-Heiligtum des Königs Ne-Woser-Re (Rathures). Band II*. Leipzig.
Blackman 1914 Blackman, A.M., *The Rock Tombs of Meir. Vol. I*. London.
Blackman 1915 ——————, *The Rock Tombs of Meir. Vol. II. The Tomb-Chapel of Senbi's Son Ukh-Hotp*. London.
Blackman1924 ——————, *The Rock Tombs of Meir. Vol. IV*. London.
Blackman and Apted 1953 Blackman, A.M. and Apted, M.R., *The Rock Tombs of Meir, Vol.V*. London.
Bodenheimer 1960 Bodenheimer, F.S., *Animal and Man in Bible Lands*. Leiden.
Boeser 1911 Boeser, P.A.A., *Beschreibung der Ägyptischen Sammlung. Leiden IV. Die Denkmäler des Neuen Reiches, I*. Den Haag.
Boessneck 1953 Boessneck, J., 'Die Haustiere in Altägypten'. *Veroff. Zool. Staatssamml. München*, 3:1-50.
Boessneck 1981a ——————, 'Gemeinsame Anliegen von Ägyptologie und Zoologie aus der Sicht des Zooarchäologen'. *Bayerische Akad. Wiss.*, 5:1-34.
Boessneck 1981b ——————, 'Der Schädel einer Streifenhyäne und Schädelknochen von Hunden aus einem Thebanischen Grab'. *Säugetierk. Mitt.*, 29 (3):67-74.
Boessneck 1988 ——————, *Die Tierwelt des Alten Ägypten*. München.
Boessneck and von den Driesch 1982 Boessneck, J. and von den Driesch, A., 'Studien an subfossilen Tierknochen aus Ägypten'. *M.Ä.S.*, 40.
Boessneck and von den Driesch 1983 ——————, 'Ein Katzenskelet der Römerzeit aus Quseir (Koser) am Roten Meer'. *Spixiana*, 6(2):211-218
Boessneck and von den Driesch 1987 ——————, 'Die Tierknochenfunde aus den Pavian- und Ibisgalerien von Tuna el-Gebel'. *H.Ä.B.*, 24:37-221.
Boessneck et al. 1984. Boessneck, J., von den Driesch, A., and Steger, U. 'Tierknochenfunden der Ausgrabungen des Deutschen Archäologischen Instituts Baghdad in Uruk-Warka, Iraq.' *Baghdader Mitteilungen*, 15:149-190.
Boessneck et al. 1992. Boessneck, J., von den Driesch, A. and Eissa, A. 'Eine Eselbestattung der 1. Dynastie in Abusir'. *M.D.A.I.K.*, 48:1-10.
Boettger1958 Boettger, C.R., *Die Haustiere Afrikas*. Jena.
Bökönyi 1974 Bökönyi, S., *History of Domestic Mammals in Central Europe*. Budapest.
Bonnet 1952 Bonnet, H., *Reallexikon der Ägyptischen Religions-geschichte*. Berlin.
Borchardt 1907 Borchardt, L., 'Drei hieroglyphenzeichen'. *Z.Ä.S.*, 44:75-79.
Borchardt 1913 ——————, *Das Grabdenkmal des Königs Sahure*. Leipzig.
Boreux 1908 Boreux, Ch., 'Les poteries décorées de l'Égypte prédynastique'. *Revue des Études ethnographiques et sociologiques*, Paris, I:1-20.
Bothmer 1949 Bothmer, B.V., 'Statuettes of *W3d t* as ichneumon coffins'. *J.N.E.S.*, VIII(2):120-123.
Bothmer and Keith 1974 Bothmer, B.V. and Keith, J.L. *Brief Guide to the Egyptian and Classical Art*. N.Y.
Bourriau 1988 Bourriau, J., *Pharoahs and Mortals. Egyptian Art in the Middle Kingdom*. Cambridge.
Boussac 1920. Boussac, P.H., 'L'animal sacré de Set-Typhon et ses divers modes d'interprétation'. *Review de l'Histoire des Religions*, Paris, 82:189-208.
Breasted 1906 Breasted, J.H., *Ancient Records of Egypt. Vol. II. The Eighteenth Dynasty*. Chicago.
Brentjes 1965 Brentjes, B., *Die Haustierwerdung im Orient*. Wittenberg Lutherstadt.
Brentjes 1966a ——————, 'Einige Bemerkungen zur Darstellung der Hyänen, Erdwölfe und Hyänenhunde in den Kulteren des Alten Orients'. Z.S., 31(44): 308-314.
Brentjes 1966b ——————, 'Kerbtierfresser, Fleder-, Nage-, und Hasentiere in der altorientalischen Kultur'. *Säugetierk. Mitt.*, 14:278-286.
Brentjes 1967a ——————, 'Zum Alter nordafrikanische Pferdedarstellung'. *Säugetierk. Mitt.*, 15:14.
Brentjes 1967b ——————, 'Füchse im Papyrusdschungel Altägyptens - ein beitrag zur Ökologie'. *Säugetierk. Mitt.*, 15:116-117.
Brentjes 1967c ——————, 'Schleichkatzen (Viverridae) und Marder (Mustelidae) in der Kultur des Alten Orients'. *Säugetierk. Mitt.*, 15:304-317.
Brentjes 1967d ——————, 'Altägyptische Hyänenhund Dartstellung'. *Säugetierk. Mitt.*, 15:172-173.
Brentjes 1971a ——————, 'Fledertiere in den Kulturen Altamerikas und des Alten Orients'. *Milu*, Leipzig, 3 (2):177-185.
Brentjes 1971b ——————, 'Der Hyänenhund als der Canidae Grundbestanteil des Seth-Tieres'. *Säugetierk. Mitt.*, XIX (4): 338-344.
Brewer and Friedman 1989 Brewer, D.J. and Friedman, R.F., *Fish and fishing in Ancient Egypt*. Warminster.
Brewer et al. 1994 Brewer, D.J., Redford, D.B., and Redford, S., *Domestic Plants and Animals. The Egyptian Origins*. Warminster.
Brink 1957 Brink, F.H. van den, *Die Säugetiere Europas*. Berlin.
Brooklyn Museum Guide see Needler 1984.
Brunner, E. 1969 Brunner, E., 'Animals of Ancient Egypt'. *Animals*, 11(12): 559-563.
Brunner-Traut 1956 Brunner-Traut, E., *Die Altägyptischen Scherbenbilder (Bildostraka) der Deutschen Museen und Sammlungen*. Wiesbaden.
Brunner-Traut 1965 ——————, 'Spitzmaus und Ichneumon als Tiere des Sonnengottes'. *N.A.W.G.*, 7:123-163.
Brunner-Traut 1968a ——————, *Ägyptische Mythen im Physiologus (zu Kapitel 26, 25 und 11)*. In: Helck, W.(ed.) *Festschrift für Siegfried Schott*. Wiesbaden.
Brunner-Traut 1968b ——————, *Altägyptische Tiergeschichte und Fabel*. Darmstadt.
Brunner-Traut 1979 ——————, *Egyptian Artist's Sketches*. Leiden.
Brunner-Traut 1981 ——————, *Die Alten Ägypter*. Stuttgart.
Brunner-Traut 1984 ——————, 'Spitzmaus'. *L.Ä.*, Vol. V, 8:1161-1162.
Brunton and Morant 1937 Brunton, G. and Morant, G.M. *Mostagedda and the Tasian Culture*. London.
Budge 1904a Budge, E.A.W., *The Gods of the Egyptians or Studies in Egyptian Mythology*. (2 Vols). London.
Budge 1904b ——————, *British Museum. A Guide to the First and Second Egyptian Rooms*. (2nd ed.). London.
Budge 1904c ——————, *British Museum. A Guide to the Third and Fourth Egyptian Rooms*. London.
Budge 1922 ——————, *British Museum. A Guide to the Fourth, Fifth and Sixth Egyptian Rooms and the Coptic Room*. London.
Budge 1926 ——————, *The Dwellers on the Nile*. London.
Budge 1930 ——————, *Amulets and Superstitions*. Oxford. (ed. 1978 by Dover Publ. Inc., N.Y.).
Budge 1934 ——————, *From Fetish to God in Ancient Egypt*. Oxford.

Budge 1967 ————, *The Book of the Dead - the Papyrus of Ani*. N.Y.
Budge 1978 see Budge 1930.
Burchardt 1914 Burchardt, M. von, 'Die Einnahme von Satuna'. *Z.Ä.S.*, 51: 106-109.
Butzer 1959 Butzer, K.W., *Studien zum Vor und Früh-geschichtlichen Landschaftswande der Sahara III*. Wiesbaden.
Butzer 1964 ————, *Environment and Archeology*. Chicago.
Butzer 1976 ————, *Early Hydraulic Civilization in Egypt*. Chicago.
Butzer 1977 ————, 'Hirsch'. *L.Ä.* II:1220.
Butzer and Hansen 1968 Butzer, K.W. and Hansen, C.L., *Desert and River in Nubia*. Madison.
Caminos 1945 Caminos, R.A., *Late-Egyptian Miscellanies*. London.
Capart 1905 Capart, J., *Primitive Art in Egypt*. London.
Capart 1907 ————, *Une Rue de Tombeaux à Saqqarah*. (2 Vols). Bruxelles.
Capart 1928 ————, *Lectures on Egyptian Art*. Chapel Hill.
Capart 1947 ————, *L'Art Égyptien, Tome IV. Les Arts Mineurs*. Brussells.
Carrington 1972 Carrington, R., *Animals in Egypt*. Chapt. 4 In: Houghton, Brodrick A. (ed.), *Animals in Archeology*, pp.69-89., N.Y.
Carter 1923, 1927, 1933 Carter, H., *The Tomb of Tut-Ankh-Amen*. (3 Vols). London.
Caton-Thompson and Gardner 1934 Caton-Thompson, G. and Gardner, E.G., *The Desert Fayum*. London.
Caulfield 1902 Caulfield, A.St.G.. *The Temple of the Kings at Abydos*. London.
Caulliaud 1831 Caulliaud, F., *Recherches sur les Arts et Métiers, les usages de le vie civile et domestique des anciens peuples de l'Égypte*. Paris.
Červíček 1974 Červíček, P., *Felsbilder des Nord-Etbai, Oberägyptens und Unternubiens*. Wiesbaden.
Červíček 1976 ————, *Catalogue of the Rock Art of the Frobenius Institute*. (Studien zur Kulturkunde, 41). Wiesbaden.
Červíček 1986 ————, 'Rock pictures of Upper Egypt and Nubia'. *Annali Instituto Univ. Orientale, Napoli*, Suppl. 46:1-115.
Červíček 1987 ————, *Zur religiössen Bedeutung der Giraffengazelle*. In: Scholz, P.O. and Stempel R. (eds.) *Nubia et Oriens Christianus*, pp.271-280, Köln.
Champollion 1845 Champollion, J.F. le Jeune , *Monuments de L'Égypte et de la Nubie. Vol.IV*. Paris.
Childe 1958 Childe, V.G. *New Light on the Most Ancient East*. London.
Churcher 1972 Churcher, C.S., 'Late Pleistocene vertebrates from archeological sites in the plain of Kom Ombo, Upper Egypt'. *Life Sciences Contributions Royal Ontario Museum*, 82:1-172.
Churcher 1974 ————, 'Relationships of the Late Pleistocene vertebrate fauna from Kom Ombo, Upper Egypt'. *Annals of the Geological Survey of Egypt*, 4:363-384.
Churcher 1980 ————, 'Dakhleh Oasis Project - Preliminary observations on the geology and vertebrate palaeontology of northwestern Dakhleh Oasis: A report on the 1979 fieldwork'. *J.S.S.E.A.*, 10(4):378-395.
Churcher 1981 ————, 'Dakhleh Oasis Project - Geology and Paleontology: interim report on the 1980 field season'. *J.S.S.E.A.*, 11(4):194-212.
Churcher 1982 ————, 'Dakhleh Oasis Project - Geology and Paleontology: interim report on the 1981 field season'. *J.S.S.E.A.*, 12(3):103-114.
Churcher 1983 ————, 'Dakhleh Oasis Project - Paleontology: interim report on the 1982 field season'. *J.S.S.E.A.*, 13(3):178-187.
Churcher 1984 ————, *The Ivory Knife-handle from Abu Zaidan*. In: Needler, W., *Predynastic and Archaic Egypt in the Brooklyn Museum*. N.Y.
Churcher 1986a ————, Oasis Project - Palaeontology: interim report on the 1985 field season'. *J.S.S.E.A.*, 16(1):1-4.
Churcher 1986b ————, *Equid Remains from Neolithic Horizons at Dakleh Oasis, Western Desert of Egypt*. In: Meadow, R.H. and Uerpmann, H.P., *Equids in the Ancient World*. Wiesbaden.
Churcher 1987 ————, (released 1991). 'Dakhleh Oasis Project, Palaeontology: Interim report on the 1988 field season'. *J.S.S.E.A.*, 17(4):177-181.
Churcher 1991 ————, 'The Egyptian fruit bat *Rousettus aegyptiacus* in Dakhleh Oasis, Western Desert of Egypt'. *Mammalia*, 55:139-143.
Churcher 1993a ————, *Dogs from Ein Tirghi Cemetery, Balat, Dakhleh Oasis, Western Desert of Egypt*. In: Clason, A., Payne, S. and Uerpmann, H.P., (eds.). *Skeletons in her Cupboard: Festschrift for Juliet Clutton-Brock*, pp. 39-59. Oxbow Monograph 34, Oxford.
Churcher 1993b ————, *Equus grevyi. Mammalian Species, No.453*, pp. 1-9. American Society of Mammalogists
Churcher et al. 1997 Churcher, C.S., Kleindienst, M.R., Wiseman, M.F., and McDonald, M.M.A., 'The Quaternary faunas of Dakhleh Oasis, Western Desert of Egypt. Abstract'. The Second Dakhleh Oasis Project Research Seminar, June 16-20, 1997, Royal Ontario Museum and University of Toronto, pp.1-3.
Clark 1971 Clark, J.D., 'A re-examination of the evidence for agricultural origins in the Nile Valley'. *Proc. Preh. Soc.*, XXXVII, Part II:34-79.
Cloudsley-Thompson 1977 Cloudsley-Thompson, J., *Man and Biology of Arid Zones*. Baltimore.
Cloudsley-Thompson 1984 ————, *Desert Life*. [Key Environments Series, Sahara Desert]. Oxford.
Clutton-Brock 1974 Clutton-Brock, J., 'The Buhenhorse'. *Journ. of Archeol. Science*, I:89-100.
Clutton-Brock 1981 ————, *Domesticated Animals from Early Times*. London.
Cobern 1913 Cobern, C.M., 'The sacred ibis cemetery at Abydos'. *Nat. Geogr. Mag.*, 24:1042-1056.
Colbert 1973 Colbert, E.H., *Wandering Lands and Animals*. N.Y.
Cooney 1965 Cooney, J.D., 'Pharaoh's rat'. *Bull. Cleveland Museum of Art*, LII(8):100-105.
Corbet 1978 Corbet, G.B., *The Mammals of the Palaearctic Region: a taxonomic review*. London.
Corbet and Hill 1991 Corbet, G.B. and Hill, J.E., *A World List of Mammalian Species*. London.
Crandall 1964 Crandall, L.S., *Wild Animals in Captivity*. Chicago.
Currelly 1904 see Ayrton et al. 1904.
Dalimier 1954 Dalimier, P., 'Quelques observations au sujet du Mouflon à Manchettes'. *Mammalia*, 18(3):331-333.
Darby et al. 1977 Darby, W.J., Ghalioungui, P. and Grivetti, L., *Food: the Gift of Osiris*. (2 Vols). London.
Daressy 1897 Daressy, G., 'Notice explicative des ruines de Médinet-Habou'. Le Caire.
Daressy 1898 ————, 'Le Mastaba de Mera'. *Mémoires l'Institut Égyptien*, Le Caire, III:521-574.
Daressy 1903 ————, 'Un modèle du signe M'. *A.S.A.E.*, 4:122-123.
Davies 1900 Davies, N. de Garis, *The Mastaba of Ptahhetep and Akhethetep at Saqqareh. Part I.- The Chapel of Ptahhetep and the Hieroglyphs*. London.
Davies 1901a ————,*The Mastaba of Ptahhetep and Akhethetep at Saqqareh. Part II.-The Mastaba. The Sculptures of Akhethetep*. London.

Davies 1901b ——————, *The Rock Tombs of Sheikh Säid*. London.
Davies 1902a ——————, *The Rock Tombs of Deir el Gebrawi. Part I.- The Tomb of Aba and Smaller Tombs of the southern Group*. London.
Davies 1902b ——————, *The Rock Tombs of Deir el Gebrawi. Part II.- Tomb of Zaw and Tombs of the Northern Group*. London.
Davies 1905 ——————, *The Rock Tombs of El Amarna. Part II.- The Tomb of Panehesy and Meryra II. Part III.- The Tombs of Huya and Ahmes*. London.
Davies 1913 ——————, *Five Theban Tombs. Being those of Mentuherkhepeshef, User, Daga, Nehemawäy and Teti*. London.
Davies 1922 ——————, *The Tomb of Puyemre at Thebes*. N.Y.
Davies 1927 ——————, *Two Ramesside Tombs at Thebes*. Robb de Peyster Tytus Memorial Series, vol.5. N.Y.
Davies 1930 ——————, *The Tomb of Ken-Amun at Thebes*, Vol.I. N.Y.
Davies 1933 ——————, 'The work of the Graphic Branch of the expedition'. In: The Egyptian Expedition 1931-1932. Section II, *B.M.M.A.*, pp.23-29.
Davies 1935 ——————, *Paintings from the Tomb of Rekh-Mi-Re at Thebes*. Vol. X. N.Y
Davies 1941 ——————, *The Tomb of the Vizier Ramose*. London.
Davies 1943 ——————, *The Tomb of Rekh-mi-Re at Thebes*. (2 Vols)., N.Y.
Davies 1942 Davies, N.M., 'Nubians in the Tomb of Amunedjeh'. *J.E.A.*, 28:50-52.
Davies 1949 ————, 'Birds and bats at Beni Hassan'. *J.E.A.*, 35:13-20.
Davies 1963. ————, *Scenes from some Theban Tombs*. Oxford.
Davies and Davies 1933a Davies, N. de Garis and Davies, N., *The Tomb of Neferhotep at Thebes*. (2 Vols). N.Y.
Davies and Davies 1933b ——————————, *The Tombs of Menkheperrasonb, Amenose, and Another*. London.
Davies and Davies 1940 ——————————, 'The Tomb of Amenmose (Nr. 89) at Thebes'. *J.E.A.*, 26:131-136.
Davies and Davies 1941 ——————————, 'Syrians in the tomb of Amunedjeh'. *J.E.A.*, 27:96-98.
Davies and Faulkner 1947 Davies, N. de Garis and Faulkner, R.O., 'A Syrian trading venture to Egypt'. *J.E.A.*, 33:40-46.
Davies and Gardiner 1915 Davies, N. de Garis and Gardiner, A.H., *The Tomb of Amenemhet (Nr. 82)*. London.
Davies and Gardiner 1920 Davies, N.M. and Gardiner, A.H., *The Tomb of Antefoker, Vizier of Sestros I, and of his wife, Senet*. London.
Davies and Gardiner 1926 ——————————, *The Tomb of Huy, Viceroy of Nubia in the Reign of Tutankhamun*. London.
Davies and Gardiner 1936 ——————————, *Ancient Egyptian Paintings*. Vol. I, II. Chicago.
Davies and Gardiner 1948 Davies, N. de Garis and Gardiner, A.H., *Seven Private Tombs at Khurnah*. London.
Davies and Gardiner 1962 Davies N.M. and Gardiner, A.H., *Tutankhamun's Painted Box*. Oxford.
Davis 1907 Davis, T.M., *The Tomb of Iouiya and Touiyou*. London.
Davis 1908 ————, *The Tomb of Siptah: The Monkey Tomb and the Gold Tomb*. London.
Dawson 1925 Dawson, W.R., 'Bats as Materia Medica'. *A.M.N.H.*, ser.9, 16:221-227.
Dawson 1927 ————, 'The earliest records of the giraffe'. *A.M.N.H.*, ser 9, 19:478-485.
Dawson 1928 ————, 'The pig in ancient Egypt. A commentary on two passages from Herodotus'. *Journ. Royal Asiatic Soc. of Great Britain and Ireland*, pp.598-608.
Dawson 1934 ————, 'Deer in Ancient Egypt'. *J. Linn. Soc.*, London, 39:137-145.
Dembeck 1965 Dembeck, H., *Animals and Men*. (transl. R. Winston and C. Winson). N.Y.
Denon 1803 Denon, V., *Travels in Upper and Lower Egypt*. Vol.II. London.
Desroches-Noblecourt 1963 Desroches-Noblecourt, C., *Leben und Tod eines Pharaoh Tut-ench-Amun*. Berlin.
Dorst 1969 Dorst, J., *A Field Guide to the Larger Mammals of Africa*. Boston.
Dorst and Dandelot, 1969 see Dorst 1969.
Driesch and Boessneck 1985 Driesch, A. von den and Boessneck, J., *Die Tierknochenfunde aus der neolithischen Siedlung von Merimde-Benisalame am westlichen Nildelta*. München.
Droste zu Hülshoff 1980 Droste zu Hülshoff, V. von, 'Der Igel im alten Ägypten'. *H.Ä.B.*, 11:1-302.
Drummond and Janssen 1990 Drummond, D.C., Janssen, R.M., Janssen, J.J., 'An ancient Egyptian rat trap'. *M.D.A.I.K.*, 46:91-98.
Dücher 1972 Dücher, G. von, *Schleichkatzen und Erdwölfe*. In: Grzimek, B. *Tierleben*, Band XII, pp.144-185, Zürich.
Duell 1938 Duell, P., *The Mastaba of Mereruka. Sakkarah Expedition Part I, II*. Chicago.
Dümichen 1869 Dümichen, J., *Historische Inschriften Altägyptischen Denkmäler*. (2nd ed). Leipzig.
Dümichen 1879 ————, *Geschichte des alten Aegyptens*. Berlin.
Dümichen and Hartman 1869 Dümichen J. and Hartman, R., *Resultate der Archäologisch-Photographishen Expedition Part I*. Berlin.
Dunbar 1941 Dunbar, J.H., *The Rock Pictures of Lower Nubia*. Cairo.
Dunham and Simpson 1974 Dunham, D. and Simpson, W.K., *The Mastaba of Queen Mersyankh III. Giza Mastabas I*. Boston.
Edel 1961 Edel, E., 'Zu den inschriften auf den Jahreszeiten- reliefs der "Weltkammer" aus dem Sonnenheligtum des Niuserre'. *N.A.W.G., Phil. Hist. Kl.*, 8:209-255.
Edel and Wenig 1974 Edel, E. and Wenig, S., *Die Jahreszeitenreliefs aus dem Sonnenheiligtum des Königs Ne-User-Re*. Berlin.
Edgerton 1936 Edgerton, W. F., 'Two notes on the flying gallop'. *J. Amer. Oriental Soc.*, 56(2):178-188.
Edwards 1955 Edwards, I.E.S., 'An Egyptian Bestiary of 5000 Years Ago', *Illustrated London News* No.6087, Vol.227 (Dec., 17, 1955), p.1061.
Edwards 1976a ————, *Tutankhamun: His Tomb and its Treasures*. N.Y.
Edwards 1976b ————, *The Treasures of Tutankhamun*. N.Y.
Edwards 1979 ————, Zoomorphic anomalies in Tutankhamun's treasures. *A.J.A.*, 83:205-206.
Eggebrecht 1984 Eggebrecht, A., (ed.). *Das alte Ägypten*. München.
Eggebrecht 1987 Eggebrecht, E. and Eggebrecht A., (eds.) *Ägyptens Aufsteig zur Weltmacht*. Mainz.
Eliez 1967 Eliez, A., *Le Lion et l'Homme*. Paris.
Ellerman and Morrison-Scott 1951 Ellerman, J.R. and Morrison-Scott, T.C.S., *Checklist of Palearctic and Indian Mammals, 1758 to 1946*. London.
Emery 1938 Emery, W.B., *The Tomb of Hemaka*. Cairo.
Emery 1939 ————, *Excavations at Saqqara 1937-1938, Hor-Aha*. Cairo.
Emery 1961 ————, *Archaic Egypt*. Middlesex.
Emery 1965 ————, *Egypt in Nubia*. London.
Emery 1971 ————, 'Preliminary report on the excavations at north Saqqara, 1969-70'. *J.E.A.*, 57:3-13.
Engelbach 1923 Engelbach, R., *Harageh*. London.

Epron et al. 1939 Epron, L. Daumas, F. and Goyon, G., *Le tombeau de Ti*. Vol. I. Le Caire.
Epstein 1971 Epstein, H., *The Origin of the Domestic Animals of Africa*. (2 Vols). N.Y.
Erman 1887 Erman, A., *Aegypten und Aegyptischen Leben im Altertum*. Tübingen.
Erman 1894 ————, *Life in Ancient Egypt*. (1971 edition, N.Y).
Erman 1971 see Erman 1894
Erman and Grapow 1926-31 Erman, A. and Grapow, H., *Wörterbuch der Aegyptischen Sprache*. (5 Vols). Leipzig.
Erman and Grapow 1950 ————, *Deutsch-Aegyptisches Wörterverzeichnis*. Vol.VI. Leipzig.
Esch 1943 Esch, H., von der. *Weenak - die Karawane ruft*. Leipzig.
Fairman 1943 Fairman, H.W., 'Notes on the alphabetic signs employed in the hieroglyphic inscriptions of the Temple of Edfu'. *A.S.A.E.*, 43:193-310.
Fakhry 1942 Fakhry, A., *The Egyptian Deserts. Bahria Oasis*. Cairo.
Fakhry 1952 ————, *The Inscriptions of the Amethyst Quarries at Wadi el Hudi*. Cairo.
Fakhry 1961 ————, *The Monuments of Snefru at Dashur. Vol. II, The Valley Temple*. Cairo.
Fakhry 1973 ————, *The Oases of Egypt. Vol. I. Siwa Oasis*. Cairo.
Faulkner 1962 Faulkner, R.O., *A Concise Dictionary of Middle Egyptian*. Oxford.
Fechheimer 1922 Fechheimer, H., *Kleinplastik der Ägypter*. Berlin.
Ferguson 1981 Ferguson, W.W., 'The systematic position of *Canis aureus lupaster* (Carnivora: Canidae) and the occurrence of *Canis lupus* in North Africa, Egypt and Sinai'. *Mammalia*, 45(4):459-465.
Fiorenza 1972 Fiorenza, P., *Encyclopédie des Animaux de Grande Chasse en Afrique*. Paris.
Firth 1927a Firth, C.M., 'Excavations of the Service des Antiquities at Saqqara'. *A.S.A.E.*, 27:105-111.
Firth 1927b ————, *The Archeological Survey of Nubia. Report for 1910-1911*. Cairo.
Firth and Gunn 1926 Firth, C.M. and Gunn, B., *Teti Pyramid Cemeteries. Excavations at Saqqara*. Le Caire.
Fischer 1958 Fischer, H.G., 'A fragment of a Late Predynastic relief from the Eastern Delta'. *Artibus Asiae, Ascona*, 21:64-88.
Fischer 1961 ————, 'A supplement to Janssen's list of dog names'. *J.E.A.*, 47:152-153.
Fischer 1975 ————, 'Two tantalizing biographical fragments of historical interest'. *J.E.A.*, 61:33-37.
Fischer 1980 ————, 'Hunde'. *L.Ä.* Band III:77-81.
Flower 1932 Flower, S.S., 'Notes on the recent mammals of Egypt, with a list of the species recorded from that kingdom'. *Proc. Zool. Soc., London*, 102:369-450.
Floyer 1887 Floyer, E.A., 'Notes on a sketch map of two routes in the Eastern Desert of Egypt'. *Proc. Royal Geogr. Soc.*, 9:659-681.
Fox 1951 Fox, P., *Tutankhamun's Treasure*. Oxford.
Frobenius 1933 Frobenius, L., *Kulturgeschichte Afrikas*. Zürich.
Gabler 1985 Gabler, K.O., Osteologische Unterscheidungsmerkmale am postkranialen Skelett zwischen Mähnenspringer (*Ammotragus lervia*), Hausschaf (*Ovis aries*) und Hausziege (*Capra hircus*). Inaugural Dissertation, Ludwig-Maxmilians-Universität, München.
Gaillard 1912 Gaillard, C., 'Les Tatonnements des Égyptiens de l'Ancien Empire à la recherche des animaux à domestiquer'. *La Revue d'Ethnographie et de Sociologie*, No.11-12:1-20.
Gaillard 1934 ————, 'Contribution à l'étude de la faune préhistorique de l'Égypte'. *Arch. Mus. Hist. nat. Lyon*, 14.
Gaillard and Daressy 1905 Gaillard, C. and Daressy, G., *La faune momifiée de l'antique Égypte*. Le Caire.
Gaisler et al. 1972 Gaisler, J. Madkour, G. and Pelikán, J., 'On the bats (*Chiroptera*) of Egypt'. *Acta Sc. Nat. Brno*, 6(8):1-40.
Gardiner 1938 Gardiner, A.H., 'The mansion of life and the master of the King's largess'. *J.E.A.*, 24:83-91.
Garnot 1937 Garnot, S.F.G., 'Le lion dans l'art Égyptien'. *B.I.F.A.O.*, 37:75-91.
Garstang 1901 Garstang, J., *El Arabah*. London.
Gautier 1976a Gautier, A., *Freshwater mollusks and mammals from Upper Paleolithic sites near Idfu and Isna*. In: Wendorf, E. and Schild, R., (eds.), *Prehistory of the Nile Valley*, pp.349-363. N.Y.
Gautier 1976b ————, *Animal Remains from Archeological Sites of Terminal Paleolithic to Old Kingdom Age of the Faiyum*. In: Wendorf, E. and Schild, R., (eds.), *Prehistory of the Nile Valley*, pp.369-382, N.Y.
Gautier 1978 ————, *La faune de vertébrés des sites épipaléolithiques d'Elkab*. In: Vermeersch, P.M., *Elkab II, L'Elkabien, Épipaléolithique de la Valeé du Nil Égyptien*, pp.103-114, Bruxelles and Leuven.
Gautier 1980 ————, *Contributions to the archaeozoology of Egypt*. In: Wendorf, F. and Schild, R., *Prehistory of the Eastern Sahara*, pp.317-344, N.Y.
Gautier 1984a ————, *Archeozoology of the Bir Kiseiba region, eastern Sahara*. In: Wendorf, F., Schild, R., and Close, A., (eds.), *Cattle Keepers of the eastern Sahara: the Neolithic of Bir Kiseiba*, pp.49-72, New Delhi.
Gautier 1984b ————, in Krzyzaniak and Kobusiewicz 1984, pp. 43-56.
Gayet 1894 Gayet, A., 'Le Temple de Louxor'. *Mémoires de la Mission Archéologique Français au Caire*, Vol. I, Paris.
Gerster 1964 Gerster, G., *Nubien Goldland am Nil*. Zurich and Stuttgart.
Ghalioungui and Dawakhly 1965 Ghalioungui, P. and El Dawakhly, Z., *Health and Healing in Ancient Egypt*. A Pictorial Essay. Cairo.
Giddy 1987 Giddy, L.L., *Egyptian Oases*. Warminster.
Gilbert et al. 1976 Gilbert, K.S. Holt, J.K. and Hudson, S., (eds.) *Treasures of Tutankhamun*. N.Y.
Glanville 1926a Glanville, S.R.K., 'A note on Herodotus II'. *J.E.A.*, 12:75-76.
Glanville 1926b ————, 'Egyptian theriomorphic vessels in the British Museum'. *J.E.A.*, 12:52-69.
Goodman 1989 Goodman, S.M., 'The occurrence of *Crocidua floweri* in Wadi el Natroun, Egypt'. *Mammalia*, 53(1):134-135.
Goodman and Helmy 1986 Goodman, S.M. and Helmy, I., 'The sand cat *Felis margarita* Loche,1858 in Egypt'. *Mammalia*, 50:120-123.
Goodman et al. 1992 Goodman, S.M. Hobbs, J.J. and Brewer, D.J., 'Nimir Cave: Morphology and fauna of a cave in the Egyptian Eastern Desert'. *Palaeoecology of Africa*, 23:73-90.
Gotch 1979 Gotch, A.F., *Mammals - Their Latin Names Explained. A Guide to Animal Classification*. Dorset.
Goyon 1957 Goyon, G., *Nouvelles Inscriptions Rupestres du Wadi Hammamat*. Paris.
Gray and Simpson 1980 Gray, G.G. and Simpson, C.D., '*Ammotragus lervia*'. *Mamm. Species*, 144:1-7.
Griffith 1892 Griffith, F.L., In: Petrie, W.M.F. *Medum*. London.
Griffith 1896 ————, *Beni Hassan* Part III. London.
Griffith 1898 ————, *A Collection of Hieroglyphs*. London.
Griffith 1900 ————, (ed.) *Beni Hassan. Part IV. Zoological and Other Details*. London.
Griffith and Newberry 1894 Griffith, F.L. and Newberry, P.E., *El Bersheh Part II*. London.
Groenewegen-Frankfort 1951 Groenewegen-Frankfort, H.A., *Arrest and movement, An Essay on Space and Time in the Representational Art of the Ancient Near East*. London.

Guilmant 1907 Guilmant, M.F., 'Le Tombeau de Ramses IX'. *M.I.F.A.O.*, vol.XV.
Hall 1913 Hall, H. R., *Catalogue of Egyptian Scarabs, etc., in the British Museum. Vol. I. Royal Scarabs.* London.
Haltenorth 1959 Haltenorth, T., 'Beitrag zur Kenntnis des Mesopotamischen Damhirsches- *Cervus (Dama) mesopotamicus* Brooke, 1875 - und zur Stammes- und Verbreitungsgeschichte der Damhirsche allgemein'. *Säugetierk. Mitt.*, VII:1-89.
Haltenorth 1961a ————, 'Lebensraum, Lebensweise und Vorkommnen des Mesopototamischen Damhirsches, *Cervus mesopotamicus* Brooke, 1875'. *Säugetierk. Mitt.* IX(9):15-39.
Haltenorth 1961b ————, 'Fruchtbare Rückkrezung eines Weiblichen Mähnenschaf-Hausziegen-Bastards mit einem Steienem Steinbock'. *Säugetierk. Mitt.* IX(3):105-109.
Haltenorth 1963 ————, *Klassifikation der Säugetiere: Artiodactyla* I (18):1-167. In: Helmcke, J.G. et al. (eds.), *Handbuch der Zoologie*, Vol.8., No.32, Berlin.
Haltenorth and Diller 1980 Haltenorth, T. and Diller, H., *Field Guide to the Mammals of Africa Including Madagascar.* London.
Hamann 1944 Hamann, R., *Ägyptische Kunst. Wesen und Geschichte.* Berlin.
Hanák 1977 Hanák, V., *A Color Guide to Familiar Mammals.* London.
Happold 1967 Happold, D.C.D., 'Guide to the natural History of Khartoum Province. Part III. Mammals'. *Sudan Notes and Records*, 48:1-22.
Harper 1940 Harper, F., 'The nomenclature and type localities of certain Old World mammals'. *Journ. Mammal.* 21(2):191-203; (3):322-332.
Harper 1945 ————, *Extinct and Vanishing Mammals of the Old World.* Spec. Publ. Amer. Comm. Inst. Wild Life Prot. No.12.
Harpur 1987 Harpur, Y., *Decoration in Egyptian Tombs of the Old Kingdom. Studies in orientation and scene content.* London.
Harrison 1967 Harrison, D.L., 'Observations on a wild goat, *Capra aegagrus* (*Artiodactyla*: *Bovidae*) from Oman, E. Arabia'. *J. Zool., London*, 151:27-30.
Harrison 1964, 1968, 1972. Harrison, D.L., *The Mammals of Arabia.* (3 Vols). London.
Hartmann 1864 Hartmann, R., 'Versuch einer systematischen Aufzählung der von den alten Aegyptern bildlich dargestellen Thiere'. *Z.Ä.S.*, 2(1):7-12, (2):19-28.
Hartmann 1869 ————, *Ueber die in Dümichen's Publication zur Mittheilung gebrachten Thierdarstellung.* In: Dümichen, J. *Historische Inschriften Altägyptischen Denkmäler*, pp.28-30, Leipzig.
Hassan 1938 Hassan, S., 'Excavations at Saqqara, 1937-1938'. *A.S.A.E.*, 38:503-521.
Hassan 1944 ————, *Excavations at Giza. Vol.V.* Cairo.
Hassan 1955 ————, 'The causeway of *Wnis* at Sakkara'. *Z.Ä.S.*, 80: 136-139.
Hayes 1951 Hayes, W.C., 'Inscriptions from the Palace of Amenhotep III'. *J.N.E.S.*, X(3):156-183.
Hayes 1953 ————, *The Scepter of Egypt Part I. From the Earliest Times to the end of the Middle Kingdom.* N.Y.
Hayes 1959 ————, *The Scepter of Egypt Part II. The Hyksos Period and the New Kingdom (1675-1080 B.C.).* N.Y.
Hayes 1964 ————, 'Most Ancient Egypt'. *J.N.E.S.*, (2-4):73-274.
Haynes 1980 Haynes, C.V., *Geological Evidence of Pluvian Climates in the Nabta Area of the Western Desert.* Appendix 6. In: Wendorf, F. and Schild, R., *Prehistory of the Eastern Sahara.* N.Y.
Heim de Balsac and Barloy 1966 Heim de Balsac, H. and Barloy, J.-J., 'Revision des Crocidures du groupe *flavenscens* - occidentalis-manni'. *Mammalia*, 30:601-633.
Heim de Balsac and Mein 1971 Heim de Balsac, H. and Mein, O., 'Les mus araignés momifiées des hypogées de Thèbes. Existence d'un metalophe chez les *Crocidurinae* (*sensu repenning*)'. *Mammalia*, 35:220-244.
Heise 1947 Heise, C.G., (ed.) *Die Sammlung Parthenon Meisterwerke Ägyptischer Plastik.* Stuttgart.
Hellström and Langballe 1970 Hellström, P. and Langballe, H., *The Rock Drawings.* (2 Vols). Stockholm.
Hemmer 1963 Hemmer, H. 'Untersuchungen über das Aussehen des altägyptischen Löven *Panthera leo nubica* (Blainville, 1843) und seine verwandtschaftlichen Beziehungen zu den benachbarten Löwen unterarten'. *Säugetierk. Mitteil.*, 11:117-128.
Hemprich and Ehrenberg 1833 Hemprich, F.W. and Ehrenberg, C.G., *Symbolae Physicae seu icones et descriptiones mammalium. Decas 2.*
Hilzheimer 1913 Hilzheimer, M., In: Borchardt, L. *Das Grabdenkmal des Königs Sahure. Band II.* Leipzig.
Hilzheimer 1926 ————, 'Säugetierkunde und Archäologie'. *Z.S.*, 1:140-169.
Hilzheimer 1927 ————, '*Dama shaeferi* Hilzh'. *Z.S.*, 2:65-73.
Hilzheimer 1928 ————, 'Nordafrikanische Schafe und ihre Bedeutung für die Besiedelungsfrage Nordafrikas'. *Z.S.*, 3:253-277.
Hilzheimer 1931 ————, 'Die Nashorndarstellung von Kerma'. *Z.Ä.S.*, 67:39-42.
Hilzheimer 1932 ————, 'Dogs'. *Antiquity*, 6:411-419.
Hinton and Dunn 1967 Hinton, H.E. and Dunn, A.M.S., *Mongooses, their Natural History and Behaviour.* Edinburgh, London.
Hobbs 1980 Hobbs, J.J., Sands of the Shore: Animals in Egyptian Life. M.A. Thesis, unpublished, Univ. Texas, Austin, pp.254.
Hobbs 1989 ————, *Bedouin Life in the Egyptian Wilderness.* Austin.
Hoffman 1982 Hoffman, M.A., 'General Summary and Conclusions - Issues in Predynastic Culture History'. Chapt. VII, pp.139-154. In: 'The Predynastic of Hierankopolis - an Interim Report'. Egyptian Studies Assoc. Publ. No.1, Cairo Univ. Herbarium, Giza and Dept. of Sociol. & Anthr., Western Ill. Univ., Macomb.
Honacki et al. 1982 Honacki, J.H. Kinman, K.E., and Koeppl, W.J., (eds.) *Mammal Species of the World.* Lawrence, Kansas.
Hoogstraal 1963 Hoogstraal, H., 'A brief review of the contemporary land mammals of Egypt (including Sinai). 2. Lagomorphs and Rodentia'. *J. Egypt. Public Health Assoc.*, 38(1):1-35.
Hoogstraal et al. 1966-1967 Hoogstraal, H. Wassif, K. Helmy, I. and Kaiser, M.N., The cheetah, *Acinonyx jubatus* Schreber, in Egypt'. *Bull. Zool. Soc. Egypt*, 21:63-68.
Hopfner 1913 Hopfner, T., *Der Tierkult der Alten Ägypter.* Wien.
Hornblower 1927 Hornblower, G.D., 'An humped bull of ivory and some Predynastic carvings'. *J.E.A.*, 13:222-225.
Hornblower 1930 ————, 'Funerary designs on predynastic pottery'. *J.E.A.*, 16;10-18.
Hornung 1967 Hornung, E., 'Die Bedeutung des Tieres im alten Aegypten'. *Studium Generale*, 20(2):69-84.
Hornung and Stachelin 1976 Hornung, E. and Stachelin, E., *Skarabäen und andere Siegelamulette aus Basler Sammlungen.* Mainz.
Houlihan 1987 Houlihan, P.F., 'Some remarks on deer (*Cervidae*) in Ancient Egypt'. *J.E.A.*, 73:238-234.
Houlihan 1996 ————, 'On Herodotus (II, 72), and the question of the evidence of the otter (*Lutra sp.*) in Ancient Egypt'. *G.M.*, 153:45-53.
Houlihan 1996 ————, *The Animal World of the Pharaohs.* London.
Houlihan 1997 ————, 'Harvesters or monkey business?' *G.M.*, 157:31-47.

Houlihan and Goodman 1986 Houlihan, P.F. and Goodman, S.M., *The Birds of Ancient Egypt.* Warminster.

Hufnagl 1972 Hufnagl, E. *Libyan Mammals.* Harrow.

Hyams 1972 Hyams, E., *Animals in the Service of Man.* London.

Ikram 1991 Ikram, S., 'Animal mating in Egyptian funerary representations'. *G.M.*, 124:51-68.

James 1953 James, T.G.F., *The Mastaba of Khentika called Ikhekhi.* London..

Janssen 1990 Janssen, J.J., 'On the scent of a fox'. *Discussions in Egyptology*, 16:43-51.

Janssen and Janssen 1989 Janssen, R. and Janssen, J., *Egyptian Household Animals.* Aylesbury.

Jarvis 1933 Jarvis, C.S., *Yesterday and Today in Sinai.* Edinburgh and London.

Jensen 1934 Jensen, A.S., 'The sacred animal of the god Set'. *Biologiske Meddelelsker*, XI(5):1-19.

Jequier 1922 Jéquier, M.G., 'Matériaux pour servir à l'établissement d'un directionaire d'archéologie Égyptienne'. *B.I.F.A.O.*, 19:1-277.

Jequier 1938 ———, *Le Monument Funéraire de Pepi II. Tome II. Le Temple.* Le Caire.

Joleaud 1935 Joleaud, L., 'Les Ruminants Cervicornes d'Afrique'. *Mémoire de l'Institut d'Égypte*, 27:1-85.

Junker 1934 Junker, H., *Giza II. Die Mastabas der beginnenden V. Dynastie auf dem Westfriehof.* Wien, Leipzig.

Junker 1941 ———, *Giza V.* Wien.

Junker 1943 ———, *Giza VI.* Wien.

Junker 1953 ———, *Giza XI.* Wien.

Kamal 1915 Kamal, M. Ahmed Bey. 'Le tombeau nouveau de Meir'. *A.S.A.E.*, 15:209-258.

Kamal 1916 ———, 'Fouilles à Deir Dronka et à Assiout (1913-1914)'. *A.S.A.E.*, 16:64-96.

Kantor 1947 Kantor, H.J. 'The Aegean and the Orient in the second millenium B.C.' *A.J.A.*, 51(1):1-103.

Kantor 1948 ———, 'A Predynastic ostrich egg with incised decoration'. *J.N.E.S.*, 7:46-51.

Kaplony 1976 Kaplony, P., *Studien zum Grab des Menthethi.* Bern.

Kees 1931 Kees, H., 'Die Befriedigung des Raubtiers'. *Z.Ä.S.*, 67:56-59.

Kees 1941 ———, *Der Götterglaube im Alten Aegypten.* Berlin.

Kees 1961 ———, *Ancient Egypt: A Cultural Topography.* London.

Keimer 1926 Keimer, L., 'Bemerkungen zur Shiefertafel von Hierakonpolis (I.Dynastie)'. *Aegyptus* Vol.VII, No.3-4, pp.169-188.

Keimer 1928 ———, 'Die Angst der Aegypter vor der Wüste. *Hamburger Fremdenblatt.* 6 janvier 1928.

Keimer 1929 ———, 'Über die Darstellung eines Kamel reiters aus ägyptischen Frühzeit'. *Kemi*, II:85-90, Cairo.

Keimer 1931 ———, 'L'Arbre IR.T [hiéroglyph] est-il réellement le saule Égyptien (Salix safsaf Forsk.)?' *B.I.F.A.O.*, 31:177-227.

Keimer 1934a ———, 'Pendeloques en forme d'insectes faisant partie de colliers Égyptiens'. *A.S.A.E.*, 34:177-213.

Keimer 1934b ———, 'Sur deux fragments de cornes de daim trouvés à Deir el- Médineh'. *M.I.F.A.O.*, 46 (Mélange Maspero Vol.I):273-308.

Keimer 1935 ———, 'Sur deux vases prédynastiques du Khozam'. *A.S.A.E.*, 35:161-181.

Keimer 1937 ———, 'Remarques sur les porc et le sanglier dans l'Égypte ancienne'. *B.I.E.*, 19:147-156.

Keimer 1938 ———, 'Remarques sur quelques représentations de divinités - beliers et sur un groupe d'objets de culte conservés an Musée du Caire'. *A.S.A.E.*, 35:297-331.

Keimer 1939a ———, 'Über zwei Fleischfresser aus der Familie der Mustelidae im Alten und Neuen Ägypten'. *M.D.A.I.K.*, 8:38-41.

Keimer 1939b ———, 'Pavian und Düm-Palme'. *M.D.A.I.K.*, 8:42-45.

Keimer 1940 ———, 'Sur un monument Égyptien au Musée du Louvre. Contribution à l'histoire de l'Égyptologie'. *Revue d'Égyptologie*, 4:45-65

Keimer 1942a ———, 'Quelques représentations rarissimes de Mustélidés conservées sur des bas-reliefs de l'ancien empire'. *Études d'Égyptologie.* Fasc.IV, Cairo..

Keimer 1942b ———, 'Deux representations Égyptiennes du Gerenuk (*Lithocranius walleri*). *A.S.A.E.*, 41:161-181.

Keimer 1943a ———, 'L'identification de l'hiéroglyphe IW'. *A.S.A.E.*, 42:257-270.

Keimer 1943b ———, 'La representation d'une antilope chevaline sur une bas-relief de Saqqarah'. *B.I.E.*, 25:101-128.

Keimer 1944a ———, 'L'Horreur des Égyptiens pour les démons du désert'. *B.I.E.*, 26:135-147.

Keimer 1944b ———, 'L'Oryctérope dans l'Égypte ancienne'. *Études d'Égyptologie*, 6:1-20.

Keimer 1947 ———, 'Interpretation de Quelques Passage D'Horapollon'. *Supplément A.S.A.E.*, 5:1-54.

Keimer 1948a ———, 'J. Vandier d'Abbadie, Catalogue des ostraca de Der el-Médineh'. *Bibliotheca Orientalis*, 5:18-25.

Keimer 1948b ———, 'INB [hiéroglyph], Le Caracal (*Caracal caracal* Schmitzi Matsch.) dans l'Égypte ancienne'. *A.S.A.E.*, 48:373-390.

Keimer 1948c ———, 'Notes sur les rhinocéros de l'Égypte ancienne'. *A.S.A.E.*, 48:47-54.

Keimer 1948d ———, 'Les 'Anes Sauvages'Abattus par Amenophis II, près de Qadesh'. *B.I.E.*, 30:117-148.

Keimer 1949 ———, 'Le porc-épic dans L'Égypte ancienne'. *A.S.A.E.*, 49:393-415.

Keimer 1953a ———, 'Les limites de l'observation naturaliste dans quelques representations animales de l'Égypte antique'. *Ann. Faculté des Lettres Univ. Ibrahim, Kairo*, 2:121-134.

Keimer 1953b ———, 'Notes prises chez les Bišarin et les Nubiens d'Assouan'. *B.I.E.*, 35:447-533.

Keimer 1954 ———, 'Jardins Zoologiques d'Égypte'. *Cahiers d'Histoire d'Égyptienne.* Ser.VI., Fasc.2:81-159.

Keimer 1955a ———, 'Interprétation de plusieurs passages contenus dans les "Histories" d'Hérédote'. *B.I.E.*, 36:455-476.

Keimer 1955b ———, 'Notes de Lecture'. *B.I.F.A.O.*, 55:7-20.

Keimer 1956 ———, 'Altägyptische, griechich-römische und byzantinisch- koptische Darstellung des syrischen Bären'. *Archiv für Orientforschung*, XVII(2):336-346.

Keimer 1957 ———, 'Notes de Lecture. II. Le sens de l'hiéroglyphe [hieroglyph]'. *B.I.F.A.O.*, 56:97-102.

Keller 1909 Keller, O., *Die Antike Tierwelt. Vol.I.* Leipzig.

Kessler 1989 Kessler, D., *Die Heiligen Tiere und der König. Vol. I: Beiträge zu Organization, Kult und Theologie der spätzeintlichen Tierfriedhöfe.* Wiesbaden.

Kingdon 1977 Kingdon, J., *East African Mammals Vol. III.* London.

Klingender 1971 Klingender, F., *Animals in Art and Thought to the End of the Middle Ages.* London.

Klunzinger 1878 Klunzinger, C.B., *Upper Egypt: Its people and its products.* N.Y.

Knault et al. 1971 Knault, W.H., (ed.) et al. *About Animals.* The 1971 Childcraft Annual. Field Enterprices Educational Corporation, Chicago.

Kock 1970a Kock, D., 'Die Verbreitungsgeschichte des Flusspherdes, *Hippopotamus amphibius* Linné,1758, im unteren Nilgebiet. Ein Beitrag zur Zoogeographie Nordafrikas'. *Säugetierk. Mitt.*, 18:12-25.

Kock 1970b ———, 'Zur Verbreitung der Mendesantilope, *Addax nasomaculatus* (De Blainville, 1816), und des Speissbockes, *Oryx gazella* (Linné,1758) im Nilgebiet. Ein Beitrag zur Zoogeographie Nordafrikas'. *Säugetierk. Mitt.*, 18:25-37.
Kock 1971 ———, 'Zur Verbreitung von Mähnenschaf und Steinbockim Nilgebiet. Ein Beitrag zur Zoogeographie Nordost-Afrikas'. *Säugetierk. Mitt.*, 19:28-39.
Kolar 1960 Kolar, H., 'Einiges über Stachelmäuse (*Acomys cahirinus dimidiatus*)'. *Die Pyramide*, 4:111-112.
Kowalski and Rzebik-Kowalska 1991 Kowalski, K. and Rzebik-Kowalska, B., *Mammals of Algeria*. Crakow.
Krebs 1973 Krebs, W., 'Nochmals die Kriegselefanten der Ptolemäer'. *Z.Ä.S.*, 100(1):41-42.
Krebs 1975 ———, 'Eine Gussform eines gesähmten Elefanten aus Ägypten'. *Z.Ä.S.*, 102(2):153-154.
Krzyzaniak and Kobusiewicz 1984 Krzyzaniak, L. and Kobusiewicz, M., (eds.) *Origin and Early Developmant of Food-producing Cultures in North-eastern Africa*. Poznan.
Kuhlman 1983 Kuhlman, K.P., *Materialen zur Ärcheologie und Geschichte des Raumes von Achmim*. Mainz.
Langton 1936 Langton, N., 'Notes on some small Egyptian figures of cats'. *J.E.A.*, 22:115-130.
Langton and Langton 1940 Langton, N. and Langton, B., *The Cat in Ancient Egypt*. Cambrigde.
Lauer 1976 Lauer, J.P., *Saqqara - The Royal Cemetery of Memphis*. N.Y.
Lawrence 1967 Lawrence, B., 'Early Domestic Dogs'. *Z.S.* 32:44-59.
Lay 1967 Lay, D.M., *A Study of the Mammals of Iran*. Fieldiana: Zoology, 54:1-282.
Leclant and Huard 1980 Leclant, J. and Huard, P., *La Culture des Chasseurs du Nil et du Sahara. Publ. du Centre de Recherches Anthropologiques, No.XXIV*. (2 Vols). Alger.
Lefebure 1903 Lefebure, E., 'Les Dieux du type rat dans le culte égyptien'. *Sphinx*, VI:189-205.
Lefebvre 1924 Lefèbvre, G., *Le Tombeau de Petosiris. Vol.3*. Le Caire.
Legge 1909 Legge, F., 'The carved slates and this season's discoveries'. *P.S.B.A.*, 31:204-211, 297-310.
Lepsius 1849-1859 Lepsius, C.R., *Denkmäler aus Ägypten und Äthiopien. Vol. I-XII*. Berlin.
Lepsius 1897 -1913 ———, *Denkmäler aus Ägypten und Äthiopien. Vol. I-III*. Berlin, Leipzig.
Loret 1907 Loret, V., 'Le Nom Égyptien de I'Oryx'. In: Lortet and Gaillard, La Faune Mommifiée de l'Ancienne Égypte'. *Arch. Mus. d'Hist. Nat. Lyon*, 9(2):174-178.
Lortet and Gaillard 1905 Lortet, L.C. and Gaillard, M.C., *La Faune Momifiée de l'Ancienne Égypte*. (Ser.2). Libr. Fac. Méd. et Fac. Droit, Lyon.
Lortet and Gaillard 1907, 1909 ———, *La Faune Momifiée de l'Ancienne Égypte*. Arch. Mus. d'Hist. Nat. Lyon.
Lucas and Harris 1962 Lucas, A. and Harris, J.R., *Ancient Egyptian Materials and Industries*. (ed.4). London.
MacDonald 1965 MacDonald, J., *Almost Human*. Phila., N.Y.
Mackenzie 1978 Mackenzie, D.A., *Egyptian Myth and Legend*. N.Y.
Macramallah 1935 Macramallah, R., *Le Mastaba d'Idout*. Cairo.
Maglio and Cooke 1978 Maglio, V.J. and Cooke, H.B.S., (eds.) 1978. *Evolution of African Mammals*. Cambridge.
Malek 1979 Malek, J., (ed.) 1979. *Topographical Bibliography of Ancient Egyptian Hieroglyphic Texts, Reliefs and Paintings III. Memphis, Part 2. Saqqara to Dashur*. Oxford.
Malek 1993 ———, *The Cat in Ancient Egypt*. London.
Marriette 1871 Marriette, A., *Denderah I,II,III*. Paris.
Marriette 1877 ———, *Deir-el-Bahari. Vol.I*. Leipzig.
Mason 1936 Mason, M., *The Paradise of Fools*. London.
Mason 1984 Mason, I.L., *Evolution of Domesticated Animals*. London and N.Y.
Maspero 1904 Maspero, M.G., 'Sur une figure de gerboise en bronze du Musée du Caire'. *A.S.A.E.*, V:205-202.
Massoulard 1949 Massoulard, E., *Préhistoire et Protohistoire d'Égypte*. Univ. de Paris. Travaux et Mémoires de l'Institut d'Ethnologie LIII.
McArdle 1982 McArdle, J., 'Preliminary report on the Predynastic fauna of the Hierakonpolis Project'. In: Hoffman, M.A. (ed.) The Predynastic of Hierakonpolis - an Interim Report, Chapt. V, pp.116-121, Egyptian Studies Assoc. Publ. No.1, Cairo Univ. Herbarium, Giza and Dept. Soc. & Anthropol. Western Ill. Univ., Macomb.
Mc Burney 1967 McBurney, C.B.M., *The Haua Fteah (Cyrenaica) and the Stone Age of the South-east Mediterranean*. London.
McDermott 1938 McDermott, W.C., *The Ape in Antiquity*. Baltimore.
McHargue 1972 McHargue, G., *Mummies*. N.Y.
McHugh 1971 McHugh, W.P., *Late Prehistoric Cultural Adaptation in the South eastern Libyan Desert*. Ph.D.Diss., unpublished, Dept.Anthrop. Univ. Wisc., Madison.
McHugh 1975 ———, 'Some archaeological results of the Bagnold-Mond expedition to the Gilf Kebir and Gebel Uweinat, southern Libyan Desert'. *J.N.E.S.*, 34(1):31-62.
Meissner 1963 Meissner, H.O., *One-Man Safari*. Chicago.
Mercatante 1978 Mercatante, A.S., *Who's Who in Egyptian Mythology*. N.Y.
Mercer 1949 Mercer, S.A.B., *The Religion of Ancient Egypt*. London.
Meyer 1904 Meyer, E., 'Die Entwickelung der Kulte von Abydos und die sogenannten Schakalsgötter'. *Z.Ä.S.*, 41:97-107.
Michaelis 1972 Michaelis, B., 'Die Schleichkatzen (Viveriden) Afrikas'. *Säugetierk. Mitt.*, 1:1-100.
Midaut-Reynes and Braunstein-Sylvestre 1977 Midaut-Reynes, B. and Braunstein-Sylvestre, F., 'Le chameau en Égypte'. *Orientalia*, 46:337-362.
Möllers 1906 Möllers, G., 'Ausgrabung der Deutsch Orient-Gesellschaft auf dem vorgeschichtlichen Friedhofe bei Abusir-el-Meleq in Sommer 1905'. *Mitt. Deutsch. Orient Ges.*, 30:1-28.
Möllers and Scharff 1926 Möllers, G. and Scharff, A, *Die Archaeologischen Ergebnisse des vorgeschichtlichen Gräberfeldes von Abusir el-Meleq*. Leipzig.
Mond and Myers 1937 Mond, R. and Myers, O.H., *Cemeteries of Armant I. The text. The plates*. London.
Mond and Myers 1940 ———, *Temples of Armant. The text. The plates*. London.
Monod 1938 Monod, T., *Contributions à l'étude du Sahara Occidental, fasc.I: Gravures, Peintures et Inscriptions rupestres*. Paris.
Montet 1910 Montet, P., 'Les scènes de boucherie dans les tombes de l'Ancienne Empire'. *B.I.F.A.O.*,7:41-65.
Montet 1937 ———, 'Les Reliques du L'Art Syrien dans L'Égypte du Nouvel Empire'. Faculté des Lettres de L'Univ. de Strassbourg. Fasc.76, pp.189.
Montet 1957 ———, *La Géographie de l'Egypte ancienne. I. To-mehu, la Basse Egypte*. Paris.
Montet 1958 ———, *Everyday life in Egypt in the days of Ramesses the Great*. London.
Montet 1961 ———, *La Géographie de l'Egypte ancienne. II. To-chema, la Heute Egypte*. Paris.
Montet 1968 ———, *Eternal Egypt*. N.Y,Toronto, London.
Morgan 1896 Morgan, J. de *Recherches sur les Origines de l'Égypte. L'Age de la Pierre et les Métaux*. Paris.

Morgan 1897 ————, *Recherches sur les Origines de L'Égypte. Ethnographie Préhistorique et Tombeau Royal de Négadah.* Paris.
Morgan 1909 ————, 'Étude sur l'Égypte primitive'. *Revue de lÉcole de Anthropologie de Paris*, 19:128-140, 263-281.
Morgan 1926 ————, *La Préhistoire Orientale. Vol. II.* Paris.
Morrison-Scott 1952 Morrison-Scott, T.C.S., The mummified cats of ancient Egypt'. *Proc. Zool. Soc., London*, 121:861-867.
Moussa and Altenmüller 1977 Moussa, A.M. and Altenmüller, H., *Das Grab des Nianchnum und Chnumhotep.* Mainz.
Moustafa 1952 Moustafa , Y.S., 'A predynastic domesticated dog'. *Bull. Inst. Desert*, 2:102-104.
Moustafa 1955 ————, '*Canis familiaris aegyptiaca* from Predynastic Maadi, Egypt'. *B.I.E.*, 36:105-109.
Müller 1964 Müller, H.W., *Ägyptische Kunstwerke, Kleinfunde und Glas in der Sammlung E. und M. Kofter-Truniger, Luzern.* Berlin.
Müller 1906 Müller, W.M., *Egyptological Researches Results of a Journey in 1904.* Carnegie Institute, Washington D.C.
Müller 1923 ————, *Egyptian Mythology.* London.
Murray 1891 Murray, J., *Handbook for travelers in lower and upper Egypt.* (8th rev. ed.). London.
Murray 1905 Murray, M.A., *Saqqara Mastabas. Part I.* London.
Murray 1937 ————, *Saqqara Mastabas. Part II.* London.
Nagel 1938 Nagel,G., *La Céramique du Nouvel Empire à Deir el Médinah.* Le Caire.
Naville 1891 Naville, E., *Boubastis.* London.
Naville 1894 Naville, E., *Ahnas el Medineh. (Heracleopolis Magna). The Tomb of Paheri at El Kab. Eleventh Memoir*, London.
Naville 1898 ————, *The Temple of Deir el Bahari. Part III.* London.
Naville 1914 ————, *Cemeteries of Abydos. Part I - 1909-1910.* London.
Needler 1984 Needler, W., *Predynastic and Archaic Egypt in the Brooklyn Museum.* N.Y..
Newberry 1892 Newberry, P.E., *El Bersheh Part I. The Tomb of Tehuti-hetep.* London..
Newberry 1893 ————, *Beni Hasan. Part I.* London.
Newberry 1894 ————, *Beni Hasan Part II.* London.
Newberry 1928 ————, 'The pig and the cult-animal of Set'. *J.E.A.*, 14:211-225.
Newberry 1944 ————, 'The elephant's trunk called its (dirt) "Maud"'. *J.E.A.* 30:75.
Newton 1924 Newton, F.G., 'Excavations at el-'Amarnah, 1923-24'. *J.E.A.*, 10:289-298.
Nibbi 1979 Nibbi, A., Some remarks on ass and horse in Ancient Egypt and the absence of the mule'. *Z.Ä.S.*, 106:148-168.
Nibbi 1980 Nibbi, A., The significance of deer in the ancient Egyptian landscape'. *Göttinger Miszellen*, 41:61-66.
Nybakken 1959 Nybakken, O.E., *Greek and Latin in Scientific Terminology.* Ames, Iowa.
Osborn 1968 Osborn, D.J., 'Hyena hunt'. *Bull. Field. Mus. Nat. Hist.*, 39(3):2-6,14.
Osborn 1977 ————, 'Animals of the Pharaohs'. Chicago Zool. Soc., Chicago, 16pp.
Osborn 1985 ————, 'A rebuttal of criticisms of identification of animals portrayed in the tomb of Tutankhamun'. *A.J.A.*, 89:157-161.
Osborn 1987 ————, 'Corrections in the identifications of the alabaster vases in Tutankhamun's treasures'. *J.E.A.*, 73:243-244.
Osborn 1988 ————, 'Zoological comments on ostracon P 2061'. *Annals of the Náprstek Museum, Prague*, 15:69-75.
Osborn and Helmy 1980 Osborn, D.J. and Helmy, I., *The Contemporary Land Mammals of Egypt (Including Sinai).* Fieldiana Zool. N.S., No.5.
Paget and Pirie 1898 Paget, R.F.E. and Pirie, A.A., *The Tomb of Ptah-hetep.* London.
Panouse 1957 Panouse, J.B., 'Les mammifères du Maroc'. *Travaux de l'Institut Scientific Chérifien, Sér. Zool.* 5:1-206.
Parker and Burkitt 1932 Parker, O.F. and Burkitt, M.C., 'Rock engravings from Onib, Wadi Allaki, Nubia'. *Man*, 32(297):249-250.
Paton 1925 Paton, D., *Animals of ancient Egypt.* Princeton.
Peet 1914 Peet, T.E., *The Cemeteries of Abydos. Part II.* London.
Peet and Loat 1913 Peet, T.E. and Loat, W.L.S., *The Cemeteries of Abydos. Part III. The Ibis Cemetery.* London.
Petrie 1891 Petrie, W.M.F., *Illahun, Kahun, and Gurob.* London.
Petrie 1892a ————, *Ten Years'Digging in Egypt.* London.
Petrie 1892b ————, *Medum.* London.
Petrie 1894 ————, *Tell el Amarna.* London.
Petrie 1896 ————, *Koptos.* London.
Petrie 1897 ————, *Deshasheh.* London.
Petrie 1898 ————, *Dendereh.* London.
Petrie 1900 ————, *The Royal Tombs ot the First Dynasty.* London.
Petrie 1901a ————, *The Royal Tombs of the Earliest Dynasties. Part II.* London.
Petrie 1901b ————, *Diospolis Parva. The Cemeteries of Abadiyeh and Hu.* London.
Petrie 1902a ————, 'Prehistoric Egyptian pottery'. *Man*, 2(83):113.
Petrie 1902b ————, 'Prehistoric Egyptian figures'. *Man*, 14:17.
Petrie 1902c ————, *Abydos. Part I.* London.
Petrie 1903 ————, *Abydos. Part II.* (with a chapter by F.L. Griffith). London.
Petrie 1906 ————, *Researches in Sinai.* London.
Petrie 1907 ————, *Giza and Rifeh.* London.
Petrie 1914a ————, *Amulets.* London.
Petrie 1914b ————, *Tarkhan II.* London.
Petrie 1917 ————, 'Egypt and Mesopotamia'. *Ancient Egypt, Part I*, Vol.16:26-36.
Petrie 1920 ————, *Prehistoric Egypt.* London.
Petrie 1921 ————, *Corpus of Prehistoric Pottery and Palettes.* London.
Petrie 1953 ————, *Ceremonial Slate Palettes.* London.
Petrie and Quibell 1896 Petrie, W.M.F. and Quibell, J.E., *Naqada and Ballas.* London.
Petzch 1958 Petzch, H., 'Reflexionen zur Phylogenie der *Capridae'. Wiss. Z. Martin-Luther Univ. Halle-Wittenberk*, 6:995-1019.
Phillips 1948 Phillips, D.W., *Ancient Egyptian Animals.* N.Y. (New ed. 1955)
Piankoff 1949 Piankoff, A., 'Les Deux papyrus "Mythologiques" de Her-Ouben au Musée du Caire'. *A.S.A.*, 49:129-144.
Piatrovski 1964 Piatrovski, B.B., (ed.) *Ancient Nubia. Results of the Archeological Expedition of the Soviet Academy of Science in the United Arab Republic 1961-1962.* Moscow. (In Russian)
Pijoan 1975 Pijoan, J., *Histoire de l'Art.* Paris.(Czech ed. Praha, 1977)

Pinney 1964 Pinney, R., *Animals of the Bible*. Phila., N.Y.
Platt 1908 Platt, A.F.R., 'The Origin of the name of the island of Elephantine'. *P.S.B.A.*, 30:206-207.
Posener 1944 Posener, G., 'La mésaventure d'un Syrien et le nom égyptien de l'ours'. *Orientalia*, 13(3):193-204.
Price 1893 Price, F.G.H., 'Notes upon some Egyptian antiquities in my collection'. *Trans. Soc. Biblical Archeol.*, 9:333-335.
Prisse d'Avennes 1847 Prisse d'Avennes, A.C., Monuments Égyptienne. Paris.
Prosper Alpin see Alpin P.
Quibell 1900 Quibell, J.E., *Hierakonpolis. Part I.* London.
Quibell 1932 ———, *Loose Ends.* In: Studies presented to F.Ll. Griffith, pp.480-484, London.
Quibell and Green 1902 Quibell, J.E. and Green, F.W., *Hierakonpolis. Part II.* London.
Quitzow 1961 Quitzow, W., 'Unsere Genette'. *Kosmos*, 57: 507-512.
Qumsiyeh 1985 Qumsiyeh, M.B., *The Bats of Egypt.* Spec. Publ. Mus. Texas Tech. Univ., 23:1-102.
Rabb 1968 Rabb, M.S., 'The sacred baboon. Brookfield Bandarlog'. The Chicago Zool. Society, No. 34:2-4.
Redford and Redford 1989 Redford, S. and Redford, D.B., 'Graffiti and petroglyphs old and new from the Eastern Desert'. *J.A.R.C.E.*, 26:3-49.
Reed 1966a Reed, C.A., 'The Yale Univ. prehistoric expedition to Nubia 1962-1965'. *Discovery*, 1(2):16-23.
Reed 1966b ———, Appendix In: Wendt, W.E., 'Two prehistoric archeological sites in Egyptian Nubia'. *Postilla*, 102:1-46.
Reed 1969 ———, *The pattern of animal domestication in the Prehistoric Near East*, pp.361-380. In: Ucko, P. and Dimbleby, G.W (eds.), *The Domestication and Exploitation of Plants and Animals.* London.
Reed and Osborn 1978 Reed, C.A. and Osborn, D.J., 1978. 'Taxonomic Transgressions in Tutankhamun's Treasures'. *A.J.A.*, 82:273-283, 1978.
Reed and Shaffer 1972 Reed, C.A. and Shaffer, W.M., The Co-evolution of Social Behaviour and Cranical Morphology in Sheep and Goats (*Bovidae, Caprini*)'. *Fieldiana Zoology*, 61:1-88.
Reed and Turnbull 1969 Reed, C.A. and Turnbull, P.F., *Late Pleistocene mammals from Nubia*, pp.55-56. In: van Zinderen Bakker, E.M. (ed.), *Palaeoecology of Africa and the surrounding islands and Antarctica. Vol. IV, covering the years 1966-1968.* Cape Town.
Reed et al. 1967 Reed, C.A. Baumhoff, M.A. Butzer, K.W. Walker, H. and Boloyan, D.S., 'Preliminary report on the archeological aspects of the Yale University prehistoric expedition to Nubia, 1962-1963'. Fouilles en Nubie (1961-1963), pp.145-156. Cairo.
Rensch and Dücher 1959 Rensch, B. and Dücher, G., 'Die Spiele von Mungo und Ichneumon'. *Behaviour*, 14(3):185-213.
Rhotert 1952 Rhotert, H., *Libysche Felsbilder.* Darmstadt.
Ricke et al. 1967 Ricke, H. Hughes, G.R. and Wente, E.F., *The Beit el Wali Temple of Ramses II.* Chicago.
Robinson 1966 Robinson, P., 'Fossil occurrence of murine rodent (*Nesokia indica*) in the Sudan'. *Science*, 154:264.
Roeder 1936 Roeder, G., 'Das Ichneumon in der ägyptischen Religion und Kunst'. *Egyptian Religion*, 4(1):1-48.
Roeder 1956 ———, 'Ägyptische Bronzewerke. Staatliche Museen zu Berlin'. *M.Ä.S.*, Band VI.
Roeder 1968 Roeder, M.G., *Temples Immergés de la Nubia VIII. Der Felsen tempel von Beit el Wali.* Le Caire.
Rommelaere 1991 Rommelaere, C., *Les Chevaux du Nouvel Empire Égyptien. Origines, Races, Harnachement.* Étude No.3. Connaissance de l'Égypte Ancienne.
Rosellini 1834 Rosellini, I., *I Monumenti dell'Egitto e della Nubia II.* Pisa.
Rosen 1994 Rosen, B., 'Mammoths in Ancient Egypt ?' *Nature*, 369:364.
Russell 1951 Russell, T., 'The fauna of the Egyptian deserts'. *Bull. Zool. Soc. Egypt*, 9:19-21.
Rzebik-Kowalska 1991 see Kowalski and Rzebik-Kowalska.
Rzoska 1976 Rzoska, J., (ed.) *The Nile. Biology of an Ancient River.* The Hague.
Saad 1951 Saad , Z., *Royal Excavations at Helwan 1945-1947.* Le Caire.
Säve-Söderbergh 1953 Säve-Söderbergh, T., 'On Egyptian representations of hippopotamus hunting as a religious motive'. *Uppsala Horae Soederblomianae*, III:56.
Säve-Söderbergh 1957 ———, *Private Tombs at Thebes. Vol.I. Four Eighteenth Dynasty Tombs.* Oxford.
Säve-Söderbergh 1970 ———, (ed.) *The Rock drawings. Scandinavian Joint Expedition to Sudanese Nubia.* (2Vols). Stockholm.
Schaller 1977 Schaller, G.B., *Mountain Monarchs.* Chicago.
Scharff 1928 Scharff, A., 'Some prehistoric vases in the British Museum and remarks on Egyptian prehistory'. *J.E.A.*, 14:261-276.
Scharff 1931 ———, 'Die Altertümer der Vor- und Frühzeit Ägyptens. Zweiter Teil'. *M.Ä.S.*, Band V.
Schmitt 1963 Schmitt, J., '*Ammotragus lervia* Pallas. Mähnenschaf oder Mähnenziege'. *Z.S.*, 28:7-12.
Schulmann 1957 Schulmann, R.A., 'Egyptian representations of horsemen and riding in the New Kingdom'. *J.N.E.S.*, 16(4):263-271.
Schweinfurth 1874 Schweinfurth, G. 'Notice sur la grande oasis du Désert Libyque'. *Bull. Soc. Geogr.* ser.7, 6:627-634.
Schweinfurth 1903a ———, 'Aegyptische Tierbilder als Kieselartefakte'. *Die Umschau*, 7:804-806.
Schweinfurth 1903b ———, 'Figures d'animaux fabriquées en silex et provenant d'Égypte'. *Rev. de l'École d'Anthrop. de Paris*, XIII:395-399.
Schweinfurth 1912 ———, 'Über alte Tierbilder und Felsenschriften bei Assuan'. *Zeitschr. f. Ethnologie*, Berlin, 44:627-658.
Schweitzer 1948 Schweitzer, U., *Löwe und Sphinx im Alten Ägypten.* Ägyptol. Forschungen, Heft 15, Hamburg.
Sclater 1900 Sclater, P.L., *The Mammals of South Africa. Vol.I: Primates, Carnivora, and Ungulata.* London.
Sclater and Thomas 1899-1900 Sclater, P.L. and Thomas, O., *The Book of Antelopes, vol.IV.* London.
Seligman 1916 Seligman, C.G., *An early representation of Taurt. Ancient Egypt, Part I:53*, British School of Archeology in Egypt, vol. 16, University College, London.
Sethe 1937 Sethe, K., In: Murray, M.A. *Saqqara Mastabas. Part II.* London.
Setzer 1956 Setzer, H.W., 'Mammals of the Anglo-Egyptian Sudan'. *Proc. U.S. Nat. Mus.*, 106(3377):447-587.
Setzer 1959 ———, 'The spiny mice (*Acomys*) of Egypt'. *The J. of Egyptian Public Health Assoc.*, 34(3):93-101.
Sharpe and Bonomi 1864 Sharpe, S. and Bonomi, J., *The Alabaster Sarcophagus of Oimenepthali I., King of Egypt.* London, 1864.
Simpson 1976a Simpson, W.K., *The Mastabas of Qar and Idu. Giza Monuments Vol.II.* Boston.
Simpson 1976b ———, *The offering chapel of Sekhem-Ankh-Ptah in the Museum of Fine Arts, Boston.* Boston.
Simpson 1978 ———, *The Mastabas of Kawab, Khafkhufu I. and II. Giza Mastabas Vol.III.* Boston.
Simpson 1980 ———, *Mastabas of the Western Cemetery. Part I.* Boston.
Smith and Dawson 1924 Smith, G.E. and Dawson, W.R., *Egyptian Mummies.* London.

Smith 1969 Smith, H.S., *Animal domestication and animal cult in dynastic Egypt*. In: Ucko, P.J. and Dimbleby, G.W. (eds.) *The Domestication and Exploitation of Animals*, pp.307-314, Chicago.
Smith 1946 Smith, W.S., *A History of Egyptian Sculpture and Painting in the Old Kingdom*. London.
Smith 1958 ————,. *The Art and Architecture of Ancient Egypt*. Middlesex.
Smith 1962 ————, 'Hatshepsut's expedition in the Land of Punt'. *J.A.R.C.E.*, I:59-61.
Smith 1965 ————, *Interconnections in the Ancient East*. New Haven.
Sonnini 1800 Sonnini, C.S., *Travels in Upper and Lower Egypt*. London.
Spence 1915 Spence, L., *Myths and Legends of Ancient Egypt*. London.
Spencer 1980 Spencer, A.J., *Catalogue of Egyptian Antiquities in the British Museum V. Early Dynastic Objects*. London.
Spinage 1968 Spinage, C.A., *The Book of the Giraffe*. London.
Steindorff 1913 Steindorff, G., *Das Grab des Ti*. Leipzig.
Steindorff 1926 ————, *Die Blütezeit des Pharaonenreiches*. (ed.2). Leipzig.
Steindorff 1928 ————, *Die Kunst der Ägypter*. Leipzig.
Stewart 1979 Stewart, H.M., *Egyptian Stelae, Reliefs and Paintings from the Petrie Collection. Part Two: Archaic Period to Second Intermediate Period*. Warminster.
Störk 1977a Störk, L., 'Fuchs'. *L.Ä.* Band II:348.
Störk 1977b ————, 'Gepard'. *L.Ä.* Band II:530-531.
Störk 1977c ————, 'Ginsterkatze'. *L.Ä.* Band II:597.
Störk 1977d ————, 'Fledermaus'. *L.Ä.* Band II:263.
Störk 1980 ————, 'Katze'. *L.Ä.* Band III:367-369.
Störk 1982 ————, 'Nashorn'. *L.Ä.* Band IV:351.
Strekalovsky 1949 Strekalovsky, N.W., *Shooting and fishing in Egypt*. Cairo.
Strouhal 1989 Strouhal, E., *Life of the Ancient Egyptians*. Praha. (In Czech)
Talbot 1960 Talbot, L.M., 'A look at threatened species'. *Oryx* 5:153-293.
Tate 1971 Tate, R., *Desert Animals*. N.Y.
Te Velde 1984 Te Velde, H., 'Seth'. *L.Ä.* Band V:908-911.
Tregenza 1958 Tregenza, L.A., *Egyptian Years*. London.
Tupinier 1984 Tupinier, D., 'Plaque à fard de l'Egypte Prédynastique representant une Chauvre- souris'. *Bull. Mensuel de la Societé Linnéenne de Lyon*, 9:296-299.
Ucko and Dimbleby 1969 Ucko, P.J. and Dimbleby, G.W., (eds.) 1969. *The Domestication and Exploitation of Animals*. London.
Uerpmann 1987 Uerpmann, H.P., *The Ancient Distribution of Ungulate Mammals in the Middle East*. Wiesbaden.
Vachala 1987 Vachala, B., 'A note on prices of oxen in Dynasty V'. *Z.Ä.S.*, 114:91-95.
Váhala 1970 Váhala, F., 'Der Elefant in Ägypten und Nubien'. *Z.Ä.S.*, 98(I):81-83.
Váhala 1971 ————, 'Zwei neue Bücher über nubische Felsbilder'. *Archiv Orientální*, 39:84-91.
Váhala (in press) ————, Large Animals in Egypt and Nubia. (in press)
Vandier 1950 Vandier, J., *Mo'alla, la Tombe d'Ankhtifi et la Tombe de Sébekhotep*. Le Caire.
Vandier 1952 ————, *Manuel d'Archéologie Égytienne. Tome I. Les Époques de Formation La Préhistorie*. Paris.
Vandier 1964 ————, *Manuel d'Archéologie Égytienne. Tome IV*. Paris.
Vandier 1969 ————, *Manuel d'Archéologie Égytienne. Tome V*. Paris.
Vandier d'Abbadie 1936, 1937, 1946, and 1959. Vandier d'Abbadie, J., *Catalogue des Ostraca Figurés de Deir el-Médineh. Fasc.1-4*. Le Caire.
Vandier d'Abbadie 1936/37 ————, 'A propos d'une chauve-souris sur un ostracon du Musée du Caire'. *B.I.F.A.O.*, 36:117-123, 1936/37.
Vandier d'Abbadie 1964 ————, 'Les singes familiers dans l'Ancienne Égypte, I. L'Éncien Empire'. *Rev. d'Égyptologie*, 16:147-177.
Vandier d'Abbadie 1965 ————, 'Les singes familiers dans l'Ancienne Égypte (Peintures et basrelief), II. Le Moyen Empire'. *Rev. d'Égyptologie*, 17:177-188.
Vandier d'Abbadie 1966 ————, 'Les singes familiers dans l'Ancienne Égypte (Pentures et bas-reliefs), III. Le Nouvel Empire'. *Rev. d'Égyptologie*, 18:143-201.
Van Noten 1978 Van Noten, F., *Rock Art of the Gebel Uweinat*. Graz.
Volf 1977 Volf, J., *Animals of the Whole World 2. Horses, Asses, and Zebras*. Praha, 1977. (In Czech)
Waddel 1939 Waddel, W.G., (ed.) *Herodotus Book II*. London.
Wassif 1954 Wassif, K., 'On a collection of mammals from northern Sinai'. *Bull. Inst. Désert Egypte*, 3(1):107-118(1953).
Wassif 1976 Wassif, K., *Mammals*. In: Rzóska, J. (ed.) *The Nile*, pp. 95-97, The Hague.
Weigall 1906 Weigall, A.E.P., 'A report on the excavation of the funeral temple of Thoutmosis III at Gurneh'. *A.S.A.E.*, 7:121-141, 1906.
Weigall 1907 Weigall, A.E.P., *A Report on the Antiquities of Lower Nubia (the First Cataract to the Sudan Frontier) and their condition in 1906-1907*. Oxford.
Wendorf 1968 Wendorf, F., (ed.) *The Prehistory of Nubia. Vol. I.* Dallas.
Wendorf and Schild 1980 Wendorf, E. and Schild, R., *Prehistory of the Eastern Sahara*. N.Y, London, etc.
Wendorf et al. 1976 Wendorf, F. Schild, R. Said, R. Haynes, C.V. Gautier, A. and Kobusiewicz, M., 'The prehistory of the Egyptian Sahara'. *Science*, 193, No.4248:103-114.
Wendorf et al. 1984 Wendorf, F. Schild, R. and Close, A., (eds.) *Cattle Keepers of the Eastern Sahara: the Neolithic of Bir Kiseiba*. New Delhi.
Wendt and Reed 1966 Wendt, W.E. and Reed, C.A., 'Two Prehistoric archeological sites in Egyptian Nubia'. *Postilla*, 102:1-46.
Westendorf 1968 Westendorf, W., *Painting, Sculpture, and Architecture of Ancien Egypt*. N.Y.
White 1920 White, H.G.E., 'The Egyptian Expedition 1916-1919, Excavations in the Asasif and Thebes'. *B.M.M.A.*, 2:3-39.
Whittemore 1914 Whittemore, T., 'The Ibis cemetery at Abydos'. *J.E.A.*, I:248-249.
Wild 1953 Wild, H., *Le Tombeau de Ti. Fasc.II La Chapelle*. Le Caire.
Wild 1966 ————, *Le Tombeau de Ti. Fasc.III La Chapelle*. Le Caire.
Wildung 1984 Wildung, D., *Ni-User-Re Sonnenkönig - Sonnengott. Schriften aus der Ägyptischen Sammlung, Heft.I*, München, 1984.
Wilkinson 1878 Wilkinson, J.G., *The manners and customs of the ancient Egyptians*. (3 Vols) London.
Williams 1980 Williams, B., 'The lost pharaohs of Nubia'. *Archeology*, 33(5):12-21.
Winkler 1937 Winkler, H.A., *Völker und Völker-bewegungen in vorgeschichtlichen Oberägypten im Lichte neuer Felsbilderfunde*. Stuttgart.

Winkler 1938 ————, *Rock Drawings of Southern Upper Egypt I*. London.
Winkler 1939 ————, *Rock Drawings of Southern Upper Egypt II*. London.
Wolf 1957 Wolf, W., *Die Kunst Aegyptens Gestalt und Geschichte*. Stuttgart.
Wreszinski 1923, 1935, and 1936 Wreszinski, W. *Atlas zur Altägyptischen Kulturgeschichte I, II, III*. Leipzig.
Zarins 1982 Zarins, J., 'Early rock art of Saudi Arabia'. *Archeology*, 35(6):20-27.
Žába 1965 Žába, Z., 'Czechoslovak discoveries of inscriptions and rock-drawings in Nubia'. *New Orient*, 4(4):110-113.
Žába 1974 Žába, Z., *The Rock Inscriptions of Lower Nubia (Czechoslovak concession)*. Prague.
Zeuner 1963 Zeuner, F.E., *A History of Domesticated Animals*. London.
Ziswiller 1967 Ziswiller, V., *Extinct and Vanishing Animals*. N.Y.
Ziccardi 1970 Ziccardi, F., 'The African wild ass'. *Afr. Wildlife*, 24:202-208, 287-292.

Index

(Synonyms are in parentheses)